Beyond the Com

PITTSBURGH STUDIES IN COMPARATIVE AND INTERNATIONAL EDUCATION

INTRODUCTION TO THE SERIES

The aim of the *Pittsburgh Studies in Comparative and International Education Series* is to produce edited and authored volumes on topics ranging from key international education issues, trends, and reforms to examinations of national education systems, social theories, and development education initiatives. Local, national, regional, and global volumes (single authored and edited collections) constitute the breadth of the series and offer potential contributors a great deal of latitude based on interests and cutting edge research. The series is supported by a strong network of international scholars and development professionals who serve on the Advisory Board and participate in the selection and review process for manuscript development. The volumes are intended to provide not only useful contributions to comparative, international, and development education (CIDE) but also possible supplementary readings for advanced courses for undergraduate and graduate students in CIDE.

BEYOND THE COMPARATIVE

Advancing Theory and its Application to Practice

Edited by

John C. Weidman

W. James Jacob

SENSE PUBLISHERS
ROTTERDAM/BOSTON/TAIPEI

A C.I.P. record for this book is available from the Library of Congress.

ISBN: 978-94-6091-720-2 (paperback)
ISBN: 978-94-6091-721-9 (hardback)
ISBN: 978-94-6091-722-6 (e-book)

Published by: Sense Publishers,
P.O. Box 21858,
3001 AW Rotterdam,
The Netherlands
www.sensepublishers.com

Printed on acid-free paper

TABLE OF CONTENTS

LIST OF FIGURES AND MAPS

LIST OF TABLES

ACKNOWLEDGEMENTS

The editors would first like to thank all the contributing authors to this volume. Each of their contributions includes reflections and new insights into multiple foundational topics expounded upon by the life works of Rolland G. Paulston. Without their unique contributions to further examining many of these topics, this project could not have occurred.

We thank Sense Publishers' Allan Pitman, Michel Lokhorst, and Peter de Liefde for their support of this research compilation endeavor. Jennifer Crandall and Chen-Jui Su provided editorial support throughout the review process and in direct correspondence with contributors.

We are especially grateful for Rolland G. Paulston, to whom the book is dedicated, for his laying a fertile foundation whereby theory can be strengthened and cultivated in comparative, international, and development education. His wife, Christina Paulston, was also very helpful as we reviewed key events in Rolland's life and works.

LIST OF ABBREVIATIONS AND ACRONYMS

A/H1N1	Swine Flu
AED	Academy for Educational Development
AFRE	All for Reparations and Emancipation
AIDS	Acquired Immunodeficiency Syndrome
APER	*Asia Pacific Education Review*
APPEP	Andhra Pradesh Primary Education Project (India)
ASHE	Association for the Study of Higher Education
AUDEM	Association of Universities for Democracy
BA	Bachelor of Arts
BBC	British Broadcasting Company
BRAC	Bangladesh Rehabilitation Assistance Committee
BRIC	Brazil, Russia, India, and China
CCIC	Canadian Council for International Cooperation
CCU	Chung Cheng University (China)
CE	*Comparative Education* (UK)
CEDAW	Convention of the Elimination of All Forms of Discrimination against Women
CEJ	*Comparative Education* (Japan)
CER	*Comparative Education Review*
CES	Comparative Education Studies
CIDE	Comparative, international, and development education
CIDA	Canadian International Development Agency
CIES	Centro de Investigación, Educación y Servicios
CIES	Comparative and International Education Society (USA)
CLUSA	Cooperative League of USA (Zambia)
CoP	Communities of Practice
CPA	Comprehensive Peace Agreement (Sudan and Southern Sudan)
CR	Critical Rationalist
CRT	Critical Race Theory
CSO	Civil Society Organizations
CUSO-VSO	Canadian University Services Overseas
DP	Deconstructive Perspectivist
DWCD	Department of Women and Child Development (India)
DNA	Discursive Network Analysis
EdD	Doctor of Education
EFA	Education for All
EMIS	Educational Management Information Systems
EPAM	Education Policy Analysis Model
ERIC	Educational Resources Information Center
EQUIP2	Educational Quality Improvement Program 2
GAD	Gender and Development

GEM	Gender Empowerment Measure
GEEP	Gender Equality, Education and Poverty
GPF	Gender Policy Framework
GATS	General Agreement on Trade in Services
GDP	Gross Domestic Product
GINIE	Global Information Networks in Education
GMR	Global Monitoring Report
GNU	Government of National Unity (Sudan)
GOI	Government of India
GOSS	Government of Southern Sudan
GPA	Grade Point Average
GPS	Global Positioning System
GRZ	Government of the Republic of Zambia
HC	Hermeneutical Constructionist
HEI	Higher education institution
HIV	Human Immunodeficiency Virus
IAU	International Association of Universities
IBE	UNESCO International Bureau of Education (Switzerland)
ICT	Information and communication technology
IDEP	International and Development Education Program, University of Pittsburgh (USA)
IDPs	Internally displaced persons
IE	International education
IER	*International Education Review*
IISE	Institute for International Studies in Education, University of Pittsburgh (USA)
IJED	*International Journal of Educational Development*
IO	International Organizations
IT	Information technology
JCES	Japan Comparative Education Society
JEP	*Journal of Education Policy*
JSIE	*Journal of Studies in International Education*
KPTIP	Consortium of Indonesian Universities-Pittsburgh
MA	Master of Arts
MBA	Master of Business Administration
MDG/s	Millennium Development Goal/s
MECS	Ministry of Education, Culture and Science (Mongolia)
MER	Monitoring, Evaluation, and Research
MEXT	Ministry of Education, Culture, Sports, Science and Technology (Japan)
MGSW&RA	Ministry of Gender, Social Welfare and Religious Affairs (Southern Sudan)
MOE	Ministry of Education
MOEST	Ministry of Education, Science and Technology (Southern Sudan)

MOH	Ministry of Health
MS	Master of Science
MSF	Médecins Sans Frontières
NAFSA[1]	NAFSA: Association of International Educators
NAFTA	North America Free Trade Agreement
NGO	Nongovernmental organization
NICs	Newly industrialized countries
NOCIES	Nordic Comparative and International Education Society
NoP	Networks of Practice
NPEW	National Policy for the Empowerment of Women (India)
NPM	New public management
NRDDB	North Rupununi District Development Board (Guyana)
NUFU	Norwegian Programme for Development, Research and Education
ODA	Official Development Aid
OECD	Organisation for Economic Co-operation and Development
OISE/UT	Ontario Institute for Studies in Education at the University of Toronto (Canada)
PhD	Doctor of Philosophy
PITT	Pre- and in-service teacher training
PISA	Program for International Student Assessment
PPI	Policy planning and implementation
Pre-K to 12	Pre-Kindergarten to twelfth grade (USA)
RAPIDS	Reaching HIV/AIDS Affected People with Integrated Support and Development (Zambia)
RICE	Research information for international and comparative education
SHEMP	Smallholder Enterprise and Marketing Program (Zambia)
SIT	School for International Training (USA)
SMART	Specific, Measurable, Attainable, Relevant and Time-Bound
SNA	Social network analysis
SSCI	Social Sciences Citation Index
TCR	*Teachers College Record*
TR	Technical Rationalist
TIMSS	Trends in International, Mathematics and Science Study
UBC	University of British Columbia (Canada)
UCLA	University of California, Los Angeles
UDHR	Universal Declaration of Human Rights
UK	United Kingdom
UN	United Nations
UNICEF[2]	United Nations Children's Fund
UNIFEM	United Nations Development Fund for Women
UNDP	United Nations Development Programme
UNESCO	United Nations Educational, Scientific and Cultural Organization
UNFPA	United Nations Population Fund

UNHCR	United Nations High Commissioner for Refugees
UNPD	United Nations Population Division
US/USA	United States of America
USAID	U.S. Agency for International Development
VDM	Verlag Dr. Müller
VSO	Voluntary Service Overseas
WBC	World Baseball Classic
WCCES	World Council of Comparative Education
WED Trust	Women's Emancipation and Development Trust (India)
WHO	World Health Organization
WID	Women in Development
WTO	World Trade Organization
WUSC	World University Service of Canada
WWII	World War II

NOTES

1. NAFSA: Association of International Educators was founded in 1948 as the National Association of Foreign Student Advisers and underwent a second name change in 1964 to the National Association for Foreign Student Affairs to reflect its growing and diverse membership. Its name was changed again in 1990 to reflect its advancement in international education.
2. UNICEF's original name was the United Nations International Children's Emergency Fund (1946–1953).

JOHN C. WEIDMAN AND W. JAMES JACOB

SERIES EDITORS INTRODUCTION

We are pleased to introduce a new book series, *Pittsburgh Studies in Comparative and International Education*, published and distributed by Sense Publishers. The issues that will be highlighted in this book series range from key international education issues, trends, and reforms to examinations of national education systems, social and educational theories, and development education initiatives. Local, national, regional, and global volumes (single authored and edited collections) are anticipated in order to offer potential contributors a great deal of latitude based on interests and cutting edge research.

PSCIE is sponsored by the University of Pittsburgh Institute for International Studies in Education (IISE) that manages review of submissions and provides editorial assistance in manuscript preparation. Selected University of Pittsburgh doctoral students have the unique opportunity to gain editing and publishing experience working or interning at IISE as a member of our editorial team.

The series is supported by a strong network of international scholars and development professionals who serve on the International Advisory Board and participate in the selection and review process for manuscript development. Working with our International Advisory Board, periodic calls will be issued for contributions to this series from among the most influential associations and organizations in international studies in education, including the Comparative and International Education Society, World Council of Comparative Education Societies, and UNESCO.

As the *PSCIE* Series Editors, we are especially pleased to introduce this inaugural volume—*Beyond the Comparative*—which expands on the life work of University of Pittsburgh Professor Rolland G. Paulston (1929–2006). Recognized as a stalwart in the field of comparative and international education, Paulston's most widely recognized contribution is in social cartography. He demonstrated that mapping comparative, international, and development education (CIDE) is no easy task and, depending on the perspective of the mapper, there may be multiple cartographies to chart. The 35 contributors to this volume, representing a range of senior and junior scholars from various CIDE backgrounds and perspectives, celebrate the life and work of Paulston by addressing issues, perspectives and approaches related to charting the future course of the field. The volume reports on new research in several genres as well as conceptual analysis. As the title suggests, authors were encouraged to go "beyond" established canons of CIDE.

In future volumes in the *PSCIE* series, we encourage the generation of exceptional CIDE scholarship from researchers, policy makers, and practitioners from around the world. We hope this initial volume will encourage prospective authors and editors to submit manuscript proposals to the *PSCIE* series about their current research and project interests.

ESTHER E. GOTTLIEB

FOREWORD

A Comparative Education Story of Maps and Mapping

> A reflexive social cartography, might serve to identify and visualize within and between disputatious communities in a way that would open space for all knowledge perspectives discovered, privilege none, yet problematize all, and promote a useful visual and verbal dialogue. (Paulston 2000, 298)

Rolland G. Paulston's work signifies the end of the old and the beginning of something new. This volume reflects the breadth of Paulston's writing over some forty years, mixing the canonical with the unexpected. Its dialogue with Paulston explores not just his writing but our own work and ideas, juxtaposing traditional modes of representation with the contemporary and reflecting the growing body of diverse research in our field. This is a conversation Paulston would have enjoyed. Pushing the envelope, or dropping a heavy rock in clear water and watching the ripples spread, was his joy and intellectual daily bread. Professor Paulston (who characteristically crossed out the title on his business cards and scribbled "Rolland" above it) wrote and re-wrote his invitation to a different social thought. Year after year, he sent us, his students and colleagues, his drawings and mappings of social and comparative education, requesting, "Please return with comments, suggestions etc." Thus, the responsibility for participating in his work and actively testing its critical implications was placed squarely on us, his readers and viewers.

So here comes this volume, the product of a "disputatious community." To publish a definitive volume dedicated to Rolland Paulston's lifework would be impossible, no matter how many chapters it included, and this volume includes plenty. Still I'm confident that he would have approved of an attempt to draw one of the many possible maps of his contribution to social foundations of education, comparative and international education.

I always like to think of Paulston dressed in white on a beach in Tangier, where he met Christina Bratt. They moved together to pursue their doctorates at Columbia University, Rolland in Comparative Education under George Bereday, Christina in Applied Linguistics. His appointment with the Teachers College's Center for Education in Latin America took them to Lima, Peru, where Paulston worked with the Ministry of Education on teacher education reform while Christina researched speakers of indigenous languages. While in Lima, their two sons Christopher and Ian were born, and in 1968 they both accepted academic positions at the University of Pittsburgh where they spent the remainder of their careers.

My own path crossed his in the mid-1980s, when the International and Development Education Program (IDEP) at the University of Pittsburgh was one of the best and largest graduate Comparative and International Education Programs in the United States. Attracting a steady stream of international students, IDEP was led by four of the most notable scholars and expert consultants in the field of development education: Don Adams, John Singleton, Seth Spaulding, and Rolland Paulston. Paulston regularly taught "Comparative Theories and Methods," one of the two mandatory courses for the graduate degree. Being contrarian among the faculty, and always up for a good intellectual argument, he was somewhat feared by students, but his demeanor softened with the years. Everyone who knew Paulston was aware of how multi-disciplinary his knowledge was, and of his phenomenal ability to stay abreast of research not just in our respective sub-fields but beyond them. There were no disciplinary boundaries to his curiosity. It helped that he was brilliant; a fast reader able to absorb new ideas quickly and to sort out what was useful from what wasn't. After my days at Pitt he used to point at me at conference presentations and say accusingly, "It's all your fault I became postmodern." We both knew the truth: he had "postmodernized" himself. Appropriately, he was both serious about "postmodernizing" comparative education and self-deprecatingly ironic about it. I'm sure he would have enjoyed (and endorsed) a passage like this one:

> It was sad to see postmodernism disappear before we could explain it, I kind of liked postmodernism, I was happy in the postmodern condition, as happy if not happier than in the previous condition, I don't remember what that was called but I was glad to get out of it, and now here we are again faced with a dilemma, what shall we call this new thing towards which we are going, this new thing I haven't seen yet, did you see it Gaston, what can we call it, postpostmodernism seems a bit too clumsy, and popomomo not serious enough, I thought of calling this new condition The People's Revolution Number Four . . . . (Federman 2001, 245)

Innovative, outside-of-the box thinking and the pursuit of alternative ways of seeing social phenomena were hallmarks of Paulston's approach. He said of his work, "I seek to make a spatial turn beyond modernist binaries and dichotomies to patterned multiplicities, a plurality of worlds" (2005, 1). Moving beyond the "two-by-two graphs" of Burrell and Morgan (who visited one of our IDEP seminars in 1985) that "mapped" out the four paradigms of social thought—Functionalist, Radical Structuralist, Radical Humanist, and Interpretive (reproduced in Gottlieb 1987; Paulston 2000, and Rust and Kenderes Chapter 2 in this volume)—Paulston began to develop his own mappings of the field, starting with his "Macro-Mapping of Paradigms and Theories of Comparative Education" (1994). The two-by-two grid of boxes becoming more and more like floating clouds, as can be seen in Figure 1.2 in the first chapter of this volume. This mapping project would engage Paulston for the remainder of his career throughout the 1990s and down to his death from cancer in 2006.

Paulston's objective was to offer comparative education a way of seeing and a research method (one that Lee and Friedrich take up in this volume). Paulston's *Social Cartography* volume was reviewed not only by the journals in our field but also in the *Cartographic Journal*, the *Journal of Historical Geography*, and the international *Journal of Qualitative Studies*. As his scholarship concentrated more and more intensively on social cartography, Paulston organized panels at each annual CIES meeting, wrote papers and chapters, offered a seminar on "mapping as a way of seeing," and gave invited talks to explore and advance his new interpretative approaches for comparative research. He went on to interrogate some sixty exemplary education texts, mapping their "theoretical perspectives onto a two dimensional field, demonstrating how such a 'social cartography,' or 'heuristic device,' might serve to identify and visualize difference within and between disputed intellectual communities . . . ." He believed that this was a "way that would open space for all perspectives in the debate" (1996, 1). In seeking to open this space for Comparative Education, he joined an exciting contemporary area of new mapping studies across disciplines, involving the mapping of many more domains of social life than ever before, and creating new forms and users of map-like diagrams. This broadening and resituating of his geographic roots (he had a degree in Geography) and his life-long mapping impulse in non- and multi-disciplinary perspectives came very naturally to Paulston.

Not everyone in the field was swept away by Paulston's repeated pleas to think more in terms of "multiple ways of seeing and multiple visual regimes," and not all scholars in comparative education saw this new space as open for their inclusion, or else they just did not accept the "place" Paulston assigned them in his drafting of "knowledge positions" (as in the map above). While it is not just in our field that some are not "postmodern yet" (Gottlieb 2000), it is nevertheless noticeable that critiques of postmodernism in our field sometimes have a hyperbolic, if not slightly hysterical flavor (MacLure 2006).

Needless to say this controversy produced many good sessions at conferences where Paulston's symposiums were always standing room only, as friends and foes alike attended, since everyone was sure that a lively discussion would develop. No matter how falsifiable and heuristic Paulston wished his maps to be, once the maps are in circulation they can be used in any number of ways, literally as well as metaphorically. There is no way the mapmaker can control the use the reader or researcher will make of his maps. Mapping is always an expression of epistemological mastery, and to map out our own intellectual field you would have to occupy a position of epistemological mastery relative to it; yet, as we know, Paulston's work calls the very idea of mastery into question. His project was to equalize all positions and place them all on a single plane. There is a contradiction here, which Paulston obviously recognized. In order to have the knowledge to make maps such as Paulston has made, you have to be Rolland Paulston; that is, "you have to have the cumulative weight of intellectual authority that someone like Paulston has exercised in theorizing comparative education over the past forty years" (Gottlieb 2002, 9).

Aware of many troubling aspects of social and comparative research, Paulston was deeply committed to the idea of his contribution to the field being a socially ameliorative one. He was thus committed to a critical rather than celebratory posture with regard to the several contexts relevant to his work.

> At the end of a long scholarly road, I opt to join those who willingly attempt what may seem to be an impossible task, to acknowledge the partiality of one's story (indeed, of all stories) and still tell it with authority and conviction, while mapping it into the debate field of comparative education. (2005, 2)

As much as Paulston's work influences us intellectually, he recognized the transient nature of his project: "Right now the mapping mode dominant for several centuries is undergoing what might be called a cartographic transformation. It is likely that the maps of the twenty-first century will look very different" (2000, 4). Indeed as you read on you will see, some of the words and maps in this volume are very different from Paulston's, and from each other.

REFERENCES

Federman, Raymond. (2001). *Aunt Rachel's Fur*. Normal, IL: FC2.
Gottlieb, Esther E. (1987). "Development Education: Discourse in Relation to Paradigms and Knowledge." PhD diss., School of Education, University of Pittsburgh, PA, USA.
Gottlieb, Esther E. (2000). "Are We Postmodern Yet? Historical and Theoretical Explorations in Comparative Education." In Bob Moon, Sally Brown, and Miriam Ben-Peretz (Ed.), *International Companion to Education* (pp. 153–175). London and New York: Routledge.
Gottlieb, Esther E. (2002). "On Becoming 'Post-': Questions of Canon in Comparative Education." Paper Presented at the CIES Eastern Regional Conference, Pittsburgh, PA, 1–2 November 2002.
Paulston, Rolland G. 1994. "Comparative and International Education: Paradigms and Theories." In T. Neville Postlethwaite and Torsten Husen (Ed.), *International Encyclopedia of Education* (pp. 923–933). 2nd ed. Oxford: Pergamon Press.
Paulston, Rolland G., ed. (1996). Social Cartography: *Mapping Ways of Seeing Social and Educational Change*. New York: Garland Publishing.
Paulston, Rolland G. (1998). *Mapping the Postmodernity Debate in Comparative Education Discourse. Pittsburgh, PA: School of Education, University of Pittsburgh. Working Paper Series No. SRF-1998–01. Pittsburgh: Institute for International Studies in Education, University of Pittsburgh.*
Paulston, Rolland G. (2000). "A Spatial Turn in Comparative Education? Constructing a Social Cartography of Difference." In Jürgen Schriewer (Ed.), *Discourse Formation in Comparative Education* (pp. 297–354). Frankfurt, Germany: Peter Lang.
Paulston, Rolland G. (2005). "Mapping Reality Turns in Western Thinking and Comparative Education Studies." Paper presented at the Comparative and International Education Society 49th Annual Conference, Palo Alto, CA, March 2005.
MacLure, Maggie. (2006). "'A Demented Form of the Familiar': Postmodernism and Educational Research." *Journal of Philosophy of Education, 40*(2), 223–239.

JOHN C. WEIDMAN AND W. JAMES JACOB

1. MAPPING COMPARATIVE, INTERNATIONAL, AND DEVELOPMENT EDUCATION

Celebrating the Work of Rolland G. Paulston

This volume celebrates and extends the scholarship of Rolland G. Paulston through a collection of essays and research studies reflecting the thoughtful approaches to the study of comparative education that he modeled, both literally and figuratively. Esther Gottlieb (2009), one of Paulston's former doctoral students, has written about the various dimensions of his career so we will not duplicate that here. Rather, we concentrate on his work focused on mapping concepts and scholars in the field of comparative, international, and development education (CIDE). It is our intent with this collection to carry the themes and approaches appearing in Paulston's work forward and, we hope, suggest new directions for CIDE that extend "beyond the comparative."

In the first section of this chapter, we show how his thinking evolved by identifying key aspects of the continuing conceptual development over his entire career that were reflected in his culminating work on social cartography of comparative and international education (Paulston 1977, 1993, 1994, 1996, 1999, 2000a, 2000b). We show how his perspectives and depictions changed over time from typological matrices and figures with very structured and impermeable boundaries based on relatively narrow paradigms in the social sciences, particularly sociology, to more whimsical maps with permeable boundaries and cloud formations representing multiple conceptual and methodological approaches that appear throughout the CIDE literature.

In the following section, we describe how the various chapters of this festschrift contribute to and extend the literature of CIDE in directions that reflect Paulston's encouragement of colleagues and students to expand their horizons, spread their wings, and accept the challenge to move their work into ever more fruitful areas. This included the work of both scholarship and practice, with the ever present caveat that to truly understand what is being presented for the consideration of others, comparative and international educators must also be very clear about the where they stand and what underlying assumptions are reflected in recommendations being made. We conclude with an invitation to readers to chart their own course, using a CIDE "theoretical compass" inspired by the work of Rolland Paulston.

It should be noted that Paulston was always "tweaking" his formulations and sometimes published very similar articles/chapters, including "maps" in different

John C. Weidman, W. James Jacob (eds.), Beyond the Comparative: Advancing Theory and Its Application to Practice, 1–16.

places (e.g., Paulston 1993, 1994, 1997, 2000a; Paulston and Liebman 1994, 1996, 2000). He was dedicated to disseminating his ideas during a period that just preceded the era of widespread electronic library access to print journals. Because Garland would not publish more copies of the 1996 hardback version of *Social Cartography*, he bought the rights to the book in 1999 and published a paperback version himself through the University of Pittsburgh Bookstore. The two books are identical except for the covers; hence, the two copyright dates (1996 and 2000), depending on which version is being referenced. Though Paulston did not use computers for his own work, preferring to write long-hand with a pencil, he also anticipated the importance of electronic bibliographic and textual databases, arranging to have the full text of a long chapter containing 29 figures and charts (Paulston 2000a: originally published in *Compare* in 1997) entered into the Educational Resources Information Center (ERIC) database where it is freely accessible online.

ROLLAND PAULSTON'S SOCIAL CARTOGRAPHIC JOURNEY

It is no stretch to suggest that the foundations for Paulston's abiding interest in cartography and pictorial representation were built during his undergraduate years at the University of California, Los Angeles (UCLA) where he majored in Geography and Art History as well as spending a year studying Anthropology and doing fieldwork at the University of Mexico. He earned a Master's degree in Economic Geography from the University of Stockholm and spent six years teaching social studies, three years in the Los Angeles Public Schools and three years in the American High School of Tangiers, Morocco.

He earned an EdD in Comparative Education from Teachers College, Columbia University, in 1966 and remained as a Visiting Assistant Professor and Research Associate with the Center for Education in Latin America until 1968, when he moved to the University of Pittsburgh as an Assistant Professor in the International and Development Education Program (IDEP) in the School of Education. Moving rapidly through the academic ranks, Paulston was appointed full professor in 1972. In 1975, he served as President of the Comparative and International Education Society (CIES), as had his IDEP colleagues, Don Adams (1965, then at Syracuse University), and William H. E. Johnson (1959–1960).

Theory Classification and Typological Development, 1970s

Arguably the first main phase of Paulston's work in the social cartography of CIDE took place during the 1970s. Always a voracious reader, he undertook two large literature reviews for the World Bank. The first (Paulston 1975) addressed theories of social and educational change, organizing and categorizing them according to major themes and perspectives. Not surprisingly, he also developed and taught a course in IDEP entitled, "Theories of Social and Educational Change," that endures to this day and is required of all doctoral students concentrating in CIDE at the University of Pittsburgh. The second volume for the

World Bank (Paulston 1978) extended the earlier work, this time focusing on theory and experience related to bringing about change in education systems. This work was exhaustive: the 1978 volume alone contains 527, single-spaced, 8.5" x 11" pages!

The first major journal article reporting on the conceptual frameworks Paulston developed from this work was included in a double issue of *Comparative Education Review* (1977, Vol. 21, nos. 2–3), entitled, "The State of the Art: Twenty Years of Comparative Education." In this article (Paulston 1977, Figure 1, 372–373), two overarching "paradigms" of social change—each encompassing four general "theories"—were presented: (1) Equilibrium Paradigm and Associated Theories (Evolutionary, Neo-Evolutionary, Structural-Functional, and Systems); and (2) Conflict Paradigm and Associated Theories (Marxian, Neo-Marxian, Cultural Revitalization, and Anarchistic Utopian).

Paulston elaborated this two-paradigm framework, showing how theories derived from social science disciplines, principally sociology, could be used to describe different types of educational change/reform. It should be noted that his "Figure 1" contained only text in matrix format and was structured as a table rather than a figure/chart, common labeling practice in journals of that era. When this matrix was republished two decades later (Paulston 1999, 443), it was labeled as "Table 1."

Mapping Theoretical Perspectives in Comparative Education, Early 1990s

In an autobiographical musing on his work, Paulston describes the events that culminated in his first "map" of the comparative education field:

> I went to the University of British Columbia (UBC) in Vancouver as a Visiting Professor in the summer of 1991 with the hope that a trip to the "frontier" might provoke some new ideas about representing knowledge and visualizing difference. Given the collapse of the cold war with its polarizing stories, and the emergence of provocative new ways of seeing in poststructuralist, postmodern feminist and postcolonial studies, the time seemed alive with opportunities to rethink our world, to sail off our brutal old maps . . .

> On returning to the University of Pittsburgh that Fall, I had begun to understand how a spatial turn in comparative studies would focus less on formal theory and competing truth claims and more on how contingent knowledge may be seen as embodied, locally constructed and visually represented as oppositional yet complementary positionings in shifting fields . . .

> At about this time, Don Adams invited me to write an encyclopedia entry titled, "Comparative Education: Paradigms and Theories" [Paulston, 1994]. I accepted, but with the proviso that the entry would in fact be post-paradigmatic, that is, it would use a perspectivist approach to "map" my view of increasingly complex conceptual relationships between the major discourse communities that compose the field. I presented this study, viewing

3

comparison as a juxtaposition of difference, in July 1992, at the 8th World Congress of Comparative Education Societies at Charles University in Prague with a title more to my liking, "Comparative Education Seen as an Intellectual Field: Mapping the Theoretical Landscape". (Paulston 2000a, 309–310, 312)

The resulting "map" (see Figure 1.1) of "paradigms and theories in comparative and international education texts" presented in Prague was included in several subsequent publications (Paulston 1993, 1994, 1997, 2000a; Paulston and Liebman 1994, 1996, 2000).

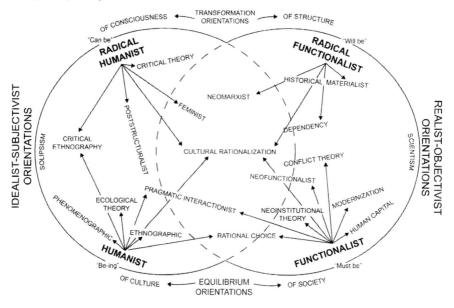

Figure 1.1. A Macromapping of Paradigms and Theories in Comparative and International Education.
Source: Reprinted from Paulston (1994, 931), with permission from Elsevier.

In this new map, Paulston moved beyond the more conventional, predominantly "objectivist" classification scheme published in his 1977 *Comparative Education Review* article, by adding a "subjectivist" dimension to the fundamentally "objectivist" dimensionality of his original two-paradigm framework. Drawing from the work of Gibson Burrell and Gareth Morgan (1979, 27), Paulston (1993, 109) elaborated his original two-paradigm classification into a four-paradigm framework that he called "a heuristic taxonomy of knowledge perspectives in comparative and international education texts."[1]

Inspired by the CIES Presidential Address by Val D. Rust (1991), he and his doctoral student, Martin Liebman, also embraced "postmodern reflection," thereby opening consideration to multiple conceptual perspectives in response what he viewed as the increasing influence of postmodernist views spanning several disciplines (Paulston and Liebman 1994, 216). Though some scholars might disagree, Paulston and Liebman (1994, 216) explained specifically that they were using postmodernism as a construct to stimulate inquiry in comparative education, opening the field to broader consideration of multiple perspectives symbolized through visual representation in conceptual maps, urging colleagues:

> to move their respective academic fields toward a postmodernist integration, to become more explicative, comparative, and open to heterogeneous orientations in their postmodern academic discourse. Postmodernism is not promoted here but, rather, the possibilities for comparative fields to expand their knowledge bases through an appropriate, thoughtful, and skillful development and application of social maps. The postmodern turn opens the way to social mapping exercises.

The resulting "map" challenged the field of comparative education by moving beyond the long-standing dominance of structural/functional perspectives. The underlying conceptual structure of this map reflected the Burrell and Morgan (1979) framework with four "root paradigms/world views." However, based on his analysis of "illustrative texts," Paulston also posited a set of "branching 'theories'" for each of the four paradigmatic constructs:

1. Functionalist ("Must be")
   - Modernisation/human capital
   - Neofunctionalist
   - Rational choice, micro-macro
   - Conflict theory

2. Radical Functionalist ("Will be")
   - Dependency
   - Historical materialist
   - Neo-Marxist, post Marxist

3. Radical Humanist ("Can be")
   - Critical theory/critical ethnography
   - Feminist
   - Post-structuralist/post-modernist

4. Humanist ("Being")
   - Pragmatic interactionist
   - Ethnographic/Ethnological
   - Phenomenographic, ethnomethodological (Paulston 1993, Table II, 109)

This map represented a significant departure from the boxed-in typological framework used by Burrell and Morgan in that the four paradigms were illustrated by two, concentric circles, into which the "branching theories" were mapped. While the external boundaries of the circles are shown as solid lines, the overlapping sections are bounded by broken lines, suggesting commonality and sharing ("communal borrowing") across theories. Paulston (1993, 106) describes this map as follows:

The four paradigmatic nodes are derived from intra-textual and cross-textual analysis. Textual dispositions regarding social and educational change (the vertical dimension) and characterisation of reality (the horizontal dimension) are the coordinates used to type and locate texts within the field. Arrows suggest the direction and extent of communal borrowing and interaction . . . . It facilitates . . . the reinscription and resituation of meanings, events and objects in the field within broader movements . . . . Comparative education is now seen as a heuristic mapping of the eclectic interweavings of knowledge communities rather than the more objectified images presented to the world in earlier foundational texts.

Metaphorical Mapping of Knowledge Positions and Communities, Mid-1990s Onward

By the latter half of the 1990s, Paulston (1999, 2000b) moved farther away from the formally structured paradigmatic views that underlay his concentric circle map of theories and texts in comparative education. He expanded his use of postmodernism as a heuristic for welcoming and embracing multiple perspectives in CIDE discourse, as shown in his cartographic representation first published in 1999 (see Figure 1.2).

Paulston seemed never to be content with the labels he used for his frameworks and continually refined and honed his descriptions of them. Consequently, when this map was republished in 2000, he added a phrase to the title ("A Web-Like Metaphorical Mapping . . . "), modified his original description of it, and issued a challenge to comparative educators (Paulston 2000b, 362):

> In this visualisation of an open intertextual field, arrows suggest intellectual flows, and proper names refer not to authors, but to illustrative texts cited in the paper and juxtaposed above. In contrast to utopias (i.e. sites with no real place) favored in modernist texts, this figure draws inspiration from Michel Foucault's notion of 'heterotopias' (Foucault, 1986, 25). These are portrayed as the simultaneously mythic and real spaces of contested everyday life. Postmodernist texts favor heterotopias, as above, because they are "capable of juxtaposing in a real place several spaces, several sites that are in themselves incompatible." Is the future of comparative education to be seen in the notion of heteropia, or utopia, or perhaps in both, or neither?

In this map, Paulston (1999, 2000b) used no fixed boundaries, employing cloud-like, irregular figures bounded by permeable, broken lines to represent each of the "knowledge positions and communities" he identified. The horizontal axis of his map showed what might be characterized as assumptions/ideologies about the nature of society, substituting "modernist certainties" for "realist-objectivist orientations" and "postmodern destabilizations" for "idealist-subjectivist orientations." The vertical axis represented the focus of inquiry and intervention, social structures ("systems problematized") or people ("actors problematized"). Within the overall space, ten "knowledge communities" were arranged in overlapping, cloud-like arrays according to their locations on the axes:

1. Modernist knowledge communities (right side of the map)
   - Metanarratives of reason, emancipation and progress
   - Rational actor gaming
   - Critical modernist appropriations
   - Reflexive modernity adaptations

2. Postmodernist knowledge communities (left side of the map)
   - Postmodernist deconstructions
   - Radical alterity
   - Semiotic society
   - Reflexive practitioner
   - Social cartography

3. "Eclectic" knowledge communities (center of the map)
   - Post paradigmatic eclecticism (Paulston 1999, 444)

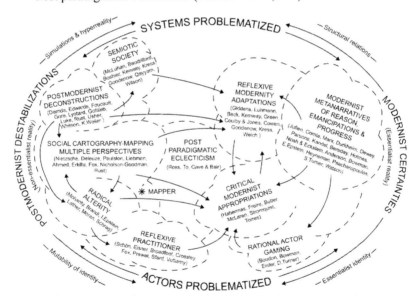

Figure 1.2. A Web-Like Metaphorical Mapping of Knowledge Positions and Communities Constructing the Postmodernity Debate in Comparative Education (and Related) Discourse.
Source: Reprinted from Paulston (1999, 445), with permission from *Comparative Education Review.*

This map represents major breakthroughs in Paulston's continually evolving conceptualization and cartographic depiction of "comparative education discourse." It illustrates the fluidity of the field and overlapping of perspectives that he had previously (Paulston, 1993) called "communal borrowing." Paulston also situates himself and posits the position of specific, representive texts on the map ("Mapper," a bit left of center), urging comparative education scholars and practitioners to be cognizant of how their own conceptual positions might influence their own work "in comparing contested realities" (Paulston, 2000b, 363).

Mapping "Representational Genres"/Methodologies in CIDE Discourse, Mid-1990s Onward

In the last of his mapping exercises, Paulston expanded his work on theoretical perspectives by considering the various forms through which they might be represented. Figure 1.3 reproduces this map (Paulston 2000b, 364).

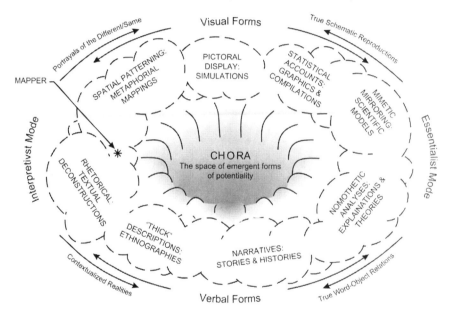

Figure 1.3. An Intertextual Mapping of Eight Representational Genres/Forms.
Source: Reprinted from Paulston (2000b, 364), with permission from *Taylor & Francis.*

In this map, the horizontal axis is an interpretivist (left side)/essentialist (right side) continuum; the vertical axis a visual (top)/verbal (bottom) continuum. At the center of this map, Paulston includes a space for new representational forms that may develop that he names "Chora: The space of emergent forms of potentiality." To him, the "chora" symbolizes the possibility (to Paulston, literally a mandate) that CIDE will be open to and welcoming of the continual evolution of new ideas and perspectives. Arrayed around the center of this map are overlapping, cloud-like formations containing different ways of representing information/data/evidence, positioned according to the underlying conceptual context.

This particular map could, in our view, also be utilized as a guide to understanding the complex linkages between theory and methodology in social science and educational research. The "visual" and "verbal" forms in the map may also be construed as representing commonly used research methodologies, with the right side (essentialist/objectivist) reflecting primarily quantitative approaches and the left side (interpretivist/subjectivist) reflecting primarily qualitative approaches. Though we are confident that Paulston would be pleased to see the continuing evolution of CIDE discourse over the past half decade, his exhortation to the field is worth repeating:

> It is now time for comparative educators (perhaps using Figures 1 ["metaphorical" map] and 2 ["intertextual" map]?) to question how our choice of ideas and forms of representation influence our views of how reality is constituted and construed, how meaning and value are created and imposed on an otherwise unruly world. (Paulston 2000b, 364)

OVERVIEW OF FESTSCHRIFT CHAPTERS IN THE CONTEXT
OF PAULSTON'S SOCIAL CARTOGRAPHY

In this section we note how each of the contributing authors in this volume add value to Paulston's notion of social cartography. They revisit, critique, and go beyond several of Paulston's seminal works. Eight chapters are included in Part I, which gives an overview and introduction to the role of social cartography in CIDE research.

In Chapter 2, Val D. Rust and Amanda Kenderes focus on defining *paradigm* as the term relates to CIDE. From a historical perspective, they note how from the natural sciences and the field of sociology, education scholars entered the paradigm discussion in the 1980s and comparative educators were among the earliest to lead this discussion. In the end, Rust and Kenderes recognize that among Paulston's greatest contributions to the literature was his commitment to allocate space through cartography to paradigmatic views of all kinds, and especially to the marginalized.

Erwin H. Epstein and Katherine T. Carroll's Chapter 3 ("Erasing Ancestry") offers a stinging critique of Martin Heideggerian-based postmodernist thought in comparative education. They argue that Paulston's call for others to pursue alternative theoretical perspectives—opening a platform for postmodernists to have a voice through social cartography—is akin to erasing decades of ancestry of comparative educationists. The chapter offers a defense of an earlier article published by Epstein and Carroll (2005) titled "Abusing Ancestors" and cautions readers of the nihilistic roots of Heideggerian postmodernism. Like Paulston, Epstein and Carroll recognize the need to prevent silencing the theoretical foundations of the comparative education field as advocated by its ancestors by encouraging open debate through critical dialogue and democratic discourse.

In Chapter 4, Richard E. Rodman presents his International Education Matrix Model as a tool for all involved in CIDE. The Matrix Model is a "self-calibrated" global positioning system that enables individuals to situate themselves and others within the greater international education community—which Rodman compares to a house with a 1,000 windows. Too often CIDE researchers act independently within their own theoretical or methodological realm; it is as if most are limited to seeing CIDE from a single window within the greater CIDE community of a 1,000 windows. Rodman argues that the Matrix Model allows individuals to break out of this isolationist tendency to recognize other perspectives and at the same time position themselves within the greater community. By breaking down the walls within the house of 1,000 windows, the CIDE community will gain greater awareness and appreciation of those with whom we work in this otherwise very diverse and multisectoral field. The Matrix Model also allows others from outside to better understand the greater CIDE community.

As part of a Comparative Education class project, W. James Jacob, Jennifer R. Crandall, Jason Hilton, and Laura Northrop examined emerging theories in CIDE in Chapter 5. Research articles from 2000 to 2010 from seven journals that focus to one degree or another on CIDE were examined for this chapter. Six emerging theories in CIDE surfaced from this literature review based upon four criteria established by the authors. After positioning each emerging theory within an adapted version of Paulston's (1993) map, Jacob and his colleagues provide a brief historical overview of each theory along with its subject of study, ontology, epistemology, and common methodologies used within each theory.

Following a call by Paulston to challenge the conventional and dare to create new ways of viewing the field of CIDE, Irving Epstein uses sports as a poignant metaphor for comparative inquiry in his Chapter 6. He draws from three social theory areas in support of this metaphor: (1) Pierre Bourdieu's concept of the social field; (2) embodiment and embodied knowledge; and (3) structure, agency, and causality. Recognizing it is not a panacea for all contexts, Epstein concludes that the sports metaphor does offer many aspects worthy of further exploration in CIDE research.

In Chapter 7, Moosung Lee and Tom Friedrich use social cartography as a research methods tool in their citation network analysis of CIES Presidential Addresses from 2000 to 2009. Spatial and structural features of social cartography are offered by the authors. They note how citation network analysis allows them to examine the sources used by individual CIES Presidents as well as the referential ties authors have with other CIES Presidents based on the citations found within their respective Presidential Addresses. Through their analysis, Lee and Friedrich depict three types of centralities in the CIES Presidential Network: degree, closeness, and betweenness. They also establish network relationships by identifying which CIES leaders connect best with others in the form of subgroups or cliques. Their chapter emphasizes the important methodological role social cartography can play in CIDE research.

In Chapter 8, Lou Sabina reflects on the works of Paulston on his current graduate studies in CIDE and also on his background as a former teacher and school principal. He describes how Paulston's social cartography is relevant for emerging scholars in CIDE. In Chapter 9, "How Can Social Cartography Help Policy Researchers?" Yukiko Yamamoto and Maureen W. McClure recognize the use of social cartography in contemporary policy analysis and research. They argue that social cartography gives a plate tectonics rationale to policy research, with four continental scholarly perspectives advocated by Paulston: technical rationalist, critical rationalist, hermeneutical constructionist, and deconstructive perspectivist. Each of these four perspectives is explored by Yamamoto and McClure with specific examples of policy framing, formation, and practice.

Six chapters comprise Part II of this volume around the theme of "Mapping Conceptual Issues in CIDE Research." Chapters 10, 11 and 12 all examine social cartography from a gender lens. Nelly P. Stromquist notes how the definition of gender has shifted over time in Chapter 10, and centers her discussion around three social cartographic concepts: space, site, and interconnection. She examines the role of gender in education, noting how schools tend to reproduce traditional societal gender norms. She also introduces from a visual standpoint the inevitable interconnections between females' private and public lives and the prominent link between women and the home (see Figures 10.1 and 10.2). Stromquist later depicts how influential local and international organizations are on public education within nation states. Her use of social cartography is depicted by size and with the intent to locate space of key actors related to gender and education.

In Chapter 11, Halla B. Homarsdottir examines the issues of equity and equality as the terms are used in key global discourses. The central focus of her chapter includes a social cartography of how these discourses relate to education policies in the local contexts of South Africa and South Sudan. Supriya Baily also advocates for greater attention to local socio-cultural contexts in her Chapter 12 titled "Trajectories of Influence." She argues that often standard education policies and practices as advocated by many international education agencies fail to take into account local contexts. In this chapter, Baily highlights the unique challenges associated with one of the most generalized marginal groups in the developing world—rural adult women. With data from a rural community in southern India, she argues that sustained and positive social change can occur only when power is given to rural women who are most marginalized. Nonformal education is one of the most practical ways to reach and empower rural adult women, and Baily introduces a power relationship map that displays education as a key element in this empowerment process.

Mina O'Dowd issues a call in Chapter 13 for the need to engage in a global project that focuses on determining whether or not comparative education is considered a stand-alone profession or not. She draws from a rich literature foundation of CIDE scholars as she stages the debate and, like Paulston and many others, cautions against exclusionary perspectives and ideologies that would seek to thwart dialogue and debate, thereby preventing alternative viewpoints from ever having a voice. She argues that there is a need for a professionalism project that allows the potential recognition of new theoretical perspectives while ensuring an academic space for diversity, especially those that have been traditionally excluded.

In Chapter 14, Gary Pluim uses social cartography to theorize and map the multitude of roles NGOs play in CIDE. He reflects on how Paulston's 1993 map

(Figure 1.1) is useful as a starting point for "plotting the roles of the great diversity of NGOs" (258). He introduces a theoretical framework of NGOs and argues NGO missions and practices can be positioned across Paulston's four primary knowledge representations (or quadrants displayed in Figure 1.1). NGOs have an important role in progressive societies, Pluim argues, but he also cautions that these organizations can also be a powerful deterrent to social progress. Being able to conceptually map NGOs is an important responsibility for policy makers, CIDE scholars and practitioners to better understand the actual contributions NGOs make to society.

Joan DeJaeghere and Lisa Vu argue for a more specific approach in explaining and understanding CIDE in Chapter 15; they argue that *transnationalism* provides the most appropriate approach. While some scholars claim transnationalism is more limited than the term *globalization*, the authors follow a more Paulstonian perspective by arguing that it provides an alternative analytic view of examining especially underrepresented and under-researched issues in CIDE. They introduce a transnationalism framework that can be used when examining the dualities or multiplicities[2] associated with diasporic groups, international organizations, and education institutions.

Part III, "Regional Perspectives of Social Cartography," is comprised of five chapters that give both case country and regional examples applying social cartography to CIDE research and practice. In Chapter 16, Sheng Yao Cheng, W. James Jacob, and Pochang Chen examine the role of social cartography from multiple regional perspectives, including East versus West, North versus South, Developed Countries versus Developing Countries and so forth. They revisit two models—Tai-Ji Model and the Education Policy Analysis Model (EPAM)— previously introduced by Jacob and Cheng (2003, 2005). The authors provide examples of how these models can be applied to CIDE research and practical purposes for policy makers and education practitioners.

Roger Boshier introduces the Maori notion of lifelong learning as a way of life in Chapter 17. He charts how in an ideal learning environment there should be a balance between learning among young and old and between formal and nonformal settings. This ideal is realized in traditional New Zealand Maori society through traditional knowledge acquisition and in more contemporary established indigenous universities or *wananga*. Boshier introduces three new figures that support his findings and in many ways expand on Paulston's (1993, 104) map of "paradigms and theories in comparative and international education texts."

In Chapter 18, Enkhjargal Adiya Diffendal and John C. Weidman examine the reverse gender gap that has existed in Mongolia, where more females than males have been enrolled in higher education since the early 1990s. Using an ethnographic approach based on face-to-face interviews, they map both the methodological process of data analysis and the results. Adiya Diffendal and Weidman describe four factors that emerged as reasons for this reverse gender gap: cultural, economic, institutional, and social. Each of these factors is closely linked to the country's transitional state from a centrally-planned to a market-oriented economy. They also argue that the decision for males not to attend higher education actually begins at a much earlier age in the primary and secondary education subsectors.

Mark Ginsburg and his colleagues in Chapter 19 report findings of a USAID-funded technical assistance project to the Zambia Ministry of Education. Ginsburg's research team focused on three questions about how much perceived progress was accomplished in the Zambian education sector from 2005 to 2009. As a team, Ginsburg and his colleagues position their research on Paulston's 1993 map (Figure 1.1) arguing that the chapter follows a functionalist paradigm by advocating a systems theory approach within the equilibrium paradigm. Ginsburg also reflects on his personal relationship as a colleague of Paulston's at the University of Pittsburgh and mentions how Paulston argued that CIDE scholars need to provide coordinates of where their research is grounded.

The concluding chapter by Shoko Yamada and Jing Liu examines research practices and emerging paradigms among Japanese comparative education scholars. Drawing largely from literature published by members of the Japan Comparative Education Society (JCES), the authors use three journals in their analysis—*Comparative Education* (*CE*) based in the UK, *Comparative Education Review* (*CER*), and the JCES-sponsored journal with the same title as the UK-based journal *Comparative Education* (*CEJ*)—to juxtapose how Japanese scholars compare with other CIDE scholars worldwide. Yamada and Liu also examine English and non-English CIDE publications written about Japan, noting that "A different language creates a different academic space" (374). They were especially interested in disseminating to a non-Japanese audience articles written in Japanese from *CEJ*. They code and map changes of Japanese comparative education scholars over time, and argue that most publications of these scholars can be grouped into two primary categories: those with a development education focus and those which focus on traditional area studies topics. In support of Paulstonian social cartography, Yamada and Liu re-issue a call for scholars to expand their borders and reconsider epistemological approaches especially from periphery, non-English CIDE perspectives.

CHARTING A COURSE: THE CIDE THEORETICAL COMPASS

Cartographers have long relied on a variety of tools to help them design the most accurate representations as possible of geographic reality. Different tools are used to establish coordinates, measure distances, and identify topography. The compass is perhaps more important than any other tool in cartography because of its innate ability to locate direction and enable mappers to establish coordinates. The compass is a tool that guides the mapper and all who use the map afterwards. A compass is reliable, tested, and able to bring a voyager through new and uncharted territory. This was the navigation tool which guided explorers and sea farers for many generations.

A compass is a tool that can also be used in social theory and social cartography in CIDE. This social compass metaphor is portrayed in Figure 1.4 as it is positioned on Paulston's (1993) concentric circle map. We call it the CIDE Theoretical

Compass. The compass metaphor is grounded firmly in the unique and rich heritage of the CIDE field and builds upon the irreplaceable foundation laid by those scholars who went before—from every region of the earth—and among whom are those listed by Epstein and Carroll as our "ancestors."

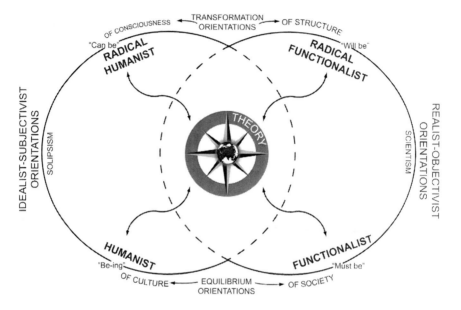

Figure 1.4. CIDE Theoretical Compass.

The CIDE Theoretical Compass has a globe at its core and the word "theory" is also shown emphasizing the need for individuals to ground their work in a theory or set of theories depending on the situation, circumstance, need, and context of their research. The CIDE Theoretical Compass can be used for *theory selection* or *theory generation*.

Theory Selection Based Upon Strategy, Need, and Context

Determining which theoretical framework is necessary to guide a research study, education reform effort, or new national education policy initiative, hinges upon the focus of the respective topic. An eclectic approach is often best because it affords individuals with the needed flexibility to select or create a theory that meets the needs of the researcher, policy maker, or education practitioner.

Charting the theoretical course is no easy task for many researchers. Graduate students often struggle to select one or more theories to guide their dissertation research. Experienced scholars may also struggle to build appropriate frameworks. Education programs or policies need periodic evaluations and theory can help guide the evaluation process. Theoretical perspectives may also provide a justification or a rationale for education practices. Following Paulston, we emphasize that researchers should situate themselves to generate an awareness of how their own perspectives influence the conclusions that might be drawn or recommendations that might be made.

The Potential for Theory Generation is a Continual Need in CIDE Research

In the absence of an existing theory to sufficiently describe a CIDE phenomenon, the CIDE Theoretical Compass can also be used to explore uncharted territory through a theory-generation process. This may entail a thorough literature review identifying theoretical gaps and detailing explanations for original thoughts and theoretical approaches. Theory generation can only exist where there simultaneously exists fertile space for alternative viewpoints. The recognition and celebration of diversity—diverse points of view, perspectives, theories, methods, ideologies, languages, cultures, identities, and peoples—are necessary for sustainable theory generation in CIDE research as well as in policy and program development.

Those who would silence diverse or alternative theoretical viewpoints in CIDE research limit the possibilities of what the field can ultimately become. We do not argue for the replacement of existing theory based on a whimsical or haphazard notion to keep CIDE research in vogue. Rather, we argue for the need for CIDE researchers to be open to use the most appropriate theoretical framework(s) for their work. In some cases this calls for theory generation. While alternative or new theories may threaten paradigmatic and conventional thought, they may also be necessary to best meet the dynamic changes occurring in education today and the unique and unforeseen challenges of tomorrow.

We encourage all those who are engaged in studying, researching, or otherwise promoting the field of comparative, international, and development education to chart a course grounded firmly in an appropriate theoretical standpoint. Where is your theoretical grounding? Do the maps presented by Paulston or others contributing to this volume provide you with sufficient space to describe your research, current policy reform initiative, administrative style, or learning philosophy? What areas of research are left uncharted on existing CIDE maps? Is a new map needed altogether? We hope the CIDE Theoretical Compass will help as you embark on your journey.

NOTES

1. Burrell and Morgan's Four Paradigms for the Analysis of Social Theory is reprinted in this volume in Val D. Rust and Amanda Kenderes' Chapter 2 (see Figure 2.1 on page 22).
2. DeJaeghere and Vu recognize that transnationalism provides alternative perspectives and a set of analytic concepts that can be used between two or more countries. In some cases "dualities" is not a sufficient term in relation to the potential space transnationalism can occupy when relating to the three categories the authors identify—migrant groups, international organizations, and education institutions. In may cases transnationalism transcends more than two countries.

REFERENCES

Burrell, Gibson, & Gareth Morgan. (1979). *Sociological Paradigms and Organisational Analysis.*Burlington, VT: Ashgate Publishing Co.

Foucault, Michel. (1986). "Of other spaces."*Diacritics,16*(1), 22–28.

Gottlieb, Esther E. (2009). " 'Somewhere better than this place/nowhere better than this place': The lifemap of Rolland G. Paulston." *Prospects, 39*(1), 91–101.

Jacob, W. James, & Sheng Yao Cheng. (2003). "Toward the Future of Education: The EPAM Approach to Educational Reform." Paper presented at the American Education Research Association National Conference, Chicago, 23 April 2003.

Jacob, W. James, & Sheng Yao Cheng.(2005). "Mapping Paradigms and Theories in Comparative, International, and Development Education (CIDE) Research." In David P. Baker and Alexander W. Wiseman (Ed.), *Global Trends in Educational Policy* (pp. 221–258). New York: Elsevier.

Paulston, Rolland G. (1975). *Conflicting Theories of Social and Educational Change.*Washington, DC: The World Bank.

Paulston, Rolland G. (1977). "Social and Educational Change: Conceptual Frameworks." *Comparative Education Review, 21*(2–3), 370–395.

Paulston, Rolland G. (1978). *Changing Education Systems: A Review of Theory and Experience.* Document RPO 671–19.Washington, DC: The World Bank.

Paulston, Rolland G. (1993). "Mapping Discourse in Comparative Education Texts."*Compare,23*(2), 101–114.

Paulston, Rolland G. (1994). "Comparative Education: Paradigms and Theories." In Torsten Husèn and T. Neville Postlethwaite (Ed.), *International Encyclopedia of Education* (pp. 923–933). New York: Elsevier Science.

Paulston, Rolland G., ed. (1996, 2000c).*Social Cartography: Mapping Ways of Seeing Social and Educational Change.* New York: Garland (1996, hardback only); Pittsburgh, PA: University of Pittsburgh Book Center (2000, paperback only).

Paulston, Rolland G. (1997). "Mapping Visual Culture in Comparative Education Discourse."*Compare,27*(2), 117–152.

Paulston, Rolland G. (1999). "Mapping Comparative Education after Postmodernity."*Comparative Education Review, 43*(4), 438–463.

Paulston, Rolland G. (2000a). "A Spatial Turn in Comparative Education?Constructing a Social Cartography of Difference."In Jürgen Schriewer (Ed.), *Discourse Formation in Comparative Education* (pp. 297–354). Frankfurt: Peter Lang. Available online at: http://www.eric.ed.gov, Accession Number: ED442711.

Paulston, Rolland G. (2000b). "Imagining Comparative Education: Past, Present, Future." *Compare,30*(2), 353–367.

Paulston, Rolland G., & Martin Liebman. (1996, 2000). "Social Cartography: A New Metaphor/Tool for Comparative Studies." In Rolland G. Paulston (Ed.), *Social Cartography: Mapping Ways of Seeing Social and Educational Change* (pp. 7–28).New York: Garland (1996, hardback only); Pittsburgh, PA: University of Pittsburgh Book Center (2000, paperback only).

Paulston, Rolland G., & Martin Liebman. (1994). "An Invitation to Postmodern Social Cartography."*Comparative Education Review, 38*(2), 215–232.

Rust, Val D. (1991)."Postmodernism and Its Comparative Education Implications."*Comparative Education Review, 35*(4), 610–626.

PART I: SOCIAL CARTOGRAPHY IN CIDE RESEARCH

VAL D. RUST AND AMANDA KENDERES

2. PAULSTON AND PARADIGMS

INTRODUCTION

Rolland G. Paulston worked for years with issues of educational and social change, non-formal and alternative education, but one of his greatest contributions was in the areas of mapping and paradigms. In doing so, Paulston wished to challenge theoretical assumptions and traditions within the field of comparative education, as well as to bring greater clarity and consciousness to the field. In this Festschrift, we intend to place Paulston within the larger academic context by exploring paradigm studies that came out of Thomas S. Kuhn's work in the social sciences, particularly sociology, in education in general, and in comparative education specifically. Paulston's work takes a creative and innovative direction that suggests he occupies a unique and exciting place in the literature of those engaged in the "paradigm dialogue"(Guba 1990).

THE PARADIGM: A MEANS OF CLASSIFICATION

There are, of course, a number of ways that ideas and objects can be classified, including simple categories, taxonomies, and classes. Some social scientists classify according to Max Weber's (1949) notion of "ideal types," a conceptual construct that serves as an instrument of research inquiry. Other social scientists rely on Michel Foucault's (1970) notion of "epistemes" that imply an underlying structure or foundation for historical inquiry. However, Paulston chose to draw largely from Kuhn's (1962) notion of paradigm. This is not entirely surprising. The impact of Kuhn was almost immediate following the publication of *The Structure of Scientific Revolutions* in 1962. Within a decade it had influenced such diverse fields as history, philosophy, theology, art and the general social sciences of sociology, political science, and anthropology (Hollinger, 1973).

While the broad concept of a paradigm is nebulous and lacks a clear definition, it remains a useful term. In fact, Egon G. Guba (1990, 17) feels its very ambiguity lends to the concept's usefulness; he claims it is most appropriate to see a paradigm as "a basic set of beliefs that guides action, whether of the everyday garden variety or action taken in connection with a disciplined inquiry." A paradigm may be considered a basic set of beliefs that guides personal and professional actions. One might thus imagine that a nuanced individual subscribes to several, perhaps dozens of paradigms, which vary by person or by circumstance. However, within the social sciences, and according to Kuhn, paradigms are usually considered

John C. Weidman, W. James Jacob (eds.), Beyond the Comparative: Advancing Theory and Its Application to Practice, 19–29.

mutually exclusive, in that they offer alternative ontological, epistemological, and metaphysical views. They are thought of as broader guiding principles or conglomerations of everything that affects how a scientific theory operates and functions. In this frame of reference, theoretical differences within a field are considered by some to be incommensurate. Erwin H. Epstein (1983) argues that within the social sciences, not only is a harmony or synthesis of individual paradigms not possible, but even a synthesis of accepted paradigms within the field is not possible, because they are based on sets of opposing meta-theoretical assumptions.

We agree with Epstein that paradigms at their broadest level may be incommensurate, but we take a more moderate position in that we believe that specific paradigms may be broadly synthesized. Furthermore, we believe it is not helpful to describe paradigms as valid or invalid, true or false, or as hypotheses of theories to be tested. Such treatment essentializes them, missing either their strengths or their weaknesses. Instead, paradigms are better described as productive, worth knowing, helpful, misleading, illuminating, or banal. Rather than highlighting truth-value, we feel the quality of a paradigm is determined by its capacity to drive discourse and shape understanding.[1]

FROM THE ABSTRACT TO THE CONCRETE: THOMAS KUHN'S PARADIGMS

According to Margaret Masterman (1970), Kuhn used the term "paradigm" in at least 21 unique ways. Despite the potential for ambiguity, however, most observers believe that Kuhn's different paradigms can be clustered around three basic categories or levels, from the abstract to the concrete. The broadest level of abstraction is at the metaphysical level, which Masterman named "metaphysical paradigms" or simply "metaparadigms." The next and more restricted category is at the theoretical level, which Masterman named "sociological paradigms." The most concrete category is at the level of what Kuhn called "exemplars."

It is at the exemplar level that Kuhn is most concerned. At this level, Kuhn (1962, 187) deals with concrete problems and their solutions, whether these are found in the laboratory or in a textbook. Physical scientists learn these exemplars in their academic studies, and they lead the science student along the path toward an understanding of a science field. Exemplars point to the theoretical and metaphysical levels to the extent that by the time the student enters the field, the contemporary world view of that field has been internalized. Kuhn identifies work at this concrete level as a type of puzzle solving, because the scientist does not challenge the basic epistemological and theoretical assumptions of the field, but attempts to solve problems and issues within the context of concrete issues.

SOCIOLOGY: A STARTING POINT

To understand Paulston's adaptation of Kuhn's paradigms within comparative education, it is helpful to look at comparative education as an outgrowth of education; and before education, sociology; as influenced by the natural sciences, where many educational paradigms emerged. As an historian of science, Thomas Kuhn focused on the way scientific knowledge is created and how it changes. We have noted that Kuhn believed most scientific knowledge creation is little more than "puzzle solving," because the scientist does not challenge the underlying paradigm but instead attempts to fill in the missing knowledge within the confines of a particular paradigm. In other words, pre-formed paradigms are given to scientists and they work comfortably within the theories, the ontological assumptions, and the approved practices and traditions of the science.

Kuhn's focus of attention was reserved to the natural sciences. He believed that a natural science community works within a single pervasive paradigm at a time, and Masterman (1970) agrees. Of course, when a scientific revolution occurred, that paradigm would temporarily break down, until a new paradigm came to dominate the field. The notion of the natural sciences as single-paradigm sciences created difficulty for the social sciences, as the social sciences in many ways looked to the natural sciences for direction to shape their legitimacy. Still, however attractive Kuhn's single-paradigm science may have been to the field of sociology, sociologists have never gained consensus in their field.

Perhaps the closest sociologists came to consensus in their theoretical orientation was the widespread acceptance of structural functionalism, or simply functionalism. It was identified with scholars such as Emile Durkheim, Herbert Spencer, and Auguste Comte, who assumed the social world is composed of concrete tangible artifacts and relationships. Through a functionalist lens, sociology was viewed as a scientific enterprise and social facts were believed to exist outside human consciousness. These facts could be measured, counted, compared, and analyzed, and in the minds of some scholars, the sociological enterprise was to be dedicated almost exclusively to this end.

However strong the effort was to craft sociology as a single-paradigm science, the reality is that sociology has never been completely dedicated to a single paradigm. Although in the first decades following World War II functionalism had come close to exercising an orthodox control over the discipline's research and publication agenda, the academic crisis of the late 1960s and 1970s brought with it challengers to this orthodoxy. The major challengers were those who espoused a "social conflict" approach, which is a macro-paradigm; those who focused on a micro-paradigm were advocates of symbolic interactionism.

By 1970, Alvin Gouldner (1970) recognized that sociology as a field was fragmenting, and he wrote an entire book emphasizing the coming crisis in Western sociology. That same year Robert Friedrichs (1970) attempted to broaden the context of the field by arguing that sociology was a "multi-paradigm science." That label is now best identified with George Ritzer (1975) who challenged Friedrich's definition of a paradigm; however, Ritzer also argued in 1975 that sociology is indeed a "multi-paradigm science."

As the sociology orthodoxy splintered, it became important to find a more appropriate mechanism to form an intellectual map of the field. Ritzer argued that even though sociology was multi-paradigmatic in nature, it was necessary to make connections between the paradigms; otherwise, the field could never maintain its coherence as a discipline.

In 1979, Douglas Lee Eckberg and Lester Hill (1979) published a study where they identified twelve sets of sociological paradigms, although none of them focused on Kuhn's primary interest in exemplars, puzzle solving, or normal science. Instead, these paradigms were all appropriately connected with what Masterman had called "sociological paradigms."

Gibson Burrell, a sociologist in Great Britain, and Gareth Morgan, a sociologist in Canada, were the first scholars who attempted to create a schema for overcoming the sources of confusion. In the process of developing a mechanism to map the theoretical landscape of sociology, they created an analytic tool that would serve the discipline and influence scholars such as Paulston (Burrell and Morgan, 1979). Though Burrell and Morgan's 1979 book, *Sociological Paradigms and Organisational Analysis,* failed to deal with exemplars, it went beyond the established sociological categories and attempted to place sociological theories within a metaparadigm context. It also set the stage for the debates that followed. Burrell and Morgan's map (see Figure 2.1) consisted of a two-dimensional matrix having an x-axis and a y-axis.

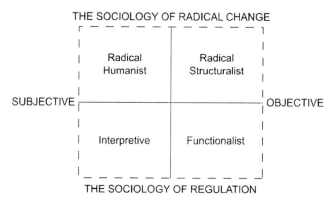

Figure 2.1. Four Paradigms for the Analysis of Social Theory.
Source: Reprinted from Burrell and Morgan (1979, 27), with permission from Ashgate Publishing Co.

The x-axis had a "subjective-objective" dimension, reflecting the extremes of philosophical assumptions related to ontology, epistemology, and methodology. The y-axis had a "regulation-radical change" dimension, reflecting the suggested ways sociologists looked at the nature of society. This matrix formed four quadrants and the authors gave each of these the descriptive titles: Radical Humanist, Interpretive, Radical Structuralist, and Functionalist.

According to Burrell and Morgan, each of the quadrants reflected a special metaparadigm within sociology. The Functionalist paradigm had dominated the field for some time until it began to fragment. Adherents of the Functionalist paradigm assumed rational human action and the ability of social scientists to understand and study society through empirical research. The Radical Structuralist paradigm represented the so-called conflict orientation that had been fundamental to followers of Marx, Engels, and Lenin, although conflict was also identified with scholars such as Ralf Dahrendorf (1957), who are advocates of participatory democracy. The Radical Humanist Paradigm was largely anti-organizational and challenged the claim that positivism is the only means toward knowledge production. Its advocates also favor radical social change, because the contemporary world is seen to constrain human potential and development. The Interpretive paradigm reflected the desires of those who did not wish to change cultures but to explain its stable and consistent dimensions. Researchers in this paradigm try to understand individual behavior within the context of behavioral and spiritual dimensions of cultures.

EDUCATION ENTERS THE PARADIGM CONVERSATION

Educationists were not among the first people outside the natural sciences to engage in the paradigm conversation. Jane Rolland Martin (1981) was among the first educationists to make reference to paradigms. She considered certain paradigms within the context of liberal education to be akin to "normal science." In the same volume where Martin's comments are found, D. C. Phillips (1981) likens a paradigm to a form of community life, where members feel a kinship with their philosophical position, just as members of a political party feel a community kinship. At that time, the intellectual community within the field of education was leaning toward positivism or empiricism.

Thomas Popkewitz (1984) published a study in 1984, where he declared that positivism indeed did not dominate the field of education. Instead, he outlined three fundamentally different paradigms in education: (1) the empirical/analytic paradigm that models itself after the physical sciences; (2) the symbolic paradigm that borrows from psychology and the social sciences, and (3) the critical paradigm that relies on political and ideological underpinnings to examine social reality. Educational scholars such as Guba (1990) soon joined the attack on positivism by pushing the constructivist paradigm as an antidote to conventional science.

The major contribution to the general paradigm conversation among educators came from the "Alternative Paradigms Conference" in 1989 under the sponsorship of Phi Delta Kappa International, a prominent educational association. The major product of this conference was Guba's (1990) *The Paradigm Dialog*, which revisited the work of Burrell and Morgan.

Echoing our previous sentiments, Guba believed each paradigm put forward by an educationist must be seen as neither true nor false, and the task is not to determine which will win out. Rather, the task is to understand each paradigm with the expectation that we become more informed and sophisticated about the total educative process (Guba 1990, 27). In his concluding remarks to the conference, Guba sounds much like Paulston as he assures us that although confusion remains rampant in the field, a fruitful dialogue is now possible. He further encourages readers to remain open to alternative paradigms and to laud the decline in confrontationalism.

COMPARATIVE EDUCATION ENTERS THE PARADIGM CONVERSATION

In his 1992 discussion of mapping, Paulston pointed out that comparative educators were among early educationists who were actively discussing issues related to paradigms, though they did not use the term until the 1980s. Scholars such as C. Arnold Anderson, for example, argued that the field should be similar to what we would describe as a "single-paradigm science," in that, like sociology, structural functionalism should dominate the comparative and international education texts (Paulston 1992, 29). Perhaps the most prominent 1980s article among comparative educators was Brian Holme's "Paradigm Shifts in Comparative Education," published in 1984. Holmes argues against the inductive approach of comparative educators, who were drawing on inductivist people such as Aristotle (1924) in attempts to make the field scientific. Holmes (1984) instead draws on Karl Popper (1963) to maintain that the field ought to turn more actively to the hypothetico-deductive methodological approach to research. In this regard, Holmes echoes the concerns of educationists more than the sociologists.

Other comparative educators relied on notions of paradigms to frame their own special interests in the field. Don Adams (1988), for example, drew from paradigms to contrast models of educational planning and to determine when each is appropriate. While he recognizes that the so-called rational model of educational planning dominates the field and he recognizes that this model is appropriate in some cases, he believes it is ill-advised to advocate for it in most cases, as most require what he calls interactive models of planning.

Paulston (1992) entered into the dialogue through mapping the theoretical landscape of comparative education which he presented at the World Congress of Comparative Education at Charles University in Prague, Czechoslovakia, from July 8–14.[2] A year later this paper was published in *Compare* (Paulston 1993). In the original paper he is somewhat historically minded in that he traces the shifting representations of knowledge in comparative education as an academic field of study as it moved from what he called "orthodoxy" following World War II, to "heterodoxy" in the 1970s, then to "emergent heterogeneity" toward the end of the 1980s. This represented a compelling effort to provide some historical context for the contemporary intellectual communities in comparative education. He then launched into a description of four contemporary intellectual communities that represent "four major root paradigms or worldviews," which, drawing from the work of Burrell and Morgan, he identifies as functionalist, radical functionalist, radical humanist, and humanist. Comparative educators since this time have also relied on the map developed by Burrell and Morgan, including Raymond A. Morrow and Carlos Alberto Torres (1995) in their study of *Social Theory and Education*.

PAULSTON'S PARADIGMS: MAPPING COMPARATIVE EDUCATION

As Paulston mapped cognitively the theories that dominate the field, he was aware that comparative education researchers ground their studies on a large number of different theories that span across the full range of social science disciplines, including political science, economics, anthropology, and particularly sociology.

Paulston recognized that the theoretical landscape of the field was so complex that anyone trying to grasp it was thrown into a tangled mess that promised frustration and likely failure. Researchers at UCLA surveyed authors of studies published in the *Comparative Education Review, Comparative Education*, and the *International Journal of Educational Development*, and identified 26 theories on which authors relied in their studies (Henrickson et al., 2003).[3] Paulston set out to classify the theories dominating the field in such a way that they could be clustered into a simple set of subgroups and anyone wanting to understand the theoretical landscape could at least grasp the basic characteristics of the subgroup to which a given theory belonged. Such a process, according to Paulston (1992), not only makes the theoretical landscape more understandable, but it gives marginal theories visibility and a more prominent place in the field.

UNIQUE CONTRIBUTIONS OF PAULSTON

While Paulston was not the first comparative educationist to address the use of paradigms within comparative education, his efforts have uniquely contributed to the paradigm debate, influencing scholars at the time of his publications and presentations and undoubtedly influencing those to come. In discussing Paulston's greatest contributions, we might synthesize his contributions related to paradigms into three broad categories: (1) dialogue, (2) dimensionality, and (3) inclusion.

1. Dialogue: Keeping the Discussion Open

Whereas many scholars argue that paradigms are so incommensurate that people talk past each other, Paulston was a firm believer in dialogue. That is, a discursive activity is a process where people having different points of view begin to discuss their differences and how to resolve them. It is a kind of puzzle-solving activity. The paradigm offers an explanation of something, and the problem for the researcher is to fill in the details. In this way, a paradigm both creates the possibility of a puzzle or question, and facilitates its resolution. Of course, Paulston is not unique in the position he takes. We might characterize his position as postfoundational or postmodern. While modernism is characterized by fragmentation, differentiation, and isolation of various discursive activities, then poststructuralism may be seen to aim at "de-differentiation" of domains. There is a kinship in thinking about poststructural deconstruction between Habermas, Rorty, and Lyotard in that they all concentrate on a dialogical process. However, Habermas differs with the neopragmatists and the poststructuralists in that he wishes dialogue to result in consensus, of members of a rational community of humankind working to understand each other and come to agreement (Habermas, 1984 and 1987). Richard Rorty (1980, 387) expresses a commitment to dialogue when he sees a sufficient aim of philosophy to be to "keeping a conversation going," and to see wisdom as consisting in the ability to sustain a conversation.

Jean-François Lyotard (1984, 55–56) also recommends dialogue but rejects the notion that the aim of dialogue ought to be consensus. He notes that the very heterogeneity of language, "the lack of a common idiom, makes consensus impossible." The very heteronomous nature of language and linguistic rules means that there is no universal discourse underlying different language games. Discussion does not have a single finality, even though "it refines our sensitivity to differences and reinforces our ability to tolerate the incommensurable" (xxv).

The dialogic process is significant in that the surface disagreements of theorists such as Habermas, Rorty, and Lyotard are set against the backdrop of a great deal of agreement. It is within this agreement that we might find the basis for ethical sensibility which appears to be neither a question of taste nor upbringing nor exhibits the heavy-handedness of absolutist moral imperatives. Paulston (1992, 18) has pointed the way away from orthodoxy toward a world where "no one knowledge community can now claim a monopoly of truth or to fill all intellectual space." We live in a world where different points of view complement each other and fill in holes that a single point of view fails to fill.

2. Dimensionality: Irregularity of Maps

Paulston found the metaparadigms of people such as Burrell and Morgan to be helpful, but he was uneasy with the "boxiness" of their construct. He was more comfortable with irregularity and movement, preferring to forgo sweeping conclusions if it ignored conflicting details. His initial map was a step away from that boxiness, in that it consisted of overlapping circles that suggested shifting theoretical orientations.

He was most comfortable with maps looking something like an island with an irregular shore-line and landscapes that indicated mountains and valleys. Of course, such a map would have coordinates indicating axes similar to north-south and east-west coordinates. The special feature of these coordinates in Paulston's maps was that they were somewhat like a Cartesian coordinate system, which indicates how far away from the center point any single point is. In contrast, the Burrell and Morgan map showed four unique quartiles without gradations in the paradigms. Paulston recognized that along each of the four lines in a two-dimensional map, the paradigms became more and more extreme as it progressed outward along the line. Conversely, as the lines converged the paradigms became more and more similar. In addition, the paradigms overlapped each other at the point of convergence creating, in Paulston's estimation, an impossible, or at least a contrived, reality.

We might illustrate Paulston's response to this concern by looking at the horizontal line of Paulston's map. At the one extreme to the left one finds "solipsism," and at the other extreme on the right, one finds "scientism." Along this line moving from left to right, one could identify Idealism, Pragmatism, Neo-Realism, and Naturalism. Each of these theoretical positions has its own metaphysical, epistemological, and axiological characteristics. That is, Idealism (consciousness is primary) has quite different metaphysical assumptions than does Pragmatism (experience is all there is), or Neo-Realism (both mind and matter exist) and Naturalism (everything is physical matter). One could identify similar shifting characteristics for epistemology and axiology.

As a consequence, Paulston located the various theories found in the field of comparative education on different places in his map, suggesting a more subtle configuration than the stark four-paradigm image created by Burrell and Morgan.

3. Inclusion: A Place for Marginalized Theories

Another crucial contribution Paulston can be said to have made is to give marginal theories visibility in the field. Whereas proponents of orthodoxy attempted to suppress theoretical competitors, Paulston refuses to judge one or another theory as worthy or unworthy of consideration. All theories are worthy of being noted and seen, and, as we have witnessed with structuralism and positivism, no one theory is safe and secure in its place in a field. No one worldview can claim to provide all the knowledge in the dialogue.

Paulston advocates a sense of goodwill among those readers of texts in the field, in that each point of view be taken seriously. He agrees with Torsten Husén (1988), who pointed out that no single paradigm can answer all questions; he believed worldviews complement each other and ought to be respected. His position is supported by Robert Cowen (1996), who argues for a more inclusive comparative education that goes beyond traditional issues and even includes poststructuralism and transitology.

Paulston could easily join with Michael Crossley (1990), a comparative education ethnographer, who argues that the "paradigm wars" be replaced by generous inclusivity. Still, much work needs to be done to overcome the theoretical and methodological separations and disparities found in the field. Paulston laments the contentious divisions in the field, particularly those representing differing disciplines and their respective methodologies. For Paulston, these divisions are not seen as the problem; rather, their presence provides a unique opportunity for comparative educators. He would join with Ronald Price (2003), who claims "It is here that comparative education, drawing on all of these disciplines but bound by none of them, offers the opportunity to discuss the real world as the whole that it is. To those who have argued the difficulty of being familiar with more than one or a few disciplines, I would counter with the difficulty of breaking out of conceptual frameworks once learned and the identification and avoidance of the game-playing nature of so much of academic disciplinary activity."

Paulston would react sympathetically to the argument of Robert F. Arnove and Carlos Alberto Torres (2003) in their edited book *Comparative Education: The Dialectic of the Global and the Local*—a primary textbook for courses in comparative education—about the importance of dialogue between various perspectives, particularly in the context of globalization forces at work in interaction with national and local forces.

Most scholars are passionate about the points of view they profess and we all tend to take our positions to some extreme limit that discounts the value and importance of other views. However, every point of view provides but a partial picture of society, and if we wish to gain perspective we must consider the virtues of those things that may challenge our particular bias and understanding. Our various commitments at times cause us to exaggerate the value of our own position and to understate the importance of those who may have other perspectives.

CONCLUSION

We have looked at Rolland Paulston's cognitive mapping of comparative education. The basic paradigms laid out in Paulston's map are derived directly from the work of social scientists, who themselves were attempting to map the social sciences through paradigms. Paulston's major contribution to the field is the creative and innovative direction he takes that gives him a special place in the literature. It is important to continue the dialogue among those professing specific paradigms, of mapping that allows for subtle gradations and variation of points of view, and the value of creating a place to highlight and recognize marginalized theories in the field of comparative education.

NOTES

1. Max Weber (1949) claimed his *ideal types* were very similar, in that their value lay in their capacity to drive discourse rather than to be proven true or false.
2. The senior author of this chapter attended that session and interacted actively with Paulston in subsequent years concerning his work. Perhaps the major publication to come out of this work was the 2000 edited book: *Social Cartography: Mapping Ways of Seeing Social and Educational Change* (Paulston 2000).
3. In Paulston's 1992 paper, he places 21 branching theories in his intellectual map of the field.

REFERENCES

Adams, Donald K. (1988). "Extending the Educational Planning Discourse: Conceptual and Paradigmatic Explorations." *Comparative Education Review, 32*(4), 400–415.
Aristotle. (1924). *Metaphysics*. Oxford: Clarendon Press.
Arnove, Robert F., & Carlos Alberto Torres, eds. (2003). *Comparative Education: The Dialectic of the Global and the Local*. 2nd ed. Lanham, MD: Rowman and Littlefield Publishers.
Burrell, Gibson, & Gareth Morgan. (1979). *Sociological Paradigms and Organisational Analysis*. Burlington, VT: Ashgate Publishing Co.
Cowen, Robert. (1996). "Last Past the Post: Comparative Education, Modernity, and Perhaps Post-Modernity." *Comparative Education, 32*(2), 151–170.
Crossley, Michael. (1990). "Collaborative Research, Ethnography and Comparative and International Education in the South Pacific." *International Journal of Educational Development, 10*(1), 37–46.
Dahrendorf, Ralf. (1957). *Class and Class Conflict in an Industrial Society*. London: Routledge and Kegan Paul.
Eckberg, Douglas Lee, & Lester Hill, Jr. (1979). "The Paradigm Concept and Sociology: A Critical Review." *American Sociological Review, 44*(6), 925–937.
Epstein, Erwin H. (1983). "Currents Left and Right: Ideology in Comparative Education." *Comparative Education Review, 27*(1), 3–29.
Foucault, Michel. (1970). *The Order of Things: An Archeology of the Human Sciences*. New York: Random House.
Friedrichs, Robert W. (1970). *A Sociology of Sociology*. New York: Free Press.

Gouldner, Alvin W. (1970). *The Coming Crisis of Western Sociology*. London: Heinemann.

Guba, Egon G. (1990). *The Paradigm Dialog*. Newbury Park, CA: Sage Publications.

Habermas, Jürgen. (1984 & 1987). The Theory of Communicative Action, trans. Thomas McCarthy. (Vol. 1: Reason and the Rationalization fo Society was published in 1984; Vol. 2: *Lifeworld and System: A Critique of Functionalist Reason was published in 1987*). Cambridge, MA: MIT Press.

Henrickson, Leslie., Steve Faison., & Val, D. Rust. (2003). "Theory in Comparative Education." *World Studies in Education*, 4(1), 5–28.

Hollinger, David A. (1973). "T. S. Kuhn's Theory of Science and its Implications for History." *The American Historical Review*, 78(2), 370–393.

Holmes, Brian. (1984). "Paradigm Shifts in Comparative Education." *Comparative Education Review*, 28(4), 584–604.

Husén, Torsten. (1988). "Research Paradigms in Education." *Interchange*, 19(1), 2–13.

Kuhn, Thomas S. (1962). *The Structure of Scientific Revolutions*. 2nd ed. Chicago: University of Chicago Press.

Lyotard, Jean-François. (1984). *The Postmodern Condition: A Report on Knowledge*, trans. G. Bennington and B. Massumi. Minneapolis, Minnesota: University of Minnesota Press.

Martin, Jane Roland. (1981). "Needed: A New Paradigm for Liberal Education." In Jonas F. Soltis. (Ed.), *Philosophy and Education: Eightieth Yearbook of the National Society for the Study of Education* Chicago: University of Chicago Press.

Masterman, Margaret. (1970). "The Nature of a Paradigm." In Imre Lakatos &Alan Musgrave (Ed.), *Criticism and the Growth of Knowledge* (pp. 59–89). Cambridge, UK: Cambridge University Press.

Morrow, Raymond A., & Carlos Alberto Torres. (1995). *Social Theory and Education: A Critique of Theories of Social and Cultural Reproduction*. Albany, NY: State University of New York Press.

Paulston, Rolland G. (1992). "Comparative Education as an Intellectual Field: Mapping the Theoretical Landscape." Paper presented at the VIIIth World Congress of Comparative Education, Prague, Czechoslovakia, 8–14 July 1992.

Paulston, Rolland G. (1993). "Comparative Education as an Intellectual Field: Mapping the Theoretical Landscape." *Compare*, 23(2), 101–114.

Paulston, Rolland G. ed. (2000). *Social Cartography: Mapping Ways of Seeing Social and Educational Change*. Pittsburgh: University of Pittsburgh Book Center.

Phillips, D. C. (1981). "Post-Kuhnian Reflections on Educational Research." In Jonas F. Soltis (Ed.), *Philsophy and Education: Eightieth Yearbook of the National Society for the Study of Education*, (pp. 237–261). Chicago: University of Chicago Press.

Popkewitz, Thomas S. (1984). *Paradigm and Ideology in Educational Research: The Social Functions of the Intellectual*. London: Falmer Press.

Popper, Karl R. (1963). *Conjectures and Refutations: The Growth of Scientific Knowledge*. New York: Harper and Row.

Price, Ronald F. (2003). "Comparative Education Redefined?" In Edward R. Beauchamp (Ed.), *Comparative Education Reader*, New York: RoutledgeFalmer.

Ritzer, George. (1975). *Sociology: A Multiple Paradigm Science*. Boston, MA: Allyn and Bacon.

Rorty, Richard. (1980). *Philosophy and the Mirror of Nature*. Princeton, NJ: Princeton University Press.

Weber, Max. (1949). The Methodology of the Social Sciences, trans. Edward A. Shils and Henry A. Finch. New York: Free Press.

ERWIN H. EPSTEIN AND KATHERINE T. CARROLL

3. ERASING ANCESTRY

A Critique of Critiques of the Postmodern Deviation
in Comparative Education

There always comes a time in history when the person who dares to say that two plus two equals four is punished with death.

And the issue is not what reward or what punishment will be the outcome of that reasoning. The issue is simply whether or not two plus two equals four. (Albert Camus 1975)

Rolland G. Paulston energetically responded to Val D. Rust's 1991 call for the implementation of postmodern theories in comparative education and for fostering studies that applied these emerging concepts and techniques (Rust 1991). He nurtured and encouraged young practitioners to develop their expertise to incorporate postmodern positions and processes in comparativist publications. However, while Paulston's project honored the tradition followed by many scholars before him of including new theoretical constructs in academic disciplines, we showed in an article entitled "Abusing Ancestors" that appeared in the *Comparative Education Review* (Epstein and Carroll 2005) that the intent of the postmodern process carries with it the very elements that will erase the openness, rational discourse, and free exchange of ideas that have characterized the field and Western scholarship for decades.

In the present chapter, we first examine a series of oppositional peer reviews that obscured key elements of our analysis in "Abusing Ancestors" as that article was still in manuscript form and being evaluated for publication. Those peer reviews and our refutation of them appeared in "Samples of Decision Letters and Reviewer Reports 2003–2009" issued by the editors of the *Comparative Education Review* (Editors 2009, 13–42), and we present them in this work with the permission of those editors. We next respond to the positioning and artifice that invoke Paulston and "social cartography" in two challenges to our earlier critique of postmodernism. Finally, we discuss the profoundly deceptive process—the deconstruction project of Martin Heidegger—and the tie of that process to Paulston's call for a "postmodern surge," together with implications of that tie for eliminating the self-cognitive "subject" and associated, fundamental attributes that are the architecture of a democratic culture. As we query whether Heideggerian thought is of conceptual value to comparative education—or, indeed, to any

John C. Weidman, W. James Jacob (eds.), Beyond the Comparative: Advancing Theory and Its
Application to Practice, 31–48.

scholarly field, we turn to the insights of Albert Camus, whose understanding of universal values kept his vision steadfast at a time of great peril to his country and the world.

INACCURACY, MISUNDERSTANDING, TRENDINESS:
COMPARATIVE EDUCATION REVIEW (CER)

In his 1982 Presidential Address (Epstein 1983), and in a follow-up essay (Epstein 1987), the senior author of the present chapter noted the introduction of phenomenology and a growing relativism in comparativist work and described insufficiencies of these approaches for comparative education studies. In later years, he continued this direction of inquiry and observed that more extreme forms of relativism and post-structuralist ideation had increasingly appeared in the field's publications. The authors of the present chapter then collaborated on the "Abusing Ancestors" manuscript and submitted it for consideration in early 2003 to the *Comparative Education Review*. The submission of "Abusing Ancestors" followed the presentation of our paper, "Understanding Ancestors: Foundations of Comparative Thought," at the 2001 annual meeting of the Comparative and International Education Society in Washington, DC. In "Understanding Ancestors," we outlined the deficits in postmodern foundational thought, identifying the source of error in Martin Heidegger's concepts of "Being" and *aletheia*, a Greek term for "revealing" or "disclosure"—interpreted by Heidegger as "truth"— that had been embraced by Rolland Paulston and others in Paulston's 1996 edited book, *Social Cartography: Mapping Ways of Seeing Social and Educational Change*. Indeed, in his earlier study, "An Invitation to Postmodern Social Cartography," written with Martin Liebman, Paulston asserted that comprehending Heidegger's use of *aletheia* and "the primordial, prereflective realm" afforded by Heidegger's interpretation of *dichtung*, or a saying, were indispensible to "the visual language," represented by social cartography that "inaugurates a world" (Paulston and Liebman 1994, 217, f.n. 8 and 218, f.n. 9; see also Paulston and Liebman 1996, 9; and Epstein and Carroll 2005, 73–75). Importantly, *aletheia*—the unveiling or unconcealment of truth—and *dichtung,* used as "it speaks," were foundational interpretations to Heidegger's own deconstructing project, introduced in his 1927 lectures, and were critically important to the thought of Michel Foucault and Jacques Derrida, whom Paulston and others liberally invoke (Carroll 2008, 29–32). Paulston's 1996 *Social Cartography* anthology included essays extolling the value of a postmodern approach in comparative education as well as his social cartography "map" to situate ideas in the field.

In our "Abusing Ancestors" study, we examined both "ancestors" in the field of comparative education and the "ancestors" from whom key postmodernist theorists derived their fundamental positioning. We noted that Heideggerian interpretations of the "self" and of "knowing" were foundational to postmodern constructs and took Paulston to task for integrating these constructs into comparative education. By the time our "Abusing Ancestors" critique was published in the *Comparative Education Review* in 2005, Paulston's *Social Cartography* had become an influential text, inspiring the inclusion in numerous comparativist studies of the ideas of Michel Foucault, Jacques Derrida, Jean-François Lyotard, Jean Baudrillard, and other theorists associated with postmodernism.

In "Abusing Ancestors" we extended our analysis of Heidegger as the central influence in the development of postmodern structures of thought. Our research identified Heidegger's opposition to rational thought, brought forward from Wilhelm Dilthey and the fundamental, anti-rational Idealism of Johannes Herder and Friedrich Schleiermacher, as key to Heidegger's disengagement from the conceptual foundations of Western rational and empirical approaches. We emphasized that this formulation of anti-rational ideation, pervasive throughout Paulston's *Social Cartography*, could serve to dissolve prior structures of analysis in comparative education and beyond.

Heidegger presented his "de-constructing" project as a tool to "uncover Being" in a set of lectures that he gave in 1927. In "Abusing Ancestors," we examined frameworks of thought in Heidegger's lectures and writings when he was a National Socialist rector and educator at the University of Freiburg, Germany and showed that his political and philosophical positioning were later embraced by Hans-Georg Gadamer and the "Big Four" in postmodern thought—Michel Foucault, Jacques Derrida, Jean-François Lyotard, and Jean Baudrillard. However, several of the *CER* reviewers, prior to publication of our manuscript, vigorously opposed our analysis (and implicitly also the challenges that had been made to the credibility of postmodern thought in the late 1980s and throughout the 1990s by, among others, Victor Farías [1989], Hugo Ott [1993], and Johannes Fritsche [1999]), showing Heidegger's integration of Nazi ideation in his philosophical interpretations. In their criticism of our analysis of Heidegger's embrace of National Socialism and the impact of that embrace on postmodernism, these reviewers asserted that Heidegger's membership in the Nazi party and his appointment as university rector by the National Socialist regime had no relationship to his philosophical constructions. One reviewer viewed our inclusion of Heidegger's early membership in the Nazi party (which Heidegger never recanted, even to the time of his death in 1976) as an *ad hominem* attack—as though Nazi party membership was akin to casual, indifferent participation in politics. Moreover, one reviewer asserted that our cautious examination of Heidegger's stated purpose to "prepare the way" for the assimilation of Wilhelm Dilthey's method of removing language obstacles to a prepredicative "entering into" of primordial, ontological Being had no analytical relevance to Heidegger's influence on postmodernism. This assessment reflected that reviewer's disinterest in Dilthey's importance in historiographic and sociological studies, his impact in comparative education, and, by way of Heidegger, his influence on Rolland Paulston. Heidegger's foundational use of *aletheia* as the "opening out" and the "unconcealment" of "truth," inserted in Paulston's configuration of social cartography, followed directly from Heidegger's intentional borrowing of Dilthey's process.

While the majority of the reviewers viewed our epistemological analysis as useful to the field overall, the *CER* editors embraced some of the reviewers' more vigorous objections. Though most of the differences between the critics and us were resolved as we neared the end of the revision process, the editors insisted that Heidegger's ideas could not "provide the explanation for why Heidegger remained committed to Hitler's project." In the final letter of acceptance of the manuscript for publication, the issue of Heidegger's cooperation with the regime was seen as tangential, and the editors maintained that the connection we made between Heidegger's Nazi political affiliation and his plausible influence on postmodernist writings in comparative education must be removed. In addition, due to an apparent lack of space, the full analysis of the structures of Heidegger's and Dilthey's thought—the epistemological heart of our piece—was eliminated in the final "tracked" version of the manuscript. A severely edited version of the analysis appeared in the final article in the February, 2005 issue of the *Comparative Education Review*, though our full discussion was featured in Katherine Carroll's 2008 book, *Does Postmodernism Compare? An Analysis of the Use of Postmodern Constructs in Comparative Education Studies*. In this study, Carroll found that, excluding social constructivism and postcolonial analysis, approximately one third of the articles published in leading comparative education journals included postmodern analytical constructs and references. In other words, Paulston's and others' ambition for these directions of thought to be embraced as analytical tools in the field was gradually being realized.

The reviewers of our manuscript for the most part believed that we overplayed the connection between Heidegger's Nazism and his philosophy, which was foundational in much of postmodernism as used by comparativists. However, the reviewers also displayed a deficiency in their knowledge of intellectual history and of major developments in comparative education, reflecting a disjunct in the knowledge they displayed. Most of all, they seemed unaware not only of Heidegger's Nazi-influenced legacy, but also of the Nazi incursion directly into the field of comparative education itself. In one of our revised versions, we described the harrowing clash with Nazi depradation experienced by Friedrich Schneider, founding editor of the *International Education Review* (*IER*), the first globally accepted journal in comparative education. Schneider had founded the *IER* in 1930 in Cologne, Germany. Paul Monroe, from Columbia University, joined Schneider as co-editor in 1931, and the joint venture was heralded as demonstrating international cooperation and great promise. Yet, within a few short years, the Hitler regime replaced Schneider with Nazi ideologue Alfred Baümler, so that for a decade beginning in 1934 the *IER* came under the influence of Nazi writers like Ernst Kreick. It is ironic that the epistemological premises and virulent program of thought of the man who sought to be the "spiritual Führer" would gain influence in Comparative Education fifty years later, through postmodernism and social cartography. (For references to Heidegger as "spiritual Führer," see Faye 2009, 146-147, 212, 220-221, 241-242.)

In response to reviewers' recommendations, the *CER* editors insisted that some important ideas and historical elements contained in our early drafts be excised. Clearly, the editors had succumbed to current trends of thought and the sensibilities of a vocal section of the comparative education community. We therefore take this opportunity to do what we could not do in "Abusing Ancestors": challenge the epistemological platform on which postmodern views, as advanced by Paulston and others, generally rest. We do so by engaging in a disputation with post-publication critics of "Abusing Ancestors."

ANALYSIS OF CRITIQUES

The Critique of Patricia A. Lather and Julie L. Clemens

We turn first to the critique of our work by Patricia A. Lather and Julie L. Clemens (2010), who discuss comparative education's willingness to incorporate Derridean techniques in writing and practice. They assert that while we (Epstein and Carroll) are "quite alert to the implications of the post for re-writing the field" (187), we apparently do not recognize the "yes of the setting to work mode of deconstruction that faces unanswerable questions" (181). Lather and Clemens base their analytical framework on Jacques Derrida's deconstruction process, derived from the de-constructing/destruktion perspective and methodology devised by Martin Heidegger's phenomenology (Bernasconi 1988, 14). This methodology provided Heidegger, Derrida, and Lather and Clemens, among others, with tools to disengage language from thought and the Cartesian understanding of self from the individual (see Epstein and Carroll 2005, 72–75). Lather and Clemens claim that Derrida's interrogation of deconstruction somehow indicates that his approach does not follow Heidegger's foundational conception and process. Indeed, in their embrace of Foucault and Derrida, Lather and Clemens try to distance themselves from Heidegger. Yet their claim is visibly refuted by their own quotation of Derrida that something "must speak from within itself" (186). Foucault and Derrida were unalterably linked to Heidegger's method, which was based on Dilthey's version of verstehen and "life"-philosophy (see Carroll 2008).

Summoning Rolland Paulston's 1999 depiction of "the 'letting go of modernity's language'," Lather and Clemens laud his description of the difficulties posed by the "poststructuralist storms" of the end of the century (186). Their jargon and clever reversals (e.g., "more is at stake than philosophy when philosophy is at stake" and "a digitalized era that interrupts the easy real") do more than bring forward the gimmicky terminology and procedures of postmodern language. Their foundation of understanding and conceptualization is based on an eager grab for an imagined aspect of "what is absent" from the apparent evidence. Lather and Clemens advance a "pop" formulation that restricts research goals to "discovering" assumed *aporias* and "openings", concentrating on what is "unsaid" and mandating that these conjectured elements are the only ones of value. Because their approach opposes accepting anything as "objective truth," it serves to institutionalize a format of pre-rehearsed techniques that excludes specificity and depth analysis. Sure that the deficiencies of this perspective will never be successfully refuted by rational means, Lather and Clemens cite Paulston's droll depiction of the anticipated configuration of thought as "the monster of a new postmodern metanarrative" (186).

We are not the first to observe such disabilities in Lather's techniques. In *Marxism Against Postmodernism in Educational Theory*, Mike Cole and David Hill (2002, 90) discuss Lather's (1998, 488) acceptance of Derrida's concepts of "undecidability," which suggests "a praxis of not being so sure." In this, Lather presages the advice of one of her collaborators, Elizabeth Adams St. Pierre (2000), to advance "rigorous confusion" that "sputters" and "makes no claim of mastery." Critiquing Lather's repeated efforts to rescue postmodernism from its own structural mandate by means of "pluralistic" communities, Cole and Hill (2002) cite Elizabeth Ellsworth, who shows that "multiple voices will be silenced" in such communities (91). Noting similar approaches in some of the essays included in *Social Cartography*, we too expressed such concern in "Abusing Ancestors" when we quoted feminist theorist Ann Oakley's caution that "postmodernism drives the enforced injustices of social inequality into the personal cupboard of privately experienced suffering" (Epstein and Carroll 2005, 86).

Regarding Lather's admonishment to "just say no to nihilism" (Lather 1991, 114), James A. (Tony) Whitson (1995, 128) observes that "the emblematic principle of postmodernism . . . may be the 'principle' of never saying 'no' to anything. This is the very principle of nihilism: that all things may be permitted when all bases for differentiating judgments are annihilated."

To be sure, Lather and her collaborators go much further than Paulston in their contorted resort to postmodern expression and techniques. Yet, their expressed reliance on Paulston to form their ideas implicates him in their postmodern intrusions into comparative education and other fields.

Marianne A. Larsen's Critique

We now examine a critique of "Abusing Ancestors" by Marianne A. Larsen (2009), who, following Paulston, embraces Foucauldian tenets in an ongoing theoretical reconfiguration of comparative education. In doing so, she applies an experiential dimension to discourse analysis that contains serious defects, especially in her manufacture of the "deconstructing" action devised by Martin Heidegger. This methodological approach is fairly new to academia; its purpose and techniques are more often seen in psychology and in training seminar formats.

Larsen bases her discourse analysis on Foucauldian premises as a historically appropriate approach to comparative studies in education. As she moves through her analysis, she employs various tactics to guide the reader through a visualization experience of the development of comparative education by "destabilizing the present moment."

Claiming that earlier comparativists wrote about factors that " 'determined' the evolutionary development of education systems" and that "extreme historicism" had prevailed, she identifies a "break" in the 1970s that brought critical analysis into the field, allowing "shifts" to bring us to a point of "discontinuities, differences, and uneven development" in approaches to comparative education (1048–1049).

Quoting Nicolas Hans (1959, 307), Larsen reminds us that " 'national character' . . . sometimes subconsciously determine[s] our present . . . (though) historical investigation can bring (it) to the surface and illuminate (its) potency" (1049). She views comparativists' contributions to education policy development in "light" of meliorists like Isaac Kandel, and she cites Keith Watson's work in "light" of sensitivity to local concerns, asserting that comparative education is challenged to "re-establish its unique role in providing comparative historical insights for future policy action." Andreas Kazamias' admonition to investigate problems "objectively" and "dispassionately" will, Larsen tells us, "illuminate certain phenomena." She argues that history can be used to "illuminate" events and "problematize . . . the world itself," and if we "shift" beyond previous ideas about comparative research our work will allow "us to 'read the world'" and achieve *verstehen.* She quotes Bloch (1964), who wrote that "understanding the living . . . is . . . the master quality of the historian" (1049–1050).

After positioning the reader, through numerous metaphors of "illumination" and "light" to develop a "master quality" and *verstehen* to perceive what opening the field further to postmodern techniques will afford, Larsen adopts an embattled posture: "Postmodernism is very much a contested terrain between those who would define and occupy it, and those who would discredit or demolish it" (1050). She then goes on to cite historian Charles Beard (1936) inaccurately, depicting his assertion that each individual had his/her own version of history, based on ideological presuppositions as confirmation that Beard believed "history functioned as cultural myth" (1051), and uses Peter Novick's dismantling of the idea of objectivity to indicate that the effort to produce reasoned, objective analysis is falling from use and "something new is emerging." Larsen then quotes Keith Jenkins' (1997) assessment that "history now appears to be just one more foundationless, positioned expression in a world of foundationless, positioned expressions." From a vision of previous thought structures that were rootless and ossified, Larsen's aim is to provide Foucault's redirection from "normal" and "old" methods of historical analysis (Larsen 2009, 1051–1052).

Larsen invokes Foucault to show that while previous historical approaches sought "'a law that accounts for [society's] cohesion'," Foucault's analytical discourse, developed from his historical approach, archeology, consists of "all that can be said and thought . . . and who has permission to speak" about a topic. It establishes "an open theoretical model to understand the rules, relations, and procedures between and among statements . . . [how] knowledge is organized or systematised" (1052–1053). His method does not "smooth over" disparities, but seeks to locate unity and disrupt it, thus "opening up spaces." Foucault writes that "History . . . introduces discontinuity into our very being—as it divides our emotions, dramatizes our instincts, multiplies our body, and sets it against itself." In this way, the "normal course of things" has become destabilized; Foucault's methodology "leaves these breaks exposed" in the "specificity of each moment or period of time" (1053). Foucault's way to view each "beginning" is contrasted with the causal interpretation of history: "determinism," "determinability," "determines," "predictability," "inevitability," and "inevitable" are heavily repeated as negative identifications of "causal privilege," often in the same sentence. However, in learning "how . . . new ideas . . . emerge and new truths [are] invented," Larsen tells us that "discourse as a practice creates objects, and by creating them, determines their nature . . . objects determine our behaviour, but our practice determines its own objects in the first place. Given that there are no things, only social practices, we need to understand the sense in which language or discourse speaks through us" (1054). She asserts that since Foucault's archeology is a "history of the present," we must set about "making the past strange" to "disturb and shake up" the given, and quotes Foucault's advice not to let history "rest comfortably in its strangeness, but . . . 'to use it, to deform it, to make it groan and protest'." We should see that the present is "unsettling" and "isolate past moments of difference or strangeness to destabilize our present moment." Larsen finally quotes Mark Poster (1997, 143), who relates that Foucault "speaks from a place that is new and strange and perhaps threatening" (1055).

Now that, for Larsen, Foucault has provided us with "a cutting edge" means to do research (1056), she employs Rolland Paulston, with whom she sat "side by side" at a comparative education conference, to guide us to what "ought" to be our response—to become those who "step out of or into different reality constructs . . . who learn to negotiate . . . the new spaces of knowledge . . . [to share in] unprecedented opportunities to . . . help to shape an interactive postmodern comparative and international education beyond our understanding today" (1055). To counteract those who would impose boundaries on the field, she urges that we engage in "challenging the barriers. . . [to accept] risk" by adopting postmodern attitudes, quoting the advice of Cowen (1999, 80) to " 'step away from our earlier confidence about . . . knowing' " (1056). Larsen asserts that Epstein and Carroll, in "Abusing Ancestors," believe that "postmodern thinkers are nothing more than 'abusing our ancestors'." Using this mischaracterization to assert that Foucault is not abusing "us" but is now, in fact, transformed into a "postmodern ancestor" she states (1057):

> [P]roposing that we engage with postmodern ideas . . . is no more an abuse to our ancestors than is the suggestion that we engage with ethnographic research or any other research methods that were foreign to early comparativists. . . . [I]t is an overstatement to accuse postmodernists such as Foucault of abusing us. . . . [B]y allowing ourselves . . . to consider the potentials of postmodernism in our historical research we honour our ancestors who drew upon a multiplicity of approaches in their research and we honour those postmodern ancestors who dared to do history differently.

What do we make of Larsen's defense of postmodernism? As an acolyte of Paulston, her discourse analysis responds to the "invitation" to implement the new modes of analysis suggested in *Social Cartography*. Following his aim to "unconceal," Paulston wrote earlier that his mapping intended to expose "knowledge . . . levels previously hidden under the shadows of modernism's metanarrative" (Paulston and Liebman, 1994, 227–228).To induce what is "hidden" in the reader, Larsen incorporates the technique of using language as a vehicle to reformulate the purpose of language and redirect thought—a technique demonstrated in several chapters in *Social Cartography* and by other comparativists who embrace Paulston's repositioning, such as Peter Ninnes, Sonia Mehta, and Leon Tikly (see especially Mehta and Ninnes 2003, 238–255; St. Pierre 2000, 25–27; Tikly 2004, 173–198; and Pillow, 2000, 21–24).

To be sure, as Lester Faigley (1992) writes, the "power to fold language back on itself makes postmodern theory . . . an extremely powerful means for exposing the political investments of foundational concepts, but the same power prevents postmodern theorists from making claims of truth or emancipatory value for this activity" (43–44). Even so, while Faigley proposed that postmodernism should begin to critique itself, since it "has been around long enough" (20), we believe that critiques like Faigley's miss the central purpose of the postmodern effort.

Faigley cites a London conference on contemporary arts whose literature stated that "postmodern theory is paralyzing in its deconstruction of all 'principled positions'" (20) and that "reflexive questioning [has now] redirect[ed] attention once again to the subject as the site where ethics enters postmodern theory" (21). It is important to understand that the elimination of the "subject" and the shift to viewing human beings by "groups" were central premises to German philosophers, including Martin Heidegger, by the mid-1930s. Arthur Liebert, writing in *The Philosophical Review* in 1936, describes Heidegger and Karl Jaspers as foundational to the new "philosophy of existence" and quotes Heinrich Rickert, a Neo-Kantian who was Heidegger's instructor, as asserting: "[T]here are no 'men in general' in the historical life and culture; there are only members of peoples and nations. If a person does not see this, or thinks it philosophically unimportant, he has not yet passed out of the 'Enlightenment' of the eighteenth century" (Rickert 1934; cited by Liebert 1936, 34).

Since they are structured, conceptual processes, the development of "ethics" and the critiquing process that Faigley recommends cannot be effected in postmodern thought, since postmodernism's process itself can only deconstruct any premise that is formulated as a *concept.* This is why the accusation of nihilism is so often directed at this approach. However, since postmodernists bring forward Heidegger's assertion of *aporia* (gap) and *aletheia* (truth; disclosure of Being), once "concepts" (thought objects) are disrupted and destroyed, "that which speaks" will make itself known. This fundamental tenet of "inner Being" and the "silence which speaks" is directly from Heidegger, and it is the core foundational assumption on which the postmodern deconstruction process is based. As we showed in "Abusing Ancestors," Heidegger wrote in *Being and Time* that his analysis was "solely concerned with preparing the way for the assimilation of the researches of W. Dilthey, which the present generation has yet to achieve" (quoted by Rickman 1962, 19). Dilthey's analysis was founded on the assumption that the "is"-predication in philosophical and metaphysical thought after the Eleatics had closed off awareness of true Being. Heidegger's fundamental process was to implement Dilthey's understanding; he developed the "disclosure process" to return to the "Being" of the pre-Socratic Greeks by deconstructing the Aristotelian/Cartesian understanding of "self" and knowledge (Carroll 2008, Chapter 3). Larsen follows Foucault's discourse process, based notably on Heidegger, when she asserts that "there are no things, only social practices, (so) we need to understand the sense in which language or discourse speaks through us" (1054).

As Cyril McDonnell (2007, 39) writes:

Heidegger's singular but characteristic hermeneutic style or "way of thinking" (*Denkweg*) about his topic in philosophy and phenomenology as he goes about "researching" and "engaging" with what is "said" and "written" about "the meaning of Being" . . . [has] particular reference to that which is left "unthought" (*ungedacht*) by the author but nevertheless implicitly expressed in the testimony of that author's text and inviting "retrieval". This is indeed, both in theory and in practice, a generous application of Dilthey's hermeneutic manner of thinking to issues in philosophy and phenomenological research, and to the topic of the question of the meaning of Being in particular, just as Heidegger intimates to his students in his 1925 lecture course.

By the time *Being and Time* was published in 1927, Heidegger had "thoroughly internalized (and advanced) Dilthey's position . . . in his own definition and *methodological practice* of phenomenology as hermeneutic phenomenology" (McDonnell 2007, 49–50, f.n. 40). The sense of dislocation created in Larsen's appropriation of Foucault, and through Foucault, Heidegger is geared to bring readers to dismantle their own relational sense of self and reality with a different reality as the procedure is completed. And, because the postmodern process does not permit its construction, there is no acceptable pattern to assess the occurrences that are described as Foucault's "archeology" that result in "discontinuity in our very being."

For Larsen, Paulston, and other postmodernist practitioners, the different reality they seek and refer to as "new knowledge", and whose roots can be traced to the ideas of Heidegger, compels that discontinuity. Indeed, Paulston refers to his "mapping" as a way to access the "new knowledge" (Paulston and Liebman 1994, 228).

In his lectures over time, Heidegger had sought ways to draw students into the experience of his ideas—foreshadowing Foucault's discourse analysis technique. Heidegger's former student, Karl Löwith (Quoted by Wolin 1995, 4), recalled:

We gave [Heidegger] the nickname of "the little magician from Messkirch." . . . He was a small dark man who knew how to cast a spell insofar as he could make disappear what he had a moment before presented. His lecture technique consisted in building up an edifice of ideas which he then proceeded to tear down, presenting the spellbound listeners with a riddle and then leaving them empty-handed. This ability to cast a spell at times had very considerable consequences: it attracted more or less psychopathic personality types, and, after three years of guessing at riddles, one woman student took her own life.

McDonnell (2007) quotes Rüdiger Safranski (1998) that "Heidegger's use of the example of perceiving a lectern, where the 'experiencing' of the lectern in terms of 'it worlds' (es weltet) . . . becomes a kind of *enactment* of a perception whereupon '(L)ooking at the lectern, we can participate in the mystery that we are and that there exists a whole world that gives itself to us' " (Safranski 1998, 94–96; quoted in McDonnell 2007, 52, f.n. 70). After the war, for the Freiburg de-Nazification committee, Karl Jaspers advised against Heidegger's re-inclusion in teaching at the university, stating that he "proceeds as if he combined the seriousness of nihilism with the mystagogy of a magician" (Quoted by Wolin 1995, 24). Even Walter Kaufmann (2005), who was one of the earliest to introduce Heidegger's thought in the United States in the 1940s, by 1980 saw Heidegger as a "pied piper" and a "false prophet," observing that many who were drawn to him were "moved by religious needs" (238). More recent students were not immune to this element of Heidegger's manipulation. Siegfried Mews (2008) reports of a student who was torn in the late sixties between "engaging in activism and his attraction to the 'great shaman' Heidegger" (311). Heidegger's delivery in his lectures also contained the erotic element that Foucault often included in his writings, as illustrated in the idea of using history, "deform[ing] it" and making it "groan", in Larsen's discourse analysis. Heidegger's purpose with his students in the 1930s was to "penetrate (their) inner life . . . by appealing to the forces of their consciousness, and especially of their eros" (Faye 2009, 133).

Larsen suggests that among comparativists who have opposed the implementation of postmodern ideas and methodology in the field, Epstein and Carroll would agree with Michael Crossley's (2000, 327) "contention that our field has responded too directly to changing disciplinary fashions, with the result that the stages of its own development indicate a rejection of past practices" (Larsen 2009, 1046). The postmodernist perspectives and methodologies that Larsen advocates, however, do not reject past *practices*; they challenge the fundamental understanding of the self, dissolving reason-based constructions on which conceptual relationships are based. This process not only "erases" the ancestors of thought in comparative education who developed those past practices; it erases the relational concept of ancestry itself. In her section on "a discontinuous history . . . in comparative education," what Larsen describes as earlier "chaos, discontinuity, and non-linearity" (1046–1047) in the field was, in fact, the diverse, investigative growth of practitioners who sought to devise multiple methods to better understand their fellow human beings. To do this, "ancestors" such as Michael Sadler, Isaac Kandel, and Nicholas Hans at no time abandoned reason-based evidence and constructions in achieving their purpose. Like all aspects of scholarship, their efforts were not linear or tidy. They were, however, based on a foundational agreement about the perceiver and the perceived and the possibility of knowledge that is antithetical to postmodernism's purpose. We contend that Paulston never intended the abandonment of our field's reason-based ancestors, but his ideas about how our field should be "mapped" and his invocation of Heidegger furnished a platform for postmodernists to advance their nihilistic agenda.

We argued in "Abusing Ancestors" that historical functionalism was both foundational to our field and continued to provide a framework of analysis that would include the rigorous, critical examination of social and cultural factors, while retaining a commitment to an epistemology that included cautious, scrupulously researched assertions about those factors. In the field of history, the debate about postmodern and constructionist frameworks is ongoing. Some view the past as "always mediated through culturally influenced narrative structures [but that] language is not a transcendent measure of truth . . . [and] deconstructionist relativism is not the only response" (Munslow 1997, 78). Historian James T.

Kloppenberg (1989, 1018) quotes John Dewey's discussion of the pragmatism of William James: "[James] asks us to look for new truth in the results of our past experiments at the same time that we continue to experiment." Kloppenberg agrees with Dewey and James:

Hypotheses—such as historical interpretations—can be checked against all the available evidence and subjected to the most rigorous critical tests the community of historians can devise. If they are verified provisionally—they stand. If they are disproved, new interpretations must be advanced and subjected to similar testing. The process is imperfect but not random; the results are always tentative, but not worthless. (1018)

Though some historians have, as Larsen relates, embraced postmodern analyses and methodologies in reconfiguring the historian's process, others have forcefully rejected the entire perspective, writing that proponents of postmodern thought are "devilish tempters who claim to offer higher forms of thought and deeper truths and insights—the intellectual equivalent of crack, in fact" (Elton 1991, 41). Indeed, Charles Beard (1936), whom Larsen cites as an early historian who abandoned objectivity as a premise, wrote about Nazi education in the mid-1930s. He stated that German schools had become "hostile to . . . free inquiry . . . [and] private opinion." His disturbing critique of German schooling under the Nazis in no way suggests that Beard declined to adhere to an understanding of "subject" and "individual" who would wish for an "independent search for truth" (Beard 1936, 439). However, like the other "new knowledge" that Paulston hoped to generate, the standards of a famous and useful historian can be repositioned to "unconceal" what this scholar did not question and challenge—and to abandon objectivity. Indeed, Beard's (1934, 222–227) speech, cited by Larsen, stated:

[T]he apostle of relativity will surely be executed by his own logic. (225)

Nor is the empirical or scientific method to be abandoned. It is the only method that can be employed in obtaining accurate knowledge of historical facts, personalities, situations, and movements. It alone can disclose conditions that made possible what happened. It has a value in itself . . . . The scientific method is, therefore, a precious and indispensable instrument of the human mind.

CONCLUSION: CAMUS AND OUR FINAL ASSESSMENT

Academic journals and books are sources of record for scholarship and healthy discourse. Without the regular presentation of many perspectives and vigorous and professional disagreements, a field will fail to create critically important distinctions among ideas that can only be made by means of public forums. Through such forums, the scholarly community is afforded the opportunity to deliberate on concepts and methodologies in the real context in which that community lives. However, when well-founded and scrupulously researched analyses are constrained from this public consideration, that absence affects the community, and opportunities to explore new or unpopular configurations of thought disappear. After reviewing the critiques of our earlier "Abusing Ancestors" essay, we have described how Lather and Clemens and Larsen disposed of our analysis of the challenge to "ancestors" of comparative education that postmodernist theorists posed. They criticized our work to help construct their own positions, using postmodern tools to "erase" analyses based on reason and logic and eschew the "knowability" of common human rights and experience. The repercussions to learning and thought produced by these critiques should alarm scholars who believe that ideas must not be isolated from real historical contexts. Events and ideas do have consequences, and historical trajectories must be remembered. The opposition to our study, which identified a relationship between an intimidating and repellant antecedent theoretical construct and current postmodernist foundations, highlights the true nature of "erasure" and "silencing."

By using the word "ancestry" rather than "ancestors" in the title of this chapter, we emphasize that the postmodern project is not simply to alter perceptions associated with words—to engage in so-called *ludic* wordplay, so that "everything is at once open and shut," as Jacques Derrida would have it. Rather, it is to abandon reason-based, Cartesian approaches to reality and replace them with the dizzying and cynical experience of the postmodern Carnival mirror-world, thus erasing the "real" things that words stand for. Success of that project would render an understanding of "ancestry"—those from whom one derives one's early direction, assumptions, and fundamental comprehension of the world—as something that will simply cease to "be", like everything or anything else not compatible with the "now-ness" of the postmodern Heteropia.

Ancestors will still *be*, of course, but they will be voiceless and no longer recognized. They, and the world of which they are a part and the structures of thought that make them comprehensible, will disappear. They will be erased, and the concept of "ancestry" itself, along with a host of other ideas, such as truth, honor, verifiability, and justice, will become unintelligible, reduced to a kind of foreign language of the mind. But, though the words will disappear, the realities will remain, waiting for another "trend of thought" to rediscover them and retrieve them from the "dustbin of history."

In the summer of 1944, in the midst of war-ravaged Europe, Albert Camus (2006) wrote in the clandestine paper *Combat* about the Vichy militia cooperating with their Nazi masters, whose ". . . job was to prove that human dignity is a lie and that the idea of a self-conscious individual, master of his own fate, is but a democratic myth . . . [They were] asked to destroy in themselves and others: confidence in man, confidence in the individual" (6–7). Later, Camus made explicit the effect of Heidegger's ideas: "The philosophy of nothingness and despair in the face of the world's absurdity and the futility of existence came from Martin Heidegger . . . (99, f.n. 212). I do not much relish the all too celebrated existential philosophy, and, to be blunt, I find its conclusions to be false." And, further, "if the age is afflicted with nihilism, it is not by ignoring nihilism we will discover the morality that we need" (100). Thus, one of the most clear-sighted and courageous members of the resistance community, at a time of mortal danger and conceptual coercion in France, understood the fraudulence of Heidegger's philosophy. Questions about phenomenology and Heidegger's configuration of it continued after World War II throughout the fields of history, sociology, and philosophy— notably, by Karl Löwith, Heidegger's former student. An animated inquiry regarding the political implications of Heidegger's analysis, raised by Victor Farías and Hugo Ott in the late 1980s, created a firestorm of scholarly discussion. Most recently, the November 2009 translation into English of Emmanuel Faye's 2005 brilliant examination of the Nazi conceptual structure implicit in Heidegger's philosophy has once again raised the challenge that "no philosophy can be based on the negation of the existence of man, as such" (314).

Ultimately, the issue of the Heideggerian foundation of postmodernism must rest on the extent to which Heidegger's legacy was infused with Nazi ideology. Our contention with Paulston is based on our conviction that incorporating Heideggerian and postmodern precepts necessarily compromises our field. And we are far from alone in asserting that the infusion of that legacy in postmodern discourse has been pervasive. Adam Kirsch (2010, 11), for example, argues:

> Heidegger's self-portrait as a misguided idealist turned dissident has been shown to be sheer fabrication. The philosopher, it is now clear, was a committed National Socialist for many years, an admirer of Hitler who purged Jewish colleagues, presided over a book-burning . . . and—unlike genuine dissidents—continued to teach, publish and travel throughout the Nazi period. At the same time, and more significantly, the alleged division between the man and the work has been thoroughly undermined, as scholars have examined the deep affinity of Heidegger's thinking with the irrationalist and chauvinist ideas of the interwar German right.

And further,

> The more familiar a reader is with Heidegger's work, the more shocking it will be to see him employ his key terms—being, existence, decision—as euphemisms for nationalism and Führer-worship. Thus we find him, in the winter of 1933–1934, declaring that "the question of the awareness of the will of the community is a problem that is posed in all democracies, but one that of course can become fruitful only when the will of the Führer and the will of the people are identified in their essence."

And, as Herman Philipse (2008, 145, 151) contends, in reference to the French postmodernists (Michel Foucault, Jacques Derrida, Jean-François Lyotard, Jean Baudrillard, et al.,), so influential in the writings of postmodern comparativists,

> [E]ven French Heideggerians will no longer be able to deny the embarrassing depth and persistence of Heidegger's philosophical involvement with Hitler's National Socialism . . . [The] important issue . . . for postwar French philosophy [is]: how to explain why since 1945 large areas of French philosophy have been dominated by a thinker who lost his chair because of his Nazi past, who never repudiated Nazism after the war, and who, from 1929 onwards, rejected rational argument, the methods of scholarly research,

and traditional philosophy in favour of an allegedly more profound style of thinking, the results of which cannot be accepted on any grounds apart from Heidegger's self-imputed authority.

Finally, let us turn to Heidegger himself in reference to how he expressed his allegiance to the Nazi state (as quoted by Cohen 2010, np):

> Only where leader and led together bind each other in one destiny, and fight for the realization of one idea, does true order grow. Then spiritual superiority and freedom respond in the form of deep dedication of all powers to the people, to the state, in the form of the most rigid training, as commitment, resistance, solitude, and love. The existence and the superiority of the Führer sink down into being, into the soul of the people and thus bind it authentically and passionately to the task.

Rolland Paulston was an important figure in the development of our field. His willingness to explore new areas of thought, evident in numerous publications, was at the time refreshing and challenging. Unfortunately, the fragmentation that extreme versions of postmodernism, advanced by some current "post-Western" or "post-Enlightenment" comparativists beyond the intent of Paulston's "maps" but drawing from his framework, brooks no structural formulation, ontologically or epistemologically, demanding a self that is "subjectless" and de-centered, incapable of originating the formulation. The vigorous challenging of Heideggerian concepts and of the related postmodern positioning of his adherents—Foucault, Derrida, Lyotard, and others—is the antithesis of "erasure" and an avowal of the integrity of academia. Failure to challenge the "postmodern experience" will, if this extreme and pernicious postmodern process moves further into the field, make the idea of "justice needs" vanish. But the needs themselves will continue to exist, just as two and two will always be four.

We have demonstrated the most recent stage of the dissolution of the connections to past scholars in comparative education that postmodern "disruption" necessarily entails. The disjoining of "self" from Cartesian "extensions" dismantles the perceptual connection of humans to their surroundings, curtailing comparative assessment and the recognition of existing meaning and significance. When the field becomes simply the observation of contemporaneous events, without judgment, what is it that practitioners will compare for clients who are not "decentered subjects" and are acutely aware of themselves in need?

As a *festschrift* to honor Rolland Paulston, *Beyond the Comparative: Advancing Theory and Its Application to Practice* affords a timely forum to continue the public debate in the field about the current and future configuration of comparative education. We have continued the debate over fundamental ideas in the field—an activity in the best tradition of scholarly discussion and one of which comparative education's "ancestors" would approve. This chapter should stimulate further critical examination of postmodern thought in comparative education and help the field to retain its integrity and usefulness in the years ahead. The "postmodern surge" that Paulston generated can benefit the field if it stimulates us to reassess our own precepts about individuality, freedom, and open inquiry. Paulston has forced us to remember both the fragility and the durability of the foundational ideas of our ancestors' thought, and the modes of inquiry inspired by those ideas.

REFERENCES

Beard, Charles A. (1934). "Written History as an Act of Faith." *The American Historical Review, 39*(2), 219–231.

Beard, Charles A. (1936). "Education Under the Nazis." *Foreign Affairs, 14*(3), 437–452.

Bernasconi, Robert. (1988). "The Trace of Levinas in Derrida." In David C. Wood and Robert Bernasconi (Ed.), *Derrida and Différence*, (pp. 13–30). Evanston, IL: Northwestern University Press.

Bloch, Marc. (1964). *The Historian's Craft.* New York: Vintage Books.

Camus, Albert. (1975). The Plague. *Trans. Stuart Gilbert.* New York: Vintage Books.

Camus, Albert. (2006). Camus at "Combat": Writings 1944–1947, ed. Jacqueline Lévi-Valensi. Trans. Arthur Goldhammer. Princeton, NJ: Princeton University Press.

Carroll, Katherine T. (2008). Does Postmodernism Compare? *An Analysis of the Use of Postmodern Constructs in Comparative Education Studies.* Saarbrücken, Germany: VDM Verlag.

Cohen, Martin. (2010). "Book of the Week: Heidegger: The Introduction of Nazism into Philosophy." *Times Higher Education, February 18.* Available online at: http://www.timeshighereducation.co.uk.

Cole, Mike, & David Hill. (2002). "'Resistance Postmodernism'—Progressive Politics or Rhetorical Left Posturing?" In Dave Hill, Peter McLaren, Mike Cole, and Glenn Rikowski (Ed.), *Marxism against Postmodernism in Educational Theory* (pp. 89–107). Lanham, MD: Lexington Books.

Cowen, Robert. (1999). "Late Modernity and the Roles of Chaos: An Initial Note on Transitologies and Rims." In Robin Alexander, Patricia Broadfoot, and David Phillips (Ed.), *Learning from Comparing: New Directions in Comparative Education Research, Vol. 1* (pp. 73–87). Oxford, UK: Symposium Books.

Crossley, Michael. (2000). "Bridging Cultures and Traditions in the Reconceptualizing of Comparative and International Education." *Comparative Education, 36*(3), 319–332.

Dilthey, Wilhelm. (1962). Pattern and Meaning in History: Thoughts on History and Society, ed. Hans Peter Rickman. New York: Harper and Row.

Editors. (2009). *Comparative Education Review: Samples of Decision Letters and Reviewer Reports 2003–2009* (pp. 13–42). Chicago: Comparative and International Education Society (CIES). Available online at: http://www.jstor.org/page/journal/compeducrevi/samples.html.

Elton, Geoffrey Rudolph. (1991). *Return to Essentials: Some Reflections on the Present State of Historical Study.* Cambridge, UK: Cambridge University Press.

Epstein, Erwin H. (1983). "Currents Left and Right: Ideology in Comparative Education." *Comparative Education Review, 27*(1), 3–29.

Epstein, Erwin H. (1987). "Against the Currents: A Critique of Critiques of 'Ideology in Comparative Education'." *Compare, 17*(1), 17–28.

Epstein, Erwin H., & Katherine T. Carroll. (2005). "Abusing Ancestors: Historical Functionalism and the Postmodern Deviation in Comparative Education." *Comparative Education Review, 49*(1), 62–88.

Faigley, Lester. (1992). *Fragments of Rationality: Postmodernity and the Subject of Composition.* Pittsburgh: University of Pittsburgh Press.

Farías, Victor. (1989). Heidegger & Nazism (Ed.), *Joseph Margolis and Tom Rockmore. Trans. Paul Burrell.* Philadelphia: Temple University Press.

Faye, Emmanuel. (2009). Heidegger: The Introduction of Nazism into Philosophy in Light of the Unpublished Seminars of 1933–1935. Trans. M. B. Smith. New Haven, CT: Yale University Press.

Fritsche, Johannes. (1999). *Historical Destiny and National Socialism in Heidegger's 'Being and Time'.* Los Angeles: University of California Press.

Hans, Nicholas. (1959). "The Historical Approach to Comparative Education." *International Review of Education, 5*(3), 299–309.

Jenkins, Keith. (1997). "Introduction: On Being Open about Our Closures." In Keith Jenkins (Ed.), *Postmodern History Reader* (pp.1–25). London: Routledge.

Kaufmann, Walter Arnold. (2005). *Nietzsche, Heidegger, and Buber: Discovering the Mind, Vol. 2.* London: Transaction Publishers.

Kirsch, Adam. (2010). "The Jewish Question: Martin Heidegger. Review of E. Faye, Heidegger: The Introduction of Nazism into Philosophy in Light of the Unpublished Seminars of 1933–1935." The New York Times Sunday Book Review, May 9, BR1.

Kloppenberg, James T. (1989). "Review: Objectivity and Historicism: A Century of American Historical Writing." The American Historical Review, 94(4), 1011–1030.

Larsen, Marianne A. (2009). "Comparative Education, Postmodernity and Historical Research: Honouring Ancestors." In Robert Cowen and Andreas M. Kazamias (Ed.), International Handbook of Comparative Education (pp. 1045–1059). London: Springer.

Lather, Patricia A. (1991). Getting Smart: Feminist Research and Pedagogy with/in the Postmodern. New York: Routledge, Chapman and Hall.

Lather, Patti. (1998). "Critical Pedagogy and Its Complicities: A Praxis of Stuck Places." Educational Theory, 48(4), 487–497.

Lather, Patricia A., & Julie L. Clemens. (2010). "Postmodern Studies in Educational Foundations." In Steven Tozer, Bernardo P. Gallegos, Annette Henry, Mary Bushnell Greiner, & Paula Groves Price (Ed.), Handbook of Research in the Social Foundations of Education (pp. 179–194). New York: Routledge.

Liebert, Arthur. (1936). "Contemporary German Philosophy." The Philosophical Review, 45(1), 26–60.

McDonnell, Cyril. (2007). "Understanding and Assessing Heidegger's Topic in Phenomenology in Light of His Appropriation of Dilthey's Hermeneutic Manner of Thinking." Maynooth Philosophical Papers 4, 31–54.

Mehta, Sonia, & Peter Ninnes. (2003). "Postmodernism Debates and Comparative Education: A Critical Discourse Analysis." Comparative Education Review, 47(2), 238–255.

Mews, Siegfried. (2008). Günter Grass and His Critics: From the Tin Drum to Crabwalk. Rochester, NY: Camden House.

Munslow, Alun. (1997). Deconstructing History. Abingdon, UK: Routledge.

Ott, Hugo. (1993). Martin Heidegger: A Political Life. Trans. Allan Blunden. London: Harper Collins Publishers.

Paulston, Rolland G., ed. (1996). Social Cartography: Mapping Ways of Seeing Social and Educational Change. New York: Garland Publishing.

Paulston, Rolland G. (1999). "Mapping Comparative Education after Postmodernity." Comparative Education Review, 43(4), 438–463.

Paulston, Rolland G., &Martin Liebman. (1994). "An Invitation to Postmodern Social Cartography." Comparative Education Review, 38(2), 215–232.

Paulston, Rolland G., & Martin Liebman. (1996). "Social Cartography: A New Metaphor/Tool for Comparative Studies." In Rolland G. Paulston (Ed.), Social Cartography: Mapping Ways of Seeing Social and Educational Change. (pp. 7–28). New York: Garland Publishing.

Philipse, Herman. (2008). "Emmanuel Faye's Exposure of Heidegger." Dialogue: Canadian Philosophical Association, 47(1), 145–153.

Pillow, Wanda S. (2000). "Deciphering Attempts to Decipher Postmodern Educational Research." Educational Researcher, 29(5), 21–24.

Poster, Mark. (1997). Cultural History and Postmodernity: Disciplinary Readings and Challenges. New York: Columbia University Press.

Rickert, Heinrich P. (1934). Grund–probleme der Philosophie: Methodogie, Ontologie, Anthropologie. Tübingen, Germany: J.C.B. Mohr.

Rickman, Hans Peter. (1962). "Introduction." In Hans Peter Rickman (Ed.), Wilhelm Dilthey Pattern and Meaning in History: Thoughts on History and Society, New York: Harper and Row.

Rust, Val D. (1991). "Postmodernism and Its Comparative Education Implications." Comparative Education Review, 35(4), 610–626.

Safranski, Rüdiger. (1998). Martin Heidegger: Between Good and Evil. Trans. Ewald Osers. Cambridge, MA: Harvard University Press.

St. Pierre, Elizabeth Adams. (2000). "The Call for Intelligibility in Postmodern Educational Research." Educational Researcher, 29(5), 25–28.

Tikly, Leon. (2004). "Education and the New Imperialism." Comparative Education, 40(2), 173–198.

Whitson, James A. (Tony). (1995). "Post-structuralist Pedagogy as Counter-Hegemonic Praxis: Can We Find the Baby in the Bath Water?" In Peter McLaren (Ed.), Postmodernism, Post-colonialism and Pedagogy. (pp. 121–143). Albert Park, Victoria, Australia: James Nicholas Publishers.

Wolin, Richard. (1995). "Karl Löwith and Martin Heidegger—Contexts and Controversies: An Introduction." In Richard Wolin (Ed.), *Martin Heidegger and European Nihilism, Karl Löwith* (pp. 1–25). Trans. Gary Steiner. New York: Columbia University Press.

RICHARD E. RODMAN

4. HOUSE OF 1,000 WINDOWS

Situating People and Perspective in Theory And Practice

The territorial "barbed wire around comparative education" (Epstein and Carroll 2005, 88) is temporarily lowered a bit to depict graphically ways in which we may see and situate ourselves, our work and the work of others in a more broadly defined field of international education. This does not diminish the ongoing lively and substantive debates of territorial ownership. It does speak to the practical advantages of periodically returning to more inclusive proxemic depictions of our community membership in international education. It is to our advantage. Inspired by Rolland G. Paulston's interest in social cartography, mapping and his keen interest in bringing international education community members into proximity to one another, we celebrate "figurative thinking using metaphors and models" (Paulston 1990, 251) in dimensional and spatial as a frontier explored here. There is always a need for new systems that may help us identify and organize operative educational variables so that we may better order material and gain fresh perspective contributing to practical (and perhaps even more sophisticated) vantage points within international education. Accordingly, the chapter introduces a rough and ready three-dimensional International Education Matrix Model, or global positioning system (GPS), that may make our work and the work of others more accessible to more people. In this way the work: (1) is a celebration of Paulston and his interest in the people, the researchers and practitioner, who comprise our international education community; and (2) attempts to further visually model and situate Paulston's postmodernist and social change cartographic inclinations in a more inclusive and accessible space for researchers and practitioner from a variety of traditions.

Our international education community and its various traditions, professional identities and territory remain the subject of considered and reconsidered definitions and debate. How we look at ourselves is important. Paulston understood this. How we see ourselves in comparative, international, and development education spurs discussion about where one specialty begins and another ends. David Phillips and Michele Schweisfurth (2008, 3) note "the sharing of international education and comparative education 'conceptual territory' creates difficulties of interpretation." It also creates distance. Perceived territorial issues, whether conceptual, definitional, professional, or practical are further exacerbated by lingering tribal suspicions and

John C. Weidman, W. James Jacob (eds.), Beyond the Comparative: Advancing Theory and Its Application to Practice, 49–67.

sufficient identity crises to suggest continued insecurity about deserved positioning in and around the social sciences. From here, we are encouraged to explore what a house might look like as a home for international education.

HOUSE OF 1,000 WINDOWS

For some, a spatial sense of our work in international education has proved useful in citing proximities of our theory and practice, and (building upon Paulston and others) encourages international education professionals to experiment with the model in their work and research. International education practitioners and researchers work and dwell under a large roof, indeed. Visualize community members from each and every definitional end of our self-identified international education professions, associations and traditions situated in a single wondrous house upon a global landscape that runs from horizon to horizon. It is nothing less than a *House of 1,000 Windows*. Within this house, comparative researchers situate themselves in certain rooms and tend to look out of certain windows through which to examine and explore the world. Development specialists favor other rooms and look out (and act upon) the world accordingly. Indeed, each of us favors certain historical, cultural, quantitative, qualitative windows that we are more comfortable with, and through which we view the world. Each of those windows offers its own clarity, uniqueness, scope, and dimensional views of portions of our external world. Each movement in front of a single window brings a slightly different perspective on the world. The windows of the international education house offer an infinite number of angles and perspectives, limited only by each window's framework.

And what of the international educators who dwell within our house? We tend to ramble blissfully around our own tribal rooms with little recognition of others in this house. Those of us who consider ourselves International Educators may attend our CIES meetings as one of the central identifying features of our professional lives. Curiously, a CIES gathering in one of our rooms, to some in research and practice, may mean a meeting of the Comparative International Education Society. To others dedicated to bringing people together across cultures, it might mean a meeting of the Council of International Exchange of Scholars, the Fulbright Program. Others still may find themselves attending as CIES associates of the Centro de Investigación, Educación y Servicios (CIES) who plan development health and educational strategies in Latin America. One would think there were enough letters in the alphabet to go round to the different international education constituencies.

Presented here certainly is less an architect's blueprint of what we should know about our house than it is an impressionistic illustration of meaning as *a community of learners, researchers, practitioners and professionals.* The demands of a cluttered, information-rich, data-driven globalized age have to do with actively extending our recognition and appreciation of the seeming strangers (Gudykunst, 1981) or the "other" (Gudykunst and Kim 1995, 450) in and beyond international education familial subcultures. Students of something we call international education, researchers and practitioners from different areas of the house need to move about the house and beyond to conferences and into the field to actively engage and open dialogue with one another. The House of 1,000 Windows promotes the need of international education professionals from the various rooms of the house to visit together in proximity. It advances the intra-cultural lessons associated with learning more about how others live within the house, what they think they see through windows they have chosen and favor, and their motivations for these choices. And even as in the mind's eye we see this imaginary three-dimensional space seeking to recognize and to know *who* walks among us, we too can visualize a similar three-dimensional space as a matrix through which to examine *what* it is that we think we see and perhaps better understand what we think others think they know.

This work does not minimize the important substance of discussions and identity differentiations that take place from room to room, floor by floor. It does shift emphasis toward the practicality of recognizing a broader, outcomes-oriented appreciation of our larger community that brings in new researchers and practitioners each year. These newcomers (as likely do we all) deserve the time and space to see some of the dimensions of our community. The model offers a sense of this dimensional cartographic space designed to help a wider community of international educationists see one another in community through our windowed perspectives, help international educators situate their thinking in the field, help international educators better see and appreciate the work of others in the field. The International Education Matrix Model is "a kind of cognitive art or 'play of figuration'" to help the international educator orient theory and practice (Paulston 1993, 101). The Matrix Model was designed as something of an international education GPS for use in the classroom or in the field to better equip international education practitioners, researchers, educators, education abroad administrators, development workers and others, experienced and new alike, along our definitional spectrum for practical, thoughtful reflection and action in real time and in nuanced educational settings. The Matrix Model is but one tool as it identifies a framework designed to help learners (visual learners in particular) situate themselves to problem solve. In application, a quick journey around the Matrix Model and the pursuant positional knowledge then offers some reasonable courage to act practically within and upon our Deweyian responsibilities to serve effectively students, adults, planners, administrators, and learning communities in formal and nonformal settings in and across cultures.

Situating one's self quickly, easily, and comfortably in something akin to a "tradition" in international and comparative education is, at best, an illusion and more likely, delusional. Surely, those who claim membership in our international education community identify themselves quite individually and according to their own selected and selective definitions of what international education is and should represent. Trained as a comparativist myself, and with experience as a practitioner in education abroad administration, graduate school teaching, and as a development education field project director in southern Africa, I anecdotally attest to the self-identification of colleagues *as* international educators and international education professionals in each of these specialties. Particularly because of the specialties at our disposal, there is no reason why we cannot be more nimble in negotiating identity and learn better how to negotiate our "house."

International education offers rich and diverse experiences grounded along a spectrum containing "schools" from area studies, comparative education and development education to education abroad, scholar exchanges and international student services. In this diversity, we reaffirm who "we" are, where we have been and where we think we are going has and like will continue. This is evidenced in comparative education, for instance, and the need to often offer an obligatory introductory case defending legitimacy by recounting a history from Marc-Antoine Jullien to Isaac Kandel, Nicholas Hans and George Z. F. Bereday. Order and historical continuity of the one hand, and reaction on the other, with new ideas and schools of thought developing that lead to this day. The essence and dynamism of an iterative process, is evidenced here in Paulston's advocacy of social change-related constructs, his emphasis upon the innate importance personal bias, postmodern contributions, and what Irving Epstein (2007) discusses as "embodied knowledge." These impulses electrify the house just as modernist theories gave the house historical structure.

It is important to know both the structure and the workings of the house. It is important that we keep the genuine dynamism of divergent and convergent, macro and micro, quantitative and qualitative, formal and nonformal, political, historical, cultural and economic-oriented international education perspectives in proximity. In any case, the various representational wings of international education offer fruitful ways, means and ends in a world that calls upon us for action, as international educators. Every day we are asked for answers, as researchers and practitioners. Each day we identify and solve problems. A constant challenge has to do then with an appreciation of the scope of reality in which we make decisions. So even with risks of illusion and delusion, researchers, students and practitioners seek scope and understanding. We seek readily accessible, practical field models that capture reasonable breadth and depth to begin one's own work and to understand others.

Rolland Paulston's mapping and ideographic representations offered fresh vantage points that have helped many of us come to better understand, if not come to terms with, the beautiful liminality that holds the quantitative and qualitative, modernist and postmodernist in the same space. The proposed International Education Matrix Model speaks to this multidimensional space we work in and must account for in our considerations, reflections and work. These "orientations . . . are not random or eclectic but rather follow from personal bias theoretical and ideological orientations to our social reality and social change" (Paulston 1976, 6). And while Paulston directs these comments to planners, the case before us here has to do with some greater applicability among us all striving to more cognizant of our tentative *situatedness* in the field and recognize the tentative *situatedness* of others.

This chapter only claims the framework though perhaps there is more here to explore, as claimed more intentionally, for instance by Paulston in social cartography maps that revealed the substantive dynamism and proximities of social change variables in our work.

Certainly, the study of comparative education and international education may be viewed from many angles (Jones 1973, 26) and experienced in an infinite number of ways. Adam Przeworski and Henry Teune (1970) even mention a vertical and horizontal dimension in comparative inquiry, though the argument was criticized as naive and antiquated in context by Epstein (2007, 3). A dimensional house is reopened especially with an academic interest and curiosity and with the very practical view of attempting solutions to educational difficulties (Jones 1973, 26). Paulston's visual mapping of some of these angles, interests and curiosities through the years suggested a sense of space. Pedro Rosselló (1963) helps us see dimensions subject, scope, range, nature and angle of comparison.

THE INTERNATIONAL EDUCATION MATRIX MODEL . . . A "GPS" SYSTEM

If the house offers some sense of living space, the Matrix Model suggests a visual working space. The Matrix Model is something of a self-calibrated international education GPS that identifies our place and that of others in the real time of thoughts, reflection and action. Its practicality builds upon the relational features of Paulston's maps, in particular, and is useful in planning and practice in the workplace and field. Paulston's invitation to place *multiple* intellectual perspectives and schools of thought onto an invented visible grid and map for the purpose of juxtaposition and to deconstruct educational phenomena offers the researcher and practitioner a refreshing sense of order and dialogical relationship to observe, reflect and launch inquiry and dialogue.

The Matrix Model (see Figure 4.1), while less focused upon Paulston's substantive social change and educational reform-oriented agendas that first stimulated interest in his map making, rather builds upon Paulston's (1993, 106) need to "make the invisible visible," to recognition of "personal bias" that separates us within our learning community and the need to bring us into the same space, and particularly "to open a way for intertextuality among competing discourses." The Matrix Model then builds on this aspect of the work to increase accessibility, community and increase mutual awareness of the spectrum of intellectual and applied pursuits in the field.

Various dimensional imagery is used here to help us here accordingly is about helping us to identify our place special *field focus interest,* with a *particular scope* and with *selected operative variables* at work, seen through a particular inquiry *lens/vantage points of inquiry* and *frame of reference.* The model places these elements from the worlds of theory and practice in proximity with available *frameworks* and *lenses* through which to view and act. This International Education Matrix Model represents a three-dimensional visual schematic designed to help the student, the practitioner, the administrator, the researcher or the visual learner situate and organize thinking when posed with the nuanced complexities found within the international education sectors.

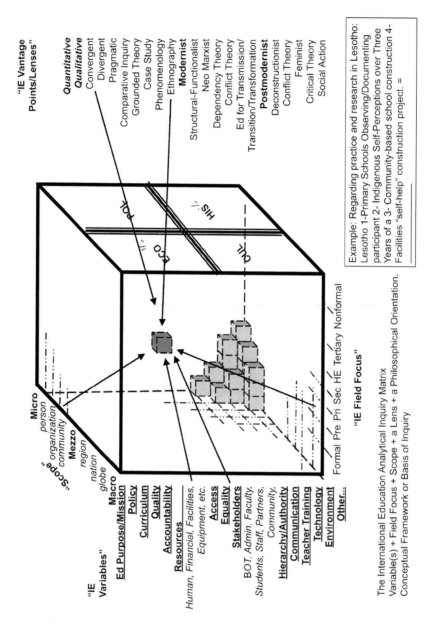

Example: Regarding practice and research in Lesotho: Lesotho 1-Primary Schools Observing/Documenting participant 2- Indigenous Self-Perceptions over Three Years of a 3- Community-based school construction 4- Facilities "self-help" construction project: =

The International Education Analytical Inquiry Matrix Variable(s) + Field Focus + Scope + a Lens + a Philosophical Orientation. Conceptual Framework or Basis of Inquiry

Figure 4.1. The International Education GPS Matrix.

A "symbiotic relationship" exists between comparative and international education (Phillips and Schweisfurth 2008, 153). And as a researcher and practitioner working across these areas, one remains less worried about the repeated claim about "its lack of tight disciplinary boundaries" and "confusion about its defining characteristics" than the more practical and immediate reality of one's situatedness in the scope of interests (Crossley and Broadfoot 1992, 99). In this regard, the Matrix Model is something of a pictorial primer about discovering a situated "place." It does not presume to mine and to manage the important and substantive details discovered within that place. The Matrix Model is focused upon finding effective ways to "practice theory." On a lighter side, such a journey thus becomes one that either takes us toward solving the riddle or just a better telling of the joke tied to the baseball player's Yogi Berra's adage: "In theory there is no difference between theory and practice. In practice there is."

The Matrix Model intentionally links research and professional practice by inviting novices and experienced international educators to identify the distinct "windows on the world" that international education presents among its different traditions. Recognizing and situating one's self in the field of international education remains an imperative, no matter what the tradition- development education, comparative education, area studies, or educational exchange research and practice. How can the development educator in southern Africa reasonably account for and situate the veritable sea of political, historical, cultural and economic variables at work in an emergent primary school system? What lenses might be used by Ukrainian university administrators seeking local, regional and international recognition for a quality academic institution? Where does the international educator begin within an American university in its internationalization efforts? Indeed, where might any of these international educators begin? What common ground might they share to recognize one another's endeavors?

One origin of the Matrix Model comes from the graduate school classroom and course in *Theory and Practice in International Education* that hosted experienced and aspiring international educators from these widely different backgrounds. Students had interests ranging from development education, to area and comparative studies, to policy planning and research, to education abroad program administration, and international student advising. Many of these modern (and impatient) students seek to acquire and possess a tangible skills set that will serve them in their international education-related work. In such a course, a basic teaching challenge becomes how to identify and honor the glorious breadth, depth and complexity of international education, while attempting to capture and communicate (in a finite time and space) the many linkages and power of theory and practice evidenced in the education phenomena, situations and problems they might face.

In this graduate course, two related illustrations were designed with this scope in mind of student interests. The illustration of our international education *House of 1,000 Windows* was constructed to help students visualize themselves and their colleagues living, working and associating together. Second, the Matrix Model was similarly designed to provide a convenient tool to consider the multi-dimensional educational problems out in the world. Each illustration provides clues and cues on how to look *within* different international education traditions. They offer international education professionals ways to better recognize and appreciate the emic perspectives of other international education colleagues who use different lenses, who look out of different windows and see the world very differently?

The Matrix Model honors the important work of Mark Bray and R. Murray Thomas (1995) in recognizing the place and power of *multi-level* (versus single-level) comparative analysis in connection with comparative research and policy analysis. The dimensional sensibilities of their work and their cube again emphasized not only the power of placing micro and macro, quantitative and qualitative variables, et cetera in proximity, but also in identifying the *perspective* of multi-level analysis suggesting a more balanced and a more comprehensive approach for research and understanding. Bray and Thomas multi-level analysis and Paulston's mapping and illustrations informed the work. In complement, the Matrix Model fills some "space between" with a practical system designed with the somewhat different purpose in more broadly identifying and situating noted multi-dimensional components of and vantage points on international education phenomena. Accordingly, the adaptable design serves to help international educators situate perspective, debate and arguments within and among international education traditions- theory and practice, practice and theory. As an example, what questions come to mind or further situated differentiations might we make, for instance, with different international educators working from modernist and postmodernist sectors of Paulston's map, in defining "quality" in connection with twenty-first century African higher education? The Matrix Model provides a framework to generate such questions and differentiations.

Beyond a certain aesthetic in being able to see visual representations of abstract ideas, the Matrix Model was invented as a practical instrument to capture graduate students' hearts and minds. It also served as a planning instrument. It represented a place where work, ideas and research could be "pinned-down" for identification, consideration and discussion. The Matrix Model represented a framework upon which to hang ordered work and to play with conceptually blended combinations. For my graduate students, anecdotal evidence showed students seemed to grasp and use ideas from our encyclopedic schools of thought that run through comparative education, area studies, intercultural communication and an international education literature dedicated to education abroad programming and internationalization in the academy. Students were able to cross-reference these schools with the modernist and postmodernist lenses and frameworks that concerned Paulston and others. The Matrix Model thus became something of a simple tracking system for ferreting through complexity. It serves to frame questions for the public dialogues we desire. It invites professional newcomers to engage and participate (with thoughtful courage) in our academic dialogues. It potentially can serve as an apparatus to assist some international educators beyond their own assertions and perhaps toward more considered thought and reflection, even across cultures.

The Matrix Model's orthodox "walls" come from the histories and traditions of Brian Holmes, E. J. King, George Z. F. Bereday, Nicholas Hans, Vernon Mallinson, Isaac Kandel, Philip Foster, and so many other foundational personages. It likewise incorporates the theory-to-practice and practice-to-theory proximities and even necessities as imperatives for substantive, demonstrable progress in development education, planning, policy development, and project implementation in a wider community of international educators. It relates to international educators working to bring people together across cultures in citizen mobility, education abroad and exchanges, and in internationalization efforts in higher education. In this regard, visually situating the possibilities of arguments on internationalization in higher education, the Bologna process or the ideas of Jane Knight, Hans de Wit, Marjik Van der Wende in proximity to other schools of thought invites the fresh picture of possibility. In addition to juxtaposed possibilities, we also more clearly come to understand other perspectives within our various international education traditions. In so doing, we recognize one another. How do we know an international education professional when we see one? Are we connected with each other, and if so, how? For some, it begins with a quick assessment and a mental tour around the various axes of the Matrix Model.

International education is multi-dimensional and its related critical variables are constantly at work at many different levels of society and across cultures. International education holds many potential definitions and a world of assumptions. And for every definition comes a host of analytical perspectives that claim to isolate, combine, mix and match educational variables and that may *conveniently* work to build systems of thought, frameworks and theories for consideration, or practical strategies for action. Just as curious, one may discover that an international educational professional from one room of the house likely may not even recognize a colleague from another room. Gaining an understanding of our field and what lies within requires combined skills in organized and critical thinking along with a sense of perspective, sensitivity and flexibility.

The Matrix Model axes identify, separate and list possible *field foci* for educational inquiry, often cited general and dynamic *issues* (variables) at play in educational inquiry, a *scope* of the educational inquiry, a *lens* or *lenses* through which to pursue inquiry, and a windowed perspective(s) through which to *frame* the inquiry. It is a simple, rough and ready GPS construct. To identify, organize and analyze international educational dilemmas/problems for research, action or policy formation, it is helpful to first answer a series of questions that may help us situate the subject for treatment within relationships.

- What educational *context* or **field focus** is being addressed? (e.g., primary schools, adult education)
- What educational *issues/variables* seem in play? (e.g., curriculum, stakeholders)
- What scope is identified? (e.g., *mezzo*-community/organizational, or *micro*-interpersonal)?
- What educational **frame(s)** will be used (e.g., *economic, cultural, historical, political*)?
- What **theories** or **theoretical lens(es)** will help explain the interaction of selected *variables,* in identified *context,* within the delimited *scope* identified, using the *frames* of history, economics, politics and culture?

As the researcher or practitioner begins to answer these questions and opens the multi-dimensional space of complex international educational phenomena (indeed even as one *creates* one's own theories in international education), fresh meaning emerges from considerations *Field Focus, Variables, Scope, Frame* and *Lens* and their possible intersections. Theory and practice mingle and knit. And while this is hardly news in our quest for meaning, the model and represents an organized construct to help identify and arrange rascally educational variables in fresh ways.

Field Focus, International Education Variables, Scope, Frame (historical, cultural, economic, political) and Vantage Point/Lens are the points of reference. Of considered importance here is the idea that each of the categorizations is open to substantive additions, changes, treatments, given the particular orientation of the practitioner researcher. The simple model is but a template. Its spatial design, and its attention to and focus upon multi-dimensional relationships primary. The listed elements of each category are neither rigid nor exclusive They rather represent ingredients with that certain elasticity, molded to the user's needs, and that when chosen, mixed and matched might lend themselves to freshly textured ideas, plans, actions and solutions. Such is the simple notion of a model that might offer the opportunity for pragmatic actions with a modicum of control and order.

The design does not pretend to offer an exhaustive review of the literature of each of the axes, but rather suggests the applicability of the underlying model. It invites researchers and practitioners to adapt existing checklist indicators, or plug-in and play their own elements. Accordingly, one draws from the various critical and operative traditions of international education, such as Patricia K. Kubow and Paul R. Fossum (2007) "issues-oriented approach" (e.g., access, equality) that lands upon an axis, to Lee Harvey and Peter T. Knight's (1996) attention to "quality" in higher education. Indeed, the myriad articulations with micro to macro foci, to formal and nonformal educational best practices, to modernist and postmodernist dynamic tension- each may deserve place in space.

THE AXES

Field Focus Axis

Samuel Enoch Stumpf (1977) depicts John Dewey's *instrumentalism* (1938) as the mind's ability to spread itself over a range of things . . . for knowledge "may very well consist of a cognitive act, but the full description of knowledge must include the environmental origin of the problem or situation that calls for the cognitive act" (410). The Matrix Model's purpose as a basic visual aid is to help frame mediation between the researcher-practitioner and a contextual environment. It is useful to acknowledge that the context of international education has expanded through the years. The community of those of us who self-identify as international educators has grown. The earlier section attests to the claims of development professionals, comparativists, area research specialist, education abroad and international student support professionals as part of this community. The further evolution of the field of intercultural communications lands within the context. Indeed, the very vocabulary of intercultural communication helps establish context. The view from our individual rooms, exclusive and unilateral research methods may well serve some *ethnocentric* orientation of an investigated phenomenon, perhaps with great success. But in terms of context it is helpful to understand the intercultural communication concept of subjective culture (Bennett 1998, 2) that establishes a necessary awareness of the varied spaces, rooms with their own furniture, adornments, preferences and taste within the house. The mere act of striving to grasp some of the grander, or at least different, context prepares us for more informed better inquiry. The context then is intercultural and intracultural.

Phillips and Schweisfurth agree that though the traditional fields of international education and comparative education are interdependent and those working each side can learn from the other, "This sharing of 'conceptual territory' (of traditional of international and comparative education arenas) and its widespread use creates more difficulties of interpretation" (Phillips and Schweisfurth 2008, 3). Certainly, in a compartmentalized ("apartmentalized") orientation to our community this seems quite correct and important. For the experienced researcher, the distinction reflects a necessary inflection of nuance and precision needed in our work. To the novice or practitioner, however, the distinction may be acknowledged but not needed in interpretation. The model presented acknowledges this interdependence. This axis identifies as useful the sectors and different levels of formal education and nonformal education. Formal early schooling, primary, secondary, higher, and tertiary education categories, along with areas in nononformal education are not siloed as exclusive categories for inquiry or consideration. Indeed, studies often cut across the sectors. At the same time, they represent convenient and obvious touchstones in research policy studies (as noted in Bray and Thomas cube focus), or in practical planning, project design and assessment.

With the identification and inclusion of this component, this offers a good opportunity to mention the utilitarian nature of the Matrix Model. The Matrix Model was first built for graduate international education students, who, under the pressures of time and schedule, needed to appreciate the essential meanings behind and beneath each of the *various* CIES camps that represent different wings in our house. The field focus axis was one of the most easily recognizable and accessible for students and mirrored a kind of categorization found in *Comparative Education Review* themes and school of education-type textbook classifications. Students identified their interest on the axis, for instance, as primary school teachers within a distinct yet kindred community of higher education. Aspiring study abroad directors and international student advisor students identified formal education and higher education, and development educators were drawn to adult, nonformal education. When encountering the Matrix Model, students (and others) naturally tend to first see and recognize "themselves" on the Matrix Model, along with their interests and components that they know. This becomes a starting point for learning.

Variables Axis

The term "variables" is borrowed from the social sciences as a useful way to identify and describe factors, components, and entities within international education that assume particular value for us. Represented as an axis and at the very heart of

59

our GPS Matrix Model (and our work) are a host of lively international education variables that are acknowledged or ignored, hidden or revealed and then considered or studied, isolated or combined, manipulated, poked and/or prodded. They represent the factors, components or entities . . . the very grist of our work in considering and managing problem analysis, policy planning, program and project design, and implementation. Rosselló (1963) (might call this "subject."

The international education variables axis list is not exhaustive. Each year my students and colleagues, depending on their inquiry interest, suggest new "variables" that fit well along on the axis. The axis listings are illustrative simply of those things we think that are at work and need our undivided attention in considering. Whether variables are identified and considered in isolation or in various combinations, we believe the selected variables critical to the phenomenon we seek to unpack and understand. In John Dewey's pragmatic world, we are brought to think of truth and value in terms of satisfactory results. In teaching and as a tool for fieldwork, the international education variable axis enables us to keep progressing in inquiry and action. It also provides a basic structure to teach and learn more about some wider, possible variety of variables that need to be considered juxtaposed to those actually selected as operative or alive for the researcher or practitioner.

Modest examples from experiences in development education activities come to mind in working with local villages and townships in Lesotho. The work required a systematic and repeated return to this axis, as a checklist, to ascertain what "variables" were coming to life in the lives of the stakeholders—parents, teachers, and students. I also could consider the design in terms of facilities construction, in isolation or in combination with various stakeholder groups.

The checklist similarly proved useful in my work in education abroad program design where college internationalization efforts lined-up with critical variables such as college mission, purpose, curriculum options, resources and various stakeholder groups. The fact that one can cognizantly link or delink these variables helped provide sensible scope for action as a college administrator.

Finally, the axis was useful as an illustrative construct for the classroom. Students actually could visualize, and hopefully better appreciate the subtlety and complexities of the aforementioned examples explained in the classroom. Certainly, this approach does not minimize in any way the power, breadth and depth of the specialized, serial, and skills-based literature that one acquires and uses in international education. The approach does have everything to do with quickly situating ourselves, some of our students and colleagues toward clear thinking and action in a fast-paced, impatient era.

Scope

A natural dimension of the Matrix Model is something that we can call scope. The Matrix Model uses categorizations previously identified by Richard Rodman and Martha Merrill (2010). They are akin in many respects to Rosselló's (1963) scope and the Bray and Thomas's (1995, 488) global/ locational dimension in illustrating the power of "different levels, different insights." The Matrix Model includes a simple incremental scale from the macro-level (globalization, international, intercultural, national) to mezzo-level (regional, community, organizational) to the micro-level (local community, school, group, individual).

Lens

The *lens* axis is Rolland Paulston-inspired territory. It is a menu representing "synchronic mapping of knowledge" (Paulston 1993, 105) for his dynamic social change-oriented constructs and captured in various mapping exercises. The matrix lens also includes additional lenses used and popularized in our modern and postmodern-related literature. Paulston's mapped lenses (1993), for instance, reads as an axis of the model (rather than as Paulston's interactive Venn diagram) from humanist ethnography, to radical humanist critical theory, to functionalist to radical functional et cetera. They also provide listings and takes on fresh meaning and perspective for application in our interconnected work in international education.

Certainly, the very reason for generating the contemporary comparative and international education textbooks such as Kubow and Fossum (2007), Robert F. Arnove and Carlos Alberto Torres (1999), and Phillips and Schweisfurth (2008) are only the latest in the long line of important attempts to capture the lightning in a bottle that sustains and powers our work. The substantive, serial and carefully constructed literature that introduces students to many aspects of our field and the different lenses we use to bring light to subject matter, are necessary but also can overwhelm the student. A single "international education" graduate classroom with its many different types of students, levels of interest, need and expectations, indeed, themselves representing different ends of our spectrum, poses challenges in meaningfully conveying the many schools of thought and perspectives in finite time and space.

Paulston's mapping discourse (1993) and phenomenography demonstrated usefulness with practical visual aids encouraging students, researchers and practitioners to think and see beyond the individual frameworks in which we work to recognize proximity among several various schools of thought, and produce "new ways of seeing" (110).

Frames

The use of *windowed frames* in the Matrix Model represents an inclusion, acknowledgement of, preoccupation with, and honoring or the traditional (and often exclusive) social science perspectives for inquiry—*historical, economic, political,* and *cultural.* Each classic window through which epic economic or political histories, sociological treatises, or anthropological field studies were written are convenient categories that students recognize and claim.

The illustrated Lesotho example (Figure 4.1) is from research conducted there a number of years ago as a field project coordinator within a large, community-based school construction project that took place throughout the country. The project priorities had to do with community involvement, planning, actions, and implementation. Critical objectives had to do with (1) erecting a primary school facility in each of the locations, and (2) community support and involvement technically equally at least 25 percent of the total project cost at each location. While the temptation here is to dig into the substance of a very real, multi-faceted and interesting development education case study, we restrict ourselves to how a purposeful and focused research endeavor first emerged. In this case, professional research interests led the researcher in this place and time and through a sea of variables to identify appropriate ways and means to examine the self-identity and impact of local community members engaged in a local primary school construction effort. Situating the research topic on such a simple but dimensional grid thus becomes a visible reference upon which clarifications, commentaries and questions may begin both on the front end of research or planning initiatives or in reviewing and analyzing completed ones. In this case, Figure 4.1 stimulated a classroom conversation of the completed project initiative, measured success, and the associated research in a case study format. A quick breakdown revealed:

- *Primary Field Foci-* Primary schooling, Formal and Non-Formal (community) and in relation to secondary foci of a Protestant, Catholic and Government school system.
- *International Education Variables-* As a project director, the entire vertical matrix menu was mined for planning and implementation. As a researcher, the vertical matrix was considered, but also the research interests emerged, in this case, the focus was upon 1-community and 2-educational facilities
- *Scope-* While the focus was upon the community (mezzo), the Matrix Model offered a constant reminder of those individual, communal, regional and national features that informed community behavior and action
- *Frame-* The project staff were attentive to the historical, political and cultural facets of community members working together in Lesotho at the time, not to mention a desperate economic environment. The education research focus landed squarely upon some historical-cultural artifacts that came to life for the community.
- *Vantage Point/Lens-* The project team stayed with a modernist, convergent, structural-functionalist orientation to the development opportunity. As a researcher, participant observation became the focus.

APPLICATIONS

C. Arnold Anderson's (1961) conventional wisdom regarding our work is about finding the right tools and finding the right questions to ask and adopt dependable research techniques. As for practice, any fine artisan will offer similar advice about producing quality results. The Matrix Model is a tool in both research and practice. While there are limits to the model, utility and accessibility are not among them. There too remains the opportunity for cross-training for the researcher and practitioner to recognize and to test different suppositions, ideas and possibilities seen through one window or another.

The Matrix Model invites us to *pentangulate* our way through observed and considered educational phenomenon—to find fresh combinations and intersections of meaning. It enables a situating GPS-type action for international educators. There are limitless possibilities. As a teaching and planning tool, it offers advantages to recognizing the interplay among active variables, within a particular context, of a particular scope, and through selected lenses and windows upon the phenomenon. As mentioned previously, the Matrix Model is more designed and attuned around relational and dimensional comprehensiveness than being an instrument to reveal deeper truths and explanations about said phenomenon. The Matrix Model is not about explanatory power. Still, the work done in negotiating the various axes of the Matrix Model invites fresh thinking for powerful analysis and explanation. Even in the seeming infinite number of possible combinations comes a sense of confidence in ways forward for inquiry in identifying and pursuing any single *pentangulated* intersection of a particular context, scope, set of international education variables, perspectives, and lens.

In teaching, the Matrix Model serves as a projected classroom map where the student, even the novice student, can see, on a single screen, the categorized menus of theories, variables, field foci, frames, and possible levels of scope related to our work in various areas of international education. One can envision that examples of model application would be as varied as the intended use in describing, reviewing or analyzing articulated case studies, applied theories, policies, or practices. Similarly, application examples may be generated in comparing and contrasting *various* lenses that might explain particular education phenomena in different ways. I particularly found lively, organic discussions emerge from class participants when the model afforded the quick opportunity to juxtapose, for instance, postmodernist, feminist, deconstructionist arguments in direct proximity with modernist, functionalist ones. Advantage here had to do with the speed with which class participants approached a warmth and eloquence in lively dialogue. Even more intriguing is the possibility of having students project *other* lenses upon selected phenomena and established arguments. At least, the modeling exercise can empower students to quickly orient and find resonant anchors and "pentangulated" considerations upon which to build a case.

Structured exercises emerged directing students to use the Matrix Model in directed case study analysis, critical reviews and comparative treatment of assigned *Comparative Education Review* articles, including the richness of our varied perspectives. As a culminating class event each year, the graduate school hosts an international education conference featuring international education student final research papers and public presentations on research ranging from area studies, formal and nonformal education, to development education studies. Each paper and presentation is introduced with a student citation of their Matrix Model "positioning," thus serving as one commonality to orient the audience.

As a teaching tool, the three-dimensional visual Matrix Model affords the instructor the advantage to identify simultaneously its living axes in isolation and in relation to one another. Along each axis alone rests the dynamic discussions and debates of our field, in the terms of the axis. Having a visual reference of where one is in instruction encourages a sense of position by the instructor, a sense of accomplishment on the part of the student and certainly a common sense of humility regarding the possibilities for fresh combinations of inquiry. These are only a few examples of how the Matrix Model has come to life in teaching and learning. One is encouraged to envision and test fresh applications.

In practice and research, any number of examples of possible applicability likely comes to mind in the sectors of comparative education, development education, international education design programming for education abroad, policy analysis. In the Lesotho example, the Matrix Model serves as a planning tool to situate a range of possible components at work in organizing the initiative. In program design and delivery education abroad professionals may use the Matrix Model to ensure that a host of international education variables are attended to for safe programming. Is it possible that the "standards" of Forum for Education Abroad's new *Standards of Good Practice for Study Abroad* be situated on the Matrix Model, or perhaps Matrix Model case studies generated from an analysis of the Association of International Educators' (NAFSA) Senator Paul Simon Campus Internationalization Award winners? The new century's higher education internationalization strategies and efforts are multi-dimensional and involve need, circumstance, vision and action (Rodman and Merrill 2010). The Matrix Model lends itself to such multi-dimensional analysis.

At a recent Association of Universities for Democracy (AUDEM) conference at Bursa, Turkey, the Matrix Model was introduced to Eastern European and Central Asian university administrators and professors, who used the mapping model to situate and differentiate perspectives regarding future accreditation and quality issues within the Ukrainian university system and the European Union. Identifying different windows used by external accrediting agencies versus Ukrainian stakeholders helped clarify considerations for Ukrainian government education planners. The presentation stimulated a conversation activity in actually adapting the model for a posed Ukrainian policy development quandry that only needed added perspective separating the dominant political frame of reference from other operative economic, cultural, and even historical ones. The exercise likewise, refocused scope from the region to the nation to the university and encouraged policy planning analysis possibilities beyond a modernist critique to ones exploring the possibilities of gender, feminist, and other less obvious (to colleagues) analysis possibilities.

The model is a means, not an end. Its "capabilities" actually only extend to the envisioned mental constructs and scenarios in research, project planning, policy analysis, training or teaching. I do not claim that the Matrix Model has the ability of interpretation nor can it supplant the substance of linear planning, monitoring or evaluating international education programming or project development, internationalization efforts, or research endeavors. It can and does serve to support and orient faculty, planners, administrators, business operators, students learning about the profession, indeed, anyone engaged in design and delivery activities.

Figure 4.2. Sako Keiichiro's "Cube Tube" Building, Jinhua, China.
Source: Courtesy of SAKO Architects, Japan.

The Matrix Model is about imagining (see Figure 4.2) and "touring the house." Making that tour and acknowledging a possible host of planning, monitoring, evaluation, et cetera scenarios and implications (whatever they may be), offers a system for utilitarian problem-solving in the field, in the classroom, in one's own intellectual life. On this last point, the Matrix Model had been demonstrated particularly effective when it is adapted with novice students and newcomers to the field in being able to reflect, articulate and argue various cases, from various positions, from around the matrix. This has been true of students coming into the graduate classroom (and a rich, diverse and vocal academic environment) straight out of undergraduate university, international field professionals returning for a credentialing and international community members gleaning sense from our western academic system. In these cases, anecdotal evidence suggests that the Matrix Model offers a system against which intellectual maturity and confidence grows. The system not only provides checkpoints for the inquirer, it also provides a rudimentary system against which the quality of other arguments (perspective, scope, variables at work, lens) can be tested.

Beyond these few examples, the practical attraction has everything to do with getting one's hands on the system for creative application and to generate one's own fresh examples. The foundation for this work is Deweyan. Application calls heavily upon the relevance and importance of experiential education (Kolb and Fry 1975). Whether it is used to frame a question addressing: "How can I better understand the perspective of a colleague from another culture?" or "What perspectives are available in framing girls basic education in Africa," the Matrix Model becomes "owner operated."

Visual modeling is useful in augmenting our intellectual discourse. It is important that international education remain as accessible as is possible to the widest audience it can reach. And where visual modeling loses in discourse for some, it gains in imaging the "picture worth a thousand words" for others. A thousand words. A thousand windows. Whether gazing out upon the twenty-first century world or peering into our international education traditions, the researcher and practitioner can become more cognizant of the various perspectives and people working in closer proximity than first imagined.

Ginsburg and Gorostiaga (2001) exhort our constituencies to remain vigilant in how our work, action and ideas *constrain* dialogue within our community, and the need to overcome constraints to dialogue. This has been one attempt encouraging *figurative, metaphors* and *modeling*, hopefully whose "florescence is not yet in sight" (Paulston 1990, 251). So before the barbed wire too quickly goes back up around our territories, perhaps fresh conversations and fresh illuminations await throughout the international education. Whether a House of 1,000 Windows, Matrix Model, or GPS system imaging can stimulate new ideas, interpretations and fresh meaning for students and colleagues. Resonant too is the sense that images can be operationalized for action.

In the house, we recognize the many rooms of international education and their windows on the world. In the Matrix Model, we recognize the many, *many* different and distinctive possible combinations. Each combination is special. Indeed, we can all take some courage in finding combinations (Rodman and Merrill 2010) that will unlock fresh thinking, robust conversation and solid planning and programming. And finally, as a GPS in a globalized world, perhaps we will be better able to disregard for a moment the metaphorical (and inevitable) *"Make a u-turn!"* just to entertain and explore intriguing intersections we have discovered and the novel possibilities and fresh avenues of thinking and inquiry newly formed in our mind's eye.

REFERENCES

Anderson, C. Arnold. (1961). "Methodology of Comparative Education." *International Review of Education, 7*(1), 1–23.

Arnove, Robert F., & Carlos Alberto Torres. (1999). *Comparative Education: The Dialectic of the Global and the Local.* Lanham, MD: Rowman & Littlefield Publishers.

Bennett, Milton J. (1998). "Intercultural Communication: A Current Perspective. In Milton J. Bennett (Ed.), *Basic Concepts of Intercultural Communication: Selected Readings.* (pp. 1–34). Boston: Intercultural Press.

Bray, Mark, & R. Murray Thomas. (1995). "Levels of Comparison in Educational Studies: Different Insights from Different Literature and the Value of Multilevel Analyses." *Harvard Educational Review, 65*(3), 472–491.

Crossley, Michael, & Patricia Broadfoot. (1992). "Comparative and International Research in Education: Scope Problems and Potential." *British Educational Research Journal, 18*(2), 99–112.

Dewey, John. (1938). *Logic:* The Theory of Inquiry. New York: Henry Holt and Company.

Epstein, Erwin H., & Katherine T. Carroll. (2005). "Abusing Ancestors: Historical Functionalism and the Postmodern Deviation in Comparative Education." *Comparative Education Review, 49*(1), 62–88.

Epstein, Irving, ed. (2007). *Recapturing the Personal: Essays on Education and Embodied Knowledge in Comparative Perspective.* Charlotte, NC: Information Age Publishing.

Ginsburg, Mark B., & Jorge M. Gorostiaga. (2001). "Relationships between Theorists/Researchers and Policy Makers/Practitioners: Rethinking the Two-Cultures Thesis and the Possibility of Dialogue." *Comparative Education Review, 45*(2), 173–196.

Gudykunst, William B. (1983). "Toward a Typology of Stranger-Host Relationships." *International Journal of Intercultural Relations, 7*(4), 401–413.

Gudykunst, William B., & Young Yun Kim. (1995). "Communicating With Strangers: An Approach to Intercultural Communication." In John Stewart (6th Ed.), *Bridges Not Walls: A Book about Interpersonal Communication*. New York: McGraw-Hill.

Harvey, Lee, & Peter T. Knight. (1996). *Transforming Higher Education*. London: Open University Press.

Jones, Phillip E. (1973). *Comparative Education: Purpose and Method*. St. Lucia, Australia: University of Queensland Press.

Kolb, David A., & Roger Fry. (1975). "Toward an Applied Theory of Experiential Learning." In C. Cooper (Ed.), *Theories of Group Process*. London: John Wiley.

Kubow, Patricia K., & Paul R. Fossum. (2007). *Comparative Education: Exploring Issues in International Context*. Upper Saddle River, NJ: Pearson Education.

Paulston, Rolland G. (1976). *Conflicting Theories of Social and Educational Change: A Typological Review*. Pittsburgh: University Center for International Studies, University of Pittsburgh.

Paulston, Rolland G. (1990). "Review: Toward a Reflective Comparative Education?" *Comparative Education Review, 34*(2), 248–255.

Paulston, Rolland G. (1993). "Mapping Discourse in Comparative Education Texts." *Compare, 23*(2), 101–114.

Phillips, David, & Michele Schweisfurth. (2008). *Comparative and International Education: An Introduction to Theory, Method, and Practice*. New York: Continuum International Publishing Group.

Przeworski, Adam, & Henry Teune. (1970). *The Logic of Comparative Social Inquiry*. New York: John Wiley and Sons.

Rodman, Richard, & Martha Merrill. (2010). "Unlocking Study Abroad Potential: Design Models, Methods and Master." In William W. Hoffa & Stephen C. DePaul (Ed.), *A History of US Study Abroad 1965-Present*. Carlisle, PA: Frontiers – The Interdisciplinary Journal of Study Abroad.

Rosselló, Pedro. (1963). "Concerning the Structure of Comparative Education." *Comparative Education Review, 7*(2), 103–107.

Stumpf, Samuel Enoch. (1977). *Philosophy: History and Problems*. New York: McGraw Hill.

W. JAMES JACOB, JENNIFER R. CRANDALL, JASON HILTON,
AND LAURA NORTHROP

5. EMERGING THEORIES IN COMPARATIVE, INTER-NATIONAL, AND DEVELOPMENT EDUCATION

INTRODUCTION

Theory building is an on-going process, a journey often undertaken by individuals and collective groups of scholars, practitioners, and policy makers. While theories often differ in their degree of validity, all theories "are associated with different truth effects" and comparative, international, and development education (CIDE) cannot "afford to neglect the insights of a range of approaches" (Marginson and Mollis 2001, 605). We define *theory* as a proposed explanation for what, when, why, and how social phenomena exist and interact. Theory can be systematic and conform to a set of rules, criteria, or principles in its attempt to describe social phenomena. It is a point of view and may have one or more alternative points of view. Theory is both a science and an art. While some social phenomena remain fairly constant, others frequently change due to societal or ideological shifts and depending on the context. Appropriate theories exist, evolve, or, if necessary, are created to help explain the dynamic nature of social phenomena.

Val D. Rust (2004) and W. James Jacob and Sheng Yao Cheng (2005) support the argument that the strength of CIDE rests on multiple theoretical perspectives, which is a particularly salient point given that CIDE draws from various disciplines and perspectives (Paulston 2000). The changing geo-political landscape of the world and advances in technology have opened doors to even more theoretical diversity within CIDE (Crossley and Tikly 2004; Jacob and Cheng 2005).

The purpose of this chapter is to compile emerging theories identified in established, peer-reviewed CIDE journals to expand on the existing conceptual literature. In this respect, we have used Rolland G. Paulston's (1994) "Macromapping of Paradigms and Theories in Comparative and International Education Texts" as a reference for determining a timeline for emerging theories before aligning the identified theories with paradigmatic positions on Paulston's map. We identify and describe six emerging theories existing in the recent CIDE literature, concluding with implications for future theory development.

METHODS

Our methodology utilizes a framework similar to that used by Val D. Rust and colleagues (1999) who examined research methodology in comparative education.

John C. Weidman, W. James Jacob (eds.), Beyond the Comparative: Advancing Theory and Its Application to Practice, 69–91.

While Rust and his colleagues focused on three core professional CIDE journals[1] and made comparisons across the journals, analyzing research strategies and their significance for comparative education, we focused on seven professional journals which are devoted exclusively to CIDE or have a significant publication focus on CIDE topics. These journals were used to identify emerging theories in CIDE. We recognize other journals associated with CIDE could have been included in this study. Where Rust and his colleagues engaged in content analysis because "authors rarely explained what their research strategy was" (92), we developed criteria centered on explicit theory identification, thus limiting the need for interpretation. If a theory was used in a study that might be new to CIDE but has a strong footing in another field, such as social capital theory, we chose to include it only if its use in a given article met our criteria. Although a limitation of this review, we felt that given the number of articles under investigation, this strategy allowed us to concentrate on those articles more clearly engaged in CIDE-related theory building or development as outlined by our criteria.

Theory-Selection Criteria

The notion of *name* carries with it a special purpose for identifying emerging theories: "it gets posited in its own account, in that it becomes a *name*; in the *name* its empirical being, as a concrete internally manifold living entity is cancelled, it is made into a strictly ideal, internally simple factor" (Hegel 1804/1979, 221). In 1804, Georg Hegel explains that giving something a name accomplishes two tasks: (1) the so named is brought into reality and (2) the so named is shaped and controlled by the name giver. The name tells us both what the entity is and what it is not. It is from this conceptualization that we may be able to begin to determine what an "emerging theory" may be.

Applying this thought to our review of the literature, the first criterion for locating an emerging theory is that the theory will have an explicit name. This name may be a modification of a previous theory that includes new characteristics or it may be something unique in its own right. In either case, it demonstrates that the author wishes to mark the theory as something new and different from something in the past. Second, the article should reference where the name has come from. The theory is either created by the author, or the author will reference the theory's creator.

Third, details of the theory must include its epistemology. This explanation would indicate that the author sees the theory as "emerging" and would wish to clarify this new or emerging way-of-knowing to provide the reader with a logic for similar understanding of what the author is studying. Once a theory has met these three criteria, the fourth criterion is to ensure the theory has not been expanded on or referenced in the work of Paulston or other CIDE social theorists before 2000.

Within our review of the seven-identified journals, we decided that editorials, commentaries, and book reviews would not be included because they lacked the substance for full descriptions of an emerging theory. We eliminated books (either edited or single-authored volumes) as data sources for our study because they might have followed peer review standards of less rigor than those adhered to by journals listed in the Social Sciences Citation Index (SSCI).

Journal Selection and Review

We decided to focus our search on peer reviewed journals rather than other publication mediums as academic journals generally provide the greatest breadth of emerging theories that have been vetted through the peer-review process. Consulting the education and educational research journal list of the Social Sciences Citation Index (SSCI), our initial journal selection included 12 journals identified as having substantial publications targeting CIDE. From this initial list we reviewed the respective journals and kept the ones that explicitly stated in their mission or description an interest in CIDE: *Asia Pacific Education Review (APER)*, *Comparative Education (CE)*, *Comparative Education Review (CER)*, *International Journal of Educational Development (IJED)*, *Journal of Education Policy (JEP)*, *Journal of Studies in International Education (JSIE)*, and *Teachers College Record (TCR)*.[2]

In determining a time frame for our review of the literature, we used Paulston's (1994) "A Macromapping of Paradigms and Theories in Comparative and International Education Texts" as a reference, tracking revisions since its publication. Paulston (1994) reviewed 60 comparative education texts to create a map illustrating the relationship between the 16 theories pulled from the texts. Two scholars have since reinterpreted Paulston's map, focusing on a more intricate analysis of the relationship between the theories (Rust 2000; Liebman 2000b), but not on the addition of emerging theories. Among the many additional maps Paulston developed over the course of his career, his 1994 map was based on the reading of 60 postmodern texts and depicted new and emerging theories in comparative education (Paulston 1999). Since the purpose of the present review is to identify emerging theories in CIDE, we decided to take Paulston (1999) as our point of departure and use 2000–2010 as the time frame for our literature review.

One member of our research team was responsible for going through each journal and identifying potential articles describing emerging theories using the criteria explained in the preceding section. After all journals had been reviewed and articles identified, two or more additional members of the research team reviewed the articles to concur with or revise if necessary the findings of the first researcher. If there was disagreement or uncertainty, all team members were consulted and came to a final decision as to whether or not the theory identified in a given article fit our criteria.

From the 2,767 articles we reviewed in the seven journals, we identified 113 articles addressing 29 potential emerging theories. After conferring with the rest of our research team, those numbers were reduced to ten articles containing six emerging theories (see Table 5.1).

Table 5.1. Emerging Theories Based on Theory-Selection Criteria, 2000–2010

Theory	APER	CE	CER	IJED	JEP	JSIE	TCR
Complexity	0	0	0	2	0	0	2
Kaupapa Maori	0	1	0	0	0	0	0
Network of Practice	1	0	0	0	0	0	0
Pedagogical Praxis	0	0	0	0	0	0	1
Public-Good Profession-alism	0	0	0	1	1	0	0
Value-Belief-Norm	0	0	0	0	0	1	0
Total No. of Articles	**1**	**1**	**0**	**3**	**1**	**1**	**3**

Note: APER = Asia Pacific Education Review; CE = Comparative Education; CER = Comparative Education Review; IJED = International Journal of Educational Development; JEP = Journal of Education Policy; JSIE = Journal of Studies in International Education; TCR = Teachers College Record.

ANALYSIS AND FINDINGS

After identifying the theories, we wanted to position them within a framework that highlights locations and relationships within a theoretical and social context. Social cartography creates a space for the depiction of such relationships, thus providing a deeper understanding of multiple perspectives (Paulston and Liebman 2000). For this we adapted Paulston's (1994) map of paradigms and theories in comparative and international education to incorporate the six identified emerging theories in this chapter (see Figure 5.1).

Paulston's 1994 map, a heuristic device meant to organize and show relationships of a growing discourse, is comprised of four paradigmatic positions and 16 theories. The arrows represent "the interparadigmatic and intertheoretic borrowing and interaction of ideas" (Liebman 2000b, 335). Paulston and Liebman (2000) caution that given the holistic nature of this map, any challenge to the space of the framework or the mininarratives as they are positioned needs to be accompanied by a thorough analysis. For us, this caveat encompasses additions to the map placed in relation to the existing theories. Since such a detailed analysis is beyond the scope of this chapter, we want to at least begin the discussion by placing the six emerging theories within one or more of Paulston's (1994) paradigmatic positions. According to our interpretation, the six theories identified in our review can be aligned with the paradigmatic positions on Paulston's map outlined in Table 5.2.

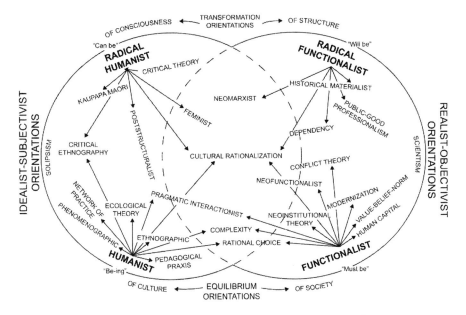

Figure 5.1. A Macromapping of Paradigms and Theories in CIDE.
Source: Adapted by the authors from Paulston (1994, 931).

Table 5.2 Positioning Identified Theories within Paulston's 1994 Map

Theory	Paradigmatic Position
Complexity	Centered between Humanist and Functionalist
Kaupapa Maori	Radical Humanist
Network of Practice	Humanist
Pedagogical Praxis	Humanist
Public-Good Professionalism	Radical Functionalist
Value-Belief-Norm	Functionalist

In connecting the theories to a paradigmatic position, we also want to identify them as either a metatheory or a microtheory. Our goal in doing so is to provide another aspect of understanding the theories in a larger theoretical landscape before moving to our discussion. As outlined in Table 5.3, three of the emerging theories could be identified as metatheories in that they are "theory about theory" (Morrow and Torres 1995, 19) while the other three could be identified as microtheories. Jacob and Cheng (2005) clarify the difference between meta- and microtheory by noting that "theoretical perspectives may differ within a given metatheory," but "the assertions within a microtheory must be mutually consistent" (237). In addition, "metatheory is an overarching theoretical paradigm that incorporates several theoretical perspectives" (237).

Table 5.3. Identified Theories as Metatheory or Microtheory

Metatheory	Complexity, Network of Practice, and Value-Belief Norm
Microtheory	Pedagogical Praxis, Public-Good Professionalism, and Kaupapa Maori

It is important to note that some theories could be perceived as both a metatheory and a microtheory. For instance, Graham Smith (2010b), who is credited with laying the groundwork for Kaupapa Maori as a theory, contends that Kaupapa Maori is an emerging theory that informs critical theory as much as critical theory informs Kaupapa Maori. At the same time, Kaupapa Maori has distinct sociocultural characteristics that make it specific to the Maori-New Zealand context. Another aspect that distinguishes Kaupapa Maori from others is the debate amongst Maori scholars whether or not to include it in Western theoretical frameworks or discourse (Smith 2000; Ratima 2008). There is concern the theory would become institutionalized, thus constraining its organic nature and potential. Such dynamics not only reflect the development of Kaupapa Maori Theory, but also highlight the dynamic nature of theory as well as CIDE.

DISCUSSION

The six emerging theories identified in our review of the literature are outlined below, moving from macro to micro; the three metatheories are presented first followed by three theories we identified as microtheories. Each description includes a brief overview, the theory's origin, subject(s) of study, ontology, epistemology, and methodology.

Metatheories

1. Complexity Theory. While more often associated with educational philosophy, our review found four instances of authors using Complexity Theory to examine issues related to overcoming the struggles associated with development education. Complexity Theory describes an approach to study that takes into account the wide range of variables within a system, with a focus on attributes of system stakeholders that can impact the functioning of the system. One of Complexity Theory's most prolific authors, Mark Mason (2009, 118) explains that, "Complexity theory concerns itself with environments, organizations, or systems that are complex in the sense that very large numbers of constituent elements or agents are connected to and interacting with each other in many different ways." While Complexity Theory has been in existence in other fields, the theory has just recently begun to be applied in CIDE in order to help researchers understand phenomena related to the creation of organizations of education in developing contexts.

1.1 Origin. Complexity Theory is an emerging theory in CIDE and could best be described as an import to educational theory from the "hard" sciences. Specifically, Complexity Theory is much more often used in the fields of physics, biology, chemistry, economics, engineering, ecology, and math and is seen as a complimentary theory to Chaos Theory (Alhadeff-Jones 2008; McQuillan 2008; Mason 2009). While a few researchers in the 1990s, most notably Ralph Stacey, began to apply Complexity Theory to social organizations (Zellermayer and Margolin 2005), we found that it was not until 2005 that Complexity Theory was first employed within the CIDE journals under review. Sometimes called "Complex Adaptive Systems" (Zellermayer and Margolin 2005), Complexity Theory is increasingly being used to explain the nature and quality of growing educational organizations, especially within the development education context. While it is often the case that hard sciences and "soft" sciences seem to be at odds with each other methodologically, Complexity Theory serves as an example of how soft sciences can learn from and adapt the processes of hard sciences to increase our understanding of social phenomena (Byrne 1998).

1.2 Subject. Within Complexity Theory, as it is applied to CIDE, educational organizations are most often seen as the subject of study. The theory is concerned with the way in which the community interacts within the education setting; a setting that would be defined in Complexity Theory as including not just the administration, teachers and students, but also the stakeholders in the process such as parents, community, government, and those who provide funding (Zellermayer and Margolin 2005; McQuillan 2008). All of these contributing members of the organization are seen as playing a role in shaping how the organization functions, with even the smallest of changes having the capacity to drastically alter the overall form of the educational setting.

Complexity Theory in CIDE seeks to explain the seemingly unpredictable facets of an ever-changing educational organization. Acknowledging that these organizations are complex and that prediction with certitude is impossible, Complexity Theory attempts to explain that certain predictable "control parameters" can be discovered and that these control parameters provide equilibrium to the system by demonstrating some level of predictability and routine to actions within the complex organization (McQuillan 2008). In other words, Complexity Theory seeks patterns of behavior within an educational organization that may help to more accurately predict the behavior of that organization.

1.3 Ontology. Reality within Complexity Theory is an interesting concept, in that it is shaped by the people within the educational organization but also exists above the individuals within the organization as a set of control parameters and routines that are theoretically discoverable (McQuillan 2008). The reality of Complexity Theory is shaped by the interconnectedness of the individuals (McQuillan 2008), as well as their diversity and creativity (Zellermayer and Margolin 2005) all working together to overcome, what Bjorn Nordtveit (2009) referred to as the "inertia" of an educational organization, or their resistance to movement toward development. While Complexity Theory allows the researcher to find facets of the educational organization that affect its growth and development, it does not presume to ever fully understand this reality. Rather, the theory seeks to enable a researcher to discover contributing factors to the current shape of an educational organization and allow the researcher to make more informed predictions about future development.

1.4 Epistemology. Because the understanding of reality in Complexity Theory reflects both subjective and objective orientations, the essence of knowledge shares an equally dual nature. On the one hand, researchers appear to study these organizations from the outside, with a clear sense of impartiality. From this outside perspective, they are attempting to uncover what they see as somewhat predictable patterns of behavior that shape the development of the educational organization (McQuillan 2008). However, researchers using Complexity Theory to study educational organizations are not attempting to describe with certainty any type of causal relationships, rather they are seeking to understand why an organization develops the way it does, how interactions of stakeholders within the educational organization shape its development, and make some limited predictions about the future behavior of the organization (Zellermayer and Margolin 2005; McQuillan 2008).

The questions asked by researchers using Complexity Theory tend to revolve around the concept of *emergence,* defined by Michal Zellermayer and Ilana Margolin (2005, 1279) as "observed phenomena that do not exist on the level of individual elements but emerge from the dynamics of the relations between different parts of the context." Researchers find themselves looking at examples of emergence in order to determine how the different aspects and actions of individual stakeholders shape the educational organization in new ways and how they combine to push an organization beyond what appears to be a sum of its parts. By exploring emergence and the organizational factors that lead to this phenomena, researchers hope to discover the control parameters operating within the educational organization, to both understand how the organization has reached its current level of development and what attributes of the organization may be able to contribute to future development.

1.5 Methodology. Complexity Theory has the possibility of using both quantitative and qualitative techniques to understand educational organizations (Byrne 1998). Because the focus of study is an educational organization, researchers lack the ability to enforce external controls, limiting the applicability of purely experimental methods of inquiry within this theory (Horn 2008). However, quasi-experimental techniques do seem possible where a theoretically impartial, outside observer can quantify certain attributes of the organization in order to look for some relationships that at least provide for some strong correlations. More often though, in order to describe the qualities of these attributes in a manner that is useful for the organization, the researcher becomes involved with the research community, where "humans are not subjected to research but, rather, are acknowledged as participants engaged in the ongoing elaboration of the communicative behaviors that include the researchers as well" (Horn 2008, 141). It appears then that Complexity Theory research, as it is applied to educational organizations, is more likely to use research methodologies that fall within the category of qualitative research.

2. *Network of Practice Theory.* Network of Practice (NoP) Theory builds on the idea of Communities of Practice (CoP), creating a superset of associations whose sharing of knowledge is greatly aided by technology, especially e-mail communication. In this instance, technology becomes a key feature in that it facilitates the creation of an expanded group that can interact across multiple sites in a collective manner. As such, the "network" serves a double meaning, both as a connected group with a shared task and as a mode of connectivity. Il-Hyun Jo (2009, 527) explains "As a loosely knit network, the [Network of Practice] has a unique structural advantage in terms of sharing knowledge both within and between networks."

2.1 Origin. The idea of NoP originated with John Seely Brown and Paul Duguid in 2001 and expands the earlier theory of CoP (Lave and Wenger 1991). A traditional CoP involves a smaller group that engages face-to-face; Brown and Duguid (2001) expand that idea to include a larger and more loosely-knit group of individuals engaged in a shared practice.

2.2 Subject. In a CoP, through group social interactions and sharing of knowledge, organizational performance can be improved. NoP extends this idea to a larger group of people who engage in shared practice; the concept of a network involves many people and includes the idea that most people in the network "will never know, know of, or come across one another" (Brown and Duguid 2001, 205). One example of a NoP is a professional organization. Jo (2009) argues that networks of practice have been aided by technological advances in communication, especially email and instant messaging.

2.3 Ontology. Reality within a NoP is created by and for the members of the network. Although members are influenced by their other associations and bring these ideas to the network, essentially within the network knowledge and perspective are created collectively and shared freely amongst the group members. Because of this collective creation of knowledge, NoP tends towards the subjective and humanist axis.

2.4 Epistemology. In both CoP and NoP, learning and the creation of knowledge is a social process; members are engaged in developing a collective outlook and creating a collective knowledge base that is available to all (Brown and Duguid 2001). According to social capital theory, participants in NoP can "enhance their personal reputation in the network" (Jo 2009) through active participation within their network. Because participation in the network is vital, it would be difficult for a researcher within the network to be impartial; thus ethnographic research would be a good fit. Researchers from outside the network may be able to separate themselves enough from the group to claim impartiality.

2.5 Methodology. In our review, we found only one article that used NoP as its theoretical base. In that research, the author, who was not a member of the network, employed a type of analysis called social network analysis (SNA) and performed a quantitative analysis on the participants' use of email. SNA comes primarily from the field of sociology from advocates Mark S. Granovetter (1973) and Barry Wellman and Stephen D. Berkowitz (1988).

3. Value-Belief-Norm Theory. The most recently introduced addition to our identified theories appeared in a November 2010 issue of the *Journal of International Studies in Education.* Value-Belief-Norm Theory (VBN) posits that "[social] movement success depends on movement activists and organizations building support by activating or reshaping personal norms to create feelings of obligation" (Stern et al., 1999, 83). In other words, the success of any social movement depends on the ability of people to align the movement with their own personal value system, thereby creating a sense of obligation to assist in the movement. VBN is specifically geared toward more casual participation in social movements—rather than an explanation of full-blown activism—and as such, proposes to explain much smaller actions that could be viewed as supporting larger social movements (e.g., recycling, petition signing, small donations, etc.). Although popular within discourses about environmental social movements and social-psychology, Michael Tarrant (2010, 434) suggests that one can apply VBN to those who participate in study abroad educational programs in order to "promote global citizenship by modifying beliefs about environmental conditions and influencing proenvironmental behaviors." It is this suggestion that brings Value-Belief-Norm Theory into the CIDE realm.

3.1 Origin. Value-Belief-Norm Theory is another theory imported into CIDE from an outside field, in this case being popular in environmentalism discourses for ten years before making its way into the CIDE literature in 2010. VBN was created in 1999 by a group of authors, led by Paul Stern, in an attempt to explain the reason for non-activist public support for environmental causes. They explain that "[w]e lack a theory of how individuals come to support movements short of committed activism" (Stern et al., 1999, 82). The theory builds heavily on moral norm-activation theory, created by Shalom H. Schwartz (1970, 1977) in the 1970s, which claims that people become involved in social movements when their values are under threat, and that these personal values can very across people leading to different amounts of participation in social movements (Stern et al., 1999). VBN goes one step further to break down the process that causes an individual to become invested in the support of a social movement in order to see how their varying values and personal norms come together to cause action on the part of the individual. Tarrant (2010) brings Value-Belief-Norm Theory to CIDE in an attempt to describe how international experiences in higher education—such as study abroad—can help to align the values and norms of participants to the cause of the global environmental movement.

3.2 Subject. In its use in CIDE, VBN has higher education students as its subject of study. More specifically, practitioners of VBN seek to analyze three values held by students in study abroad programs in order to determine their likelihood of acting in a more or less environmentally responsible way. These values "include a concern for the self (egoistic value) and the nonhuman/living world (biospheric value), in addition to a concern for the welfare of others (altruistic value)" (Tarrant 2010, 437). In analyzing these three values in a student, VBN suggests that one can determine a measure of general environmental concern that the student would normally display. This makes the theory useful in selecting students who may best fit a particular pro-environmental educational program.

Tarrant (2010) goes on to suggest that VBN is not only useful for finding students who may have the most concern for the environment, but that the theory can be used to help design study abroad programs that would focus on changing the underlying values, beliefs and norms of students to make them more environmentally conscious and active after their educational experience. In this case, the approach favored by Tarrant in applying VBN to design more effective environmental study abroad programs is one in which students would have direct experiences with the environment. By having direct experiences with the environment, students may become more personally aware and invested in the fragile nature of the environment and its importance to our planet, increasing their level of concern for insuring its safety. While the focus of VBN is not to create environmental activists, it does suggest that as more individuals begin to show concern for protecting the environment, this concern becomes incorporated into our societal and cultural norms, perhaps leading to a major cultural shift away from environmentally damaging practices.

3.3 Ontology. In Value-Belief-Norm Theory, researchers are concerned with providing measurements of three values—egoistic value, biospheric value, and altruistic value—in order to determine a subject's likelihood of embracing pro-environmental behaviors (Stern et al., 1999). This means that reality in this theory is something that can be discovered and measured in a quantitative way and actions can be taken to alter these values and, consequently, the likelihood of environmental action on the part of the subject. This places VBN within the functionalist quadrant of social theory, with both an objective reality to be discovered and the theoretical tendency to make causal links between characteristics of a person and their later social actions. Adherents to VBN believe that they can not only make predictions about the likelihood of human social behavior based on measurements of a subject's personal values, but that by attempting to alter these values, they might also increase or decrease the likelihood of engagement in certain social behaviors in the future.

3.4 Epistemology. Value-Belief-Norm Theory has at its core a concern for inspiring others to take up the cause of environmentalism by internalizing values that would make them see threats to the environment as threats to their personal value system. As such, the knowledge that VBN practitioners are most concerned with are ways in which changes to values can result in changes to behaviors, what VBN practitioners refer to as the "causal chain." Stern and colleagues (1999, 86) explain that

> the causal chain moves from relatively stable, central elements of personality and belief structure to more focused beliefs about human-environment relations, the threats they pose to valued objects, and the responsibility for action, finally activating a sense of moral obligation that creates a predisposition to act in support of movement goals.

Therefore, knowledge claims within VBN relate to increased understanding of the functioning of this causal chain and improvement of the chain's predictive abilities.

Researchers employing VBN tend to raise questions that result from different parts of the theory. In the original formulation of VBN, the authors were interested in determining the link between the beginning of the chain and the end, so they chose to measure the personal values of study participants and relate them to their overall desire to contribute to the environmental movement (Stern et al., 1999). Tarrant (2010), in applying VBN to CIDE, instead chose to use the causal chain in a reverse order, suggesting that study abroad programs that desire to instill pro-environmental behaviors in students ought to question ways in which they can seek to change students' personal values.

3.5 Methodology. Research in Value-Belief-Norm Theory most often centers on the measurement of these personal values and the relation of different degrees of those values to a propensity for small-scale involvement in the environmental movement. Stern and colleagues (1999), made use of survey questions with likert scale responses (strongly agree, somewhat agree, somewhat disagree, strongly disagree) in order to determine the levels of egoistic, biospheric and altruistic values, which they then attempted to link to pro-environmental behaviors that study participants had been engaging in. Within CIDE, Tarrant (2010) makes use of two case studies as examples of study abroad programs that appear to effectively inspire pro-environmental behaviors in their students, and then highlights aspects of these programs that influence the personal values and norms of the study abroad students, causing them to become more concerned for the environment. While these studies represent different approaches to a methodology for analysis under VBN, they both have at the core an inquiry into the causal links between personal values and pro-environmental actions.

Microtheories

1. Pedagogical Praxis Theory. Pedagogical Praxis is a theory related to an adaptation of the practice of teaching that includes fusing new information technology with experiences that simulate real world applications in order to both educate and motivate students. The goal of Pedagogical Praxis Theory is to allow students to adapt to life in a postindustrial society by proposing substantive changes to the way students are educated that account for increasing levels of globalization and technological development. The goal of Pedagogical Praxis is to increase the level of complexity of the learning process to incorporate "emerging social, economic and technological forces and their implications for cognition and citizenship" (Shaffer 2004, 1402).

1.1 Origin. Pedagogical Praxis originates in *Teachers College Record* in a July 2004 article written by David Williamson Shaffer (2004) in which he is proposing this new theory to try to embrace the trends in technological growth and problems he sees with current pedagogy in the classrooms of postindustrial nations. While he is the first to name and elucidate this theory, he also explains some of the theoretical links for his thinking. Pedagogical Praxis builds heavily on a theory called "Reflective Practice" which suggests that professionals learn best by action focused on professional experiences in their fields (Schön 1983, 1991). Shaffer takes this concept and applies it to children in a classroom, reasoning that if adults can learn by doing on the job, children can as well. Additionally, Pedagogical Praxis recognizes the increasing growth and incorporation of new technology in the workplace and is reacting to this growth by calling for similar growth and technological usage in the classroom setting.

1.2 Subject. The subject of Pedagogical Praxis is the methodology employed by teachers in the classroom and how this pedagogy applies to students in their future adult lives. Shaffer (2004, 1403) explains, "pedagogical praxis investigates the nature of learning and its relationship to the central cultural, social, and economic practices of the post-industrial era." Essential to this investigation is the incorporation of emerging technological advancements into the practices of classroom teachers and their use by students. Shaffer argues that creating classrooms that allow students to use technology to engage in activities that simulate those that might be found in their adult working lives will compel children to learn and prepare them for the increasingly globalized world marketplace.

1.3 Ontology. Reality within the theory of Pedagogical Praxis is one that is constructed by teachers and students in a classroom setting, and while teachers may begin the process by adapting their pedagogy to such a theory, it is the involvement of the students that shapes the reality within the classroom itself. Pedagogical Praxis seeks to create, for and with the students, an environment that authentically aligns classroom activities with: (1) goals important to the outside community, (2) goals that are meaningful to the students, (3) ways of knowing present in an established field, and/or (4) a way of assessment the students will be subject to (Shaffer 2004). Essential to this reality creation is the incorporation of technology into the classroom. The goal is to use technology to "create experimental learning environments designed to develop life skills through participation in a community of practice" (Shaffer 2004, 1405). Whereas Pedagogical Praxis is concerned with aligning student learning with advancements in technology and outside professions, it is clear that to some degree the reality of this theory is also shaped by shifting elements of globalization and their impact on the workplace.

1.4 Epistemology. Knowledge within Pedagogical Praxis is shaped by influences from outside of the classroom and by the students and teacher within the classroom. This knowledge focuses on "learning and the conditions and processes of learning that facilitate learning in technology-rich contexts writ large" (Shaffer 2004, 1402). This includes a focus on activities within the school, as well as after school activities where school, family, mass media, friends and the community all connect (Shaffer 2004). A formal researcher in Pedagogical Praxis would naturally need to be immersed within the setting in order to gain a full understanding of the process, making impartiality highly unlikely. Additionally, Pedagogical Praxis is a theory that appears to empower the students and teachers in the classroom to become active investigators of the types and content of knowledge created in the class. To question this knowledge, researchers would most often concern themselves with issues related to the use of technology, the building of global connections, and the relevancy of classroom practices to real world settings.

1.5 Methodology. Shaffer (2004), as the originator of Pedagogical Praxis, seems very concerned about clarifying the methodology of his theory. He explains that the methodology contains five key steps to enacting new pedagogy based on this theory. First, a baseline study is concerned with piloting a set of learning practices to explore how students relate to professional ways of working and thinking. Second, ethnographic studies should be conducted to determine how professionals learn in the field. Third, technology should be developed to bring this outside professional world into the classroom. Fourth, the technology should be used to construct a learning environment in which the students simulate the practices found in the ethnographic studies. Lastly, outcomes-based measurements should be developed to evaluate progress in the learning environment and connection to the outside communities. While the steps appear to function in a linear manner, it is reasonable to expect that these processes would need to be repeated regularly in order for the classroom to continue to adapt to the ever-changing composition of our globalized world.

2. Public-Good Professionalism Theory. Public-Good Professionalism is a theory in its initial stages. It combines the ideas of human development as capability building with a social obligation to others in the hope that "professionals would contribute in different ways to expanding and securing comprehensive capabilities to all in society, but especially those living in conditions of poverty and vulnerability" (Walker and McLean n.d.). Although originally contextualized at the university level—due to the role universities play in the preparation of professionals—it could potentially be expanded to cover multiple levels of educational settings and a variety of professional development situations.

2.1 Origin. Public-Good Professionalism was first theorized as pro-poor professionalism in 2009 by researchers investigating the contribution South African universities can make toward poverty reduction in that country (Walker and McLean n.d.; Walker et al., 2009). The idea of Public-Good Professionalism builds on the capability approach pioneered by Amartya Sen (1988, 1989, 1993), specifically focusing on a university education as the means of building capabilities and the transformation of society. Public-Good Professionalism combines the ideas of human development as capability building with a social obligation to others in the hope that "professionals would contribute in different ways to expanding and securing comprehensive capabilities to all in society, but especially those living in conditions of poverty and vulnerability" (Walker and McLean n.d.).

2.2 Subject. Public-Good Professionalism builds on Sen's capability approach, in particular that Public-Good Professionalism is "the expansion of people's capabilities—both the people to whom professionals provide a service and the professionals themselves" (Walker et al., 2009, 567). This dual layer of capability building focuses on development at the individual level, while at the same time aiming to increase development at the societal level through the reduction of poverty.

Public-Good Professionalism is focused on university institutions, and maintains that if universities work to provide transformational teaching through critical awareness of society then a professional who is able to reduce poverty through praxis will be formed. For the creators of this theory, poverty reduction means "capability expansion" (567) and offers a "generative approach to equality, advantage and social change" (571).

2.3 Ontology. Reality within the theory of Public-Good Professionalism is one that is constructed by the university's policies and practices, and although the student is creating and enhancing their individual professional values, it is the university that determines what that knowledge will be. The originators of the theory explain that "when universities do certain kinds of things, certain kinds of student professionals are formed" (566). Despite the fact that professional capabilities are seen as created through the actions of the university, without the students' input, Public-Good Professionalism advocates for poverty reduction through social change and thus orientates itself toward the radical change dimension.

2.4 Epistemology. Knowledge building in Public-Good Professionalism aims to be both transformative and critical, encompassing three main areas: contextual knowledge, identity development, and transformative learning (568). In the case study conducted by the original researchers, the focus is at the institutional level, not the individual level, and aims to determine what institutions should do to create professionals who have the capability to be a change agent and the capability for affiliation. Researchers could find themselves operating from an external point of view, maintain their impartiality as observers, or they could find themselves operating from an internal point of being the change agent for the university.

2.5 Methodology. The originators of Public-Good Professionalism used a qualitative study consisting of interviews at professional education sites within South African universities (i.e., social work schools, law schools, etc.) and supplemented these interviews with statistical information and university policy documents. Building from the list of comprehensive capabilities compiled by Martha Nussbaum (2000) and Jonathan Wolff and Avner de-Shalit (2007), the originators of the theory created a professional capabilities index that identifies eight professional capabilities that can be applied to the university setting for planning or evaluative purposes.

3. Kaupapa Maori Theory. Translated as "Maori philosophy and principles," Kaupapa Maori Theory is a worldview or way of knowing the world that advocates "increased self-determination of Maori people as equal partners in the formation of the modern nation-state of New Zealand" (Bishop 2003, 223). This involves the coming together of *whakapapa* (genealogy) and *whanau* (kinship) in reformulating the Maori identity, an identity that is Maori owned and controlled. Such transformative action looks to the past to develop "an equitable present and future" (Fitzsimons and Smith 2000, 39).

3.1 Origin. After formal colonization by the British, marked by the signing of the Treaty of Waitangi in 1840, the promise of cultural and linguistic protection was established. This paved the way for future reparations and redress after Maori people had experienced decades of subjugation. It was not until the 1980s that Maori began to assert their rights to self-development within and through alternative education and schooling initiatives (Fitzsimons and Smith 2000; Smith 2003; Motohashi 2007). Smith (2010a) emphasized this shift

> toward self-development in education was accompanied by a simultaneous shift in thinking about the politics of knowledge; Maori began to understand the social construction of knowledge and subsequent ability of dominant groups to manipulate knowledge. Critical understandings related to the 'control over knowledge' led to Maori reclaiming and asserting the validity of Maori language, knowledge, and culture. The changes occurring in this contested space between dominant and subordinate[d] interests needs to be understood both theoretically and practically.

Unpacking the dialectal relationship between theory and practice laid the groundwork for Kaupapa Maori to be identified as a theory of transformative praxis (Smith 1997).

While the principles of Kaupapa Maori are based on traditional knowledge and cultural values, it was first argued as a theory in 1997 by Graham Smith in his unpublished PhD thesis *The Development of Kaupapa Maori: Theory and Praxis* and is not prevalent in the literature as such until after 2000. While praxis *is* fundamental, Smith (2003) argues the need for theory as a portable tool to assist in the positive and proactive transformation of indigenous groups. Furthermore, Smith (2010a) contends that theorizing Kaupapa Maori opens up space in the academy to develop a canon that is based on and reinforces the validity of indigenous knowledge. In Smith's (1997) view, Kaupapa Maori Theory and Praxis need to align with critical theory. While critical theory engages dominant hegemony and allows space for the existence of Maori knowledge forms (Smith 2010a), Kaupapa Maori Theory focuses on transformative action through the revitalization and maintenance of Maori language, culture and identity to form new power relationships (Fitzsimons and Smith 2000; Bishop 2003; Smith 2003; Pihama et al., 2004; Mane 2009).

3.2 Subject. In theorizing Kaupapa Maori, Smith (1997) identified six intervention principles[3] core to the success of the Maori alternative education and schooling initiatives in the 1980s that have since been successfully applied to other areas (Fitzsimons and Smith 2000). As a result, Kaupapa Maori Theory is not bound to education or a particular age group. It has the capacity to address Maori inequalities in various sectors (e.g., education, health, justice, housing, etc.) and work with all age groups (Fitzsimons and Smith 2000; Smith 2003; Pihama et al., 2004) as it "challenges, questions, and critiques expressions of the dominant White New Zealander hegemony" (Pihama in Pihama et al., 2004, 10–11).

3.3 Ontology. Reality is to be shaped by Maori for Maori, the process for which involves intervention and resistance strategies. According to Smith (2003), intervention strategies involve a non-linear and recursive cycle of conscientization, resistance, and transformative action. Maori, who are knowingly or unknowingly engaged in struggle, enter the cycle at any point and can engage with more than one state at a time. This inclusive cycle of transformative praxis is an extension of a critical pedagogy by which Maori might liberate "themselves from multiple oppression(s) and exploitation" (Smith 2003, 8).

3.4 Epistemology. Knowledge is a complex conceptualization in Kaupapa Maori Theory. Leonie Pihama and colleagues (2004) state that three types of knowledge exist: celestial knowledge, esoteric knowledge, and knowledge as it relates to the physical world. Kaupapa Maori itself is knowledge acquired based on experiences of Maori throughout history, informed by "the world 'behind' this world of constructed reality" (Marsden as cited in Pihama et al., 2004, 19). As a result, knowledge has "a dual structure, a sacred inner corpus and a general or every day corpus of knowledge" (Pihama et al., 2004, 19).

These beliefs are reflected in Smith's (1997) intervention principles, the two more central ones being mediation of socio-economic and home circumstances and collective vision or philosophy (Smith 2010b). The former, *kia piki ake i nga raruraru o te kainga,* acknowledges the socio-economic difficulties and other disadvantages Maori have faced yet stresses the ability to overcome them through an extended family network. The latter intervention principle stresses the need for a collective vision or commitment. Described as a "utopian vision," this principle is important as it "is able to provide impetus and direction to struggle" (Smith 2003, 8).

3.5 Methodology. Kaupapa Maori epistemology influences research in that researchers are expected to have a critical understanding not only of themselves (as Maori) but of Maori they research. While non-Maori can carry out research, it is doubtful their role would be a significant one. Several Maori scholars argue that "being Maori, identifying as Maori and as a Maori researcher, is a critical element of Kaupapa Maori research" (Smith 2000, 229).

Other elements key in undertaking Kaupapa Maori research include, but are not limited to, knowledge of the language, cultural sensitivity, collaboration, empowerment, and reciprocity. Research itself is often multi-disciplinary and not reliant on a single method or approach. It is viewed as a "social project" (Smith 2000, 233), the nature of which is participatory with attention to shared power and control (Mane 2009).

CONCLUSION

Researchers and practitioners in CIDE can utilize and apply these six new theories in a multitude of ways, thus enriching and expanding our knowledge of education in comparative, international and developmental contexts. Possible applications of these emerging theories include: examining instruction and learning at the classroom level, examining and building capacity at the organizational level, enhancing teacher professional development, using teaching as a transformative practice, and enhancing education development efforts. While the theories could have several, overlapping applications and warrant a richer discussion, we briefly describe how they are applicable to the area(s) we feel each one more closely aligns with.

Applications at the Classroom Level

At the heart of education are interactions between students and teachers in the classroom. Three of the emerging theories—Pedagogical Praxis, Kaupapa Maori, and VBN—are concerned with *what* students learn in the classroom. Pedagogical Praxis, with its dual focus on reflexive learning and incorporation of technology, can be used by researchers and practitioners when making instructional decisions. Kaupapa Maori Theory, which grew in part from concern that Maori values and knowledge were not being incorporated into classroom practice, could be used to consider how instruction can or does address the interests of minority students.

Although Value-Belief-Norm Theory is currently more associated with international education program design, it could be applied at the classroom level through a curriculum designed to instill increased pro-environmental sentiment and action in students. By designing programs or curricula that cause students to experience and interact with the environment in meaningful ways, CIDE practitioners of VBN aspire for students to more fully incorporate protection of the environment into their personal value system. Following this process, students should be more apt to engage in small-scale activities that benefit the environmental movement.

Applications at the Organizational Level

Most classroom teaching and learning is supported at the organizational level, by the school or district, or by larger organizations at the regional and national levels. Researchers and practitioners studying education at the organizational level can apply several of the emerging theories to their work in two distinct areas: first, by studying how and why an organization functions the way it does; and secondly, as a tool to build the organization's knowledge capacity.

Complexity Theory can be used to study the behavior of organizations. Complexity Theory, with its focus on multiple variables within a system, can be used to look at the interaction of different parts of a system, and the effect of a part on the whole. Although it is important to note that in our review of the CIDE literature, most researchers using Complexity Theory chose to theorize about potentials, rather than actual study of a specific educational organization, it is not difficult to see how this theory could be applied to a practical setting.

The emerging theories can also be used in organizational capacity building. NoP, with its focus on using technology to link together a great number of professionals, can give expanded international reach to its workers. Jo (2009, 533) argues that "little has been done to develop systematic ways of working with the knowledge that is embedded in social networks" leaving open many vast possibilities for policy makers and researchers.

Applications for Teacher Professional Development

Similar to building capacity at the organizational level, several of the theories described can be used to improve teacher practice through teacher professional development. Public-Good Professionalism, and the creation of a professional capabilities index, offers a concrete framework for the development of professional capabilities. NoP can have a substantial effect on teacher professional development by allowing geographically segregated, but professionally linked, colleagues to work together and share best practices. NoP can also be used to link effective and experienced teachers with newer, less experienced teachers to engage in mentoring activities.

Applications for Transformative Teaching

Kaupapa Maori Theory and Public-Good Professionalism both expand on the idea of teaching as a means for social transformation. Kaupapa Maori Theory, according to Smith (2009, 1), "confronts hierarchies of knowledge that are a fundamental, 'taken for granted' premise within the Western academy." It can contribute to CIDE discourse by opening up what has been primarily Eurocentric, to include alternative traditions and ways of knowing. When we understand the symbiotic relationship between the local and global, our capacity to engage in dialogue and transform increases, which is paramount given the socio-cultural differences that exist within and across borders (Kamel 1990). Public-Good

Professionalization also focuses on equalizing power relationships, but pays particular attention to teacher training programs in the hope that the newly graduated teachers will "choose to be professionals responsibly committed to pro-poor human development" (Walker et al., 2009, 565).

Applications for Education Development

Although the emerging theories are different from each other, one commonality exists—they can all be applied to the study of educational development efforts across the globe (see Table 5.4). Kaupapa Maori Theory, for example, can inform other indigenous contexts. It focuses on the process of transformative action and outcomes embedded in a culturally specific epistemology and framework others can build upon and modify to address their cultural preferences and conditions.

Table 5.4. Application of Emerging CIDE Theories

Theory	Classroom Level	Organization Level	Teacher PD	Transform. Practice	Develop. Education
Complexity		X			X
Network of Practice		X	X		X
Value-Belief-Norm	X				X
Pedagogical Praxis	X				X
Public-Good Profess-ionalism			X	X	X
Kaupapa Maori	X			X	X

As CIDE continues to evolve, so too do CIDE theories, allowing researchers and practitioners to draw from an array of theoretical approaches to help them best explain what, when, why, and how social phenomena interact and exist. Time, however, will determine how valuable of a tool any of the emerging theories identified in this chapter will become. "The ultimate test of a theory," Mark Fettes (1998, 251) asserts, "will be whether it can be picked up and applied, criticized, revised, and extended as an evolving guide to practice."

NOTES

1. The three journals Rust and his colleagues examined include *Comparative Education, Comparative Education Review,* and *International Journal of Educational Development.*
2. The five journals we dropped from our final list were *British Educational Research Journal, Harvard Educational Review, Journal of Philosophy of Education, Oxford Review of Education,* and *Theory into Practice.*
3. Smith's six principles guide the transformative praxis of Kaupapa Maori Theory. While these principles were initially created as intervention principles for Maori alternative education and schooling initiatives in the 1980s, they are applicable to other areas. The six principles are as follows: The self-determination principle (*tino rangatiratanga*) stresses autonomy and the ability to take control over one's life and cultural well being. The cultural aspirations principle (*taonga tuku iho*) reinforces that to be Maori is a given, which makes it possible for a spiritual and emotional factor to be incorporated into various settings. There is no need for Maori to justify their identity

(Smith 2003; Pihama et al., 2004). The culturally preferred pedagogy principle (*ako Maori*) emphasizes reciprocal learning that is active and connects with one's cultural backgrounds and life experiences (Bishop, 2003). The meditation of socio-economic and home difficulties principle (*kia piki ake i nga raruraru o te kainga*) acknowledges the socioeconomic difficulties and other disadvantages Maori have faced yet stresses the ability to overcome them through collective commitment and intervention. The extended family structure principle (*whanau*) is fundamental to Maori identity and cultural aspirations and practices; it highlights commitment, connectedness, responsibility, and collaboration (Bishop 2003). The collective vision or philosophy principle (*kaupapa*) stresses the need for a collective vision or commitment as it "is able to provide impetus and direction to struggle" (Smith 2003, 8).

REFERENCES

Alhadeff-Jones, Michel. (2008). "Three Generations of Complexity Theories: Nuances and Ambiguities." *Educational Philosophy and Theory, 40*(1), 66–82.

Bishop, Russell. (2003). "Changing Power Relations in Education: Kaupapa Maori Messages for 'Mainstream' Education in Aotearoa/New Zealand." *Comparative Education, 39*(2), 221–238.

Brown, John Seely, & Paul Duguid. (2001). "Knowledge and Organization: A Social Practice Perspectives." *Organizational Science, 12*(2), 198–213.

Byrne, David. (1998). *Complexity Theory and the Social Sciences: An Introduction.* New York: Routledge.

Crossley, Michael, and Leon Tikly. (2004). Postcolonial Perspectives and Comparative and International Research in Education: A Critical Introduction." *Comparative Education, 40*(2), 147–156.

Fettes, Mark. (1998). "Indigenous Education and the Ecology of Community." *Language, Culture and Curriculum, 11*(3), 250–271.

Fitzsimmons, Patrick, & Graham H. Smith. (2000). "Philosophy and Indigenous Cultural Transformation." *Educational Philosophy and Theory, 32*(1), 25–41.

Granovetter, Mark S. (1973). "The Strength of Weak Ties." *American Journal of Sociology, 78*(6), 1360-1380.

Hegel, Georg W. F. (1979). *Systems of Ethical Life and First Philosophy of Spirit*, trans H. S. Harris and T. M. Knox. Albany: State University of New York Press.

Horn, James. (2008). "Human Research and Complexity Theory." *Educational Philosophy and Theory, 40*(1), 130–143.

Jacob, W. James, & Sheng Yao Cheng. (2005). "Mapping Paradigms and Theories in Comparative, International, and Development Education (CIDE) Research." *International Perspectives on Education and Society,* (6), 231–268.

Jo, Il-Hyun. (2009). "The Effect of Social Network Diagrams on a Virtual Network of Practice: A Korean Case." *Asia Pacific Review, 10,* 525–534.

Kamel, Rachael. (1990). *The Global Factory: Analysis and Action for a New Economic Era.* Philadelphia, PA: American Friends Service Committee.

Lave, Jean, & Etienne Wenger. (1991). *Situated Learning: Legitimate Peripheral Participation.* Cambridge: Cambridge University Press.

Liebman, Martin. (2000a). "Envisioning Spatial Metaphors from Wherever We Stand." In Rolland G. Paulston (Ed.), *Social Cartography: Mapping Ways of Seeing Social and Educational Change* (pp. 191–215). Pittsburgh: University of Pittsburgh Book Center.

Liebman, Martin. (2000b). "Social Mapping: The Art of Representing Intellectual Perception." In Rolland G. Paulston (Ed.), *Social Cartography: Mapping Ways of Seeing Social and Educational Change* (pp. 327–340). Pittsburgh: University of Pittsburgh Book Center.

Lyotard, Jean-Francois. (1984). *The Postmodern Condition: A Report on Knowledge*, trans. Geoff Bennington and Brian Massumi. Minneapolis: University of Minnesota Press.

Mane, Jo. (2009). "Kaupapa Maori: A Community Approach." *MAI Review,* (3), 1–9.

Marginson, Simon, & Marcela Mollis. (2001). ""The Door Opens and the Tiger Leaps": Theory and Method in Comparative Education in the Global Era." *Comparative Education Review, 45*(4), 581–615.

Mason, Mark. (2009). "Making Educational Development and Change Sustainable: Insights from Complexity Theory." *International Journal of Educational Development, 29*(2), 117–124.

McQuillan, Patrick J. (2008). "Small-School Reform Through the Lens of Complexity Theory: It's "Good to Think With"." *Teachers College Record, 110* (9), 1772–1801.

Morrow, Raymond, & Carlos Torres. (1995). *Social Theory and Education: A Critique of Theories of Social and Cultural Reproduction.* New York: State University of New York Press.

Motohashi, Ellen. P. (2007). "Despair Turned to Hope: A Theoretical Reconsideration of the Maori as a Caste Minority." *Educational Foundations* summer-fall: 73–88.

Nordtveit, Bjorn Harald. (2009). "Development as a Complex Process of Change: Conception and Analysis of Projects, Programs and Policies." *International Journal of Educational Development, 30*(2), 110–117.

Nussbaun, Martha C. (2000). *Women and Human Development.* Cambridge: Cambridge University Press.

Paulston, Rolland G. (1994). "Comparative and International Education: Paradigms and Theories." In ed. T. Neville Postlethwaite and Torsten Husen (2nd ed.), *International Encyclopedia of Education,* Oxford: Pergamon Press.

Paulston, Rolland G. (1999). "Mapping Comparative Education After Postmodernity." *Comparative Education Review, 43*(4), 438–463.

Paulston, Rolland G. (2000). "Editor's Forward." In Rolland G. Paulston (Ed.), *Social Cartography: Mapping Ways of Seeing Social and Educational Change,* Pittsburgh: University of Pittsburgh Book Center.

Paulston, Rolland G., & Martin Liebman. (2000). "Social Cartography: A New Metaphor/Tool for Comparative Studies." In Rolland G. Paulston (Ed.), *Social Cartography: Mapping Ways of Seeing Social and Educational Change,* Pittsburgh: University of Pittsburgh Book Center.

Pihama, Leonie, Kaapua Smith, Mereana Taki, & Jenny Lee. (2004). *A Literature Review on Kaupapa Maori and Maori Education Pedagogy.* Auckland: The International Research Institute for Maori and Indigenous Education, University of Auckland.

Ratima, Matiu. (2008). "Making Space for Kaupapa Maori Within the Academy." *MAI Review,* (1), 1–3.

Rust, Val D. (2004). "Postmodernism and Globalization: The State of the Debate." Presented at the Comparative and International Education Society Annual Conference, Salt Lake City, Utah.

Rust, Val D. (2000). "From Modern to Postmodern Ways of Seeing Social and Educational Change." In Rolland G. Paulston (Ed.), *Social Cartography: Mapping Ways of Seeing Social and Educational Change,* Pittsburgh: University of Pittsburgh Book Center.

Rust, Val D., Aminata Soumare, Octavio Pescador, & Megumi Shibuya. (1999). "Research Strategies in Comparative Education." *Comparative Education Review, 43*(1), 86–109.

Schön, Donald A. (1983). *The Reflective Practitioner: How Professionals Think in Action.* New York: Basic Books.

Schön, Donald A. (1991). *The Reflective Turn: Case Studies In and On Educational Practice.* New York: Teachers College Press.

Sen, Amartya. (1988). "The Concept of Development." In Hollis Chenery and T. N. Strinivasan (Ed.), *Handbooks of Development Economics* (pp. 9–26). Amsterdam: Elsevier, North-Holland.

Sen, Amartya. (1989). "Development as Capability Expansion." *Journal of Development Planning, 19*(1), 41–58.

Sen, Amartya. (1993). "Capability and Well-Being." In Martha Craven Nussbaum and Amartya Sen (Ed.), *The Quality of Life* (pp. 30–53). Oxford, UK; New York: Clarendon Press; Oxford University Press.

Shaffer, David Williamson. (2004). "Pedagogical Praxis: The Professions as Models for Postindustrial Education." *Teachers College Record, 106*(7), 1401–1421.

Smith, Graham H. (2010a). Correspondence with Jennifer R. Crandall, Whakatane, New Zealand to Pittsburgh, Pennsylvania, 11 May 2010.

Smith, Graham H. (2010b). Interview with Jennifer R. Crandall, Colorado Convention Center, Denver, CO, 2 May 2010.

Smith, Graham H. (2009). "Indigenous Knowledges: Transforming Higher Education, Transforming Society." Presentation at Sydney Ideas: International Public Lecture Series at the University of Sydney, Sydney, 15 December 2009.

Smith, Graham H. (2003). "Indigenous Struggle for the Transformation of Education and Schooling." Keynote address to the Alaskan Federation of Natives (AFN) Convention, Anchorage, October 2003.

Smith, Graham H. (1997). "The Development of Kaupapa Maori: Theory and Praxis." Unpublished PhD diss., Education Department, University of Auckland, Auckland, New Zealand.

Smith, Linda. T. (2000). "Kaupapa Maori Research." In Marie Battiste (Ed.), *Reclaiming Indigenous Voice and Vision*, British Columbia: UBC Press.

Stern, Paul C., Thomas Dietz, Troy Abel, Gregory A. Guagnano, & Linda Kalof. (1999). "A Value-Belief-Norm Theory of Support for Social Movements: The Case of Environmentalism." *Human Ecology Review, 6*(2), 81–97.

Schwartz, Shalom H. (1970). "Moral Decision Making and Behavior." In Jacqueline Macaulay and Leonard Berkowitz (Ed.), *Altruism and Helping Behavior: Social Psychological Studies of Some Antecedents and Consequences* (pp. 127–141). New York: Academic Press.

Schwartz, Shalom H. (1977). "Normative Influences on Altruism." In Leonard Berkowitz (Ed.), *Advances in Experimental Social Psychology*, New York: Academic Press.

Tarrant, Michael A. (2010). "A Conceptual Framework for Exploring the Role of Studies Abroad in Nurturing Global Citizenship." *Journal of Studies in International Education, 14* (5), 433–451.

Walker, Melanie, & Monica McLean. (n.d.). *Making Lives Go Better: University Education and 'Professional Capablities'*. Unpublished paper.University of Nottingham.

Walker, Melanie, Monica McLean, Arona Dison, & Rose Peppin-Vaughan. (2009). "South African Universities and Human Development: Towards a Theorization and Operationalism of Professional Capabilities for Povery Reduction." *International Journal of Educational Development, 29*, 565–572.

Wellman, Barry, & Stephen D. Berkowitz. (1988). *Social Structures: A Network Approach, Structural Analysis in the Social Sciences*. Cambridge, UK; New York: Cambridge University Press.

Wolff, Jonathan, & Avner de-Shalit. (2007). *Disadvantage*. Oxford: Oxford University Press.

Zellermayer, Michal, & Ilana Margolin. (2005). "Teacher Educators' Professional Learning Described Through the Lens of Complexity Theory." *Teachers College Record, 107*(6), 1275–1304.

IRVING EPSTEIN

6. SPORTS AS A METAPHOR FOR COMPARATIVE INQUIRY

INTRODUCTION: ROLLAND G. PAULSTON'S CHALLENGE

Few scholars working in the field of comparative education have understood the importance of social theory as well as did Rolland G. Paulston. His general interest in social theory and his focus upon the importance of social mapping more specifically, addressed a number of conundrums scholars within the comparative education field commonly confront. But the contributions Paulston made in that area need to be seen within his larger body of work that included important empirical studies too. Because he was a scholar who was as eclectic in his interests as he was persuasive in his argumentation, his prescient analyses of the nuances of educational policies in areas as far-reaching as Scandinavia and Cuba (Paulston 1972, 1976, 1980) stood as models of case study inquiry for generations of comparative educators. In his later writings, Paulston (1996, xv-xxiv) returned to long-standing interests in the study of geography so as to apply the principles of social mapping to comparative education scholarship. Such a commitment could only have been successfully pursued by a scholar with an active as well as encyclopedic mind, as evidenced by the range of empirical studies he conducted earlier on.

Although comparative education can best be described as a field rather than a discipline, its evolution has mimicked the familiar intellectual and ideological conflicts representative of twentieth century social science research, including those expressed by advocates of various schools including positivism, methodological empiricism, policy analysis, structuralism, post-structuralism, neo-Marxism, feminist theory, postmodernism, and cultural studies. Proponents of broadly conceived survey research have shared space with those who construct case studies bounded by the conventions of area, culture, and religion. Practitioners of quantitative research publish their work side by side their qualitative counterparts, and the editors of the leading journals in the field have regularly published studies that have intentionally emphasized differing degrees of theoretical grounding or empirical depth.

Paulston helped us make sense this cacophony of voices in unique and creative ways. His understanding of the broad trends and specific nuances of social theory led him to conclude that the assumptions which characterized social science research from the 1950s through the late 1970s and 1980s had limited utility. His enthusiasm for postmodernist perspectives was grounded in his frustration with

John C. Weidman, W. James Jacob (eds.), Beyond the Comparative: Advancing Theory and Its Application to Practice, 93–112.

those limitations. At the same time, he was conversant with the weaknesses certain postmodernist perspectives possessed: a fetishized adherence to abstraction, an uncritical embrace of situational relativism, solipsistic perspectives of meta-narration, et cetera.

His embrace of social cartography was thus meant to reconcile contradictory perspectives while acknowledging newer advances in social theory to which the mainstream comparative education audience had had little exposure. The idea of the conceptual map was an effort to illustrate how the relationship between theoretical movements and the concepts they espoused were related to one another in concrete form. It was clear that for Paulston, mapping was not the same thing as diagramming or categorizing. The subjectivity implicit in creating the conceptual map was always readily acknowledged. Indeed, the diagramming that was constructed always included symbolic arrows indicating the dynamic nature of the relationships between the ideas that were depicted. Such relationships were spatially illustrated in vertical and horizontal terms, but were never constructed so as to embrace hierarchical authority. Postmodern notions of time as flux, with an ensuing dissolution of temporal fixedness, were thus applied to conventional notions of space, in recognition of the challenges globalization theory was presenting to conventional understandings of the state, and of political, economic, social, and cultural borders. In short, Paulston's call was for all of us to become cognizant of the limitations of the conventional, understand the challenges posed by recent advances in social theory, and dare to create new ways of seeing our field that are as approachable as they are provocative. It is within this spirit that I propose that we examine the sports metaphor as a way of clarifying many of the salient issues that mark the comparative education field while raising new and important questions for further consideration.

GENERATIVE NARRATIVES

It behooves us to further address the role of metaphor and allegory in Paulston's thinking before considering the specific utility of the sports metaphor. Metaphors by their nature can be limiting or generative. They can elucidate or clarify meanings that are common-sensical or taken for granted, compelling us to re-examine unchallenged assumptions, or they can force us to extend ourselves so as to synthesize familiar elements into a new whole. For Donald Schön (1993), a key element to the comprehension of social policy formation lies in the understanding of those assumptions that frame the problem to be solved, or the act of problem setting, as opposed to problem solving. Insofar as generative metaphors encourage us to re-conceive of the ways in which we frame problems in new ways, an appreciation for their formation lies at the heart of successful policy making. At the same time, metaphors can also help us to clarify our understandings by forcing us to focus upon those concepts that are essential to the construction of new meanings. They allow us to make abstractions concrete so as to encourage us to see such meanings in familiar lights that clearly resonate with previously shared experiences. Rolland Paulston and Martin Liebman (1996, 22) recognized the dual functions of metaphorical analysis in discussing the nature of narrative in relation to his social cartography project, viewing the process of social cartography as one involving "mininarrativization," without excluding the "metanarrative." In so doing, their discussion of these differing forms of narration give further support to what I contend is the more general power of metaphorical construction and analysis.

> It is our thesis that when scholars address the cultural values and differences revealed by different and often competing knowledge claims, they can enhance their research by developing and including in their findings a cognitive map showing their perceptions of how these multiple knowledge claims interrelate. Social cartography rejects no narrative, whether it is a metanarrative or that of a localized culture. Although metanarratives are accepted and mapped, they are neither privileged nor accepted in their previous role of dominating other narratives. Rather than legitimizing metanarratives—and their ideologies—in their modernist form, our mapping project introduces the concept of the mininarrativization of the metanarrative. Thus the breadth of research possibilities and understandings that social cartography envisions recognizes ... all points of view. Their general validity opens opportunities for comparison because mapping does not 'deny integration of cultures and harmonizing values.' (Rust 1991, 616)

> Social cartography arises from what Rust notes are the possible 'metanarratives . . . [that] open the world to individuals and societies, providing forms of analysis that express and articulate differences and that encourage critical thinking without closing off thought and avenues for constructive action'. (Rust 1991, 616)

In this chapter, through invoking the formation of metaphor as a process similar to what Paulston describes as meta and mini narrativization, we will examine ways in which employing the sports metaphor can be used to both clarify salient concepts in social theory and generate new questions and areas of exploration for comparative education scholars and practitioners.

SPORT AND SOCIAL THEORY

Three broad areas of social theory whose meanings I believe can be clarified through the use of the sports metaphor include Pierre Bourdieu's concept of the social field, notions of embodiment and embodied knowledge as generally expressed within educational practice, and the nature of causality as defined according to the interplay between social structure and agency, a continuing area of discussion for social theorists of all bents. Bourdieu's notion of the field has important ramifications for the ways in which we understand social and more specifically educational inequality. The sociological literature on embodiment and embodied knowledge speaks to the ways in which we artificially construct certain educational practices and categories, and a discussion of the nature of causality within the context of structure and agency has important implications for the ways in which we view globalization trends. It thus makes sense to frame examinations of specific educational policies and practices within these larger lenses.

The "Field" as a Metaphor for Sport or a Game

Few sociologists have had as significant an impact within the discipline over the past three decades as has Bourdieu, having written on fields as diverse as education, the arts, globalization, and French colonialism in Algeria. His seminal works including *The Logic of Practice* (1980), *Reproduction and Education* (1970), and *Distinction: A Social Critique of the Judgment of Taste* (1984), are foundational writings that clearly delineate post-structuralist concepts that have been adapted in numerous disciplines. He clearly enhanced our understanding of the ways in which the mechanism through which social reproduction operates, and his use of terms such as cultural and social capital has been so influential, that these words have become common parlance within most sociological discourse. Other concepts, reflective of Bourdieu's originality, but essential to our understanding of his views include habitus and symbolic violence. But all of these concepts cannot be appreciated without considering his view of the social field, a term that that was consciously developed with the sports or game metaphor in mind.

For Bourdieu, an understanding of the exercise and negotiation of power in social settings is crucial to a larger comprehension of social reproduction processes. And in this vein, the concepts of habitus, cultural and social capital, are key. In his use of the term habitus, Bourdieu referred to the dispositions and interactions we internalize on the basis of our interactions with our environment. From the very start, then, Bourdieu viewed the distinction between the personal, individual, or private, and the social as a conceptually problematic artificial social construction. To conceive of thoughts or emotions as operating in a way that is independent of their social origins made no sense to him. At the same time, the employment of habitus to acquire cultural capital, or the formal thoughts, beliefs and values we come to possess, and social capital, or the networking and friendship ties we cultivate throughout our lives, is never a process that occurs in a standardized fashion. On the one hand, the process of acquiring cultural and social capital is strategic, insofar as it involves accumulating and exchanging ideas, beliefs, friendships, that we perceive to hold value. On the other hand, the value we associate with cultural and social capital is at least in part determined by their scarcity and the conditions of their distribution, which are neither equalized nor fair.

To be sure, Bourdieu viewed the privileging of some forms of cultural and social capital over others as evidence of the unequal power relations that mark all social interactions, and pointed to their fundamental irrationality as a demonstration of symbolic violence. He listed as concrete examples of the process, the ways in which higher education institutions or museums would reify certain forms of knowledge or selected cultural artifacts to the exclusion of others. The process of questioning the legitimacy of various knowledge forms within the academy, so as to exclude their presence, as being unworthy of systematic study by higher education gatekeepers, while promoting inquiry as a generically inclusive series of actions in the abstract, was a specific case of symbolic violence prevalent within French higher education. And, following the earlier work of French anthropologist Marcel Mauss, Bourdieu noted how the intertwining of gift exchange among peoples of various wealth and social standing not only reiterated one's social position to the exclusion of the other (albeit in the name of philanthropy or charity), but in so doing, constituted another fundamental example of symbolic violence, expressed within social landscapes (Epstein 2007, 10–14).

However, none of these concepts can in themselves explain how class, status, and power are universally reproduced until one examines Bourdieu's unifying notion of the field. Bourdieu defines field

> as a network, or a configuration of objective relations between positions. These positions are objectively defined, in their existence and in the determinations they impose upon their occupants, agents or institutions, by their present and potential situation (*situs*) in the structure of the distribution of species of power (or capital) whose possession commands access to the specific profits that are at stake in the field, as well as by their objective relation to other positions (domination, subordination, homology, etc.). (Bourdieu and Wacquant 1992, 97)

While the positions of which he speaks are determined by the cultural, social, or economic capital one accumulates, invests in, or distributes, as well as by one's habituses or those dispositions that influence one's willingness to use these forms of capital in various ways, it is in the field where the space in which these relations are situated and are defined. And, it is the notion of the game (or for our purposes, sport), that best describes the characteristics of the field.

> We can indeed, with caution, compare a field to a game (*jeu*) although, unlike the latter, a field is not the product of a deliberate act of creation, and it follows rules, or better, regularities, that are not explicit and codified. Thus we have *stakes (enjeux)* which are for the most part the product of the competition between players. We have an investment in the game, *illusio* (from *ludus*, the game): players are taken in by the game, they oppose one another, sometimes with ferocity, only to the extent that they concur in their belief (*doxa*) in the game and its stakes; they grant these a recognition that escapes questioning. Players agree, by the mere fact of playing, and not by way of a 'contract,' that the game is worth playing, that it is 'worth the candle,' and this collusion is the very basis of their competition . . .

> at bottom, the value of a species of capital (e.g., knowledge of Greek or of Integral calculus) hinges on the existence of a game, of a field in which this competency can be employed: a species of capital is what is efficacious in a given field, both as a weapon and as a stake of struggle, that which allows its possessors to wield a power, an influence, and thus to exist, in the field under

consideration, instead of being considered a negligible quantity. (Bourdieu and Wacquant 1992, 98)

What then, is clarified through using the metaphor of "game" or "sport" to understand Bourdieu's view of the social field? First, the sport metaphor emphasizes the fact that a field is comprised of activities that are relational and are subject to change and reinvention. While individual games or sports have common sets of rules that their participants accept as a condition of their participation, their rule governing characteristics never preclude evolution and change, both internally but also in relation to other games or sports. A social field thus, is not bounded or separated in ways that are always clear or distinct from other fields, and the internal dynamics involving participation within the field are fluid rather than static. In the same way that a sporting contest is never simply made up of discrete entities: players, managers/coaches, fans, owners, et cetera but involves the interplay amongst all of these actors, social fields are constructed in an equally elastic fashion (Bourdieu and Wacquant 1992, 100–101). The "field of education," for example, is comprised of more than a set of institutions (schools), actors (teachers, parents, students), and other stakeholders (community members, researchers), but involves the relationships they form with one another and with those in other fields (politics, law, medicine, the arts, etc.). Through using the metaphor of sport to clarify Bourdieu's notion of the field as constituting a series of social relations, we are compelled to re-evaluate how we define terms such as "the school," "the community," or the state, for they can no longer be accurately described as fixed entities with independent meanings.

As is true of sport, competition, for power, influence, prestige, exists among participants within fields and amongst the fields themselves. And, as is true of sports contests, even though participants agree to play by a set of re-determined rules, they bring to the contexts specific assets that contribute to their chances of success. So, the universality or seeming inclusivity of the rules of the game do indeed masks the unequal opportunities for successful outcomes afforded its participants. Finally, it is important to note that the outcome of a sports contest is never predetermined as the chance of unexpected triumph or failure is always a possibility.

These factors clarify aspects of social reproduction as evidenced within the educational field in important ways. First, the social field that Bourdieu describes does not operate in overly mechanistic ways (Bourdieu and Wacquant 1992, 102–104), and offers a compelling alternative to the functionalist and radical functionalist paradigms Paulston and Liebman (1996, 15) describe in their social cartography project. Educational institutions, to Bourdieu (1970), for example, perform social acts that are more complicated than those that simply certify class privilege. The process through which cultural capital is distributed within the educational system is intricate. A set of universal rules or principles that appear to inclusively apply equitably to all students, while simultaneously fostering a competition for the allocation of that cultural capital is created. This results in the reproduction of unequal power relationships with participants strategically positioning themselves within the field to compete according to the forms of capital they possess or view themselves as in a position to acquire. Because not all participants are offered the same chances of success, the chances of their efforts resulting in lasting success differ according to the forms of capital they have acquired and the habituses they bring to the game (or the field). Yet the willingness to continue to play and invest in the game in part is affected by one's understanding that the outcome is to at least a limited degree uncertain and non-predetermined, even if the chances of success are slight. It is only through such analysis that one can understand how and why one's class privilege influences one's educational achievement, often but not all of the time. And it's only through such an analysis that one can appreciate the impact of individualist achievement ideology that is so characteristic of modern forms of schooling, whereby students are seductively more willing to accept the proposition that academic failure can be explained by personal rather than structural incompetence.

It should be reiterated that Bourdieu's concept of the field cannot be divorced from his other concepts that we have identified, for to do so would seriously misrepresent his view of the field as being intrinsically social. Unlike game or rational choice theory, whereby individual behavior is simplistically attributed to one's calculation of the costs and benefits of pursuing a particular course of action, and where fixed reward structures are viewed as influencing predictable individual behaviors, Bourdieu's view of the field does not invoke a similar view of instrumental rationality that is de-contextualized and separated from the contingencies that involve social relationships. The conditions under which the various forms of capital are acquired, invested, and exchanged, the habituses that influence one's outlook on the field (or the rules of the game or the sport) are of intrinsic importance in understanding his frame of reference. But as has also been noted, the meaning of these terms is closely tied to the concept of the field, which makes it easier for us to interpret their meaning according to an appropriate context.

Embodiment and Embodied Knowledge

Although the literature focusing upon the sociology of the body has a long and distinguished history (Epstein 2007, 5), its prominence coincided with the growth of cultural studies in the 1970s and 1980s, and more recently, with the awareness of consumerism as a driving characteristic of globalization. Scholars have employed this area of inquiry to study the relationship of "the body" to the social construction of identity, with "the body" viewed as a social site, subject to manipulation and reinvention, with regard to notions of gender, race, sexual orientation, et cetera. Others have examined efforts to control the body from external sources, with Michel Foucault's writings (1977; 1978; 1984) serving as a pioneering framework in this regard. Still others have examined the use of body terminology for the purposes of engaging in metaphoric construction, with regard to preservation, safety, boundedness, containment, contamination, et cetera. Finally, the examination of cognition as a holistic bodily function, rather than being reserved for the brain as a separate entity is a prominent area of study within the sociology of the body literature.

Theoretical as well as empirical discussions of sport address these themes in direct and concrete ways, and they speak in general ways to the concerns of educational scholars. In this vein, the works of two scholars that I find to be particularly compelling are Loïc Wacquant (2004) and John J. MacAloon (2008). Wacquant, who worked closely with Pierre Bourdieu on a number of projects, trained for the Golden Gloves amateur boxing tournament while a graduate student at the University of Chicago. His book, *Body and Soul* is not simply a personal memoir of that experience, but a deeper investigation of the ways in which his companion athletes living in the inner city, generate, invest in, and trade physical capital as a means of surviving in a difficult external environment. Wacquant's conclusions are therefore quite fascinating. First, he learns that the popular perception that views the sport of boxing as especially attractive to the most poor and indigent inner city youth is in fact mistaken, for the vast majority of the youth who attend training gymnasiums come from working class backgrounds, having acquired the degree of self-discipline necessary to succeed in a sport marked by its asceticism. Its popularity as an endeavor that promises upward social mobility amongst those with no reasonable alternative is thus overstated. Second, Wacquant notes that the physical aggression associated with the sport allows its practitioners to respond to the violence of street life through internalizing its effects; exerting control over one's body represents safely negotiating the unpredictability of life on the street. It is noteworthy that at its essence, boxing is a defensive sport; one trains so as to avoid being hit, a much more important goal than inflicting direct punishment upon one's opponent. At the same time, the training techniques that are employed, involving a serious disciplining of the body so as to demand control over diet, sexual activity, and alcohol and drug use prior to a match, speak eloquently to Foucault's writings regarding the interplay between education (in this case training), and discipline. Another theme that Wacquant emphasizes is the nature of the mentoring relationship between trainer and boxer. He observes that the expert trainer whom he profiles never tries to teach a novice boxer too much too soon. Mastery of the "sweet science" requires that one repeatedly learn through acting and reacting to an opponent's moves and strategy, but such learning occurs concurrent with repeated practice. Learning and practice are inter-related; one does not predetermine the other. But it is self-reflection and recognition that serve as indicators as to when new skills should be introduced. Finally, Wacquant reaffirms the views of others in asserting that notions of "pure" talent and ability really are artificial constructions that dismiss the importance of focus, repetitive training, and the resources to pursue such training at the earliest of ages in influencing in this case athletic prowess (Chambliss [1989] quoted in Wacquant 2004, 68). The differences in performance between ordinary and world-class athletes cannot be explained simply by comparative assessments of their physical differences in athletic skill levels.

To be sure, there are many studies that have focused upon the nature of the coaching and mentoring processes, experiential learning and reflective practice (Schön 1983), and the ways in which youth utilize their abilities (Csikszentmihalyi et al., 1996) or world-class geniuses succeed through the efforts of outstanding teachers (Arnove 2009). In addition, the connection between pedagogy, curriculum, student social class background, and their ultimate educational success is well-established (Bernstein 1977). But the boxing metaphor is especially powerful insofar as it brings together many of these findings and compels us to address specific imperatives that have cross-cultural and global currency. For example, being mindful of the social class influence upon those inner city youth who pursue boxing activity and comparing Wacquant's findings to the formal educational field, we can legitimately ask if there are ways in which educational practices involving student selection, assessment, and retention can be constructed so as to limit the social class bias that too often accompanies their implementation? Following this line, we can further inquire as to whether there are curricular and pedagogical assumptions that need to be rethought, as they, although universally applied, inherently affect diverse groups of students in negative ways? Are there more flexible and accurate but less arbitrary methods for determining and then cultivating student talent and ability? And, if the cultivation of individual talent is so dependent upon resource availability distributed in extremely selective ways, how can we implement more equitable forms of educational resource allocation? Furthermore, if the power of the learning process lies at least in part, in structuring situations whereby the learner perceives immediate consequence to her/his decision-making (as seems to be true of most high impact learning events [Kuh et al., 2010]), what would have to happen in order to ensure that such situations were intentionally made part of formal curricula? Finally, does what we know about high impact learning, as reiterated through the boxing metaphor, have larger implications as to how we understand the interplay between formal, informal, non-formal, and hidden curricular experiences? As has been previously argued, not only do robust metaphors clarify our understanding of existing concepts by making their premises more explicit, but they also challenge us to revisit comfortable assumptions by expanding the conditions that influence their applicability. Clearly, the boxing metaphor speaks to those of us who view the sociology of the body as a fruitful and relevant area of exploration with reference to educational issues.

A second text that I believe speaks to issues of embodiment through the metaphor of sports is MacAloon's (2008) *This Great Symbol: Pierre de Coubertin and the Origins of the Modern Olympic Games.* This work, which is part biography, part history, and part ethnography, is a classic work that details the growth of the modern Olympic movement through analyzing the life of its founder. De Coubertin was born of French aristocratic lineage in 1863, and thus experienced the influences of nineteenth century industrialization and republican liberalism that characterized much of the history of the Third Republic. Such influences had an effect upon de Coubertin insofar as they shaped his quest to find and assert a personal identity based upon *prouesses* (feats of prowess) rather than simple privilege (6–7). His thinking, informed by classicist and Christian values, was shaped by the ideology of muscular Christianity as espoused by Matthew Arnold and his disciples, Thomas Hughes in the popular novel, *Tom Brown's School Days* and A. P. Stanle. It was also influenced by his travels to England where he visited Rugby and other public schools where he solidified his faith in these principles that he hoped could be employed to reform French state operated lycees. During his travel to the United States, he was duly impressed with the New York Athletic Club (146), whose organizational form was later parroted in the establishment of national bodies reporting to an International Olympic Committee. In a curious way, de Coubertin thus mimicked the views of early comparative educators who as a result of their travels, sought to selectively borrow elements of foreign national education systems and graft them onto one's own (52–69). In his case, his hope was that French lycees would be reformed according to what he viewed as the laudatory characteristics of the English public schools, and would thus become models of patriotism and moral training (72).

MacAloon notes that athletics, as promoted in the elite male schools to which de Coubertin was so enamored, focused less upon organized sports and more upon bodily and athletic training. The growing popularity of British sport outside of the confines of such schooling coincided with an expanding middle class; practices within the Rugbys, Harrows, and Etons of the world reflected their traditional class character. Thus, it was de Coubertin himself, who made the strong connection between sport as a vehicle for moral education, character building, et cetera for all citizens. At the same time, his embrace of sport was accompanied by a reaffirmation of his own belief in the power of a classical formal education that, if at least partially defined by athletic engagement, would further promote growth in both mind and body, entities that he viewed as inseparable.

Of course, a large component of the ideology to which de Coubertin espoused, involved an idiosyncratic merging of a worship of Ancient Greece with a faith in the type of internationalism that would promote cooperation and end conflict. In reality, the expectation that the Games could ever be separated from political considerations was grossly naïve; nationalist sentiments accompanied the construction of the movement from its inception, and overshadowed their planning and execution after the initial modern games were held in 1896, and plagued subsequent games held in Paris in 1900 and London in 1908 (302). The distinction de Coubertin made in his own mind between patriotism (a positive virtue), and nationalism (a negative one), was lost upon his external audience (299). In addition, the importance of spectacle, so prevalent in the creation of world expositions during the late nineteenth century, came to overshadow the second two Olympic Games themselves, as they were held in conjunction with such events (313).

The fact that the influences of nineteenth century nationalism hijacked de Coubertin's dream of promoting individual character building through acknowledging athletic excellence is not surprising, given our understanding of twentieth century European history. Nor is it shocking to note how a person of aristocratic privilege attempted, without success, to popularize a worldview that promoted an idealized humanism, unable to acknowledge the existence of social class or ethnic division as a natural part of social relations. But de Coubertin's views, and the growth of the Modern Olympic movement also have implications for the comparative education field too.

As was true of de Coubertin's investigations of school athletics, early comparative educators writing in the nineteenth and early twentieth centuries lacked the tools of the modern social sciences to pursue focused research regarding educational practice and policy, resulting in writings that were overly descriptive and subject to broad generalizations regarding the ascribed characteristics of national education systems (Kelly, Altbach and Arnove 1982, 510). Certainly, they failed to construct a sophisticated analysis of the nature of the nation-state, or of the complexity involved in the educational sector's role in furthering state legitimation, through shaping the nature of one's citizenry, delivering a basic public good, et cetera. However, in pursuing analyses that were grossly holistic, they shared de Coubertin's aversion to notions of social conflict or the embrace of cultural difference. The repercussions for creating educational structures that would adequately address the differing needs of those who were socially and politically marginalized, or the difficulties of developing universal institutional structures that were *both* cross-cultural and locally relevant, were never directly nor fully addressed. But, the sentiments of muscular Christianity, which were so influential to de Coubertin's thinking, were echoed among early comparative educators as well, albeit in a more general form, whereby educational reform became viewed as a moral imperative and an inherent good, a vehicle for building personal character and cultivating intellectual talent.

Of course, the discipline associated with what many characterize as educational training bears some resemblance to the physical training that accompanies athletic preparation, and such an association is certainly not limited to late nineteenth and early twentieth century discourses. Such an association was explicitly expressed in the early 1980s as post-Cultural Revolution Chinese educators claimed that resurrected national examinations would encourage the creation of well-rounded future leaders in all domains including the physical as well as the intellectual (Pepper 1984, 45-68). The pressures for increased accountability that have more recently resulted in the barrage of testing that has accompanied neo-liberal educational reforms globally have also created test preparation and training sessions that mimic the rigorous preparation that is expected prior to major athletic contests. Indeed, the traditional role of university entrance examinations in Japan, as a spectacle designed to publicly displaying one's social worth (Rohlen 1983), is not unlike the use of international sporting competitions to engender mechanical solidarity and national cohesiveness. Not surprisingly, for almost three decades, the use of international achievement examinations to determine a country's global educational standing has been connected to the heightened global competition of the Olympics Movement (Inkeles 1982). In these instances, expressions of collective pride or shame are articulated in forceful ways, even though their duration is of a relatively short period and the means through which such expressions are voiced are artificial and external to the operations of regular institutional practices.

Although their levels of analysis differ, both Wacquant and MacAloon compel us to examine conventional assumptions regarding categorizations of the physical as opposed to the mental, the relationship between education, morality, and discipline, and the roles of competition and cooperation in defining what constitutes educational value. The Olympic Movement became professionalized and commercialized during the latter part of the twentieth century, of course, ironically creating a more powerful global spectacle than the type that overshadowed its uniqueness when it was first created. In a similar vein, the commercialization or McDonaldization of educational practices, including the explosion of for-profit online delivery learning based upon pure business oriented cost effective efficiency models, the international ranking of higher education institutions according to the presumed scholarly productivity of faculty (Altbach 2006), admissions selectivity, et cetera, or the hoopla attached to Nobel Prize awards, demonstrates that similar processes involving the creation of spectacle, the overt commercialization of what one delivers and the means of its delivery, and the heightened importance of determining winners and losers on an international basis so as to gain global prominence, are influential trends affecting both domains.

Structure, Agency, and Causality

Questions about cause and effect, the relationship between history and culture, and the degrees of freedom that mark our decision-making capabilities in various social settings lie at the heart of our understanding of historical method and the social sciences. In *Apologies to Thucydides*, renowned anthropologist Marshall Sahlins (2004) investigates these questions by initially comparing the similarities and differences in the political and social structures of two incredibly disparate societies: the ancient Greek city states of Athens and Sparta, and the inhabitants of the islands that comprise what we today identify as Fiji. Later, he examines an assassination that influenced the course of modern Fijian history. But interspersed among these studies is a lengthy exposition regarding the nature of historical action and contingency as expressed through baseball history, for in his chapter "Culture and Agency in History," Sahlins compares the exploits of the 1939 New York Yankees with those of the 1951 New York Giants, referencing an analysis first articulated by the Yale historian, J. H. Hexter.

The 1939 New York Yankees were one of the more dominant teams in baseball history, leading their competitors from the start of the season, winning the American League Pennant by seventeen games. There was no one moment when the Yankees transformed themselves into the winners they had become, and in looking at their winning trajectory, it is difficult to distinguish any particular event that was so influential or unique so as to dictate the future course of events during that season. On the other hand, the 1951 New York Giants won the National League Pennant in the last half of the last inning of a three game playoff series, when outfielder Bobby Thompson hit a homerun off Brooklyn Dodger pitcher Ralph Branca. Hexter's point is that these cases represent different ways of examining the historical record; in the former case, as there are no specific events that can be characterized as exceptional, and as a result, one would be likely to employ a systematic if general analysis of the strengths of the team, in explaining their comparative excellence. In the latter case, we tend to focus upon the individual acting within the moment: Bobby Thompson's talent, his ability to rise to the occasion, Ralph Branca's mistaken pitch, et cetera. In short, one can easily juxtapose a view of agency and structure that parallels traditional notions of great men independently shaping historical events with those whereby fundamental structural change occurs during specific time periods (the Industrial Revolution, the Age of Exploration, for example) independent of historical personality.

For Sahlins (2004), however, such an explanation is overly simplistic, as it fails to account for the structural factors that place a hero or celebrity in a situation whereby one is in a position to effect change. More importantly, the entire process through which the individual becomes an object of cultural focus is part of what Sahlins labels, "the structuring of agency," or the ways in which "history makes the history makers" (155). In this vein, Sahlins argues that there are two structures of agency, systemic and conjunctual. Napoleon would be an example of the former, given the fact that his power derived from the nature of the hierarchically powerful institutional position he held, which allowed him to implement his will (157). The political and military structure of the French government thus created the probability for the excessive exercise of state power that was present regardless of the peculiarities of the individual leader. Historical characters such as Bobby Thompson, or Elian Gonzales (the Cuban boat refugee who was returned to his home over the objection of distant relatives and members of the Cuban-American community in Florida), or Katherine Harris (the Florida Secretary of State involved in the 2000 Bush vs. Gore presidential election certification dispute), demonstrate conjunctual agency, insofar as their agency is derived from the "circumstances of a particular historical conjuncture" (157). In these cases, the contingent situation dictates the nature of the agency that is expressed and is non-systemic and non-institutional. But what is most important, for Sahlens, is his conclusion that the making of history as a cultural process, involves symbolic representations that fuse the "national with the personal," allowing us to create symbolic meanings that address deeply felt needs (169). Thus, the importance we attach to those who attain a manufactured celebrity status is as much derived from the social construction of their role as it is to their unique personalities.

History, unlike the other social sciences, is much more messy when efforts are made to impugn cause-effect relationships or to control for selected factors or variables. But the questions the Sahlins raises have significance for comparative educators of all types, regardless as to whether or not they employ historical narratives in their analyses, for we also struggle with issues involving the roles of systems as opposed to individuals in shaping educational outcomes, the nature of contingency and determinism in understanding knowledge flows and trends, and the role of culture in providing symbolic meanings that draw us to specific events or individuals.

For example, how do we analyze the power of Paulo Freire's legacy? Was Freire simply a "one hit wonder," who in 1971 hit the pop charts around the world with the publication of *Pedagogy of the Oppressed* (Freire 1971)? One can address this question through examining in a systemic fashion, the corollary growth and popularity of liberation theology in the 1960s and 1970s in Latin America (Gutiérrez 1973), or one can focus upon Freire's own gifts of personal and political engagement. To do the latter would raise questions regarding his less than stellar success as Minister of Education in Sao Paolo (Torres 1994); to do the former would force us to address reasons for the decline in popularity of liberation theology while Freire's writings continue to hold near universal appeal among educators. Indeed Thomas S. Popkewitz (2000) has written specifically about the tendency to promote the writings of "indigenous foreigners," (e.g., John Dewey, Paulo Freire, Lev Vygotsky, Jürgen Habermas, and Michel Foucault) without appropriately contextualizing their views. In so doing, the social construction of these educational personalities is similar to the cultural meanings attached to the personalities Sahlins discusses, only for Popkewitz, such an exercise allows policymakers to negotiate global and local tendencies so as to legitimize their own policy choices.

The systemic versus conjunctual forms of analysis Sahlins' mentions can also be loosely applied to the case study vs. cross-national survey research extremes that characterize much of the empirical work in the comparative education field. Case study analyses tend to be country, region or culturally specific; their architecture includes rather thick description of factors that make the case unique, with references to broader themes and concepts that situate the case within larger frameworks that match context with generalizable principle. Cross-national studies offer systemic overviews of trends that are viewed as widely applicable regardless of local context. The call for empirical work that would employ levels of analysis that incorporate the both of these categories has been longstanding, if often ignored (Przeworski and Teune 1970).

Of course, issues involving the nature of causality and determinism, with reference to comparative education policy-making and curricular reform have also marked empirical studies in the field for over five decades. The justification for engaging in efforts to determine co-variation among selected factors or characteristics analyzed cross-nationally formed an important part of the comparative education theoretical literature during the 1960s and early 1970s (Noah and Eckstein 1969). Later, proponents of institutional theory examined the ways in which global educational expansion with regard to enrollments, organizational components, and curricula coalesced around similar sets of cultural norms that became widely diffused (DiMaggio and Powell 1983; Meyer et al., 1992; Scott 2001). More recently, globalization theorists both inside and outside of the comparative education field have offered more complicated and nuanced views as to how ideas are globally transmitted, affirmed, resisted, or reconfigured, with particular respect to the variations of neo-liberal policies that mark the interactions between the state, its elites, and its citizenry (Harvey 2005; Carney 2009). Needless to say, issues involving determinism, contingency, causality, and the appropriate level and type of empirical analysis to be conducted continue to influence inquiry involving comparative education issues even if the approaches to these issues vary and the methods employed offer answers that may be characterized as only partially satisfactory.

Of course, a fair understanding of the dynamics of neo-liberal principles as expressed in support of global capitalist initiatives necessitates an appreciation for both the rules of engagement to which nation-states conform, and the means through which they position themselves in relation to one another. Anthropologist John Kelly (2006) makes another striking analogy to baseball in explaining what he views to be the fundamental nature of global capitalism. By examining the development of the Major League Baseball minor league system in the 1930s, Kelly explains how US baseball teams created a minor league system through which they were able to cultivate and monopolize athletic talent for their own purposes. Although often operating independent of their major league counterparts, minor league teams are contractually obligated to furnish players to their parent teams, who keep, trade, or return the players according to their needs. The creation of the World Baseball Classic (WBC) in 2006, whereby Major League Baseball manufactured a competition between professional baseball players representing their home countries can be viewed as a global extension of this process. International talent is showcased and US teams can then invest in those players whom they deem useful to their needs, all the while encouraging nation-state visibility on an international stage. In both of these instances, Kelly reminds us that there is a vertical hierarchical organizational structure that is formed between the core US major league club and its farm team(s) or between the Major League organization and the baseball associations in other countries participating in the WBC. Competition between teams is not only allowed to exist but is encouraged, so long as such competition enhances the cultivation of athletic talent that can later be monopolized. However, the expansion of vertical organizational hierarchies that serves to privilege major league clubs remains uncontested.

For Kelly, such are the rules of global capitalism. The fact that economic competition between nation-states exists belies the contention that Western core countries have simply succeed in expanding their domination of the world economy through the expansion of empire. Alternatively, the rules through which such competition exists are written by Western powers whose long-term interests are never seriously threatened. During the 1970s and 1980s, the use of world systems analysis became a compelling framework for understanding issues including Western domination of academic publishing and the brain drain (Altbach 1982; Arnove 1982) and the roles of US-dominated international organizations such as the U.S. Agency for International Development, the International Monetary Fund, and the World Bank (Klees 1986; Berman 1992) in dictating the terms of bilateral educational assistance, and consequently, educational policy in receiver countries. More recently, comparativists have examined the impact of European educational reforms such as the Bologna Process and the Lisbon Accords in standardizing the European higher education system for purposes of enhancing the global competitiveness of the region (Dale 2009). At the same time, the increasing privatization of higher education on a global level, the impact of technological change upon course delivery as evidenced through the explosion of online learning, and the franchising of established higher education institutional brands (prominent Western research universities) onto foreign terrain (new branch campuses in China, Dubai, etc.), give evidence as to how basic principles of neo-liberalism are being expressed in new ways within the educational field (Croom

2008). Standardization, competition, and privatization are not new trends in and of themselves. The ways in which they have found expression in global rather than simply bilateral frameworks necessitates a re-conceptualization of their dynamics however. And, it is in this vein that Kelly's baseball metaphor is both clarifying and provocative.

CAVEATS AND CONCLUSIONS

We have employed the use of sports metaphors to both raise and clarify issues relating to the nature of education as a social field, the ways in which educational practices serve to categorize, nee discipline physical and intellectual activities, the use of schooling to promote synthetic nationalism as constructed for global audiences, the nature of causality, determinism, and contingency as related to the framing of educational personalities, issues, and systems, and the interplay between competition and power within educational contexts as characteristics of neo-liberalism and global capitalism. In so doing, we have argued that used as a generative metaphor, sports is useful because it compels us to re-evaluate and reconsider the contexts in which such issues arise. But what are the limitations of using the sports metaphor as a generative, analytic tool to be applied to comparative education inquiry?

Three potential objectives immediately come to mind. First, we make a natural association with sports activities and play/leisure. Their attraction lies in the fact that for most of us, who are neither professional athletes nor employees of sports businesses, their appeal is due to the fact that they are not work related. Although the ways in which professional sports structure themselves can be influenced by the ways in which formal work is organized, along with other factors including consumerist desire, marketing techniques, media influences, et cetera. involvement in sports as a participant or an observer tends to be less consequential than one's associations with family, occupation, governmental institutions, church, et cetera. The "playful" essence of sports distinguishes it from what we might consider to be more serious endeavors. It is for this reason that de Coubertin's effort to attach the ethical and moral imperatives he associated with muscular Christianity to the Olympic movement seem so contradictory and out of place according to twentieth and twenty-first century sensibilities. But for those of us who work in the comparative education field, the ethical consequences of the policies and practices we scrutinize are important (or at least we view them as being so), insofar as they directly affect people's lives and life chances, from childhood through adulthood and beyond. While it is a useful corrective to evaluate assumptions regarding the inherent benefit of programs and policies we promote, we view our roles as policymakers, teachers, and educational scholars as being more than simply performing a set of academic exercises. It is thus justifiable to question whether or not the use of the sports metaphor as a tool of analysis for comparative educators creates a gaze that trivializes the importance of the intellectual and policy-oriented work that we pursue. And, does the use of that gaze further legitimize the role of the comparative educator as a distant observer rather as engaged scholar? One response to this objection though, would be to counter-argue that it is as a result of the use of the sports metaphor that we are compelled to fundamentally re-examine the relationship between leisure, play, and work, and that such a reassessment has the potential to further our contextual understanding of the issues we passionately believe are worth exploring. And, far from legitimizing a role for the comparativist that eschews emotional distance, the concrete nature of the sports metaphor actually helps to illustrate the ease with which engagement can occur and the imperative to do so.

A second objection involves the closed nature of the sports activity or the game. Sports and games are bounded by time and place; they have beginnings and outcomes that are discrete in ways that do not mirror the real life ambiguities of the educational policies and practices that we study. Can their use create artificial perceptions regarding the nature of those educational issues that are worth exploring? This argument mirrors the previous distinction that was noted regarding the use of metaphors that may not generate new inquiries but inadvertently limit them and it closely follows Bourdieu's previously noted distinction between the rules of the game and the nature of the social field. One response to this objection would simply counter- argue that it is not only useful, but imperative, that questions are raised involving the extent to which specific educational practices/policies are bounded as opposed to being open-ended or ambiguous, with regard to their finality of duration or consequence. When such questions are raised in conjunction with the use of the sports metaphor, then the use of the metaphor becomes generative in a positive manner. Metaphors should not be construed as duplicate imagery and those who offer an objection to their use on the basis of their inherent closed nature make such an error.

A final potential objection to the sports metaphor criticizes its use as being too vague, internally inconsistent, and context specific to be analytically powerful. In this essay, for example, we have touched upon a wide-ranging set of issues varied in their content, yet linked to one another indirectly. In so doing, we have used the Olympic Games, boxing, and baseball as metaphors for the issues that we have discussed. Indeed, sociology of sports scholars have certainly gone beyond these themes in their writings as studies of race, gender, and consumerist consumption have become part of the scholarly canon in this field (Carrington and McDonald 2009; Smith 2010). But if the sports metaphor can be applied to every social (or for our purposes educational) phenomenon, at what point does it lose its uniqueness and its power as an explanatory device?

In addition, one needs to be reticent in one's choices of examples that illustrate the metaphor. The "Western" influences of the sports events that have been chronicled in this essay should certainly be acknowledged. One can add parenthetically, that other popular metaphors, such as George Ritzer's coinage of "McDonaldization," as a political, social, and global process have been attacked for only selectively explaining all aspects of globalization while focusing upon decidedly Western consumption patterns (Veseth 2006; Waters 2006). Although I believe such concerns hold potential legitimacy, the field of comparative education in my opinion, does not at this time suffer from an overuse of metaphor as an analytic tool, quite the opposite. One may with a certain degree of legitimacy criticize the specific examples used in this essay as overly narrow illustrations of the sports metaphor that do little more than replicate the author's Western bias. However, the purpose here is to make the plea for an eclectic approach to the use of generative metaphors generically, and the examples offered in this essay are meant to function only as illustrative examples of the principle being defended. Although there have been occasional direct uses of the sports metaphor within the field to examine issues of education and national identity (Epstein 2002) and citizenship education with reference to the contemporary Olympic Games (Law 2006), the contention that the invocation of metaphors has already exhausted its usefulness through over-employment is difficult to defend.

A discussion of the power of the sports metaphor inevitably leads us back to an appreciation of Paulston's efforts to extend the boundaries of comparative education inquiry through use of the social cartography metaphor. Social cartography as an analytical tool was never meant to be all encompassing but was instead meant to offer a stimulating and provocative method of viewing the comparative education field. It was further devised as a means of encouraging the construction of alternative metaphors that might also further advance the field. In this essay, I have proposed the use of the sports metaphor as one potential tool for fulfilling this aim. Others, have in equally compelling ways, examined the use of visual imagery (Fischmann 2001) and the artifacts of material culture (Lawn and Grosvenor 2005) to accomplish a similar purpose. All scholars who are concerned about questioning existing categories and extending the borders of comparative education scholarship owe a debt to Paulston, for his passionate advocacy for the furthering of intellectual inquiry within the comparative education field. It is for this reason that the legacy of his work will continue to find expression in the writings of current and future scholars in new and creative ways.

REFERENCES

Altbach, Philip G. (1982). "Servitude of the Mind? Education, Dependency, and Neocolonialism." In Philip G. Altbach, Robert F. Arnove, and Gail P. Kelly (Ed.), *Comparative Education* (pp. 469–484). New York: Macmillan.

Altbach, Philip G. (2006). "The Dilemmas of Ranking." International Higher Education 42 (Winter): 2–3. Available online at: http://www.bc.edu/research/cihe.html.

Arnove, Robert F. (1982). "Comparative Education and World Systems Analyis." In Philip G. Altbach, Robert F. Arnove, and Gail P. Kelly (Ed.), *Comparative Education* (pp. 453–468). New York: Macmillan.

Arnove, Robert F. (2009). *Talent Abounds: Profiles of Master Teachers and Peak Performers.* Boulder, CO: Paradigm Publishers.

Berman, Edward H. (1992). "Donor Agencies and Third World Educational Development, 1945–1985." In Robert F. Arnove, Philip G. Altbach, & Gail P. Kelly (Ed.), *Emergent Issues in Education: Comparative Perspectives* (pp. 57–74). Albany, NY: State University of New York Press.

Bernstein, Basil B. (1977). *Class, Codes and Control, Vol. 3.* London: Routledge and Kagan Paul.

Bourdieu, Pierre. (1970). *Reproduction and Education.* Beverly Hills, CA: Sage Publishing.

Bourdieu, Pierre. (1980). *The Logic of Practice.* Palo Alto, CA: Stanford University Press.

Bourdieu, Pierre. (1984). *Distinction: A Social Critique of the Judgment of Taste.* Cambridge, MA: Harvard University Press.

Bourdieu, Pierre, & Loïc J. D. Wacquant. (1992). *An Invitation to Reflexive Sociology*. Chicago: University of Chicago Press.

Carney, Stephen. (2009). "Negotiating Policy in the Age of Globalization: Exploring Educational 'Policyscapes' in Denmark, Nepal and China." *Comparative Education Review, 53*(1), 63–88.

Carrington, Ben, & Ian McDonald. (2009). "Marxism, Cultural Studies and Sport: Mapping the Field." In Ben Carrington & Ian Mcdonald (Ed.), *Marxism, Cultural Studies and Sport* (pp. 1–12). New York: Routledge.

Chambliss, Daniel F. (1989). "The Mundanity of Excellence: An Ethnographic Report on Stratification and Olympic Swimmers." *Sociological Theory, 7*(1), 70–86.

Croom, Patricia. (2008). "Branch Campuses in a Neo-liberal Context." Paper presented at the Annual Meeting of the Comparative and International Education Society, New York, 17 March 2008.

Csikszentmihalyi, Mihaly, Kevin Rathunde, & Samuel Whalen. (1996). *Talented Teenagers: The Roots of Success and Failure*. New York: Cambridge University Press.

Dale, Roger. (2009). "Studying Globalisation and Europeanisation in Education: Lisbon, the Open Method of Coordination and Beyond." In Roger Dale and Susan L. Robertson (Ed.), *Globalisation and Europeanisation in Education* (pp. 121–140). Oxford, UK: Symposium Books.

DiMaggio, Paul J., & Walter W. Powell. (1983). "The Iron Cage Revisited: Institutional Isomorphism and Collective Rationality in Organizational Fields." *American Sociological Review, 48*(2), 147–160.

Epstein, Irving. (2002). "Education and Work in Embargoed Cuba." *Educational Practice and Theory, 24*(1), 39–60.

Epstein, Irving. (2007). "Education, Comparison, and the Challenges of an Embodied Perspective." In Irving Epstein (Ed.), *Recapturing the Personal: Essays on Education and Embodied Knowledge in Comparative Perspective* (pp. 1–21). Charlotte, NC: Information Age Publishing.

Fischmann, Gustavo E. (2001). "Reflections about Images, Visual Culture and Educational Research." *Educational Researcher, 30*(8), 28–33.

Foucault, Michel. (1977). *Discipline and Punish: The Birth of the Prison*. New York: Pantheon Books.

Foucault, Michel. (1978). *The History of Sexuality: An Introduction, Vol. 1*. New York: Random House.

Foucault, Michel. (1984). "Right of Death and Power over Life." In Paul Rabinow (Ed.), *The Foucault Reader* (pp. 258–272). New York: Pantheon Books.

Freire, Paulo. (1971). *Pedagogy of the Oppressed*. New York: Continuum.

Gutiérrez, Gustavo. (1973). *A Theology of Liberation: History, Politics, and Salvation*. Maryknoll, NY: Orbis Books.

Harvey, David. (2005). *A Brief History of Neoliberalism*. New York: Oxford University Press.

Inkeles, Alex. (1982). "National Differences in Scholastic Performance." In Philip G. Altbach, Robert F. Arnove, and Gail P. Kelly (Ed.), *Comparative Education* (pp. 210–231). New York: Macmillan.

Kelly, Gail P., Philip G. Altbach, & Robert F. Arnove. (1982). "Trends in Comparative Education: A Critical Analysis." In Philip G. Altbach, Robert F. Arnove, and Gail P. Kelly (Ed.), *Comparative Education* (pp. 505–533). New York: Macmillan.

Kelly, John D. (2006). *The American Game: Capitalism, Decolonization, World Domination and Baseball*. Chicago: Prickly Paradigm Press.

Klees, Steven J. (1986). "Planning and Policy Analysis in Education: What Can Economics Tell Us?" *Comparative Education Review, 30*(4), 574–607.

Kuh, George D., Jillian Kinzie, John H. Schuh, & Elizabeth J. Whitt. (2010). *Student Success in College: Creating Conditions That Matter*. San Francisco, CA: Jossey-Bass.

Law, Wing-Wah. (2006). "Citizenship, Citizenship Education and the State in China in a Global Age." *Cambridge Journal of Education, 36*(4), 597–628.

Lawn, Martin, & Ian Grosvenor. (2005). "Introduction: The Materialities of Schooling." In Martin Lawn & Ian Grosvenor (Ed.), *Materialities of Schooling: Design, Technology, Objects, Routines* (pp. 7–17). Oxford, UK: Symposium Books.

MacAloon, John J. (2008). *This Great Symbol: Pierre de Coubertin and the Origins of the Modern Olympic Games*. New York: Routledge.

Meyer, John W., David H. Kamens, Aaron Benavot, Yun-kyung Cha, & Suk-Ying Wong. (1992). *School Knowledge for the Masses: World Models and National Primary Curricular Categories in the Twentieth Century*. London: Falmer Press.

Noah, Harold J., & Max A. Eckstein. (1969). *Toward a Science of Comparative Education*. New York: Macmillan.

Paulston, Rolland G. (1972). "Cultural Revitalization and Educational Change in Cuba." *Comparative Education Review, 16*(3), 474–485.
Paulston, Rolland G. (1976). "Ethnic Revival and Educational Conflict in Swedish Lapland." *Comparative Education Review, 20*(2), 179–192.
Paulston, Rolland G. (1980). "Education as Anti-Structure: Non-formal Education in Social and Ethnic Movements." *Comparative Education, 16*(1), 55–66.
Paulston, Rolland G., & Martin Liebman. (1996). "Social Cartography: A New Metaphor/Tool for Comparative Studies." In Rolland G. Paulston (Ed.), *Social Cartography: Mapping Ways of Seeing Social and Educational Change* (pp. 7–28). New York: Garland Publishing.
Paulston, Rolland G. (1996). "Preface: Four Principles for a Non-Innocent Social Cartography." In Rolland G. Paulston (Ed.), Social *Cartography: Mapping Ways of Seeing Social and Educational Change* (pp. xv–xxiv). New York: Garland Publishing.
Pepper, Suzanne. (1984). China's Universities. *Post-Mao Enrollment Policies and Their Impact on the Structure of Secondary Education: A Research Report.* Ann Arbor, MI: University of Michigan Press.
Popkewitz, Thomas S. (2000). "National Imaginaries, the Indigenous Foreigner, and Power: Comparative Educational Research." In Jürgen Schriewer (Ed.), *Discourse Formation in Comparative Education* (pp. 261–294). Frankfurt am Main, Germany: Peter Lang.
Przeworski, Adam, & Henry Teune. (1970). *The Logic of Comparative Social Inquiry.* New York: John Wiley and Sons.
Rohlen, Thomas P. (1983). *Japan's High Schools.* Berkeley, CA: University of California Press.
Rust, Val D. (1991). "Postmodernism and its Comparative Education Implications." *Comparative Education Review, 35*(4), 610–626.
Sahlins, Marshall David. (2004). *Apologies to Thucydides: Understanding History as Culture and Vice Versa.* Chicago: University of Chicago Press.
Schön, Donald. (1983). *The Reflective Practitioner: How Professionals Think in Action.* New York: Basic Books.
Schön, Donald. (1993). "Generative Metaphor: A Perspective on Problem-Setting in Social Policy." In Andrew Ortony (Ed.), *Metaphor and Thought,* (pp. 137–163). 2nd ed. New York: Cambridge University Press.
Scott, W. Richard. (2001). *Institutions and Organizations.* Thousand Oaks, CA: Sage Publications.
Smith, Earl, ed. (2010). *Sociology of Sport and Social Theory.* Champaign, IL: Human Kinetics.
Torres, Carlos Alberto. (1994). "Paulo Freire as Secretary of Education in the Municipality of São Paulo." *Comparative Education Review, 38*(2), 181–214.
Veseth, Michael. (2006). "Globaloney." In George Ritzer (Ed.), *McDonaldization: The Reader* (pp. 350–357). 2nd ed. Thousand Oaks, CA: Pine Forge Press.
Wacquant, Loïc. (2004). *Body & Soul: Notebooks of an Apprentice Boxer.* New York: Oxford University Press.
Waters, Malcolm. (2006). "McDonaldization and the Global Culture of Consumption." In George Ritzer (Ed.), *McDonaldization: The Reader* (pp. 284–290). 2nd ed. Thousand Oaks, CA: Pine Forge Press.

MOOSUNG LEE AND TOM FRIEDRICH

7. CITATION NETWORK ANALYSIS OF COMPARATIVE EDUCATION TEXTS

A Methodological Consideration for Micro Social Cartography

Researchers in the field of comparative education have long been interested in charting emerging and competing educational discourses. James Gee (1996, 131– 132) defines a discourse as a "socially accepted association among ways of using language, other symbolic expressions, and 'artifacts,' of thinking, feeling, believing, valuing and acting . . . [that] involve[s] a set of values and viewpoints about the relationships between people and the distribution of social goods." Each discourse is a sign-mediated, communicative means that is not an individual invention but a social practice; therefore, comparative education researchers study discourse to understand life in social contexts such as a classroom, a meeting of policy sponsors, or an educational journal. Amid various methodological approaches, Rolland G. Paulston's social cartography has been regarded as one of the most innovative (Epstein n.d.). However, despite the promise of Paulston's research, social cartography is rarely used as a research tool or perspective in educational research. With this in mind, we provide in this article a methodological consideration for social cartography as a research tool in comparative education research. We do so by using citation network analysis as a social cartography research method. As an applied method of social network analysis, citation network analysis charts a citation network among actors (e.g., authors or articles) generated from a particular boundary of texts (e.g., journals in comparative education). In this way, a citation network analysis represents the discursive interactions and relationships (i.e., citing authors or their work) generated by a set of actors. As a result, citation network analysis may illuminate a particular individual or subgroup's ontological and epistemological perspectives, her theory or their theories of what it means to be and know, by revealing her or their position(s) in the citation practices of researchers in a particular intellectual community. In this regard, citation network analysis of a particular discipline is in effect a genealogical study of discourses or knowledge within that discipline (de Nooy et al., 2005).

Based on these characteristics of citation network analysis, we view citation network analysis as a robust method for analyzing the "structural" and "spatial" features of social cartography, both a network's general themes and its actor-to-actor relations at the micro level.[1] Rolland Paulston and Martin Liebman (1996, 7,

John C. Weidman, W. James Jacob (eds.), Beyond the Comparative: Advancing Theory and Its Application to Practice, 113–144.

italics added) define "[s]ocial cartography as a *space* of juxtapositions [that] suggests an opening of dialogue among diverse *social players*, including those *individuals and cultural clusters* who want their 'mininarratives' included in the social discourse." To the extent that social cartography is spatial, it is formed from a "space" that harbors "diverse social players." Social cartography is also structural because its "diverse social players," such as "individuals" and "cultural clusters," interact with each other because they "want their mininarratives included in the social discourse." These interconnections and interactions among diverse social players are meaningfully patterned, or structured.

These two features of social cartography—the spatial and structural—describe citation network analysis equally well. A citation network consists of actors and ties. Actors refer to individual actors (i.e., diverse social players) within the network (i.e., a space), and ties represent structural relationships or citations between these actors. That is, a citation network serves as a channel or conduit, conveying various mininarratives. As such, the most distinctive feature of citation network analysis is that it particularly represents certain citation patterns among individuals who (and groups that) influence their ontological and epistemological views.

With this in mind, we have two aims in this chapter. First, we show that citation network analysis is one method for conducting micro social cartography research through demonstrating how to conduct a small-scale citation network analysis of comparative education texts. Using this exploratory citation network analysis as evidence, we discuss how citation network analysis extends the scope of Paulston's social cartography research. Second, based on our exploratory citation network analysis, we suggest how citation network analysis may be expanded as a micro social cartography research method by being combined with discourse analysis.

AN ILLUSTRATION OF ANALYSIS USING CITATION NETWORK ANALYSIS AS A TOOL FOR MICRO SOCIAL CARTOGRAPHY

The Boundary Specification of Comparative Education Texts

The first step for conducting a citation analysis is to construct a database that contains target archival data. Given that there are various comparative education texts, we confined our data mining to a set of Presidential Addresses in *Comparative Education Review (CER)* from 2000 to 2009. As a result, the citation network data in this study are ten Presidential Addresses. There are several important reasons why we chose those ten particular texts only. First, while there is some variation among the ten texts in terms of content or topics they cover, all of the Presidential Addresses have a commonality: each attempt to clarify, critique, et cetera, the identity of comparative education as a discipline to some extent. Second, in terms of data analysis, choosing Presidential Addresses as a source of data mining secured a clear analytical boundary (i.e., citation network from Presidential Addresses). Third, confining our data source to ten Presidential Addresses within a particular time period (i.e., 2000–2009) reflected this study's purpose of proposing a methodological consideration. Providing a clear demonstration was important to us, and a smaller network seemed likely to make our method more transparent than a larger one. Therefore, we preferred the Presidential Address network to, say, the citation network embedded in all comparative education texts from *CER*.

The Procedure of Data Mining

To generate network data, we coded the ten Presidential Addresses by taking several systematic steps. To make our procedure clear, let us describe how we coded Henry M. Levin's 2009 Presidential Address. In his text, he cites several authors. For example, he cites (or nominates) Martin Carnoy (1974), Carnoy and Derek Shearer (1980), and Donald Schön (1983), to name a few. Therefore, citation ties were generated from Levin to those authors. We will call these "directional" ties.

Self-nominations (i.e., the author cites his/her work) were, however, not included to avoid lopsided citation data mining; if self-nominations had been included, those ten presidents' influence on comparative education's identity would possibly have been overestimated. For the same reason, each president's nominations of his or her co-authored work were also not included (e.g., Levin's nomination of Carnoy and Levin's work in 1985).

Multiple nominations of the same author in one Presidential Address were treated as one nomination but weighted. For example, Levin cites Carnoy's two different works (e.g., Carnoy 1974; Carnoy and Shearer 1980) in his Presidential Address; as a result, this nomination was coded as "1" to indicate a citation tie between Levin and Carnoy, but it was weighted as "2" given Levin's citing of two of Carnoy's works. Because of this weighting, the network data in our citation analysis illustrate "valued" networks.

This also means that Carnoy's two different works were coded as "M.Carnoy74/80" under his name. Notably, since other former presidents also nominate Carnoy's other texts, the coding ended up taking the form "M.Carnoy74/80/94/95/96/98/99/06." Additionally, co-authors (i.e., Carnoy and Shearer (1980), whom Levin cites) were coded separately if they were cited again in other Presidential Addresses. Otherwise, a co-author was not coded because she or he was cited only one time as a co-author.

It should also be noted that Levin, in fact, mentions Carnoy more than two times (in fact, lots of times) in his address. However, our data coding used a "publication-oriented" principle. That is, we did not code when the presidents mentioned a scholar's name only. Our data were constructed only when authors and years are mentioned together in the Presidential Addresses. We adopted this principle because we encountered some statements concerning personal relationships between some authors. While we admit that these may be important relationships, we focused particularly on building a network of scholarly ties. Additionally, even though some authors and years are cited by some presidents, if the citations were collateral (i.e., a string of classic texts on a research topic) or not specifically related to a president's point at a given moment in his/her text, then they were deleted (see the case of Karl Popper cited by Ruth Hayhoe 2000).

Finally, as some presidents cite several different works from particular international organizations such as the World Bank and UNESCO, those citations were coded under the heading of those international organization's names. These sources included policies or technical reports that had been prepared by different authors but published in the name of those international organizations.

The Overall Feature of the Constructed Data

All the coding was done with the use of Excel sheets. As a result, we constructed 304 actors (authors) and 370 ties (citation links) among those actors. The network is loosely connected given such a low ratio between actors and their ties. As seen in Figure 7.1, the network includes many actors who are connected with only one other actor. This is not surprising because the citation network is based on the ten presidents' "ego-centric networks." By ego-centric networks, we mean networks showing all the social ties surrounding one particular actor, a so-called focal node or actor (Scott 1991). As such, the network data we constructed combines the ego-centric networks of the ten presidents (i.e., 10 focal nodes), encompassing the various actors surrounding these ten Comparative International Education Society (CIES) presidents.

It should be recalled that the main purpose of our data mining of the ten Presidential Addresses was to secure a clear network boundary (i.e., citation networks within CIES Presidential Addresses from 2000 to 2009). While useful, as ego-centric network data, our data have a clear limitation; because the collected network data are based on the citations of the ten former presidents only, the data do not include the relationships among authors cited by the ten presidents. This issue could be substantially mitigated in a future study by expanding the scope of data mining. For example, building a citation network from all the texts from *CER* would be a way to solve this problem.

Despite the limitations noted above, we note that this chapter aims to provide a small-scale example of citation network analysis of comparative education texts in order to present a methodological approach to micro social cartography.

Analysis 1: Who Is Cited Most?

Paulston and Liebman (1996, 8) point out that their aim with social cartography is to unfold comparative discourse as representing "a visual dialogue." This resonates with a key feature of citation network analysis: the fact that citation network analysis visualizes who is connected to whom. In this regard, one obvious way to visualize scholarly dialogues or relationships at the micro level is to investigate who is citing whom. To this end, we used the concept of centrality, which refers to "the degree to which an actor is in a central role in the network" (Fredericks and Durland 2005, 18). According to Linton Freeman (1977, 1979) there are three distinctive ways of measuring central roles of actors in a network: *degree*, *closeness*, and *betweenness* centrality. In what follows, we define and present descriptive tables on each measure in what follows.

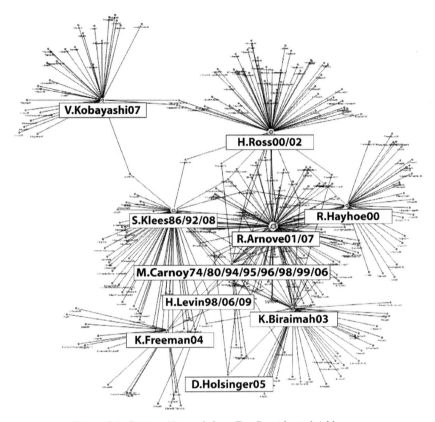

Figure 7.1. Citation Network from Ten Presidential Addresses.

Degree centrality captures the central role of a focal actor by simply measuring the degree of the actors who are adjacent to her or him. We let $C_D(a)$ denote degree centrality of one particular actor. The formula for a particular actor's degree centrality was, then,

$$C_D(a) = \frac{d(a)}{g-1}$$

where g is the group size (the total number of actors in the group) and d is the number of other actors (alters) who are adjacent to the focal actor (Wasserman and Faust 2007). Notably, we used "in-degree" centrality, which shows actors frequently nominated/cited by other actors. In this regard, we assumed that important scholars in our network would be actors with high in-degree centrality.

Table 7.1 lists the top 20 authors in terms of in-degree centrality, showing who are most frequently cited by other scholars; the work of scholars with higher in-degree centrality is highly recognized by their peers. Carnoy is the most cited scholar, represented by various works (1974, 1980, 1994, 1995, 1996, 1998, 1999, 2006). Carlos Alberto Torres and Vandra Masemann are the second most cited scholars. Scholarly works of David N. Wilson, Mark B. Ginsburg, Nelly P. Stromquist, and Stephen P. Heyneman are also frequently mentioned.

Table 7.1. List of the 20 Highest In-Degree Centrality Authors

Rank	Author	In-Degree Centrality
1	M.Carnoy74/80/94/95/96/98/99/06	0.019802
2	C.Torres98a/98b/07	0.016502
3	V.Masemann82/97/99/90	0.016502
4	D.Wilson94	0.013201
5	M.Ginsburg88/91/92/01/08	0.013201
6	N.Stromquist95/97/98/99/01	0.013201
7	S.Heyneman76/81/84/93/95/99	0.013201
8	H.Noah68/69/74/84/98	0.009901
9	J.Farrell79/85/92/99	0.009901
10	M.Eckstein68/69/98	0.009901
11	R.Arnove01/07	0.009901
12	R.Paulston77/99/00	0.009901
13	R.Torres00/01	0.009901
14	UNESCO98/03	0.009901
15	V.Rust91/99/00	0.009901
16	B.Fuller86/87/99	0.006601
17	B.Holmes65/83/84	0.006601
18	C.Bowers93/95/97/06	0.006601
19	D.Kelly96/00	0.006601
20	E.Epstein83/92/05 *and 28 more authors*	0.006601

Analysis 2: Who Is Located in the Center?

Guided by Pierre Bourdieu's work, Paulston (1993, 102) states that intellectual fields or discursive communities are formed by "dialectical interaction with objective structures and actors' views of the world." In response to his statement, we introduce another important concept of centrality called *closeness centrality* that enabled us to chart scholarly interactions based upon ties and actors. Closeness centrality can be used as a crucial instrument in micro social cartography because it reveals the degree to which one particular actor gets to other actors along the shortest path:

> This measure [closeness centrality] has also been described as a measure of efficiency or the ability to get to others without interference, along the shortest possible path available. Persons with closeness are productive in getting communication to others and getting feedback to them. Closeness is defined as the shortest path (geodesic) connecting one person to another. (Durland 2005, 37)

Closeness centrality is calculated with the use of the following equation (Wasserman and Faust 2007):

$$C_C(n_i) = \left[\sum_{j=1}^{g} d(n_i, n_j) \right]^{-1} .$$

In the equation, d denotes the geodesic distance (i.e., the shortest path between two actors) from a focal actor (i.e., ego) to another actor j. The denominator represents the sum of geodesic distances from a focal actor to all the other actors. Based on this, closeness centrality is calculated by the inverse of the sum of the geodesic distances from a focal actor to all the other actors (Wasserman and Faust 2007). Therefore, larger distances between a focal actor and others generate lower closeness centrality scores (de Nooy et al., 2005).

For a directional network in this study, we considered each in-closeness and out-closeness centrality score separately, because the distances between a focal actor and another actor can be measured either "from" or "to" each actor. In this study we focused particularly on in-closeness centrality on the assumption that certain key scholars with short paths to other scholars in the network (i.e., scholars with high in-closeness centrality) were more likely to be accessed from other scholars.[2]

Table 7.2 lists the top 20 authors in terms of in-closeness centrality. Carnoy is again ranked as the top scholar in terms of having the shortest paths connecting to the rest of the scholars in the network; that is, he is the author most likely to be accessed from other scholars because of his central location. The second to the fourth most frequently cited scholars are also the same as in the results for in-degree centrality. This is partly because the influence of degree centrality overshadowed the closeness-centrality measure.

At the same time, however, the rest of the scholars listed in Table 7.2 are somewhat different from those in Table 7.1 in two distinctive ways. First, while some of the scholars (e.g., Stromquist, Ginsburg, Heyneman, Val D. Rust, Joseph P. Farrell, and R. Torres) were identified both by in-degree and in-closeness centrality measures, other scholars (e.g., Bruce Fuller, Brian Holmes, and David H. Kelly) identified from the in-degree centrality measure were not identified through the in-closeness centrality measure. Instead, scholars such as Paulo Freire, George Psacharopoulos, David Plank, Noel F. McGinn, and William Cummings were newly listed by the in-closeness centrality measure. This suggests that the newly identified scholars' works are more likely than their counterparts' works to be accessed by the rest of the scholars in the networks in terms of network distance (that is, they have shorter paths) although the newly identified scholars' works are less frequently cited than those of their counterparts. In other words, the works of Freire, Psacharopoulos, Plank, McGinn, and Cummings are less cited, but their works are located in a more central position in the entire network.

Another interesting feature is that even though almost all actors are individual scholars in the network, UNESCO as an international organization is positioned in this highly cited group by both in-closeness as well as in-degree centrality measures.

Table 7.2. List of the 20 Highest In-Closeness Centrality Authors

Rank	Author	In-Closeness
1	M.Carnoy74/80/94/95/96/98/99/06	0.019802
2	C.Torres98a/98b/07	0.019202
3	V.Masemann82/97/99/90	0.019202
4	D.Wilson94	0.017602
5	N.Stromquist95/97/98/99/01	0.016172
6	M.Ginsburg88/91/92/01/08	0.015087
7	P.Freire70/73	0.015087
8	R.Paulston77/99/00	0.014701
9	S.Heyneman76/81/84/93/95/99	0.014701
10	V.Rust91/99/00	0.014701
11	J.Farrell79/85/92/99	0.014081
12	R.Torres00/01	0.014081
13	UNESCO98/03	0.014081
14	G.Psacharopoulos90/93	0.013476
15	N.McGinn96	0.013476
16	W.Cummings99	0.013476
17	R.Arnove01/07	0.013201
18	D.Plank&G.Sykes03	0.01244
19	H.Noah68/69/74/84/98	0.01244
20	M.Eckstein68/69/98 *and 3 more authors*	0.01244

Analysis 3: Who Bridges Different Scholars?

In his classic research, Paulston (1993) presents a heuristic taxonomy of knowledge perspectives in comparative education texts, including functionalist, radical functionalist, radical humanist, and humanist views. Interestingly, Paulston locates himself in three out of the four categories. This suggests that there are key scholars whose works bridge different scholarly groups. *Betweenness centrality*, suggested by Freeman (1979), can be utilized to identify those bridging actors.

According to John Scott (1991, 89), betweenness centrality measures "the extent to which a particular point lies 'between' the various other points in the graph [network]." In other words, betweenness centrality shows "how much an individual is indirectly linked to other members of the group and is a measure of to what extent an individual is between two others" (Durland 2005, 37). In this sense, it is often regarded as a measure of information control or conversely norm pressure (Lee 2009). Although betweenness centrality is more appropriate for analyzing non-directional ties in general, we used betweenness centrality for the directional network in this study by symmetrizing directional ties—converting directional ties into non-directional ones when we found reciprocal ties or one tie between two actors. Table 7.3 presents the top 20 authors' betweenness centrality. Nine out of the ten former presidents bridge different scholars.

Table 7.3. List of the 20 Highest Betweenness Centrality Authors

Rank	Author	Betweenness Centrality
1	R.Arnove01/07	0.546768
2	H.Ross00/02	0.361159
3	S.Klees86/92/08	0.333446
4	K.Biraimah03	0.179334
5	V.Kobayashi07	0.17127
6	R.Hayhoe00	0.152692
7	M.Carnoy74/80/94/95/96/98/99/06	0.095686
8	K.Freeman04	0.091891
9	D.Orr91/04	0.079024
10	C.Bowers93/95/97/06	0.044358
11	M.Bateson79/87/91/99	0.044358
12	C.Torres98a/98b/07	0.033516
13	V.Masemann82/97/99/90	0.026158
14	M.Ginsburg88/91/92/01/08	0.02216
15	S.Heyneman76/81/84/93/95/99	0.015717
16	H.Levin98/06/09	0.013977
17	M.Miles93/94	0.01095
18	R.Torres00/01	0.01095
19	D.Wilson94	0.009708
20	J.Farrell79/85/92/99	0.00969

This is not surprising in that the network was constructed by combining their ego-centric networks. Despite this, betweenness centrality captured several interesting patterns from a different conceptual angle. Robert F. Arnove plays a key role in bridging different members. He is ranked 11th in in-degree centrality and 17th in in-closeness centrality, but he is the most active in bridging different scholars. Likewise, Heidi Ross, Steve Klees, Karen Biraimah, Victor Kobayashi, Ruth Hayhoe, Martin Carnoy, and Kasie Freeman are key authors whose works connect different groups of scholars' work. Other than the ten former presidents, scholars such as David Orr, C. A. Bowers, Mary Catherine Bateson, C. A. Torres, Masemann, Ginsburg, and Heyneman also serve as bridges in the network. In sum, these authors were found to be influential in bridging different groups of authors in comparative education texts.

Analysis 4: Who Is Closely Grouped Together?

Turning again to Paulston to guide our work, we note that Paulston's (1993) heuristic taxonomy categorizes the following group of scholars' works into one group under the heading of functionalist: John Boli, Francisco O. Ramirez, and John W. Meyer (1985); Philip H. Coombs (1985); Theodore Schultz (1989); Donald K. Adams (1988); Plank (1990); Dennis Rondinelli and colleagues (1990); James S. Coleman (1987); and others cited in Paulston (1993). Paulston further divided these functionalists into several sub-groups, with one including Adams (1988), Plank (1990), and Rondinelli and colleagues (1990) that Paulston considered neofunctionalist. This suggests that there may be cohesive subgroups in discursive communities in comparative education texts.

Following suit, we employed the concept of "cliques," which are essential for understanding the dynamics of citation network structures. In general, cliques refer to "subgroups where all members connect to each other" (Durland 2005, 30). That is, a clique is a subgroup in a network, and all members in a clique are mutually connected by each other. In this sense, cliques are fundamental for analyzing the cohesion structure of a network (i.e., cohesive subgroups). Specifically, in citation network analysis, a clique is defined as a maximal complete sub-network of at least three actors (Wasserman and Faust 2007). Notably, since our network data were coded by directional ties between actors, we symmetrized our sociomatrix to include cliques.

Table 7.4 presents the nine cliques identified. Notably, several authors belong to more than one clique. It is quite common for different actors to have different social or discursive boundaries. In particular, Arnove and Carnoy belong to all the cliques, showing their mutual relationships with particular authors. Other key authors contributing to more than two cliques are Hayhoe and Biraimah.

However, caution should be exercised in interpreting this table. In identifying the cliques, we took the "maximum" of the entries in corresponding off-diagonal cells, although conceptually cliques are identified through "reciprocated links" between actors. In other words, for illustrative purposes, we transformed non-reciprocal ties into reciprocal ties even when two actors had only one directional tie. In this sense, cliques identified in this chapter are based on relatively a less strict definition of the concept.

Table 7.4. List of the Nine Cliques and Members

Cliques	Members
Clique1	R.Arnove, S.Klees, M.Carnoy, C.Torres
Clique2	R.Arnove, S.Klees, M.Carnoy, N.Stromquist
Clique3	R.Arnove, D.Wilson, K.Biraimah, M.Carnoy
Clique4	R.Arnove, K.Biraimah, M.Carnoy, N.Stromquist
Clique5	R.Arnove, K.Biraimah, M.Carnoy, V.Masemann
Clique6	R.Arnove, R.Hayhoe, M.Carnoy, C.Torres
Clique7	R.Arnove, R.Hayhoe, M.Carnoy, R.Paulston
Clique8	R.Arnove, R.Hayhoe, M.Carnoy, V.Masemann
Clique9	R.Arnove, R.Hayhoe, M.Carnoy, V.Rust

Figure 7.2. 2-Clique with 33 Actors.

Furthering our analysis of cliques we used *n*-cliques, which also reflect a somewhat relaxed concept of cliques. In fact, cliques are sometimes not identified in some networks when the strict definition is used; in our network data, when we took the "minimum" of the entries in corresponding off-diagonal cells, no cliques were identified. When they are used, and in the case of this study, *n*-cliques include an actor as a member of a particular clique if the actor is connected to every other member of the group at a path distance of *n*. That is, *n* as in *n*-cliques means the length of the path (Wasserman and Faust 2007). For example, in a friendship network, a *2*-clique means a friend of a friend.

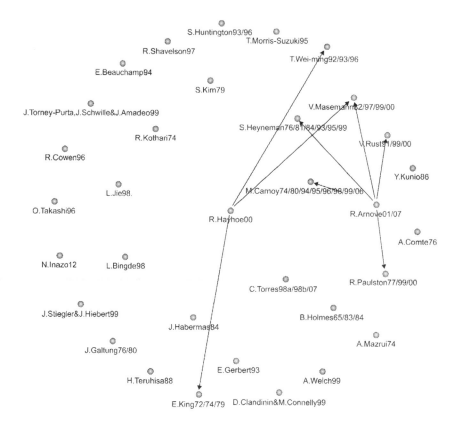

Figure 7.3. 2-Clique with 33 Actors Based on Weighting.

Using 2-cliques, we sought to identify larger sized but less cohesive subgroups. We again took the maximum of the entries in corresponding off-diagonal cells and set the minimum size of 2-cliques as 4.[3] We found 30 2-cliques. The minimum and maximum sizes of the 2-cliques are 4 and 107, respectively. For illustrative purposes, we present a 2-clique (i.e., including 33 actors) below. The density of this clique is 0.081, which is quite low given that the definition of density is the proportion of present ties to the maximum possible number of ties in a network (Scott 1991); therefore, density ranges from 0 (minimal density) to 1 (maximal density). The reason for the low density is that the clique is predominantly based on Hayhoe's ego-centric network. This suggests that as the scope of data mining expands, *n*-cliques capture cohesive groups consisting of various actors who are not from a particular actor's ego-centric network only.

Analysis 5: Who Is More Emphasized than Whom?

As mentioned earlier, the network data in our citation analysis include information about how particular scholars (or their works) are cited more than one time in particular Presidential Addresses. This is valuable information for helping us visualize the different features of particular authors' works. Again, for illustrative purposes, we used the 2-clique presented in Figure 7.2 to create a measure of emphasis. Specifically, we only selected ties where particular presidents cite the same author(s) more than two times in their Presidential Addresses. As Figure 7.3 shows, a majority of ties disappeared when we used the threshold of three (citing three times or more). Only a few ties (e.g., Hayhoe's citations of Edmund King and Vandra Masemann, and Arnove's citations of Carnoy, Heyneman, Masemann, Rust, and Paulston) still remained, which shows these cited authors or works are particularly influential. As this shows, using "valued" networks can be useful in charting a particular quality of scholarly relationships or discursive interactions.

LIMITATIONS OF THE ILLUSTRATIVE ANALYSIS

We acknowledge several limitations in our analysis. As mentioned earlier, the scope of our data mining was quite limited; specifically, we studied only ten Presidential Addresses from 2000 to 2009. This hindered us from mapping out precise network structures of scholarly relationships or dialogues on a larger scale; this effort did not seem necessary, however, given that our main intention was to provide a methodological consideration through our small-scale analysis.

Another limitation is also linked to the scope of data mining. Given that the first issue of *CER* was published in 1957, we believe there likely are particular, historical patterns or trends in *CER*'s citation networks. Following the same logic, Paulston (1993) periodizes changing representations of knowledge in comparative education texts from the 1950s to 1990s as linear and orthodoxy (1950s–1960s), heterodoxy (1970s–1980s), and intertwined (1990s). Reflecting Paulston's periodization, we believe that future research should pay attention to longitudinal citation network analysis by studying more comprehensive comparative education texts than we have done.

Finally, while our citation network analysis revealed whose works are regarded as important or influential within the ten Presidential Addresses, we know little about what kinds of discourses or scholarly dialogues are positioned as central or peripheral within the citation network. This limitation, in fact, is not simply a weakness of the current study; it is a limitation that any study utilizing citation data analysis faces.

FUTURE RESEARCH: TOWARDS DISCURSIVE NETWORK ANALYSIS (DNA) FOR MICRO SOCIAL CARTOGRAPHY

The final limitation mentioned above is inherent to citation network analysis as a method. Given that citation network analysis is a branch of social network analysis, which focuses mostly on structural and functional features of social relationships, the limitation is understandable. At the same time, however, drawing from our analysis, we conclude that citation network analysis may be complemented by other methodological approaches to serve as an enhanced tool for micro social cartography. As mentioned above, the kinds of discourses that are interacted in our citation network data remain unclear. With this in mind, we propose discursive network analysis (DNA), which combines citation network analysis and discourse analysis, as an enhanced approach for future research on micro social cartography. Let us briefly discuss the conceptual linkages of discourse analysis with social cartography first. We will then discuss the analytically complementary features of discourse analysis and citation network analysis in order to further validate DNA as an enhanced approach for micro social cartography research that may be used in the future.

THE CONCEPTUAL LINKAGES OF SOCIAL CARTOGRAPHY WITH DISCOURSE ANALYSIS

We return once more to Paulston and Liebman's (1996, 7, italics added) definition of social cartography: "[s]ocial cartography . . . [is] a space of juxtapositions [that] suggests an opening of *dialogue* among diverse social players, including those individuals and cultural clusters *who want their "mininarratives" included in the social discourse.*" This definition suggests a key characteristic of social cartography is charting "individuals and cultural clusters' mininarratives in the social discourse." In social cartography, mininarratives are viewed as a way individuals and cultural clusters exist in social discourse (or in the world) in that such mininarratives reveal individuals' and cultural clusters' ontological status and epistemological positions within social discourse. That is, social cartography is viewed as an intellectual project for mapping out various mininarratives in social discourse.

From a discourse analysis perspective, articulating mininarratives is a particular way of being in the world that involves "language use" in a situational and cultural context (Kinneavy 1971). Articulating mininarratives is a "mode . . . of thinking" that refers to language used by historically specific subjects and "'the ideas and philosophies they propagate'" (van Dijk 1997 quoted in Grant et al., 2001, 7). Furthermore, articulating mininarratives in social discourse is a "mode of action" and therefore a form of social practice (Fairclough 1992, 63–64).

As this examination of the act of articulating mininarratives shows, we believe that discourse analysis is analytically paralleled with social cartography. Discourse analysis performs social cartography because it reveals (1) how discourses as a form of social practice entailing language use are "produced, consumed and distributed" (Fairclough 1992, 71) and (2) how discourses are "constituted and constitute . . . dialectically." That is, as with social cartography, discourse analysis refers to and signifies, a "condition for, and an effect of" social structure (Fairclough 1992, 64). In addition, discourse analysis is an acceptable means for studying postmodern lived experience on the grounds that it accepts that (1) knowledge is socially constructed, and therefore dynamic; that (2) lived reality is organized not so much in relatively stable, larger social structures (such as recognizable "status groups") but in highly flexible networks; and that (3) network-based subjects do not so much possess "essences" but are beings-in-the-world interpenetratively constituting and constituted by one another. As this discussion shows, discourse analysis treated as a research tool for conducting social cartography can reveal how various mininarratives are contested by individuals and cultural clusters and their ontological and epistemological relationships.

ANALYTICALLY COMPLEMENTARY FEATURES SHARED BY DISCOURSE ANALYSIS AND CITATION NETWORK ANALYSIS

Discourse dialogically constitutes and is constituted by connected individuals and interactive cultural clusters. This is one reason why discourse is rule-governed yet has an open structure. This ordered, dynamic structure of discourse can also be seen in its dialogic relation with context. Discourse is "controlled, selected, organized and redistributed according to a certain number of procedures" or rules; these rules direct discourse production in order to "avert. . .[nature's] powers and its dangers, to cope with chance events" (Foucault 1972, 222–223). At the same time, each discourse presents not an inflexible set of values but is, rather, partially open, an "interpretive repertoire" (Bacchi 2000, 53) that affords room for "fresh propositions" (Foucault 1972, 22–23) made possible because individuals and cultural clusters are interconnected, interdependent, and interactive.

These characteristics of discourse analysis described above complement citation network analysis in valuable ways. We believe that this proposed combination of discourse analysis with citation network analysis can provide researchers with a methodologically-enhanced approach to social cartography for this reason: social cartography is a "space" where diverse individuals and cultural clusters function as channels and/or generators of "mininarratives." In other words, social cartography maps out mininarratives that are conveyed through citation networks. The point here is that there are three features of social cartography (i.e., discursive, spatial, and structural) that are conceptually integrated into a "discursive network" in that a structural, spatial network within social cartography serves as a channel or conduit, conveying mininarratives (or discourses) that form intellectual communities and their relationships. This is also an analytical interface between discourse and citation network analysis with regard to social cartography. This analytical interface is implied in Paulston and Lieberman's (1996, 7, italics added) following statement: "It [social cartography] offers comparative educators a new method for *visually* demonstrating the sensitivity of postmodern influences in order to open *social dialogue*." In this regard, we propose DNA as a future direction for micro social cartography, a combined approach based on discourse analysis and citation network analysis. DNA is a research method integrating discursive, spatial and structural dimensions of social cartography that may indeed contribute to what Paulston and Liebman intended social cartography to do: unfold comparative discourse as a visual and heuristic dialogue.

CONCLUDING REMARKS

This chapter sought to illuminate how citation network analysis could pave a methodological route for using micro social cartography to study comparative education texts. Based on the ten key texts from *CER* from 2000 to 2009, we sought to identify authors and their relationships with other authors by employing network analysis techniques such as centrality and cliques. We believe that citation network analysis is a useful tool for identifying key actors and subgroups in a citation network. We also believe our illustration of citation network analysis provides several methodological and analytical insights from which future comparative research may benefit. First, citation network analysis precisely captures who is related to whom so long as data mining is done on a larger scale. Second, future research is likely to benefit from our proposal for DNA because it is intended to capture who is related to whom (through citation network analysis) in certain discursive contexts (through discourse analysis), enabling researchers to unveil how, why, and where mininarratives are formulated, disseminated, reproduced, and transformed. That is, through being combined with discourse analysis, we propose that citation network analysis can contribute more to creating the kind of social map Paulston and Liebman (1996, 14) aimed for (i.e., a social map that identifies "intellectual communities and relationships, illustrates domains, suggests a field of interactive ideas and opens space to all propositions and ways of seeing in the social milieu"). Finally, while DNA is novel and conceptually sound, the analytical combination of citation network analysis with discourse analysis remains to be articulated. Future research would benefit by focusing on developing more specific guidance in maximizing analytical advantages from both citation network analysis and discourse analysis with regard to social cartography.

NOTES

1. Once Val D. Rust (1996) mentioned the benefit of using social network analysis for social cartography research. He briefly introduced basic concepts of social network analysis for possible utilization.
2. For a disconnected network, closeness centrality sometimes cannot be computed because there are no paths between some actors (i.e., unreachable or isolated actors). However, the network in this study did not include any isolate actors.
3. Typically, the minimum size of cliques is 3.

REFERENCES

Adams, Donald K. (1988). "Expanding the Educational Planning Discourse." *Comparative Education Review, 32*(4), 400–415.
Bacchi, Carol L. (2000). "Policy as Discourse: What Does It Mean? Where Does It Get Us?" *Discourse: Studies in the Cultural Politics of Education, 21*(1), 45–57.
Boli, John, Francisco O. Ramirez, & John W. Meyer. (1985). "Explaining the Origins and Expansion of Mass Schooling." *Comparative Education Review, 29*(2), 145–170.
Coleman, James S. (1987). "Micro-foundations and macro-social behavior." In Jeffrey Alexander, Bernhard Geisen, Richard Munch, and Neil J. Smelser (Ed.), *The Micro-Macro Link* (pp. 153–173). Berkeley, CA: The University of California Press.
Coombs, P. (1985). *The World Crisis in Education.* London: Oxford University Press.

de Nooy, Wooter, Andcj Mrvar, & Vladimir Batagelj. (2005). *Exploratory Social Network Analysis with Pajek.* New York: Cambridge University Press.

Durland, Maryann M. (2005). "Exploring and Understanding Relationships." *New Directions for Evaluation, 107,* 25–40.

Epstein, Irving. n.d. Book Review of *Social Cartography: Mapping Ways of Seeing Social and Educational Change,* ed. Rolland G. Paulston. *Education Review.* Available online at: http://edrev.info.

Fairclough, Norman. (1992). *Discourse and Social Change.* Cambridge: Polity Press.

Foucault, Michel. (1972). *The Archaeology of Knowledge.* New York: Pantheon.

Fredericks, Kimberly A., & Maryann M. Durland. (2005). "The Historical Evolution and Basic Concepts of Social Network Analysis." *New Directions for Evaluation, 107,* 15–23.

Freeman, Linton C. (1977). "A Set of Measures of Centrality Based on Betweenness." *Sociometry, 40,* 35–41.

Freeman, Linton C. (1979). "Centrality in Social Networks: I. Conceptual Clarification." *Social Networks, 1,* 215–239.

Gee, James P. (1996). *Social Linguistics and Literacies: Ideology in Discourses.* London: Routledge.

Grant, David, Tom Keenoy, & Cliff Oswick. (2001). "Organizational Discourse: Key Contributions and Challenges." *International Studies of Management and Organization, 31*(3), 5–24.

Kinneavy, James L. (1971). *A Theory of Discourse.* New York: Norton.

Lee, Moosung. (2009). "Decoding Effects of Micro Social Contexts on the Academic Achievement of Immigrant Adolescents From the Poor Working Class: Peers, Institutional Agents, and School Contexts." PhD diss., University of Minnesota-Twin Cities, Minneapolis, MN, USA.

Paulston, Rolland G. (1993). "Mapping Discourse in Comparative Education Texts." *Compare, 23*(2), 101–114.

Paulston, Rolland G., & Martin Liebman. (1996). "Social Cartography: A New Metaphor/Tool for Comparative Studies." In Rolland G. Paulston (Ed.), *Social Cartography: Mapping Ways of Seeing Social and Educational Change* (pp. 7–28). New York: Garland Publishing.

Plank, David. (1990). "The Politics of Basic Educational Reform in Brazil." *Comparative Education Review, 34*(4), 538–560.

Rondinelli, Dennis, John Middleton, & Adrian Vespoor. (1990). *Planning Educational Reforms in Developing Countries.* Durham, NC: Duke University Press.

Rust, Val D. (1996). "From Modern to Postmodern Ways of Seeing Social and Educational Change." In Rolland G. Paulston (Ed.), *Social Cartography: Mapping Ways of Seeing Social and Educational Change* (pp. 29–51). New York: Garland Publishing.

Schultz, Theodore. (1989). "Investing in People: Schooling in Low Income Countries." *Economics of Education Review, 8*(3), 219–240.

Scott, John. (1991). *Social Network Analysis: A Handbook.* London: Sage Publications.

van Dijk, Teun. A. (1997). "The Study of Discourse." In Teun A. van Dijk (Ed.), *Discourse as Structure and Process* (pp. 1–34). London: Sage Publications.

Wasserman, Stanley, & Katherine Faust. (2007). *Social Network Analysis: Methods and Applications.* New York: Cambridge University Press.

APPENDIX: BIBLIOGRAPHY USED FOR CITATION NETWORKS

Akkari, Abdeljalil, & Soledad Perez. (1998). "Educational Research in Latin America: Review and Perspectives." *Educational Policy Analysis Archives, 6*(7), 1–10.

Albright, Madeline K. (2000). "Statement on International Education Week (November 13–17, 2000)." *Office of the Spokesman.* Washington, DC: U.S. Department of State. September 26, 2000.

Alger, Chadwick F., & James E. Harf. (1986). *Global Education: Why? For Whom? About What?* Columbus, OH: Ohio State University.

Alperovitz, Gar. (2004). *America beyond Capitalism: Reclaiming Our Wealth, Our Liberty, and Our Democracy.* New York: Wiley.

Altbach, Philip G., & Gail P. Kelly. (1978). *Education and Colonialism.* New York: Longman.

Altbach, Philip G. (1998). *Comparative Higher Education: Knowledge, the University and Development.* Hong Kong: University of Hong Kong.

Altbach, Philip G. (1998). "The University as Center and Periphery." In Philip G. Altbach (Ed.), *Comparative Higher Education: Knowledge, the University, and Development* .(pp. 19–36). Norwood, NJ: Ablex.

Anderson, Arnold. (1977). "Comparative Education over a Quarter Century: Maturity and Challenges." *Comparative Education Review, 21*(2&3), 405–416.

Apple, Michael W. (1999). *Power, Meaning and Identity: Essays in Critical Educational Studies.* New York: Peter Lang.

Apple, Michael W. (2000). "Can Critical Pedagogies Interrupt Rightist Policies?" *Educational Theory, 50*(2), 229–255.

Apple, Michael W. (2001). *Educating the "Right" Way: Markets, Standards, God, and Inequality.* New York: Routledge-Falmer.

Arnot, Madeleine, & Jo-Anne Dillabough. (2000). *Challenging Democracy: International Perspectives on Gender, Education and Citizenship.* New York: Routledge-Falmer.

Arnove, Robert F., & Carlos Alberto Torres, eds. (2007). *Comparative Education: The Dialectic of the Global and the Local. 3rd ed.* New York: Rowman & Littlefield.

Arnove, Robert F.. (2001). "Comparative and International Education Society Facing the Twenty-first Century: Challenges and Contributions." *Comparative Education Review, 45*(4), 477–503.

Assie-Lumumba, N-Dri Therese. (2000). "Educational and Economic Reforms, Gender Equity and Access to Schooling in Africa." *International Journal of Comparative Sociology, 41*(1), 39–120.

Ayers, William, & Janet Miller, eds. (1998). *A Light in Dark Times: Maxine Greene and the Unfinished Conversation.* New York: Teachers College Press.

Bakhtin, Mikhail. (1968). *Rabelais and His World.* Trans. H. Iswolsky. Boston: MIT Press.

Banks, James, ed. (1996). *Multicultural Education, Transformative Knowledge, and Action: Historical and Contemporary Perspectives.* New York: Teachers College Press.

Banks, James. (2001). "Citizenship Education and Diversity: Implications for Teacher Education." *Journal of Teacher Education, 52*(1), 5–16.

Barricada. (1992). "Falso y Peligroso Dilemma." *Barricada*, March 12, 3.

Bateson, Gregory, & Mary Catherine Bateson. (1987). *Angels Fear: Towards an Epistemology of the Sacred.* New York: Macmillan.

Bateson, Gregory. (1979). *Mind and Nature: A Necessary Unity.* New York: E. P. Dutton.

Bateson, Gregory. (1991). *A Sacred Unity: Further Steps to an Ecology of Mind.* Rodney E. Donaldson (Ed.), New York: Harper Collins.

Bateson, Gregory. (1999). *Steps to an Ecology of Mind.* Chicago: University of Chicago Press.

Bateson, Mary Catherine. (1984). *With a Daughter's Eye: A Memoir of Margaret Mead and Gregory Bateson.* New York: Morrow.

Bateson, Mary Catherine. (1995). *Peripheral Visions: Learning along the Way.* New York: Harper Collins.

Bateson, Mary Catherine. (2000). *Full Circles, Overlapping Lives: Culture and Generation in Transition.* New York: Random House.

Beauchamp, Edward. (1994). "Introduction: Japanese Education since 1945: The Development of Postwar Education Policy." In Edward R. Beauchamp and James M. Vardaman, Jr. (Ed.), *Japanese Education since 1945: A Documentary Study* .(pp. 3–33). New York: Sharpe.

de Beauvoir, Simone. (1952). *The Second Sex.* New York: Knopf. de Beauvoir, Simone. 1952. *The Second Sex.* New York: Knopf.

Beck, E. M., Patrick Horan, & Charles Tolbert. (1980). "Social Stratification in Industrial Society: Further Evidence for a Structural Alternative; A Reply to Hauser." *American Sociological Review, 45,* 712–719.

Belenky, Mary Field, Lynne A. Bond, & Jacqueline S. Weinstock. (1997). *A Tradition That Has No Name: Nurturing the Development of People, Families, and Communities.* New York: Basic.

Berliner, David C., & Bruce J. Biddle. (1995). *The Manufactured Crisis: Myths, Fraud, and the Attack on America's Public Schools.* Reading, MA: Addison-Wesley.

Bigelow, William. (1990). "Inside the Classroom: Social Vision and Critical Pedagogy." *Teachers College Record, 91*(3), 437–448.

Biraimah, Karen. (2003). "Transforming Education, Transforming Ourselves: Contributions and Lessons Learned." *Comparative Education Review, 47*(4), 423–443.

Blaug, Mark. (1975). "Kuhn versus Lakatos, or Paradigms versus Research Programmes in the History of Economics." *History of Political Economy, 7,* 399–433.

Bloom, Allan. (1988). *Closing of the American Mind.* New York: Simon and Schuster.

Bloom, Leslie Rebecca. (1998). *Under the Sign of Hope: Feminist Methodology and Narrative Interpretation*. Albany, NY: SUNY Press.

Blum, Lawrence A. (1994). *Moral Perception and Particularity*. Cambridge, MA: Cambridge University Press.

Blunt, Alison, & Gillian Rose, eds. (1994). *Writing Women and Space: Colonial and Postcolonial Geographies*. New York: Guilford.

Blunt, Alison, & Gillian Rose. (1994). "Introduction." In Alison Blunt and Gillian Rose (Ed.), *Writing Women and Space: Colonial and Postcolonial Geographies* . (pp. 1–25). New York: Guilford.

Boli, John, Francisco O. Ramirez, & John W. Meyers. (1985). "Explaining the Origins and Expansion of Mass Education." *Comparative Education Review, 29*(2), 145–170.

Bourdieu, Pierre, & Loïc J. D. Wacquant. (1992). *An Invitation to Reflexive Sociology*. Chicago: University of Chicago Press.

Bowen, Howard R. (1977). *Investment in Learning*. San Francisco: Jossey-Bass.

Bowers, Chet A. (1993). *Education, Cultural Myths, and the Ecological Crisis: Toward Deep Changes*. Albany, NY: State University of New York Press.

Bowers, Chet A. (1995). *Educating for an Ecologically Sustainable Culture: Rethinking Moral Education, Creativity, Intelligence, and Other Modern Orthodoxies*. Albany, NY: SUNY Press.

Bowers, Chet A. (1997). *The Culture of Denial: Why the Environmental Movement Needs a Strategy for Reforming Universities and Public Schools*. Albany, NY: SUNY Press.

Bowers, Chet A. (2006). *Revitalizing the Commons: Cultural and Educational Sites of Resistance and Affirmation*. Lanham, MD: Lexington Books.

Bowles, Samuel, & Herbert Gintis. (1986). *Democracy and Capitalism: Property, Community, and the Contradictions of Modern Social Thought*. New York: Basic.

Boyd, William, & Edmund. J. King. (1972). *History of Western Education*. 10th ed. New York: Barnes & Noble Books.

Bracey, Gerald W. (1998). "The Eighth Bracey Report on the Condition of Public Education." *Phi Delta Kappan, 80*(2), 112–131.

Bracey, Gerald W. (1998). "Tinkering with TIMSS." *Phi Delta Kappan, 80*(1), 32–35.

Bracey, Gerald W. (2002). *The War against American's Public Schools: Privatizing Schools, Commercializing Education*. Boston: Allyn & Bacon.

Bradshaw, York, & Michael Wallace. (1991). "Informing Generality and Explaining Uniqueness: The Place of Case Studies in Comparative Research." *International Journal of Comparative Sociology, 32*(1–2), 154–171.

Brantmeirer, Edward J., Jing Lin, & C. Bruhn, eds. (2008). *Transforming Education for Peace: Educators as Peace Makers*. Greenwich, CT: Information Age Publishing.

Bray, Mark, & R. Murray Thomas. (1995). "Levels of Comparison in Educational Studies: Different Insights from Different Literatures and the Value of Multilevel Analysis." *Harvard Educational Review, 65*(3), 472–490.

Bray, Mark. (1998). "Comparative Education Research in the Asian Region: Implications for the Field as a Whole." *Comparative Education Bulletin, ,* 6–9.

Brembeck, Cole S. (1975). "The Future of Comparative and International Education." *Comparative Education Review, 19*(3), 369–374.

Broadfoot, Patricia. (1977). "The Comparative Contribution: A Research Perspective." *Comparative Education, 13*(2), 133–137.

Brock-Utne, Birgit. (1997). "The Language Question in Namibian Schools." *International Review of Education, 43*(2/3), 241–260.

Brock-Utne, Birgit. (2000). *Whose Education for All? The Recolonization of the African Mind*. New York: Falmer.

Brown, Elsa Barkley. (1990). "African American Women's Quilting: A Framework for Conceptualizing and Teaching." In Patricia Hill Collins (Ed.), *Black Feminist Thought*. (pp 41–73). New York: Routledge.

Buber, Martin. (1967). *A Believing Humanism*. New York: Simon & Schuster.

Buber, Martin. (1970). *I and Thou*. New York: Scribner.

Bucur, Marie, & Ben Eklof. (1999). "Russia and Eastern Europe." In Robert F. Arnove and Carlos A. Torres (Ed.), *Comparative Education: The Dialectic of the Global and the Local* (pp. 371–392). New York: Rowman & Littlefield.

Cain, Glen. (1976). "The Challenge of Segmented Labor Market Theory to Orthodox Theory." *Journal of Economic Literature, 14*, 1215–1257.

Campbell, Donald T., & Julian Stanley. (1963). *Experimental and Quasi-Experiemntal Designs for Research.* Chicago: Rand McNally.

Cannon, Walter B. (1932). *The Wisdom of the Body.* New York: Norton.

Carasco, Joseph, Nancy Clair, & Lawrence Kanyike. (2001). "Enhancing Dialogue among Researchers, Policy Makers, and Community Members in Uganda: Complexities, Possibilities, and Persistent Questions." *Comparative Education Review, 45*(2), 257–279.

Carnoy, Martin. (1974). *Education as Cultural Imperialism.* New York: MacKay.

Carnoy, Martin. (1980). "Segmented Labor Markets." In UNESCO (Ed.), *Education, Work, and Employment.* (pp. 9–122) Paris: International Institute for Educational Planning.

Carnoy, Martin. (1994). *Faded Dreams: The Politics and Economics of Race in America.* Cambridge, MA: Cambridge University Press.

Carnoy, Martin. (1995). "Structural Adjustment and the Changing Face of Education." *International Labour Review, 134*(6), 654–673.

Carnoy, Martin. (1996). "Rates of Return to Education." *In* Martin Carnoy (Ed.), *International Encyclopedia of the Economics of Education.* 2nd ed. Oxford: Pergamon.

Carnoy, Martin. (1998). "National Voucher Plans in Chile and Sweden: Did Privatization Reforms Make for Better Education?" *Comparative Education Review, 42*(3), 309–337.

Carnoy, Martin. (1999). *Globalization and Educational Reform: What Planners Need to Know.* Paris: UNESCO. Available online at http://www.unesco.org.

Carnoy, Martin. (2006). "Rethinking the Comparative—and the International." *Comparative Education Review ,50*(4), 551–570.

Carnoy, Martin, Lynn Fendler, Thomas Popkewitz, Robert Tabachnick, & Kenneth Zeichner. Sectoral Activities Programme, and Joint Meeting on the Impact of Structural Adjustment on Educational Personnel (1996). *Impact of Structural Adjustment on the Employment and Training of Teachers.* Geneva: International Labor Office.

Carnoy, Martin, & Derek Shearer. (1980). *Economic Democracy: The Challenge of the 1980's.* White Plains, NY: M. E. Sharpe.

Carson, Rachel. (2002). *Silent Spring.* Boston: Houghton Mifflin.

Cavanagh, John, & Jerry Mander, eds. (2002). *Alternatives to Globalization: A Better World Is Possible.* San Francisco: Berrett-Koehler.

CEPAL, (1991). *Educacio'n y Conocimiento, eje de la Transformacio'n Productiva con Equidad.* Santiago, Chile: Economic Commission for Latin America.

Chan, Jennifer. (2006). "Between Efficiency, Capability, and Recognition: Competing Epistemes in Global Governance." *Comparative Education, 43*(3), 359–376.

Clandinin, D. Jean, & F. Michael Connelly. (1999). *Narrative Inquiry: Experience and Story in Qualitative Research.* San Francisco: Jossey-Bass.

Clinton, William J. (2000). *Memorandum for the Heads of Executive Departments and Agencies: International Education Policy.* Oklahoma City, OK: The White House Office of the Press Secretary.

Cockburn, Cynthia. (1998). *The Space between Us: Negotiating Gender and National Identities in Conflict.* London: Zed.

Coleman, James S. (1966). *Equality of Educational Opportunity.* Washington, DC: U.S. Government Printing Office.

Collins, Patricia Hill. (1998). *Fighting Words: Black Women and the Search for Justice.* Minneapolis, MN: University of Minnesota Press.

Comte, Auguste. (1976). *Introduction to Positive Philosophy.* ed. and trans. Frederick Ferre. Indianapolis, IN: Bobbs-Merrill.

Connolly, William E. (1991). *Identity/Difference: Democratic Negotiations of Political Paradox.* Ithaca, NY: Cornell University Press.

Coombs, Phillip H. (1985). *The World Crisis in Education: The View from the Eighties.* New York: Oxford.

Cowen, Robert. (1996). "Last Past the Post: Comparative Education, Modernity and Perhaps Postmodernity." *Comparative Education, 32*(2), 165–166.

Crossley, Michael. (2000a). "Bridging Cultures and Traditions in the Reconceptualisation of Comparative and International Education." *Comparative Education, 36*(3), 319–332.

Crossley, Michael. (2000b). "Research, Education and Development: Setting the Scene." In Robin Alexander, Marilyn Osborn, and David Phillips (Ed.), *Learning from Comparing: New Directions in Comparative Educational Research*. Vol. 2. *Policy, Professionals and Development*. (pp. 73–79). Oxford: Symposium.

Cummings, William. (1999). "The Institutions of Education: Compare, Compare, Compare!" *Comparative Education Review, 43*(4), 413–437.

Daly, Herman E. (1996). *Beyond Growth: The Economics of Sustainable Development*. Boston: Beacon Press.

Daly, Herman E., & J. Cobb. (1994). *For the Common Good: Redirecting the Economy Toward Community, the Environment, and a Sustainable Future*. Boston: Beacon Press.

Davenport, Melanie. (1998). "Asian Conceptions of the Teacher Internship: Implications for American Art Education." Unpublished manuscript. Indiana University, School of Education, May 1998.

Denzin, Norman, Yvonna Lincoln, & Linda Smith. (2007). *Handbook of Critical and Indigenous Methodologies*. Thousand Oaks, CA: Sage.

Dewey, John. (1916). *Democracy and Education*. New York: Macmillan.

Diamond, Jared. (1992). *The Third Chimpanzee: The Evolution and Future of the Human Animal*. New York: HarperCollins.

Diamond, Jared. (1997). *Guns, Germs, and Steel: The Fates of Human Societies*. New York: Norton.

Diamond, Jared. (2005). *Collapse: How Societies Choose to Fail or Succeed*. New York: Penguin Group.

Diaw, Codou. (2005). "Gender and Education in Sub-Saharan Africa: The Women in Development (WID) Approach and Its Alternatives." In A. Abdi and A. Cleghorn (Ed.), *Issues in African Education: Sociological Perspectives*. (pp.175–192). New York: Palgrave Macmillan.

Diaz, Carlos A., Byron G. Massialas, & John A. Xanthopoulos. (1999). *Global Perspectives for Educators*. Boston: Allyn & Bacon.

Donmoyer, Robert. (1990). "Generalizability and the Single-Case Study." In Elliot W. Eisner & Alan Peshkin (Ed.), *Qualitative Inquiry in Education*. (pp. 175–200). New York: Teachers College Press.

Dore, Ronald. (1976). *The Diploma Disease: Education, Qualification and Development*. Berkeley, CA: University of California Press.

Easton, Peter, & Simon M. Fass. (1989). "Monetary Consumption Benefits and the Demand for Primary Schooling in Haiti." *Comparative Education Review, 33*(2), 176–193.

Easton, Peter, & Steven Klees. (1992). "Conceptualizing the Role of Education in the Economy." In Robert F. Arnove, Philip G. Altbach, & Gail P. Kelly. Albany (Ed.), *Emergent Issues in Education*, NY: State University of New York Press.

Eckstein, Max A., & Harold J. Noah. (1968). *Toward a Science of Comparative Education*. New York: MacMillan.

Ehrenreich, Barbara. (1997). *Blood Rites: Origins and History of the Passions of War*. New York: Henry Holt.

Ehrenreich, Barbara. (2006). *Dancing in the Streets: A History of Collective Joy*. New York: Henry Holt.

Eisenhart, Margaret. (2001). "Educational Ethnography Past, Present, and Future: Ideas to Think With." *Educational Researcher, 30*(8), 16–27.

Elley, Warwick B., ed. (1997). *The IEA Study of Reading Literacy: Achievement and Instruction in Thirty-Two School Systems*. 1st ed. Oxford: Pergamon.

Epstein, Erwin H. (1983). "Currents Left and Right: Ideology in Comparative Education." *Comparative Education Review, 27*(1), 3–29.

Epstein, Erwin H. (1992). "Editorial." *Comparative Education Review, 36*(4), 409–416.

Epstein, Erwin H., & Katherine Carroll. (2005). "Abusing Ancestors: Historical Functionalism and Postmodern Deviations in Comparative Education." *Comparative Education Review, 49*(1), 62–88.

Farrell, Joseph P. (1979). "The Necessity of Comparisons in the Study of Education: The Salience of Science and the Problem of Comparability." *Comparative Education Review, 23*(1), 3–16.

Farrell, Joseph P. (1992).. "Conceptualizing Education and the Drive for Social Equality." In Robert F. Arnove, Philip G. Altbach, and Gail P. Kelly (Ed.), *Emergent Issues in Education: Comparative Perspectives*. (pp. 107–122) Albany, NY: State University of New York Press.

Farrell, Joseph P. (1999). "Changing Conceptions of Equality of Education: Forty Years of Comparative Education." In Robert. F. Arnove and Carols. A. Torres (Ed.), *Comparative Education: The Dialectic of the Global and the Local.*. Lanham, MD: Rowman & Littlefield.

Farrell, Joseph P., & Ernesto Schiefelbein. (1985). "Education and Status Attainment in Chile: A Comparative Challenge to the Wisconsin Model of Status Attainment." *Comparative Education Review, 29*(4), 490–506.

Fine, Michelle. (1994). "Working the Hyphens: Reinventing Self and Other in Qualitative Research." In Norman K. Denzin and Yvonna S. Lincoln (Ed.), *Handbook of Qualitative Research.*. Thousand Oaks, CA: Sage.

Finkelstein, Barbara. (2002). "Dwelling in the Experience of Others: Reflections on Culture in Education after September 11." Presidential symposium at the American Educational Research Association, New Orleans, 4 April 2002.

Finn, Chester E. Jr., & Diane Ravitch. (1996). "Is Educational Reform a Failure?" *USA Today Magazine, 125*(2618), 22–24.

Fischman, Gustavo E. (2000). *Imagining Teachers: Rethinking Gender Dynamics in Teacher Education.* New York: Rowman & Littlefield.

Flemming, Ted. (2002). *Habermas on Civil Society, Lifeworld and System: Underrating the Social in Transformational Theory.* New York: Teachers College Record. Available online at www.tcrecord.org.

Fletcher, Todd V., & Darrell L. Sabers. (1995). "Interaction Effects in Cross-National Studies of Achievement." *Comparative Education Review, 39*(4), 455–467.

Flinders, David J., & Michael W. Apple. (2001). "Forum: What Should Schools Teach?" *Journal of Curriculum and Supervision, 16*(2), 112–136.

Foster, Philip. (1971). "The Revolt against the Schools." *Comparative Education Review ,15*(3), 267–275.

Fox, Christine. (2007). "The Question of Identity from a Comparative Education Perspective" In Robert F. Arnove and Carlos A. Torres (Ed.), *Comparative Education: The Dialectic of the Global and the Local.* (pp. 117–128). New York: Rowman & Littlefield.

Fraser, Stewart. (1964). *Jullien's Plan for Comparative Education.* New York: Columbia University, Teachers College.

Freeman, Kassie. (2004). "Looking at and Seeing Possibilities: The Compelling Case for the Use of Human Potential." *Comparative Education Review, 48*(4), 443–455.

Freire, Paulo. (1970). *Pedagogy of the Oppressed.* New York: Herder & Herder.

Freire, Paulo. (1973). *Pedagogy of the Oppressed.* New York: Seabury.

Fukuyama, Francis. (2006). *The End of History and the Last Man.* New York: Simon & Schuster.

Fuller, Bruce, Lucia Dellagnelo, Annelie Strath, Eni Santana Barretto Bastos,Maurício Holanda Maia, Kelma Socorro Lopes de Matos, Adélia Luiza Portela, & Sofia Lerche Vieira. (1999). "How to Raise Children's Early Literacy? The Influence of Family, Teacher, and Classroom in Northeast Brazil." *Comparative Education Review, 43*(1), 1–35.

Fuller, Bruce. (1987). "What Factors Raise Achievement in the Third World?" *Review of Educational Research, 57*, 255–292.

Fung, Archon, & Erik Olin Wright. (1999). *Experiments in Empowered Deliberative Democracy.* Madison, WI: Social Science Computing Cooperative, University of Wisconsin at Madison. Available online at: www.ssc.wisc.edu.

Galtung, Johann. (1972). "A Structural Theory of Imperialism." *Journal of Peace Research, 8*(2), 81–117.

Galtung, Johann. (1976). "Conflict on a Global Scale: Social Imperialism and Sub-imperialism-Continuities in the Structural Theory of Imperialism." *World Development, 4*(3), 153–165.

Galtung, Johann. (1980). *The True Worlds: A Transnational Perspective.* New York: Free Press.

Geertz, Clifford. (2000). *Available Light: Anthropological Reflections on Philosophical Topics.* Princeton, NJ: Princeton University Press.

Gerbert, Elaine. (1993). "Lessons from the Kokugo (National Language) Readers." *Comparative Education Review, 37*(2), 152–180.

Gilford, Dorothy M., ed. (1995). *A Collaborative Agenda for Improving International Comparative Studies in Education: How Can International Comparative Studies Be Improved?* Washington, D.C: Commission on Behavioral and Social Sciences and Education and National Research Council, National Academy Press.

Gill, Stephen. (1992). "Economic Globalization and the Internationalization of Authority: Limits and Contradictions." *Geoforum, 23*(3), 269–283.

Gilligan, Carol. (1982). *In a Different Voice.* Cambridge: Harvard University Press.

Ginsburg, Mark, Susan Cooper, Rajeshwari. Raghu, & Hugo Zegarra. (1991)."Educational Reform: Social Struggle, the State and the World Economic System." In Mark Ginsburg (Ed.), *Understanding*

Educational Reform in Global Context: Economy, Ideology, and the State. (pp. 33–47). New York: Garland.

Ginsburg, Mark B. (1988). "Teachers, Economy, and the State: An English Example." *Teaching and Teacher Education, 4*(4), 317–337.

Ginsburg, Mark B., & Jorge M. Gorostiaga. (2001). "Relationships between Theorists/Researchers and Policy Makers/Practioners: Rethinking the Two-Cultures Thesis and the Possibility of Dialogue." *Comparative Education Review, 45*(2), 173–196.

Ginsburg, Mark B., Sangeeta Kamat, Rajeshwari Raghu, & John Weaver. (1992). "Educators/Politics." *Comparative Education Review, 36*(4), 417–445.

Ginsburg, Mark B., & Alison Price-Rom. (2008). "Comparative and International Education." In Eugene Provenzo (Ed.), *Encyclopedia of the Social and Cultural Foundations of Education* (pp. 938–939) Thousand Oaks. CA: Sage.

Giroux, Henry A. (1992). *Border Crossing.* New York: Routledge.

Giroux, Henry A. (2002). "Democracy, Freedom, and Justice after September 11th: Rethinking the Role of Educators and the Politics of Schooling." New York: Teachers College Record. Available online at: www.tcrecord.org.

Glewwe, Paul, & Meng Zhao. (2006). "Attaining Universal Primary Education Schooling by 2015: An Evaluation of Cost Estimates." In Joel Cohen, David Bloom, and Martin Malin (Ed.), *Educating All Children: A Global Agenda* (pp. 415–454). Cambridge, MA: American Academy of Arts and Sciences.

Gore, Al. (2006). *An Inconvenient Truth: The Planetary Emergency of Global Warming and What We Can Do about It.* Emmaus, PA: Rodale.

Gould, Stephen Jay. (1996). *The Mismeasure of Man.* Rev. and expanded ed. New York: Norton.

Gutek, Gerald L. (1993). *American Education in a Global Society: Internationalizing Teacher Education.* White Plains, NY: Longman.

Habermas, Jürgen. (1984). *Theory of Communicative Action.* 2 vols. Boston: Beacon.

Hackett, Peter. (1988). "Aesthetics as a Dimension for Comparative Study." *Comparative Education Review, 32*(4), 389–399.

Hahnel, Robin. (2005). *Economic Justice and Democracy: From Competition to Cooperation.* New York: Routledge.

Hall, Budd. (1982). "Breaking the Monopoly of Knowledge: Research Methods, Participation and Development." In Budd Hall, Arthur Gillette, and Rajest Tandon (Ed.), *Creating Knowledge: A Monopoly? Participatory Research in Development.* (pp. 13–25). New Delhi: Society for Participatory Research in Asia: International Council for Adult Education.

Hansen, David T. (2001). *Exploring the Moral Heart of Teaching: Toward a Teacher's Creed.* New York: Teachers College Press.

Hanushek, Eric. (1979). "Conceptual and Empirical Issues in the Estimation of Educational Production Functions." *Journal of Human Resources, 14*(3), 351–388.

Hanushek, Eric. (2004). "What if There Are No 'Best Practices'?" *Scottish Journal of Political Economy, 51*(2), 156–172.

Hanvey, Robert. (1975). *An Attainable Global Perspective.* Denver, CO: University of Denver, Center for Teaching International Relations/New York Friends Group Center for War/Peace Studies.

Hauser, Robert. (1980). "On 'Stratification in a Dual Economy': a Comment on Beck, Horan, and Tolbert 1978." *American Sociological Review, 45*(4), 701–712.

Hayhoe, Ruth. (2000). "Redeeming Modernity." *Comparative Education Review ,44*(4), 423–439.

Hearn, James C. (1991). "Academic and Nonacademic Influences on the College Destinations of 1980 High School Graduates." *Sociology, 64,* 158–171.

Hegel, Georg W. F. (1992). "1809 Address." In Johannes Hoffmeister (Ed.), *Nu"rnberger Schriften,..* Leipzig: Felix Miner.

Henry, Jules. (1965). *Culture against Man.* New York: Vintage.

Herstein, R. J., & C. Murray. (1996). *The Bell Curve: Intelligence and Class Structure in American Life.* New York: Simon and Schuster.

Heyman, Richard. (1979). "Comparative Education from an Ethnomethodological Perspective." *Comparative Education, 15,* 241–249.

Heyneman, Stephen P. (1976). "Influences on Academic Achievement: A Comparison of Results from Uganda and More Industrialized Societies." *Sociology of Education, 49*(3), 200–211.

Heyneman, Stephen P. (1993). "Quantity, Quality, and Source." *Comparative Education Review, 37*(4), 372–388.

Heyneman, Stephen P. (1995). "Economics of Education: Disappointments and Potential." *Prospects, 25*(4), 557–583.

Heyneman, Stephen P. (1999). "The Sad Story of UNESCO's Statistics." *International Journal of Educational Development, 19*, 65–74.

Heyneman, Stephen P., Dean Jamison, & Xenia Montenegro. (1984). "Textbooks in the Philippines: Evaluation of the Pedagogical Impact of a Nationwide Investment." *Educational Evaluation and Policy Analysis, 6*(2), 139–150.

Hickling-Hudson, Anne, & Roberta Ahlquist. (2003). "Contesting the Curriculum in the Schooling of Indigenous Children in Australia and the United States: From Eurocentrism to Culturally Powerful Pedagogies." *Comparative Education Review ,47*(1), 64–89.

Hickling-Hudson, Anne. (2007). "Beyond Schooling: The Role of Adult and Community Education in Postcolonial Change." In Robert F. Arnove and Carlos Alberto Torres (Ed.), *Comparative Education: The Dialectic of the Global and the Local.* (pp. 197–216). 3rd ed. New York: Rowman & Littlefield.

Hirsch, E. D. Jr., (1987). *Cultural Literacy: What Every American Needs to Know.* New York: Houghton Mifflin.

Hirst, Paul, &Grahame Thompson. (1999). *Globalization in Question: The International Economy and the Possibilities of Governance.* 2d ed. Cambridge, MA: Polity Press.

Holland, Dorothy, Debra Skinner, & Carole Cain. (1998). *Identity and Agency in Cultural Worlds.* Cambridge: Harvard University Press.

Holmes, Brian. (1965). *Problems in Education: A Comparative Approach.* London: Routledge & Kegan Paul.

Holmes, Brian. (1983). *Comparative Education: Some Considerations of Method.* London: Allen & Unwin.

Holmes, Brian. (1984). "Paradigm Shifts in Comparative Education." *Comparative Education Review, 28*(4), 584–604.

Holsinger, Donald B. (2005). "Inequality in the Public Provision of Education: Why It Matters." *Comparative Education Review, 49*(3), 297–310.

Hooks, Bell. (2000). *Feminist Theory from Margin to Center,* 2nd ed. Cambridge, MA: South End.

Hooks, Bell. (1994). *Teaching to Transgress: Education as the Practice of Freedom.* New York: Routledge.

Hossler, D., & K. Gallagher. (1987). "Studying Student College Choice: A Three-Phase Model and the Implications for Policymakers." *College and University, 62*(3), 207–221.

Huntington, Samuel. (1993). "The Clash of Civilizations?" *Foreign Affairs, 72*(3), 22–28.

Huntington, Samuel. (1996). *The Clash of Civilizations and the Remaking of World Order.* New York: Simon & Schuster.

Hurston, Zora Neale. (1990). *Their Eyes Were Watching God.* New York: Harper & Row.

Husén, Tosten. (1987). "Policy Impact of IEA Research." *Comparative Education Review, 31*(1), 29–46.

Illich, Ivan. (1970). *Deschooling Society.* New York: Harper & Row.

Imberman, Scott A. (2007). "Achievement and Behavior in Charter Schools: Drawing a More Complete Picture." Occasional Paper No. 142. National Center for the Study of Privatization in Education. New York: Columbia University.

Inazo, Nitobe. (1912). *The Japanese Nation, Its Land, Its People and Its Life, with Special Consideration to Its Relations with the United States.* New York: Putnam.

Jacobs, Jane M. (1994). "Earth Honoring: Western Desires and Indigenous Knowledges." In Alison Blunt and Gillian Rose (Ed.), *Writing Women and Space: Colonial and Postcolonial Geographies.* (pp. 169–196). New York: Guilford Press.

Jamison, Dean, Barbara Searle, Klaus Galda, & Stephen P. Heyneman. (1981). "Improving Elementary Mathematics Education in Nicaragua: An Experimental Study of the Impact of Textbooks and Radio on Achievement." *Journal of Educational Psychology, 73*(4), 556–567.

Jansen, Jonathan D. (1995). "Understanding Social Transition through the Lens of Curriculum Policy: Namibia/South Africa." *Journal of Curriculum Studies, 27*(3), 245–261.

Jarvis, Peter. (1999). *The Practitioner Researcher.* San Francisco: Jossey-Bass.

Jencks, Christopher, Marshall Smith, Henry Acland, Mary Jo Bane, David Cohen, Herbert Gintis, Barbara Heyns, & Stephanie Michelson. (1972). *Inequality: A Reassessment of the Effect of Family and Schooling in America.* New York: Basic Books.

Jie, Lu, ed. (1999). *Education of Chinese: The Global Prospect of National Cultural Tradition.* Nanjing, China: Nanjing Normal University Press.

Johns, Roe L., Edgar L. Morphet, & Kerin Alexander. (1983). *The Economics and Financing of Education*. 4th ed. Englewood Cliffs, NJ: Prentice-Hall.

Jones, Lyle V. (1998). *National Tests and Education Reform: Are They Compatible?* William H. Angoff Memorial Lecture Series. Princeton, NJ: Educational Testing Service. Available online at: http://www.ets.org.

Josselson, Ruthellen. (1992). *The Space between Us: Exploring the Dimensions of Human Relationships*. San Francisco: Jossey-Bass.

Ka, Fernando. (1997). "Black People's Situation in Portugal." Paper presented at the Fisk University Race Relations Institute Conference, Nashville, TN, 5–8 July 1997.

Kandel, Isaac L. (1933). *Studies in Comparative Education*. Boston: Houghton Mifflin.

Kazamias, Andreas. (1972). "Comparative Pedagogy: An Assignment for the 70's." *Comparative Education Review ,16*(3), 406–411.

Kellner, Douglas. (2000). "Globalization and New Social Movements: Lessons for Critical Theory and Pedagogy."In Nicholas C. Burbules and Carlos Alberto Torres (Ed.), *Globalization and Education: Critical Perspectives*. (pp. 299–322). New York: Routledge.

Kelly, David H., ed. (1996). *International Feminist Perspectives on Educational Reform: The Work of Gail Paradise Kelly*. New York: Garland.

Kelly, Gail P. (1992). "Debates and Trends in Comparative Education." In Robert F. Arnove, Philip G. Altbach, and Gail P. Kelly (Ed.), *Emergent Issues in Education: Comparative Perspectives..* Albany, NY: State University of New York Press.

Kim, Samuel. (1979). *The Quest for a Just World Order*. Princeton, NJ: Princeton University Press.

King, Edmund J. (1979). *Other Schools and Ours: Comparative Studies for Today*. 5th ed. London: Holt, Rinehart & Winston.

King, Edmund J., Christine Moor, & Jennifer Mundy. (1974). *Post-compulsory Education: A New Analysis in Western Europe*. London: Sage.

King, Kenneth. (2007). "Multilateral Agencies in the Construction of the Global Agenda on Education." *Comparative Education, 43*(3), 377–391.

Kirschenbaum, Howard, & Valeri Land Henderson, eds. (1989). *Carl Rogers: Dialogues, Conversations with Martin Buber, Paul Tillich, B. F. Skinner, Gregory Bateson, Michael Polanyi, and Rollo May, and Others*. Boston: Houghton Mifflin.

Klak, Thomas. (1998). "Thirteen Theses on Globalization and Neoliberalism." In Thomas Klak. (Ed.), *Globalization and Neoliberalism: The Caribbean Context..* Boulder, CO: Rowman & Littlefield.

Klees, Steven J. (1986). "Planning and Policy Analysis in Education: What Can Economics Tell Us?" *Comparative Education Review, 30*(4), 574–607.

Klees, Steven, J. (2008). "Reflections on Theory, Method, and Practice in Comparative and International Education." *Comparative Education Review, 52*(3), 301–328.

Kothari, Rajni. (1974). *Footsteps into the Future*. New York: Free Press.

Kobayashi, Victor. (2007). "Patterns That Engage and Disengage: Comparative Education, Research, and Practice." *Comparative Education Review , 51*(3), 261–280.

Kuhn, Thomas. (1962). *The Structure of Scientific Revolutions*. Chicago: University of Chicago Press.

Kunio, Yanagita. (1986). *The Yanagita Kunio Guide to the Japanese Folk Tale*, trans. Fanny Hagin Mayer. Bloomington, IN: Indiana University Press.

Kuwako, Toshio. (1999). *Kankyo˚ no tetsugaku: Nihon no shiso˚ wo Gendai ni Ikasu Environmental Philosophy: Reviving Japanese Thought*. Tokyo: Kodansha Gakujutsu Bunko.

Lala, Vinay, & Ashis Nandy. (2005). *The Future of Knowledge and Culture: A Dictionary for the 21st Century*. New Delhi: Penguin-Viking, Penguin Group.

Leamer, Edward E. (1983). "Let's Take the Con Out of Econometrics." *American Economic Review, 73*1), 31–43.

Lee, Wing On. (2007). "Lifelong Learning in Asia: Eclectic Concepts, Rhetorical Ideals, and Missing Values: Implications for Values Education." *Paper for keynote address at the Biennial Conference of the Comparative Education Society of Asia and the Comparative Education Society of Hong Kong Annual Conference*, Hong Kong, 8–11 January 2007.

Levin, Henry M. (1998). "Educational Vouchers: Effectiveness, Choice, and Costs." *Journal of Policy Analysis and Management, 17*, 373–392.

Levin, Henry M. (2006). "Déjà Vu All Over Again." Our Schools in the Year 2030 Forum: How Will They Be Different? *Education Next* 6 (2): 20–24. Available online at: http://www.educationnext.org.

Levin, Henry M. 2009. "My Comparative Education, 1970–1975." *Comparative Education Review, 53* (3), 315–327.

Levinson, Bradley. (2001). *We Are All Equal: Student Culture at a Mexican Secondary School, 1988–1998.* Durham, NC: Duke University Press.

Levitan, Sar, Garth Mangum, & Ray Marshall. (1972). *Human Resources and Labor Markets: Labor and Manpower in the American Economy.* New York: Harper & Row.

Lewis, Anthony. (2001). "Abroad at Home: The Inescapable World." *New York Times,* October 20, A23.

Lightfoot, Sara Lawrence. (1999). *Respect: An Exploration.* Reading, MA: Perseus Books.

Lockheed, Marlaine E., Adriaan M. Verspoor, Deborah Bloch, Pierre Englebert, Bruce Fuller, Elizabeth King, John Middleton, Vicente Paqueo, Alastair Rood, Ralph Romain, & Michel Welmond. (1991). *Improving Primary Education in Developing Countries.* Washington, DC: Oxford University Press.

Lockheed, Marlaine E., Stephen C. Vail, & Bruce Fuller. (1986). "How Textbooks Affect Achievement in Developing Countries: Evidence from Thailand." *Educational Evaluation and Policy Analysis, 8*(4), 379–392.

Luhmann, Niklas. (1990). *Essays on Self-Reference.* New York: Columbia University Press.

Lutjens, Sheryl L. (1996). *The State, Bureaucracy, and the Cuban Schools: Power and Participation.* Boulder, CO: Westview.

Lyotard, Jean-François. (1984). *The Postmodern Condition: A Report on Knowledge.* Vol. 10. *Theory and History of Literature,* trans. Geoff Bennington and Brian Massumi. Minneapolis, MN: University of Minnesota Press.

Mabokela, Reitumese Obakeng, & Kimberly Leanese King, eds. (2001). *Apartheid No More: Case Studies of Southern African Universities in the Process of Transformation.* Westport, CT: Bergin & Garvey.

Mackinnon, Allan. (1996). "Learning to Teach at the Elbows: The Tao of Teaching." *Teaching and Teacher Education, 12,* 633–664.

Manning, Rita C. (1992). *Speaking from the Heart: A Feminist Perspective on Ethics.* Lanham, MD: Rowman & Littlefield.

Martin, Jane Roland. (2000). *Coming of Age in Academe: Rekindling Women's Hopes and Reforming the Academy.* New York: Routledge.

Masemann, Vandra. (1999). "Culture and Education." In Robert F. Arnove and Carlos Alberto Torres (Ed.), *Comparative Education: The Dialectic of the Global and the Local.* (pp. 101–116). New York: Rowman & Littlefield.

Masemann, Vandra. (1982). "Critical Ethnography in Comparative Education." *Comparative Education Review , 26*(1), 1–15.

Masemann, Vandra. (1990) "Ways of Knowing: Implications for Comparative Education." *Comparative Education Review, 34*(4), 465–473.

Masemann, Vandra. (1997). "Recent Directions in Comparative Education." *Paper presented at the Comparative and International Education Society Annual Conference,* Mexico City, Mexico, 1997.

Mazrui, A. Ali. (1974). *A World Federation of Cultures.* New York: Free Press.

McCarthy, Thomas. (1984) "Translator's Introduction." In *The Theory of Communicative Action,* Vol. I: *Reason and Rationalization of Society,* Jurgen Habermas. Boston: Beacon Press.

McCarty, Luise. (1993). "Out of Isolation: Philosophy, Hermeneutics, Multiculturalism." In Audrey Thompson (Ed.), *Philosophy of Education.* Urbana, IL: Philosophy of Education Society.

McCarty, Luise. (1992). "On Internationalizing a Curriculum: Some Philosophical Considerations." *Paper presented for Brescia College Professional Development Day,* Bloomington, IN, 16 March 1992.

McGinn, Noel F. (1996). "Education, Democratization, and Globalization: A Challenge for Comparative Education." *Comparative Education Review, 40*(4), 341–357.

McLaren, Peter, & Joe Kincheloe, eds. (2007). *Critical Pedagogy: Where Are We Now?* New York: Peter Lang.

McLaren, Peter, & Ramin Farahmandpur. (2001). "Teaching against Globalization and the New Imperialism." *Journal of Teacher Education, 52*(2), 136–150.

Merisotis, J. P. (1998). "Who Benefits from Education? An American Perspective." *International Higher Education, 12,* 2–3.

Mertens, Donna. (2005). *Research Methods in Education and Psychology: Integrating Diversity with Quantitative and Qualitative Approaches.* 2nd ed. Thousand Oaks, CA: Sage.

Metcalf, Barbara, D. (1995). "Presidential Address: Too Little and Too Much: Reflections on Muslims in the History of India." *Journal of Asian Studies, 4*, 951–967.

Meyer, John W., & David P. Baker. (1996). "Forming American Educational Policy with International Data: Lessons from the Sociology of Education." *Sociology of Education, 69*, 123–130.

Mies, Maria, & Shiva Vandana. (1993). *Ecofeminism*. London: Zed.

Miles, M., & A. Huberman. (1994). *Qualitative Data Analysis*. 2nd ed. Newbury Park, CA: Sage.

Millman, Jason, & Linda Darling-Hammond. (1990). *The New Handbook of Teacher Evaluation: Assessing Elementary and Secondary School Teachers*. Newbury Park, CA: Sage.

Mok, Ka Ho. (2007). "Policy Learning or Policy Copying: Critical Reflections on Internationalization of Universities in East Asia." *Paper presented at the Biennial Conference of the Comparative Education Society of Asia*, Hong Kong, 8–11 January 2007.

Moncada-Davidson, Lillian. (1995). "Education and Its Limitations in the Maintenance of Peace in El Salvador." *Comparative Education Review, 39*(1), 54–75.

Morrison, Toni. *Jazz*. New York: Knopf.

Morris-Suzuki, Tessa. (1995). "The Invention and Reinvention of 'Japanese Culture'." *Journal of Asian Studies ,54*(3), 759–780.

Muskin, Joshua A. (1999). "Including Local Priorities to Assess School Quality: The Case of Save the Children Community Schools in Mali." *Comparative Education Review ,43*(1), 36–64.

Myers, Robert G. (1995). *The Twelve Who Survive: Strengthening Programs of Early Childhood Development in the World*. 2nd ed. Ypsilanti, MI: High Scope.

Narayan, Uma. (1989). "The Project of Feminist Epistemology: Perspectives from a Non-Western Feminist." In Alison M. Jaggar and Susan R. Bordo (Ed.), *Gender Body/Knowledge: Feminist Reconstructions of Being and Knowing*. (pp. 256–269). New Brunswick, NJ: Rutgers University Press.

Nga, Nguyen Nyuyet. (2001). "Viet Nam: Trends in the Education Sector during 1993–98." Washington, DC: The World Bank.

Nickell, Stephen, & Brian Bell. 1996. "Changes in Distribution of Wages and Unemployed in OECD Countries." *American Economic Review, 86*(2), 302–314.

Nickell, Stephen. (1997). "Unemployment and Labour Market Rigidities: Europe versus North America." *Journal of Economic Perspectives, 11*(3), 55–74.

Noah, Harold J. (1974). "Fast-Fish and Loose-Fish in Comparative Education." *Comparative Education Review, 18*(4), 341–347.

Noah, Harold J. (1984). "The Use and Abuse of Comparative Education." *Comparative Education Review, 28*(4), 550–562.

Noah, Harold J., & Max A. Eckstein. (1969). *Toward a Science of Comparative Education*. New York: Macmillan.

Noah, Harold J., & Max A. Eckstein. (1998). "The Two Faces of Examinations." In Harold J. Noah and Max A. Eckstein (Ed.), *Doing Comparative Education: Three Decades of Collaboration.*. Hong Kong: University of Hong Kong.

Noddings, Nel. (1992). *The Challenge to Care in Schools*. New York: Teachers College Press.

Noddings, Nel. (2002). *Educating Moral People: A Caring Alternative to Character Education*. New York: Teachers College Press.

Nussbaum, Martha. (2000). *Women and Human Development: The Capabilities Approach*. New York: Cambridge University Press.

Odora Hoppers, Catherine A. (2000). "Globalization and the Social Construction of Reality: Affirming or Unmasking the Inevitable?" In Nelly P. Stromquist and Karen Monkman (Ed.), *Globalization and Education, Integration and Contestation across Cultures* (pp. 99–119). Lanham, MD: Rowman & Littlefield.

Office of the High Commission for Human Rights (OHCHR). (2002). *Draft Guidelines: A Human Rights Approach to Poverty Reduction Strategies*. New York: United Nations.

Orlando Sentinel. (2003). February 1, A1, A8.

Orr, David. (1991). "What Is Education For? Six Myths about the Foundations of Modern Education, and Six New Principles to Replace Them." *In Context* 27, 52–55.

Orr, David. (2004). *The Nature of Design: Ecology, Culture, and Human Intention*. New York: Oxford University Press.

Paige, Ron. (2002). "An Overview of America's Education Agenda." *Phi Delta Kappan, 83*(9), 708–713.

139

Paine, Lynn Webster. (1990). "The Teacher as Virtuoso: A Chinese Model for Teaching." *Teacher College Record*, *92*(1), 49–81.

Palley, Thomas. (2008). "Breaking the Neoclassical Monopoly in Economics." Washington, DC: Thomas Palley. Available online at http://www.thomaspalley.com.

Parrado, Emilio A. (1998). "Expansion of Schooling, Economic Growth, and Regional Inequalities in Argentina." *Comparative Education Review*, *42*(3), 338–364.

Paulston, Rolland G. (1977). "Social and Educational Change: Conceptual Frameworks." *Comparative Education Review*, *21*(2/3), 370–395. Paulston, Rolland G. (1999). "Mapping Comparative Education after Postmodernity." *Comparative Education Review*, *43*(4), 438–463.

Paulston, Rolland G. (2000). "Imagining Comparative Education: Past, Present, Future." *Compare*, *30*(3), 353–367.

Peirce, Charles Saunders. (1955). *Philosophical Writings of Peirce*, Justus Buchler (Ed.). New York: Dover Publications.

Pereira, Ruth Da Cunha. (1997). "Teachers' In-Service Education: A Proposal for Turning Teachers into Teacher-Researchers." In Vandra Masemann and Anthony Welch (Ed.), *Tradition, Modernity and Post-Modernity in Comparative Education* (pp. 569–579). Boston: Kluwer.

Petchesky, Rosalind. (2001). "Phantom Towers." *Women's Review of Books*, *2*(2), 3–4.

Phillips, David. (1999). "On Comparing." In Robin Alexander, Patricia Broadfoot, and David Phillips (Ed.), *Learning from Comparing: New Directions in Comparative Educational Research*. Vol. 1. *Contexts, Classrooms and Outcomes*,. (pp. 109–111). Oxford: Symposium Books.

Phillips, David. (2000). "Introduction" In Robin Alexander, Marilyn Osborn, and David Phillips (Ed.), *Learning from Comparing: New Directions in Comparative Education Research*. Vol. 2. *Policy, Professionals and Development*. (pp. 11–12). Oxford: Symposium Books.

Piore, Michael. (1983). "Labor Market Segmentation: To What Paradigm Does It Belong?" *American Economic Review*, *73*(2), 249–253.

Piscitelli, Barbara. (1997). "Children's Art Exhibitions and Exchanges: Assessing the Impact." *SEA News*, *4*, 1.

Piscitelli, Barbara. (1997). "Culture, Curriculum, and Young Children's Art: Directions for Further Research." *Journal of Cognitive Education*, *6*(1), 27–39.

Plank, David, & Gary Sykes. (2003). *Choosing Choice*. New York: Teachers College Press.

Plowden, Bridget, et al., (1967). *Children and Their Primary Schools: A Report of the Central Advisory Council for Education, England*. London: Her Majesty's Stationery Office.

Polanyi, Michael. (1958). *Personal Knowledge: Towards a Post-critical Philosophy*. Chicago: University of Chicago Press.

Popkewitz, Thomas S. ed. (2000). *Educational Knowledge: Changing Relationships between the State, Civil Society, and the Educational Community*. Albany, NY: SUNY Press.

Post, David. (2001). *Children's Work, Schooling, and Welfare in Latin America*. Boulder, CO: Westview.

Postlethwaite, T. Neville, & David E. Wiley. ed. (1992). *The IEA Study of Science II: Science Achievement in Twenty-Three Countries*. Oxford: Pergamon.

Power, Samantha. (2002). *"A Problem from Hell": America and the Age of Genocide*. New York: HarperCollins.

Preston, Rosemary. (1997). "Integrating Paradigms in Educational Research: Issues of Quantity and Quality in Poor Countries." In Michael Crossley and Graham Vulliamy (Ed.), *Qualitative Educational Research in Developing Countries: Current Perspectives*. (pp. 31–64). New York: Garland.

Pritchett, Lant. (1996). *Where Has All the Education Gone?* Policy Research Working Paper No. 1581. Washington, DC: World Bank.

Psacharopoulos, George. (1990). "Comparative Education: From Theory to Practice. Or Are You A: \neo.* or B: *.ist?" *Comparative Education Review*, *34*(3), 369–380.

Psacharopoulos, George. (1993). *Returns to Investment in Education: A Global Update*. Policy Research Working Paper No. 1067. Washington, DC: World Bank.

Puchner, Laurel. (2001). "Researching Women's Literacy in Mali: A Case Study of Dialogue among Researchers, Practitioners, and Policy Makers." *Comparative Education Review*, *45*(2), 242–256.

Ragin, Charles C. (1987). *The Comparative Method: Moving Beyond Qualitative and Quantitative Strategies*. Berkeley, CA: University of California Press.

Rakowski, James. (1980). "The Theory of the Second Best and the Competitive Equilibrium Model." *Journal of Economic Issues ,14*(1),197–207.

Rappaport, Roy A. (1979). *Ecology, Meaning and Religion.* Richmond, CA: North Atlantic Books.

Rappaport, Roy A. (1999). *Ritual and Religion in the Making of Humanity.* Cambridge, MA: Cambridge University Press.

Rappaport, Roy A. (2000). *Pigs for the Ancestors: Ritual in the Ecology of a New Guinea People.* 2nd ed. Long Grove, IL: Waveland.

Ravitch, Diane. (1990). "Multiculturalism Yes, Particularism No." *Chronicle of Higher Education, 37*(8), A44.

Ravitch, Diane. (1991/1992). "A Culture in Common." *Educational Leadership ,49*(4), 8–21.

Razquin, Paula. (2000). "The Attractiveness of Teaching in Argentina, Chile, and Uruguay: How Has Seniority Been Rewarded Compared to Other Selected Occupations?" *Paper presented at the Comparative and International Education Society 44th Annual Conference,* San Antonio, Texas, 8 March 2000.

Reder, Stephen M. (1987). "Comparative Aspects of Functional Literacy Development: Three Ethnic American Communities." In Daniel Wagner (Ed.), *The Future of Literacy in a Changing World.* (pp. 250–270). New York, Pergamon.

Reimers, Fernando. (2000). *Unequal Schools, Unequal Chances: The Challenges to Equal Opportunity in the Americas.* Cambridge, MA: Harvard University Press.

Riker, James. (2005). "Promoting Visions and Strategies to Advancing Global Democracy." *Unpublished paper. The Democracy Collaborative,* University of Maryland, College Park.

Rizvi, Fazal. (2000). "International Education and the Production of Global Imagination." In Nicholas C. Burbules and Carlos Alberto Torres (Ed.), *Globalization and Education: Critical Perspectives.* (pp. 205–226). New York: Routledge.

Rodrik, Dani. (2007). *One Economics, Many Recipes: Globalization, Institutions, and Economic Growth.* Princeton, NJ: Princeton University Press.

Rondinelli, Dennis, John Middleton, & Adrian Verspoor. (1990). *Planning Educational Reforms in Developing Countries: A Contingency Approach.* Durham, NC: Duke University Press.

Ross, Heidi A. (2000). "In the Moment: Discourses of Power, Narratives of Relationship. Framing Ethnography of Chinese Schooling. 1981–1997." In Judith Liu, Heidi Ross and Donald Kelly (Ed.), *The Ethnographic Eye: Interpretive Studies of Education in China.* (pp. 123–152). New York: Falmer Press.

Ross, Heidi A. (2002.) "The Space between Us: The Relevance of Relational Theories to Comparative and International Education." *Comparative Education Review, 46*(4), 407–432.

Rothstein, Richard. (2008). *Holding Accountability to Account: How Scholarship and Experience in Other Fields Inform Exploration of Performance Incentives in Education.* National Center on Performance Incentives Working Paper 2008–04. Washington, DC: Economic Policy Institute.

Rummel, R. J. (1994). *Death by Government.* New Brunswick, NJ: Transaction.

Rust, Val D. (1991). "Postmodernism and its Comparative Education Implications." *Comparative Education Review, 35*(4), 610–626.

Rust, Val D. (2000). "Education Policy Studies and Comparative Education." In Robin Alexander, Marilyn Osborn, and David Philips (Ed.), *Learning from Comparing: New Directions in Comparative Education Research.* Vol.2. *Policy,Professionals and Development.* (pp. 13–39). Oxford: Symposium Books.

Rust, Val D., Aminata Soumaré, Octavio Pescador, & Megumi Shibuya. (1999). "Research Strategies in Comparative Education." *Comparative Education Review, 43*(1), 86–109.

Sachs, Wolfgang. (1992). *The Development Dictionary: A Guide to Knowledge as Power.* New York: Zed.

Sadler, Michael E. (1912). "The History of Education." In *Germany in the Nineteenth Century: Five Lectures,* J. H. Rose, C. H. Herford, E. C. K. Gooner, and M. E. Sadler (pp. 101–127). Manchester, UK: University Press.

Sadler, Michael. (1900). "How Far Can We Learn Anything of Practical Value from the Study of Foreign Systems of Education." In J. H. Higginson (Ed.), *Selections from Michael Sadler: Studies in World Citizenship..* (1900 original; 1979 reprinted in Liverpool, UK: Dejalle & Meyorre).

Samir. Amin. (1998). *Spectres of Capitalism.* New York: Monthly Review Press.

Samoff, Joel. (1991). "The Façade of Precision in Education Data and Statistics: A Troubling Example from Tanzania." *Journal of Modern African Studies, 29*(4), 669–689.

141

Samoff, Joel. (1999). "No Teacher Guide, No Textbooks, No Chairs: Contending with Crisis in African Education." In Robert F. Arnove and Carlos Alberto Torres (Ed.), *Comparative Education: The Dialectic of the Global and the Local.* (pp. 409–445). 2nd ed. Boulder, CO: Rowman & Littlefield.

Samoff, Joel. (2007). "Institutionalizing International Influence." In Robert F. Arnove and Carlos Alberto Torres (Ed.), *Comparative Education: The Dialectic of the Global and the Local.* (pp. 47–78). 3rd ed. New York: Rowman & Littlefield.

Sandel Michael. (1998). *Liberalism and the Limits of Justice.* New York: Cambridge University Press.

Santibanez, Lucrecia. (2000). "Relative Teacher Salaries in Mexico: Wage Premiums and Other Considerations." *Paper presented at the Comparative International Education Society 44th Annual Conference*, San Antonio, Texas, 8 March 2000.

Saunders, K., ed. (2002). *Feminist Post-development Thought.* New York: Zed.

Saxe, Geoffrey B. (1988). "Candy Selling and Math Learning." *Educational Researcher, 17*(6), 14–21.

Schapiro, H. Svi. (2000). "Empowerment." In David A. Gabbard (Ed.), *Knowledge and Power in the Global Economy, Politics and the Rhetoric of School Reform.* (pp. 103–110). Mahwah, NJ: Erlbaum.

Schlefer, Jonathan. (1998). "Today's Most Mischievous Misquotation: Adam Smith Did Not Mean What He Is Often Made to Say." *Atlantic Monthly, 121*(3), 16–19.

Schmidt, William H., Curtis C. McKnight, Richard T. Houang, Hsing Chi Wang, David E. Wiley, Leland S. Cogan, & Richard G. Wolfe. (2001). *Why Schools Matter: A Cross-National Comparison of Curriculum and Learning.* Hoboken, NJ: Jossey-Bass.

Schön, Donald. (1983). *The Reflective Practitioner: How Professionals Think in Action.* New York: Basic Books.

Schriewer, Jürgen. (1990). "The Method of Comparison and the Need for Externalization: Methodological Criteria and Sociological Concepts." In Jürgen Schriewer in cooperation with Brian Holmes (Ed.), *Theories and Methods in Comparative Education.* (pp. 25–83). Frankfurt: Peter Lang.

Schultz, Theodore W. (1961). "Investment in Human Capital." *American Economic Review, 51*(1), 1–17.

Schwarcz, Vera. (1998). *Bridge across Broken Time: Chinese and Jewish Cultural Memory.* New Haven: Yale University Press.

Sen, Amartya. (1999). *Development as Freedom.* New York: Knopf.

Serpell, James. (1996). *In the Company of Animals: A Study of Human-Animal Relationships.* Cambridge, MA: Cambridge University Press.

Shavelson, Richard. (1997). *Learning from TIMSS: Results of the Third International Mathematics and Science Study: Summary of a Symposium*, Alexandra Beatty (Ed.) . Washington, DC: National Academy.

Sigurdsson, Geir. (2004). "Learning and Li: The Confucian Process of Humanization through Ritual Propriety." *PhD diss.*, Department of Philosophy, University of Hawaii, Hawaii, USA.

Sleeter, Christine E., & Carl A. Grant. (2003). *Making Choices for Multicultural Education: Five Approaches to Race, Class, and Gender.* 4th ed. New York: Wiley.

Smith, John, & Louis Heshusius. (1986). "Closing Down the Conversation: The End of the Quantitative-Qualitative Debate among Educational Inquirers." *Educational Researcher, 15*(1), 4–13.

Snauwaert, Dale. (2001). "Cosmopolitan Democracy and Democratic Education. " *Current Issues in Comparative Education, 4*(2), 5–15.

Soudien, Crain, Peter Kallaway, & Mignonne Breier, eds. (1999). *Education, Equity and Transformation.* Dordrecht: Kluwer.

Spivak, Gayatri Chakravorty. (1993). *Outside in the Teaching Machine.* New York: Routledge.

Spivak, Gayatri Chakravorty. (1999). *A Critique of Postcolonial Reason: Toward a History of the Vanishing Present.* Cambridge, MA: Harvard University Press.

Spring, Joel. (1994). *Wheels in the Head: Educational Philosophies of Authority, Freedom, and Culture from Socrates to Paulo Freire.* New York: McGraw-Hill.

Steele, Claude. (1999). "Thin Ice: 'Stereotype Threat' and Black College Students." *Atlantic Monthly, 284*, 44–54.

Steiner-Khamsi, Gita, & Hubert O. Quist. (2000). "The Politics of Educational Borrowing: Reopening the Case of Achimota in British Ghana." *Comparative Education Review, 44*(3), 272–299.

Steingraber, Sandra. (2001). *Having Faith: An Ecologist's Journey to Motherhood.* Cambridge, MA: Perseus.

Stewart, Abigail J., & David G. Winter. (1977). "The Nature and Causes of Female Suppression." *Signs: Journal of Women in Culture and Society, 2*(3), 531–555.

Stiegler, James W., & James Hiebert. (1999). *The Teaching Gap: Best Ideas from the World's Teachers for Improving Education in the Classroom.* New York: Free Press.

Stiglitz, Joseph. (2003). *Globalization and Its Discontents.* New York: Norton.

Street, Brian, V. (1987). "Literacy and Social Change: The Significance of Social Context in the Development of Literacy Programmes." In Daniel Wagner(Ed.), *The Future of Literacy in a Changing World.* (pp. 48–64). New York: Pergamon.

Stromquist, Nelly P. (1995). "Romancing the State: Gender and Power in Education." *Comparative Education Review, 39*(4), 423–454.

Stromquist, Nelly P. (1998). "The Institutionalisation of Gender and Its Impact on Education Policy." *Comparative Education, 34*(4), 85–100.

Stromquist, Nelly P. (1999). "Editorial." *Comparative Education Review, 43*(4), 3–5.

Stromquist, Nelly P. (2001). "Preface." *Comparative Education Review, 45*(2), iii.

Stromquist, Nelly P. (1997). *Increasing Girls' Participation in Basic Education.* Paris: International Institute for Educational Planning.

Strouse, Joan H. (2001). *Exploring Socio-Cultural Themes in Education: Readings in Social Foundations.* 2nd ed. Columbus, OH: Merrill Prentice-Hall.

Subotzky, George. (1999). "Beyond the Entrepreneurial University: The Potential Role of South Africa's Historically Disadvantaged Institutions in Reconstruction and Development." In Crain Soudien, Peter Kallaway, and Mignonne Breier (Ed.), *Education, Equity and Transformation.* (pp. 507–527). Hamburg: UNESCO Institute for Education.

Sutton, Margaret. (1998). "Global Education and National Interest: The Last Fifty Years." *International Journal of Social Education ,13*(2), 6–28.

Swing, Elizabeth Sherman. (1997). "From Eurocentrism to Post-colonialism: A Bibliographic Perspective." *Paper presented at the Comparative International Education Society Annual Conference*, Mexico City, Mexico, 1997.

Taylor, Jill McLean, Carol Gilligan, & Amy M. Sullivan. (1995). *Between Voice and Silence, Women and Girls, Race and Relationship.* Cambridge, MA: Harvard University Press.

Teruhisa, Horio. (1988). *Educational Thought and Ideology in Modern Japan: State Authority and Intellectual Freedom.* Tokyo: University of Tokyo Press.

Theisen, Gary L. (1997). "The New ABCs of Comparative and International Education." *Comparative Education Review, 41*(4), 397–412.

Theisen, Gary L., Paul P. W. Achola, & Francis Musa Boakari. (1983). "The Underachievement of Cross-National Studies of Achievement." *Comparative Education Review, 27*(1), 46–68.

Thurow, L. C. (1972). "Education and Economic Equality." *Public Interest, 28*, 66–81.

Tietjen, Karen. (1999). *Community Schools in Mali: A Comparative Cost Study.* SD Publication Series Technical Paper No. 97. Washington, DC: U.S. Agency for International Development, Bureau for Africa.

Tikly, Leon. (1999). "Postcolonialism and Comparative Education." In Crain Soudien, Peter Kallaway, and Mignonne Breier (Ed.), *Education, Equity and Transformation.* (pp. 603–621). Hamburg: UNESCO, Institute for Education.

Tomasevski, Katarina. (2003). *Education Denied: Costs and Remedies.* London: Zed Books.

Torney-Purta, Judith, John Schwille, & Jo-Ann Amadeo. (1999). "Mapping the Distinctive and Common Features of Civic Education in Twenty-Four Countries." In Judith Torney-Purta, John Schwille, and Jo-Ann Amadeo (Ed.), *Civic Education across Countries: Twenty-Four National Case Studies from the IEA Civic Education Project.* (pp. 18–19). Amsterdam: International Association for the Evaluation of Educational Achievement.

Torres, Carlos Alberto. (1998a). "Democracy, Education and Multi-Culturalism: Dilemmas of Global Citizenship." *Comparative Education Review, 42*(4), 421–447.

Torres, Carlos Alberto, & Mitchell Theodore R, eds. (1998). *Sociology of Education: Emerging Perspectives.* Albany, NY: State University of New York Press.

Torres, Rosa Maria. (2000). *One Decade of Education for All: The Challenge Ahead.* Buenos Aires: International Institute of Education Planning.

Torres, Rosa-Maria. (2001). *What Works in Education: Facing the New Century.* Baltimore, MD: International Youth Foundation.

Tremmel, Robert. (1993). "Zen and the Art of Reflective Practice in Teacher Education." *Harvard Educational Review, 63*(1), 434–458.

UNESCO. (1998). *Primer Estudio internacional Comparativo sobre Lenguaje, Matemática y Factores Asociados en Tecero y Cuarto Grado*. Santiago, Chile: Oficina Regional de Educación Para Américal Latina y EL Caribe.

UNESCO. (2003). *EFA Global Monitoring Report 2003/4, Gender and Education for All: The Leap to Equality*. Paris: UNESCO.

United States Department of Labor. (1999). *Future Work: Trends and Challenges for Work in the 21st Century: Labor Day 1999 Executive Summary*. Washington, DC: U.S. Department of Labor.

Walker, Decker, & Jon Schaffarzick. (1974). "Comparing Curricula." *Review of Educational Research 44*,(1), 83–111.

Walker, David C., Arnold Anderson, & Richard M. Wolfe. (1976). *The IEA Six Subject Survey: An Empirical Study of Education in Twenty-One Countries*. Stockholm: Alquist & Wiksell.

Waller, James. (2002). *Becoming Evil: How Ordinary People Commit Genocide and Mass Killing*. Oxford: Oxford University Press.

Wallerstein, Immanuel. (2004). *World-Systems Analysis: An Introduction*. Durham, NC: Duke University Press.

Wallraff, Barbara. (2000). "What Global Language?" *Atlantic Monthly, 286*(5), 52–66.

Ward, Janie Victoria. *The Skin We're In: Teaching Our Children to Be Emotionally Strong, Socially Smart, Spiritually Connected*. New York: Free Press.

Watson, Jean. (1999). *Nursing: Human Science and Human Care, a Theory of Nursing*. New York: Jones & Bartlett.

Weiler, Hans. (1984). "The Political Economy of Education and Development." *Prospects, 19*(4), 468–477.

Wei-ming, Tu, ed. (1996). *Confucian Traditions and East Asian Modernity: Moral Education and Economic Culture in Japan and the Four Mini-Dragons*. Cambridge, MA: Harvard University Press.

Wei-ming, Tu, Milan Hejtmanek, & Alan Wachman, eds. (1992). *The Confucian World Observed: A Contemporary Discussion of Confucian Humanism in East Asia*. Honolulu, HI: Institute of Culture and Communication East-Asia Center.

Wei-ming, Tu. (1993). "Towards a Third Epoch of Confucian Humanism." In *Way, Learning, and Politics: Essays on the Confucian Intellectual* (pp. 141–160). Albany, NY: SUNY Press.

Weis, Lois. (1996). "Foreword." In Bradley Levinson, Douglas E. Foley, and Dorothy C. Holland (Ed.), *The Cultural Production of the Educated Person: Critical Ethnographies of Schooling and Local Practice*. (pp. ix–xiv). Albany, NY: SUNY Press.

Welch, Anthony. (1999). "The Triumph of Technocracy or the Collapse of Certainty? Modernity, Postmodernity and Postcolonialism in Comparative Education." In Robert F. Arnove and Carlos Alberto Torres (Ed.), *Comparative Education: The Dialectic of the Global and the Local*. (pp. 25–50). Lanham, MD: Rowman & Littlefield.

Wilson, David N. (1994). "Comparative and International Education: Fraternal or Siamese Twins: A Preliminary Genealogy of our Twin Fields." *Comparative Education Review, 38*(4), 449–486.

World Bank. (1995). *Priorities and Strategies for Education*. Washington, DC: The World Bank.

World Bank. (2000). *Higher Education in Developing Countries: Peril and Promise*. Joint Task Force on Higher Education and Society, Discussion Paper No. 14630. Washington, DC: World Bank.

World Conference on Education for All. (1990). *Final Report of the World Conference on Education for All*. New York: UNICEF, World Conference on Education for All.

World Development Report. (2000). *2000/2001: Attacking Poverty*. Washington, DC: The World Bank and Oxford University Press.

Wypjewski. Jo Ann. (2001). "GE Brings Bad Things to Life: For Downsized Workers in Bloomington, It's Time to Start Thinking Globally." *The Nation 272*,(6), 18–23.

Yuval-Davis, Nira. (1997). *Gender and Nation*. Thousand Oaks, CA: Sage.

LOU SABINA

8. TEACHER, PRINCIPAL, PROFESSOR?

. . . An Ongoing Journey in the Shadow of Rolland Paulston

Unlike many of the authors in this book, I have never had the privilege of meeting Rolland G. Paulston. Despite this, his writings and work in social cartography were the primary catalyst for helping me as I struggled to bridge the gap between the worlds of a school principal and graduate student in a major research university. While Paulston's work clearly represents the power that theory can hold for scholars, I found its concrete terms and clear presentation to be an inspiration to me as a school practitioner. My goal for this chapter is to reflect on how Paulston's work has had a lasting impact on my journey in education as a teacher, school administrator, and doctoral student aspiring to become a professor.

What separates education from other academic fields is the school practitioner environment that the majority of undergraduate and master's level programs preparing teachers and principals focus on rather than more abstract theory and research. The traditional path for teachers tends to be to complete a bachelor's degree in education, obtain a teaching position, and then pursue a master's degree while teaching. Negotiating a university can be a daunting task for a school practitioner because it is beyond an individual classroom or school district, has a very different cast of characters, and different expectations for graduate students. Some individuals pursue an advanced degree and obtain principal, curriculum, or superintendent certification in order to become a school leader, but on this path, too, courses based on theoretical frameworks that encourage research are rare. Instead, aspiring principals and superintendents end up taking classes to advance their practice that do little to address the theory on which education is built. Only by pursuing a PhD in a theoretically-oriented program can one obtain the deep conceptual knowledge to transition from practitioner to professor and scholar. Addressing that challenge becomes one of the most important elements in completing a doctoral program and ultimately preparing for the rigors and responsibilities of academia.

MY JOURNEY

I spent seven years as a high school business teacher, and finally ended my career in public education as an elementary school administrator. While teaching, I earned a master's degree and obtained certification to become a K-12 school principal. My experiences were diverse and comprehensive enough that I felt confident in my

John C. Weidman, W. James Jacob (eds.), Beyond the Comparative: Advancing Theory and Its Application to Practice, 145–151.

ability to transition into a major research university to pursue my PhD. My time in public education was predicated on a belief that when I had accomplished everything I hoped to, I would prepare to move into a career in academia. Upon receiving an appointment as a school administrator, I knew if an opportunity presented itself to transition into a doctoral program on a full-time basis it would be in my best interest to pursue that opportunity, as it would be more closely aligned with my ultimate career goals.

In the Fall Term of 2007, I chose to enter the University of Pittsburgh's Social and Comparative Analysis in Education Program as a full-time PhD student. My choice of the Social and Comparative Analysis degree over the doctoral degree in School Leadership was because of the flexibility with the program, the awarding of a PhD as opposed to an EdD, and the opportunity to obtain international experience, which would increase my qualifications for becoming a professor. This was also the program where former presidents of the Comparative and International Education Society (CIES), Mark B. Ginsburg, Donald K. Adams, and Rolland G. Paulston had been professors. I was fortunate enough to obtain part-time teaching positions at a few different colleges and universities to continue gaining teaching experience in higher education. Also, I participated in a multi-state funded research project that studied the theory of cohesive leadership in K-12 schools. Although I was gaining applied research experience, teaching experience, and progressing through my course work, I still lacked the theoretical background necessary to make the transition from practitioner to scholar.

My time as a school administrator taught me a great deal that I felt would be useful for doctoral level work such as technical writing, presentation to multiple stakeholders in an organization, and dealing with a wide array of conflicts, including finding resolutions to benefit all involved parties. What I did not have was the capability and experience to look at problems in society in terms of broader patterns, both historical and conceptual, and use those patterns to understand the bigger picture.

At this point, I felt intimidated by people in my doctoral program who had extensive backgrounds in history, philosophy, English, or global and international studies—people who were comfortable when faced with questions of a theoretical nature. Instead, I was locked into the pattern of attempting to solve a question as quickly and efficiently as possible, in short, a school administrator's mentality. The ability to reflect, and use my knowledge to understand myself before I knew others was not a skill I had acquired. Through reading Paulston's work, I experienced a scholar who presented reflection in every aspect of his scholarship.

My first exposure to Paulston and his work was in September 2008, when I read "Social Cartography: A New Metaphor/Tool for Comparative Studies" (Paulston and Liebman 1996). This chapter introduced the idea of social cartography in very easy-to-understand terms, included four conceptual maps, and explained how the maps were developed. Paulston's writing was the first theoretical piece I had encountered that "made sense" to this school practitioner in the world of academia. Although Paulston's wording was still just as technical as the other theoretical writers to whom I had been exposed, his use of social cartography and the graphical representation of those theories made his work infinitely more accessible.

Paulston (1996, 15) fascinated me because he married a broad range of relevant social and educational theories and placed them in one clear visualization of their inter-relationships. Very similar to how a teacher would utilize multiple intelligences in a classroom environment, Paulston's graphical and written representations work in conjunction to stimulate discussion.

Paulston's work introduced the concept of scholarly reflection to me and motivated me to continue my exploration. I moved on to his article in the *International Encyclopedia of Education* (Paulston 1994, 931). This particular article placed all of the various theories I had seen previously in their various conceptual domains and was probably the best piece for a beginner to read. It served as a starting point for me to begin developing an understanding of the paradigms and theories that exist not only in the field of education, but in others as well. Two years later, Paulston (1996, 23) argued that "the map provides the comparative researcher a better understanding of the social milieu and gives all persons the opportunity to enter a dialogue to show where they believe they are in society." This particular piece enhanced my understanding of challenging dialogue and suggested important issues in not only comparative education, the intended domain of Paulston's research, but also in educational administration research.

HOW PAULSTON INFLUENCED MY RESEARCH

The articles by Paulston helped my understanding of social theories and, more importantly, identify other authors' theoretical perspectives in their educational research. This newfound understanding of theoretical literature was especially helpful when a publication released in 2005 helped catalyze a shift in the literature of educational administration. The report, titled "Educating School Leaders," by Arthur Levine (2005), a former president and professor of education at Teacher's College of Columbia University, incited furor in the education community. Levine wrote about how disenchanted he was with school leadership training providers, and encouraged them to increase their standards in accepting students by limiting graduate admissions and refocusing on strengthening the research in school leadership. In his study, Levine claimed that he found an irrelevant curriculum, low admission and graduation standards, weak faculty, inadequate clinical instruction, inappropriate degrees, and poor research across all principal training programs in the United States. Many researchers and professors at leading universities felt the need to address Levine's criticisms by suggesting improvements in the structure of educational leadership programs (Fossey and Shoho 2006; Shulman et al., 2006; Goduto et al., 2008; Young and Brewer 2008). An indirect result was the increased use of theoretical frameworks and conceptual mapping in research on school leadership.

One of the conclusions that Paulston regularly presented throughout his work was that theory drives methodology, and not the reverse. Some might argue that Paulston's work, embedded in international and comparative research, might serve better for aspiring researchers in this particular education domain. While Paulston might not have intended for his work in social cartography to be utilized by individuals in school leadership programs, the call for advanced research and increased dedication to theory lends itself to Paulston's model of scholarship.

<h2 style="text-align:center">HOW PAULSTON INFLUENCED MY PRACTICE</h2>

Paulston's work has also influenced my teaching practice as well. While embedding social theory in education curricula is far easier than doing so in the business curricula to which I was accustomed, the inclusion of such a unit in the business courses I teach is also important. While the integration of Paulston's work into other disciplines is not always straightforward or easily done, I have found it applicable in one way or another to all of the classes that I teach. Paulston's social cartography has informed my interactions with students as well.

I have found that teaching social theories in both verbal and graphical form is invaluable, for it speeds the learning process and deepens the comprehension of my students. To accomplish this, I have used Paulston's 1993 map (see Figure 1.1) as a regular tool in my classes.

As part of the Pennsylvania state requirements to obtain teacher certification, each candidate is required to compose a one-page "philosophy of education" which is then submitted as part of their standard application for teaching. I use Paulston's work to help candidates with this requirement, simply because of his use of quadrants in identifying four different perspectives on theory. I have found that most education students have heard of popular theories such as Marxism, functionalism, feminism, and social capital, but until given a visual representation of those theories, it can be unclear how those theories are aligned with others. By having a graphical representation, students can both familiarize themselves with popular theoretical frameworks and also see each theoretical perspective in juxtaposition to one another. After they have a visual understanding, the students can more effectively use these positions to tie theory into practice.

Another approach that I incorporate is to classify each local school district's community on selected dimensions, and debate income level, cost of property, education level, and increasing or decreasing populations in the school district. This exercise is helpful in determining which of the theories on Paulston's map represent the dominant paradigm for a particular school district, which in turn furthers students' understanding of whether or not their philosophy of education would fit into a particular school district. Since Pennsylvania has 500 school districts, having an understanding of districts as separate entities is important for prospective teachers to identify the particular characteristics of each district and assist them when applying for employment.

I also make a point of integrating Paulston's work into my non-mathematical business courses such as Organizational Behavior, Marketing, and Human Resource Management. By encouraging my students to have a micro-level understanding of theories I empower them with the knowledge necessary for facilitating interactions in organizations and mediating potential conflict. It is important that students understand the differences between privately owned businesses, small businesses, large businesses, and corporations. From a critical standpoint, individuals have to understand how big systems work and interact with each other, how the world views a business or a particular segment of a business, and how individuals and society interact. From a consumer standpoint, Paulston's theories can also be utilized to provide students with an understanding of consumer behavior in terms of dependency and independency on a social system. These systems and behaviors can all be looked upon from a larger, global scale, but can also be examined at the national, state, or even community level.

Implementing Paulston's work in my business courses has been challenging, especially with some of the more abstract concepts and ideas. For the ethical components that are now required in accounting and human resource management programs, Paulston's graphical representations of the objectivist theories can be used by instructors to better explain the relationships that exist in business. Paulston's theoretical work is even useful in dissecting current events, and many of the issues concerning "whistleblowers" featured in the media today can even be cross-referenced with the concepts of radical vs. non-radical functionalism.

Not only has Paulston had a great influence on my research and teaching practice, but his work has also had an immeasurable influence over my professional practice and associations with others. At various times in my career I have found myself peering through a lens that no one else seems to share and interpreting issues as critical that the rest of the world seems to overlook. Such was the case during my tenure as a school administrator, when I felt pressures from many different directions—from my superiors, peers, and staff, and also from outside stakeholder groups such as parents, school board members, and community leaders—and disagreed with many of them. It was difficult for me to compare and chart experiences I had over that period of time, since the moment one problem was resolved, another would emerge that always managed to be even more urgent than its predecessor. Now that I have the ability to reflect and look back on all of the conflicts that I experienced, I am able to note that performing a thoughtful and engaging critique of each situation upon resolution would have benefited my future practice tremendously.

The reflective element of understanding others and their unique experiences to better understand oneself is something that Paulston always chose to include as a part of his research, for as he said, "The social world cannot be measured, but it can be experienced, reported and compared" (Paulston 1996, 22). Paulston (1999, 462) would encourage his readers to understand environments where they would encounter allies and favorite experiences in their quest to obtain knowledge. Translating this to practice means having the ability to actively reflect upon and document each experience through a general framework and prepare for the inevitable occurrence of similar situations.

HOW PAULSTON INFLUENCED MY SCHOLARSHIP

Paulston's aptitude for crafting a concise piece that clearly targeted a particular audience was remarkable, and such ability is a key component to successful writing for scholarly publications that is too often overlooked. When coming from a background of traditional graduate school writing, where writings and research are designed for a particular class, writing for academic scholarship presents a challenge as publications have different themes and objectives depending on issue, location of publication, methodology utilized, region of research, and any number of other criteria. Paulston's work, however, transcended many of these difficulties because his ideas span multiple disciplines and are accessible to more researchers than just comparative education.

The concept of a social cartography that maps social and educational change occurred toward the end of Paulston's career. He can be an inspiration for those entering academia with the fear of pigeonholing themselves in one particular type of scholarship for the entirety of their career. Some might argue that Paulston's best work occurred after the age of 60. Just as Paulston was able to reflect upon his life's work in a manner that left a significant contribution to the academic world, scholars can use this as a takeaway message. The potential for scholarship is without bound for an academic, and obstacles and the opportunities that spring from them are abundant in all aspects of the profession.

Rolland Paulston's work in social cartography created a gateway to theoretical debate and discourse for aspiring scholars of many ability levels. Because of the influence of Paulston's writing on both my professional career and the field of education, his work is an integral component of the courses that I teach, especially my Foundations of Education and Introduction to Education courses. Through this, I can help preserve the legacy of a University of Pittsburgh scholar that came before me and opened up the doors for a neophyte to gain confidence in his understanding of the theories that encompass education and other disciplines. And so I leave as I began with a final statement from Paulston:

Sharing and critiquing our interpretive and cartographic collaborations will help us to better know ourselves, others, and the world we jointly construct. The point to remember here is that my purpose is to read and interpret written and figural texts, not authors. This requires that, to the extent possible texts be allowed to speak for themselves, to tell, with the use of quotes their own stories. (Paulston 1999, 439)

REFERENCES

Fossey, Richard, & Alan Shoho. (2006). "Educational Leadership Preparation Programs: In Transition or in Crisis?" *Journal of Cases in Educational Leadership, 9*(3), 3–11.

Goduto, Leonard, Gini Doolittle, & Donald Leake. (2008). "Forming Collaborative Partnerships on a Statewide Level to Develop Quality School Leaders." *Theory Into Practice, 47*(4), 345–352.

Levine, Arthur. (2005). *Educating School Leaders.* Washington, DC: Educating Schools Project.

Paulston, Rolland G. (1994). "Comparative and International Education: Paradigms and Theories." In T. Neville Postlethwaite and Torsten Husen (Ed.), *International Encyclopedia of Education.* (pp. 923–933). 2nd ed. Oxford: Pergamon.

Paulston, Rolland G. (1996). *Social Cartography: Mapping Ways of Seeing Social and Educational Change.* New York: Garland Publishing.

Paulston, Rolland G. (1999). "Mapping Comparative Education After Post Modernity." *Comparative Education Review, 43*(4), 438–463.

Paulston, Rolland G., & Martin Liebman. (1996). "Social Cartography: A New Metaphor/Tool for Comparative Studies." In Rolland G. Paulston (Ed.), *Social Cartography: Mapping Ways of Seeing Social and Educational Change*. New York: Garland Publishing.

Shulman, Lee S., Chris M. Golde, Andrea Conklin Bueschel, & Kristen J. Garabedian. (2006). "Reclaiming Education's Doctorates: A Critique and a Proposal." *Educational Researcher, 35*(3), 25–32.

Young, Michele, & Curtis Brewer. (2008). "Fear and the Preparation of School Leaders: The Role of Ambiguity, Anxiety, and Power in Meaning Making." *Educational Policy, 22*(1), 106–129.

YUKIKO YAMAMOTO AND MAUREEN W. MCCLURE

9. HOW CAN SOCIAL CARTOGRAPHY HELP POLICY RESEARCHERS?

PROLOGUE: A PANEGYRIC FOR PAULSTON

Social cartography research in education, sometimes called "mapping," has often been written in an exclusive, exhausting language constructed by careful intellectuals. Rolland G. Paulston was one of them. His thoughtful choice of each word has opened up new ways of thinking about education policy research. His mapping of multiple perspectives is particularly well suited for the contested and/or fragmented policy problems so common in contemporary education policy internationally. Comparative education traditionally spans not only international boundaries, but also complex historical, political, cultural, economic and philosophical points of view. An understanding of multiple valid perspectives, therefore, is required. Social cartography visually organizes these different policy research perspectives so that they can be compared. In so doing, it compels us as researchers to more transparently reveal our own points of view. Given the deep political waters of contemporary education policies within and across the sector, even the crudest of maps for policymakers can be better than none at all.

Rolland Paulston's context-embedded scholarship arrived at a propitious time. Today a focus on globalization in policy often promotes the reduction of international educational reforms into "plug and play" algorithms, such as designing curriculum around literacy and math skills, or framing schools as "accountable businesses." In contrast, Rolland painted a different, more arduous path. His work was fundamentally about education for the nuances of the human condition (Ninnes 2008, 347). To him comparative education meant an immersion in the very constructions of self and other.

> As the field increasingly welcomes more and more comparativists, especially from mainland China, Hong Kong, Taiwan and the Philippines (Bray, Adamson, and Mason 2007), Paulston's challenge appears even more relevant than when it first was made: "By using maps as a part of our comparative studies we may provide an insider view, a visual dialogue of cultural flow and changing influences appropriate for future work in comparative education, particularly in those instances where cultural values and differences are revealed by competing knowledge claims" (Paulston and Liebman 2000, 244). (Holmarsdottir and O'Dowd 2009, 3)

John C. Weidman, W. James Jacob (eds.), Beyond the Comparative: Advancing Theory and Its Application to Practice, 153–170.

At the heart of Paulston's work was his clear, strong affirmation of the strength and value of comparative education. He repeatedly rejected contemporary notions that education can and should be reduced to skills defined by causal algorithms and engineered into generic interventions and treatments. He refused the dominant narrative that objectivity and universality could marginalize historical, ideological and cultural knowledge. To him, being educated first meant owning one's own agency and creative voice, and respecting the personal agency of others. This meant taking responsibility for the messy contexts generated by a comparative education that acknowledged multiple perspectives and the multiple validities they generated. This chapter centers somewhat, but not exclusively on Paulston's Multiple Perspectives research project in the International and Development Education Program (IDEP) at the University of Pittsburgh in the 1990s (Paulston, Liebman, and Nicholson-Goodman 1996).[1] The project grew slowly over time out of Paulston's continuing work, Esther Gottlieb's dissertation using discourse analysis (Gottlieb 1987), and growing interest in the quadrant mapping of perspectives in Gibson Burrell and Gareth Morgan's (1979) *Sociological Paradigms and Organizational Analysis*.

Acknowledging the traditional value of multiple academic traditions for comparative education, he increasingly turned toward the problems of multiple validity and inadvertent marginalization created by intellectual inclusion (Mehta and Ninnes 2003). He created maps that included even those who would have sought to exclude him. The scholarly inclusion required by social cartography has important implications both for education policy researchers and the future of comparative education.

Paulston's work persists. A Google Scholar search of "social cartography" and "Paulston" returned 267 hits in multiple languages since his death in 2006. His scholarship extended not only to his role as a groundbreaking scholar, but also to his role as a teacher who influenced students both in Pittsburgh and elsewhere. Martin Liebman (Liebman and Paulston 1992, 1993), Jo Victoria Nicholson-Goodman (1996), Esther Gottlieb (1987, 2009; Gottlieb and La Belle 1990), Kristiina Erkkilä (2000), and Katsuhisa Ito (2001) together with other colleagues and heirs, used social cartography in education both as a method of study and as a moral or ethical *stance* that required the inclusion of the most marginal voices, even those with whom they intensely disagreed. As good empiricists they carefully represented the relative positions of different actors and their points of view by focusing on their texts, leaving their maps open for discourse, debate and revision. We are all the wealthier for it.

Paulston was an esurient scholar, speaking and reading in multiple languages. He devoured the texts of scholars, intellectuals and artists who wrote history, sociology, philosophy, technology, politics, literature, theater, cultural and media studies, as well as education. He made more of a turn into the humanities than most in the field. He would make copies of turgid articles he found interesting, put them in our mailboxes, and commanded the program faculty to read and digest them. And yes, there was always a test. And yes, we read them to vexation and took the test. And no we didn't always pass.

The Paulston test was always the same. Not how could an article help us first to become better scholars; rather, how could it help us become intellectually riper and more humane persons, and thus more creative scholars? This was rare. Even with all of his intense attention, replete with lots of little stickies on the drafts of ours that he returned and still turn up in our files, each of us today remains a paler but still hopeful version of what he thought we could be. Paulston's work was often too opaque for many policy researchers. When this was repeatedly pointed out to him, he would turn and say coolly that this was our task. So here we are joining others that have taken up Val D. Rust's challenge (Mehta and Ninnes 2003; Mehta 2009).

Rust, over time, challenged Paulston's assertion that comparative education was opening up to new perspectives with methods to challenge the orthodoxy of technical rationalism.

> These new developments have been mapped by people such as Rolland Paulston, who maintains that comparative education is now composed of a whole array of theoretical points of view; however, he has not addressed the methodological implications of this recent development in the field. (Rust, Johnstone, and Allaf 2009, 88)

We have tried here to translate a few of the complex ideas of social cartography into methods for policy use; much, however, still awaits translation.

PAULSTON'S SOCIAL CARTOGRAPHY: MULTIPLE PERSPECTIVES' CENTRALITY

Social scientists often create maps in order to view, report, and compare social realities. The purpose of these maps is to bring to light differences between or among social groups (Seppi 2000). A social map is a representative methodological work, especially for those conducting authoritative research that seeks to include contested voices in the research (Ito 2001). Paulston, and even more so his student, Martin Liebman, broke with more traditional educational policy reform thinking, stating that "The social world cannot be measured, but it can be viewed, reported, and compared" (Liebman and Paulston 1993, 10).

As a qualitative research method, mapping allows viewers to tell their stories from their particular points of view. Because it usually balances multiple valid and often competing points of view, it cannot and does not claim one ultimate and objective truth. Sometimes policy solutions can converge on standard agreements, such as the need for poor children's safety in schools. They are, however, unlikely to converge on who should pay or how much they should pay. More often than not, policy issues have stakeholders with competing claims and interests, leading to different interpretations of the same events. Called the Rashomon effect, most policymakers and executives intuitively understand how people with different interests not only have different interpretations of the same events; they also come to believe their positions to be true (Roth and Mehta 2002).

Thus traditional educational policy goals based on issues of access, equity, adequacy or sustainability need more than technical solutions. They also need nuanced political balances across stakeholder groups. Here, by mapping key texts and ideas, mappers may be able to help find where there are breakdowns in communications or where bridges may be built (Huff 2000).

THE FEATURES OF SOCIAL CARTOGRAPHY FOR POLICY USE

What makes social cartography similar to more traditional forms of cultural geography is that it attempts to locate complex relationships. What makes social cartography different from traditional geography is that it often *intends* to reflect the perspective of its producer (Stromquist 2000), because informed hunches may be all that are currently available to serious scholars. We attend to two of social cartography's specific characteristics: (a) the *spatial relationship* and (b) *open-ended results*.

Nelly Stromquist (2000) complements Paulston's work by discussing in detail the value of boundary identification. It can be useful for policy researchers. She states that borders not only protect and preserve identities, but also function as lines to indicate separations or cooperation. Separating borders, sometimes called borderwork, can strengthen the boundaries of a particular space, whereas, crossing borders, which lead the viewer from one sphere to another, can create opportunities for developing shared values (Stromquist 2000). Border-crossing is especially important because it means that different entities (i.e., cultures), come into contact, and there is the possibility of finding a place to recognize differences (Stromquist 2000). Finding this space might be a critical policy opportunity, since it indicates a possibility of bridging these two cultures. In addition, using critical perspectives, map borders are sometimes drawn in an attempt to break down what might be seen as established but unjust boundaries (Paulston 1993).

Mapping requires the analyses of interpretations through traditional methodological processes of acquiring, coding, decoding, aggregating, recalling, amalgamating, and storing information. *An interpretive map, therefore, is not replicable by other social mappers* (Liebman and Paulston 1993). What the social mapper must lose in the power of replication may be balanced by boundary setting, the visibility of juxtaposition, the authenticity of voice, dialogue and debate, the entrance of multiple mappers, and ongoing revisions.

The Spatial Relationship: What Is and Is Not There?

A graphic representation can systematically reduce complexity by creating meaningful images out of the original data (Huff and Fletcher 1990). Even the most traditional maps are more than a portrait of a physical area. For instance, a geographical map for tourists can show how far one restaurant is located from a landmark building (i.e., it illustrates its distance, direction, or points of interest between them). In order to make a map more easily understood, the mapper often excludes less significant information, such as the locations of the private homes in the area. This logic applies to conceptual maps as well. When a mapper chooses what to include in or exclude from the map in a meaningful way, a cognitive map can become a useful tool to understand complex and often confusing realities (Huff and Fletcher 1990).

One critically different feature of social cartography apart from traditional geographic map is its use of *negative space*, of examining what has *not* been placed on it. For this reason, *maps are particularly well suited for analyzing gaps in policy research, both to situate them and to reveal negative spaces.*[2] For example, we are interested in education and youth policy, with a particular interest in the problems of countries with "youth bulges." The answers to questions about what educational options are available to youth across the education sector cannot be located in any one field of scholarship, as relevant development policy research reaches across the fields of education, sociology, economics, history, political science, psychology, public health, social work, business, public administration, security studies and other fields. It is a problem well suited for comparative education policy research. We found, for example, that while many people were writing about the problems of youth bulges for education and employment policies, few authors cited others who were working outside of their own disciplines, policy positions or national debates, even though a little on-line searching could have been helpful.

With maps, this integration of conceptual distance and physical connections are drawn in order: (a) to clarify positions, (b) to identify relationships between and among entities, and (c) to explore the convergence and divergence of ideas. Maps can illustrate how and why the represented spaces of entities are placed, crossed, or hardly crossed (Stromquist 2000). Simply knowing what is outside of the boundaries of current policy dialogues can be helpful.

Open-ended Results

Maps Can be Redrawn. This makes them temporary. A map can open dialogues and deepen contemporary understandings of unknown and contested relationships (Mausolff 2000). *Here, the resolution of ideological and theoretical controversies is not a primary goal* (Paulston and Liebman 2000). Viewers who disagree with the mapper are encouraged to redefine the space, debate, and even personalize it (Liebman and Paulston 1992, 1993; Nicholson-Goodman 1996). Liebman and Paulston (1993) further claim that social maps cannot be finalized with any exactitude. This open-endedness can be particularly useful in policy formation. A map allows readers to deliberate the momentary relationships of the current situation, as well as wider, longer-term pictures. Paulston (1996, 35) wrote that "every social map is the product of its makers and open to continuous revision and interrogation" (Nicholson-Goodman 1996, 2). Conditions change and actors change their minds.

In a policy world in which little is known and much is contested, social cartographers begin by examining existing texts and mapping their central ideas and knowledge. As more researchers enter the map area with additional texts and ideas, a clearer picture of the terrain may be constructed. Policy analysts may search this terrain for gaps, for connections, and for possible bridging language across contested interpretations. This requires a map that cannot close its boundaries (Paulston and Liebman 1994).

USING PAULSTON'S MAPS

Mapping stakeholders' texts allows the researcher to better understand the foundational thinking, clear, tangled or lacking, that rests underneath many policy positions. An understanding of these intellectual and cultural "tectonic plates" is important to policy framing and formation. Each of the four scholarly perspectives used here occupies a scholarly "continent" with its own boundaries, logic, "language," and "culture." It is often important for policy researchers to identify how others are framing issues. Policy framing in a language that potential allies can't "hear" is unlikely to create or sustain needed alliances.

Social cartography often begins with the choice of a type of visual representation. Over the years Paulston used four major intellectual perspectives that require separate visual spaces: Technical Rationalist (TR), Critical Rationalist (CR), Hermeneutical Constructionist (HC), and Deconstructive Perspectivist (DP). These terms evolved over the decades (Paulston 1996). If he were still writing, he would be regularly updating these constructs against his interpretations of new work. Each of the four has a strong intellectual foundation. Together their traditions span the arts and sciences. Their boundaries are porous and shifting, nevertheless, they provide a place to start. We cautiously suggest alternative titles that we think capture the spirit of the perspective and may be easier to remember. We are unsure of Rolland's approbation, however, as we can no longer stuff our comments under his door.

Technical Rationalists (TR): The Bean Counters

The technical rationalists (TR) point of view has been the dominant and the most profitable narrative in comparative education, particularly in the US and Great Britain since the 1960s. It is so dominant that many researchers and policymakers are unaware of other intellectual traditions. It attempts to mirror nature and consequently is called a corresponding or mimetic view, meaning that it mimics reality. Here the viewer is assumed to be an observer relatively independent of history and culture. Here education policy heavily focuses on the most efficient and effective ways for institutions, governments and markets to get results.

The TR visual representation insists on the literality of realism, and is the one that we are most used to "seeing." Policy analysts, for example, regularly map lines of authority. Organization charts are simple TR representations. TRs have an assumption, not universally shared, that their work does not burden readers with a responsibility for cultural interpretation. As policy comparativists, we may need to respectfully disagree, as one might ignore the cultural dimensions of authority at one's own peril. Of course all causal modeling is TR, and so the graphic outputs of statistical analyses will be found here. New statistical mapping packages, for example, are opening up new ways of visually presenting complex data in multiple dimensions. Figure 9.1 is one example of a simple TR representation, displaying levels and stages of a national education sector, using vertical and horizontal lines.

Classification of vertical and Horizontal Relationships

Level	Age	Range	
IV	(25)	STAGE 6 Postgraduate Study	
III		STAGE 5	
		Examples Professional Schools	Higher Stage of University Study, Teacher Training
	(21/22)	STAGE 4	
		Examples Advanced Technical Schools	Lower Stage of University Study, Teacher Training
	(18/19)	Undergraduate Colleges	
II		STAGE 3	
		Examples Full-time and part-time Vocational Schools	Upper Section of High Schools, Grammar Schools, Gymnasium Teacher Training
	(14/15)	STAGE 2	
		Examples Upper Section of Elementary Schools	Lower section of High Schools, Grammar Schools Gymnasiums
	(10/11)	Intermediate Schools	
I		STAGE 1	
		Examples	
	(5/6/7)	Primary Schools	
Compulsory School begins ↑		Pre-School Education	
		Examples	
		Nursery and Kindergarten	

Figure 9.1. Example of TR Visual Representation.
Source: Reprinted from Franz Hilker (1963, 57), with permission from UNESCO.

As you can see in this figure, the visual representation simply categorizes different institutional domains in order to show their relationship to one another. This figure shows how many school systems are organized based on children's development. The map attempts to "mirror" reality as closely as possible. It is interesting to note, however, that it is the mapper who chose to orient the institutional levels from the youngest and most students at the bottom; and where the structures rise pyramid like to the oldest and fewest students at the top. The mapper could have chosen, for example, a more horizontal, time-line approach that shows students flowing in from one side and flowing out the other. But most of us would not consider this option, assuming instead that the chart "mirrors" reality.

Critical Rationalists (CR): The Righteously Indignant

What if I want to direct people's attention to educational inequalities, not only so that people "see" them, but also so they are also moved to do something about it? Then I may need a map that demonstrates these inequalities by including those, if any, who are benefitting from existing conditions and who are not. Paulston regularly peppered both students and faculty with Antonio Gramsci's (1957) grand "*Cui bono?*" or "Who stands to benefit?" question.

According to Critical Rationalists (CR), people act rationally, but in their own self-interests, giving rise to chronic conflicts (Paulston 1996). Those who benefit from the status quo, will, acting in their own self-interests, allocate resources to sustain their position, and not necessarily for the common good. This results not in the equilibrium hoped for by the neoclassic economists, but rather in the persistence of comparative advantage, mostly historical.

For example, a dark side of educational policy rarely discussed is the politics of the self-interested rich. Within the narrow logic of sustaining comparative advantage, it is, therefore, not in their self-interest to allow themselves to be taxed in order to subsidize the education of poor children. Why? First, it reduces the amount that they can invest in a high quality education for their own children. Second, it subsidizes children who will then grow up to compete in the marketplace with their own children. Yes, there are many arguments for the need for taxation for public security and private prosperity, but taxes are short-term, concentrated costs, and public security and private prosperity are long-term, diffused benefits. This rationally biases choices toward the shorter-term.

Critical rationalists (CR) in education problematized and critiqued both hierarchies and the problems created by unregulated self-interest (Paulston 1996). CR, who appeared during 1970s, focused, for example, on the bi-polar center and periphery thinking found in de-colonization and civil right movements. Some mapped social networks to describe relative power access (Paulston 1996). CR visual representation tended to display inequality issues and elicit a level of judgment from the viewer. Social activists and related NGOs interested in social justice policies will find this kind visualization of inequity helpful.

Figure 9.2 is an example, showing global wealth distribution. Notice that it is both rationalist and ideological. The facts are meant to speak for themselves. If the world were a village of 100 people, six of the villagers, would own the front of the oil-drenched piggy bank with 59 percent of the wealth, 74 of them would own the middle rear with 39 percent of the wealth, and 20 of them would share only 2 percent of the wealth, symbolized by the small tail. Notice that the statistics are presented in a horizontal and not vertical orientation.

If the world were a village of 100 people

MONEY

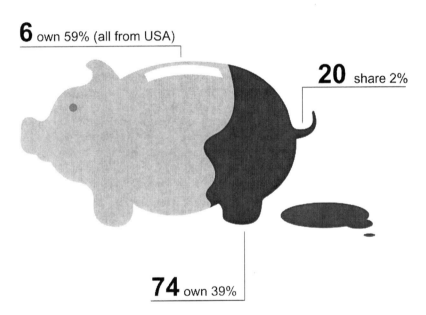

Figure 9.2. Example of CR Visual Representation.
Source: Reprinted from Toby Ng Design (2009), with permission from Toby Ng.

The "map's" purpose was to provide an awareness of what CRs think is a problematic hierarchy. The mapper then hoped this visualization could not only make readers more aware of inequalities, but also to be moved to support policies that address these inequalities. Note that both TRs and CRs focus on social structures, not personal points of view. Here education policy focuses on fairness.

Hermeneutical Constructivists (HC): The Poets

In contrast, during the 1980s, Hermeneutical Constructivists (HC) attempted to find patterns and meaning in "voice" i.e., the experience of personal meaning in situations. HC scholarship grows out of the humanities, and focuses on stories and images that possess the power to change minds and bodies. Unlike much in the social sciences, HC in education, among other things, seek personal experiences and their meanings because they are so foundational in the shaping of personal identities. Here education policy tends to focus on the importance of individual rights and responsibilities.

Hermeneutical constructivists shifted thinking about policy away from mapping social structures to mapping understandings of people as persons with experiences that they need to understand. This major shift to "voice" underscores the centrality of personal meaning in education policy. According to Peter Hackett (1988), most people use framing metaphors and allegories to shape how they think in their daily lives (Paulston and Liebman 2000, 8). They may or may not yet, however, own their own metaphors or therefore their own thinking; thus they may not yet be able to think or act in their own rational self-interest. This educated, rational self-interest is a cornerstone to self-governance in both democracies and markets.

Metaphors can become powerful sources of miscommunication when different people use different frames for the same thing or event. The problems can quickly escalate when researchers work in complex cultural environments internationally. The Rashomon effect can complicate policymaking as one person's policy solution generates another person's policy problem, with each believing that their position is the correct one.

Education today is increasingly a highly charged political issue in most countries. For example, children and schooling can be viewed through the metaphors of assets, investments, liabilities or choices. Some farmers may think of children as assets for their farm. The more they have, the more cheap labor they will have. Education may not be as valuable to them as child labor because school takes children away from the fields. In addition, educated children may leave their parents on the farm and move into the cities. Urban dwellers, on the other hand, may see children as expensive investments, requiring long-term education for jobs in cities. They may have fewer children. Those who frame children as liabilities may be disinclined to subsidize the children of others. "Why should I pay for another man's mistakes?"[3]

Finally, widespread access to birth control has given rise to thinking of children as consumer choices, as parents decide how many they want. This thinking has important potential consequences for public education. Policy formation based on notions of public ownership and responsibility for children's education and welfare will necessarily differ from policy formation based on notions of private, consumption-based ownership and responsibility for children's education and welfare.

Narratives, or the stories that we tell each other, often use words and images that act as shortcuts to other, larger meanings, and are standard fare in policy. These shortcuts, such as metaphors or the use of irony, are sometimes called *tropes.* For example, advocates for the poor are likely to create narratives around solving the educational problems by building on tropes of poverty and social justice. Meanwhile, middle class taxpayers may ignore these tropes, focusing instead almost exclusively on narratives built on tropes of achievement and accountability. A map can help policy researchers see where these tropes are located and if any bridging language can be built. Mapping can also reveal what has not yet been framed.

In Kristiina Erkkilä's work on the problems of education and entrepreneurship, she discovered that research about the relationships between entrepreneurship and education policy were not well developed (Erkkilä 2000). Even a general definition of "entrepreneurship" had not reached any kind of consensus in an international level. This situation made it difficult to pursue her comparative study across the UK, US, and Finland. She approached the problem by mapping the relative locations of supporting and oppositional discourse within each country's policy context, based on her analysis of available texts. She then overlay her national maps in order to define the general boundaries of the policy discourse. Erkkilä discovered that even though the policy debates were similar across countries, the policy spaces they occupied were different.

Figure 9.3 is an example of this approach in the Finnish context. First, she analyzed arguments from the Finnish literature and categorized them according to whether or not: (a) the texts indicated supporting or opposing policy language, and (b) they considered entrepreneurship education as a benefit for individuals or for society. The cloud size portrayed the frequency of concept use in the policy text. Distance portrayed the relative relationships among the concepts. In addition, the mapper located herself in the map, so that viewers can see where she stood. As you can see, there is no overlap between the supporting and opposing tropes that frame the policy narrative, meaning that bridging language would need to be constructed. Figure 9.3, later overlain to show multiple cultural contexts, enabled her to frame the policy climates internationally. Note that her original intention was to map differences in meaning across different countries. What she also created was a map of the domestic policy discourse, badly fragmented with no overlapping room for bridging dialogue. This juxtaposed and fragmented national policy discourse analysis now shifts our thinking toward the value of deconstruction.

Deconstructive Perspectivists (DP): The Puzzle Masters

Paulston's late works for social mapping made room for Deconstructive Perspectivists (DP). Their approach came into the comparative education discourse in the 1990s (Paulston 1996, 1997). As Nicholson-Goodman (1996, 9) notes, "the postmodern era began with a dawning awareness that "reality" is composed of disconnected fragments," not universal truths. As she suggested, mapping was a way of connecting and reconnecting the discontinuities that comprised reality. DP turned away from the technical rationalists' promises of causality as the explanation of social behavior.

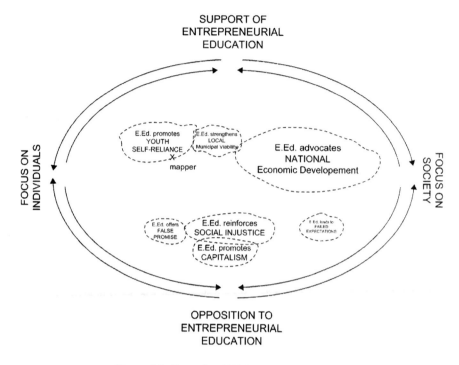

Figure 9.3. Example of HC Visual Representation.
Source: Reprinted from Erkkilä (2000, 166), with permission from Taylor & Francis.

More than framing narratives, DP argued that since we can't achieve an objective social reality about which we can all agree because our individual experience gets in the way, we now needed something like Foucault's genealogies and archaeologies to map the roots of our tangled points of view (Gottlieb and La Belle 1990). If those who are attempting to influence policy are unable to construct themselves and others with coherent ideas that are clearly understandable to others, then they are likely to generate incoherent policy with unhappy and unexpected outcomes.

Here Paulston used DP's visual theorizing to draw maps that portrayed how major fragmented and contesting educational theories were related to each other. He first identified the philosophical locations of these theories along floating axes. He then juxtaposed comparative education scholarship within "clouds" of texts and ideas. Finally, he located himself where he stood as scholar. This allowed others to use this work as a template to understand in what ideas he thought other authors grounded themselves. It was also an open-ended map and subject to change. These changes included not only the content of the map, but also its very structure, the criteria used to choose and locate texts. Figure 9.4 contains a simplified map of the conceptual spaces occupied by these different approaches to policy research.

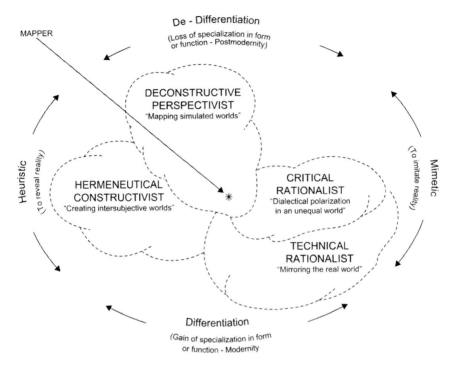

Figure 9.4. Example of DP Visual Representation.
Source: Reprinted from Paulston (1997, 118), with permission from Taylor & Francis.

In Figure 9.4, Paulston divided the comparative and international education field into four different conceptual clouds. Like Erkkilä, he included only himself on the map, leaving the clouds to define the space occupied by many authors. He summarized decades of framing core tropes. Technical rationalists tried to mirror reality. Critical rationalists were close by, dividing reality into two unequal parts, and then addressing the problems created by these divisions. Hermeneutic constructivists preferred to reveal personal reality rather than imitate nature, using concepts such as metaphors to explain and share meaning, not through the authority of natural laws, but through the authority of human rights and the "authenticity" of personal experiences. Not too far away, Deconstructivists tried to piece together fragmented realities through juxtapositions in order to reveal new meanings and powerful contradictions. In a discussion with the authors on 22 September 2010, Ted Serrant, a former graduate student advisee of Paulston, commented that:

[Paulston] proposed, like Val Rust (Rust 1991), the dismantling of the metanarratives of modernity in order to reveal the small narratives that lie obscure within the space of modern society, hence truth for him was the "absence of concealment" (Paulston and Liebman 2000, 9) and that constituted personal location within that space.

The social cartography project, launched in the 1990s at the University of Pittsburgh, still persists there as well as elsewhere in the world. Picking up on the value of reconstructing culture, James Jacob, now directing the school's Institute for International Studies in Education (IISE), and Sheng Yao Cheng used Paulston's work to deconstruct the familiar Yin/Yang or traditional Tai-Ji icon. They reached into the strengths of Chinese culture to reinterpret its appropriateness for contemporary Western use. It is a powerful symbol that reflects a deep philosophical view of life and the world. It requires the observer to attend to multiple points of view through the endless ebb and flow of the universe. It constructs opposites not as enemies to be eliminated, but complementary ends of the same pole. Which theoretical perspectives to use then becomes a contextually-embedded choice. In arguing for its use in comparative, international, and development education (CIDE), they posited:

> The Tai-Ji Model . . . is an excellent tool for helping determine which type of theoretical framework and methodology to use in CIDE research. Yet it differs from an altogether postmodern perspective that provides no literal theoretical foundation. The Tai-Ji Model urges CIDE scholars to be aware and knowledgeable of the broad range of theories and metatheories at our disposal; yet we must also be able to ascertain which one or set of theories would be most appropriate for a given study. (Jacob and Cheng 2005, 251)

The Tai-Ji symbol defined the world through a concept of universality as eternal flow and harmonized balance. This differs somewhat from Western neoclassical views of universality as equilibrium. In the Tai-Ji symbol for example, space and negative space can only exist in relationship to each other. This duality cannot be resolved, so the world must be constructed in balance, not in the final resolution of Western equilibrium. By drawing on the images' central focus on balancing space and its negative, Jacob and Cheng construct a next step in the mapping literature by offering two increasingly important concepts in education policy analysis.

First, change, not equilibrium, is a permanent condition; therefore policy solutions can only be temporary. This apparently small point can make large differences in policy choices. Instead of arguing for private or public sector funding, policy reformers may be better off first learning more about the contexts in which today's children live, and then designing policies that can work for specific children as their generation grows up over the next ten to twenty years. Policy balance within a particular context then becomes a goal. Policy formation focuses not only on the proper engineering of effective solutions, but also on the shifting balances and harmonies of sustainable alliances among stakeholders.

Second, the growing complexity of contemporary policy can also make it increasingly important to analyze the Yin, or negative space. This means that what is not yet visible is central to the policy formation process. Scholars need to examine multiple theoretical perspectives to better understand the ebbs and flows that created both the visible and the not or not yet visible. This fits. Paulston repeatedly told his students to attend to what was not on the table, because what people wanted to avoid, or couldn't help avoiding, mattered. Now we have a better way to map it.

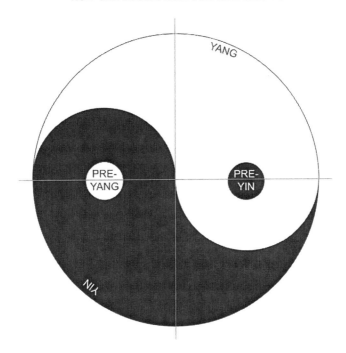

Figure 9.5. Tai-Ji Model for Framing Comparative, International, and Development Education Research Paradigms.
Source: Reprinted from Jacob and Cheng (2005, 248), with permission from Elsevier.

DÉNOUEMENT

In sum, social cartography can be meaningful in specific educational policy research environments. Mapping is particularly well suited for policy environments that:

1. Contain many unknown and complex relationships
2. Require a consideration of multiple perspectives
3. Require an ideological or moral stance
4. Are important, but lack measurable data
5. Address policy consequences that require personal points of view, especially those that are marginalized

The use of social cartography, especially in conjunction with three of Paulston's perspectives—Critical Rationalist, Hermeneutic Constructivist, and Deconstructive Perspectivist—help re-embed comparative education policy in the contested, fragmented and messy contexts that drew us to it in the first place. Paulston believed, like others, in the opportunities for conflict to be reduced when every voice is included in one place (Hall 2002). Comparative educators today are challenged to contribute to the messy politics of education reform policies in many countries. In the past, we may have been most visible when we explained the reform failures we predicted. We need to be a bit further ahead of the policy curve. We have much to offer and must stop allowing our tumid prose to send education policy analysts constantly diving for their dictionaries.

Over the years Paulston revisited his mapping spaces, changing both content and criteria as his understanding deepened. We need to do likewise. In later years, his spaces were no longer rigid quadrants; they became instead clouds of problems, ideas and language that floated in variable proximity to each other. For example, the critical theorists of the 1970s, were, by the 1990s, seen as close to the technical rationalists of the 1960s because they both focused on the problems of social structures and institutions as well as on data that corresponded with nature. Later newer perspectives in the field studied the consequences of education for personal experience and identity formation. Now newer work that focuses on the use of social cartography for policy outreach won't supplant older thinking; we hope that it will just open up new spaces and bump the clouds around.

NOTES

1. In addition to students, department faculty members who became engaged in the multiple perspectives project to varying degrees included Don Adams, Seth Spaulding, John Singleton, Thomas LaBelle, Mark Ginsburg, John Weidman, James Mauch, Noreen Garman, and Maureen McClure, and sundry well-known visiting faculty members including Manzoor Ahmed and Vandra Masemann.
2. Sometimes mappers create negative spaces to show current gaps by drawing attention to 'what is not there,' inviting the viewer to deliberate its meaning. Other times negatives spaces are created when they lie beyond the boundaries of the mappers' own frameworks. For example, mappers who believe that development is basically getting the mathematics right and tidy will need to discount the value of what others see as the untamable torrents of histories and cultures.
3. A serious question posed to one of the authors.

REFERENCES

Bray, Mark, Bob Adamson, & Mark Mason, eds. (2007). *Comparative Education Research: Approaches and Methods*. Hong Kong: Comparative Education Research Centre, University of Hong Kong, Springer.

Burrell, Gibson, & Gareth Morgan. (1979). *Sociological Paradigms and Organizational Analysis: Elements of the Sociology of Corporate Life*. New Hampshire: Heinemann Educational Books Inc.

Erkkilä, Kristiina. (2000). *Entrepreneurial Education: Mapping the Debates in the United States, the United Kingdom and Finland*. New York: Garland Publishing.

Gottlieb, Esther E. (1987). "Development Education: Discourse in Relation to Paradigms and Knowledge." PhD diss., Administrative and Policy Studies, School of Education, University of Pittsburgh, Pittsburgh, USA.

Gottlieb, Esther E. (2009). "'Somewhere Better than This Place/Nowhere Better than This Place': The Lifemap of Rolland G. Paulston (1929–2006)." *Prospects, 39*, 91–101.

Gottlieb, Esther E., & Thomas J. La Belle. (1990). "Ethnographic Contextualization of Freire's Discourse: Consciousness-Raising, Theory and Practice." *Anthropology & Education Quarterly, 21*(1), 3–18.

Gramsci, Antonio. (1957). *The Modern Prince and Other Writings*. New York: International Publishers.

Hackett, Peter. (1988). "Aesthetics as a Dimension for Comparative Study." *Comparative Education Review ,32*(4), 389–399.

Hall, Roger I. (2002). "Gaining Understanding in a Complex Cause-Effect Policy Domain." In Anne Sigismund Huff and Mark Jenkins (Ed.), *Mapping Strategic Knowledge*. (pp. 89–111). Thousand Oaks, CA: Sage.

Hilker, Franz. (1963). "Classification of Vertical and Horizontal Relationships." In *Relevant Data in Comparative Education: Report on Expert Meeting March 11–16, 1963*, presented by Brian Holmes and Saul Robinson (p. 57). Hamburg, Germany: UNESCO Institute for Education.

Holmarsdottir, Halla B., & Mina O'Dowd. (2009). "Introduction." In Halla B. Holmarsdottir and Mina O'Dowd. Rotterdam (Ed.), *Nordic Voices: Teaching and Researching Comparative and International Education in the Nordic Countries.*. The Netherlands: Sense Publishers.

Huff, Anne Sigismund. (2000). "Ways of Mapping Strategic Thought." In Rolland G. Paulston (Ed.), *Social Cartography: Mapping Ways of Seeing Social and Educational Change.*. Pittsburgh: University of Pittsburgh Book Center.

Huff, Anne Sigismund, & Karen E. Fletcher. (1990). "Conclusion: Key Mapping Decisions." In Anne Sigismund Huff (Ed.), *Mapping Strategic Thought.*. New York: John Wiley & Sons, Inc.

Ito, Katsuhisa. (2001). "Spatial Representation in Comparative Education and Geography: A Social Cartography Analysis." *PhD diss., Administrative and Policy Studies, School of Education*, University of Pittsburgh, Pittsburgh, USA.

Jacob, W. James, & Sheng Yao Cheng. (2005). "Mapping Theories in Comparative, International, and Development Education (CIDE) Research." In David P. Baker and Alexander W. Wiseman (Ed.), *Global Trends in Educational Policy.* (pp. 221–258). New York: Elsevier Science, Ltd.

Liebman, Martin, & Rolland G. Paulston. (1992). "Mapping the Postmodern Turn in Comparative Education." Paper presented at the *Comparative and International Education Society.* Pittsburgh, PA, 6 November 1992.

Liebman, Martin, & Rolland G. Paulston. (1993). Social Cartography: "A New Methodology for Comparative Studies." In Rolland G. Paulston. (Ed.), *Conceptual Mapping Project Research.* Pittsburgh: University of Pittsburgh.

Mausolff, Christopher. (2000). "Postmodernism and Participation in International Rural Development Projects." In Rolland G. Paulston (Ed.), *Social Cartography: Mapping Ways of Seeing Social and Educational Change.*. Pittsburgh: University of Pittsburgh Book Center.

Mehta, Sonia (2009). "Big Stories, Small Stories: Beyond Disputatious Theory Towards 'Multilogue'." In Robert Cowen and Andreas M. Kazamias (Ed.), *International Handbook of Comparative Education.*. New York: Springer Science + Business Media B. V.

Mehta, Sonia, & Peter Ninnes. (2003). "Postmodernism Debates and Comparative Education: A Critical Discourse Analysis." *Comparative Education Review, 47*(2), 238–255.

Nicholson-Goodman, Jo Victoria. (1996). "Mapping/Remapping Discourse in Educational Policy Studies." In Rolland G. Paulston (Ed.), *APS Conceptual Mapping Project.*. Pittsburgh: University of Pittsburgh.

Ninnes, Peter. (2008). "Fear and Desire in Twentieth Century Comparative Education." *Comparative Education, 44*(3),345–358.

Paulston, Rolland G. (1993). "Mapping Knowledge Perspectives in Studies of Social and Educational Change." In Rolland. G. Paulston (Ed.), *APS Conceptual Mapping Project.*. Pittsburgh: University of Pittsburgh.

Paulston, Rolland G. (1996). "Opening the Development Debate with Maps of Multiple Perspectives." Paper presented at the *Moving Beyond the Poverty of Developmentalism Conference*, Pittsburgh, PA, 8–9 November 1996.

Paulston, Rolland G. (1997). "Mapping Visual Culture in Comparative Education Discourse." *Compare: A Journal of Comparative and International Education, 27*(2), 117–152.

Paulston, Rolland G., & Martin Liebman. 1994. "An Invitation to Postmodern Social Cartography." *Comparative Education Review, 38*(2), 215–232.

Paulston, Rolland G., & Martin Liebman. (2000). "Social Cartography: A New Metaphor/Tool for Comparative Studies." In Rolland G. Paulston (Ed.), *Social Cartography: Mapping Ways of Seeing Social and Educational Change.*. Pittsburgh: University of Pittsburgh Book Center.

Paulston, Rolland G., Martin Liebman, & Jo Victoria Nicholson-Goodman. (1996). "Mapping Multiple Perspectives: Research Reports of the University of Pittsburgh Social Cartography Project, 1993–1996." In Rolland G. Paulston (Ed.), *Social Cartography Project.*. Pittsburgh: University of Pittsburgh.

Roth, Wendy D., & Jal D. Mehta. (2002). "The Rashomon Effect: Combining Positivist and Interpretivist Approaches in the Analysis of Contested Events." *Sociological Methods & Research, 31*(2), 131–173.

Rust, Val D. (1991). "Postmodernism and its Comparative Education Implications." *Comparative Education Review, 35*(4),610–626.

Rust, Val D., Brian Johnstone, & Carine Allaf. (2009). "Reflections on the Development of Comparative Education." In Robert Cowen and Andreas M. Kazamias (Ed.), *International Handbooks of Education.*. New York: Springer Science + Business Media B.V.

Seppi, Joseph R. (2000). "Spatial Analysis in Social Cartography." In Rolland. G. Paulston (Ed.), *Social Cartography: Mapping Ways of Seeing Social and Educational Change.*. Pittsburgh: University of Pittsburgh Book Center.

Serrant, Ted. (2010). *Interview with Maureen* McClure and Yukiko Yamamoto, University of Pittsburgh, Pittsburgh, PA, 22 September 2010.

Stromquist, Nelly P. (2000). "Mapping Gendered Spaces in Third World Educational Interventions." In Rolland G. Paulston (Ed.), *Social Cartography: Mapping Ways of Seeing Social and Educational Change.*. Pittsburgh: University of Pittsburgh Book Center.

Toby Ng Design. (2010_. *The World of 100*. Hong Kong: Toby Ng Design 2009. Available online at: http://www.toby-ng.com.

PART II: MAPPING CONCEPTUAL ISSUES IN CIDE RESEARCH

NELLY P. STROMQUIST

10 A SOCIAL CARTOGRAPHY OF GENDER
IN EDUCATION

Visualizing Private and Public Spheres and Interconnecting Forces

INTRODUCTION

In this chapter I discuss how gender manifests itself in the educational field, examining how this phenomenon is framed in public policy and how in fact it functions. I will present its features employing a social cartography framework. My basic argument is that since gender is a pervasive social phenomenon—which implies that it operates at multiple levels—it must be examined holistically if we are to advance in the modification of gender beliefs and dynamics.

NATURE OF THE DATA ANALYTICAL METHODS

The analytical framework used for this study builds on social cartography. Originally developed in the discipline of geography, this framework enables the researcher to consider territory, location, the institutional and individual actors that inhabit a particular social space, the way these actors define problems and solutions, and the interrelationship between all of these (Siekierska c1995).[1]

Social maps are selective representations of reality and thus simplify the world (Black 1997; Ruitenberg 2007). At the same time, they serve valuable functions in identification and classification. Social cartography enables the visualization of relations between and among groups and institutions. Its descriptive capability allows one to view the complexity of perspectives by identifying the points of contact and distance between varying spaces and social sites. To talk about space implies recognition that social life is embedded in concrete terrains. Robert Sack (1986, 9), a pioneer in the use of social cartography, argues that territoriality is "an effort by an individual or a group to affect, influence, or control people, phenomena or relations through the delimitation and control over a given geographical area." Sack further argues that territoriality is a strategy "completely within the context of human motivation and objectives" (21). In examining social space, we must acknowledge that it is not a natural cultural outcome but rather a political outcome. Spaces therefore should be seen both as effects and causes of conscious social action.

It has been observed that "the axes of identity . . . never function outside space but rather are linked to particular spaces and sites within which and in relation to

John C. Weidman, W. James Jacob (eds.), Beyond the Comparative: Advancing Theory and Its Application to Practice, 173–192.

which people live" (Bondi and Rose 2003, 232). At the same time, as Richard Peet (1998) tells us, spaces must be thought of as differentiated and not homogeneous, as dynamic and not static, and as active both in the material sense and in ideological representations. Three key concepts in social cartography refer to space, site, and interconnection. Thus, there are distinct and distant spaces as there are also overlapping spaces. In a given space, there can be several sites, each of which maintains diverse levels of relation/communication with the others. In these sites, power relations are played out, generating constant political struggle. Essentially, the gender analysis I propose decomposes space into private and public. For the discussion of the private space, this study relies on the theoretical literature and addresses concepts that apply to sociocultural contexts across the world. For discussion of the public space, the study focuses on gender and education and relies primarily on data coming from a cross-national study of public policies in education of three countries: Costa Rica, Brazil, and Peru (Stromquist 2006).[2] I use social cartography to locate space (represented by that occupied by key social actors) and to depict the relative size of the multiple social actors implicated in gender in society and to show the overlapping spaces occupied by them. I also use social cartography to show the relative distance among actors that seek to influence the state regarding gender issues as well as to express in graphic form the degree of influence non-state actors have on national states.

UNDERSTANDING GENDER

Gender theory initially addressed the power asymmetries between women and men, but over time it has become increasingly complex and fractured by growing differences in its basic premises. There exist differences in the perception of the nature of gender oppression: some view gender subordination as due to ideological and material conditions linked to patriarchy; others see it as the result of socially constructed binary categories of women and men and assert that discourse and representation are the main processes by which oppression is created and exercised. Significant tensions can be detected between the principle of equality and the right to be different, between individual and collective rights, between public responsibilities and respect for privacy and intimacy, and between values rooted in universal rights and a perspective grounded in systems of social relationships (Dore 1997; Redclift 1997).

Important changes are happening within gender theories. Today, more than in the past, emphasis is being placed on aspects of identity, the body, and desire. There is also much greater recognition of the simultaneous impact on gender within multiple social markers, such as race, ethnicity, and social class, among others (i.e., the growing emergence of intersectionality as an analytical concept in gender studies).

Despite the diversity in gender theories, all of them seek to unmask the existence of the uncontested oppression of women. A prevailing understanding of the gender system contends that it is constructed at three levels: *structural*—supported by the social division of labor, *institutional*—shaped by norms and regulations that guide the distribution of resources and opportunities among men and women, and *symbolic*—framed by conceptions, mentalities, and collective representations of femininity and masculinity (Stromquist 1995; Guzmán 2003). The concept of patriarchy is not used by several feminist theories. However, this concept continues to be useful in enabling us to capture a pervasive gender ideology that places men as the key referent. Patriarchy refers not only to the power that men derive from their ascribed role as heads of family but also to the privileges they derive from state allocations in multiple areas of social and political life.

GENDER IN EDUCATION

Theories of gender in education assert that schools—more than many other social institutions—are actively engaged in the construction of gender. Moreover, because of their *educational* nature, schools play a socially sanctioned ideological role. Theories of gender in education also acknowledge the reproductive nature of schooling, by which knowledge and everyday practice build upon traditional norms and values that position masculinity and femininity in starkly oppositional ways (Davies 2000; Dillabough and Arnot 2000; Lee 2000). These theories, however, also consider that schooling can be transformational through the possibilities that it offers for constant dialogue and consciousness-raising in young and thus malleable minds.

Education exposes individuals to cosmopolitan ideas, rules of evidence, and ethical considerations. Training people to think analytically always carries a revolutionary potential. But you need supportive *content* and *context* to make these ideas flourish. Research on schools identifies them as key sites for the creation of masculinity (Connell 1995, 2000). The evidence from industrialized countries—which can be considered the most democratically advanced societies in terms of gender—signals that gender construction in primary and secondary school remains polarized as boys continue to dominate classroom space and teacher attention while girls' contributions are still discounted. Sexual harassment remains a problem and there is a persistent clustering of field-of-study choices in higher education between women and men (Dillabough 2001; Francis and Skelton 2001).

Schools are unquestionably difficult to change and they tend to reproduce masculinity and femininity through the creation of a variety of same-age and same-sex peer groups whose members spend significant amounts of time together and use one another as main referent individuals.[3] While schools generally tend to maintain traditional norms, some groups of teachers in them challenge tradition and provide mutual support. Unfortunately, they are the few. Not surprisingly, then, many of those who pursue the emancipatory possibilities of education devote attention to the education of adult women in nonformal education settings and through informal learning.

MAPPING GENDER IN SOCIAL SPACE

Gender encounters space in unique ways: both men and women inhabit private and public spaces but those spaces produce starkly differential impacts. There are spatial differences between production and reproduction tasks, between house and work, between remunerated and non-remunerated work. Private spaces are those affecting individual and family lives. Public spaces are those created by the state and non-state actors in broader society (Harcourt 2001).

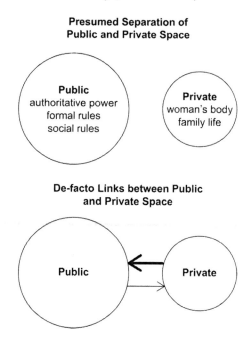

Figure 10.1. Public and Private Space In The Social Construction of Gender.

Despite their different locations, both spaces are deeply interconnected, with the private space strongly affecting the public world. The top half of Figure 10.1 depicts the commonly assumed separation between the public and private space. On the bottom half, the figure shows that there is an interconnection between the two, with the influence of the private sector over the public being the stronger force. Basic as it is, the depiction on the bottom should serve to remind us of the intimate connection between the two spaces.

Private Space

For women, the first type of private space is their body; the second is the domestic place of the home. Women live in spaces that are much more restricted than those of men, predominantly in the home, to which women are tied in their roles as wives, mothers, and household managers.

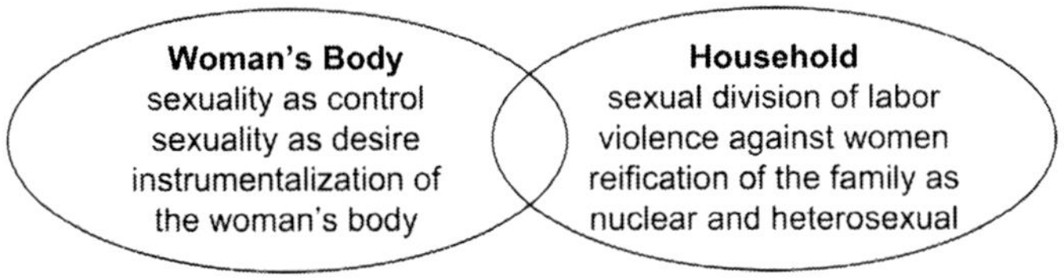

Figure 10.2. The Deep Linkages of Private Space.

Figure 10.2 highlights how a woman's body results in a number of consequences and conditions at the household level; in other words, the household is not just a collective of individuals under the same roof but depends on attributions of the women who occupy this space, particularly on the domestication of women and their subsequent place in management and caring tasks.

Women's Bodies. The body is a critical micro-space through which women emerge both as reproductive beings and as subjects and objects of sexual desire. Dominant social norms tend to repress women's sexuality and frame it mostly in its reproductive, maternal dimension. Although the media portrays cases of women with a great deal of agency, it often treats women as sexual objects, thus presenting contradictory messages. Overall, the social control of women's bodies shapes women's sexuality as submissive and receptive while men's sexuality is naturalized as aggressive and instinctual (and thus uncontrollable); this double standard in the conceptualization of sexuality deeply affects women's life chances because it becomes expanded to other forms of social behavior. In recent years, progress has been made in several nations (usually through the women's movement) to establish more definite legislation against rape and spousal violence; in a handful of countries, legislation against marital rape has been enacted.

Women's bodies are not only contested spaces but spaces that the state and educational policies in particular expressly avoid. The elimination of violence against women and denial of their reproductive rights—including the prerogative to avoid unwanted pregnancies and to have abortions—are part of women's political agendas worldwide. A key difficulty in dealing with the body is that women have been socialized to reserve this space for their most intimate relationships and therefore many avoid problematizing it.

The Household. Domesticity is culturally and economically specific, but women tend to be much more responsible than men for nurturing the family (Ashfar 1987). In the domestic place of the home, social constructions of femininity assign women as full-time mothers, household managers, and wives on an everyday basis. The kitchen is seen as one of the most gendered spaces, in which even women create barriers to the entrance of husbands and sons. Other strongly gendered spaces, especially in less industrialized countries, are the areas where clothes are washed and ironed.

It is now recognized that rules of domestic living reinforce advantages for men and these advantages are extended to institutions outside the home. It was a key insight of the women's movement in the 1960s to realize that "the personal is political."[4] The demands of time and effort required by the household result in multiple and recurrent practices that affect women's capability to enter and act in the public world. Clearly, politics do not exist only outside the home; they derive from transactions that originate at micro levels, including those in the home (Pateman 1988; Giddens 1995; Bowser and Patton 2004). So, in fact, the private and the public world are deeply interconnected. Many issues are yet to be resolved within the family: the structure of family patterns, the sexual division of labor, and the control by others of women's bodies. Consequently, as Anthony Giddens (1995) and many feminist thinkers argue, it is indispensable to politicize the family and not to consider it as a natural institution.

The separation between private and public space is enforced by the state. It is not that the state does not influence the private space; it does in important ways through measures regarding welfare benefits, family law, and marriage conventions. Yet, there still remain a host of issues affecting the private space that are considered out of bounds by the state. These include seemingly innocuous tasks such as the sexual division of labor at home, particularly childcare, but which produce significant time and space constraints for women.

Public Space

The public space encompasses both the state and civil society. The state occupies public space in the form of (a) local governments, the national state, and (b) actors external to the nation state but that seek to influence it. The latter include international financial institutions, bilateral development agencies, and multilateral agencies; these agencies are not autonomous institutions, as their behavior "is conditioned and delimited by state decisions and state power" of their respective member states (Krasner 1985, 28). Civil society occupies the public space in the form of organized nongovernmental organizations (NGOs) such as women's advocacy groups, institutionalized religion, and—in the context of educational issues—teachers' unions.

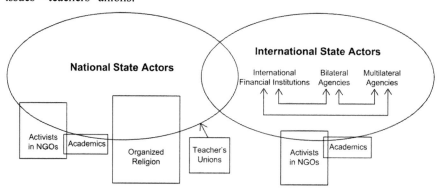

Figure 10.3. Public Space and Education.
Note: Based primarily on three Latin American country studies: Costa Rica, Brazil, and Peru (Stromquist 2006). The overlapping represents roughly the degree of association and influence between and among the entities shown.

Figure 10.3 attempts to depict the overlapping terrain among state actors on the issue of gender. There is a strong interconnection between national and international actors, as well as there are constant connections among bilateral agencies, multilateral organizations, and international financial institutions. The representation of a set of non-state actors (activists working in NGOs, academics working on gender issues, groups representing the dominant religion in a particular country, and teachers' unions) shows starkly different proximity to the state, with organized religion in Latin America occupying the greatest overlap and thus influence on national state actors, and the teachers' unions functioning as a marginal entity. Activists in NGOs do have an impact on the state while academics barely affect it.

State Actors. In the area of education, national governments and international agencies are crucial state actors.

National Governments. Some observers maintain that states have complex and different formations and thus no generalizations are possible (Ashfar 1987). Others further explain that the state comprises a differentiated set of institutions and is a site of constant struggle (Alexander 1991; Rai and Lievesley 1996; Molyneux 2000). In my view, the empirical evidence suggests a less ambiguous picture, with states readily agreeing on the importance of paying attention to gender in their respective societies. A number of positive "global commitments" have been enacted by state organizations, commitments that, at first face, seem solid. However, the set of intentions these commitments ought to encompass is vague and missing procedures for their implementation and monitoring.

Even though feminist theories have expanded the understanding of schooling by recognizing that the curriculum functions as a powerful ideological discourse and that the educational experience of girls and boys is highly gendered, educational policies continue to sidestep around issues of gender ideology and limit themselves to the much safer expedient of equal opportunity, framing it as access to education, particularly access to primary education. Because equality of opportunity concentrates on the access of women to school and women's completion of their education, these policies reduce *gender* to *sex*. Measures to increase access sometimes include social marketing campaigns by which the community and family are told that it is important to allow girls to obtain an education. Such campaigns, however, do not attempt to modify gender ideologies about the sexual division of labor and conceptions of femininity and masculinity. In several countries, particularly in Latin America, girls' enrollment is surpassing that of boys (albeit in small percentages) at the secondary and tertiary levels; consequently, governments in that region are taking the position that gender is *not* an educational problem in their countries. Confusing equal access with equity assumes that school knowledge is gender-neutral and, thus, this policy fails to problematize the nature of the schooling experience.[5]

The policy discourse of governments increasingly proposes "equity." But equity should mean differentiated provision, not just acceptance of the principle of equality of opportunity. True equity, as compensatory measures to attain changes in the condition of girls in education, has been enacted by only a handful of states. What is more, when these compensatory measures are proposed, they focus on vulnerable groups of women: rural girls, poor girls, and illiterate women. This fragments the notion of gender into women/girls with special needs. Again, these compensatory measures do not address discriminatory notions of gender in society but rather result in delimiting the concept.

The school avoids questioning of the private space, despite the fact that such space produces and maintains strong gender ideologies. It has been empirically demonstrated that the family is a critical site for gender socialization and that powerful persuasive and dissuasive messages are emitted there, messages that influence the conceptions and expectations regarding ways of life, work, social relations, and women's and men's education. Likewise, the school avoids discussion of women's bodies and intimate relations between men and women. The physicality of women and men is studied superficially in classes of sexual education, the experience of domestic violence seems to exist only as rumors or in police accounts, and the sexuality of adolescent girls and boys is reduced to disciplinary advice. The responsibilities and expectations linked to a differentiated domestic life for women and men are rarely covered in discussions about civic education and citizenship. The school's failure to consider the citizenship dimensions in the private life is reflected in the persistent disregard of personal relations in the discourses about civic behaviors and procedures (Arnot 2006). By not considering the family/household as a gendered space, the school misses a significant opportunity to question its contribution to the formation of representations of femininity and masculinity and does not prepare young girls and men to construct alternative views of gender.

National policies for social change in gender tend to disregard both gender theories and research findings and, judging from their persistently poor implementation, exist mostly for symbolic purposes (i.e., to generate grounds for state legitimacy). Great importance is attached today to the concept of democratic governance: the need for people to have access to human rights, to engage in decisions that affect their lives, to hold their decision-makers accountable, and to have access to inclusive and fair rules, institutions, and practice. It is also generally acknowledged that women should be equal partners with men in private and public spheres of life (UNDP 2002). Despite these progressive signs, ensuing discussions of democracy consider neither gender nor the gendered nature of contemporary democracy, particularly how the private world intertwines with the public world and thus with citizenship. Moreover, with the emergence of a single major global power in the past two decades—the US—there has been a regression in the conceptualization and support of women's rights. Most notable in this regard, was the US position at the Beijing+10 meeting (held in New York in March 2005) to evaluate progress in the Platform for Action (a document that proposes specific areas for state action, including education). The US sought to introduce an amendment to affirm that the objectives of the Platform for Action "do not create any new international human rights and that they do not include the right to abortion." It eventually dropped the amendment for lack of support by other countries, notably those of the European Union.

There have been, however, improvements in the nature of the school curriculum globally, as many of the most egregious forms of sexual stereotypes have been deleted from textbooks. Educators and policy makers have become more conscious of the sexist practices in school, especially sexual harassment. There has also been progress in the provision of new knowledge, as a number of school systems are moving into the provision of comprehensive sexual education. While the state increasingly addresses sexuality in the public school curriculum, it tends to see it as a matter of health and control, particularly in the face of HIV/AIDS. Moreover, the construction of compartmentalized and mutually exclusive forms of femininity and masculinity are not only taken for granted but persistently supported by the school content and experience.

In short, on the issue of gender, states are rich in policy discourse, poor in theories of action (i.e., the logic that sustains specific interventions), weak in implementation efforts, and stingy in the allocation of resources to promote changes in the social relations of gender. Feminist theory is not used by state actors; the state's avowed interest in gender has not been translated into a theoretical effort to understand and alter it (see Unterhalter 2000). The problems women encounter in the educational arena are reduced to problems of access and completion, thus by implication treating schooling as gender-neutral. The evidence shows that the state keeps a wide distance from non-state actors when addressing gender issues.

International State Actors. These operate in education through the provision of international assistance, which is currently accompanied by global policies. Two major global policies in education today are represented in Education for All (EFA, adopted unanimously by all participating governments in Dakar in 2000) and the Millennium Development Goals (MDGs, adopted by the United Nations, also in 2000). EFA has six objectives, two of which explicitly address gender (Goal No. 2, which seeks universal primary education for all by 2015, and Goal No. 5, which seeks gender parity at primary and secondary education levels by 2005 and at all levels of education by 2015). Both goals reflect one more time an exclusive concern with access and thus the implicit assumption that access, regardless of content, will generate change in the social relations of gender. The MDGs also seek universal primary education for women and men and have an explicit gender-related goal, Goal No. 3, which calls on countries "to promote gender equality and empower women." This goal offers no definition of empowerment, much less from a feminist perspective. The MDGs were decided by state actors without the participation of the women's movement.

The positions of states tend to be in high congruence with those of international financial institutions, bilateral development agencies, and multilateral organizations. This congruence occurs through the frequent contact between these institutions, which share ideas, reports, perspectives, and analyses of educational conditions and problems, as well as the role that gender plays in them. Constant contact creates and strengthens the formation of social networks that reinforce the members' perspectives. Currently, a number of multi-lateral agencies include a gender specialist in most projects; however, their work seldom reflects a "feminist" perspective inasmuch as emphasis is on integration of women in development rather than on questioning of and reframing the conditions under which this integration takes place.

Non-State Actors. Although they occupy spaces outside the state, these entities function within a nation-state. Concerning gender specifically, four groups emerge as key actors: the women's movement and feminist NGOs, academics working on gender issues, the teachers' unions, and religious groups (especially those representing Christian, Islamic, and Hindu ideologies). Some of these actors favor gender changes; others are quite opposed to them. They have different ways of acting on gender concerns, ranging from physical mobilization and lobbying the state to producing transformational knowledge. The influence of this set on non-state actors is much greater at the national level than in the international arena.

Women's Movements and Feminist Organizations. Activists in these groups promote women's collective action. Although women are fractured by differences in race, class, and sexuality, the category "women" has proven to be an adequate basis for mobilization. These groups concentrate on adult women and their claim to material benefits and citizenship rights. They have also advocated the incorporation of gender in all areas of decision-making, a position adopted at the Fourth World Women's Conference (held in Beijing in 1995) and known as gender mainstreaming. These groups pay considerable attention to the private space women experience in their everyday life and attempt to expand women's rights in these spheres by demanding sexual and reproductive rights and striving to eliminate domestic violence against women. Generally, the educational work of these groups focuses on issues of empowerment and income-generation. They uphold formal education as a human right, which means that they assign it a for-granted value and thus fail to question the knowledge and experiences schooling provides (and fails to provide).

The physical spaces provided by NGOs and grassroots groups constitute important venues where gender problems and agendas are shaped. The issues for action involve both distributive policies—those providing new symbolic and material benefits to all within designated categories—as well as redistributive or structural policies—those that seek reallocation of benefits between or among classes, ethnic, racial, gender, or other collectivities (Barnett 1986; Fraser 1997, 1998; Stromquist 2004). In general, feminist NGOs constitute sites that question the status quo while promoting collective action. Since they function outside state control and even surveillance, they can develop into strong sites for emancipatory gender projects. These institutions thus create sites of resistance.

Most of the rights women have achieved in the past three decades can be traced to the activism of the women's movement and the established feminist NGOs. With their sensitivity to and knowledge of the private space, these groups have expanded the view of the political, going beyond electoral politics and the politics of public office to include the power and powerlessness that exists at the micro levels in intimate relationships and the household. Women's groups, especially in Latin America, have made major contributions to the intellectual construction of an "amplified" or "full" citizenship. The women's movement and feminist organizations seek to influence the state through advocacy and lobbying actions but, since they operate with substantial external financial support, they function under a certain amount of political dependency; they must rely upon other groups, such as the international NGOs and some progressive bilateral agencies, for continued assistance. The latter groups, unfortunately, often shift their attention to new issues and thus render the actions of women's groups highly vulnerable to unrenewed funding.

A notable contribution of women's and feminist NGOs is their ability to engage in scalar politics, a term used by Helga Leitner and colleagues (2008) to highlight that, as part of a broader social movement, they can transform local issues into regional, national and global concerns, thus expanding their power. The existence of simultaneous scale levels is difficult to capture in a mapping exercise.

The state, typically, does not consider women's groups as important interlocutors and deals with them only in exceptional instances (generally in response to studies and positions in which the feminist NGOs question state action) and primarily by relying on certain activists as individual consultants rather than as representatives of their organizations (Stromquist 2007). The distance between the state and feminist NGOs is not conducive to social change for key actors are prevented from discussion and participation. The absence of feminist NGOs from dialogue with state actors makes it difficult for the private world to be considered. In the three Latin American countries on which my analysis of the public space is based, no substantial participation of the feminist movement in educational matters was observed, except in the case of Brazil, where there was strong participation to obtain pre-school education although they exerted no pressure to modify school curricula or textbooks at higher levels of schooling.

Feminist Academics. This space is occupied mostly by women and increasingly by pro-feminist men (i.e., men who are able to acknowledge their advantage and to work to modify gender relations).

Feminist academics have contributed the analytical change from *women* (with a focus on disadvantage and discrimination) to *gender* (underscoring the construction of asymmetries, the role of ideology, and power), as well as explorations that go *beyond* gender dichotomies. Their research on education has registered shifts from first centering on the gendered nature of school curricula in the 70s to sexist practices in the school in the 80s to construction of gender identities in the 90s, and now to the role of schools in the development of an amplified citizenship (Dillabough 2001; see also Arnot et al., 1999; Arnot and Dillabough 2000; Moore 2004).

At present, feminist academics can be categorized into two groups: (1) Those in education and such disciplines as sociology, economics, and political science who are concerned with issues of equality, equity, and transforming the relations between women and men in society. These academics endorse collective action as a means to change asymmetries in gender construction. (2) Those in fields such as cultural studies and the humanities, who avoid binary categories such as women and men and seek to develop new conceptualizations that go beyond sex and gender. They give preference to individual action and resistance, and prefer postmodern approaches. Postmodernism is a form of critical theory with considerable influence in gender studies, bringing subjugated knowledges to the fore through the deconstruction of existing texts. Judith Butler (1993, 1999), one of the most influential postmodern gender theoreticians, proposes that women engage in individual performance (or performativity) that goes against social expectations concerning women's behaviors and norms. Postmodernism does not confront subordination through collective political action. Consequently, there is a division among feminist academics in terms of analysis and proposed solutions. The division is often left unspoken, a situation that does not contribute to making the academy a strong site for feminist action.

Important theoretical debates have come up in the academic world involving such questions such as the notion of diffuse power, the possibility of individual agency through performativity as opposed to collective action, the concept of identity construction versus fluid identities, and the use of binary categories versus multiple variations of gender. In the area of citizenship, in particular, the debate going on in the women's movement about its expanded nature is blending public and private areas to consider not only *access* to civil rights (linked to individual freedoms such as the freedoms of speech, thought, and religion as well as the rights to justice, private property, and respect for contracts) but also the *capacity to engage* in civil rights. These debates only marginally pierce state boundaries.

The three Latin American countries upon whose data the discussion of the public space of this study is founded do not reveal participation by feminist scholars in questions regarding formal education. This happens not only because the state keeps a distance from feminist scholars but also because feminist scholars have yet to effectively expose the educational sector as a source of deeply engrained gender ideologies. Occasionally, academics in education influence the state through consultancies. To my knowledge, state agencies do not habitually read articles produced by feminist academics and thus do not keep up to date with ongoing intellectual debates. Postmodern feminists have no contact with the state nor do they seek it.

Institutionalized Religion. There is considerable evidence of the influence of religious authorities in public policies affecting gender. In the case of Latin America, a large number of countries establish in their constitutions a separation between religious and secular power. Nonetheless, the Catholic Church has intervened in subtle yet decisive maneuvers to defend the status quo, particularly to support traditional family values (e.g., motherhood), to promote a single model of family, and to attack any deviation from heterosexuality. The Catholic Church has also played a decisive role in vetoing the development and use of progressive sex-education materials. The Church maintains close contact with state officials through formal liaison mechanisms and abundant informal contacts; further, it influences school curricula through the design and implementation of courses on Catholic religion that cover both primary and secondary school levels.

Teachers' Unions. Professional organizations representing teachers tend to wield significant amounts of power through strikes and support for particular candidates to political office. However, they have not crossed boundaries to influence the state in the area of gender. The teachers' unions' agenda includes the defense of free and high-quality public schools, and they frequently favor issues of personal vindication, such as increased national resources for public education, higher teacher salaries, and limits on the evaluation of teacher performance.[6] It should be recognized that, although teachers' unions do influence the state, they focus on matters linked to their professional performance and status, and thus their demand for a higher public investment in education, better remuneration, and limits to interventions such as teacher evaluations. The country studies of Costa Rica, Peru, and Brazil evinced an absence of teachers' union involvement regarding gender issues, be they related to students or to conditions facing female teachers, such as sexual harassment. Contact between state and teachers' unions is regular, yet it is weakly linked to pedagogical or educational content issues.

UNCERTAIN CONCEPTUAL PROGRESS

Aristotle said in *Ethics* that "reasoning is imperfect if it needs one or more propositions which have not been expressly stated as premises." The exclusion of the private world represents one of the most egregious unstated premises in the treatment of gender by those who hold formal power. In gender and education, stark boundaries have been erected between public and private space. The private world, with its personal mix of the body and household relations, is persistently avoided by the state and various state-related agencies.

The failure to address the inequities of the private sphere and to establish connections with the women's movement and feminist activists and academics signals that the state prefers to do gender without feminism and to pursue gender equality without its main advocates—those in the women's movement. Relations between the state and the women's movement occur through interstices, rather than through established and stable connections as is the case with international state actors. Aggravating this situation is the limited circulation of ideas from theories produced in the academy among feminist NGOs or members of the women's movement—and vice versa, as actions and products of the women's movement and feminist NGOs are seldom utilized by academic feminists. This tends to establish a barrier to a possible mutual enrichment between these two important non-state actors.

Many terrains exist and they are diverse and crossed on an everyday basis, but such boundary crossing is done much more frequently by individuals and activists from civil society than by institutions and state officials. The public space is dominated by state actors, which prefer to decide and plan by themselves rather than—especially in the case of gender—to seek the participation of the women's movement or feminists in the academy.

There is significant overlapping among national and international state actors, which show consensus in defining gender issues in fragmented ways ("indigenous women," "rural girls," "poor families") and through responses that leave the ideological constitution of gender untouched. Two consequences result: First, the state's response focuses mostly on formal education, thus missing the mode of education most likely to facilitate social change—nonformal education. Second, within formal education gender issues are defined as equality of opportunity and linked only to conditions of particularly disadvantaged groups of women. This conjunction is no accident but rather reflects the state's willingness to protect the patriarchal nature of subordination and continued control of women. Since there is little boundary crossing by state actors, limited circulation of gender theories or feminist perspectives reaches the government. Contentious politics need to pay attention to socio-spatial organization; organizations shape one another through their co-presence and affect the trajectory of contentious politics (Leitner et al., 2008).

Despite the fact that the state *avoids* terrains such as the private space and explicitly *ignores* locations such as the women's NGOs and the university (where most feminist academics reside), there has been discernable progress in the improvement of women's conditions and in the move toward greater gender equality. Among the gains, we can list the increased presence of organized and informed women's groups, a growing social acceptance of women's rights as fundamental human rights, greater understanding of the factors related to gender inequalities and their interconnection and reinforcement, a growing number of pro-feminist men—aware of their privilege and willing to modify it, and a larger and more comprehensive body of laws that secure women's political and economic rights such as those governing property rights, divorce, electoral quotas, and various forms of violence against women.

In balance, there has been greater progress for women in the securing of attention and rights in the public rather than the private space. The public space, however, comprises multiple actors and divergent views, and is characterized by little communication between state actors and the non-state actors that represent women's interests. Some patterns are visible: among those entities with power—the national state and the bilateral/multilateral agencies—there is movement toward convergent positions best defined as a modest understanding of gender and limited action to address it, namely, more emphasis on expanding access to schooling but much less on questioning and transforming the content of what is learned and the nature of the schooling experience. Among those without formal political power (the feminist NGOs and the feminist academics) there is an increasingly divergent understanding, with NGOs tending to advocate equality for women and men (and thus deploying binary categories such as "women" and "men"), and many in the academic world moving into discourse or a "cultural turn" (i.e., privileging the impact of language in the formation of identities), while minimizing the impact of differences in material conditions and being hesitant about endorsing dichotomies such as women and men.

Men continue to dominate the public space and, while in popular culture women are said to dominate the private space, they in fact are relegated to it. It would seem that men have not had the opportunity to reflect on alternative masculinities. Why? Nobody has prevented them. Perhaps they have not had the motivation to explore these matters from their position of privilege. At present there is very little training of male authorities in gender issues and thus their lack of understanding about the impact of various policy interventions (or lack of interventions) on gender. The patriarchal model of governance and authority has not been totally eradicated even though it continues to lose its legitimacy in a stronger discourse of democracy. There have been changes in public discourses so that equality has gained terrain in the symbolic dimension, which helps individual capacities to monitor public action. But effective efforts to make equality real are still a handful.

Linking gender theories to government policies and practices also remains sorely needed. For women there are very few spaces where they encounter state agents. Articulation of the academic debate with personnel in governmental offices and community leaders is practically non-existent. Moreover, with some precious exemptions, academics working on gender are by and large physically and cognitively distant from the women's movement. An essential part of the new consensus must bring back into the analysis and political project the critical importance of the material and practical dimensions of gender inequality.

Understanding gender means both *recognizing* complex relations and *changing* unfavorable situations and perceptions. But let us not allow complexity to render political action remote or unlikely. Women need to give special attention to politics and women need to receive special attention in theories of politics. Women, particularly Third World women, including Blacks and Latinas in US society, pertain to disadvantaged groups—those with limited power and for whom the normal political process (especially voting for male candidates) has not worked to their favor. Therefore, women must act through alternative political mechanisms, such as protest and alliance-formation (Barnett 1986). The pending feminist agenda is large: more attention to women's reproductive health and sexual rights, the introduction of electoral quotas to ensure women's participation in formal political office, better alliances between government and civil society, and more sustained gender training for state officials. The state must continue to be a target of feminist action and strong efforts to link the public and private space must be made. A strategic alliance between feminist NGOs, feminist scholars in the academy, and teachers' unions will be more able to develop clearly gender-related objectives, maximizing the fact that the majority of primary school teachers—in most regions of the world—are women and an increasing number of those at the secondary school level are also women.

CONTRIBUTIONS AND LIMITATIONS OF SOCIAL CARTOGRAPHY

When applied to the analysis of gender in education, social cartography explains the influence of various actors upon each other. This influence is affected by the distance they keep from each other, which in turn facilitates or makes difficult engagement in discussions of varying points of view. The tenuous linkage between feminist NGOs and state actors enables national governments to persist in frames of educational issues in ways that do not contest gender ideologies. Certainly, the distance does not emerge by chance but is the product of studied avoidance.

Social cartography has enabled us to explore the various space linkages affecting gender in education. Social mapping enables us to detect space, sites, and social actors in interaction. We can represent solid and blurred boundaries among institutions, show their overlapping, and the partition of social space as a whole. At the same time, the graphic device does not enable us to capture differences in scale and power. Therefore, visualization of social phenomena must be, by force, accompanied by a detailed narrative. The two approaches are very complementary, for narrative discourse emphasizes temporality and pays less attention to spatiality (Ruitenberg 2007).

Social cartography is less also successful in incorporating the time dimension. Yet, space and time are closely interconnected. Any temporal dimension is connected to its space and the space of social phenomena depends in turn on temporal dimensions. The inability of social cartography to represent time results in somewhat static depictions of reality; also, this inability does not enable researchers to incorporate key events that might have significantly altered existing relations. The time dimension can only be captured through a detailed narrative.

While multiple spaces usually emerge within a single frame of time, some spaces tend to have their own time and some institutions located in them become prisoners of their own initial perception. Sites do not produce identities independent of time; identities become altered or questioned by changing contexts and ideas over different historical periods. As Richard Teese (2007) admonishes us, it is crucial not only to consider contemporary barriers but to be sensitive to the accumulation of advantage or disadvantage over time, as historical patterns that create hierarchies of knowledge and power are imposed on each new generation of students. On the other hand, although time affects all social actors and institutions inasmuch as organizations—particularly state actors—recognize only certain forces and influences, it is possible for their positions to become frozen in time (i.e., to lag behind conceptual developments in sectors with whom state actors have no contact).

This study has been based on a social cartography to enable us to illuminate the relations between spaces and sites that construct gender in society and especially in the area of education. Through the use of social cartography, the fragility of the dichotomous nature of public and private space is exposed, and connections between mutually supportive and opposing institutions are put in evidence. At the same time, the limitation of social cartography in capturing time dimensions and multilayered dynamics is acknowledged. In balance, social cartography serves a crucial function by enabling the clear identification of sites of gender reproduction as well as gender transformation. This methodology permits the identification of key spaces and the connections between various sites, connections that, when close, facilitate convergence and, when distant, reinforce different perspectives in framing the problematique of gender. The mapping of private and public spaces we have attempted in this chapter contributes to discovering similarities and differences between social actors and also within them. This is not an empty exercise as it leads to carefully assessing the possibilities for social and cultural change.

Key social institutions act in unison to produce dominant views of gender. Their strong collaboration is reflected in close communication between them and frequent joint action. Institutions that hold counter-hegemonic views of gender are distant and marginalized. States and international agencies consider each other implicitly the only legitimate interlocutors and thus are distant from being democratic; this pushes aside the role of women and feminist NGOs, which tend to be institutions with the strongest drive to alter perceptions and practices regarding gender in society. The framing of gender by states and international agencies tends to conceptualize gender problems essentially as those linked to access, thus leaving untouched questions of ideology and self-interest in the preservation of the status quo. Applied to the educational arena, both national budgets and international loans and grants focus on issues of educational parity, which involves increasing the educational supply and, in a few instances, altering the educational demand by making it easier for poor families to invest in their daughters' education. Little attention is paid to the reproductive role of the formal educational system through the hidden curriculum and through the still gender-biased educational materials and practices. Unfortunately, the consensus on the part of these national and international actors in framing gender issues exclusively as one of social and economic inequality blinds them to a deeper understanding of the ideological foundations of this inequality and prevents them from reaching individuals and groups with alternative understandings of the functioning of gender.

The distance created between state and certain non-state actors is considerable, impervious to change, and unproductive. It tends in this case to preserve the status quo of gender in society and accounts for the enduring characteristics of conventional education policies. The careful mapping of distances, locations, and interconnections, as well as the identification of multiple actors and the terrains they occupy in the public spheres enables scholars to highlight intense points of gender reproduction as well as likely sites through which gender notions may be reconceptualized and transformed. In the same way that unequal geographies are produced between urban and rural sites, with the latter operating in greater isolation and thus less advantaged than urban sites (Teese 2007), unequal geographies also emerge between the private and the public sphere, with the latter commanding more attention, more protection, and more resources.

The sites in which gender is created and reproduced on a daily basis are multiple. At the same time, the key sites are a small number. The interaction between state-controlled sites gives them mutual support to resist efforts from the challenging feminist sites. The identification of public and private spaces as well as of the actors that inhabit them is fundamental to the framing and design of public policies. To carry out successful actions in this regard it will be necessary to cross certain boundaries, especially those that will permit the construction of new alliances—as would be the case between feminist NGOs and feminist scholars working in universities.

Societies are constituted by multiple overlapping and intersecting socio-spatial networks of power. This applies with great relevance to the issue of gender. Expanding on the notion of intersecting spaces, Randall Collins (2004) notes that ideas themselves are the product of social networks. The use of space as an analytical construct in discussing gender is not merely a metaphor but in key instances stands for real terrains and locations. I have sought to widen our understanding of gender in society and gender in education by demonstrating the existence and differential power of different social actors and their location. Those who seek a transformation in the social relations of gender inhabit spaces quite distant from those who hold formal power, with substantial boundaries between them. The development of convergent positions among these non-state actors emerges as an unavoidable step if women are to move from the margins into the center.

NOTES

1. The American scholar who introduced social cartography to comparative education is Rolland G. Paulston (1996), in honor of whom this book has been produced.
2. The study was conducted by national researchers of those three countries and involved content analysis of national education policy documents and interviews of policy-makers and those with implementing responsibilities.
3. In many parts of the world, certainly in the US and in Latin America, schools use the space and time of physical education to transmit gender values and ideologies that tend to divide girls and boys in different fields of physical force and aggression through games, exercises, and dances. Aisenstein and Scharagrodsky (2006) present valuable related insights in their study of Argentinean schools.
4. The author of this phrase is Carol Hanisch (1975) who, in a brief essay entitled "The Personal is Political," first expressed the concept in 1969 in the Redstockings Collection entitled *Feminist Revolution*, reprinted in 1975. Earlier, sociologist C. Wright Mills had remarked on the intersection between public issues and personal problems in his classic, *The Sociological Imagination* (1959), although it seems women arrived at the same conclusion independently.
5. In the US gender parity in basic education was reached in 1850. If access to education is the entire solution to gender inequalities there would have been no women's movement in this country in the twentieth century.
6. The reader should remember that I am describing the situation in Latin America. In countries such as Canada and the UK, women teachers, building on the fact they constitute the majority of teachers' union members—have engaged in political action toward gender change.

REFERENCES

Alexander, Jacqui. (1991). "Redrafting Morality: The Postcolonial State and the Sexual Offences Bill of Trinidad and Tobago." In Chandra Talpade Mohanty, Ann Russo, and Lourdes Torres (Ed.), *Third World Women and the Politics of Feminism.* (pp. 133–152). Bloomington, IN: Indiana University Press.
Aisenstein, Angela, & Pablo Scharagrodsky. (2006). *Tras las Huellas de la Educación Física Escolar Argentina. Cuerpo, Género y Pedagogía,. 1880–1950.* Buenos Aires: Prometeo Libros.
Arnot, Madeleine. (2006). "Freedom's Children: A Gender Perspective on the Education of the Learner-Citizen." *International Review of Education, 52*(1), 67–87.
Arnot, Madeleine, Miriam David, & Gaby Weiner. (1999). *Closing the Gender Gap in Education.* Cambridge, UK: Polity Press.

Arnot, Madeleine, & Jo-Anne Dillabough, eds. (2000). *Challenging Democracy: International Perspectives on Gender, Education and Citizenship.* London: Routledge/Farmer.

Ashfar, Haleh, ed. (1987). *Women, State, and Ideology.* Albany, NY: State University of New York Press.

Barnett, Marguerite. (1986). "The Politics of Scarcity: New Directions for Political Science Research on Gender, Race and Poverty in America." In Marguerite R. Barnett, Charles C. Harrington, and Philip V. White (Ed.), *Readings on Equal Education,* Vol. 9: *Education Policy in an Era of Conservative Reform.* (pp. 213–230). New York: AMS Press.

Black, Jeremy. (1997). *Maps and Politics.* London: Reaktion Books.

Bondi, Liz, & Damaris Rose. (2003). "Constructing Gender, Constructing the Urban: A Review of Anglo-American Feminist Urban Geography." *Gender, Place and Culture, 10*(3), 229–245.

Bowser, Brenda, & John Patton. (2004). "Domestic Spaces as Public Places: An Ethnoarchaeological Case Study of Houses, Gender, and Politics in the Ecuadorian Amazon." *Journal of Archaeological Method and Theory, 11*(2), 157–181.

Butler, Judith. (1993). *Bodies That Matter. On the Discursive Limits of Sex.* New York: Routledge.

Butler, Judith. (1999). *Gender Trouble and the Subversion of Identity.* London: Routledge.

Collins, Randall. (2004). *Interaction Ritual Chains.* Princeton, NJ: Princeton University Press.

Connell, Robert. (1995). *Masculinities.* St. Leonards, Australia: Allen & Unwin.

Connell, Robert. (2000). *The Men and the Boys.* Cambridge, UK: Polity Press.

Davies, Lynn. (2000). "The Civil School and Civil Society. Gender, Democracy and Development." In Madeleine Arnot and Jo-Anne Dillabough (Ed.), *Challenging Democracy: International Perspectives on Gender, Education and Citizenship.* (pp. 278–296). London: Routledge/Farmer.

Dillabough, Jo-Anne. (2001). "Gender Theory and Research in Education: Modernity Traditions and Emerging Contemporary Themes." In Becky Francis and Christine Skelton (Ed.), *Investigating Gender: Contemporary Perspectives in Education.* (pp. 11–26). Buckingham, UK: Open University Press.

Dillabough, Jo-Anne, & Madeleine Arnot. (2000). "Feminist Political Frameworks." In Madeleine Arnot and Jo-Anne Dillabough (Ed.), *Challenging Democracy: International Perspectives on Gender, Education and Citizenship.* (pp. 21–40). London: Routledge/Farmer.

Dore, Elizabeth. (1997). "The Holy Family. Imagined Households in Latin American History." In Elizabeth Dore (Ed.), *Gender Politics in Latin America: Debates in Theory and Practice.* (pp. 101–117). New York: Monthly Review Press.

Francis, Becky, & Christine Skelton. (2001). "Introduction." In Francis Becky and Christine Skelton (Ed.), *Investigating Gender: Contemporary Perspectives in Education.* (pp. 1–7). Buckingham, UK: Open University Press.

Fraser, Nancy. (1997). *Justice Interruptus: Critical Reflections on the "Postsocialist" Condition.* New York: Routledge.

Giddens, Anthony. (1995). *Affluence, Poverty and the Idea of a Post-Scarcity Society.* Discussion Paper 63. Geneva, Switzerland: United Nations Research Institute for Social Development.

Guzmán, Virginia. (2003). *Gobernabilidad Democrática y Género, una Articulación Posible.* Santiago: Unidad Mujer y Desarrollo, UN Economic and Social Commission.

Hanisch, Carol. (1975). "The Personal is Political." In *Redstockings of the Women's Liberation Movement. Feminist Revolution.* New York: Random House.

Harcourt, Wendy. (2001). "Rethinking Difference and Equality: Women and the Politics of Place." In Roxann Prazniak and Arif Dirlik (Ed.), *Places and Politics in an Age of Globalization.* (pp. 299–322). Lanham, MD: Rowman & Littlefield.

Krasner, Stephen. (1985). *Structural Conflict: The Third World against Global Liberalism.* Berkeley, CA: University of California Press.

Lee, Sue. (2000). "Sexuality and Citizenship." In Madeleine Arnot and Jo-Anne Dillabough (Ed.), *Challenging Democracy: International Perspectives on Gender, Education and Citizenship.* (pp. 259–277). London: Routledge/Farmer.

Leitner, Helga, Eric Sheppard, & Kristin Sziarto. (2008). "The Spatialities of Contentious Politics." *Transactions of the Institute of British Geographers, 33*(2), 157–172.

Mills, C. Wright. (1959). *The Sociological Imagination.* New York: Oxford Press.

Molyneux, Maxine. (2000). "Twentieth-Century State Formations." In Elizabeth Dore and Maxine Molyneux (Ed.), *Hidden Histories of Gender and the State in Latin America.* Durham, NC: Duke University Press.

Moore, Rob. (2004). *Education and Society: Issues and Explanations in the Sociology of Education.* Cambridge, UK: Polity Press.

Pateman, Carole. (1988). *The Sexual Contract.* Cambridge, UK: Polity Press.

Paulston, Rolland G., ed. (1996). *Social Cartography: Mapping Ways of Seeing Social and Educational Change.* New York: Garland Publishing.

Peet, Richard. (1998). *Modern Geographical Thought.* Oxford, UK: Blackwell Publishers.

Rai, Shirin, & Geraldine Lievesley. (1996). "Women and the State." In Shirin Rai (Ed.), *Women and the State: International Perspectives..* New York: Taylor & Francis.

Redclift, Nanneke. (1997). "Conclusion: Post Binary Bliss: Towards a New Materialist Synthesis?" In Elizabeth Dore (Ed.), *Gender Politics in Latin America: Debates in Theory and Practice* (pp. 222–236). New York: Monthly Review Press.

Ruitenberg, Claudia. (2007). "Here be Dragons: Exploring Cartography in Educational Theory and Research." *Complicity: An International Journal of Complexity and Education, 4*(1), 7–21.

Sack, Robert. (1986). *Human Territoriality: Its Theory and History.* Cambridge, UK: Cambridge University Press.

Siekierska, Eva. C(1995). "From the Task Force on Women in Cartography to the ICA Working Group on Gender and Cartography: What We Learned." Ottawa: Geomatics Canada, National Resources Canada. Available online at: http://www.geo.ar.wroc.pl.

Stromquist, Nelly P. (1995). "Romancing the State: Gender and Power in Education." *Comparative Education Review, 39*(4), 423–454.

Stromquist, Nelly P. (2004). "The Impact of Globalization on Gender and Education: An Emergent Cross-National Balance." *Keynote speech delivered at the Kenton Conference*, Drakensberg, South Africa, 30 September-3 October 2004.

Stromquist, Nelly P., ed. (2006). *La Construcción de Género en las Políticas Públicas: Perspectivas Comparadas desde América Latina.* Lima: Instituto de Estudios Peruanos.

Stromquist, Nelly P. (2007). *Feminist Organizations and Social Transformation in Latin America.* Boulder, CO: Paradigm Publishers.

Teese, Richard. (2007). "Time and Space in the Reproduction of Educational Inequality." In Richard Teese, Stephen Lamb, and Marie Duru-Bellat (Ed.), *International Studies in Educational Inequality, Theory and Policy*, Vol. 2,. (pp. 1–21.). Dordrecht, The Netherlands: Springer.

Unterhalter, Elaine. (2000). "Transnational Visions of the 1990s: Contrasting Views of Women, Education and Citizenship." In Madeleine Arnot and Jo-Anne Dillabough (Ed.), *Challenging Democracy: International Perspectives on Gender, Education and Citizenship.* (pp. 87–102). London: Routledge/Farmer.

United Nations Development Programme (UNDP). (2002). *Human Development Report 2002: Deepening Democracy in a Fragmented World.* New York: UNDP.

HALLA B. HOLMARSDOTTIR

11. MAPPING THE DIALECTIC BETWEEN GLOBAL AND LOCAL EDUCATIONAL DISCOURSES ON GENDER EQUALITY AND EQUITY

INTRODUCTION

It may be argued that in 1990 the global campaign on education began with the start of the Education for All (EFA) movement, a result of the World Conference on Education for All in Jomtien, Thailand. This brought about a new era in educational research focusing on issues such as the "world institutionalization of education" (Meyer and Ramirez 2000), "global governance" (Mundy 2006), or more recently the "harmonization of education" (Tröhler 2010).

> In the past two or three decades we have been witnessing an ongoing worldwide assimilation of the different national educational systems. This process has been promoted by international organizations such as the World Bank or the International Monetary Fund investing millions of dollars in the school systems of poorer countries on the condition that organizational structures and governance systems that proved to be successful in the rich countries are implemented. The effects of this global governance are quite tangible. (Tröhler 2010, 5)

The result has not only been the way in which education systems are affected, but also involves how we view various issues within education (Meyer and Ramirez 2000). Linked to the idea of global governance in education Karen Mundy (2006, 24) points out that EFA "has steadily built momentum as a focus for discussion and action within the international community." As a result, EFA and other global agendas have "become part of a broadly based consensus about 'what works' among bilateral and multilateral development agencies." One of the key issues found within the EFA movement, which has been accepted as part of the global consensus of "what works" is the emphasis on gender within education. This emphasis has, however, mainly focused on the quantitative aspects of gender, namely gender parity. Accordingly, we currently have significant knowledge about the causes and consequences of the low participation rates for girls and young women in education, with much of the research data consisting of evidence collected through large scale quantitative studies focusing on the numbers of girls in school (Colclough et al., 1998; Wiseman 2008). Consequently, a considerable amount of research has focused on access to education and to some degree on retention (King and Hill 1993; Brock

John C. Weidman, W. James Jacob (eds.), Beyond the Comparative: Advancing Theory and Its Application to Practice, 193–215.

and Cammish 1997; Colclough et al., 1998; Swainson et al., 1998; Bendera 1999; Wiseman 2008; Baker and Wiseman 2009). There have, however, been fewer studies that have taken a more in-depth qualitative approach in examining the local realities of the school environment and the community.

Accordingly, this chapter is an attempt to understand the key issues related to gender and education as part of a larger research project entitled Gender Equality, Education and Poverty (GEEP), funded by the Norwegian Programme for Development, Research and Education (NUFU). The project encompasses critical questions surrounding gender equality, equity, and education within a context of poverty in post-conflict South Africa and Sudan. The understanding is that the social production of gender is inseparable from that of race, sexuality, class, nationality, ability and other categories of difference. The project places feminist concerns within a transnational context, while respecting the need for geographic and historical specificity. Thus, the understanding in the GEEP project is that gender equality in education is a challenging issue in both South Africa and Sudan and as such our focus is on both the similarities and differences in these two contexts. The ways in which gender issues are understood globally and, in particular, in these two contexts depend on how gender, equality, and education are defined and how the consequences of this are assessed.

According to the global discourses surrounding gender within education, education is about the school system and as a result the focus has primarily been on counting the number of girls and boys enrolled in different phases of education. However, as Elaine Unterhalter (2005a, 77) argues this is "a descriptive and primarily biological meaning of gender and a very simple understanding of equality as equal numbers." This criticism suggests that the simplistic focus on numbers has not encouraged us to "understand education much more broadly than schooling." Furthermore, she points out that our challenge then remains to "look at processes of developing political and cultural understandings and the capacity for action between different socially situated gendered groups in a range of different settings, including, but not only comprising schooling," the equity issues. In taking up this challenge I will attempt to examine what we know and do not know within the theory domain on gender and education, focusing specifically around the concepts of equality and equity and using South Africa and Sudan as examples of how global policy initiatives are interpreted and acted upon in local contexts; the local context at this juncture will be focused on the policy level. In doing so my concern is to provide a critical analysis of how the global consensus to advance gender equality and equity in education are understood. This will be achieved through a visualizing exercise in which I will map the discourses surrounding the key issues mentioned above. Ultimately, the goal is for this analysis to serve as an exchange of ideas to build upon and thus increase global awareness around the issue of gender within education.

MAPPING—WHY AND HOW

In this chapter, I attempt to respond to Rolland G. Paulston's (2005, 2) impossible challenge which is: "to acknowledge the partiality of one's story (indeed, of all stories) and still tell it with authority and conviction." Overall the chapter focuses on how the global discourses surrounding gender within education can be visualized through Paulston's (1996) mapping method and how these are interpreted and acted upon in local contexts.

According to Rolland G. Paulston and Martin Liebman (1996, 7) "the writing and reading of maps . . . [addresses] questions of location in the social milieu." Thus social cartography illustrates the use of metaphor as a visual way of constructing meaning, a visual dialogue. However, maps are never neutral documents. Since the process of mapping encourages personal interpretation of specific criteria in representing spatial relationships among differing ideas, social cartography relies heavily upon the use of the visual metaphor as an explanatory device to bring about further discussion. Hence, by conducting this mapping exercise it is not my intention to suggest that my views are necessarily shared in the broader social context, but it is simply to visualize the discourses in the field in order to initiate a dialogue between the research group which I am part of and between this group and the larger research community involved in gender-based research. Furthermore, such mapping exercises are a useful device for summarizing and communicating information and it is argued that some individuals may encode information more effectively as images rather than words (Paivio 1986; Clark and Paivio 1991).

In addition to seeing maps as a way of communicating information, we may also see them as a methodological tool. Borrowing from social network theory Val D. Rust (1996) explains how maps consist of nodes (represented by points in the diagram) and ties (represented by lines in the diagram). A node represents the actors and lines represent the ties between actors. Rust (45) argues that "in mapping the intellectual landscape . . . a node is not necessarily a person, but can be either a text or a particular theoretical orientation. Lines represent the kind of interactions or relationships that exist between different texts or theoretical orientations." The nodes in my mapping represent the discourses, located in policy documents, surrounding gender within education, both at the global and local levels with the lines representing the ties between these discourses. In attempting to conceptualize what maps are Anne S. Huff (1996, 163–164) suggests that: "maps can be placed on a continuum . . . and that the relationships ultimately chosen for mapping depend upon the purpose of the map. . . . It is possible, however, to group the purposes of mapping . . . into at least five 'families'." The five "families" suggested by Huff are: maps that assess attention, association and importance of concepts; maps that show dimensions of categories and cognitive taxonomies; maps that show influence, causality and system dynamics; maps that show structure of argument and conclusion; and maps that specify schemas, frames and perceptual codes. Given that there are a range of techniques available within each of these families it is also believed that "in practice map makers often use more than one approach to mapping" (165). Ultimately, my maps fall into Huff's first category as I attempt to assess the attention, association and importance of the concepts equality and equity in terms of gender.

Having discussed the why and how with regard to my mapping exercise I would also like to reflect on the usefulness of maps in what is described by Paulston (1996) as a postmodern exercise. Steven Best and Doug Kellner (n.d.) argue that:

Maps and theories provide orientation, overviews, and show how parts relate to each other and to a larger whole. If something new appears on the horizon, a good map will chart it, including sketches of some future configurations. And while some old maps and authorities are discredited and obsolete, some traditional theories continue to provide guideposts for current thought and action.

Yet we also need new sketches of society and culture, and part of the postmodern adventure is sailing forth into new domains without complete maps, or with maps that are fragmentary and torn. Journeys into the postmodern thus thrust us into new worlds, making us explorers of uncharted, or poorly charted, domains. Our mappings can thus only be provisional, reports back from our explorations that require further investigation, testing, and revision. Yet the brave new worlds of postmodern culture and society are of sufficient interest, importance, and novelty to justify taking chances, leaving the familiar behind, and trying out new ideas and approaches.

Before I journey into the uncharted territory I have discussed above I will first explore the waters of the postmodern world, which I believe will provide me with some direction in trying out my new ideas.

POSTMODERN REFLECTIONS

In the last few decades, postmodernist critiques have increasingly dominated scholarship in the social sciences and humanities. Postmodernism is not easily summarized in a single idea as it has been conceptualized by various theorists in several disciplines. The overall focus of postmodernists is their questioning of "metatheories" (Rorty 1989), "regimes of truth" (Foucault 1980) or avoidance of what Jean-Francois Lyotard (1984) refers to as "grand narratives." Lyotard questions the attempt of grand narratives to explain everything and in a sense simply argues that no theory is able to explain everything. "These theories, whether in the Marxist or the liberal tradition, are no longer seen as "the truth" but simply as privileged discourses that deny and silence competing, dissident voices" (Connelly et al., 2000, 136). Reflecting on dissident voices Lyotard (1984, xxv) suggests that "postmodern knowledge is not simply a tool of the authorities; it refines our sensitivity to differences and reinforces our ability to tolerate the incommensurable."

The use of the term postmodern in this chapter as can be seen as a family resemblance (Wittgenstein 1953) or a hybrid (Popkewtiz 2000) of the different literature presented, which have certain epistemological assumptions in analyzing knowledge, change and power. One particular feature of postmodernism is the "linguistic turn" highlighting the interplay of various signs and symbols. The linguistic turn was apparent in Foucault's (1989) analysis of the past generation, which involved calling into question the control of speakers and writers over their own discourse. In his work Foucault centered his attention on knowledge and power, demonstrating that power is exercised not by force and instead "through the practices by which knowledge (the rules of reason) structures the field of possible action and inscribes the principles of performance and modes of subjectification" (Popkewtiz 2000, 262).

Reflecting on knowledge, language and truth Andrew Uduigwomen (2005) argues that:

> Lyotard and Foucault, for instance, reject any attempt to ground reality in one all-encompassing theory or system of thought. . . . Reality or truth thus ceases to be defined in terms of a correspondence to a fixed entity that the descriptions and manipulations provided in our language must perfectly fit. Rather the preponderant view is that reality both conforms to language and is shaped by it. Language, as it were, is the repository of a people's culture. Culture itself is a complex phenomenon which revels variety. . . . The epistemological and metaphysical implication of this is that truth or reality is neither one nor objective but subjective and many. Lyotard posits that there are many discourses and the rules governing these discourses differ in corresponding proportion to socio-cultural and linguistic variations. Thus, our understanding of reality and interpretation of truth must differ in accordance with and reflect the linguistic and cultural variations.

Thus, it is argued that culture is a field of struggle and as a result language, culture and education should include a plurality of values, voices and intentions. This plurality of voices is seen in postmodernism's "questioning of totalizing, universalizing theory . . . situated [not only] within a post-imperialist world where colonial 'others' have emerged as subjects in their own right" (Lather 1991, 31), but also in postmodern feminist questioning of universalist knowledge.

Hence, postmodern scholarship has also manifested itself in feminist research (Lather 1991) focusing on, for example, women's lived experiences (Harding 1991). At the heart of postmodern feminism is the sensitivity to the multiple voices of "women" and the recognition of manifold perspectives. For Patti Lather (1991, 21) the "essence of the postmodern argument is that the dualisms which continue to dominate Western thought are inadequate for understanding a world of multiple causes and effects interacting in complex ways." More recently postmodernism (also poststructuralism) has moved away from the idea of speaking for *all* women. Lather (27) points out that in essence the speaking for *all* women "was disrupted by the political pressures put upon such theorizing by those left out of it—poor and working-class women, women of color, lesbians." This criticism of the production of grand narratives in speaking for *all* women corresponds with the developments over the last 10–15 years in which gender and language have been reconceptualized (e.g., Butler 1990).

> The assumption of women as an already constituted, coherent group with identical interests and desires, regardless of class, ethnic, or racial location, or contradictions, implies a notion of gender or sexual difference or even

patriarchy that can be applied universally and cross-culturally. (Mohanty 2004, 21)

Accordingly postmodernism coincides with a move from focusing exclusively on women and speaking for *all* women to postcolonial critiques of Western feminism and the tendency to assume that the experiences of Western women are the same for *all* women. Postmodernism has also signalled a move from focusing primarily on women to that of gender.

Gender has come to be seen not as a prior category that affects how people speak, but as a contextualized achievement brought into being in particular contexts. The focus is on how aspects of gender are produced as salient, represented and given meaning and significance within everyday life across various cultural and social settings.

Gender is also seen not so much as an independent category, but rather as intricately embedded in other social divisions: race, class, age, sexuality and so on, all of which are in turn embedded within—and (re-)produced by— structures of power, authority and social inequality. (Swann and Maybin 2008, 23)

The frequently cited claim that gender is socially or discursively constructed finds one of its homes in postmodernism (Butler 1990). However, postmodernism has figured more prominently in its overall questioning of power and authority (Foucault 1980). In attempting to question power and authority in my mapping I place my work within Habermas' (1971) reasoning that there are three categories of human interest that underscore knowledge claims: prediction, understanding, emancipation. Lather (1991, 6) adds a fourth category of deconstruction arguing that each of these "postpositivist 'paradigms' offers a different approach to generating and legitimating knowledge." Accordingly, my mapping exercise is placed both within understanding and deconstruction as the actual map will help to comprehend the dialectic between the global and the local through a deconstruction of how the various texts function (Derrida 1991). Deconstruction is then "a way of thinking ... about the danger of what is powerful and useful. ... You deconstruct-ively critique something which is so useful that you cannot speak another way" (Rooney 1989, 135, 151). Moreover, Lather (1991, 13) argues that "deconstruction foregrounds the lack of innocence in any discourse by looking at the textual staging of knowledge, the constitutive effects of our uses of language."

MAPPING THE GLOBAL DISCOURSES ON GENDER EQUALITY AND EQUITY

Recovering the lives of women from the neglect of historians was the goal of women's history from its inception. Its methodology and interests have evolved over time as it has become established as an academic discipline. From its early origins in cataloguing great women in history, in the 1970s it turned to recording ordinary women's expectations, aspirations and status. Then, with the rise of the feminist movement, the emphasis shifted in the

1980s towards exposing the oppression of women and examining how they responded to discrimination and subordination. In more recent times women's history has moved to charting female agency, recognising women's strategies, accommodations and negotiations within a male dominated world. Although it developed out of the feminist agenda, gender history has somewhat different objectives. Recognising that femininity and masculinity are to some extent social constructs, it investigates how institutions are gendered and how institutions gender individuals. In a short space of time gender has become an indispensable category for historical analysis alongside class and race. (Bailey 2005)

In the quote above Joanne Bailey demonstrates that there is no single agenda or mode of discourse linked to feminist research. Instead the women's movement opened up new questions and strategies for change by expanding and building gender differentiated meanings and positions on a number of issues. Furthermore, postcolonical feminists have more recently brought to light issues of "diversity and difference as central values" suggesting that these should be "acknowledged and respected and not erased in the building of alliances" (Mohanty 2004, 7). The result is a postmodern questioning of totalizing, universalizing theory. At the same time it is also important to consider the argument by Clifford Geertz (1973, 21) that women and gender historians deal with the same "grand realities . . . Power, Change, Faith, Oppression, Work, Passion, Authority, Beauty, Violence, Love, [and] Prestige." The key is to explore how such realities influence and affect women and men in numerous ways in different settings. By conducting this mapping exercise I hope to come closer to achieving this goal while simultaneously acknowledging and respecting the diversity and difference that exists at the local levels. This will be achieved by first mapping the global discourses surrounding gender and education, which do not necessarily take note of diversity and difference, and as mentioned earlier my main focus is on the concepts of equality and equity. This will be followed by another mapping of the local gender and education discourses, at the policy level, in which I will attempt to heed Chandra Mohanty's (2004) call for acknowledgement and respect in the building of alliances within the research group of which I am a part of and between this group and others conducting research on gender and education.

The global discourses surrounding gender and education found in the map below (Figure 11.1) are a result of an analysis of various global governance documents. What my analysis shows is that there are various interpretations of the term equity, but that equality appears to have a much more stable meaning. The mapping below is constructed on the basis of a thorough analysis of the texts and an interpretation made by the mapper, Holmarsdottir. In recognition of intertextuality and what it entails (Allen 2000), the interpretation is based on the mapper's analysis of the texts.

As a starting point in mapping the global discourses I began with the Universal Declaration of Human Rights (UDHR) (United Nations 1948) in which neither equity nor equality are mentioned, instead the term equal is found throughout the document, related to equal rights. The key issue being that of equal access to rights for both men and women.

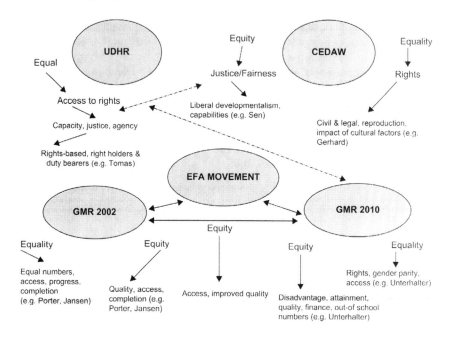

Figure 11.1. Mapping the Global Discourses on Equality and Equity in Gender.

Although human rights are not necessarily new, particularly within the field of education and development, recent focus suggests a systematic application and increased relevance of human rights standards. Some of the recent literature on human rights suggests that the goal is to "develop poor people's capacities to demand justice" (Tomas 2005, 174). Thus, a rights-based approach with a focus on equality allows us to see people as active agents. Moreover, Amparo Tomas (2005, 174) argues that "a rights-based approach facilitates the analysis of how justice systems deal with poverty-related inequalities, and thus the extent to which they may be 'biased' against the poor." A rights-based approach basically means to address simultaneously two separate, yet interacting, parties—the right holders and the duty bearers.

In the Convention on the Elimination of All Forms of Discrimination against Women (CEDAW) (United Nations 1979) the issue of equity has only one mention in which it is linked to justice. Julio Teehankee (2007) *argues that j*ustice is a "contested concept that evokes varied claims to fairness, equality, impartiality and appropriate rewards or punishments." Furthermore, he argues that there are three liberal conceptions of justice, namely: libertarianism, liberal egalitarianism, and liberal developmentalism. Given constraints of space in this chapter I will focus on the latter as it links with the underlying theoretical foundation of the GEEP project.

It is argued that "liberal developmentalism is a fairly new dimension to the liberal concept of justice that emerged from the writings of Amartya Sen" (Teehankee 2007). Founded on the Aristotelian concept of the "good life," Sen (1992, 1999) emphasizes that the goal of both justice and poverty reduction should be to expand the *functional* capability people have to enjoy. For Sen (1999, 75) functionings are "valuable beings and doings," such as being nourished, being confident, or taking part in group decisions. It is also acknowledged that certain capabilities, particularly education, enlarge each other. The word, functionings, is of Aristotelian origin[1] and, like Aristotle, this approach claims that "functionings are constitutive of a person's being" (73).

In addition to equity mentioned in the CEDAW, the term equality stands as a central theme in the document. Equality here refers to the issue of rights, similar to that found in the Universal Declaration of Human Rights. CEDAW argues that the theme of equality found in the 14 articles of the document cover three dimensions: civil rights and legal status of women, human reproduction, and impact of cultural factors on gender relations (United Nations 1979). The main thrust of the document thus appears to be on rights, non-discrimination and participation. Ute Gerhard (2001), however, points out that there appears to be some confusion in the use of the term equality in Western discourse, which comes from its origins.

> In Western discourse equality is derived from Aristotle's concept of equality of justice, which has caused conceptual confusion in modern times. According to this rule, only "things that are alike should be treated alike, while things that are unalike should be treated unalike in proportion to their unalikeness." . . . In terms of legal equality between men and women . . . the principle of equality assumes that men and women are different and that they will not become identical as a result of equal treatment, but will be able to preserve their difference. The 1949 Basic Law . . . of the Federal Republic of Germany explicitly guaranteed the legal equality of man and woman, including private law for the first time, and thus invalidating the Aristotelian rule. (Gerhard 2001, 7–8)

Moving from the CEDAW to the EFA movement, I first focus on the World Conference on EFA, which brought about a focus on gender in education, aiming to reduce gender disparity by focusing on women and girls (UNESCO 1990). One of the main goals in the EFA documents (the World Declaration on EFA and the Framework for Action) is to universalize access and to promote equity. My initial analysis of these documents shows that equity involves access to education in order to "achieve and maintain an acceptable level of learning." Moreover, access is also linked to the idea of "improved quality in education . . . [and the removal of] obstacles that hamper active participation" (UNESCO 1990). Looking further into the EFA movement, particularly the global monitoring reports (GMR) published by UNESCO since 2002, I have chosen to focus only on the first report from 2002 and the latest report from 2010 (UNESCO 2002, 2010). My brief analysis of how these reports use the terms equality and equity show an interesting pattern. First the term equality appears to have been much more prominent in the earlier report than equity. On the other hand, in the 2010 report equity appears to have just as much significance as equality/inequality.

Analyzing how these terms have been used and if the way in which they are used has changed from the 2002 to the 2010 GMR a noticeable pattern emerges. In the 2002 GMR equality is linked to the idea of equal numbers in education. Thus equality is associated with access and disparities within education (e.g., progress and completion) whereas equity appears to be looked at in terms of both quality in education, but it is also linked to access and completion. Thus early in the EFA movement the use of the two terms (equality and equity) appears to focus much more on the numbers game. In an article analyzing target setting within EFA Jonathan Jansen (2005) is critical of the numeral focus and our "trust in numbers" (Porter 1995).

> I want to suggest that the very practice of measurement has taken on meanings and significance well beyond the specific concerns which it is supposed to illuminate. It is part of being modern, that pretence that we can be precise and exact in measuring our reality; it is part of our faith in measurement technologies, that we can with constant fine-tuning make at least "informed judgments" about performance—the overwhelming problems notwithstanding. It comes from our quest for economy captured in "SMART" targets defined as specific, measurable, attainable, relevant and time-bound. (Jansen 2005, 372)

Driven by our "trust in numbers," quantification "goes beyond the boundaries of locality and community . . . [that is] quantification is a technology of distance . . . [resulting in a] reliance on numbers and quantitative manipulation [which] minimizes the need for intimate knowledge and personal trust" (Porter 1995, ix). Furthermore, the quality of a quantitative "evidence base, suggests that its appeal has as much to do with our psychological needs as our economic aspirations" (Fielding 1999, 277). In his investigation Theodore Porter (1995) invokes the work of Michael Oakeshott, Max Horkheimer and Theodor Adorno in order to provide him with a "critical view of modern, positivistic rationalism" (Porter 2001, ix). Thus within the EFA movement it may be argued that it is in the numbers that we trust, and scientific credibility is vested in apparent objectivity, achieved through quantification. As mentioned earlier a questioning of this apparent objectivity and trust in a single universalizing theory is the key objective of postmodernism.

Moving to the 2010 GMR equity has taken on as much importance as equality/inequality. At times in the report the use of the term equity appears problematic as it often lacks a clearer definition. The term is used in relation to several issues: disadvantage (e.g., language, gender, ethnicity, etc.), educational attainment (particularly in terms of gender parity), quality, educational finance and cost-effectiveness, in addition to a decline in out-of-school numbers. Thus despite the increased prominence in the use of term in the recent report equity appears to be more of a catch all term.

Equality, on the other hand, is found less often; instead the term inequality is referred to more often than in the earlier GMR (UNESCO 2002). The use of equality/inequality is much more clearly linked to issues concerning the right to education, gender parity and access. The conclusion is that this term still reflects the focus of the EFA targets and, in particular, a clearer focus on numbers.

In a review of different frameworks used to understand the "nature of the challenge to achieve gender equality in education" Unterhalter (2005b, 15) argues that the women in development (WID) framework linked to the expansion of education for women and girls as well as efficiency and economic growth has concentrated on the simple counting of girls in and out of school clearly found in much of the EFA literature (UNESCO 1990, 2002, 2010). The research utilizing this approach has been mainly led by economists working for IOs, such as the World Bank, UNESCO and UNICEF. Another framework analyzed by Unterhalter (2005b) is the gender and development (GAD) approach, which includes concerns about empowerment. For Unterhalter empowerment is often "called 'equity', an approach to instituting fairness (23)." Here equity is linked to justice and thus similar to how equity is understood in the CEDAW.

Referring back to the map (see Figure 11.1) surrounding the global discourses on equality and equity we can see that the overriding concern appears to be one of justice and fairness in relation to the UDHR and CEDAW, whereas within the EFA movement there is more of a numbers focus in relation to access, completion, gender parity, et cetera. Despite the fact that equity is also linked to quality in education it still appears that the quality aspect is couched within a quantitative evidence base (Porter 1995). The 2010 GMR is interpreted as linking equality to a rights-based philosophy and therefore moving slightly away from the sole numerical focus in the earlier GMR.

If an overall conclusion can be drawn from the mapping of how the global consensus, the discourses, to advance gender equality and equity in education are understood it is clear that these concepts reflect different aspects in relation to gender and education. The question we are left with is how this global consensus is understood and acted up locally. In pondering this question Joel Samoff and Carol Bidemi (2003, 51) speculate on the behavior of national states in relation to EFA:

> Ultimately, notwithstanding what its leaders or educators might say privately, no country wanted to be the lone and lonely nay-sayer, arguing an alternative perspective or different priorities. If the major players were putting their money on basic education, those seeking funds clearly had to do likewise. Not only the broad basic education message but also interpretations and implementation were communicated and given official sanction through the conference process. Education for All was to focus on expanding access, primarily to formal schools. . . . So too were equity and quality issues, though girls' education achieved some prominence. Critics quickly raised these and other concerns, with an even louder voice in the 2000 conference. The evidence suggests, however, that the original framework has proved quite durable.

MAPPING THE LOCAL DISCOURSES ON GENDER EQUALITY AND EQUITY

In this section I attempt to take into consideration the challenge posed by Mohanty (2004, 7) in which she reminds us of the centrality of "diversity and difference" and that it is imperative that these are "acknowledged and respected and not erased in the building of alliances." Thus I now focus my analysis on the way gender equality and equity in education is understood within the local contexts of South Africa and Sudan. This will be accomplished through a document analysis of the various educational policies in the two countries focusing on how gender equality and equity are interpreted in these local contexts. As my main goal is to assess how the concepts of equality and equity are understood in relation to gender and education I limit my attention to education policy documents and to documents that focus on gender in general. Given the space constraints in this chapter I will be unable to present how these are acted upon in the local contexts (cf. Holmarsdottir et al., 2011), but instead I will aim my focus on the discourse found within policy documents.

South Africa

> Everyone is equal before the law and has the right to equal protection and benefit of the law. Equality includes the full and equal enjoyment of all rights and freedoms. To promote the achievement of equality, legislative and other measures designed to protect or advance persons or categories of persons disadvantaged by unfair discrimination, may be taken. (Republic of South Africa 1996a, Act 108)

The 1996 Constitution of post-apartheid South Africa embraces equality as a basic human right with a particular focus on those who were previously disadvantaged; along with this came the dismantling of the apartheid education system. The goal was to transform the previous apartheid education system into a diversifying one, where a "rainbow" of identities is accepted, and to construct a national identity that acknowledges and respects diversity. Such diversity and difference constitute ideological paradoxes which are often a challenge to implement. Since the first democratic elections in South Africa, legislation has been passed to implement a new school system resulting in a flurry of policy changes in 1994 and 1995, often by policymakers with very limited sensitivity to those in the townships or rural areas. The new Constitution of South Africa included a commitment to democracy, and, since 1996, education policy has aimed to contribute to this new democratic society. However, it must be noted that the dramatic changes in policy have met with both success and failure (Holmarsdottir 2005) and one cannot underestimate the destructive wake of four decades of oppression and division within the society. The inherited legacy of apartheid is thus seen as one in which:

> The new government of national unity assumed responsibility for a society systematically fractured across a range of divisions: not only by race, class and gender, but also by ethnicity and language, and between rural and urban dwellers as well as between those with land and the landless. The divisions were a consequence not only of apartheid but also of the exigencies of the struggle against it. (Enslin 2003, 73)

In attempting to analyze how gender equality and gender equity are interpreted in South Africa I limited myself to only a few key documents as post-apartheid

South Africa includes an overflow of various legislative policies, focusing on both education and society in general, which I do not have the space to tackle here. Given that the overall aim in this chapter is on gender and education I have chosen to look at three particular education policies: *National Education Policy No. 27 of 1996* (Republic of South Africa 1996b), *South Africa Schools Act No. 84 of 1996* (Republic of South Africa 1996c), and *Higher Education Act No. 101 of 1997* (Republic of South Africa 1997). Furthermore, as an all encompassing policy I chose to briefly look at South Africa's National Policy Framework for Women's Empowerment (Office on the Status of Women 2000). These four documents I believe will provide a snapshot of how gender equality and equity are envisioned in post-apartheid South Africa.

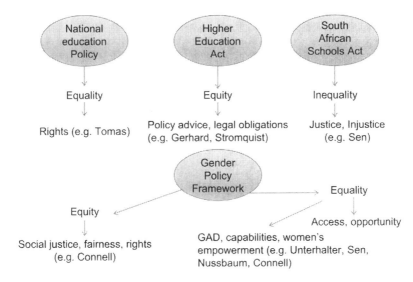

Figure 11.2. Mapping the Local (South African) Discourses on Equality and Equity in Gender.

To begin with I focus my initial attention on the *National Education Policy* (Republic of South Africa 1996b, Section 4c), which states the following in relation to equality:

achieving equitable education opportunities and the redress of past inequality in education provision, including the promotion of gender equality and the advancement of the status of women.

This section is the only place in the document where either equality or gender is mentioned. Equity, on the other hand, is completely absent, but there is a linking of the right to education as stated in the Constitution. Thus, as found in the global discourse and in particular the CEDAW, the idea of human rights is evoked and as such equal opportunities within education is seen as a key point in the document.

With respect to the link between both the global and local focus on a rights-based approach to education, Tomas (2005, 171–172) reminds us that:

> approaches to justice reform have traditionally underestimated the complex social processes involved in rule-making and institutional development. This has resulted in an overemphasis on formal institutions. . . . Much justice-related . . . work takes for granted that law and institutions provide opportunity, empowerment and security, through which they promote economic growth. However, laws and institutions cannot provide security and opportunity by themselves; it is the application of those laws and the actual functioning of those institutions that can.

Thus for Tomas it is not a question of the existence of policies or the institutions that are responsible for implementing these policies—in this case educational institutions. Instead it is how these policies and institutions interact with people and "how people perceive, use, change and develop them" (172). This interaction between policy and individuals on the ground will be the next step in the research project discussed in this chapter and will therefore not be taken up at this point.

In addition to the *National Education Policy* (Republic of South Africa 1996b) the *South African Schools Act* (Republic of South Africa 1996c, Preamble) makes only one mention of the word inequality—as opposed to equality—in which a reference to past injustices is made:

> the achievement of democracy in South Africa has consigned to history the past system of education which was based on racial inequality and segregation.

Furthermore, as in the *National Education Policy* the *African Schools Act* also makes no mention of equity. Thus it appears that the term equity during the early post-apartheid period was non-existent. Ultimately, it may be argued that early post-apartheid education policies did not take into account or were not influenced by the global agenda surrounding gender and education and in particular the question of equality and to a lesser degree equity. Furthermore, this almost invisible focus on equality, equity and even gender in the early educational policies is also evident in the Higher Education Act (Republic of South Africa 1997, Section 31a) in which the focus on the institutional forum of a public higher education institution is required to "advise the council on issues affecting the institution, including race and gender equity policies." Again this is the only place in the document that gender and equity are found, while equality is once more completely absent.

Given the limited focus on the issues of gender equality and gender equity in the three education policy documents discussed above it was deemed useful to also consider a more comprehensive policy. As a result of a thorough search of the numerous post-apartheid policy documents, I located South Africa's National Policy Framework for Women's Empowerment, often referred to as the Gender Policy Framework (Office on the Status of Women 2000). Given that this document was specifically focused on the issue of women's empowerment—focusing not only on education but all sectors of the society—I believed this document would provide me with a broader understanding of if and how the global gender agenda has impacted the South African policy arena.

As this document is comprehensive, covering all sectors of the society, I chose to mainly focus my attention on the executive summary and the areas in which education was the specific focus. In the beginning of the document it is stated that the "Gender Policy Framework [GPF] outlines South Africa's vision for gender equality and for how it intends to realise this ideal" (Office on the Status of Women 2000, Executive Summary 1.1). The opening section, therefore, clearly points to the main thrust of the document, one in which gender equality is central and where the term equality has been mentioned well over 200 times. What I find unique about this document in comparison to some of the global documents is that equality is linked not only to issues of access and opportunity, as was the case with the 2002 GMR, but that the term equality also appears to be used much more broadly. For instance, it is linked to some of the frameworks discussed by Unterhalter (2005b), in particular GAD; however the GPF goes further than most of the global policies by linking together GAD and women's empowerment arguing that:

> the "women's empowerment" approach tends to focus more on practical needs which in themselves are complementary to the "basic needs" approach reflected in the situational analysis. On the other hand, the "Gender and Development" (GAD) approach focuses on 'strategic needs,' the goal of which is gender equality. Given the high levels of inequalities which pertain in the South African context, the focus on women's empowerment in this document affirms the satisfaction of 'basic needs' ('practical needs') as a necessary precondition towards the identification and attainment of 'strategic needs'. (Office on the Status of Women 2000, Executive Summary 1.3)

In addition to linking together the different frameworks in achieving gender equality (Unterhalter 2005b) the GPF brings in the idea of capabilities (Sen 1999), specifically linked to the concept of equality, arguing that the "expansion of capabilities . . . [is] reflected in the emphasis on access to resources while the key element of the GEM [Gender Empowerment Measure] is the use of these capabilities" (Office on the Status of Women 2000, Executive Summary 1.7). Thus capabilities are seen as a central concern of the GPF, linked to among other things "equality of access to the means of developing basic human capabilities" (Office on the Status of Women 2000, 49). In the GPF capabilities goes hand in hand with equality and the idea of access. The "capabilities approach" (Sen 1999) allows for new ways to measure the quality of life and simultaneously argues against the "still-dominant economic growth paradigm" (Nussbaum 2004, 329) and as such it is seen as questioning the "numbers game." The question that remains is if the understanding of capabilities in the GPF has in reality moved beyond a mere "trust in numbers" (Porter 1995) and simple access and instead attempts to implement deeper changes. The capabilities approach challenges us to "examine real lives in their material and social settings" (Nussbaum 2000, 71), which I am unable to do here given space constraints, but it is something that is required in order to ascertain whether or not the GPF has achieved the deeper changes necessary to achieve real gender equality and equity. Thus, understanding not only what is done but the way in which it is done. However, the document, already in 2000, reflects on these more recent issues, which suggests that the South African GPF was at the forefront in envisioning gender equality in a more comprehensive way than the global documents.

In addition, the document also considers gender equity issues, although equity is not dealt with as exhaustively as equality. However, it appears that equity reflects much of the same understanding as was found in the global documents where it is linked to issues of social justice, fairness and rights. In a recent article by Raewyn Connell (2010, 607) it is argued that feminism in South Africa includes "the most progressive equality guarantees in the world written into the 1996 Constitution; and has struggled to turn this into economic and social reality." Perhaps it might be concluded that the goal of the GPF was one way in which to achieve this. However, what remains to be considered is whether or not the economic and social changes that South African feminists have strived for and which are reflected in the GPF have actually taken place. Having briefly looked at the South African context I would now like to move my attention to the policies in Sudan.

Southern Sudan

> [Southern] Sudanese of school going age over the past 21 years have had no chance whatsoever to attend any school, much less complete their primary education. Many have been fortunate to survive at all, or have been thrown into the business of fighting or sustaining some sort of livelihood at a very early age. Others have had chances to go to school, but school itself has been so unstable and of such low quality that it received low priority. Even when the prospect of attending a school has become a reality, the chances of remaining in school long and consistently has constituted a truly daunting challenge for many schoolchildren. (Sommers 2005, 26)

The work in the GEEP project is embedded in the context described above. The main focus of the project is on the education of the most marginalized Sudanese communities, which mainly include Southern Sudanese, but also nomadic groups in Sudan and other Internally Displaced Peoples (IPDs) in the country (e.g., various groups of people currently displace in the Darfur conflict and Southerners living in camps in and around the capital Khartoum). Thus it must be understood that "war, isolation and instability have dominated Southern Sudan since 1955 and the countless events as a result have left Southern Sudanese as one of the most undereducated populations in the world" (15).

The Comprehensive Peace Agreement (CPA), signed in January 2005, resulted in the establishment of a plural democratic system of governance and ultimately self-determination as a result of the referendum that took place on 9 January 2011 (BBC News 2011).

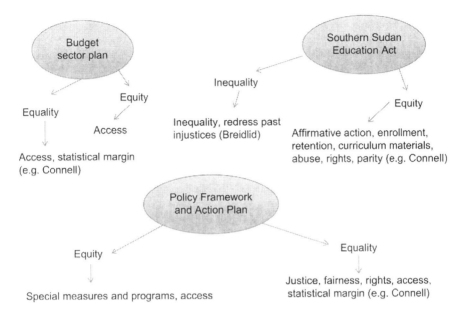

Figure 11.3. Mapping the Local (Southern Sudanese) Discourses on Equality and Equity in Gender.

While acknowledging the unity of the Sudanese State the CPA draws out plans for an interim administration for the whole of Sudan with the division of power between different levels of government. This includes a Government of National Unity (GNU) alongside an autonomous Government of Southern Sudan (GOSS), giving the people of Southern Sudan the right to manage their own affairs and to participate equitably in the National Government. Amongst the powers of the Southern Government is the authority over basic education in the South. This requires the development of several education policies for Southern Sudan. In this chapter I focus only on Southern Sudan since this is where the new policy developments are currently taking place. Given the scenario described above and the tenuous government capacity for policy development, I was only able to locate a few documents that relate to education in Southern Sudan; moreover I was only able to obtain these documents firsthand while conducting fieldwork in Sudan in the latter part of 2008 and 2009.

The first document is the budget sector plan (2010–2012) which does provide some discussion on how and why funds are to be spent (GOSS 2009). The second document which I will focus on is the *Southern Sudan Education Act* (Ministry of Education, Science and Technology [MOEST] 2008). The final document, which is similar to South Africa's National Policy Framework for Women's Empowerment in terms of being a comprehensive document, is the Policy Framework and Action Plan from the Ministry of Gender, Social Welfare and Religious Affairs (MGSW&RA 2009).

The budget sector plan (2010–2012) appears to immediately reflect on the global gender goals and the relevance of these goals in terms of education in Southern Sudan:

> While Southern Sudan has achieved remarkable increase in primary school enrolment since the signing of the Comprehensive Peace Agreement . . . the challenge remains enormous. There is an estimated 1.3 million children in schools in Southern Sudan which represents 32% of the school going age. However out of the estimated 1.3 million children who are at school only 36 percent are girls and the great majority of those who remain out of school are equally girls. If Southern Sudan is to make any significant improvement towards achieving the Millennium Development Goals (MDGs) of Universal Primary Education and Gender Equality and Empowerment of Women by 2015, there is need by the Government and the Development Partners to invest heavily in these areas of education. (GOSS 2009, 3)

Thus, initially it appears that gender equality in Southern Sudan is linked to the idea of access and the "statistical margin" of difference between boys and girls and the result is that this ultimately *"becomes* the meaning of gender" (Connell 2010, 604). The mention of gender equality is otherwise absent in the document as this is the only time it is specifically mentioned. Moreover, the term gender equity is limited to a brief mention in the introduction section as well and it is likewise only linked to the idea of access.

The second document which I have analyzed as part of the local education discourses on gender equality and gender equity is the *Southern Sudan Education Act* (MOEST 2008). In this document there is an understanding of the need to redress past inequality in terms of education in general and with regard to gender more specifically. Thus equality in the document is not solely limited to gender issues, but instead is seen as an overall goal of education. Certainly the "strong feeling of marginalisation and subordination underlines the minority status of the Southerners in the Sudan" (Breidlid 2005, 260), which necessitates the need to redress the inequalities that have existed between the north and the south in terms of education.

While equality is seen as a more general aspect in the *Education Act*, equity is more specifically linked to gender. Furthermore, the term is dealt with more comprehensively in the document than equality. In particular in "Chapter IV: Provision of Education Section 26: Gender Equity in Education" includes ten specific points of focus and embraces issues such as: affirmative action linked specifically to female enrolment and retention, gender responsive curriculum materials, abuse and sexual relationships particularly between teachers and pupils, and pregnancy where female students "shall have the right to remain in school or gain re-entry after delivery" (MOEST 2008, 30). Again despite the reference made to prohibiting abuse and sexual relationships between teachers and pupils and the need for gender sensitive curriculum materials no concrete options are drafted on how this is to be accomplished. Accordingly, the main focus once again seems to be on gender parity where gender policy:

targets women and girls, and includes men and boys only in a shadow sense. Men and boys figure as the statistical norm against which the position of women and girls is measured, or as the perpetrators (in policy about violence or harassment). (Connell 2010, 604)

The final document analyzed as part of the Sudan context is the Policy Framework and Action Plan (MGSW&RA 2009). In the document the minister links equality with that of justice and fairness in terms of the distribution of resources in Southern Sudan. The document also includes a section where both gender equality and gender equity are defined specifically. This is something which has not been found in other documents in Sudan, South Africa or the global documents. These are defined as follows:

- **Gender Equality** refers to several rights, which ascertain to men and women. It is a basic human rights equalization whereby women and men are treated equally.
- **Gender Equity** is a set of policy measures/special programs targeting women with aims of compensating them for the historical and social disparities that deprive them of enjoying access to equal opportunities.

Gender equality in this document therefore is linked specifically to a rights-based philosophy couched in the same understanding as is found in both the UDHR and CEDAW documents. However, when analyzing the document further with a focus of how equality is understood the results show gender equality seen in terms of the statistical margin with a focus on girls' access to education is the key point (Connell 2010). Thus, a rights-based philosophy is linked to access and the numbers game.

On the other hand, the definition of gender equity found in the Policy Framework and Action Plan is centered on affirmative action and specifically targets women in terms of measures to be taken or special programs to make up for past inequalities. However, equity is only found twice in the document suggesting that this concept is less important than equality and our "trust in numbers" (Jansen 2005). One final point that suggests a heavy influence of the global discourses in the development of policy in Southern Sudan is the specific reference to many of the global governance documents:

Ministry's role, performance and effectiveness in implementing the Millennium Development Goals (MDGs), the Beijing platform for Action 1995 and the CEDAW (Commission for Elimination of all Forms of Discrimination Against Women) for the advancement of gender equality within their specific sector (e.g., Education, Health, Water and Agriculture). (MGSW&RA 2009, 3)

It may be concluded that the government of Southern Sudan might have willingly committed itself to gender equity as a result of the influence of these global discourses and in doing so they have mainly focused on issues of equal access in their policies, while simultaneously they may have been reluctant to take "steps that would transform schools" (Connell 2010, 611) in terms of practice. Certainly the reality of what is taking place in schools in Southern Sudan is the next step that needs to be taken.

CONCLUSION

There seems to be a general consensus that the way to reconciliation, justice and equality at least also passes through education if in the quest for a new South Africa and a new Southern Sudan are to be achieved. Accordingly, Connell (2010, 611) argues that the "dynamics of the state now come into view as part of the story of education." To use the words of Stromquist (1995), perhaps the global gender goals have been involved in "romancing the state" and as a result have sought to influence educational reform through persuading reluctant governments to include gender equality and equity which Connell (2010, 611) argues results in "readily committing to equal access, [but] much less willingly taking steps that would transform schools, and least of all changing gender content of the curriculum." It is this change that needs to be considered in future research to see if the local policy is actually implemented.

What I have attempted to do in this chapter is to shed light upon the dialectic between global and local educational discourses in terms of gender equality and equity. What has come to light is that despite some attempts to view equality and equity as more than just access and a focus on numbers the reality in terms of policy suggests that governments still rationalize education in terms of a "modern, positivistic rationalism" (Porter 1995, ix) where access and gender parity take precedence over real structural changes needed in order to transform education into a real tool for gender equality and equity. Furthermore, my analysis confirms that "there is no consensus as to the precise difference between these two terms, exactly what they mean, or how they should be used" (Aikman and Unterhalter 2007, 23). The result is an ambiguous understanding of these concepts in relation to gender in education, which can be problematic in achieving the necessary changes in education in order to achieve true functional capability. As Connell (2010, 613) reminds us:

> The case for gender justice in education has often been made on the basis of 'rights'. The global agenda in education can draw on a tradition of international rights statements, from the Universal Declaration of Human Rights, to the Convention on the Elimination of All Forms of Discrimination Against Women, to the Declaration of the Rights of the Child. Yet ultimately, the case has to be an educational one, reflecting ideas of what makes good education. Good education is education that is just; the quality of education is defined by the quality of social life generated by the capacities [capabilities] that education yields.

NOTE

1. Sen traces the roots of this approach to Aristotle's writings in both *The Nicomachean Ethics* and *Politics.*

REFERENCES

Aikman, Shelia, & Elaine Unterhalter, eds. (2007). *Practising Gender Equality in Education.* Oxford, UK: Oxfam Publishing.

Allen, Graham. (2000). Intertextuality: *The New Critical Idiom.* London: Routledge.

Bailey, Joanne. (2005). *Is the Rise of Gender History 'Hiding' Women from History Once Again?* London: Institute of Historical Research. Available online at: http://www.history.ac.uk.

Baker, David P., & Alexander W. Wiseman, eds. (2009). Gender, *Equality, and Education from International and Comparative Perspectives.* Bingley, UK: Emerald/JAI.

BBC News. (2011). "South Sudan Referendum: 99% Vote for Independence." *London: BBC News Africa.* Available online at: http://www.bbc.co.uk.

Bendera, Stella. (1999). "Promoting Education for Girls in Tanzania." In Christine Heward and Shelia Bunwaree (Ed.), *Gender, Education, and Development: Beyond Access to Empowerment* (pp. 117–132). London: Zed Books.

Best, Steven, & Douglas Kellner. n.d. *The Postmodern Turn in Philosophy: Theoretical Provocations and Normative Deficits.* Los Angeles: Graduate School of Education and Information Studies, University of California, Los Angeles. Available online at: http://www.gseis.ucla.edu.

Breidlid, Anders. (2005). "Sudanese Migrants in the Khartoum Area: Fighting for Educational Space." *International Journal of Educational Development, 25*(3), 253–268.

Brock, Colin, & Nadine K. Cammish. (1997). *Factors Affecting Female Participation in Education in Seven Developing Countries.* Education Research Series 9. London: Department for International Development (formerly Overseas Development Administration).

Butler, Judith. (1990). Gender Trouble: *Feminism and the Subversion of Identity.* New York: Routledge.

Clark, James, & Allan Paivio. (1991). "Dual Coding Theory and Education." *Educational Psychology Review 3*(3), 149–210.

Colclough, Christopher, Pauline Rose, & Mercy Tembon. (1998). Gender Inequalities in Primary Schooling: *The Roles of Poverty and Adverse Cultural Practice. Working Paper No. 78.* Brighton, UK: Institute of Development Studies.

Connell, Raewyn. (2010). "Kartini's Children: On the Need for Thinking Gender and Education Together on a World Scale." *Gender and Education 22*(6), 603–615.

Connelly, Patricia M., Tania M. Li, Martha MacDonald, & Jane L. Parpart. (2000). "Feminism and Development: Theoretical Perspectives." In Jane L. Parpart, Patricia Connelly, & Eudine Barriteau (Ed.), *Theoretical Perspectives on Gender and Development.* (pp. 51–160). Ottawa: International Development Research Centre.

Derrida, Jacques. (1991). "A Letter to a Japanese Friend." In Peggy Kamuf (Ed.), *A Derrida Reader: Between the Blinds* (pp. 269–276). New York: Harvester Wheatsheaf.

Enslin, Penny. (2003). "Citizenship Education in Post-Apartheid South Africa." *Cambridge Journal of Education, 33*(1), 73–83.

Fielding, Michael. (1999). "Target Setting, Policy Pathology and Student Perspectives: Learning to Labour in New Times." *Cambridge Journal of Education 29*(2), 277–287.

Foucault, Michel. (1980). Power/Knowledge: *Selected Interviews and Other Writings 1972–1977,* ed. and trans. Colin Gordon. New York: Pantheon Books.

Foucault, Michel. (1989). *The Archaeology of Knowledge.* London: Routledge.

Geertz, Clifford. (1973). *The Interpretation of Cultures:* Selected Essays. New York: Basic Books.

Gerhard, Ute. (2001). *Debating Women's Equality: Toward a Feminist Theory of Law from a European Perspective. Piscataway,* NJ: Rutgers University Press.

Government of Southern Sudan (GOSS). (2009). *Education Sector: Budget Sector Plan 2010–2012.* Juba, Southern Sudan: GOSS.

Habermas, Jürgen. (1971). *Theory and Practice.* Boston: Beacon Books.

Harding, Sandra. (1991). *Whose Science? Whose Knowledge? Thinking from Women's Lives.* Ithaca, NY: Cornell University Press.

Holmarsdottir, Halla B. (2005). From Policy to Practice: *A Study of the Implementation of the Language-in-Education Policy (LiEP) in Three South African Primary Schools.* Oslo: Unipub.

Holmarsdottir, Halla B., Ingrid B. M. Ekne, & Heidi L. Augestad. (2011). "The Dialectic between Global Gender Goals and Local Empowerment: Girls' Education in Southern Sudan and South Africa." *Research in Comparative and International Education (RCIE), 6*(1), 14–26.

Huff, Anne S. (1996). "Ways of Mapping Strategic Thought." In Rolland G. Paulston (Ed.), *Social Cartography: Mapping Ways of Seeing Social and Educational Change*. (pp. 161–190). New York: Garland Publishing.

Jansen, Jonathan D. (2005). "Targeting Education: The Politics of Performance and the Prospects of 'Education For All'." *International Journal of Educational Development*, 25(4), 368–380.

King, Elizabeth M., & Anne Hill, eds. (1993). *Women's Education in Developing Countries: Barriers, Benefits, and Policies*. Baltimore, MD: Johns Hopkins University Press.

Lather, Patti. (1991). Getting Smart: *Feminist Research and Pedagogy within/in the Postmodern*. New York: Routledge.

Lyotard, Jean-Francois. (1984). The Postmodern Condition: *A Report on Knowledge*. Trans. Geoff Bennington and Brian Massumi. Minneapolis, MN: University of Minnesota Press.

Meyer, John W., & Fransico O. Ramirez. (2000). "The World Institutionalization of Education." In Jürgen Schriewer (Ed.), *Discourse Formation in Comparative Education*. (pp. 111–132). New York: Peter Lang.

Ministry of Gender, Social Welfare & Religious Affairs (MGSW&RA). (2009). *Policy Framework and Action Plan*. Juba, Southern Sudan: GOSS. Available online at: www.goss-online.org.

Ministry of Education, Science & Technology (MOEST). (2008). *Southern Sudan Education Act, 2008*. 4th ed. Juba, Southern Sudan: MOEST.

Mohanty, Chandra. (2004). *Feminism without Borders: Decolonizing Theory, Practicing Solidarity*. Durham, NC: Duke University Press.

Mundy, Karen. (2006). "Education for All and the New Development Compact." *International Review of Education*, 52(1), 23–48.

Nussbaum, Martha. (2004). "Women's Education: A Global Challenge." *Signs: Journal of Women in Culture and Society*, 29(2), 325–356.

Nussbaum, Martha C. (2000). Women and Human Development: *The Capabilities Approach*. Cambridge, UK: Cambridge University Press.

Office on the Status of Women. (2000). *South Africa's National Policy Framework for Women's Empowerment and Gender Equality*. Pretoria, South Africa: Republic of South Africa. Available online at: http://www.info.gov.za.

Paivio, Allan. (1986). Mental Representations: *A Dual Coding Approach*. Oxford, UK: Oxford University Press.

Paulston, Rolland G., ed. (1996). Social Cartography: *Mapping Ways of Seeing Social and Educational Change*. New York: Garland Publishing.

Paulston, Rolland G. (2005). "Mapping Reality in Western Thinking and Comparative Education." Paper presented at the *49th Comparative and International Education Society Annual Meeting, Beyond Dichotomies*, Stanford University, Palo Alto, CA, 22–26 March 2005.

Paulston, Rolland G., & Martin Liebman. (1996). "Social Cartography: A New Metaphor/Tool for Comparative Studies." In Rolland G. Paulston (Ed.), *Social Cartography: Mapping Ways of Seeing Social and Educational Change*. (pp. 7–28). New York: Garland Publishing.

Popkewtiz, Thomas S. (2000). "National Imaginaries, the Indigenous Foreigner, and Power: Comparative Educational Research." In Jürgen Schriewer (Ed.), *Discourse Formation in Comparative Education*. (pp. 261–294). New York: Peter Lang.

Porter, Theodore. (1995). Trust in Numbers: *The Pursuit of Objectivity in Science and Public Life*. Princeton, NJ: Princeton University Press.

Porter, Theodore. (2001). "On the Virtues and Disadvantage of Quantification for Democratic Life." *Studies in History and Philosophy of Science*, 32(4), 739–747.

Republic of South Africa. (1996)a. *Constitution of the Republic of South Africa*. Pretoria, South Africa: Republic of South Africa. Available online at: http://www.info.gov.za.

Republic of South Africa. (1996)b. *National Education Policy Act No. 27 of 1996*. Pretoria, South Africa: Republic of South Africa.

Republic of South Africa. (1996)c. *South African Schools Act No. 84 of 1996*. Pretoria, South Africa: Republic of South Africa. Available online at: http://www.education.gov.za.

Republic of South Africa. (1997). *Higher Education Act No. 101 of 1997*. Pretoria, South Africa: Republic of South Africa. Available online at: http://www.education.gov.za.

Rooney, Ellen. (1989). "In a Word: An Interview with Gayatri Spivak." *Differences*, 1(2), 124–156.

Rorty, Richard. (1989). *Contingency, Irony, and Solidarity*. Cambridge, UK: Cambridge University Press.

Rust, Val D. (1996). "From Modern to Postmodern Ways of Seeing Social and Educational Change." In Rolland G. Paulston (Ed.), *Social Cartography: Mapping Ways of Seeing Social and Educational Change.* (pp. 29–51). New York: Garland Publishing.

Samoff, Joel, & Carol Bidemi. (2003). From Manpower Planning to the Knowledge Era: *World Bank Policies on Higher Education in Africa. UNESCO Forum Occasional Paper Series.* Paris: UNESCO. Available online at: http://unesdoc.unesco.org.

Sen, Amartya. (1992). *Inequality Reexamined.* Cambridge, MA: Harvard University Press.

Sen, Amartya. (1999). *Development as Freedom.* New York: Knopf.

Sommers, Marc. (2005). *Islands of Education: Schooling, Civil War and the Southern Sudanese* (1983–2004). Paris: International Institute for Educational Planning (IIEP), UNESCO.

Stromquist, Nelly P. (1995). "Romancing the State: Gender and Power in Education." *Comparative Education Review, 39*(4), 423–454.

Swainson, Nicola, Stella Bendera, Rosemary Gordon, & Esme Kadzamira. (1998). Promoting Girls' Education in Africa: *The Design and Implementation of Policy Interventions. Education Research Papers No. 12840.* London: Department of International Development.

Swann, Joan, & Janet Maybin. (2008). "Sociolinguistic and Ethnographic Approaches to Language and Gender." In Kate Harrington, Lia Litosseliti, Helen Sauntson, & Jane Sunderland (Ed.), *Gender and Language Research Methodologies.* (pp. 21–28). Hampshire, UK: Palgrave Macmillan.

Teehankee, Julio C. (2007). "Equity and Justice in a Globalized World: A Liberal Review." *Seminar Report.* Makati City, Philippines: Friedrich Naumann Foundation for Liberty. Available online at: http://www.fnf.org.ph.

Tomas, Amparo. (2005). "Reforms that Benefit Poor People: Practical Solutions and Dilemmas of Rights-based Approaches to Legal and Justice Reform." In Paul Gready & Jonathan Ensor (Ed.), *Reinventing Development? Translating Rights-based Approaches from Theory into Practice* (pp. 171–184). London: Zed Books.

Tröhler, Daniel. (2010). "Harmonizing the Educational Globe: World Polity, Cultural Features, and the Challenges to Educational Research." *Studies in Philosophy and Education 29*(1), 5–17.

Uduigwomen, Andrew. (2005). "Philosophical Objections to the Knowability of Truth: Answering Postmodernism." *Quodlibet Journal 7*(2). Available online at: http://www.quodlibet.net.

UNESCO. (2002). *Education for All: Is the World on Track?* Paris: UNESCO Publishing.

UNESCO. (2010). *Reaching the Marginalized.* Paris: UNESCO Publishing.

UNESCO. (1990). UNESCO Education for All. Background Documents – World Conference on EFA – World Declaration. *Paris: UNESCO. Available online at: http://www.unesco.org.*

United Nations. (1948). *The Universal Declaration of Human Rights.* New York: United Nations. Available online at: http://www.un.org.

United Nations. (1979). "Convention on the Elimination of All Forms of Discrimination against Women." *New York: United Nations.* Available online at: http://www.unhcr.org.

Unterhalter, Elaine. (2005a). "Gender Equality and Education in South Africa: Measurements, Scores and Strategies." In Linda Chisholm and Jean September (Ed.), *Gender Equity in South African Education 1994–2004: Perspectives from Research, Government and Unions: Conference Proceedings.* (pp. 77–91). Cape Town, South Africa: HSRC Press.

Unterhalter, Elaine. (2005b). "Fragmented Frameworks? Researching Women, Gender, Education, and Development." In Sheila Aikman and Elaine Unterhalter (Ed.), *Beyond Access: Transforming Policy and Practice for Gender Equality in Education* (pp. 15–35). Oxford, UK: Oxfam.

Wiseman, Alexander W. (2008). "A Culture of (In)Equality? A Cross-national Study of Gender Parity and Gender Segregation in National School Systems." *Research in Comparative and International Education 3*(2), 179–201.

Wittgenstein, Ludwig. (1953). *Philosophical Investigations.* New York: Macmillan.

SUPRIYA BAILY

12. TRAJECTORIES OF INFLUENCE

Extending Paulston's Ideas to Gender, Empowerment,
and Community Development

INTRODUCTION

For over 30 years Rolland G. Paulston's focus on social change, social movements and social mapping helped to frame the discourse in comparative, international and development education. He began his career by exploring educational change and reform and the role of "ideology, power . . . and group self-interest" in education (Paulston 1977, 371). His culminating works highlight how the absence of cultural options prevented the power of imagination to counter "modernity's insistence on linear certainty and univocality" (Paulston 2000, 362). Paulston's ideas leave ripples in the work of modern scholars who talk about power, hidden curricula, indigenous rights, and the complexity of advocating for education alongside issues related to development in the twenty-first century. With the ever present challenges of conflict, poverty, human rights violations, trade issues, marginalization and discrimination, it becomes all the more important to leave linear thinking and a single mindedness approach to change behind.

This chapter seeks to bridge the past and the future with the intent that current international scholars—who on paper might be considered somewhat of an antithesis to Paulston—are able to relocate his ideas to better understand the "feasibility, processes and outcomes for educational change" (Paulston 1977, 370). By juxtaposing Paulston's views of education and power in a theoretical framework, this chapter attempts to do two things as it relates to gender and education. The first is to articulate a need for an increased understanding of local contexts and cultures within which educational change operates. The second is to advocate for some consideration of how the history of linear and uniform expectations, often mandated by international entities and supported by international experts, fail to take into account the local views and experiences. Though Paulston stressed the importance of processes and outcomes, it is vital to explore the environment and the social dynamics that affect the role of education especially as it relates to women.

According to Paulston, theories of education are manifested in *process*. Implementation of these processes must be deconstructed for social change to make a difference for those marginalized by the structures of power (Paulston 1996). One such marginalized group remains rural adult women in the developing

John C. Weidman, W. James Jacob (eds.), Beyond the Comparative: Advancing Theory and Its Application to Practice, 217–233.

world. Though 50 percent of the world's population now resides in urban areas (United Nations Population Fund [UNFPA] 2007), women disproportionally continue to live in rural areas where they often face safety and discrimination issues (United Nations 2007). Rural women face significant challenges where besides "burdensome and time-consuming chores," they also face the specter of low paying, low technology, manual jobs with little stability and even less room for growth and opportunity (Lahiri-Dutt and Samanta 2002, 138). Rural women also face greater forms of structural oppression than their peers in urban centers (Bosch 1998).

Opportunities to improve the lives of rural women have often fallen beneath an overarching theme of empowerment. This chapter emerges from a larger research study conducted in India on how community members perceived the role of rural women after they had been involved in nonformal education programs (Baily 2008). By building on Paulston's foundation where education must "represent our separate truths . . . to be less parochial and more self-knowledgeable in comparing contested realities" (2000, 363), this chapter outlines some of the "contested realities" of rural women. By understanding the experiences of women, this chapter theorizes how the role of nonformal education affects social change in a dynamic and conflicting social environment.

CONCEPTUAL FRAMEWORK

Paulston's name may be more familiar to scholars, researchers, and intellectuals who were schooled in the traditions of comparative and international education in Western Europe and North America. Today, however, international and comparative researchers come from diverse countries and carry with them their lived experiences as immigrants, global nomads, expatriates, and often with bicultural/bi-national or multicultural/multi-national allegiances. In spite of these alternate identities the trajectory of Paulston's theories continue to have broad impact. His influence stretches through his initial work on issues of power and nonformal education to his later work on social cartography—the mapping of social spaces, milieus, and relationships in a given time and/or space (Paulston 1996). Much of Paulston's work on mapping tried to assure a more effective way to portray the links and relationships between education and other critical dimensions influencing human development, all of which lie at the fulcrum of social change.

One of Paulston's legacies to the scholarship of comparative education is his conceptualism of mapping diverse, embedded and complex layers, which reveal how social change occurs. Paulston grapples with social change and social mapping as a way to include issues of power, intersectionality and multiperspectivism in education. Beyond the physical, material and tangible changes that are needed to afford social change, people must also "shift the point of view" (Paulston 2000, 358). Doing so, however, requires some understanding of how underlying relationships and structures promote the status quo.

Social Change and Social Mapping

Today the face of international education is global in representation as well as interdisciplinary in scope; integrating the field with the scholarship of political science, economics, anthropology, sociology, gender studies, and business. Predicting the synthesis of education with other fields of study, Paulston suggested that comparative education was beginning to share common interdisciplinary theories, alongside "knowledge-generation processes as well as . . . traditional cross-cultural comparison of national practices" (Paulston 1996, xx). It seemed significant to him that such blending would have positive and useful effects on education, thus ultimately influencing social change.

Social change has broad connotations that reverberate with both positive and negative attributes depending on the nature of the conversation, the perspective taken, the experience had, or even the specific moment in time. All of these positive and negative attributes are linked, but their disentanglement is far more complicated, often depending on the same factors that affect social change. The relevance of common meanings takes a more central role as multiple actors enter into the field and the nature of large-scale change necessitates the need for visual descriptions of roles, players and goals. Unfortunately, in the continued push for education, the challenges and hazards of promoting education for all is not one that is either simple or complete. Social mapping allows for the opportunity to "develop a methodology . . . in a time when people now realize their potential and place in the world quite differently than they did a few decades ago" (Paulston 1996, xviii). Social mapping has been suggested to provide for a visual articulation that allows "for the beginning of a more open social dialogue . . . representing different ways of seeing" (Rust 1996, 36). This can help provide both order and a lens for interpretation that can be increasingly complicated in today's diverse social environments (Paulston and Liebman 1996).

Paulston recognized that education is constantly in flux and altering education occurs on a consistent and constant basis in every society (Paulston 1977). Mapping, he conjectured, would allow for multiple viewpoints to be taken into consideration while also offering an opportunity for cultures and local contexts to be recognized.

The development of narratives true to the individual's experiences is a thoughtful shift towards reducing the influence of the narratives of the powerful over the powerless (though I will argue that we are far from close to done). Support for social mapping emerges from the criticism of limited admittance of personal values that is significant in propping up and facilitating the establishment of beliefs systems that are particularly in synch with one ideology or the other (Epstein 1983). Additionally, social mapping allows for fluidity in the development and maintenance of the maps, where "people whose concerns include social positions, the perspectives others have of them, and how they fit into society" (Liebman 1996, 203). It is these concepts of position, perspective and fit that affect hierarchies of power that allow the voices of the marginalized to emerge.

If social change is what we are seeking (and one could argue that my requirements for social change could be very different from yours, and at that moment our narratives would diverge), the ways in which we strive for that change may also differ. Understanding these differences leads to interesting questions. Does social mapping take into account the multiple narratives that are to be unpacked? Do the representations of how webs of relationships are woven adequately capture the reach of comparative and international education? Does social mapping allow for the nuances of an increasingly dependent and interdependent world? Are the voices of hegemony and power exercising a dominant force on the work we are attempting?

Power, Women and Education

The role and influence of power in education is still hidden and often ignored at the different levels of educational implementation. Forty years ago Paulston appealed to scholars to understand how structural change in education is manipulated by "power and power-based activities" (Paulston 1977, 394). Education in the hands of the powerful promotes the continued dominance of those in power and maintains the status quo. The highlighting of world statistics of access, enrollment and numbers of schools does little to promote the equitable distribution of education, especially for those historically marginalized populations.

At this juncture, women play a critical role. Education is a necessary and vital component of a woman's development and is a human right. Unfortunately, women have been marginalized in almost every society and from the longest reaches of human memory. Often stripped of agency and power, the status of women was, and often is, equated with that of children. Though governments have signed international mandates to promote the empowerment of women, the focus on improving statistical markers to illustrate gains in women's development does not tell the complete story. In spite of national and international enthusiasm, educational mandates often sacrifice a greater understanding of the challenges of local level implementation in the name of statistical expediency. There are three issues that play a role in how such policies continue to limit women's access to power while also ignoring the local context and culture.

The first significant issue is that the push for women's rights has evolved from a Western framework and has been limited in terms of understanding women's voices from the perspective of their local and cultural contexts. The influence of the west in spearheading these ideas can be understood by reading Christine Fox's (1996, 291) comment on the dilemma involving indigenous communities and the promotion of education: "Members of indigenous societies responsible for schooling and education in their own countries face some fundamental choices between what is often proffered as knowledge in industrial systems, and what is understood as knowledge in its local cultural context." The conflict here lies between the expectations of education to promote employment and gainful participation in the market place versus education that might be of value and importance to the local culture and environment.

Second, women are often considered a homogenous and massive group, for whom Western feminists have been spearheading movements to empower their "sisters in the global south." Amartya Sen's theory of personal capabilities promotes the idea that development of society occurs through the overall well being of every individual in that society (Sen 1996). Yet there is something lacking in the narratives of power that represent the true needs and desires of women in diverse spaces, cultures and life experiences. Often, these interpretations do not adequately convey perspectives beyond "western cultural mini-narratives and Third World political and economic independence" (Liebman and Paulston 1994, np).

Finally, the use of law as a vehicle of social change continues to discount the fact that in most countries women are not socialized to be comfortable with the law—historically considered the bastion of men and authority (Stromquist 1995). Law also remains a concept that is synonymous with power and structure—both of which disallow the reality that women have had limited experience with power, authority and mandates. This makes the international focus on women's education relatively disconnected from local level implementation. Nowhere is this disconnect more clearly visible than in India which has developed a national level policy for women that depends almost completely on local level acceptance in order to be implemented.

SETTING THE STAGE

As a theoretical exercise of how power and women's development intersects with Paulston's ideas of social change and mapping, I draw upon data gathered during 2007–2008 in rural India. Using a qualitative research methodology, and interacting with one rural community in southern India, the research explored how community members and women understood the hierarchies of power and the renegotiation of roles between men and women as a result of the women's participation in a nonformal education, empowerment-focused program. The voices of the community members are well documented in the dissertation and in forthcoming articles (Baily 2008), but this chapter uses the data as an anchor to build a theoretical argument rather than further analyze the situation in the context of development and gender.

In 2001, the Government of India (GOI) recognized that there existed a large gap between the principles of gender equity, as enshrined in the Constitution, and the practice of gender equity (Department of Women and Child Development [DWCD] 2001). By developing the National Policy for the Empowerment of Women (NPEW), the GOI put the abstract concept of empowerment at the center of their strategies for gender equity. The main goal of the NPEW is to address the advancement, development and empowerment of women by:

1. Creating an environment to encourage beneficial policies that would allow for women to attain their full potential;
2. Reiterating the provision of human rights in all arenas including political, economic, social, cultural and civil;

3. Allowing equal access to participation and decision making of women in the social, political and economic life of the nation;
4. Challenging societal attitudes and community practices by encouraging the active participation and involvement of both men and women in all aspects of life; and
5. Mainstreaming a gender perspective in the development process. (DWCD 2001)

Carol C. Mukhopadhyay and Susan Seymour (1994) theorize that there is an inherent tension between the desirability of education for women in India and the constraints foisted on the preservation of social institutions and ideologies. They argue first that India, as an "intensive agriculture, socially stratified, state level (society)," has produced a system of "predominant kinship and family structures and beliefs (which give) precedence to men over women—sons over daughters, fathers over mothers, husbands over wives, and so on" (3). Second, their theory maintains that these relationships manifest themselves in decisions made surrounding education for women in the society. Education in India is a decision that is primarily directed by the male figure in the home, and decisions on allocating family resources (no matter whether the resources are extensive or meager), setting familial goals, and maintaining familial commitments are related to decisions about access to education. Finally, women are faced with alternate obligations towards their family, and to the families in which they will marry. The type of education that is provided to women is dependent on the priority women have in being married (Mukhopadhyay and Seymour 1994).

What would motivate a country such as India to embark on an ambitious agenda focusing primarily on the empowerment of women? Practical, ideological, and national self-interest arguments could be made and any combination of all or some of the reasons could be cobbled together for a correct answer. The main issue here is to illustrate how Paulston's ideas can intersect with this momentum to empower women to facilitate a more local and less linear model of development.

PAULSTON'S REACH—CONNECTING GENDER TO POWER AND EDUCATION

By reframing Paulston's ideas to the context of the development of education for women, I seek to map new connections to enhance our understanding of local contexts of education and empowerment for women. Education for women is still largely a hegemonic exercise that is conceived and implemented at the largest macro levels of educational planning and development. For social change to occur in the lives of the women who are directly impacted by these efforts, the community itself has to play a part in the mapping of that change. Such partnerships between the women and the community link Paulston's ideas of power and nonformal education and allow for a greater understanding of relationships of power in women's development.

Tracing Paulston's Vision to Women's Empowerment

As early as 1977, Paulston argued that power plays a central role in the "theoretical and ideological axes ground in educational change" (1977, 394). His point particularly contends that the redistribution of power is especially salient to marginalized groups in any population. Degrees of marginalization aside, I argue that women have been by far, and in the most uniform patterns across the globe, the most marginalized of peoples. Gender "is one of the few modes of differentiation that has social, cultural, political, and economic implications everywhere in the world" (Gray et al., 2006, 294). This universality of gender juxtaposed with the different ways it is perceived in the world leads to inconsistencies in the understanding of gender equity and empowerment. These inconsistencies limit meaning since the measures to combat inequity are dependent on each individual context, history and policy focus.

Paulston supported the overarching goal of education as a means towards social justice (1990). Early on he determined there were limited studies that "come to grips with the concept of power in either the political and administrative or research and development phases of national reforms" (Paulston 1976, 51). He further argued that major reforms were almost always a "partisan, political process implying the redistribution of power" (1976, 51). Over the past 30 years, world leaders have pushed for national reforms to support gender equity. Education continues to be seen as the lynchpin around which women can seek some redistribution of power. Nonetheless, there still exists a limited exploration of what role power plays in the call for greater empowerment for women.

It is beyond the scope of this chapter to trace if and how Paulston's emerging ideas of power were connected to concurrent scholarship on gender. It can however be concluded that by the early 1970s, an empowered woman was one who was aware of her status, informed of choices to appeal a subordinate status, and held a sense of liberation from within (Kindervatter 1979). It was around the same time that Paulston called for a better understanding of change processes influencing educational reform. Over the last 30 years development professionals have tried to explore how girls and women's lives have explicitly changed as a result of the educational outreach, processes, and efforts.

Rather than tracing the history and evolution of empowerment in Western feminism, this brief framework on empowerment is contained within the scholarship of international development. As mentioned earlier, there is a critical difference between the conceptions of empowerment from Western and non-Western perspectives. Empowerment in Western philosophy is rooted in the rights and roles of women as individuals (Rowlands 1998), while empowerment in the context of international development is beginning to stress the social nature of women and highlights the importance of culture in tandem with women's empowerment (Reza 2003).

Researchers and development practitioners are becoming increasingly aware of how empowerment programs allow marginalized individuals the ability to tap into resources and place a value on their own experiences. The term "empowerment," however, remains ambiguous and difficult to define since the basis of empowerment is contextualized by one's own experiences and choices (Afshar and Alikhan 2002). This becomes increasingly complicated when the oppression of women is layered with other factors including poverty and low levels of education (Afshar and Alikhan 2002).

In an early exploration in the dialogue on empowerment and nonformal education, Suzanne Kindervatter (1979) describes the process of empowerment as one where individuals gain insight of and control over social, economic and/or political entities that could potentially lead to improvements in their social standing. This early definition highlights the fluid nature of empowerment and introduces the focus on process, which subsequent scholars continued to apply to their own definitions of empowerment. Paulston (1976) also supported this focus on process in his exploration of the systemic theories of social and educational change. In his later works he spoke of problematizing knowledge and the systemic notion of process which he considers "mythic and real spaces of contested everyday life" (Paulston 1999, 445).

Within the development context, empowerment has been defined as a "process whereby women become able to organize themselves to increase their own self-reliance, to assert their independent right to make choices and to control resources which will assist in challenging and eliminating their own subordination" (Keller and Mbewe 1991, 78). Jo Rowlands (1995, 102) described empowerment as "bringing people who are outside the decision making process into it," and categorized empowerment into three broad areas: (1) personal empowerment, where it is about a sense of self; (2) close relationship, where empowerment is about negotiating relationships in close structures; and (3) collective empowerment, where people work together to accomplish wide-ranging goals (see also Ugbomeh 2001).

Lutfun N. K.Osmani (1998) argues that women are limited in their own bargaining power in familial relationships and subsequently play a limited or negligible role in decision-making. Osmani's argument stems from a philosophy that the lack of power itself defines empowerment. From Kindervatter's (1979) definition, others argue that empowerment is a process that needs to emerge from within oneself, and cannot be imbued from any outside entity (Afshar 1998). These definitions imply that there is some imbalance of power and the deficiency of power is a result of circumstances, denial or default (Olakulein and Ojo 2006). An extension of this idea is that if there is an imbalance of power to be balanced, there are individuals, who either in perception or reality, stand to be affected during the process of "rebalancing" thus leading to both positive and/or negative repercussions for both the beneficiaries and non-beneficiaries of empowerment related programs.

Empowerment programs have not always emerged championing the weakest in society or leading to exclusively positive results. Claire Mercer (2002) showed how women's participation in local organizations was used as a strategy to increase social standings while concurrently increasing economic standing. Access to these programs are protected by the more privileged in the community, who recognize their power can be expanded as a result of participation, while limiting access to those who they perceive as less desirable. This results in the continued marginalization of the poorest of the poor (Mercer 2002). Additionally, the over-representation of women of higher social and economic status excluded women to whom the program may have had the most meaningful impact—resulting in women's groups legitimizing and perpetuating the inequalities within that society (Mercer, 2002).

Another criticism leveled at empowerment programs is the potential danger of reducing women to objects of, rather than agents for, their own liberation. As countries and international organizations increasingly adopt the language of empowerment, it may have the opposite effect of substituting one oppressor with another (Parmar 2003). This criticism underpins other significant constraints that still hinder the empowerment of women in developing countries. Some of the constraints include:

1. Limited institutional capacity of government to address the needs of women;
2. Top-down development approaches that leave little room for grassroots mobilization;
3. Lack of skills for women to maximize earnings to alleviate poverty; and
4. Shortage of support services to lift burdens of childcare, health, and education; and continued dominance of social inhibitions. (World Bank 1997)

In summary, empowerment remains a process through which women have sought to increase their agency and opportunities for choice, resulting in improved social, economic and political status. Empowerment occurs at the individual level, the familial level, and at the community level, serving as a catalyst for further change and development, not only for women and their children, but also for the broader community within which they live. The process of empowerment can be manifested in various forms, including through health programs, economic programs and through building skills and knowledge through nonformal education programs.

Tracing Paulston's Vision to Women's Nonformal Education

The second point to consider is Paulston's recognition of the growing importance of nonformal education as a tool to support social change. Appearing to build on Paulo Freire's earlier work on grassroots movements and the role of nonformal education, Paulston recognized that for change to occur, researchers and scholars in international education could not neglect the changes happening at the local level (1980). He premised that formal education tended to support the replication of powers that maintains control in society, but that nonformal education programs seeking social change could be the type of "autonomous change-oriented education . . . to facilitate . . . a wide variety of individual and structural change" (Paulston 1980, 64).

Though Paulston was looking at North American and Scandinavian formal and nonformal educational institutions, the spread of nonformal education as a tool for change and for women's empowerment is evolving. It important to note how

Paulston's notions of power and support for nonformal education have been directly or indirectly adapted in the movement for greater equity and equality for women. Today, for good or ill, nonformal education is often tied to microcredit and income-generating programs.

The emergence of nonformal education as a practical solution in the field of education began in 1968, but it was not until Phillip H. Coombs and Manzoor Ahmed's influential work in 1974 that attention shifted to nonformal education. To define nonformal education, Coombs and Ahmed (1974) classified the three main categories of education, namely, formal, informal and nonformal. In their eyes, formal education is characterized by the institutionalized, "chronologically graded and hierarchically structured system" that spans education from primary to university level schooling. Nonformal education is "any organized, systematic, education activity carried on outside the framework of the formal schooling system to provide selected types of learning to particular sub-groups in the population" (8). Informal education is concerned with lifelong learning where "every person acquires and accumulates knowledge, skills, attitudes and insights" (8) from a combination of their lived experiences and their exposure to the outside world.

In his synthesis of nonformal education, Alan Rogers (2004) described the system Coombs and Ahmed (1974) outlined for nonformal education as one part system and one part process. Nonformal education emerged with a scope that was on one hand, short-term and systematic, dealing primarily with adults, to long-term and flexible, addressing the needs of various diverse populations who may or may not continue on to higher education. As a tool for the poor, nonformal education needed to be integrated both "vertically" and "horizontally" (236). The vertical integration would complement activities and organizations to nourish those participating in nonformal education as they progressed to higher levels of education. The horizontal integration occurred to provide complimentality to education programs and "noneducation factors in the same geographic area" such as employment and other social and cultural opportunities (Ibid.).

In an alternate evolution, and separate from the development discourse where Coombs and Ahmed placed it, nonformal education is also tied to empowerment literature through its roots in Freire's work on empowerment with the peasants in Brazil (Moulton 1997). Education, or those engaged in learning, in Freire's (1985, 14) mind, "contribute to their own ability to take charge as the actors of the task." It is the process of knowing one's world that allows for the change in control of that same world. Freire argues "the culture of silence, generated by the objective conditions of an oppressive reality, not only conditions behavior patterns . . . while they are living in the infrastructure that produces oppression but also continues . . . well after the infrastructure has been modified" (30).

It is through this discussion of power, oppression and infrastructure, that Moulton (1997, 13) applies Freire's concepts of empowerment to women, where she notes "Freire was concerned with empowering groups of men to take charge of their political and social environment. . . . Groups are not empowered until their individual members gain the sense of efficacy and understanding to act together." Though early iterations of nonformal education were primarily aimed at men

(Rogers 2004), it was not until 1979 that Kindervatter included women in the dialogue that the role of nonformal education and women. Nelly P. Stromquist (1988) expanded the debate on nonformal education and its impact on and women, but to a great extent, in the early years, nonformal education was limited to sustaining women's subordinate roles rather than focusing on women's empowerment and liberation (Rogers 2004).

If power is one facet of Paulston's work that connected directly to the research and scholarship on gender, education through movements has been a point of intersection as well. His recognition that attention needed to be paid to bottom up, grassroots education to understand the "greater or lesser effectiveness of collective change efforts in a variety of settings" (Paulston 1980, 55) has been the hallmark of how we need to look at women's development. His exploration of Scandinavian nonformal education programs draws direct connections between the uses of alternate forms of education to discount and dismantle structural forms of oppressive behavior, all the while becoming structures of power themselves. He states that these organizations can "become part of the structural obstacle that new groups seeking to realize other dreams must oppose with new educational strategies, as anti-structure consistent with their perceptions of structural bonds and social justice" (65).

COMMUNITY DEVELOPMENT AND THE EMPOWERMENT VACUUM

I draw attention to the parallel and congruent patterns between the work of Paulston and others in the field of gender and education to highlight how both power and nonformal education are relevant facets of women's development. Education for women, especially in the developing world, has focused on increasing the power women have over themselves and their lives. What is missing in the conversation is the role of relationships beyond those in the family, which are also central to the notions of agency and voice. The importance of relationships has been an aspect of Paulston's conceptualization of power in educational change and community development through the development of his theories of social mapping. Similarly relationships are also pivotal and undergird any successful and effective change for women.

As scholars and students of comparative and international education, it is not possible to view the field as a "natural object outside of human experience . . . (but to realize it) is constituted by what people in and around the field say about its nature, origins, purposes, futures . . . (and) by the truths people promote" (Mehta and Ninnes 2003, 240). Though it is popular to use women's empowerment as an overarching theme to address women's education, there is not often a clear understanding of the impact these changes have on the broader community within which women reside.

In spite of the many studies that address the impact education and empowerment programs have had on women, most continue to highlight the changes that occur within the women themselves or within the confines of their family (Colletta et al. 1982; Aksornkool 1993; Jones 1995; Lephoto 1995; Moulton 1997; Bosch 1998;

Mfum-Mensah 2003). This focus on the family highlights the growing importance to "admit that power transactions occur at all levels of society and that the lower levels are equally important" (Stromquist 1995, 433). In her article on power and education, Stromquist discusses Foucault's conception of micropower, which has helped feminists define "that power is not always power over but also power with and that it is not only public but mostly private" (Ibid.). It is their exploration of local power that is both public and private that bears the greater scrutiny.

More recent community related empowerment measures have taken a broader look at how women and education programs have sought to take collective action or had some representation in politics (Snyder 2003; Tesoriero 2006; Chatterjee 2008). Again, this falls far short of mapping the complex and interrelated lives which are at the heart of altering structures of power. There have been calls to understand the role of men as gatekeepers in women's development (Connell 2005). Nonetheless, these ideas have not been systematically studied or even mapped to the extent that we can visualize the complex nature of the interactions.

These relationships can hinder, hamper or help in the alteration of women's roles, yet limited efforts have been expended on exploring how these relationships are transformed as a result. I would argue that empowerment does not occur in a vacuum and it is in our best interest as educational researchers and scholars to recognize that the effectiveness of such programs depends in great part on the interaction of relationships.

The paradoxical nature of empowerment is that though it is conceptualized at the national and international levels of policy-making, the operations of empowerment occur predominantly at the grassroots level (Parpart 2002). This has led to an increase in the number of theories on women's empowerment and subsequently, movement at the policy levels (both nationally and internationally) to embrace empowerment as an overarching development goal around which to rally (Añonuevo and Bochynek 1993). Yet, it is the engagement or disengagement of community members that affect how women translate knowledge related to empowerment into action. Paulston's point on educational movements impresses upon scholars the need for complimentary approval by structures of power related to and surrounding the change agent. According to Paulston (1980, 58), "social movements are tolerated only when their potential threat to the status quo is in some degree acceptable to those in control of the polity, the military, the courts and the police." Similarly, the push for women's empowerment could easily be categorized as a movement requiring the same level of permissions from the structures of power surrounding them.

The argument for the need to understand this empowerment vacuum and to work cohesively and systematically with structures of power emerges out of the aforementioned qualitative study conducted in rural India in late 2007. A critical perspective was used to provide a detailed exploration into the nuances of relationships and the nature of altering the dynamics of power in one particular case. The key findings that emerged from the data was that women who were growing more cognizant of their power in the community, renegotiated new roles for themselves in the village, and were actively engaged in the development of their village. What was evident was that though empowerment was defined through the perspective of the individual, the impact of the women's participation altered their community. By hypothesizing that this is not an unusual occurrence, what appears unusual is that there has been limited interest in exploring the broader social and structural ramifications of what happens beyond the individual and the family. The broad social indicators are considered of value to national and international entities in holding a linear and univocal accountability among unequal participants.

The women and the power holders showed how their thinking changed over the course of time as well as defined how their complimentary expectations of the role of woman and her empowered behavior within the community also changed. Some of the negative considerations of the community towards the women signaled the fragile nature of the willingness to "accept" the more vocal and active women. The still high levels of control over the women at the hands of the power holders in the village emphasized that there is also a pervading wariness that too much freedom and opportunity for the women might not be welcomed as easily. The overall poverty of the whole community caused strife among those who could not understand why the women were only being singled out when all could benefit from certain programs. The relative fear of women being taken to trainings by men unknown to the community could have led to tragic consequences if there was any semblance of "irregular" behavior (perceived or actual) (Baily 2008). All these complexities are impossible to disentangle without accepting the empowerment vacuum and the systematic need to understand how the multiple actors, actions, cultures, roles, and outputs are integrated. The long-term change in how the community views empowered women will require more research in the years to come. Thus, it becomes critical to highlight the theoretical framework of how the community affects and influences the rebalancing of power. These intricate renegotiations and understandings of separate truths are well-suited to Paulston's support of social cartography where the "social map (might even reflect) the perceived efforts of social changes in real space . . . (and even represent) that space through the creation of multiple social maps" (Paulston and Liebman 1996, 23).

CONCLUDING DISCUSSION

In the spirit of Paulston, it becomes an imperative to view women's empowerment as a map where the "cyclic pattern of individual cognitive development and the cyclic pattern of social development are interrelated; (and where) education, the link between individual and social development are investigated" (1996, 5). Mapping is not easy and in attempting to do so, one might only provide a framework that does not effectively illustrate the "fragmentation of societies, (the) fluid relationship between societies and groupings" (Watson 1998, 12).

In an effort to move beyond that simple framework, Figure 12.1 represents the transformation of perceptions and willingness to renegotiate roles as a result of education and empowerment-related efforts to facilitate the use of women's voice and agency.

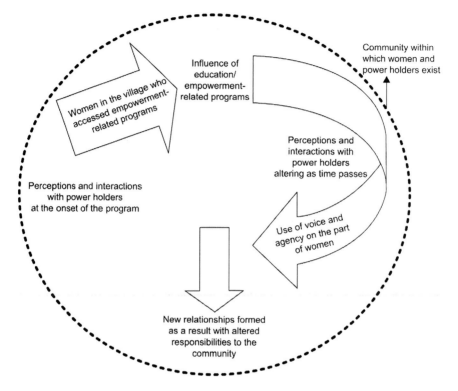

Figure 12.1. Changing Perceptions of Powerholders as
Women Access Empowerment Programs.

The empowerment vacuum focuses attention on the fact that there is a necessary rebalancing of power in formal, informal, or undercover ways. There is also a level of change to be anticipated when power relations are altered. As feminist scholars, development professionals, and educational experts work to influence the balance of women's equity in communities, there is a need to understand what happens to the moving parts and players who are in contact with the women. Empowerment is dynamic. The significance of shifting points of view cannot be understated; yet, the reality is that empowerment for women can be manifested in many different ways. Disentangling these manifestations is complicated. National and international measures that appear relatively "simple" and limited in meaning and scope, often fail to adequately gauge levels of empowerment among women. To understand what is really unfolding in the engagement of women in their communities, a further exploration of the relationships developed within *and* without the family is paramount.

By ignoring these relationships, we are left with the empty promise that empowerment remains merely a philosophical and personal bent that has little to do with altering a women's status in the community. Ignoring the impact women have on the community further complicates the situation as it pits men against women in communities where there are already limited resources and where poverty is a greater handicap for all people in the community.

This chapter traces a parallel track between the works Paulston presented over his 30 plus years in the field, and the movement to engage women with greater voice and agency. I also highlight a breach in efforts around understanding empowerment and gender and make the case that by ignoring the empowerment vacuum we only limit opportunities communities have to transform based on the participation of all adults in the community. If Paulston's work "contributes to a more open social and intellectual dialogue with theoretical orientations that have heretofore been marginalized and excluded from social discourse" (Rust 1996, 29), we must not allow kudos to ourselves about how far women have come when we have a limited and/or unclear understanding of the impact women have had outside of the confines of their households. Our ability to map the transformation of communities relies on the development of a research agenda that explores the broader impact women have had, and by taking notice of the vacuum, we might actually be able to begin a conversation that moves us to understand how and why the balance of power might better be shared.

REFERENCES

Afshar, Haleh, ed. (1998). *Women and Empowerment: Illustrations from the Third World*. Basingstoke, UK: Macmillan Press.

Afshar, Haleh, & Fatima Alikhan. (2002). "Age and Empowerment amongst Slum Dwelling Women in Hyderabad." *Journal of International Development*, 14(8), 1153–1161.

Aksornkool, Namtip. (1993). "Educate to Empower." In *Women's Education and Empowerment, by UNESCO*. Hamburg, Germany: UNESCO.

Añonuevo, Carolyn, & Bettina Bochynek. (1993). "The International Seminar on Women's Empowerment." In *Women's Education and Empowerment, ed. UNESCO*. Hamburg, Germany: UNESCO.

Baily, Supriya. (2008). "Negotiating for Power: Women and Nonformal Education in India." PhD diss., Graduate School of Education, George Mason University, Fairfax, USA.

Bosch, Anna E. (1998). "Popular Education, Work Training, and the Path to Women's Empowerment in Chile." *Comparative Education Review*, 42(2), 163–182.

Chatterjee, Piya. (2008). "Hungering for Power: Borders and Contradictions in Indian Tea Plantation Women's Organizing." *Signs: Journal of Women in Culture and Society*, 33(3), 497–505.

Colletta, Nate J., Reed T. Ewing, & Terry A. Todd. (1982). "Cultural Revitalization, Participatory Nonformal Education and Village Development in Sri Lanka: The Sarvodaya Shramadana Movement." *Comparative Educational Review*, 26(2), 271–285.

Connell, Robert W. (2005). "Change among the Gatekeepers: Men, Masculinity, and Gender Equity in the Global Arena." *Signs: Journal of Women and Culture in Society*, 30(3), 1801–1825.

Coombs, Philip H., & Manzoor Ahmed. (1974). *Attacking Rural Poverty: How Non-Formal Education can Help*. Washington, DC: World Bank.

Department of Women and Child Development (DWCD). (2001). National Policy for the Empowerment of Women. New Delhi, India: DWCD. Available online at http://wcd.nic.in/empwomen.htm.

Epstein, Erwin H. (1983). "Currents Left and Right: Ideology in Comparative Education." *Comparative Educational Review*, 27(1), 3–29.

Fox, Christine. (1996). "Listening to the Other: Mapping Intercultural Communication in Postcolonial Educational Consultancies." In Rolland. G. Paulston (Ed.), *Social Cartography: Mapping Ways of Seeing Social and Educational Change*. New York: Garland Publishing.

Freire, Paulo. (1985). *The Politics of Education: Culture, Power and Liberation*. South Hadley, MA: Bergin & Garvey Publishers.

Gray, Mark M., Miki Caul Kittilson, & Wayne Sandholtz. (2006). "Women and Globalization: A Study of 180 Countries, 1975–2000." *International Organization, 60*(2), 293–333.

Jones, Adele. (1995). "Nonformal Education and Women's Empowerment: Perspective on South Pacific Praxis." *ASPABE Courier, 61,* 32–36.

Keller, Bonnie, & Dorcas C. Mbewe. (1991). "Policy and Planning for the Empowerment of Zambia's Women Farmers." *Canadian Journal of Development Studies, 12*(1), 75–88.

Kindervatter, Suzanne. (1979). *Nonformal Education as an Empowering Process with Case Studies from Indonesia and Thailand.* Amherst, MA: Center for International Education, University of Massachusetts.

Lahiri-Dutt, Kuntala, & Gopa Samanta. (2002). "State Initiatives for the Empowerment of Women of Rural Communities: Experiences from eastern India." *Community Development Journal, 37*(2), 137–156.

Liebman, Martin. (1996). "Envisioning Spatial Metaphors from Wherever We Stand." In Rolland G. Paulston (Ed.), *Social Cartography: Mapping Ways of Seeing Social and Educational Change* (pp.191–215). New York: Garland Publishing.

Liebman, Martin, & Rolland G. Paulston. (1994). "Social Cartography: A New Methodology for Comparative Studies." *Compare, 24*(3), 233–245.

Lephoto, Hyacinth M. (1995). "Empowering Women for Development through Non-formal Education: The Case of Lesotho." PhD diss., University of Southern California, Los Angeles, USA.

Mehta, Sonia, & Peter Ninnes. (2003). "Postmodernism Debates and Comparative Education: A Critical Discourse Analysis." *Comparative Educational Review, 47*(2), 238–255.

Mercer, Claire. (2002). "The Discourse of Maendeleo and the Politics of Women's Participation on Mount Kilimanjaro." *Development and Change 33*(1), 101–127.

Mfum-Mensah, Obed. (2003). "Fostering Educational Participation in Pastoral Communities through Non-formal Education: The Ghanaian Perspective." *International Journal of Educational Development 23*(6), 661–677.

Moulton, Jeanne. (1997). *Formal and Nonformal Education and Empowered Behavior: A Review of the Research Literature.* Washington, DC: USAID.

Mukhopadhyay, Carol C., & Susan Seymour, eds. (1994). *Women, Education, and Family Structure in India.* Boulder, CO: Westview Press.

Olakulein, Felix K., & Olugbenga D. Ojo. (2006). "Distance Education as a Women Empowerment Strategy in Africa." *Turkish Online Journal of Distance Education, 7*(1), 149–154.

Osmani, Lutfun N. K. (1998). "The Grameen Bank Experiment: Empowerment of Women through Credit." In Haleh Afshar (Ed.), *Empowerment and Women: Illustrations from the Third World* (pp.67–85). Basingstoke, UK: MacMillan Press.

Parmar, Aradhana. (2003). "Micro-credit, Empowerment, and Agency: Re-evaluating the Discourse." *Canadian Journal of Development Studies, 24*(3), 461–476.

Parpart, Jane L., Shirin M. Rai, & Kathleen Staudt. (2002). *Rethinking Empowerment: Gender and Development in a Global/Local World.* New York: Routledge.

Paulston, Rolland G. (1976). *Conflicting Theories of Social and Educational Change: A Typological Review.* Pittsburgh, PA: University Center for International Studies, University of Pittsburgh.

Paulston, Rolland G. (1977). "Social and Educational Change: Conceptual Frameworks." *Comparative Education Review, 21*(2&3), 370–395.

Paulston, Rolland G. (1980). "Education as Anti-structure: Non-formal Education in Social and Ethnic Movements." *Comparative Education, 16*(1), 55–66.

Paulston, Rolland G. (1990). "From Paradigm Wars to Disputatious Community." *Comparative Education Review, 34*(3), 395–400.

Paulston, Rolland G., ed. (1996). *Social Cartography: Mapping Ways of Seeing Social and Educational Change.* New York: Garland Publishing.

Paulston, Rolland G. (2000). "Imagining Comparative Education: Past, Present, Future." *Compare, 30*(3), 353–367.

Paulston, Rolland G., & Martin Liebman. (1996). "Social Cartography: A New Metaphor/Look for Comparative Studies." In Rolland G. Paulston (Ed.), *Social Cartography: Mapping Ways of Seeing Social and Educational Change* (pp. 7–28). New York: Garland Publishing.

Reza, Md. Hasan. (2003). "When Culture Trumps Ideology: Micro-enterprise and the Empowerment of Women in Bangladesh." *Canadian Journal of Development Studies, 24*(3), 439–459.

Rogers, Alan. (2004). Non-formal Education: Flexible Schooling or Participatory Education? Hong Kong: Comparative Education Research Centre (CERC) and Kluwer Academic Publishers.

Rowlands, Jo. (1995). "Empowerment Examined." *Development in Practice, 5*(2), 101–107.

Rowlands, Jo. (1998). "A Word of the Times, but what does it Mean? Empowerment in the Discourse and Practice of Development." In Haleh Afshar (Ed.), *Empowerment and Women: Illustrations from the Third World* (pp. 11–34). Basingstoke, UK: Macmillan.

Rust, Val D. (1996). "From Modern to Postmodern Ways of Seeing Social and Educational Change." In Rolland G. Paulston (Ed.), *Social Cartography: Mapping Ways of Seeing Social and Educational Change* (pp. 29–51). New York: Garland Publishing.

Sen, Amartya. (1996). *Development as Freedom.* New York: Anchor Books.

Snyder, Margaret. (2004). "Women Determine Development: The Unfinished Revolution." *Signs: Journal of Women in Culture and Society, 29*(2), 619–632.

Stromquist, Nelly P. (1995). "Romancing the State: Gender and Power in Education." *Comparative Education Review, 39*(4), 423–454.

Stromquist, Nelly P. (1990). "Women and Illiteracy: The Interplay of Gender Subordination and Poverty." *Comparative Education Review, 34*(1), 95–111.

Tesoriero, Frank. (2006). "Strengthening Communities through Women's Self Help Groups in South India." *Community Development Journal 41*(3), 321–333.

Ugbomeh, George M. M. (2001). "Empowering Women in Agricultural Education for Sustainable Rural Development." *Community Development Journal, 36*(4), 289–302.

United Nations. (2007). Rural Women Face Problems of Discrimination and Manifold Disadvantages. *General Assembly held on 16 October 2007 (GA/SHC/3887).* New York: United Nations.

United Nations Development Programme (UNDP). (2006). *Millennium Development Goals.* New York: UNDP.

United Nations Population Fund (UNFPA). (2007). *Linking Population, Poverty and Development.* New York: UNFPA. Available online at: http://www.unfpa.org.

Watson, Keith. (1998). "Memories, Models and Mapping: The Impact of Geopolitical Changes on Comparative Studies in Education." *Compare, 28*(1), 5–31.

World Bank. (1997). *Staff Appraisal Report.* Washington, DC: World Bank.

MINA O'DOWD

13. DEVELOPMENT AND HUMANIST CONCERNS

A Professionalism Project for Comparative Education?

At the end of a long scholarly road, I opt to join those who willingly attempt what may seem to be an impossible task, "to acknowledge the partiality of one's story (indeed, of all stories) and still tell it with authority and conviction" while mapping it into the debate field of comparative education. (Paulston 2005, 1)

Increasingly attention has focused, not least through the work of Rolland G. Paulston, on what constitutes or does not constitute comparative education, what the rules are, who are entitled to identify themselves as comparative educators, and what kind of theories, methods and data are considered appropriate. It has become compelling to clarify for oneself and others what the underlying premises for one's work as a comparative educator are, as neo-liberal agendas and imperatives become more powerful. It is maintained in this chapter that comparative education can no longer maintain that it is a value-free, objective and non-political enterprise. Audrey Osler and Hugh Starkey (1999), Lynn Davis (2008), Caroline Dyer (2010), Madeleine Arnot (2009) and Susan Robertson (2010) argue convincingly that education is a human right, while the practice and policy implementation of education undermines human rights. Moreover the argument can be advanced that development can only be justified in terms of the extent to which it promotes and preserves human rights. In this chapter it is argued that it follows that we as researchers become obliged to identify our agendas and justify what we do and how we perceive our work in terms of the promotion and preservation of human rights.

The aim of this chapter is to raise a number of issues with relevance to comparative education. First, the aim is to address the increasingly difficult relation between education and development, questioning its veracity and its legitimacy, as education increasingly is seen as instrumentalism[1] and an expression of a neoliberal agenda. Or as Anne Hickling-Hudson (2006, 194) writes,

the central facts in development are international capital, regional power blocs, and the position of nation states, but its metanarratives and its assumptions of superiority have racial undertones. . . . Although "race" has no biological validity, it is a socio-historical construct which is an important aspect of identity, as well as being a principle influencing particular types of social structures, transforming physical space, the human body, consciousness,

John C. Weidman, W. James Jacob (eds.), Beyond the Comparative: Advancing Theory and Its Application to Practice, 235–252.

institutions, and contributing to the concept and techniques of modernist development.

Education, seen as a human right, entails a number of far-fetching consequences for research and practice, policy and implementation. It follows, then, that it also entails some re-thinking as regards comparative education. Is comparative education a discipline as Donatella Palomba (2010) maintains? If so, is it a social science; is it multi-disciplinary? Or is it, as Palomba maintains, a humane science? Re-thinking comparative education as a humane science has the advantage of putting people back into the discourse, a discourse that for all intents and purposes appears to have displaced them. What is a humane science, if not a multidisciplinary field, in which all human endeavours are included (Cassirer 1957)?

What distinguishes comparative education from the vast field of educational research? Is it enough to insist that comparative education is that which uses a comparative perspective, when more and more research is being conducted in political science, sociology, legal studies, and economics, to name but a few fields in which a comparative perspective is used? Is what we do as academics, as comparative educators, professional? On one hand, "academic professionals" are identified in relation to three aspects (i.e., academic discipline, career stages and institutional type) (Teichler 2010, 161). On the other hand, academics are categorized as "semi-professional"[2] (Brante 2010, 97). Recent discussions with comparative educators from England reveal that it is becoming increasingly difficult in that national context to justify teaching comparative education, a trend that may eventually reach other nations. It was maintained that the existence of the World Council of Comparative Education Societies (WCCES) serves as a means of legitimizing the need for comparative education nationally. This discussion and others have encouraged me to outline the scape of comparative education as a profession. What can characterize comparative education as a profession? Do we have one identifiable knowledge base? What are the standards that characterize our profession? What are our goals and what are the ontological models that guide our work? Or do any of the aforementioned traditional criteria apply to the field of comparative education, when considered a profession?

At the same time, it should be noted that "de-professionalization" is increasingly being discussed, related often to New Public Management (NPM). While Karin Healy (2009) reports on effects of NPM on social welfare professionals in Australia, Hanne Dahl (2009) addresses the same issues in relation to care professionals in Denmark. What these two discussions have in common is what is termed de-professionalization (i.e., the process by which professional identity and influence are challenged), often related to gendered assumptions about professional identity. At this particular time in history, it seems appropriate to discuss a professionalism project (Scuilli 2005) for comparative education. Rather than relying on Anglo-American or Continental Sociology of Professions, a professionalism project for comparative education entails formulation of a globalized comparative education professionalism project, in much the same way as Shailaja Fennel and Madeleine Arnot (2008) argue for a "globalized feminism": to counter-act hegemony through education.

A globalized comparative education professionalism project entails the following components:

- Acknowledging, first, that professionals occupy *in their occupational field entrenched positions of power, trust and discretion*, and that these positions of power obligate professionals to *acknowledge their clients' positions of dependence, vulnerability and apprehension*
- Second, professions and their associations bear *structurally* two fiduciary responsibilities simultaneously. A failure to bear this fiduciary responsibility, whether consciously or inadvertently, results in what can be called the immediate externalities of the professional—client relationship. *Immediate harm is done to the clients, workplaces and communities directly involved in and affected by professional services. Professions and their associations bear a fiduciary responsibility for institutional design that is inherent in the governance, regulation and activities of any structured situation in civil society.*
- Third, professions and associations that exhibit ongoing behavioral fidelity to these two fiduciary responsibilities find it necessary structurally, to this end, *to establish and maintain ongoing deliberation.* Professionals bearing both fiduciary responsibilities, that is, have no alternative other than to *ceaselessly scan their environments for any changes in their knowledge base or in client needs that bear on the positional interests of anyone in their entrenched position of power.* This is why professional instruction includes a learned or theoretical component and also why professions and their associations are uniquely organized in a collegial form rather than others. (Sciulli 2005, 936–937, italics added)

A globalized comparative education professionalism project is suggested herein as a way forward for comparative education. It can, however, be argued that how we define the field and how we define what we do has consequences for our profession and whether or not our efforts have value, relevance and impact both in and outside of the comparative education field itself.

BACKGROUND

Over the years comparative and international education has experienced conflicts. One of these is the conflict that has arisen around the "shrill debate over the objectivity of knowledge and science" (Lynch 1998, 2). This debate has never been resolved, nor have the central issues and their ramifications been adequately addressed. We have experienced, on the one hand, a power manifestation, which often has said more about authors' vested professional/occupational interests than the scientific implications of the objectivity of knowledge and science. On the other hand, efforts have been made to redefine the field, with comparative education being the central category and International Education being one of many sub-fields belonging to this category (Phillips and Schweisfurth 2006). Moreover, attempts have been made to clarify what comparative education is through the purpose and intentions of research conducted in the field (Nóvoa and

Yaruv-Mashal 2003). Frustration and disillusionment have also been expressed, with regard to the discourses of fear and desire that characterize the field of comparative education:

> First, they act to prescribe the boundaries of the field and its future possibilities, in terms of aims, methods, and purposes and so on. Second, they act to position authors and readers within and outside of the field. By analysing these discourses of fear and desire, we begin to recognize how authors in the field either contribute to its growth and development or alternatively seek to limit, preserve or contain it. (Ninnes 2008, 346)

Among those who have contributed to the growth and development of comparative education, Rolland G. Paulston and Val D. Rust stand out. Paulston (1996, 9) has consistently rejected metanarratives, viewing them as "totalizing, standardizing and predominating." Rust (1996, 31) concurs: "The danger of grand narrative developers is that they and their devotees continue to overstate the potential of their narrative. They play a power game in that they would exclude other narratives, claiming that only their narrative is legitimate." The field of comparative education is not without both "grand narrative developers" and "their devotees," a fact of which one can assume Rust was well aware when he gave his 1991 presidential address to the Comparative and International Education Society. Allowing space for multiple perspectives and multiple voices would appear to be a prerequisite for research, teaching and training in comparative education. However, this appears not to be the case. The knowledge base that is comparative education has been constructed over the years on the exclusion of others and the perspectives and experiences of so many different groups. As innocent as the claim for the necessity to allow space for difference to enter the discourse might first appear, it ultimately has consequences for the scientific project itself. The cumulative process by which our knowledge claims are assumed to be developed, maintained and defended is questioned when the process is viewed as an exclusive process, that is, when we take into consideration that the cumulative process has rested on the inclusion of only a portion of the voices, perspectives and experiences concerned. This poses a serious challenge to what we assume to be "the known," to what we are prepared to acknowledge as "knowledge" and to whom we view as legitimate knowledge producers who are thus vested with the status and power associated with this designation (see Latour 1990, 1993, 1999; Lynch 1998; Paulston 1996, 2005).

SCIENTIFIC KNOWLEDGE AND THE MARKET

> The relationship between researchers and industry is undoubtedly one of the most striking trends of recent years, and it significantly characterizes the current organization and policy of research. In areas like microelectronics, nanotechnology and biotechnology, especially, one witnesses an unprecedented interweaving between research and the market whereby 'scientific knowledge' is transformed into economic activity. (Bucchi 2008, 135)[3]

In the field of comparative education research, Antonió Nóvoa and Tali Yaruv-Mashal (2003, 423) identify a similar trend where "comparative educational studies are used as a political tool creating education policy, rather than a research method or an intellectual inquiry." With education undergoing a redefinition and reconceptualization as instrumentalism (O'Dowd 2009, 2010), voices can be heard of those who reject this perception of the goals and purpose of education (Harris 2007; Buras and Apple 2008; Standish 2008; O'Dowd 2009, 2010), while expressing concern for the practice of education and the training of future generations Susan Harris (2007, 354) expresses her concern in the following manner:

> The value of education as important in itself is not recognised. There is no recognition of the purpose of education as a means of questioning the self and society. There is no space to think about difference and what it means in a globalised economy.

Expressing his concern with "the importance of questions of naming" with reference to new philosophies of learning, Paul Standish (2008, 352) states that there is reason "to question how far accounts of emotional intelligence, well-being and self-esteem, fight shy of direct considerations of ethical matters, becoming in the process a conceptual muddle and offering no more than a panacea." In the wake of new learning philosophies, Standish sees as inevitable the categorizing of people as a result of the new learning becoming "jargon." Suggesting that the use of such familiar terms as "intelligent" or "non-intelligent," as "normal" or "abnormal," can lead to educational deprivation, Standish asks: "what impoverishments may that new jargon hold in store?"

In the United States, Kristen Buras and Michael Apple (2008) discuss the problematic issue of neoconservatism in the United States and its impact on contemporary schooling. Tracing the history of neoconservatism[4] in the United States, the authors maintain that: "the unimaginative emphasis of neoconservatives on enforcing academic standards while dismissing the difficult but essential work of debating whose standards count (and to which effect) is narrow and politically naïve" (297).

At the same time, the authors question the redefinition of utopianism in the neoconservative context of the United States, a redefinition which they claim robs utopianism of its visionary power. Buras and Apple stress that transformations are necessary to bring about "more just and humane social arrangements" than those which constitute knowledge in schools at present, urging us to engage in a continued process of "debating, envisioning and re-envisioning" to counteract "the deadening standardisation, 'security' and 'stability' endorsed by neoconservatives" who have rejected the utopian ideals (299).

The importance of utopian ideals is stressed by Buras and Apple who see history as a means by which to "re-educate desire, initiate the infinite process of re-thinking schools and ignite a renewed confidence in the possibilities of imagination," thereby stressing the marginalizing effect neoconservativism is having on imagination (299). What is utopianism? Briefly, it is "[T]he idea that we can possibly go somewhere that exists only in our imagination. . . . The map to a new world is in the imagination, in what we see in our third eyes rather than in the desolation that surrounds us" (Kelley 2002, 2). If we together view a new world with our third eye, we may envision a new world in which there are new structures of knowledge. What more appropriate time to begin seeing less unimaginatively, than when we are faced with the "global economic crisis," and the danger posed by the AIDS and the A/H1N1[5] pandemics, their causes and consequences for our own lives and the lives of countless others. Immanuel Wallerstein (1997, 10) identifies this as a time when "[T]he modern world-system has developed structures of knowledge that are significantly different from previous structures of knowledge." He urges us to consider the implications of these new structures of knowledge:

> What is specific to the structures of knowledge in the modern world-system is the concept of the "two cultures." No other historical system has instituted a fundamental divorce between science and philosophy/humanities, or what I think would be better characterized as the separation of the quest for the true and the quest for the good and the beautiful. . . . The idea that science is over here and socio-political decisions are over there is the core concept that sustains Eurocentrism, since the only universalist propositions that have been acceptable are those which are Eurocentric.

Wallerstein's claims echo Esther Gottlieb's (2000, 171) vision for the future of comparative education, in which she sees

> a [different] construction of knowledge. The destabilization of the dominant modernist genres of discourse and the opening up of space for the actors' voices and authority will introduce indigenous knowledge and new categories into the semantic universe of comparative education, through the typical interpretative underlying metaphors of culture as text, metaphor and game.

SOCIAL CARTOGRAPHY

As a response to demands for space for actors' voices and indigenous knowledge, Paulston (1996, 319) developed social cartography mapping and published a seminal work on the topic. In *Social Cartography: Mapping Ways of Seeing Social and Educational Change*, different mappings are presented by cartographers and comparativists alike, providing insight into how mapping social and educational change can be done. In the same context, Paulston defines social cartography as seeking to "visualize and re-present the simultaneity, diversity and power inherent in all the social 'scapes' that can be seen to constitute our world today."

Each of the contributors to the volume on *Social Cartography* has shown how they have made use of this methodology. This volume signals a new way of seeing comparative education, its role, its goals and its legitimacy. Hence, old problems can be "seen" in new and different ways, offering greater possibilities to resolve these same problems and to address new problems.

Over the years education has been defined in numerous and often contradictory ways. As definitions have become more elaborate and expansive, in the wake of globalization and neoliberalism, it appears that human beings have become displaced, as the priorities and goals of nation-states, supranational regimes,[6] and the market have redefined education. It is argued here that this might be an appropriate time in which to get back to basic, as it were, re-instating humans and humanist concerns in education. Indeed, one can even argue as does Robertson (2010) that there is a need for us as educators to investigate whether there are "spaces for citizens' voices" today, defining education as the site at which social relations are learned and social order is taught. This argument appears to also require that we study the demands that have been made and continue to be made on education to become more efficient. As education over the years increasingly was viewed from an economic perspective, not least due to its proposed usefulness in promoting development, a number of concerns have arisen. Despite claims that education can and should be effective, other voices have been raised to challenge this assumption. Notable is that of Everett Reimer (1971, 13):

> Schools in all nations, of all kinds, at all levels, combine four distinct social functions: custodial care, social-role selection, indoctrination, and education as usually defined in terms of the development of skills and knowledge. . . . It is the conflict among these functions which makes schools inefficient. It is the combination of these functions which tends to make school a total institution . . . and which makes it such an effective instrument of social control.

Reimer's thoughts are expressed by Michel Foucault (1977, 304) in the following manner:

> The judges of normality are present everywhere. We are in the society of the teacher-judge, the doctor-judge, the educator-judge, the 'social-worker' judge; it is on them that the universal reign of the normative is based; and each individual, wherever he may find himself, subjects it to his body, his gestures, his behavior, his aptitudes, his achievements.

ANOTHER FORM OF SCHOOLING

Sciulli describes in detail what he terms as the first example of professionalism in Europe, maintaining that the lack of attention that this example has received has affected and continues to influence the sociological understanding of professions. Rather than set as its starting point four particular occupational fields (law and medicine, science and engineering), Sciulli (2010, 41, emphasis in the original) proposes that "in unthinkably approaching the *historiographic* record of the entire occupational order with these four *modern* occupations in mind, this invariably yields indefensible Whiggish misreadings of this record." Tracing the advent and development of visual culture in mid-seventeenth century Europe, Sciulli shows how the establishment of a visual *Academie*—the *Academie Royale de Peinture et de Sculpture* in Paris in 1648 by Louis XIV and Jean-Baptiste Colbert can be seen to clarify what constitutes professionalism. Three major steps are undertaken, which, according to Sciulli (2010, 44–46), distinguish "the Paris visual *Academie* from all other expert occupations in any field":

- In 1660 the first "professional graduate school" in Western history is established, through the opening in Rome of the *Academie de France*. Admission was based on "merit and success in student competitions," rather than "nepotism, patronage or venality;
- Students submit drawings or other works that they have completed unsupervised over the course of several months. Then three judges administer the *prove*, an extemporaneous drawing exercise used for comparison to the submission, to ensure that instructors or masters had not assisted the contestants. Only now does the actual competition begin, among students who survive this screening. Now assigned the same subject, all drawings submitted for the next round are executed on site, in separated work areas, and submitted numbered, not signed, all for purposes of anonymous scoring;
- The founding guidelines for the new student competition apply principles and precepts of narrative painting which the *Academie* is simultaneously identifying and standardizing, through a new series of formal *conferences* initiated in 1667. With this the Academie initiates and sustains learned—intellection-based— discussions and debates which simultaneously advance its instructional and occupational ends;
- In the *Academie's* case, one academician each month analyzes before the entire assembly one exemplary painting (or sculpture) borrowed from the royal collection. Interested amateurs are also invited to participate fully and freely during the discussion period;
- The *Academie* refines, standardizes and disseminates the first *visual-based* lexicon—as opposed to literary-based, strictly oral vocabulary—in Western history; and
- The success of the satellite visual school in Rome is already sufficiently notable by 1676 that the older *Accademia di San Luca* in Rome formally merges with the parent, still upstart, visual *Academie* in Paris . . . an unprecedented organizational development in any field of occupational activity.

The *Academie Royale de Peinture et de Sculpture* is not only another form of schooling than that which Reimer describes above, but also, according to Sciulli the first example in Europe of professionalization, in which instructional, organizational and occupational upgrading is undertaken: the Paris *Academie* was "a reason-giving collegial formation which, as such, institutionalized both disinterestedness and ongoing deliberation" (46–47).

Professionalism

The fifth constant of a profession requires an ideology "asserting greater devotion to doing good work than to economic reward" (Freidson 2004, 180). What of, professionalism, then? To what extent can comparative education be conceived of as a profession? What, if so, does viewing comparative education as a professionalism project entail? First a brief account for professions will be given, singling out the concept of profession itself and discussing it in relation to collegiality and discretion.

Scuilli (2010) argues that research on the sociology of professions has thus far lacked the adequate theoretical and conceptual tools for understanding the complexity of professionalism. Towards this end a discussion is undertaken of what is termed the structural and institutional invariance of professions and professionalism, in which the distinctions between Anglo-American and European understandings of these concepts is underlined. Tracing the development of the sociology of professions from the 1930s to present, Scuilli reminds us of the lists of "traits" and "qualities" first devised to distinguish professions from occupations, such as those produced by Ronald Pavalko (1971).[7] Later Randal Collins (1990) questions the basis for the sociology of professions, as laid out by Talcott Parsons (1937, 1939, 1952) arguing for a narrower perception of professions (i.e., as the "structure of privilege"). Scuilli (2010, 37), on the other hand, terms the absence of research on what Parsons and others viewed as the contribution of professionalism to social integration as "disastrous":

> Yet, if Parsons and other functionalists were correct, if professions do contribute uniquely to social integration under modern conditions, and thereby ameliorate the negative effects of state bureaucracy and market commercialism, then this oversight in this literature is nothing short of disastrous. It draws attention away from the factors potentially vital in integrating new democracies, and, equally vital, in retaining or increasing integration in established democracies.

Proposing that a convergence has occurred between Anglo-American and European sociology of professions, and rejecting new efforts in the 1980s to return to list-making, Scuilli proposes a conceptual and theoretical framework for the sociology of professions.[8] By identifying eight structural qualities constitutive of professionalism, the contours of professionalism are presented:

> providing expert services within structured situations on the basis of an independent socio-cultural authority and consistently with positional interests, fiducial[9] responsibilities, occupational orientations and other invariant qualities, only professions introduce into the larger society structurally and positionally both immediate consequences and institutional consequences. (57)

Of central importance in Scuilli's description of professionalism is location in structured situations:

> Only professionals, whether practitioners or researchers, earn their livelihoods by providing expert services within what contemporaries believe *universally,* as a literal cultural truism of *their* society and era, to be *structured situations* in civil society or the state. (65)

To be noted here is the distinction between fiduciary law and contractual law, which Scuilli maintains is highly relevant in the discussion as to what characterizes structured situations:

Just as there are no possible contractual terms that protect stakeholders fully from the moral hazard intrinsic in their position of dependence vis-à-vis corporate officers and shareholders majorities, so, too, clients or patrons of professional services provided within structured situations cannot avoid trusting strangers impersonally. They cannot avoid trusting particular practitioners or researchers to exhibit some fiducial responsibility for their wellbeing or investments. (65)

Explicit in fiducial responsibility is an understanding that professional practitioners or researchers exercise their positional power relatively "disinterestedly and deliberatively" and conduct themselves "in ways that peers, association leaders and interested outsiders are both willing and able to defend openly and publically—including on epistemological and didactic ground—as acceptable, legitimate and, indeed, exemplary" (69).

At this point the relation of professionalism to civil society, which is here defined in broad terms is important to note. Parsons (1939) was explicit as to the value of professionalism and its significance for social order and stability. Eliot Freidson (2001, 34–35) reaffirms this view, calling professionalism a "third logic: The ideal typical position of professionalism is founded on the official belief that the knowledge and skill of a particular specialization requires a foundation in abstract concepts and formal learning." Julia Evetts (2010, 124) asserts that this view is no longer self-evident: "It seems that professionalism is no longer a distinctive 'third' logic since the exercise of professionalism is now organizationally defined and includes the logics of the organization and the market, managerialism and commercialism." Rather than viewing professionalism in individual terms, the relationship between professionalism and civil society rests on professional positional interests and positional power incumbent in structured situations.[10] Lennart Svensson (2010, 148) stresses that professions are "strongly organization-dependent," which he underlines is something that is "often underestimated in studies of professional work." Inherent in professional work is, then, an organizational context, control of professional practice is undertaken and responsibility is claimed. Evetts (2010, 134) maintains that professionalism as an occupational value is challenged, on the one hand, by organizational professionalism, and, on the other hand, has provided opportunities for professionalism. Changes and continuities are traced by Evetts in the following manner:

Evetts' systematization in Table 13.1 of the changes and continuities in professionalism as occupational value fails to include race and class in the continuities that affect, not only professionalism, but also research and education in this field and others. Such an exclusion of the significance of race and class can be seen as "compounded by cultural and racial oppression" (Hickling-Hudson 2006, 205). "Eurocentric education is stratifying and racist. It suppresses knowledge, distorts learning and persuades Europe and its diaspora of their putative superiority. The experience of education in the era of decolonisation indicates that socialisation in neo-colonial ideas of race is still hegemonic" (205).

Table 13.1. Changes and Continuities in Professionalism as Occupational Value

Changes	Continuities
Governance	Authority
Management	Legitimacy
External forms of regulation	Prestige, status, power, dominance
Audit and measurement	Competence, knowledge
Targets and performance indicators	Identity and work culture
Work standardization Financial control	Discretion to deal with complex cases, respect and trust
Competition, individualism, stratification	Collegial relations and jurisdictional competitions
Organization control of the work priorities	Gender differences in careers and strategies
Possible range of solutions/procedures defined by the organization	Procedures and solutions discussed and agreed within specialist teams

Collegiality

A discussion of collegiality is necessary at this point to tease out the distinction between occupational and organizational professionalism (Evetts 2010; Svensson 2010). The former concept of occupational professionalism has to do with professionalism in relation to the collegial authority of professional associations, while the latter has to do with the rational-legal authority of work organizations (Svensson 2010, 145). Freidson (2001, 2) maintains that "professionalism, as a means of controlling certain occupational activities, has again been strongly challenged by the free market's logic and the logic of rational management." What, then, of professional collegiality? Has it also been strongly challenged? Svensson (2010, 159) maintains that this is the case, citing such factors as accountability, evidence-based work and new forms of governance, including "de-regulation, goal-governance, and framework laws." But first, what is the significance of collegiality as regards professionalism? Svensson (2010, 149) suggests that in contrast to "the Weberian concept of collegiality as a negative pole to bureaucratic efficiency" collegiality can be seen as that which emphasizes what Waters (1989, 961) argues is the "processes of equality, consensus and autonomy in which decisions emerge as a collective product and are morally binding only on members; bureaucracy emphasizes processes of hierarchy, delegation, and accountability in which decisions are matters of individual responsibility and imperatives for subordinates." A characteristic feature of professional work organization is collegial organization, signalling the difference between professions and other occupations. "The collegial form of organization is the foundation of professional work, and differs from bureaucratic rules and market demands, where managers and customers, respectively, control the work rather than professional occupational practitioners" (Freidson 2001, 12). Hans Grimen (2008, 144–145) maintains that "professions administer a certain type of knowledge in a collegial form of organization with political legitimacy to perform a certain social assignments."

Important terms as regards collegiality are reciprocity and solidarity, with an emphasis upon lateral, rather than hierarchical, relations among professionals.[11] Grimen describes four traits that characterize collegial organizations: "equality of power and influence, inequality or meritocracy concerning competence and expertise, and an association by reasoning and self-control, and democratic deliberation with one vote for each member. Further, the essential properties of the collegial organization, according to Malcolm Waters (1989, 956) and Emmanuel Lazega (2001, 2), are:

- application of theoretical knowledge,
- professional career with selection and security of tenure,
- formal egalitarianism with prestige-based stratification,
- formal autonomy and self-regulation,
- scrutiny and peer review of openly accessed products, and
- collective decision making striving for consensus (but often replaced by democratic voting).

The role of responsibility in collegial organizations cannot be underestimated, and shall be discussed below in relation to the concept of discretion.

Discretion

"Responsibility calls for independence or discretion in exercising the profession" (Svensson 2010, 151). Over the last few decades, forms of control and regulation have been implemented, focusing on "control and responsibility claims in retrospect of work performed" (151). As diverse forms of control increase, less responsibility can be claimed from occupational practitioners, according to Svensson. It has been maintained that as forms of governance alter and shift, the relation between four different forms of legitimacy also change and shift.[12] Professional legitimacy is based on "knowledge and competence grounded in collegially developed and controlled science and proven experience. The competence may be recognized by the citizens and the state, and in the form of legitimation and authorization it confers a monopoly on certain occupational practice" (152–153). Professional work is usually more independent at the same time as it proceeds from a social assignment. Thereby it requires

> ethically grounded judgments and justifications or legitimations that give greater responsibility. The legitimations may in principle be based on administrative rules in combination with professional ethical codes and values that one has to obey or comply with, or—typically in professional work—knowledge and proven experience in a collegial context, of taking account of professional ethics. (151)

As is clear from the above, discretion is related to responsibility and the legitimacy of one's actions: "To have discretion is then to have a liberty that has been delegated by an authority and is relative to standards set by the same authority. Thus, someone who has discretion is accountable for and must justify discretionary decisions to the authority, which has set the standards and delegated the powers of discretion" (Molander and Grimen 2010, 171). This definition entails, however, an understanding of the tension between what Rothstein (1998, 14) has termed "the black hole of democracy," on the one hand, and, on the other hand, the principle of formal justice (see Molander and Grimen 2010, 167 for a comprehensive discussion). While discretion is necessary and appropriate as regards professional work, it is both associated with autonomy and arbitrariness, and dependent upon what Anders Molander and Hans Grimen (2010, 183) term the normative contexts of discretion.[13] Given the normative contexts of discretion, it follows that a feature of discretion is that different conclusions can be reached, even if individual reasoning is thorough and conscientious. Therefore, the authors go on to describe the burdens of discretion, based on the work of John Rawls (1993) as the following:

1. Relevant facts in a case can be complex, contradictory, and difficult to assess because they point in different directions.
2. Even if we agree about which considerations are relevant in a case, we can disagree about their weight and, therefore, arrive at different conclusions.
3. To a certain degree, all our concepts are indeterminate and vulnerable to hard cases. The use of concepts much therefore be based on judgements and interpretations, where reasonable persons can disagree.
4. The experiences we have had during our lives shape how we select facts and how we weigh moral and political values. Because modern societies comprise many different positions, ethnically and socially diverse groups, and kinds of division of labor, people's experiences are varied enough to make assessments different, at least in cases with some complexity.
5. Most often, there are normative considerations with different forces on all sides of a case; thus, an overall assessment of these considerations can be difficult.
6. Systems of social institutions have a limited social space. One cannot realize all positive values simultaneously. Then one must rank values, which per se can be equally good. For such rankings, we mostly lack clear and uncontroversial criteria.

Given the complexity of discretion, its normative contexts and the need to fully understand the consequences of discretionary judgements, the authors propose that the problem of discretion "must be anchored in communities of argumentation which make the burdens of discretion an issue of continuous discussion" (Molander and Grimen 2010, 186–187).

A PROFESSIONALISM PROJECT FOR COMPARATIVE EDUCATION?

In this chapter an attempt has been made to discuss conflicts, changes and continuities that effect education as well as issues that effect comparative education, its goals and purposes. This has been done against the backdrop of the Sociology of Professions. As has become apparent, this field has severe limitations, as it is ethnocentric. However, using Scuilli's example of the Paris visual *Academie* we can reject lists, categories and explanations based on the English mid- or late-nineteenth century law (and American a generation later) as a prototype for professions, opening up the discourse on professionalism. Again using Scuilli's example, we can venture outside of continental Europe to find better theoretical and conceptual tools for understanding professionalism. Scuilli (2010, 40) stresses that one of the major problems with the entire Sociology of Professions is that "all participants—Talcott Parsons included—proceeded and continue to proceed too directly on the basis of empirical generalizations, a crude and lowly level of conceptual abstraction" Given this criticism, a professionalism project for comparative education is advanced. In such a project discussions on collegiality and discretion are suggested, especially given Foucault's reminder of our role as "judges of normality." A professionalism project for comparative education entails that we take gender, race and class seriously, especially in light of Freidson's fifth constant. If we define comparative education as a humane science, a professionalism project for comparative education appears to require that we clarify the ideological grounds for our profession: "asserting greater devotion to doing good work than to economic reward" (Freidson 2004, 180).

Lest we construct yet another ethnocentric account, replete with lists and categories, with hidden measurements for inclusion and exclusion, marking out the parameters for superiority and subordination, perhaps we can engage as colleagues in an attempt to clarify the professional landscape of comparative education as a worldwide organization of educators, the purpose of which would be to counteract de-professionalization processes that are occurring, to counteract hegemony in education and to promote human rights. For such a project much appears to be in place already. Many of the essential properties of the collegial organization cited by Svensson (2010, 149) are to be found in 37 national and regional societies that constitute the members of WCCES. As a group we provide "expert services within structured situations on the basis of an independent socio-cultural authority and consistently with positional interests, fiducial responsibilities, occupational orientations and other invariant qualities" (57). Moreover, participation in comparative education societies, conferences and congresses provides us with opportunities to discuss the problem of discretion in "communities of argumentation" where "the burdens of discretion" can become "an issue of continuous discussion" (Molander and Grimen 2010, 186–187).

A professionalism project for comparative education entails that consideration be given to developing new theoretical and conceptual tools for understanding what it means to be a professional comparative educator in a global world where continuities matter, despite changes that affect practice and research. Hickling-Hudson's (2006) description of the Yolgnu philosophy of education[14] can provide a starting point for finding such new theoretical and conceptual tools. First and foremost, a professionalism project for comparative education requires that we include multiple perspectives, appreciating and celebrating difference, recognizing the value of other perspectives and providing space for the voices of those who have thus far been excluded. Such a project can ultimately result in the construction of a fluid concept (O'Dowd 2000), opening up the discourse of comparative education to put "a human face on comparative education" (Hickling-Hudson 2006, 195).

Amidst all the changes that have occurred, I see with optimism the opportunities that these changes make possible. This is my "story," to use Paulston's words, and I hereby acknowledge its partiality, hoping that I have managed to tell it with "authority and conviction, while mapping it into the debate field of comparative education" (Paulston 2005, 1).

NOTES

1. *Instrumentalism* is defined as "an antirealist philosophy of science that holds that theories are not true or false but are merely tools for deriving predictions from observational data" (Dictionary.com 2011).
2. Brante clarifies that there are two general reasons for distinguishing semiprofessions from the classic professions: "(1) Knowledge and authority are subordinated to another profession, implying that the profession is not the primary point of access to the highest knowledge in the area, e.g., nurses. (2) There is no basic, robust, systemized, replicable and generally recognized model of performance, or core. Hence it is easily questioned by laymen as well as politicians; cf. teachers and social workers" (Brante 2010, 96–97).
3. Bucchi calls contemporary Science an "academic-industrial -governmental complex." At present 64 percent of research funding on a global scale is financed by private companies and approximately 70 percent of the research worldwide is conducted by private companies (Bucchi 2008, 134–135).
4. *Neo-conservatism* is defined as "an approach to politics or theology that represents a return to a traditional point of view (in contrast to more liberal or radical schools of thought of the 1960s)," according to Dictionary.com (2011).
5. According to the World Health Organization (WHO 2009), the A/H1N1 influenza has spread with "unprecedented speed": "In past pandemics, influenza viruses have needed more than six months to spread as widely as the new H1N1 virus has spread in six weeks."
6. I wish to acknowledge the work of Johanna Kallo and Risto Rinne (eds.) from whose volume entitled *Supranational Regimes and National Educational Policies: Encountering Challenges* I have borrowed the concept of supranational regimes.
7. Leadership research thus far appears to have undergone a similar development process, with lists of "traits" and "qualities" first identifying this sub-field of research.
8. Sculli thereby rejects as the basis for the sociology of profession that which has previously been proposed, i.e., the history and development of law, medicine, science and engineering, focusing instead on the Paris visual *Academie*: "No other seventeenth century Academy of any kind anywhere in Europe professionalized similarly, not in painting, not in writing or letters and, most certainly, not in 'science'—experimental natural philosophy." The Paris visual *Academie* nonetheless professionalized by 1680, and remained professionalized for two full centuries" (Sculli 2010, 47).
9. According to Law.com (2011), *fiduciary* is defined as "(1) n. from the Latin fiducia, meaning 'trust,' a person (or a business like a bank or stock brokerage) who has the power and obligation to act for another (often called the beneficiary) under circumstances which require total trust, good faith and honesty. The most common is a trustee of a trust, but fiduciaries can include business advisers, attorneys, guardians, administrators of estates, real estate agents, bankers, stockbrokers, title companies or anyone who undertakes to assist someone who places complete confidence and trust in that person or company. Characteristically, the fiduciary has greater knowledge and expertise about the matters being handled. A fiduciary is held to a standard of conduct and trust above that of a stranger or of a casual business person. He/she/it must avoid 'self-dealing' or 'conflicts of interests' in which the potential benefit to the fiduciary is in conflict with what is best for the person who trusts him/her/it. For example, a stockbroker must consider the best investment for the client and not buy or sell on the basis of what brings him/her the highest commission. While a fiduciary and the beneficiary may join together in a business venture or a purchase of property, the best interest of the

beneficiary must be primary, and absolute candor is required of the fiduciary. (2) adj. defining a situation or relationship in which a person is acting as a fiduciary for another."

10 Sculli (2010, 69) goes on to point out: "the central question in a scientific, thus conceptually grounded and critical, sociology of professions cannot be whether or how professionals become altruistic or service-oriented at dispersed worksites, as properly socialized or inculcated individuals. Such motivations or orientations would require individual professionals—somehow—to disregard their positional interest and, as a result of this, to relinquish or abnegate their positional power. Our point is that such abiding self-control is simply not an available option structurally, irrespective of what professionals' motivations and orientations as individual happen to be. It cannot become an available option unless and until fluid sites or embedded exchanges displace structured situations. As a result of this displacement at a structural level, professionalism then gives way to de-professionalization; and simple contractual and statutory relationships displace demands of impersonal trust or fiducial responsibilities."

11 For more information see Svensson (2010, 145).

12 Svensson (2010, 152–153) describes the four forms of legitimacy as political legitimacy, professional legitimacy, bureaucratic legitimacy and the market.

13 The authors stipulate the following normative contexts: "(1) between contexts that demand *comparative consistency* and those that require individualization; and (2) between two kinds of comparative consistency (one is entitled by the principle of formal justice, or the formal principle of *equal treatment*; the other is entailed by the demand for *reproducibility*).

14 From his work with Aboriginal educators and community members, Michael Christie (2000) has been able to identify the Yolgnu philosophy of education, which departs fundamentally from the modernist Western school, according to Anne-Hickling-Hudson (2006, 203).

REFERENCES

Arnot, Madeleine. (2009). "A Global Conscience Collective? Incorporating Gender Injustices into Global Citizenship Education." *Education, Citizenship and Social Justice, 4*(2), 117–132.

Brante, Thomas. (2010). "State Formations and the Historical Take-off of Continental Professional Types: The Case of Sweden." In Lennart G. Svensson & Julia Evetts (Ed.), *Sociology of Professions: Continental and Anglo-Saxon Traditions* (pp. 75–122). Borås, Sweden: Daidalos.

Bucchi, Massimiano. (2008). *Science in Society: An Introduction to Social Studies of Science.* London: Routledge.

Buras, Kristen L., & Michael W. Apple. (2008). "Radical Disenchantments: Neoconservatives and the Disciplining of Desire in an Anti-utopian Era." *Comparative Education, 44*(2), 291–304.

Cassirer, Ernst. (1957). *The Philosophy of Symbolic Forms*, Vol. 3: *The Phenomenology of Knowledge.* London: Yale University Press.

Christie, Michael. (2000). "Galtha: The Application of Aboriginal Philosophy to School Learning." *New Horizons in Education, 103*, 3–19.

Collins, Randal.(1990). "Changing Conceptions in the Sociology of Professions." In Rolf Torstendahl and Michael Burrage (Ed.), *The Formation of Professions: Knowledge, State and Strategy.* London: Sage.

Dahl, Hanne. M. (2009). "New Public Management, Care and Struggles about Recognition." *Critical Social Policy, 29,* 634–654.

Davies, Lynn. (2008). "Gender, Education, Extremism and Security." *Compare, 38*(5), 611–625.

Dictionary.com. (2011). "Instrumentalism" and "Neo-conservatism." Oakland, CA: Dictionary.com. Available online at: http://www.dictionary.com.

Dyer, Caroline. (2010). "Education and Social (in)Justice for Mobile Groups: Re-framing Rights and Educational Inclusion for Indian Pastoralist Children." *Educational Review, 62*(3), 301–313.

Evetts, Julia. (2010). "Reconnecting Professional Occupations with Professional Organizations: Risks and Opportunities." In Lennart G. Svensson and Julia Evetts (Ed.), *Sociology of Professions: Continental and Anglo-Saxon Traditions .* Borås, Sweden: Daidalos.

Fennell, Shailaja, & Madeleine Arnot. (2008). "Decentring Hegemonic Gender Theory: The Implications for Educational Research." *Compare, 38*(5), 525–538.

Foucault, Michel. (1977). *Discipline and Punish.* New York: Vintage.

Freidson, Eliot. (2001). *Professional Powers: A Study of the Institutionalization of Formal Knowledge.* Chicago: The University of Chicago Press.

Freidson, Eliot. (2004). *Professionalism. The Third Logic.* Cambridge: Polity Press.

Gottlieb, Esther E. (2000). "Are We Post-modern Yet? Historical and Theoretical Explorations in Comparative Education." In Bob Moon, Miriam Ben-Peretz, and Sally Brown (Ed.), *Routledge International Companion to Education* (pp. 153–179). London: Routledge.

Grimen, Hans. (2008). "Profesjon og Profesjonsmoral" ["Profession and Professional Moral"]. In Anders Molander Lars-Inge Terum (Ed.), *Profesjonsstudier [Studies of Profession]* (pp. 144–159). Oslo: Universitetsforlaget.

Harris, Susan. (2007). "Internationalising the University." *Educational Philosophy and Theory, 40*(2), 346–357.

Healy, Karin. (2009). "The Case of Mistaken Identity: the Social Welfare Professions and New Public Management." *Journal of Sociology, 45*(4), 401–418.

Hickling-Hudson, Anne. (2006). "Cultural Complexity, Post-colonialism and Educational Change." In Joseph Zajda, Susan Majhanovich, Val D. Rust, & E. Martin Sabina (Ed.), *Education and Social Justice* (pp. 191–208). Dordrecht, The Netherlands: Springer.

Kelley, Robin D. G. (2002). *Freedom Dreams: The Black Radical Imagination.* Boston: Beacon Press.

Latour, Bruno. (1990). "Drawing Things Together." In Michael Lynch and Steven Woolgar (Ed.), *Representation in Scientific Practice* (pp. 19–68). London: MIT Press.

Latour, Bruno. (1999). *Pardora's Hope: Essays on the Reality of Social Studies.* Cambridge, MA: Harvard University Press.

Latour, Bruno. (1993). *We Have Never Been Modern.* Cambridge, MA: Harvard University Press.

Law.com. (2011). "Fudiciary." New York: Law.com, ALM Media, LLC. Available online at: http://www.law.com.

Lazega, Emmanuel. (2001). *The Collegial Phenomenon. The Social Mechanisms of Cooperation among Peers in a Corporative Law Partnership.* New York: Oxford University Press.

Lynch, Michael P. (1998). *Truth in Context. An Essay on Pluralism and Objectivity.* Cambridge, MA: MIT Press.

Ninnes, Peter. (2008). "Fear and Desire in Twentieth Century Comparative Education." *Comparative, Education, 44*(3), 345–358.

Nóvoa, Antonió, & Tali Yariv-Mashal. (2003). "Comparative Research in Education: A Mode of Governance or a Historical Journey?" *Comparative Education, 39*(4), 423–438.

Molander, Anders, & Hans Grimen. (2010). "Understanding Professional Discretion." In Lennart G. Svensson and Julia Evetts (Ed.), *Sociology of Professions Continental and Anglo-Saxon Traditions.* Borås, Sweden: Daidalos.

O'Dowd, Mina. (2000). *The Changing Nature of Knowledge. Mapping the Discourse of the Malmö Longitudinal Study 1938–1995.* Stockholm: Institute of International Education, Stockholm University.

O'Dowd, Mina. (2009). "The God that Failed. Lifelong Learning: From Utopianism to Instrumentalism." In James Ogunleye, Bruno Leutwyler, Charl Wolhuter, and Marinela Mihova (Ed.), *The Bulgarian Comparative Education Society Conference Proceedings* Vol. 7. Sofia: Bulgarian Comparative Education Society.

O'Dowd, Mina. (2010). "The Bologna Process and the Re-structuring of Higher Education: Who Will Bear the Brunt of 'Unexpected Outcomes'?" In *Papers in Memory of David N. Wilson: Clamouring for a Better World,* ed. Vandra Masemann, Suzanne Majhanovich, Nhung Truong, and Kara Janigan. Rotterdam: Sense Publishers.

Osler, Audrey, & Hugh Starkey. (1999). "Rights, Identities and Inclusion: European Action Programmes as Political Education." *Oxford Review of Education, 25*(1&2), 199–215.

Palomba, Donatella. (2010). "Exploring the Problematic Meaning of "Education" in Comparative Education." Presentation at the WCCES Congress, Istanbul, Turkey, 18 June 2010.

Parsons, Talcott. (1937). *The Structure of Social Action.* 2nd ed. New York: Free Press.

Parsons, Talcott. (1939). "The Professions and Social Structure." In *Essays in Sociological Theory.* 2nd ed. New York: Free Press.

Parsons, Talcott. (1952). "A Sociologist Looks at the Legal Profession." In *Essays in Sociological Theory.* 2nd ed. New York: Free Press.

Paulston, Rolland G., ed. (1996). *Social Cartography: Mapping Ways of Seeing Social and Educational Change.* London: Garland Publishing.

Paulston, Rolland G. (2005). "Mapping Reality Turns in Western Thinking and Comparative Education." Paper presented at the 49th Comparative and International Education Society Annual Meeting, Stanford University, Palo Alto, CA, March 2005.

Pavalko, Ronald M. (1971). *Sociology of Occupations and Professions.* 2nd ed. Ithaca, NY: F.E. Peacock Publishers.

Phillips, David, & Michele Schweisfurth. (2006). *Comparative and International Education. An Introduction to Theory, Method and Practice.* London: Continuum International Publishing Group.

Rawls, John. (1971). *A Theory of Justice.* Cambridge, MA: Harvard University Press.

Reimer, Everett. (1971). *School is Dead.* New Delhi, India: Gyanpedia. Available online at: http://www.gyanpedia.in.

Robertson, Susan. (2010). "The New Spatial Politics of (Re) Bordering and (Re) Ordering the State-Education-Citizen Relation for the Global Economy." Keynote presentation at the WCCES Conference, Istanbul, Turkey, 14 June 2010.

Rust, Val D. (1996). "From Modern to Postmodern Ways of Seeing Social and Educational Change." In Rolland G. Paulston (Ed.), *Social Cartography: Mapping Ways of Seeing Social and Educational Change* (pp. 29–52). London: Garland Publishing.

Scuilli, David. (2005). "Continental Sociology of Professions Today: Conceptual Contributions." *Current Sociology, 53*(6), 915–942.

Scuilli, David. (2010). "Structural and Institutional Invariance in Professions and Professionalism." In Lennart G. Svensson and Julia Evetts (Ed.), *Sociology of Professions. Continental and Anglo-Saxon Traditions.* Borså, Sweden: Daidalos.

Svensson, Lennart G. (2010). "Professions, Organizations, Collegiality and Accountability." In Lennart G. Svensson and Julia Evetts (Ed.), *Sociology of Professions: Continental and Anglo-Saxon Traditions.* Borås, Sweden: Daidalos.

Standish, Paul. (2008). Preface. *Journal of the Philosophy of Education, 42*(3–4), 349–353.

Teichler, Ulrich. (2010). "The Diversifying Academic Profession?" *European Review, 18* (Supplement 1), S157–S179.

Wallerstein, Immanuel. (1997). *Eurocentrism and Its Avatars: The Dilemmas of Social Science.* Keynote Address at the ISA East Asian Regional Colloquium, Seoul, Korea, 22–23 November 1996. Available online at: http://www.binghamton.edu.

Waters, Malcom. (1989). "Collegiality, Bureaucratization, and Professionalization: A Weberian Analysis." *American Journal of Sociology, 94*(5), 945–972.

World Health Organization (WHO). (2009). "Changes in Reporting Requirements for Pandemic (H1N1) 2009 Virus Infection." Pandemic (H1N1) 2009 Briefing Note 3 (revised). Geneva, Switzerland: WHO. Available online at: http://www.who.int.

GARY W. J. PLUIM

14. THEORIZING THE NGO THROUGH CONCEPTUAL MAPPING

Mapping offers comparative educators a valuable tool to capture the rhetoric and metaphor of texts, to make the invisible visible, and to open a way for intertextuality among competing discourses. And, when needed, they provide a way to see all knowledge thoroughly enmeshed in the larger battles that constitute our world space. We should also note the maps are practical. *They provide orientation to and in practice, and they help us see, contextualize and organise proliferating intellectual communities producing an ever expanding textual discourse.* (Paulston 1993, 106, emphasis added)

THEORIZING THE NGO

In this passage from "Mapping Discourses in Comparative Education Texts," Rolland G. Paulston (1993) points to the valuable role that conceptual mapping plays in bridging theory with practice. For over a century, theory has been famously applied to constructs in education and development. Consider, for example, theories of the school (Sandison 1886), the city (Jacobs 1961), the university (Robbins 2008), and the state (Bluntschli 1891; Bosanquet 1899). A theory, applied to a social construct, is a powerful analytical tool in explaining life's phenomena. Theorizing various social actors has allowed for the articulation, definition, and development of these institutions, and has helped sustain a focus on central values of education and development, such as equity, justice, and learning. Yet, the nongovernmental organization (NGO) has notoriously defied theorization. Although there have been several scholarly efforts (Ahmed and Potter 2006; DeMars 2005) and many reasons suggested for this dearth (such as their diversity in nature, and the basic problem of defining the unit itself), elaborate and popular theories have largely evaded NGOs. The importance of theorizing the NGO would help to distinguish it from other organizations and actors in education and development, and an accepted, underpinning theory of the NGO would contribute to its legitimacy as an actor.

However the ontological shifts of recent decades suggest that the period for ascribing a singular theory of the NGO may well be behind us. Given its comparative youth as an actor in education—it was only in 1950 that UNESCO introduced to the popular lexicon the term "non-governmental organization" (Vakil 1997)—and its rapid proliferation around the globe, the theorizing of these previously untheorized actors has swiftly become a complicated endeavor.

John C. Weidman, W. James Jacob (eds.), Beyond the Comparative: Advancing Theory and Its Application to Practice, 253–268.

Although up until the1960s there was a great deal of homogeneity in the nature and role of the NGO (Clark 1991), the diversity of the institution known today creates numerous problems for theorization. For one, the NGO does not fit tightly or clearly into a single theoretical discipline. Many bodies of literature address the NGO from their own particular vantage points, in, among others, political science, sociology, international relations, non-profit management, and theories of social movements. Second, the NGO as a unit of analysis is notoriously hard to define. Defining a negative ("non") entity is inherently problematic, while the reality of whether individual NGOs are actually nongovernmental or non-profit further complicates this definition (in many environments, for example, NGO connections with the government and market are commonplace). Finally, there is an incredible variation among NGOs in their functionality: international vs. grassroots-orientations; advocacy vs. service provisions; religious vs. secular bases; humanitarian vs. developmental focuses; and so on. They differ on the basis of their primary issues of education, agriculture, health, children, environment, rights, and sport, to name a few. There is also an immense range in organizational size. While thousands of NGOs rely simply on a volunteer base or only a handful of paid employees, some individual, international NGOs employ tens of thousands worldwide. The issue of variation makes theorizing difficult, especially as new NGOs emerge on a daily basis. With conservative estimates suggesting upwards of fifty thousand NGOs worldwide (Edwards and Hulme 1995), the prevalence and impact of NGOs—combined with their variety of political positions, ontological stances, and shifting global dynamics—necessitate a more sophisticated means of understanding the positions and potential of the organization.

Therefore, rather than conceptualizing a single notion of the NGO, a more useful exercise might be a theoretical charting of its possibilities. The use of social mapping and the contributions of Rolland Paulston to comparative education suggest a practical avenue for social analysis of the NGO. With an expanding heterogeneity of perspectives of social actors in education, "cognitive mapping is . . . necessary to provide theoretical and political orientation as we move into a new and confusing social terrain" (Kellner 1990, 281–282). Thus the goal of this chapter is to situate the multiple discourses of the NGO within the conceptual maps provided by Paulston, guided by two central questions: (1) What roles do NGOs fulfill around the world, and what are the varying discourses that serve to conceptualize NGO approaches? (2) How might these theories of the NGO be mapped against Paulston's knowledge representations in comparative and international education?

THE DOMINANT FRAMING OF THE NGO

The contemporary, dominant discourse would lead one to assume a singular, theoretical position of the NGO as a modernist, functional organization. In such a structural orientation, the NGO has been defined as a self-governing, private, independent, not-for-profit organization geared to improving the quality of life of disadvantaged people in international development contexts (Vakil 1997). Much of this discourse stems from the realities of practice, in which NGO officials are focused on issues such as results, impact and accountability. Debates in the dominant literature either note the challenges of NGOs in ensuring this accountability, or cite problems with how accountability is demonstrated (Edwards 2002). In this context, the NGO is reduced to a citizen-level implementation agency that enables cost-effective projects (Edwards 2000) in which accountability is ensured by establishing the achievement of "results for money spent" (Hudock 2000, 16), by delivering the terms of contracts (Edwards 2002), or by demonstrating output to donors (Collingwood and Logister 2007). More broadly, accountability is demonstrated to NGO supporters (Edwards 2002), to their members, (Collingwood and Logister 2007), to local communities (Schwarz and Worthington 2006), or through the representation and satisfaction of NGO "beneficiaries" and "stakeholders"—increasingly framed through a discourse of "democracy" that conflates citizens with clients (Scholte 2005). These notions, according to Steven Klees (2008), are part of a structure that furthers a neoliberal agenda in which citizens are re-framed as investors, beneficiaries and stakeholders. In this context the NGO is seen to sustain and support existing structures of society through ideals of "democracy," "governance," and "entrepreneurship." The very fact that NGOs are bound largely by empiricist methodologies takes its root in their structural-functional position in society. Understandably, given their tangible nature, their need for resources, and the predominance of structural thought, such paradigms tend to prevail. Yet, despite what this dominant discourse would suggest, there exists a much broader vision for the NGO, an organization that is fundamentally heterogeneous (Grzybowski 2001). This chapter seeks to broaden the perspective of the NGO by highlighting the growing diversity of NGO paradigms.

SOCIAL CARTOGRAPHY FOR A BROADER PERSPECTIVE

The overt and necessary political orientation of the NGO necessitates a social map reflective of these characteristics. Rolland Paulston's theoretical maps are useful for the analysis of the position of NGOs precisely because they open up spaces beyond the dominant discourse and introduce areas for a multiplicity of conceptions of the NGO. The strengths of cartography, as Paulston (1993, 106) has suggested, lie in the ability of the conceptual map to portray

> a dynamic and rhizomatic field of tangled roots and tendrils. Comparative education is now seen as a heuristic mapping of the eclectic interwearvings of knowledge communities rather than the more objectified images presented to the world in earlier foundational texts. The strength of social theory in the field today is in fact firmly grounded in this very multiplicity of its perspectives and tools known through intertextual composition.

Paulston proposes a "mapping of paradigms and theories in comparative and international education texts seen as an intellectual field" that continues to be useful in today's global arena of education (104). Relating broad paradigms to historical periods of epistemological orthodoxy and heterodoxy, Paulston suggests the emergent heterogeneity of knowledge representation is moving to a "new and confused terrain of disputatious yet complementary communities as the use of knowledge becomes more eclectic and reoriented by new ideas and new knowledge methods in, for example, interpretations, simulations, translations, probes, and conceptual mapping" (105). In the complex reality of the internationalized era of education in national and global development, such broader theoretical frames are useful for conceptualizing global actors such as the NGO.

Paulston's (1993, 106) specific paradigmatic map of comparative and international education texts locates theories in a conceptual map of two axes. A vertical axis considers "textual dispositions of social and educational change," with points of transformation at one end of the axis, and equilibrium at the other. A horizontal axis evaluates "characterizations of reality", polarizing orientations of solipsism ("idealist-subjectivist") and scientism ("realist-objectivist") at opposite ends of the continuum. Located in this map are twenty-one different theories, included within their "direction and extent of communal borrowing and interaction" (106), alongside which NGOs and other actors in international education might be plotted. Anchoring the map are four paradigms situated in the theoretical corners of the map. Corresponding to a historical analysis of knowledge representation in the social sciences, these paradigms include functionalism and its radical response, and humanism with its radical response (see Table 14.1).

Table 14.1. Paradigms and Theories in Comparative Education

Functionalist	A perspective characterized by a scientific, realist, objectivist, and equilibrium orientation of society. This world view suggests that things "must be."
Radical Functionalist	A perspective characterized by a scientific, realist, objectivist, and transformative orientation of structures. This world view suggests a way that things "will be."
Radical Humanist	A perspective characterized by a solipsistic, idealist, subjectivist, and transformative orientation of consciousness. This world view suggests how things "can be."
Humanist	A perspective characterized by a solipsistic, idealist, subjectivist, and equilibrium orientation of culture. This world view suggests a way of "be-ing."

These four positions are useful for plotting the roles of the great diversity of NGOs because of their capacity to locate distinct actors, and to help make sense of a multi-oriented world. Because it is also useful to follow trends in historical perspective, what follows is a historical-chronological examination of theories of the NGO through the past century, with a particular focus on their role in education. Of note is the traditional pull towards functionalist ideologies, but also of interest are the non-dominant paradigms and examples of radical responses— both functionalist and humanist. The chapter concludes with a discussion of contemporary theories that characterize an emerging humanist theorization of the NGO. Different conceptions of civil society, and the role of power and politics that have also informed our understanding and positioning of the NGO, are also be addressed in this chapter.

Functionalism in the Early Twentieth Century

Once viewed as panaceas in overseas development, NGOs were the original players in international education. Many of these early organizations in the West were extensions of the overseas, Christian missionary movement and had functionalist, evangelical and *salvational* missions. Much of the focus of these NGOs was on China, India, and Sub-Saharan Africa, and they often represented the foremost relations that Western nations had abroad. Faith-based NGOs that remain prominent today originated in the early part of the twentieth century and the religious orientation of many NGOs from this era was entrenched in ideologies supporting a modernist process of development. To some extent these premises underpin the ideologies of modern NGOs such as Christian Aid or World Vision that ground their international work in a moral imperative based on Christian doctrine.

Reflections on the disastrous effects of the World Wars spurred a realization that a much greater involvement in international development by the West was needed (Esteva 1995), and the NGO became viewed as an actor to mobilize this development. Indeed, Paulston (1993, 103) notes the dominant functionalist perspective of this era:

Following the Second World War with the crises of decolonization and cold war competition, comparative education studies, and especially those in North America, continued to be framed in evolutionary and functionalist perspectives while moving closer to the social sciences and their concerns to explain and inform social and economic development using the vocabulary, if not the rigour, of the natural sciences.

The 1950s and 1960s witnessed a tremendous expansion in the number of NGOs working in education for development. Volunteer-sending organizations such as the US-based Peace Corps, Britain's Voluntary Service Overseas (VSO), and the Canadian University Services Overseas (now known as CUSO-VSO in Canada) were formed in the early 1960s and drew on the zeal of Western youth to respond to education and development needs abroad. One aspect of this arrangement was (and is) the benefit incurred back to the citizens of the volunteer-sending nation. In Canada, for example, NGOs amassed Canadian paper for book production, shipped prefabricated schools, and sent Canadian experts and volunteer teachers abroad (Mundy and Bhanji 2005). Engagement focused on post-secondary level education, was largely represented by the Canadian supply of volunteers and/or teachers, by Canadian books and curriculum, and by Canadian school materials and technology. And yet, internally, NGOs were recognized for their central role in addressing the educational needs of the marginalized through an *instrumentalist* perspective. As Marcel Massé, the then president of the Canadian International Development Agency (CIDA), observed, "the NGO projects that have been executed in the last few years—and those that I've seen that are presently being planned—are better instruments to realize . . . development as we now understand it, than almost any other channel of delivery in the agency" (Canadian Council for International Cooperation [CCIC] 1982, 7). Clearly, a human capital development orientation of the NGO was solidly entrenched during this era.

Variations of the modernization agenda can be seen through examples of NGOs that target marginalized groups in supporting the ability of individual citizens to produce resources to sustain a living. The Foundation for International Training and Street Kids International are several examples of NGOs that draw on a brand of compensatory liberal structuralism in their international work. Street Kids supplies youth-at-risk with "practical solutions needed to give street kids around the world the choices, skills, and opportunities to make a better life for themselves" (Street Kids International 2010), educating and training street youth to succeed in market-driven environments. Founded as the result of a transformative life experience of a young Canadian lawyer travelling in famine-stricken Sudan, Street Kids grew out of a grassroots endeavor that began as a bicycle courier service in Khartoum run entirely by street children. Transferring entrepreneurial ideals to a segment of the population that is routinely disregarded, Peter Dalglish started Street Kids with "$200, a borrowed office, and an American Express card" (Dalglish 1983, 3). This type of intrepid entrepreneurialism has endured at Street Kids and is a good example of the NGO in a framework of *social liberalism* in which a fundamental liberal market orientation chiefly addresses issues of social justice.

An extension of human capital theories of the NGO is evident in William Easterly's (2006, 18) distinctions between "searchers" and "planners" in development projects. In this dichotomy distinguishing between two dominant approaches to development, Easterly proposes that "working level people in non-governmental organizations are more likely to be searchers than planners," attending to local conditions and the reality at the "bottom", and attempting to understand the demand and level of satisfaction of participants, thereby assuming responsibilities and gaining rewards for their activities. The way in which such NGOs as *Umoja wa Watu wenye Ulemavu* (Zanzibar Association of People with Disabilities) and the Kastom Gaden Association (Solomon Islands) have emerged as a response to local conditions are representative of the searcher mentality framed by Easterly. Taken structurally, the collectivity of searchers come together in a *piecemeal, neoliberal* arrangement in which NGOs work in an unorchestrated, functional environment.

The planners in Easterly's dichotomy are best illustrated using a *globalist* theoretical framework. Globalism is a perspective that envisions NGO participation in a world government as a way to enforce the global norms proposed by supranational bodies such as the United Nations. William DeMars (2005) has likened this relationship as a global government where multilateral organization officials constitute the upper house chamber, and the meetings of NGOs as the lower house. The limits of this paradigm confine NGOs to either agents of or becoming co-opted by the United Nations or an emerging new world order. Indeed, proponents of mainstream structuralism suggest that the NGO seen through the globalist lens is limited to a supporting role of legitimizing the United Nations (DeMars 2005). Some of the most visible products of the globalist paradigm in education are the growing initiatives to form global coalitions. A prominent example of this was the 1990 commitment to Education for All (EFA) made in Jomtien, Thailand, "the first time that NGOs acted as fully credentialed participants in a major international conference" (Brinkerhoff et al., 2007, 156). Actors in international education were encouraged to sign and support this declaration, and today a large proportion of NGOs make clear their normative claim to engage in education as a right for all. Civil society umbrella organizations such as the Global Campaign for Education or the Tanzania Education Network are associations that represent hundreds of NGOs which support the goals of EFA.

As this section illustrates, the focus of NGOs of the past century largely involved optimistic, charitable and highly functionalist approaches, highlighting the possibilities for NGOs to contribute to the educational, economic and social development of southern societies.

Critiques of the Functionalist Approach

While elements of the structural-functional perspective provide a basis for understanding a perspective of NGO, the futility of certain offshoot theories and the depth of their critiques suggest that more thorough and progressive frameworks are necessary. "Functionalist theory", as Paulston (1993, 103) notes, "proved unable to adequately predict or control frequent development failures." Among the most persuasive critiques of NGOs are the contribution of NGOs to a global hegemony, their perpetuation of unequal development (Klees 1998), and their reinforcement of neoliberalism (Archer 1994) through exacerbating economic and technological dependency through capitalist structures (Harrington 1977). The NGO has been accused of encouraging imperialism (Tikly 2004) and neo-colonialism (Gary 1996; Hearn 1998) through their neglect of indigenous knowledges, individual perspectives, and grassroots movements. As Paul Wangoola (1995, 68) proposes:

NGOs are one of the instruments for the continued conquest and occupation of the South. They join in the marginalization of Third World governments and indigenous NGOs and leadership, so as to directly rule the people at the grassroots. This way, the North's latest conquest would be complete: the World Bank [and] big powers and transnational rule from above, while NGOs govern from below. Needless to say, all of this is usually done in the name of empowering the grassroots.

As the equilibrium, functionalist, "must be" quadrant theories of the NGO have received a great increase of conceptual, empirical and critical attention, transformative orientations of functionalism have arisen as possibilities to respond to the role of NGOs in education for development.

Transformative, Functionalist NGO Orientations

Many of the critical and radical responses to the positioning of the NGO began during the civil rights era of the 1960s and 1970s. The World University Service of Canada (WUSC), for example, had become more radical in their approach as it began to focus both on knowledge sharing through an international seminar program, and on providing post-secondary opportunities for youth from war-torn countries through a student refugee program. Macro theories such as dependency, post-colonialism, and Gustavo Esteva's notion of post-development were influential for thinking about the role of NGOs, as they critically examined the consequences of embedding Eurocentric, equilibrium-oriented, structural-functional ideals in other societies. Orientations specific to NGOs supported to these ideals through transformative, functionalist perspectives. A *fourth-position* orientation, for example, is a realistic-objectivist theory that resists the equilibrium orientation of Paulston's functionalism. While traditional structural conceptualizing of the NGO has envisioned the NGO in a "third space" between the government and market, Alan Fowler (2002) suggests that this perspective is too simplistic, that NGOs are often more likely to resemble governments (by delivering public goods) and private-sector bodies (by self-financing) than other actors within civil society in which they are grounded. Thus, Fowler sees NGOs consciously located between state, market and civil society in a fourth position. In this structural arrangement, the NGO begins with an explicit value position, and negotiates between the three sectors to mediate and advocate for the poor and excluded, using as its prime justification universal human rights-based principles. The role that the Bangladesh Rehabilitation Assistance Committee (BRAC) pioneered in South Asia is representative of ways in which NGOs are fulfilling a fourth, structural position. While maintaining a realist orientation, this fourth position suggests that more transformative outcomes are a potential role for the NGO.

Cândido Grzybowski's (2001, 220) proposition of *international solidarity* as a principle framework is representative in the work of NGOs such as Partners in Health (in Haiti) and the Cuba Solidarity Campaign. For Grzybowski the NGO's chief role is to strengthen the chain of solidarity between local communities and international NGOs. As a direct challenge to the modernist-oriented pressure for achievement, the international solidarity orientation does not require immediate results to be achieved by the NGO. Instead, the NGO looks to strengthen global diversity through upholding rights of minorities and providing access to impoverished citizens, advocating for "citizenship against all forms of destruction and social exclusion." Grzybowski uses a unique metaphor of animals with fleas to conceptualize the NGO: as miniscule creatures, NGOs disturb and unsettle the structural elephants of states, corporations, international organizations (IOs), and even large media through rooting out the causes of social ills and forming "colonies" with local civil society organizations (CSOs) and other agencies for greater effectiveness.

An Emerging Humanist Perspective

In opposition to the functionalist spectrum, Paulston positions humanism as a framework in which the inherent dignity of the individual is recognized; one which focuses on human values, rights, and concerns. An equilibrium orientation of this ideal was captured by Cranford Pratt's (1990, 5) philosophy of *humane internationalism*, a position that charges "citizens and governments of the industrialized world [to] have ethical responsibilities towards those beyond their borders who are suffering severely and who live in abject poverty." As early as the 1930s, secular NGOs such as the Red Cross and the International Student Service originated, the former providing basic and emergency needs on an impartial basis; the latter focusing on student issues, such as aiding fleeing student refugees, facilitating book donations, organizing study tours and coordinating overseas seminars (World University Service of Canada 2010). More recently the broader discourse of *universal* human rights has extended the notion of humane internationalism by ensuring fundamental entitlements such as speech, health and education to all human beings. In Canada, several NGOs have emerged with an explicit focus on the human rights of citizens worldwide. Two such examples are Right to Play in 2003, growing out of a gathering of high level athletes that extended fundamental human rights to recognize the importance of play in war-torn areas and War Child in 1999, born out of medical doctor Samantha Nutt's pursuit for human rights in conflict and post-conflict regions.

An increasing number of NGOs are operating from a *transnationalist* perspective in which "at least one actor is a non-state agent or does not operate on behalf of a national government or international organization" during regular interactions across national boundaries (Risse-Kappen 1995, 12). The ability of grassroots movements to mobilize transnationally, and in particular, the linking of like-minded organizations previously unable to connect in sustainable ways across international borders, is a growing phenomenon of development NGOs. At its purest, transnationalism envisions a united, global government that replaces our current configuration of nation states (Weiss and Jacobsen 2000), building on a philosophy of cosmopolitanism. But more commonly, advocates of moderate transnational perspectives continue to view the state as the principal actor, with the NGO playing an increasingly complex role in a larger, non-hierarchical global community. NGOs such as Greenpeace or Médecins Sans Frontières (MSF), which operate internationally with strategic inattention to national politics, are examples of transnationally-orientated NGOs.

Humanist positions begin to become increasingly radical and transformative through orientations such as *constructivism*, a perspective founded on the idea that structural roles are socially defined and can be changed through norms, ideas, and power. Constructivism demonstrates that knowledge about our world is socially constructed as opposed to being discovered through macro, scientific or quantitative theories. Constructivists believe that no single methodology is validated, a position that opposes positivism, realism, liberalism, and socialism. Thus the core notion in this paradigm is that ideas hold the power to shape the world. Constructivist-oriented NGOs assume a great deal of influence through the ideas, pressure and advocacy of their staff. NGOs such as Activists without Borders and Earth Rights International focus much of their work on changing the ways in which people view the constructs of citizenship, rights and education. The "power of NGOs," describe Shamima Ahmed and David Potter (2006, 15), "is the power to persuade." The constructivist perspective submits that the NGO as an actor in development aims to make changes in society by its ability to leverage through persuasion, relationships, and grassroots action. The NGO acting through a constructivist lens is interested in education as a tool to change norms in order to create a society of our own choosing. Indeed, new ideas are evolving regarding the rights of animals, and the roles of NGOs in advocating for and protecting these rights are laying a foundation for generation of *post-humanist* organizations in global relations. Meanwhile, in education for development, this forum can be a basis for deconstructing the reality of the world we live in, for NGOs to critically analyze what is worth learning, and for building new thoughts and ideals for a more just society.

Increasingly, *emancipatory* approaches by NGOs are occupying Paulston's humanist realm including those assumed by the Women's Emancipation and Development Trust (WED Trust) in India or the Atlanta-based All for Reparations and Emancipation (AFRE). Following Laurel Richardson's (2000, 928) doubt that any theory "has a universal and general claim as the 'right' or the privileged form of authoritative knowledge," advocates of emancipatory paradigms respond to the call for new ways of thinking about society, and look beyond the structures of status-quo and its conflict response. Paulston (1993, 105) agrees that "the collapse of grand theory in the social sciences means that today no one knowledge community can claim a monopoly of truth or claim to fill all intellectual space." Viewed through this lens, the NGO responds to development issues by turning to issues of culture, gender and the individual, thus prioritizing a qualitative methodology in its mission. Emancipatory perspectives draw on post-structural theory to shift thinking away from the dominant discourse in order "to liberate human beings from the circumstances that enslave them" (Horkheimer 1982, 244). Concurs Paulston (1993, 105):

> Knowledge has become more 'textual'. It is increasingly seen as construction employing a conventional sign system where even non-book texts such as icons, architectural structures, musical compositions, or graphic texts such as maps are seen to "presuppose a signifying consciousness that it is our business to uncover" (Barthes 1979). With the appearance of feminist, post-structural and post-modern studies, among others, comparative education discourse has also begun this excavation with a shift in knowledge-framing perspectives from traditional natural and social science models to those of the interpretive humanities and linguistics.

A privileging of *indigenous* worldviews is an underrepresented perspective in social theorizing and education for development alike. For indigenous orientations, post-structuralism has been long been an embedded paradigm. As Linda Tuhiwai Smith (1988, 33) notes in *Decolonizing Methodologies*, "for indigenous peoples, the critique of history is not unfamiliar, although it has now been claimed by postmodern theories. The idea of contested stories and multiple discourses about the past, by different communities, is closely linked to the politics of everyday contemporary indigenous life." Smith continues by asserting that:

> While acknowledging the critical approaches of post-structuralist theory and cultural studies, the arguments which are debated at this level are not new to indigenous peoples. There are numerous oral stories which tell of what it

means, what it feels like, to be present while your history is erased before your eyes, dismissed as irrelevant, ignored or rendered as the lunatic ravings of drunken old people. The negation of indigenous views of history was a critical part of asserting colonial ideology, partly because such views were regarded as clearly 'primitive' and 'incorrect' and mostly because they challenged and resisted the mission of colonization. (29)

The proliferation of indigenous NGOs around the world can be seen by examples such as the North Rupununi District Development Board (NRDDB) in Guyana or Ghost River Rediscovery in Canada. Ghost River has a rediscovery focus on empowering people of all ages and cultures through "the strength of Indigenous culture, the wisdom of the Elders [and] a philosophy of love and respect for the Earth and all peoples" (Ghost River Rediscovery 2010). Founded in 1994, Ghost River's particular approach is the development of young, largely aboriginal leaders through cultural outdoor education, and the fostering of ties with other indigenous groups around the world, assisting them in the establishment of their own rediscovery programs. Especially through partnerships such as that between Ghost River and the NRDDB, indigenous NGOs are growing in prominence and visibility.

A *pluralist* perspective of the NGO attempts to uphold and recognize all non-dominant orientations. In pluralism, NGOs "speak truth to power" through the claims made on behalf of citizens through the NGO (De Mars 2005). Representing and legitimizing alternative ideas are central to the role of NGOs in the construction of new or non-Eurocentric worldviews, including indigenous and aboriginal perspectives (Lickers 2007), feminist-inspired orientations (Vakil 1997; Alvarez 1999), and those advocating for people with disabilities living in low income countries. Research on alternative, decolonizing forms of organization development also suggests promising new ways of conceptualizing NGOs. For example, recent work on Afrocentric organizational development paradigms has examined and highlighted the role of indigenous knowledge, Afrocentric perspectives and values, de-colonization, and personal reflection in organizational approaches (Gibson 1999). In comparative education, Michael Crossley and Keith Watson (2003, 82) point out the transformative, humanist arrival of the field to a point in which the outlook toward the future will rely as "much on theory and methodology as they do to the emergence of new substantive issues." In this way they note the importance of ensuring constant reflexivity of researcher; a more "culturally sensitive reconsideration of the concept and use of time," beyond Western notions of scheduling and progress; and the commitment to a democratic, trans-disciplinary sustainability (80). Indeed, Michael Edwards's (2002, 59) assertion on the reciprocal imperative of theorizing the NGO speak to the role of *hermeneutic* theory in current conceptions of the NGO: "We cannot change the world unless we understand how it works, but neither can we understand the way it works unless we are involved in some way with the processes that change it."

The varying orientations discussed in this chapter have been introduced in an order that roughly corresponds to the historical development of the NGO. However this order more closely parallels the sequencing on Paulston's knowledge representation map, progressing from the functionalist "must be" and "will be" quadrants, to the humanist "be-ing" and "can be" positions (see Figure 14.1). As theoretical orientations evolve with time and complexity of thought, it follows that the historical and conceptual tracts are reasonably well aligned.

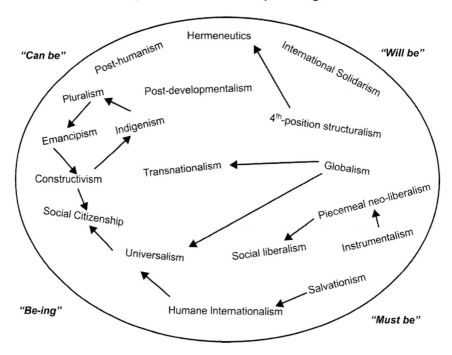

Figure 14.1. Theoretical Frameworks of the NGO Superimposed on Paulston's Knowledge Representations.

NGO Relationships with Civil Society, the Political Economy, and the Global Community

Because concepts of the NGO necessarily depend on how civil society is understood, a word might be said about this social space in which NGOs are strategically located. The theorizing of civil society dates back to political philosophers as Cicero, Locke, Hegel, and Gramsci, and has been defined as the space that mediates between the excesses of state and market (Van Rooy 2000; DeMars 2005). In such a structural-functional orientation, civil society actors are supporters, partners, and executers of various facets of development including certain brands of democracy, governance, and enterprise. In my recent research on Canadian, education-oriented NGOs, I found that directors held an overwhelming structural-functional perspective of civil society. One director in my study described the role of democracy as a factor for enabling a place for NGOs in civil society:

> There is the philosophical belief . . . that NGOs are part of healthy functioning democracy, that civil society has a significant role to play in

development, not only in the increase of democratic space and in decision making, but also in the ability of NGOs to actually deliver and execute. (quoted in Pluim 2008, 23)

By contrast, in a conflict-based orientation the perception of civil society as critical space reflects Immanuel Kant's notion that civil society is a domain that should "guard against the domination of a single interest and check the tyranny of the majority" (Alagappa 2004, 30). NGOs functioning through a conflict theory lens defend citizens against the market by fostering "democratic will to influence the state" (30). Accordingly, this view of civil society might be best positioned in Paulston's "will be" quadrant. In humanist orientations, by contrast, civil society can be conceptualized as a space to strategically construct an alternative social order. It can be an environment that creates an atmosphere for NGOs to envisage global relationships which challenge popular structures such as modernity, positivism, and neoliberalism, and which can be conducive for fostering societal change through the construction of new norms, new ideas, and new relationships of power. Karen Mundy's (2008) proposal of *social citizenship* as a lens through which to evaluate NGOs engagement in education for all is a good example of a framing of new relationships of power where citizen voice, opportunity and rights are prioritized across local, national and global levels.

Unquestionably, the role of power is a certain factor in our understanding of the NGO. As the dominant discourse suggests, NGOs are not apolitical bodies (Klees 2008), and are most likely to be particularly concerned with issues of public image, public engagement, public support, their portrayal and exposure in the media, and the relationship between their perceived performance and public support (Smillie 1995). By examining the NGO through a political perspective, one can appreciate the relative dearth of theorizing. In the past, there have been two main strategies to deal with the lack of theory ascribed to the NGO. The first is avoidance and/or acceptance of this absence. With the absence of connection to a substantive theory, it is simply assumed that the NGO is naturally beneficial to society, and to theorize its existence is of negligible use. Obviously, the consequence of this approach is the relative ease with which the values of NGOs might be compromised, a potentiality that has been widely asserted. In this vein, Klees (2008) has recently remarked that NGOs have been "temp workers" in development education. The second strategy has been to propose a theory on a case-by-case instance (Vakil 1997). In this process, the NGO is analyzed in connection with other constructs or phenomena, perhaps a greater societal movement, larger educational institutions, or a political party. The malleability of the NGO employing this strategy also leaves it open for co-optation by more powerful organizations, an eventuality that might be diminished through the consistency and certainty of theorization.

CONCLUSION

This chapter proposes that the theorization of the NGO is not just an academic exercise; it is an ethical responsibility for scholars and practitioners. By conceptually positioning these organizations in the greater context of human and global development, an examination of their specific contributions to society might be better assessed. The goal of this chapter has been to move us closer toward various understandings of the societal location, the political actions, and the organizational behavior of the NGO. These conceptualizations cut across different disciplines and inform not only present situations, but more importantly, future possibilities for the NGO. The journey toward theorizing the NGO is evidently multi-faceted, controversial and complex. It involves overcoming various barriers implicit in the nature of the organization, and the recognition of vastly different paradigms of the NGO, and of civil society. As Paulston (1993, 101) remarks, "Today, no one world view or way of knowing can claim to fill all the space of vision or knowledge. Rather, it would seem we are in for an extended period of learning to work together as a diverse yet interactive global community of scholars." Indeed, the ability of conceptual mapping to facilitate the interactivity between practitioners and scholars working within the diverse context of the construct of the NGO may be an invaluable tool for us to chart the potential of this organization.

REFERENCES

Ahmed, Shamima, & David M. Potter. (2006). *NGOs in International Politics.* Bloomfield, CT: Kumarian Press.

Alagappa, Muthiah. (2004). *Civil Society and Political Change in Asia.* Palo Alto, CA: Stanford University Press.

Alvarez, Sonia E. (1999). "The Latin American Feminist NGO 'Boom'." *International Feminist Journal of Politics, 1*(2), 181–209.

Archer, David. (1994). "The Changing Roles of Non-governmental Organisations in the Field of Education." *International Journal of Educational Developmen,t 14*(3), 223–232.

Barthes, Roland. (1979). "From Work to Text." In Josue Hariri (Ed.), *Textual Strategies: Perspectives in Poststructural Criticism.* Ithaca, NY: Cornell University Press.

Bluntschli, Johann C. (1891). *The Theory of the State.* Heidelberg, Germany: Oxford Press.

Bosanquet, Bernard. (1899). *The Philosophical Theory of the State.* Kitchener, Canada: Batoche Books.

Brinkerhoff, Jennifer, Stephen Smith, & Hildy Teegen. (2007). *NGOs and the Millennium Development Goals: Citizen Action to Reduce Poverty.* New York: Palgrave Macmillan.

Canadian Council for International Cooperation (CCIC). (1982). *Consultation on Country Focus: Report on the Proceedings of the NGO-CIDA Meeting.* Ottawa, Canada: CCIC.

Clark, John. (1991). "What are Voluntary Organisations and Where Have They Come From?" In John Clark (Ed.), *Democratising Development: The Role of Voluntary Organisations.* London: Earthscan Publications.

Collingwood, Vivien, & Louis Logister. (2007). "Perceptions of the Legitimacy of International NGOs." In Anton Vedder (Ed.), *NGO Involvement in Governance and Policy.* Leiden, The Netherlands: Martinus Nijhoff Publishers.

Crossley, Michael, & Keith Watson. (2003). *Comparative and International Research in Education: Globalisation, Context and Difference.* New York: Routledge Falmer.

Dalglish, Peter. (1998). *The Courage of Children: My Life With the World's Poorest Kids.* Toronto, Canada: Harper-Collins.

DeMars, William E. (2005). *NGOs and Transnational Networks: Wild Cards in World Politics.* London: Pluto.

Easterly, William. (2006). "Planners Versus Searchers in Foreign Aid." *Asian Development Review, 23*(2), 1–35.

Edwards, Michael. (2000). *NGO Rights and Responsibilities: A New Deal for Global Governance*. London: Redwood Books.

Edwards, Michael. (2002). "Are NGOs Overrated? Why and How to Say 'No'." *Current Issues in Comparative Education, 1*(1), 3–5.

Edwards, Michael, & David Hulme. (1995). *Nongovernment Organizations: Performance and Accountability Beyond the Magic Bullet*. London: Earthscan Publications.

Esteva, Gustavo (1995). Development. In Wolfgang Sachs (Ed.), *The Development Dictionary: A Guide to Knowledge as Power*. London: Zed Books.

Fowler, Alan. (2002). "NGO Future – Beyond Aid: NGDO Values and the Fourth Position." In Michael Edwards and Alan Fowler (Ed.), *The Earthscan Reader on NGO Management* (pp. 13–26). London: Earthscan Publications Ltd.

Gary, Ian. (1996). "Confrontation, Co-operation or Co-optation? NGOs and the Ghanaian State During Structural Adjustment." *Review of African Political Economy, 68*, 149–168.

Ghost River Rediscovery. (2010). *History*. Calgary, Canada: Ghost River Rediscovery. Available online at: http://www.ghostriverrediscovery.com.

Gibson, Catherine. (1999). *Afrocentric Organization Development? Shifting the Paradigm from Eurocentricity to Afrocentricity*. MA thesis, Ontario Institute for Studies in Education, University of Toronto, Canada.

Grzybowski, Cândido. (2001). "We NGOs: A Controversial Way of Being and Acting." In Deborah Eade and Ernst Ligteringen (Ed.), *Debating Development: NGOs and The Future*. London: Oxfam.

Harrington, Michael. (1977). *The Vast Majority: A Journey to the World's Poor*. New York: Simon & Schuster.

Hearn, Julie. (1998). "The NGOization of Kenyan Society: USAID and the Restructuring of Health Care." *Review of African Political Economy, 75*, 89–100.

Horkheimer, Max. (1982). *Critical Theory*. New York: Seabury Press.

Hudock, Ann C. (2000). "NGOs' Seat at the Donor Table: Enjoying the Food or Serving the Dinner?" *IDS Bulletin, 31*(3), 14–18.

Jacobs, Jane. (1961). *The Death and Life of Great American Cities*. New York: Random House.

Kellner, Douglas. (1990). "The Postmodern Turn: Positions, Problems, and Prospects." In George Ritzer (Ed.), *Frontiers of Social Theory: The New Syntheses* (pp. 255–286). New York: Columbia University Press.

Klees, Steven J. (1998). "NGOs: Progressive Tool or Neoliberal Force?" *Current Issues in Comparative Education, 1*(1), 49–54.

Klees, Steven J. (2008). "NGOs, Civil Society and Development: Is There a Third Way?" *Current Issues in Comparative Education, 10*(1&2), 22–25.

Lickers, Michael. (2007). *Urban Aboriginal Leadership*. Calgary, Canada: VDM Verlag.

Mundy, Karen E. (2008). "From NGOs to CSOs: Social Citizenship, Civil Society and 'Education for All' – An Agenda for Further Research." *Current Issues in Comparative Education, 10*(1&2), 32–40.

Mundy, Karen E., & Zahra Bhanji. (2005). *Canadian Aid to Education: The What, Why and How of Education Now*. Background paper for the Canadian Global Campaign for Education Forum. Toronto: Ontario Institute for Studies in Education, University of Toronto.

Paulston, Rolland G. (1993). "Mapping Discourse in Comparative Education Texts." *Compare: A Journal of Comparative Education, 23*(2), 101–114.

Pluim, Gary W. J. (2008). *Prospects for Education for Development in Canada: The Role of Small Non-governmental Organizations from the Perspectives of their Directors*. MA thesis, Ontario Institute for Studies in Education, University of Toronto, Canada.

Pratt, Cranford. (1990). "Middle Power Internationalism and Global Poverty." In Cranford Pratt (Ed.), *Middle Power Internationalism: The North-South Dimension*. Montreal, Canada: McGill-Queen's University Press.

Richardson, Laurel. (2000). "Writing: A Method of Inquiry." In Norman K. Denzin and Yvonna S. Lincoln (Ed.), *Handbook of Qualitative Research*. (pp. 923–948). 2nd ed. Thousand Oaks, CA: Sage Publications.

Risse-Kappen, Thomas. (1995). *Bringing Transnational Relations Back In: Non-State Actors, Domestic Structures and International Institutions.* Cambridge, UK: Cambridge University Press.

Robbins, Jane. (2008). "Toward a Theory of the University: Mapping the American Research University in Space and Time." *American Journal of Education, 114*(2), 243–272.

Sandison, Howard. (1886). *The Theory of the School.* 3rd ed. Terre Haute, IN: C. W. Brown.

Scholte, Jan Aart. (2005). "Civil Society and Democracy in Global Governance." In Rorden Wilkinson (Ed.), *The Global Governance Reader.* London: Routledge.

Schwarz, Eric, & Samuel Worthington. (2006). *NGO Impact Initiative: An Assessment by the International Humanitarian NGO Community.* London: Active Learning Network for Accountability and Performance in Humanitarian Action. Available online at: http://www.alnap.org.

Smillie, Ian. (1995). *The Alms Bazaar: Altruism Under Fire—Non-Profit Organizations and International Development.* London: IT Publications.

Smith, Linda Tuhiwai. (1988). *Decolonizing Methodologies: Research and Indigenous Peoples.* New York: St. Martin's Press.

Street Kids International. (2010). *Our Philosophy.* Toronto, Canada: Street Kids International. Available online at: http://www.streetkids.org.

Tikly, Leon. (2004). "Education and the New Imperialism." *Comparative Education, 40*(2), 173–198.

Vakil, Anna C. (1997). Confronting the Classification Problem: Toward a Taxonomy of NGOs. *World Development, 25*(12), 2057–2070.

Van Rooy, Alison. (2000). "Good News! You May Be Out of a Job: Reflections on the Past and Future. 50 Years for Northern NGOs." *Development in Practice, 10*(3&4), 300–318.

Wangoola, Paul. (1995). "The Political Economy of Nongovernmental Organisations." In Beverly Benner Cassara (Ed.), *Adult Education Through World Collaboration.* Malabar, FL: Krieger.

Weiss, Edith B., & Harold K. Jacobson. (2000). *Engaging Countries: Strengthening Compliance with International Environmental Accords.* Cambridge, MA: MIT Press.

World University Service of Canada (WUSC). (2010). *Student Refugee Program.* Ottawa, Canada: WUSC. Available online at: http://www.wusc.ca/en.

JOAN DEJAEGHERE AND LISA VU

15. TRANSNATIONALISM AND ITS ANALYTIC POSSIBILITIES FOR COMPARATIVE, INTERNATIONAL, AND DEVELOPMENT EDUCATION

INTRODUCTION

Globalization has been a dominant force affecting conceptual frameworks, empirical studies and policy research in comparative, international and development education (CIDE) particularly in the past two decades. Functionalist perspectives of globalization, such as neoliberal and neo-institutional perspectives, have had a strong influence on the field, particularly in creating and advancing global agendas, policies, standards, and practices. Jason Beech (2009, 351), in a call for new ways of examining policies in the field, reminds us that most of the literature on global education policy "tends to associate globalisation and global networks with neoliberalism and the promotion of pro-market reforms." Critics of this perspective of globalization are present, though less dominant in the field, drawing from other fields such as critical studies, feminist studies, history and sociology (e.g., Rizvi 2000; Stromquist and Monkman 2000; Arnove and Torres 2003). For example, Fazal Rizvi (2000) notes the narrow ways in which globalization has been defined and used in the field of CIDE, and he calls for greater analytical application of cultural flows and arrangements across nation-state borders. These neoliberal and critical perspectives of globalization have often been used to reinforce binary approaches to understanding globalization and its relation to educational policies and practices. Nicholas C. Burbules and Carlos A. Torres (2000) note the dualities created in the scholarship on globalization: globalization from above and below, global and local, economic and cultural, homogenization and diversification.

The nation-state, its conceptualizations and actions have tended to be overlooked within these binaries, particularly in relation to phenomena that transcend borders. Globalization with an assumption of greater deterritorialization and denationalization is invoked without examining how the nation-state adapts and reformulates itself in relation to global forces. In addition, the influences that the nation-state continues to have in the lives of people and in systems, such as education, need to be re-examined. We suggest that perspectives of globalization are limited in understanding and explaining cross-border phenomena as it affects education and that transnationalism provides another perspective and set of analytic concepts by which to understand emerging educational issues in a globalizing world.

John C. Weidman, W. James Jacob (eds.), Beyond the Comparative: Advancing Theory and Its Application to Practice, 269–291.

Rolland G. Paulston's use of social cartography to map various theories and perspectives applicable to the field of CIDE is useful for examining the usages of approaches and perspectives of globalization and also for identifying emerging perspectives that problematize globalizing phenomena in new ways. We suggest a reconceptualization of how globalizing phenomena link to nation-states and how nation-states respond to and influence these global flows. Transnationalism, like globalization, is concerned with the movement of people, capital and ideas across borders, and it has been most often associated with the migration of people. It is distinct from globalization, however, in that it aims to understand, explain and critique trans-border movements as being both anchored in and transcending nation-states (Kearney 1995). Whereas Michael Kearney (1995, 548), in a seminal piece on transnationalism and globalization, suggests that transnationalism "has a more limited purview" than globalization, we put forth in this chapter how transnationalism, and particularly recent critical perspectives and uses of it, offers an alternative to dominant perspectives of globalization by examining and problematizing transnational phenomena in relation to the nation-state. As Thomas Faist (2000b, 210–211) argues in his distinction of globalization and transnationalism, "transnational processes are anchored in and span two or more nation-states and thus are not 'denationalized'." Transnationalism examines the nation-state and does not assume that it is essentialized in its borders. Analytic concepts of transnationalism offer possibilities for understanding globalization differently. We argue in this chapter that transnationalism, and particularly emerging concepts developed and used in other fields, offers another important analytical framework for examining under-researched issues in the field of CIDE. Paulston (2000, 297-298) reminds us that "a reflexive social cartography might serve to identify and visualize between disputatious communities that would open space for all knowledge perspectives discovered, privilege known, yet problematize all, and yet promote a useful visual and verbal dialogue." In this chapter, we aim to identify the various perspectives of transnationalism used in scholarship in CIDE and to offer additional perspectives on transnationalism as used in other disciplines and fields to create spaces for understanding globalization, education and development in new ways.

Transnationalism, as it problematizes the nation-state's roles in and responses to globalizing phenomena such as migration of learners and the mobility of educational policies and practices, is an important framework for examining education. The state and its education systems are invariably linked, as Burbules and Torres (2000) note, albeit with great variation in this relationship historically and politically. Nevertheless, overlooking this relationship, as too often occurs in analyses using globalization frameworks, is problematic. Many studies in CIDE use the nation-state as the unit of analysis when examining global phenomena rather than problematizing it as a concept. Important recent works that examine educational phenomena globally or across borders, such as Gita Steiner-Khamsi's (2004) *The Global Politics of Educational Borrowing and Lending* do not necessarily problematize and reconceptualize the nature of the nation-state within cross-border educational linkages. Similarly, Frances Vavrus and Lesley Bartlett's (2009) work on multi-level cases uniquely positions educational research in the linkages among global agendas, nation-states, and local contexts. They do not utilize, however, the analytic contributions of transnationalism.

Given its limited use to date and the possibilities to inform new ways of examining education in CIDE, we provide an analytical summary of how transnationalism has been used in our field by reviewing articles published in flagship journals of the field.[1] We find that the uses of transnationalism in CIDE, similar to globalization, tend to be functionalist, with some scholars using critical approaches. In addition, transnationalism is not well conceptualized and utilized in many studies. Transnationalism is sometimes used to refer to people or organizations, while in other studies, it refers to the processes by which trans-border phenomena occur. Drawing on the emerging scholarship on transnationalism in other fields and disciplines, we suggest key concepts that can clarify the uses of transnationalism and expand our "visual and verbal dialogue" (Paulston 2000, 298) in comparative, international and development education. Analytical concepts such as linkages, reciprocity, solidarities, hybridities, and social and political fields can be potentially useful for examining and thinking about education and development transnationally. In addition, new concepts are needed to describe and explain the nation-state and its transnational policies and practices. Using these concepts and approaches emerging in studies of transnationalism, we pose several areas and questions for further study in the field.

One area for further research resides in transnationalism, migrant networks and development. We suggest a need for further inquiry on how transnational migrants influence country of origin and receiving country development. This line of inquiry challenges common assumptions about the roles and prominence of transnational organizations and overseas development assistance, as well as the roles of civil society in development. A second area for inquiry resides in the purposes and practices of education as informed by transnational perspectives. Research in this area includes examining and problematizing assumptions about education for mobile populations, as well as for those who are not mobile but are transnationally connected. It raises questions about the roles of nation-states in education, and it calls for further inquiries toward education's role in fostering civic and social/cultural identities, and in workplace development.

PERSPECTIVES ON TRANSNATIONALISM ACROSS THE DISCIPLINES

The disciplines of sociology, anthropology and political science, as well as the fields of migration, ethnic and diaspora studies, have developed the analytical perspectives and uses of transnationalism. Each of the disciplines has advanced different concepts and uses in the inquiry of transnationalism. Figure 15.1 maps analytical concepts related to transnationalism that are also pertinent to our field. Transnationalism is generally conceptualized as the metaphorical overlap between sending and receiving nation-states. Social, cultural and economic ties link internationally mobile populations and nation-states. The dotted lines that bound the transnational space serve two purposes. First, they help to signify the porous geographical boundaries of countries. Second, they denote the indefinite nature of transnational ties. This is to say that not every migrant will maintain transnational ties, and transnational relationships may change over time. In the transnational space, we mapped key concepts found in the transnationalism literature utilizing Michael Smith and Luis Guarnizo's (1998) conceptualization of transnationalism from above and transnationalism from below to organize these terms. Thus, the concepts found in the top half of the transnational space relate to Smith and Guarnizo's (1998) schemata of transnationalism among nation-states and organizations whereas the concepts found at the bottom are more closely connected to the lives of migrants.

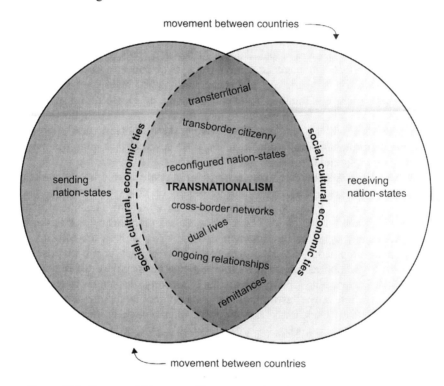

Figure 15.1. Conceptual Mapping of Transnationalism from the Current Scholarship.

In the 1990s, though the concept was used to describe cross-border phenomena before that, sociologists and anthropologists expanded the usage of transnationalism to understand and explain recent immigration as distinct from immigration and immigrant experiences historically. Scholars using transnationalism attempted to push the conceptual thinking in these fields to explain new ways that immigrants are incorporated into societies in which they settle and how they develop networks in societies of origins (e.g., Glick Schiller et al., 1992; Basch et al., 1994; Portes et al., 1999). While they developed new metaphors and concepts, these perspectives were mostly functional in attempting to explain social relations in and between two societies (see Kivisto 2001 for a critique of the theoretical perspectives of transnationalism and its explanatory uses for migration). Linda Basch and colleagues (1994, 7) describe transnationalism as "the processes by which immigrants forge and sustain multi-stranded social relations that link together their societies of origin and settlement." Alejandro Portes, Luis E. Guarnizo, and Patricia Landolt (1999) describe these relations as economic, social, cultural and political networks that affect the environments in country of origins. Both the sociological perspective of Portes and colleagues and the anthropological one of Basch and colleagues utilize the concepts of society of origin and receiving society, and they aim to position the two societies in relation to each other, or as Nina Glick Schiller and colleagues (1992, 1) note, "Their lives cut across national boundaries and bring two societies into a single social field." This conceptualization suggests that transnationalism is useful for examining nation-states not only within their distinct borders but also as a single social field, in effect, permeating and remaking borders of the state's territory and authority.

From these perspectives, transnationalism has been used to understand the dual lives that migrants lead whether in economic, social, cultural and educational spheres (Portes et al., 1999). These perspectives allow us to examine the dialectical interplay between homeland concerns and receiving nation realities and the impact this interplay has on immigrants and nations (Kivisto 2001, 553). Transnationalism from these perspectives provides analytic concepts to examine relations that immigrants have between states and processes of acculturation and incorporation, including resistance and adaptation. While immigrant is a common term used in much of this transnationalism research, it is used to refer to their integration into the receiving society. Other scholars, such as Sofia Villenas (2007), make a distinction between migrants and immigrants in that migrant signifies mobile populations who live and imagine their lives between nation-states. With regard to comparative, international and development education, these perspectives frame questions about how education is an institution that aims to integrate immigrants into the receiving society. These analytical concepts also allow an understanding of how immigrants resist and adapt educational practices for their purposes, including their identity, and social, cultural and economic relations (see Hall 2002; Murillo 2002). The unit of analysis is often the individual student or immigrant/sojourner; in fact, Portes and colleagues (1999) called for limiting the unit to individuals rather than groups or the nation-state. Additionally, the debates within these approaches have focused on the concepts used to define the individual (migrant, immigrant) and how to conceptualize the social, economic, cultural and political relations and spaces of nation-states.

Another perspective is developed in Michael Smith's (1994) work and is exemplified in the edited volume *Transnationalism from Below* by Smith and Guarnizo (1998). This work examines transnationalism through migrant experiences in locally situated contexts and therefore is similar to the approaches above in examining the individual, though it also addresses collective groups or mass movements (e.g., mass migrations) as the unit of analysis. This work attempts to problematize the idea of sending and receiving countries by reconceptualizing locality and translocality. As Smith and Guarnizo (1998, 11) state: "Transnational practices do not take place in an imaginary 'third space' (Bhabha 1990; Soja 1996) abstractly located 'in-between' national territories. Transnational practices, while connecting collectivities located in more than one national territory, are embodied in specific social relations established between specific people, situated in unequivocal localities, at historically determined times." Here, transnationalism is less concerned with abstract networks and activities and more with understanding the meaning of linkages and activities in specific contexts and times. While addressing the micro-level processes of transnationalism, this book recognizes and attempts to understand and place into a dialectic relationship transnationalism from below with that from above. Guarnizo and Smith (1998) state that future research in transnationalism needs to address the challenge of integrating macro- and micro-determinants into analysis and to better explicate the units of analysis, of which they do not explicitly include the nation-state. In referring to the consequences of transnationalism for the nation-state, they suggest the nation-state is undergoing a reformation and reconstitution in relation to the transterritorialization of these phenomena.

Another analytic contribution to transnationalism is put forth by Faist (2000a, 2000b) in his conceptualization of nation-states as new social spaces, which expands on the earlier usage of social fields by Glick Schiller and colleagues (1992). Faist (2000a) regards transnationalism as boundary-breaking and creating new social spaces, as distinct from places. His approach does not position the nation-state as a political project with inherent political hegemonic interests and it diverges from a world-systems approach of core and periphery relations between nation-states. These transnational spaces represent new social meanings based on reciprocity and solidarity, as he states:

> Space here does not only refer to physical features, but also to larger opportunity structures, the social life and the subjective images, values, and meanings that the specific and limited place represents to migrants. Space is thus different from place in that it encompasses or spans various territorial locations . . . . Space has a social meaning that extends beyond simple territoriality; only with concrete social or symbolic ties does it gain meaning for potential migrants. (45–46)

Peter Kivisto (2001) argues that Faist's conceptualization allows for linking transnationalism from below with transnationalism from above by focusing not only on individuals, but individuals in relation to these social spaces. This analytic concept extends and reformulates the unit of analysis by which to understand transnational phenomena, such as migrating individuals' lives. It extends the analysis of nation-states as reconfiguring their bordered spaces and the linkages between them. Faist (2000b) also suggests how cultural and political factors affect the nature of transnational social spaces, and he provides a thorough explanation of the role of reciprocity, solidarity and circuits as they relate to these spaces.

Aihwa Ong (1999), Ritty Lukose (2007), and Villenas (2007) call for alternative concepts to the functionalist perspectives of receiving and sending states and networks to understand transnationalism and migrants' lives. They suggest that transnational studies need to problematize the nation-state and borders with regard to how migrants live and imagine their transnational lives. To examine nation-states as political and cultural projects as they reformulate themselves in relation to globalizing phenomenon is to follow Lukose's (2007) call for examining the nation-state as an object of analysis, not the unit of analysis. Such an analysis, however, is not abstract but rather is situated in the specific cultural, historical and political projects of people's daily lives and in the daily practices and interactions in schools and education more broadly. Lukose's approach to transnationalism calls for "an interrogation of educational spaces as sites for a complex encounter between diasporic longings and belongings, powerful processes of national racial formation, and state practices in ways that are producing new forms of cultural production and experiences between diaspora and nation" (412).

Meanwhile, Ong (1999, 13) takes up the issue of the role of the nation-state not only in terms of the consequences of transnationalism that affect it, but as an actor in these processes of transnationalism. In her book on the cultural logics of transnationality, Ong asserts that the connections between nation-states are often ignored and "local-global structural articulations that materially and symbolically shape" lives in places and spaces are overlooked. Different from the approaches above, Ong aims to understand the local subjectivities in transnational social spaces and the nation-state as a powerful actor in those social spaces. Ong argues that "the nation-state—along with its juridical-legislative systems, bureaucratic apparatuses, economic entities, modes of governmentality and war-making capacities—continues to define, discipline, control and regulate all kinds of populations, whether in movement or in residence" (15). This conceptualization follows Kearney's (1995, 548) statement that transnationalism "calls attention to the cultural and political projects of nation-states as they vie for hegemony in relations with other nation-states, with their citizens and 'aliens'." This conceptualization complicates and examines the tensions between and within nation-states in relation to global flows and migrating peoples, and it calls for new ways of rethinking the concept of the nation-state as a bordered and autonomous entity.

In this section, we have mapped how various perspectives of transnationalism are explicated in the fields of sociology, anthropology and political science. These various approaches tend to focus on either transnationalism from below or from above while attempting to understand the dialectical relationship and the influence of the nation-state in that relationship. The analytic uses of transnationalism from below are often linked to migrating individuals and their cultural and social networks. Transnationalism from above tends to examine and problematize the political and economic roles of nation-states in the lives of mobile populations and in other nation-states. These different analytic approaches of transnationalism vary in the concepts used, their explanatory power and their application to various global phenomena; nonetheless, transnationalism aims to reexamine and reformulate

J. DEJAEGHERE AND L. VU

our conceptualizations about the nation-state as an actor in trans-border phenomena and in the lives of mobile people.

PERSPECTIVES OF TRANSNATIONALISM IN CIDE

In this section, we will map and critique the uses of transnationalism in the scholarship of comparative, international and development education. This is a partial mapping, as most developing scholarship requires time to emerge, coalesce, and be articulated in new ways. In addition, such a mapping cannot do full justice to a field that is global and that takes up these concepts in varying ways through multiple languages. Our mapping and analysis focus on articles written within the last 15 years in the major journals (published in English) of the field, including *Compare, Comparative Education, Comparative Education Review, International Journal of Educational Development* and *Journal of Studies in International Education*. Our search utilized the concepts of transnationalism, international mobility, networks, hybridity, and solidarities. Some articles may use the term globalization alongside concepts related to transnationalism (e.g., Rizvi's chapter in Burbules and Torres [2000] discussing globalization and referencing concepts of hybridity and solidarity). Conversely, some articles that use the term transnationalism without explicit definitions or those with implicit references to globalizing phenomenon were not included. We also omitted articles referring to migrants, migration, identity, and similar concepts if they did not also use the concept of transnationalism even in a limited way.

In addition to scholarship published within the field of CIDE, we reviewed at least 18 articles concerning transnationalism and education in a variety of journals of education, migration, ethnic, diasporic and transnational studies. The educational journals included *Harvard Educational Review, Higher Education Policy, International Journal of Lifelong Education* and *The High School Journal*. Journals outside the field of education include: *Journal of Ethnic and Migration Studies, International Migration Review, Global Networks, Ethnic and Racial Studies*, and *Diaspora*. We have also referred to select chapters from books that specifically use transnationalism.

In this section, we present selections of the main conceptualizations and usages of transnationalism from 12 articles found in the CIDE flagship journals. Though the conceptualizations and usages of transnationalism are quite disparate, the literature can be grouped into three broad categories based on the central focus of study, which include: migrant/mobile populations, educational systems, and international development organizations. We find that transnationalism and some of its key concepts have not been well distinguished from globalization in the CIDE literature. These studies also tend to follow a pattern in the broader transnational literature: transnationalism from below focusing on individuals and migrating students and transnationalism from above illustrating the state-led influences in creating networks and in controlling mobilities and migrating peoples.

Transnationalism and Mobile Populations

A set of studies in the CIDE literature describes individuals as transnational and focuses on transnationalism as it affects either migrant students in K-12 education or higher education (in higher education the term international student is employed). Concepts of transnationalism are explored in terms of identity and learning processes related to education across national boundaries. They most closely align with the sociological and anthropological origins of transnationalism in their focus on the individual migrant's dual lives and how this affects the migrant's education and learning. For example, Karen Monkman (1999) offers a piece about the learning experiences of transnational adults while Victor Zúñiga and Edmund Hamann (2009) examine school-age students with experience in multiple educational contexts.

Monkman (1999, 368) refers to transnationalism as "the processes that link together societies and cultures of origin and settlement, revealing a multifaceted context of life based in two nations simultaneously," which harkens to Basch and colleagues (1994) and Kearney's (1995) usages of transnationalism. Her study utilizes the concepts of social networks and transnational social dynamics and relations, particularly as they are formed, fostered and transformed in transnational learning contexts. Setting out these concepts as occurring in transnational spaces or in two nations simultaneously, Monkman also delineates the learning that occurs at different phases, referencing the sociological literature on separation, transition and incorporation of migrants. Adult migrants are the primary unit of analysis in this study with some examination of the state in terms of how it develops and supports different modes of learning and education (e.g., establishing nonformal programs). The analysis of these adult migrants' lives is situated in a framework of orientation to the country of origin or the country of settlement while at times illustrating the difficulty in positioning these as binaries since some of the adults' lives are more multidimensional than is captured by relating them to nation-states. Monkman (1999) concludes the need for researchers and educators/education systems to utilize a broader frame for understanding transnationalism. She states:

> So often the lives of immigrants are viewed as deficient in skills and knowledge valued in the country of residence. Only part of their lives is visible when looking through only one national lens. By re-drawing life's boundaries to reveal a broader frame, we can more easily recognize the richness and complexities of constructing lives in transnational contexts. (381)

In calling for other frames to understand the dialectical between individuals and nation-states and reconceptualizing the nation-state, this study's conceptualization of transnationalism is later extended by Smith and Guarnizo's (1998) and Ong's (1999) scholarship on the transnational role of the nation-state and individuals in specific localities.

Zúñiga and Hamann (2009) provide another example of transnationalism as it relates to students in public schools. The authors focus on the transnational movements of students, thus referencing the action of moving between two nation-states and using students as the unit of analysis. The study provides an exploration of student identities and the ways that schools construct the identities of these students. The authors differentiate immigrant students who settle permanently in a country and sojourner students who may live in a country for a limited amount of time before returning to the country of origin. Of particular concern for the authors are sojourner students whose learning is disrupted by the multiple relocations. As sojourners, the students' experiences cannot be framed in terms of adaptation or integration because their schooling cannot be described in a linear pattern. For some students, the authors view transnational experience as a state of in-betweenness that poses challenges for schools. In their recognition of the challenges of transnationalism for schools, the authors seem to suggest that schools often follow a national script that territorializes knowledge and students' experiences.

In the realm of higher education, Terri Kim (2009) provides a historical account of the mobility of academics while Terra Gargano (2009) and Katalin Szelényi and Robert Rhoads (2007) discuss international students. Like Monkman (1999) and Zúñiga and Hamann (2009), the authors focus on individuals, although they conceptualize transnationalism as being fostered through educational hiring and exchanges rather than as an effect of migration for other purposes. These latter articles serve as reminders that education may not only be reactive to students with transnational experience but that it may also be a mode through which certain forms of transnationalism are fostered.

Academics, rather than the more commonly discussed student population, are the focus of Kim's (2009, 387) study. Her analysis frames academics' international mobility within broader historical forces rather than as individual choices, which suggests a world systems approach to explaining transnational phenomenon. Describing the patterns of movement during several historical periods, beginning with the medieval period and ending with the neoliberal ideologies of today, the author tries to show that academic movements are "transnational" and occur "'between' or 'above' territorial boundaries . . . and not on official interaction between nations." She emphasizes the "simultaneity of interlocking relations . . . national and supranational policy frameworks; and institutional networks of universities" that characterize today's academic movements (400), which reflects transnationalism's focus on global networks and linkages as they interact with the nation-state and its educational institutions. The political, economic and institutional linkages described in the article relate to transnationalism from above, contrasting with Smith and Guarnizo's (1998) conceptualization of transnationalism from below. In the conclusion, however, Kim (2009) calls for more research into the lived experiences of academics that would align more with Smith and Guarnizo's research. Although she does not explicitly discuss transnationalism in Smith and Guarnizo's (1998) terms, she seems to recognize the difference between the two levels of transnationalism in her acknowledgement that her research examines the broader context while there is a need for further research at the micro-level.

In contrast to Kim's study of academics, Gargano (2009) focuses on international students' identity construction while Szelényi and Rhoads (2007) examine how experience as international graduate students in the US changed notions of citizenship for the 30 students that they interviewed. Both studies reference transnational lives fostered by participation in cross-border educational programs, but Gargano (2009) explores the intricacies surrounding her usage of transnationalism while Szelényi and Rhoads (2007) use the term transnational with little analysis of its conceptual evolution. Similar to our objectives of highlighting the possible uses of transnationalism for CIDE, Gargano (2009) sees potential for utilizing concepts from transnationalism for studies of international students, or students participating in cross-border programs. She argues that the current scholarship on international students does not sufficiently utilize analytic concepts of transnationalism to explain the processes of identity negotiation and construction, nor does the research on transnationalism often examine educational contexts or lived experiences of university students. Citing Georges Fouron and Glick Schiller's (2001) definition of transnational social field, Gargano (2009, 544) states that it is "an unbounded terrain of interlocking egocentric networks that extends across the borders of two or more nation-states and that incorporates its participants in the day-to-day activities of social reproduction in these various locations." Transnational social fields affect and are created by those who travel abroad, those who remain in contexts of origin, and those from the new context. Rather than regarding international students as moving between bounded territories, transnational social fields are spaces for the exchange, organization, and transformation of ideas, practices, and social networks.

Gargano (2009) distinguishes her approach from that of globalization and international education in its explanation of international students' cross-border education and experiences. She argues that the foci of these approaches tend to focus on national or institutional level trends, or global influences on institutions and nation-states, and does not sufficiently examine the students' experiences as constructed in and beyond the nation-state contexts. It appears that Gargano grounds her approach in Smith and Guarnizo's (1998, 6) concept of transnationalism as a dynamic, "multifaceted, multi-local process" in which students' experiences are constructed in specific and multiple local settings. Gargano (2009) suggests that transnationalism allows for research on international students or mobile students to be understood for their multiple and variable trajectories rather than as a homogenous group or as equivalent to other border crossers such as immigrants. This analytic lens allows for research to unbind these students' experiences from the primacy of national origin and still understand how nation-states and nationality may affect their lives and identities. Though this article focuses primarily on the individual student in higher education and the student's identity construction in transnational social fields, it also briefly discusses the importance of examining the social, political, cultural and economic contexts of nation-states as they affect students' experiences.

Transnationalism and Educational Institutions

The second set of articles in CIDE journals focuses on transnationalism as it affects educational systems rather than individuals. Rieko Fry (2009), Debora Hinderliter Ortloff and Christopher Frey (2007), and Ana Bravo-Moreno (2009) utilize transnationalism to examine nation-state policies and institutional responses to the influx of students who cross borders. In comparing countries' differing conceptualizations and responses to transnationalism, these studies use the nation-state as a unit of analysis. In addition, they problematize the nation-state as an object of analysis particularly in the promotion of a singular national-identity.

Like Zúñiga and Hamann (2009), Fry (2009) writes about the education of sojourner students, but in the Japanese context and as a policy critique rather than as an explanatory piece. Unlike the Mexican context that Zúñiga and Hamann study, the Japanese government provides support and Japanese-style schooling for children who accompany their parents on extended overseas business stays. Fry outlines a shift in the Japanese government's strategies, from providing remedial education to help the sojourner students stay on par with their peers who never left Japan, to a more receptive outlook leading towards the promotion rather than downplay of the students' international experience. While transnationalism tends to emphasize the sojourner's successful negotiation of both the current and home societies, Fry's interviews and tests of students' competencies in the home and host languages led her to conclude that the students retain strong attachments to Japan and may not be so integrated into the host society. Consequently, Fry argues that the Japanese government's remedial policies that deem sojourner students as lagging behind their national peers are unnecessary; meanwhile, the promotion of the students' international competence may be overestimating the students' knowledge of the host culture. In essence, she finds incongruence between the Japanese policies toward sojourner students and their actual lived experience. Fry challenges the assumption that migrants are equally integrated or competent in both cultures (sending and receiving) and suggests that in the case of Japanese students who attend Japanese schools while living abroad, there is more competence in the home culture than in the host culture. The Japanese schools, therefore, seem to succeed in linking students to Japan despite the students' physical absence from the country. The article illustrates a case in which a nation-state—Japan—utilizes education as a means to foster ties with its overseas community. It shows that transnational ties to Japan do not solely arise from the overseas Japanese community but can also be attributed to the existence of the Japanese schools overseas.

Whereas Fry (2009) provides an example of how education may be used to foster transnational ties, Hinderliter Ortloff and Frey (2007, 461) provide a comparative study of educational policies of Germany and Japan as they respond to increasing populations with transnational experience. Their article discusses ethnic Germans and Japanese who have spent the majority or all of their time in another country, but, for various reasons, are returning to Germany and Japan. Hinderliter Ortloff and Frey refer to the "transnational lives" of a particular group of returnees, the *kikokushijo*, and suggest that while they are ethnically Japanese, they do not have a strong Japanese cultural or national identity. This group does not possess "home country" linguistic and cultural competencies, which the authors assert is their primary challenge for integrating into the German or Japanese society. It was suggested that the *kikokushijo's* transnational experience marked their status as outsiders and resulted in the government's underinvestment in their education. In contrast, the education of business people's children as sojourners (who were the subjects in Fry 2009) is a higher priority and receives more resources. The differentiation between the two groups by the Japanese government indicates the government's mixed conceptualizations of what constitutes transnational experience and transnational migrants. On one hand, transnational experiences of sojourners are viewed as helping Japan to internationalize (children of businesspeople), while on the other hand, transnational kikokushijos are seen as outside the national and cultural identity of Japan. Taken together, the articles by Fry (2009) and Hinderliter Ortloff and Frey (2007) reveal the contradictory response of the Japanese government towards transnationalism in two different circumstances.

Bravo-Moreno (2009, 420) offers another article that examines immigration and educational policies as they shape and respond to transnational lives of students. Without explicit use of transnationalism conceptually, Bravo-Moreno contextually and historically situates contemporary immigration in Spain and the US in terms of how education and nationhood are conceived. Different from the preceding studies, her article examines how immigration complicates the traditional notion of citizenship as tied to a single territory. Bravo-Moreno uses transnationalism to refer to migrant students and references transnational studies as having examined "how migrant groups have historically reconstituted belonging, mobilised territory-based identities across geopolitical borders, and challenged existing pedagogies in the education systems of host countries." She appears to take an approach that problematizes nation-states as objects of analyses, as Ong (1999) and Lukose (2007) propose, although her theoretical framing does not refer to this and is situated in literature on immigration and critical multiculturalism, such as how opportunity structures and racism in societies and systems affect immigrant identity and schooling opportunities. By focusing primarily on the nation-state, this study does not provide the micro-level analysis that Smith and Guarnizo (1998) and Ong (1999) call for in understanding the localized ways in which transnationalism is lived and materialized in the daily lives of students. Instead, the article takes a structural approach to how schools perpetuate hegemonic ideas of the nation-state despite the transnational lives of students while also acknowledging the dynamic nature of schools and the education systems. Bravo-Moreno (2009, 430) concludes that researchers and educators need to broaden the conceptualization of schools as dynamic institutions that adapt to new demographic shifts rather than as fixed entities. She introduces the concept and metaphor "shape-shifting" "as one that facilitates purposive, interactive and (re)construction of education systems." She suggests that immigration and transnational experiences require "shifting concepts of nationhood and the challenges that transnational mobilities pose to ideas of cultural homogeneity in education and feelings of belonging" (419–420).

Transnationalism and International Development Organizations

Complicating the traditional international-national dichotomy, the third group of articles utilizes transnationalism to denote a new political space within which international organizations and institutions operate. As Stephen Carney (2009, 65) explains, "a focus on transnational relations opens new empirical lenses that uncover a multitude of practices in government at the top and within grassroots organizations at the bottom that are actually deeply connected to and formed by global and cross-national phenomena." Rather than transnational ties and lives of individuals, Carney writes about the linkages between nation-states and the global educational policies set forth by international agencies like the European Union and Organisation for Economic Co-operation and Development (OECD) that are nonetheless still grounded in nation-state politics and power. These educational policies and practices are transnational because they bind nation-states to global agendas, or what Carney refers to as the "global national script" (79). He shows how policies are translated in different country contexts even though they are linked to a larger global agenda (i.e., an agenda that transcends nation-states). In his study of Denmark, Nepal and China, he emphasizes the countries' autonomy in the interpretation of the global neoliberal policy agenda in ways that fit each country's political, historical and cultural context. According to his conceptualization, the agenda set forth by international organizations are separate from the political, cultural and social structures of a country, and when they mix, hybrid policies are formed that contain elements of both the global agenda and the country-specific interpretations. Hybridity is a key concept of transnationalism and is one that needs further explanation in specific contexts and spaces, but Carney only implicitly alludes to it in the article.

The topic of transnational relations between nation-states and international organizations also gets taken up by Stavros Moutsios (2009) who uses transnationalism to describe the process in which the educational development agenda of international organizations, such as the World Bank, the International Monetary Fund, the World Trade Organization and the Organisation for Economic Co-operation and Development is formulated. Moutsios differentiates this "transnational policy making" process from international relations because it goes beyond the nation-state-to-nation-state interaction (471). In other words, the process transcends nation-states while also being grounded in them. Citing Ulrich Beck (2005), he characterizes the process to be the flow of global policies into nation-states so that "nation-state politics is becoming the arena where transnational politics is elaborated" (Moutsios 2009, 471). Within his framework, nation-states are not conceptualized as separate units that make their own educational policies and practices but are influenced instead by global agendas propagated by multilateral organizations. This conceptualization of national boundaries being blurred by transnational relations mirrors the earlier work of Glick Schiller and colleagues (1992); however, unlike Glick Schiller and colleagues who view the complete subjugation of the nation-state to transnational processes, Moutsios (2009) retains the nation-state as the site where global policies are debated and adapted to fit the local context. He does not focus on how the global policies get translated into the local context, which is the issue discussed in Carney (2009), but he does offer criticisms of the transnational policy making process itself and the consequent ideologies that are formed.

One criticism discussed by Moutsios (2009) is that the educational development agenda of international organizations continues to be shaped by economic and political interests of the individual nation-state members of the organizations. The transnational policy making process is, in essence, wrought with unequal networks and alliances among nation-states. Moutsios offers a deconstruction of power differentials in the transnational policy making process, which is rarely done in transnational studies; however, he reserves his analysis to each individual organization rather than theorizing about power differentials in the broader process. The transnational policy making process involves multiple actors, from those that participate in the making of the policies to those who only respond to policies and also those who play dual roles. More could have been said about the positionality of nation-states and how that undermines or facilitates their participation in the transnational policy making process, as well as the reformulation of the nation-state as a political space that is both bounded and moves beyond boundaries.

Like Moutsios (2009), Jonathan Jansen (2005) problematizes the transnational policy making process and discusses one particular practice, target setting. While describing the fallacies associated with target setting, Jansen also theorizes that it is a strategy for checking the accountability of nation-states. Control of this surveillance process, as Jansen refers to it, occurs transnationally, or beyond nation-state boundaries and through the activities of international organizations in relation to nation-states. Jansen believes that developing nation-states participate in the practice for both financial incentives and to avoid negative political consequences. Like the two previous articles, transnationalism is used to denote a political space that transcends national borders and is also linked with the political space within these boundaries.

Whereas Carney (2009), Moutsios (2009) and Jansen (2005) focus on the relationship between multilateral organizations and nation-states, Karen Mundy and Lynn Murphy (2001) discuss the growing prominence of transnational civil society in the setting of global educational agendas. In their view, transnational refers to an arena for political action across nation-state boundaries and in relation to global phenomena. They draw on works in international relations that have conceptualized transnational civil society as expanding beyond the nation-state. Citing Clark and colleagues (1998), Mundy and Murphy (2001, 92) state that "theories of international civil society . . . 'envision a dense exchange among individuals, groups, and organizations in the public sphere, separate from state dominated action'." The Global Campaign for Education, with the goal of spotlighting education among the plethora of other international development issues, serves as their example of a movement that is supported by civil society. Joining this campaign allows individuals from around the world to become part of a network that advocates for education. The authors conclude that the movement has the potential to change the decision-making landscape of educational development.

Unlike some of the sociological and anthropological works on transnationalism that focus on individuals and their personal networks and linkages, Mundy and Murphy (2001) discuss individuals linking up with organizations and developing a political agenda that affects interests within a nation-state and across nation-states, in this case educational development. While the article contains a comprehensive discussion of the historical context from which today's transnational advocacy movements arose, its macro-level analysis does not explain why individuals are supporting such groups, or why one group receives support over another. The multiple localities from which such transnational movements draw support bring up the question of whether the movements are democratic, or whether there could be power differentials similar to what exists in the transnational policymaking of multilateral organizations discussed in Moutsios (2009). In addition, analysis of these transnational movements could be better linked to how they relate to and reconfigure the nation-state, as well as the global agendas. Lastly, the authors do not provide a conceptual grounding for their use of transnational, and the term is used interchangeably with international throughout the article.

As evidenced by the articles discussed above, scholars in CIDE have taken up the notion of transnationalism to explain a variety of issues, including the education of immigrants and mobile populations, impacts of international education programs on individuals, and the role and relations of citizens and nation-states in multilateral organizations and the global educational agenda. The challenge in using and critiquing transnationalism in CIDE literature is that the term is most often equated with groups—migrant students, international students, and institutions—rather than explicated as analytic concepts that explain education in transnational contexts and processes. Relatedly, when using concepts of transnationalism, such as social spaces, solidarities, and linkages, an explanation of the meaning of these concepts in the contexts of study is necessary to advance our thinking about the nation-state, global phenomena and explanations of and implications for education.

Figure 15.2 maps our suggestions for the use of the transnationalism in future studies within CIDE. We see the utility in examining the space between sending and receiving nation-states. Situated in this between space, research could investigate the relationships among international organizations, mobile populations, and educational institutions. For example, the use of transnationalism to examine relations between international organizations and mobile populations may yield understanding and explanations of the role of diasporic communities in educational development in the societies of origin. Meanwhile, transnationalism can be used to illuminate the complex web of social relationships and practices affecting education for mobile populations. Finally, the transnationalism framework may be used to examine the role of the nation-state as an actor in shaping and creating hybridities of external development policies and practices.

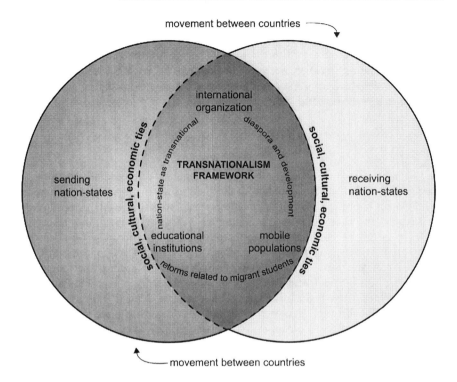

Figure 15.2. Analytical Possibilities of Transnationalism for Comparative, International, and Development Education.

Based on this analysis and mapping, we offer a few suggestions for furthering the field's analytic usage of transnationalism. First, scholars need to provide clearer definitions of transnationalism and reference the intellectual history of ideas from which they are drawing. Do the usages of transnationalism refer to sending and receiving nation-states and that body of literature? How does transnationalism explain processes of identity construction beyond national identity, and which bodies of literature should we reference? Also, how do our uses of transnationalism problematize the nation-state and examine new social and political spaces? Second, we might better explicate how transnationalism differs from globalization, or how it informs an analysis of globalizing phenomena. Given the ubiquity of international organizations, transnational organizations and global agendas in our field, studies need to better explain what distinguishes transnationalism, particularly in relation to conceptualizations of nation-states, from that which is understood as international or global phenomena. We should consider more explicitly the relationship between the nation-state and global phenomena and how the concept of the nation-state is shifting and adapting in these contexts. Finally, more conceptual clarity is needed in how transnationalism relates to postcolonial perspectives. In CIDE, we might ask how transnational relations between the former colonized and colonizer can be examined through transnationalism concepts, and/or the postcolonalism or neo-colonialism perspectives. In addition, we should problematize the concept of the nation-state in these contexts. In the next section, we provide examples of research outside CIDE that use transnationalism in order to illustrate the analytic meanings and uses of concepts that could be better taken up in our field.

ANALYTICAL POSSIBILITIES FOR COMPARATIVE, INTERNATIONAL,
AND DEVELOPMENT EDUCATION

How might analytic concepts of transnationalism be useful in providing explanations for phenomena studied in the field of comparative, international and development education? We offer several considerations for using perspectives of transnationalism from the related literature, as well as areas for further research in CIDE. It is not uncommon for theories from other disciplines to be adapted to CIDE. In their review of the ways that dependency theory is applicable to CIDE, Harold Noah and Max Eckstein (1992) suggested two criteria for judging the relevance of an outside theory for education: explanatory power and capacity to inform policies. Transnationalism meets both criteria. First, it offers explanatory power that globalization perspectives do not with regard to understanding global phenomena in relation to nation-states, as well as individuals who reside among nation-states and who create new identities and social spaces. It allows us to examine and provide explanations for education as it is situated both within nation-states and as a global phenomenon, and it can further explain the role of nation-states in education and development agendas. The second criterion is a functionalist approach that seeks a translation of theory into practice. In regards to international and development education, transnationalism is highly relevant as a tool that informs policies as they are created in and through the interstices of nation-state contexts and transnational organizations.

Drawing on research using transnationalism outside of our field, we suggest analytic uses of it and research questions that need further examination. From the functionalist approaches of transnationalism, studies in anthropology and sociology have meticulously documented and explained the types of activities that connect mobile populations socially, economically, and politically to their countries of origin, such as through visits or remittances sent to relatives and communities of origin (Levitt 2001; Portes 2009). For example, in an article published in Social Text, Smith (1994, 27) discusses political actions resulting from transnational ties. He gives the example of students of Latin American heritage at the University of California, Berkeley who, drawing from their transnational ties, organized a trip to El Salvador to deliver medical and other needed supplies. Smith describes these students as "thinking transnationally and acting multilocally," meaning that the students utilized their transnational knowledge to determine which exact supplies were most needed in El Salvador and how to mobilize support in the US to complete the task. This example illustrates that transnationalism is a theoretical construct that could illuminate small-scale development practices. In another study published in

International Migration Review, the social anthropologist Steven Vertovec (2004) offers a typology of ways that emigrants change their countries of origin socially, politically and economically. He claims that through remittances and the establishment of hometown associations, emigrants are engaging in the economic transformation of the country of origin. Like Smith (1994), the focus is on the general development capabilities of the migrant population; thus, it remains the task of CIDE scholars to adapt these concepts to educational issues and education policies within the nation-state.

Smith (1994) and Vertovec (2004) draw on the analytic concepts of networks, linkages and solidarities. What remains under-researched is how those ties affect educational development. Not only are investigations of development by migrant communities with transnational ties in order, but also needed are comparative studies that examine migrants' activities and influences as development actors against the work of powerful bilateral and multilateral organizations and large international nongovernmental organizations. Whereas nation-states donate money to support national interests (Alesina and Dollar 2000), emigrants seem to be personally committed to building or sustaining community relationships in their country of origin. The inclusion of emigrants/diasporas as stakeholders in educational development processes alongside bilateral agencies and multilateral agencies allows for alternatives to the dominant discourses and research in international development education. The World Bank and similar institutions have long acknowledged the importance of remittances to the economies of developing countries with a sizeable diaspora population, but their work tends to be at the macro level, which lacks the richness and depth offered by ethnographic studies. CIDE scholars could utilize transnationalism to portray and explain a detailed picture of the involvement of diaspora groups in educational development projects. This strand of research would build on Mundy and Murphy's (2001) discussion of civil society in which they documented how civil organizations are taking more ownership of the development process in education. Whether as advocates or funders of educational development programs, an understanding of diasporic populations and their role in educational development needs to be expanded in CIDE for the field to obtain a more complete picture of who the actors are, how they positively and/or negatively impact and transform education, and the implications of these linkages for policies and practices related to development work and diasporic communities.

Critical approaches of transnationalism that problematize the nation-state as a transnational actor and a reconfigured entity both in relation to global agendas of education and individual students' lives in schools offer analytic possibilities for research in CIDE. These studies have particularly examined how language of instruction, teachers' knowledge of students' transnational lives, and education content and knowledge are areas of consideration and contestation in policies and practices for the education of transnational students. Villenas (2009) uses transnationalism as a way to understand the complex educational lives of Latinos/as through their locally situated and hybrid cultural practices. Transnationalism refers to the lived experience created in spaces that are situated in historical and cultural realities of nation-states. The concept of solidarities also provides analytic possibilities for understanding both individuals and educational practices in transnational spaces. Villenas refers to solidarities in terms of the shared experiences and close relationships that develop between individuals in these transnational spaces, both across nation-states and within nation-states. Solidarities, she suggests, present tensions of negotiating differences in these contexts and powerful counter-stories that help shape a sense of belonging.

Patricia Sanchez (2001, 376) offers another useful conceptualization of transnationalism, which is that it "unbinds binationalism through a complex understanding of global economic, cultural and political processes." She argues that to understand mobile students (whether children of migrants or international students), one needs to comprehend the transnational spaces in which they live and not to see them as binational, or bounded in relation to two nation-states. In particular, she argues that we need to examine what is not seen or what is hidden in transnational lives, in part due to the nation-state structures and discourses that hide transnationality, not to mention the lack of analytic concepts to signify the experiences. She illustrates through her own experience how schooling is a public space that is imbued with national ideals, and yet her transnational life experiences were not given a public face (377). Her knowledge of Mexico, the Spanish language, and experiences in transnational spaces with her family and friends were not seen or understood in the school.

Scholarship in CIDE could more fruitfully use these analytic concepts from transnationalism to understand, challenge and reconfigure educational policies as it relates to the lives of students in basic, secondary, or post-secondary education systems. We need to ask how nation-state educational policies enacted in national and local contexts are affected by the movement of students across borders and how these policies are adapting, or not, to these transnational phenomena.

CONCLUSION

This chapter has mapped the various analytical perspectives of transnationalism and called for the comparative, international and development education field to re-imagine what and how it compares, to rethink units of analysis, and to critically examine the theoretical and ideological borders and maps that are used to understand education, learning and students. The uses of transnationalism in CIDE scholarship include those describing and explaining mobile populations' incorporation into societies, as well as approaches that problematize nation-states and schools as institutions of the state for the ways in which they make and respond to phenomena that transcends national borders. These approaches to transnationalism call for problematizing the nation-state and schools and how migrants and non-migrants imagine and live the complexities in transnational spaces.

Transnationalism can offer an alternative to examine local/national/ transnational/ global relations and responses to the flow of knowledge and people, particularly as they affect education and development policies and practices. The analytic possibilities of transnationalism allow us to rethink the methodologies common in comparative, international and development education. It problematizes the idea of comparisons between nation-states, which are common units of analysis, and it situates nation-states as both concrete entities and fluid imaginaries in relation to each other. In other words, transnationalism seeks to problematize the nation-state as comprised of fluid relations between individuals and yet as a concrete actor in global phenomena. It challenges us to rethink what we understand and accept as global agendas and phenomena and again, examine the role of nation-states in making and remaking of "global" agendas of education. Finally, transnationalism offers ways to rethink development as being tied to the nation-state as a unit, to reevaluate relations between nation-states—such as bilateral aid—and to consider how individuals situated in and transcending nation-states create and impact dynamic processes of development.

NOTE

1. The articles reviewed for this chapter are all written in English. We are aware that scholarship by non-English speaking scholars and in non-English journals have made contributions to the study of transnationalism. A subsequent review of these works is also critical to understanding how transnationalism is conceptualized and used in our field.

REFERENCES

Alesina, Alberto, & David Dollar. (2000). "Who Gives Foreign Aid to Whom and Why?" *Journal of Economic Growth, 5*, 33–63.

Arnove, Robert F., & Carlos Alberto Torres. (2003). *Comparative Education: The Dialectic of the Global and the Local.* Lanham, MD: Rowman & Littlefield Publishers.

Basch, Linda, Nina Glick Schiller, & Christina Blanc-Szanton. (1994). *Nations Unbound: Transnational Projects, Post-colonial Predicaments, and De-territorialized Nation-States.* Langhorne, PA: Gordon and Breach.

Beck, Ulrich. (2005). *Power in the Global Age: A New Global Political Economy.* London: Polity.

Beech, Jason. (2009). "Policy Spaces, Mobile Discourses, and the Definition of Educated Identities." *Comparative Education, 45*(3), 347–364.

Bhabha, Homi K. (1990). "DissemiNation: Time, Narrative and the Margins of the Modern State." In Homi K. Bhabha (Ed.), *Nation and Narration.* New York: Routledge.

Bravo-Moreno, Ana. (2009). "Transnational Mobilities: Migrants and Education." *Comparative Education, 45*(3), 419–433.

Burbules, Nicholas C., & Carlos Alberto Torres, eds. (2000). *Globalization and Education: Critical Perspectives.* New York: Routledge.

Carney, Stephen. (2009). "Negotiating Policy in an Age of Globalization: Exploring Educational 'Policyscapes' in Denmark, Nepal, and China." *Comparative Education Review, 53*(1), 63–88.

Clark, Anne Marie, Elisabeth J. Friedman, & Kathryn Hochstetler. (1998). "The Sovereign Limits of Global Civil Society: A Comparison of NGO Participation in UN World Conferences on the Environment, Human Rights, and Women." *World Politics, 51*(1), 1–35.

Faist, Thomas. (2000a). *The Volume and Dynamics of International Migration and Transnational Social Spaces.* Oxford, UK: Oxford University Press.

Faist, Thomas. (2000b). "Transnationalization in International Migration: Implications for the Study of Citizenship and Culture." *Ethnic and Racial Studies, 23*(2), 189–222.

Fouron, Georges, & Nina Glick Schiller. (2001). "All in the Family: Gender, Transnational Migration, and the Nation-state." *Identities, 7*(4), 539–582.

Fry, Rieko. (2009). "Politics of Education for Japanese Returnee Children." *Compare, 39*(3), 367–383.

Gargano, Terra. (2009). "(Re)conceptualizing International Student Mobility: The Potential of Transnational Social Fields." *Journal of Studies in International Education, 13*(3), 331–346.

Glick Schiller, Nina, Linda Basch, & Christina Szanton Blanc, eds. (1992). *Towards a Transnational Perspective on Migration: Race, Class, Ethnicity, and Nationalism Reconsidered.* New York: New York Academy of Sciences.

Hall, Kathleen D. (2002). *Lives in Translation: Sikh Youth as British Citizens.* Philadelphia: University of Pennsylvania Press.

Hinderliter Ortloff, Debora, & Christopher J. Frey. (2007). "Blood Relatives: Language, Immigration, and Education of Ethnic Returnees in Germany and Japan." *Comparative Education Review, 51*(4), 447–470.

Jansen, Jonathan D. (2005). "Targeting Education: The Politics of Performance and the Prospects of 'Education for All'." *International Journal of Educational Development, 25*(4), 368–380.

Kearney, Michael. (1995). "The Local and the Global: The Anthropology of Globalization and Transnationalism." *Annual Reviews in Anthropology, 24*(1), 547–565.

Kim, Terri. (2009). "Shifting Patterns of Transnational Academic Mobility: A Comparative and Historical Approach." *Comparative Education, 45*(3), 387–403.

Kivisto, Peter. (2001). "Theorizing Transnational Immigration: A Critical Review of Current Efforts." *Ethnic and Racial Studies, 24*(4), 549–577.

Levitt, Peggy. (2001). "Transnational Migration: Taking Stock and Future Directions." *Global Networks, 1*(3), 195–216.

Lukose, Ritty A. (2007). "The Difference that Diaspora Makes: Thinking through the Anthropology of Immigrant Education in the United States." *Anthropology & Education Quarterly, 38*(4), 405–418.

Monkman, Karen. (1999). "Transnational Migration and Learning Processes of Mexican Adults Constructing Lives in California." *International Journal of Educational Development, 19*(4&5), 367–382.

Moutsios, Stavros. (2009). "International Organisations and Transnational Education Policy." *Compare, 39*(4), 469–481.

Mundy, Karen, & Lynn Murphy. (2001). "Transnational Advocacy, Global Civil Society? Emerging Evidence from the Field of Education." *Comparative Education Review, 45*(1), 85–126.

Murillo, Enrique G. (2002). "How Does it Feel to be a Problem: Disciplining the Transnational Subject in the American South." In Stanton Wortham, Enrique G. Murillo Jr., and Edmund Hamann (Ed.), *Education in the New Latino Diaspora: Policy and the Politics of Identity* (pp. 215–240). Westport, CT: Ablex Publishing.

Noah, Harold J., & Max A. Eckstein. (1992). "Dependency Theory in Comparative Education: Twelve Lessons from the Literature." In Jürgen Schriewer and Brian Holmes (Ed.), Theories and Methods in Comparative Education (pp. 165–192). Frankfurt, Gemany: Peter Lang.

Ong, Aihwa. (1999). *Flexible Citizenship: The Cultural Logics of Transnationality.* Durham, NC: Duke University Press.

Paulston, Rolland G. (2000). "A Spatial Turn in Comparative Education? Constructing a Social Cartography of Difference." In Jürgen Schriewer (Ed.), *Discourse Formation in Comparative Education* (pp. 297–354). Frankfurt, Germany: Peter Lang.

Portes, Alejandro, Luis E. Guarnizo, & Patricia Landolt. (1999). "The Study of Transnationalism: Pitfalls and Promise of an Emergent Research Field." *Ethnic and Racial Studies, 22*(2), 217–237.

Portes, Alejandro, & Rubén G. Rumbaut. (2006). *Immigrant America: A Portrait.* Berkeley, CA: University of California Press.

Portes, Alejandro. (2009). "Migration and Development: Reconciling Opposite Views." *Ethnic and Racial Studies, 32*(1), 5–22.

Rizvi, Fazal. (2000). "International Education and the Production of Global Imagination." In Nicholas C. Burbules and Carlos Alberto Torres (Ed.), *Globalization and Education: Critical Perspectives* (pp. 205–226). New York: Routledge.

Sanchez, Patricia. (2001). "Adopting Transnationalism Theory and Discourse: Making Space for a Transnational Chicana." *Discourse: Studies in the Cultural Politics of Education, 22*(3), 375–381.

Smith, Michael P. (1994). "Can You Imagine? Transnational Migration and the Globalization of Grassroots Politics." *Social Text, 39,* 15–33.

Smith, Michael P., & Luis Eduardo Guarnizo, eds. (1998). *Transnationalism from Below.* New Brunswick, NJ: Transaction Publishers.

Soja, Edward. (1996). Thirdspace: Journeys to Los Angeles and Other Real-and-Imagined Places. Cambridge, MA: Blackwell.

Steiner-Khamsi, Gita, ed. (2004). *The Global Politics of Educational Borrowing and Lending*. New York: Teachers College Press.

Stromquist, Nelly P., & Karen Monkman. (2000). *Globalization and Education: Integration and Contestation across Cultures*. Lanham, MD: Rowman & Littlefield Publishers.

Szelényi, Katalin, & Robert A. Rhoads. (2007). "Citizenship in a Global Context: The Perspectives of International Graduate Students in the United States." Comparative Education Review, 51(1), 25–47.

Vavrus, Frances, & Lesley Bartlett, eds. (2009). *Critical Approaches to Comparative Education: Vertical Case Studies from Africa, Europe, the Middle East, and the Americas*. New York: Palgrave Macmillan.

Vertovec, Steven. (2004). "Migrant Transnationalism and Modes of Transformation." *International Migration Review*, 38(3), 970–1001.

Villenas, Sofia A. (2007). "Diaspora and the Anthropology of Latino Education: Challenges, Affinities, and Intersections." *Anthropology & Education Quarterly*, 38(4), 419–425.

Villenas, Sofia A. (2009). "Knowing and Unknowing Transnational Latino Lives in Teacher Education: At the Intersection of Educational Research and the Latino Humanities." *The High School Journal*, 92(4), 129–136.

Zúñiga, Victor, & Edmund T. Hamann. (2009). "Sojourners in Mexico with U.S. School Experience: A New Taxonomy of Transnational Students." *Comparative Education Review*, 53(3), 329–353.

PART III: REGIONAL PERSPECTIVES OF SOCIAL CARTOGRAPHY

SHENG YAO CHENG, W. JAMES JACOB, AND POCHANG CHEN

16. METATHEORY IN COMPARATIVE, INTERNATIONAL, AND DEVELOPMENT EDUCATION

Dialectics Between the East and West and Other Perspectives

INTRODUCTION

Changes in travel, communication, and technology have continuously brought our world closer together. These changes have escalated in recent centuries and especially in the latter-part of the twentieth century and continue at a rapid pace at the beginning of the twenty-first century. Communicable diseases that were at one time contained within geographic regions are now able to travel at the speed of a single passenger to almost any place on the earth within a 24-hour time period. The traditional definition of war has also transitioned from battles fought against militias to include international terrorism. The academic field of education continues to adjust to meet the dynamic needs of these rapid changes across the earth. Comparative, international, and development education (CIDE) and research are shaped by global history, culture, economy, and social context changes.

CIDE research has kept pace with the many changes over the past century. The theoretical underpinnings of CIDE research have also required similar changes to explain many education phenomena. Social theories have undergone a number of changes over time. Contemporary mainstream CIDE research is based largely on a Western theoretical foundation but other theoretical perspectives can add to this legacy (Phillips and Schweisfurth 2008). In this article, we revisit two CIDE models that can be used by researchers to emphasize how important it is to take an eclectic stance to determine which theory/ies and policy/ies are most appropriate to meet dynamic needs and various education contexts.

A review of "classical" comparative education literature emphasizes the reliance of most research products on "traditional" Western epistemology and largely ignores the importance of Eastern and other theoretical perspectives. We begin by introducing differing theoretical perspectives based on geography, economy, and theory. Third, we introduce the Tai-Ji Model as an essential tool for CIDE researchers in selecting an appropriate theory and research method for a given study or project. The Education Policy Analysis Model (EPAM) is also introduced as a framework for advancing educational reform efforts based on equity and with an end goal toward excellence. The article concludes with a discussion of how both the Tai-Ji Model and EPAM can serve policy makers,

John C. Weidman, W. James Jacob (eds.), Beyond the Comparative: Advancing Theory and Its Application to Practice, 295–314.

government planners, scholars, graduate students, and educators in their ongoing CIDE research.

We define *metatheory* as an "overarching theory or framework used to analyze theoretical systems" (Jacob and Cheng 2005, 227). A metatheory is comprised of multiple theories that are linked together by a common political concept or framework. Metatheories can be found at local and global levels and often transcend boundaries that delimit singular theoretical concepts or ideologies. We argue that CIDE encompasses multiple theoretical perspectives and paradigms. These theoretical perspectives are increasing in number and have evolved over time based on changes in culture, context, political situation, and economics. The CIDE theoretical landscape has been categorized and mapped in the past; we aim to add to this list of previous literature by emphasizing that one of the primary strengths of CIDE "lies in its multi-theoretical reservoir. This depth allows researchers to draw from a broad theoretical base, necessary to analyze a number of complex and evolving contemporary issues" (p. 227). We also advocate that theory creation in CIDE is an ongoing process that builds upon the rich foundation of previous educators who advocated various global standpoint theoretical perspectives. In this regard we support Val D. Rust's (2004) assertion that CIDE research hinges on the need for inclusion of a variety of research methods, approaches, and theories. No single theoretical perspective reigns supreme in the CIDE research literature.

DIFFERING CIDE PERSPECTIVES BASED ON GEOGRAPHY, ECONOMY, AND THEORY

Geographic delimitations relating to national boundaries are often social constructions established to meet the needs of those who are in "power" to enforce the boundaries (Jacob and Ouattara 2009). Border disputes still exist between countries and in some cases within nation states. Often boundaries are established on economic interests in order to maintain political dominance or hegemonic clout. Trade agreements such as the China-ASEAN Free Trade Area, the General Agreement on Trade in Services (GATS), and the North American Free Trade Agreement (NAFTA) often provide benefits to some countries or regions while limiting trade from others. Theories are often established based on the paradigmatic philosophies that shape the social sciences including CIDE research. In this section we provide definitions of several dialectical perspectives that define a significant portion of historical and contemporary CIDE research. These perspectives highlight comparisons and differences that inevitably exist between dialectical notions of East versus West, North versus South, and developed versus developing countries. In addition to their dialectic counterpart terms, often CIDE researchers use the terms West, North and developed countries interchangeably. Others hold firm to only using one "politically correct" dialectic term based largely on a theoretical standpoint. It is beyond the scope of this article to determine which set of dialectic terms is most appropriate; rather we strive to outline common uses of these terms as a background to the rest of our article that focuses on metatheory in CIDE research.

East versus West

The *West* derives its name primarily from influential thinkers who transitioned philosophical thought and the philosophical paradigms of their day and resided primarily in Europe. Leading philosophers and thinkers who influenced the daily philosophy included Pythagoras, Socrates, Aristotle, Epictetus, Roger Bacon, Galileo Galilei, John Locke, Adam Smith, and Immanuel Kant. Later Western thinkers who influenced international education included Karl Marx, Emile Durkheim, Max Weber, John Dewey, Frank Charles Laubach, Michel Foucault, Karl Popper, John Rawls, Paulo Freire, and James Coleman. The East has its own long line of prestigious thinkers that have helped shape the CIDE landscape. These thinkers include Siddhartha Gautama, Laozi, Confucius, and Sun Yat-Sen.

With the rise of global colonialism based largely in Western Europe, the definition of West and Western thought underwent further revision to include the United States, Canada, Australia, and New Zealand. Western cartographers often positioned Western Europe in the center of global maps and bisected Asia into the Near East and Far East. This cartographic denotation of Asia as *East* positioned it in an opposite to the *West*.

East to those who live in Japan refers to locations on the eastern line of the Pacific Rim. Devote Christians look to the Mount of Olives as the future location of the Second Coming of Jesus Christ. The Mount of Olives lies in a general eastern direction from where most traditional Christians resided in Europe, and afterwards in North and South America. Yet for Christians residing in India, Australia, or Vietnam, the most likely direction toward the Mount of Olives is in a general western direction. Muslims face Mecca when they pray, but many Westerners believe that the Muslims face east merely because their Muslim friends pray in a general eastern direction when living in Western Europe or North America.

What constitutes "East" versus "West" is also arbitrary and hinges upon the point of view of each CIDE researcher. Much like the geographic dialectic between East and West, often philosophical thought between East and West were at odds or opposition with each other as well. No other Eastern philosopher contributed more to education than Confucius whose contributions offer a counter perspective to much of the Western-dominated theoretical perspectives. Confucius has been regarded as a prominent teacher and education researcher in history. He saw education is the key developer and stabilizer of society. To desire to do right and to seek what is good would give a person a little reputation but would not enable him to influence the masses. To associate with the wise and able, and to welcome those who come from distant countries may enable a person to influence the masses but would not necessarily enable him to civilize the people. The only solution for an individual to civilize the people and establish good social customs is through education. Compared with Western ideas of education, we can juxtapose it with transformation orientation vs. equilibrium orientation and idealist-subjectivist orientation vs. realist-objectivist orientation.

Confucius taught that only through education does one come to be dissatisfied with his own knowledge, and only through teaching others does one come to realize the uncomfortable inadequacy of his knowledge. Being unsatisfied with his own knowledge, one then realizes that the trouble lies with him and realizing the uncomfortable inadequacy of his knowledge, one then feels stimulated to improve himself. This philosophy supports the notion that the processes of teaching and learning stimulate one another. That is the meaning of the passage in the Advice to Fu Yueh which says, "Teaching is half of learning." The Eastern educational concepts above could correspond directly to critical, human capital, and functionalist theories.

Confucius identifies four characteristics of ideal teachers. First, he emphasized *prevention*, or preventing bad habits before they are given a chance to arise. Second, *timeliness* or giving students information as soon as they are ready for it. Third, *order* or teaching subjects in proper sequence. Fourth, *mutual stimulation* or letting the students admire the excellence of other students (Lin 2009, p. 487). These four characteristics ensure the success of education. Even though Confucian education ideology originated several thousand years ago, the theories have significant relevance to CIDE research today.

North versus South

East versus West leaves out much of the global terrain and other perspectives or concepts help fill this void. One such perspective is the *North-South* dialectic where the *North* relates to more affluent countries predominantly in Europe and North America. Nations in the *South* include those which are less affluent and that are still in the process of economic development and transition (UNESCO 2001; Peters 2009). The South provides a voice to those from Africa, Latin America, and other less affluent nations and regions (Mbabuike 2004).

There are increasing South-South partnerships in education research that provide countries of the South opportunities to collaborate together and establish their own theoretical perspectives (World Bank 2009). North-North relationships also exist that provide similar opportunities to those from more affluent countries in Europe and North America. Most CIDE research endeavors are based on North-to-South international collaborations that include co-researchers from both affluent and less affluent countries. South-South partnerships are rare but increasing (Cronin 2008; Jacobsen 2009). Often funding drives these dialectic CIDE research relationships between North and South collaborators, which frequently provide researchers from North countries opportunities to dominate or shape the theoretical debate.

Developed versus Developing

Based primarily on an economic theoretical perspective, the terms *developed* and *developing countries* are conceived from the notion that countries can evolve, transition or "develop" from an inferior state to one that is more advanced or economically prosperous. Walt W. Rostow (1960) and other functionalists were prominent in advancing the dialectical relationship between advanced, transitioning, and traditional societies or countries (see also Inkeles and Holsinger 1973; Ish-Shalom 2006). The terms developed and developing countries became especially prominent toward the end of the Cold War Era rendering the terms *first*, *second*, and *third-world countries* obsolete.

The World Trade Organization (WTO) allows each member country to self-announce whether they are a developed or developing country, but there are certain advantages linked to a developing country status. A third term used by WTO and other UN agencies includes *least-developed* countries which provide even greater flexibility and advantages in international trade agreements (United Nations Population Division [UNPD] 2009). UNPD designates all countries in Europe, Australia, Canada, Japan, New Zealand, and the United States as the more developed countries. They also provide definitions for *less-developed* and least-developed countries.

What constitutes a developed versus a developing country is determined in the eyes of the beholder, researcher, policy maker, or UN officer. Low- and middle-income countries are often grouped in the category of developing countries. Newly industrialized countries (NICs)—including Brazil, Russia, India, and China (BRIC)—are often grouped in developing country status but are fast becoming global leaders in trade and human resource production powerhouses. Still the education disparities that exist between developed, developing, and least-developed countries are significant. This inequality in education is highlighted by global rankings of higher education institutions and the number of top academic journals in most fields, both published in English and located in so-called developed countries (Maddison 1983; UNESCO 1995; Holsinger and Jacob 2009; Mok 2010).

The Role of Cartography in Comparative, International, and Development Education

Perhaps no contemporary CIDE scholar has influenced the categorizing of CIDE metatheory more than Rolland G. Paulston. With an academic background in geography, Paulston focused his work during the final stage of his career on mapping theories in comparative education. In his book *Social Cartography*, Paulston set the stage for CIDE scholars to examine theory from a variety of visual perspectives and encouraged seasoned and young scholars alike to embark on a journey of theory creation (Rust 1996; Stromquist 1996; Chapter 1 of this volume). Thinking outside of the box or beyond theoretical paradigms was at the root of Paulston's latter works (see for instance Paulston 1999, 2000; Chapter 1) and he often encouraged CIDE scholars to expand their theoretical horizon.

Regardless of the perspective, we argue scholars should take an eclectic theoretical stance that provides CIDE researchers with the ability to choose an existing theory (or set of theories) depending on the relevant needs or topic of study associated with local, national, and international contexts (Jacob and Cheng 2005; Jacob and Holsinger 2009). The next section introduces two theoretical models developed and adapted to the dynamic contexts in CIDE research.

TAI-JI MODEL

Almost four thousand years age, Chinese philosopher Fu-Xi created a model to interpret the evolution of the universe, and he called it *Tai-Ji* (Shen et al., 1988). Along with the very beginning of Tai-Ji, *Supreme Ultimate*, Fu-Xi indicates *Yin* and *Yang* are two fundamental elements in the universe (Zhang and Ryden 2002).

Similar to the traditional Western binary idea, after Fu-Xi observed the movement of the sun, moon, and stars for more than 40 years, he interpreted the regulation of life and nature with two dichotomous characters: *Yin* and *Yang*. Yin means the dark side, the moon, female, and negative; Yang refers to the light side, the sun, male, and positive.

To figure out the multifaceted dynamics and complications of real life, Fu-Xi continued to interpret Tai-Ji as a combination of four semi-sectors including Yin, Yang, *pre-Yin*, and *pre-Yang*. Pre-Yin is located in the era of Yang but represents the possibility of Yin. Following the same vein, pre-Yang is situated in the area of Yin but represents the appearance of Yang. There are no obvious borders between Yin and Yang, and no absolute direction between them. Unlike the Western traditional binary, Tai-Ji emphasizes the importance of continuous, border-crossing, and dynamic dimensions.

For instance, when people see the sun at noon they know that this constitutes day and not night. From a global perspective, you would see that when it is day in the Western hemisphere it is night in the Eastern hemisphere. There are similar dichotomies portrayed throughout the universe. The Tai-Ji concept has significance to social theory and education. Multiple perspectives are often used to examine the same educational phenomenon, depending on the standpoint of the policy maker, researcher, participant, teacher, student, or parent of student. With multiple ways of seeing the world or educational phenomena, there are also often multiple social theories that undergird these phenomena. The Tai-Ji Model was first introduced in relation to CIDE research and theory in W. James Jacob and Sheng Yao Cheng (2005), recognizing that no singular theory or perspective dominates in CIDE (see Figure 16.1).

Based on a non-linear framework, the Tai-Ji Model has the ability to span time, space, and theoretical paradigms. Its strength lies in its ability to adapt to the need of the research/study, depending on the context of a given situation or country.

The Tai-Ji Model supports an eclectic approach to CIDE studies in that one, two, or several theoretical approaches may be appropriate for a given study, depending on the context and nature of the research being conducted. Different or even multiple theoretical approaches may be appropriate. If you select a given theoretical perspective, it may be important to supplement this with additional points of view, thus maximizing the effect of synergistic perspectives. (249)

The Tai-Ji Model serves as a filter mechanism in determining which theory or research method is appropriate to use in a given CIDE study, policy document, or geographic or cultural context. For instance, if a researcher were examining higher education quality assurance in the Middle East, she may want to include one or more functionalist theories that would help determine how Middle Eastern universities operationalize the strategic planning process. Another scholar may examine the same topic from a critical theory framework offering a counter-theoretical balance to the previous study.

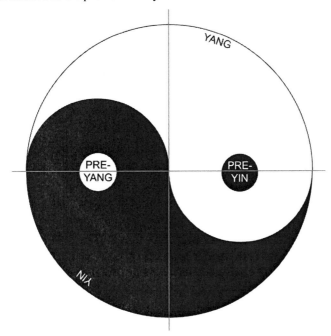

Figure 16.1. Tai-Ji Model for Framing Comparative,
International, and Development Education.
Source: Reprinted from Jacob and Cheng (2005, 248), with permission from Elsevier.

The Tai-Ji Model is also an ideal theoretical framework and research methods filtering mechanism for graduate students determining which theory/ies and research method/s to use to guide their thesis and doctoral research. Using the Tai-Ji Model in the theoretical selection process of one's own research can be done similarly to using a Venn diagram to hone in on the most appropriate theory/ies for the study's topical focus. For instance, if a student was interested in applying critical race theory (CRT) in examining issues of equity and access to higher education of Native Americans, the Tai-Ji Model could be used to help the student identify alternative perspectives that would either compliment or provide an alternative perspective to CRT. Alternative theoretical perspectives that could be examined in the same dissertation may include human capital, rational choice, or dependency theory. Other theories the scholar may consider that are more closely associated with a radical humanist perspective include feminist, Freirian, or poststructuralist theory. Unlike the traditional dualism in the Western culture, the Tai-Ji Model pays more attention to interactive, dynamic, and border-crossing processes. The methodology is dynamic, providing an avenue for both theory selection based upon need and theory generation where opportunities demand a new way of answering questions to educational phenomena (see Figures 16.2 and 16.3).

Figure 16.2. Example of Using the Tai-Ji Model to Select an Appropriate Theory for Graduate Research: Proposed Thesis/Dissertation Theory.

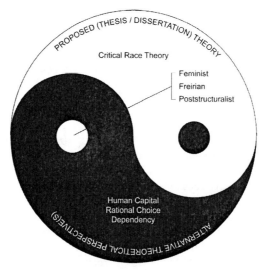

Figure 16.3. Example of Using the Tai-Ji Model in Examining Alternative Theoretical Perspectives.

The primary strength of applying the Tai-Ji Model in the theory selection process is it forces graduate students to consider alternative perspectives to the theoretical stance they choose for their research. Acknowledging alternative theoretical viewpoints does not necessarily diminish one's own theoretical stance but in many cases can enhance one's standpoint. It also emphasizes the notion that in the social sciences there is often more than one way of examining any one situation.

The Tai-Ji Model can easily be used by a team of government planners, development aid officers, and education consultants who are establishing the policy framework for a multi-year education sector development program at the national level. In addition to applying principles of good governance, the team also needs to ensure ownership and buy-in from top-level government policy makers as well as those who will be implementing the education reforms once they become law. Multiple research methods could benefit this type of a development education program. Ample quantitative data at all levels would help inform the team of longitudinal trends and help identify social justice gaps. This quantitative data could be triangulated and substantiated by months of qualitative focus groups, in-depth interviews, and observations with groups of students, teachers, administrators, and local and national government education planners. Using the Tai-Ji Model as a filtering mechanism, the team could determine which method or group of methods are most appropriate and under which contexts. The Tai-Ji Model reminds us to reflect on the continuous, border-crossing, and dynamic dimensions of comparative education theories.

EDUCATION POLICY ANALYSIS MODEL (EPAM)

Another way of examining theory in CIDE research is through an education policy lens. The Education Policy Analysis Model (EPAM) was first presented by Jacob and Cheng (2003) and published in the *Journal of Education Research* (Cheng and Jacob 2005). EPAM offers scholars a way of reviewing current CIDE research from a policy analysis framework and includes four areas of education reform: equity, choice, efficiency, and excellence; and two areas of dichotomous comparison: neo-right vs. neo-left and globalization vs. localization (see Figure 16.4). Furthermore, EPAM emphasizes differences of perspectives and practices. Debates between equity and excellence remain constant in many education circles. Ideological struggles also exist between choice and efficiency. The dialectics between Neo-Right and Neo-Left are common in politics and discourse. Moreover, the dynamic relationship between globalization and localization remain at the forefront of education discourse and political reforms worldwide. EPAM is grounded in one or more metatheory or multiple perspectives that help support the four criteria of education policy reform as well as the two dichotomous political comparison areas. Many of these theoretical perspectives are further explained in Jacob and Cheng (2005) and W. James Jacob and Donald B. Holsinger (2009) but will be introduced in the following sections along with definitions of each EPAM component.

Equity

Confucius taught that *equity* of education opportunity could be interpreted into "educating everyone, and discriminating against none" (Tong 1970). Similar to

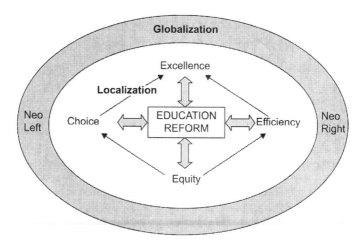

Figure 16.4 Education Policy Analysis Model.
Source: Reprinted from Cheng and Jacob (2005, 146), with permission from the *Journal of Education Research.*

Confucius, John Rawls (1972) argued in his *Theory of Justice* the important role positive discrimination can play in education contexts. James S. Coleman (1990) interpreted equality as the opportunity for students to receive equal treatment in regards to access, schooling, and outcome. A complete review of the comparison between the terms equity and equality is found in Jacob and Holsinger (2009) and will not be replicated here. We prefer the term equity rather than equality because it focuses on the "social justice ramifications of education in relation to fairness, justness, and impartiality of its distribution" (4). Equity is grounded in the radical humanist metatheory. Critical, equilibrium, Freirian, and feminist theories all provide avenues for explaining equity according to our definition.

Since *Brown v. Board of Education*, the *Civil Rights Act*, *Public Law 94–142*, the Head Start Program, the *No Child Left Behind Act*, and the so-called "War on Poverty," the standpoint of equity and equality of educational opportunity continues to preoccupy education reform efforts in the United States. Two Millennium Development Goals emphasize education equity at the global level: universal education and gender equality.

Equity underpins all other aspects of education reform listed in the EPAM framework. Without equity it is difficult if not impossible to achieve ideal levels of choice, efficiency, and excellence. Equity implies that all individuals have an equal opportunity to access education at all levels and to ultimately succeed in their education aspirations. We recognize that this is the ideal and far from reality in some contexts, but education equity can lead to optimal education reform efforts at local, national, regional and global levels.

Choice

Choice may be regarded as making a decision according to one's own desire and will (Billingsley 1994; Devine 2004; Scott 2005). As our second criterion of education policy reform, we also define choice as meaning that students should not be treated as mere objects during instructional procedures; educators must share the decision-making power vested in pedagogy, curricula, and school selection with students and their parents. This is supported by several scholars who recognize that, while choice is important and should be shared by multiple stakeholders (Rees 2000; Chapman et al., 2010), it is not always a panacea (Vranish et al., 2010). Although the school-choice movement spread rapidly in multiple countries, little time has been taken by CIDE researchers to assess whether the claimed benefits of school choice have actually been realized. Choice remains a political debate issue in many countries and education choice reform efforts often vary depending on the context (Wu 2008; Kim et al., 2009; Forsey 2010; West and Ylonen 2010).

There remain great disparities that prevent students from continuing their education even when they would choose to continue if they could. This inequality in education access and attainment is apparent in multiple global regions (Jacob and Holsinger 2009). In China, for instance, only a fraction of the eligible cohort of student graduates from secondary education have access to higher education; this access and attainment restriction is generally exacerbated for ethnic minorities and migrant workers due to several factors that include sociocultural limitations unique to these populations (Jacob 2006; Hawkins, Jacob and Li 2009; Mok 2010). Other countries in East Asia have reached virtual universal higher education—a feat not realized in most other areas of the earth. Students may not want to choose to pursue a higher education degree in Taiwan or South Korea but recognize that without this education their employment opportunities are severely hampered. Gender remains a barrier for many individuals in determining which career path to take or accessing education altogether (Hyer et al., 2009; Maslak 2009). Gender career path barriers differ depending on the geographic and sociocultural contexts that are often difficult to overcome.

Like the other three education policy reform criteria, choice can be explained by more than one theoretical perspective. Perhaps the most common metatheory often associated with education or school choice is the functionalist metatheory. Conflict, cultural rationalization, human capital, modernization, neofunctionalist, rational choice, and social choice theories all lay claim to this metatheoretical umbrella and all relate to individual and social choice.

Efficiency

According to Bosker and colleagues (1999), the conventional concept of education *efficiency*, adapted from the technical-industrial sector, is inappropriate for public schools. In the technical industrial sector, there is widespread agreement about desired outcomes and profits. Furthermore, it is difficult to measure school efficiency since the influence of outside environmental and socioeconomic factors on achievement is so significant. Efficiency is increasingly linked to issues of decentralization and privatization as these are market-guided signals that lead to more efficient and effective schools. When we juxtapose choice and efficiency in the discussion of comparative education, we recognize the potential struggles among parental choice, students' wills, and administrative accountability.

Much of the education efficiency literature is based on a functionalist metatheory that includes human capital, social efficiency, and neoinstitutional theories. Radical functionalist perspectives are also important in providing alternative viewpoints that include Marxist and Neo-Marxist theories. Ministries of education often strengthen their pre- and in-service teacher training (PITT) programmes through an emphasis on quality improvement to increase efficiency (Ayodele and Akindutire 2009). Higher education institutions are also under increased pressure from stakeholders to improve their overall efficiency through a series of quality assurance measures (Bigalke and Neubauer 2009).

Excellence

The concept of education *excellence* can be interpreted in a number of ways (see Deem and Kelly 1984; Mangieri 1985; Crossley and U.S. Department of Education 1990; Gillies 2008). From a Western perspective, there has been difficulty in defining and agreeing on what constitutes "the good" since the time of ancient Greece. The meaning of excellence implies quality and is thus regarded as one of the most difficult education concepts to define from a global lens. What constitutes excellence in Eastern contexts may not be the same in other regions of the earth. Several scholars recently gathered to deliberate the definition of excellence in CIDE from areas of student learning and curriculum relevance to the economic, social, and cultural demands of local and global forces (Bigalke and Neubauer 2009). Since the era of international competition and marketization, along with the rise in education competition, education excellence is measured or compared by several standardized tests or ranking systems. These include the Trends in International, Mathematics and Science Study (TIMSS), Program for International Student Assessment (PISA), ranking of world universities, the criteria of excellence tends to become convergent (Cheng 2009; Portnoi, Rust and Bagley 2010).

The border between equity and excellence was regarded as well defined and strictly identified. When we review the educational thoughts from the East and the West, how to cross the borderline between equity and excellence becomes a major factor in CIDE. Choice, efficiency, and educational excellence without equity is hollow and prevents the realization of the Millennium Development Goals for universal education and gender equality. Too often excellence, or quality of education, suffers because of limitations in the other three education reform criteria (Inoue and Oketch 2008). Still government policy makers, planners, and educators are increasingly aware that these limitations must be overcome in order to achieve education quality improvement and excellence in education.

Quality and educational excellence can be measured from multiple perspectives and using multiple research methods. Depending on the need, and following a truly Tai-Ji Model selection process, CIDE scholars could argue multiple metatheoretical angles for determining educational excellence. Thus we argue that excellence is grounded in the functionalist, radical functionalist, radical humanist, and humanist metatheories identified in Jacob and Cheng (2005).

Globalization versus Localization

Multiple CIDE scholars have discussed the dialectic relationship of the global and the local (Stromquist and Monkman 2000; Apodaca 2002; Watson 2002; Rust and Jacob 2005; Abdi et al., 2006). There is an increasing and intensification of worldwide social relationships, in which local happenings are often shaped by events occurring thousands of kilometers away and vice versa. Globalization has been and continues to be defined in many ways (Guillen 2001; de Wit 2002; Mok and Chan 2002; Uvalic-Trumbic, UNESCO and IAU 2002). Mauro Guillen (2001) provides a historical overview of the term globalization and introduces five key questions or "debates" that are worthy of note: (i) is globalization really happening?, (ii) does it produce convergence?, (iii) Does it undermine the authority of nation-states?, (iv) Is globality different from modernity?, and (v) Is a global culture in the making? Henrike Donner (2008) defines globalization as a "set of processes" where the world is rapidly becoming a global society, with homogenous economic, cultural, and technological contexts.

Nicholas C. Burbules and Carols Alberto Torres (2000) provide several definitions of globalization around certain dualities. One definition argues that globalization includes two primary forces at work, globalization from above (a process effecting elites within and across national contexts) and globalization from below (drawing from the masses of society). A second definition examines the inevitable conflicts globalization breeds between the global and the local; between the economic and the cultural; and homogenized norms and culture (which is sometimes interpreted as Western or American). At the very least a definition of globalization should include economic, political, and cultural terms. The discourse of globalization can be articulated with both modern and postmodern theories because we are currently involved in an interregnum period between an aging modern and an emerging postmodern era (Best and Kellner 1991; Stromquist and Monkman 2000).

Localization is the process of adapting not only language, but also graphics, technology and any other communications media of a region or country (Stromquist and Monkman 2000). Localization refers to an emphasis on traditional ways of knowing, medicine, cultures, traditions, and indigenous languages. Localization can take the form of a general demand for broader popular participation in politics such as the democracy movements in Eastern Europe in the 1980s, the former Union of Soviet Socialist Republics in the 1990s, and many other countries throughout the world today. Or it can take the form of demands for greater local autonomy, which may lead to decentralization or greater recognition of a local cultural identity and nationalism, as in Japan, New Zealand, and Venezuela. Either way, localization can be a mixed blessing.

In the dialectic between the global and the local, scholars introduce the hybrid terms *glocalization* and *glocal* which include the dialectic dimensions of global and local in one concept (see for instance Sewpaul 2006; Sarroub 2008; Hatoss 2009). The notion "think global, act local" is a common phase in recent globalization literature and has relevance to EPAM and education policy reform efforts (Friedman 2004; *Economist* 2006). Sometimes offering an alternative perspective to Immanuel Wallerstein's (1974) classical World Systems Theory, many recent globalization and localization theories focus on developing a global education norm in terms of structure and the dominant educational paradigm (Hawkins 2007; Portnoi, Rust and Bagley 2010).

Neo-Right versus Neo-Left

We now look at education reform from two extreme positions, the political concepts of the *Right* and the *Left*. The concepts have different historical roots depending on the country. In the United States, the Right has been defined as conservative, middle class, and representative of the dominant group. In opposition to the Right, the Left has focused on radicalism, critical ideology, minorities, and the oppressed. But these mainstream ideological concepts change over time and it is not as easy to ascertain between the Right and the Left (Jacob and Cheng 2005).

With the evolution of the dialectical concepts we prefer to use the terms *Neo-Right* and *Neo-Left*. The Neo-Right is predominantly based on the ideas represented by the dominant group(s), but can also be disaggregated into two sub-tendencies. The first is called the *neoliberal* perspective which focuses on market economics and stresses the influence of globalization. Following this vein, educational reforms like school vouchers, magnet schools, charter schools, national curriculum, national tests, and school choice emerged. The second New Right sub-tendency is the *neoconservative* perspective that emphasizes traditional values and moral preservation of societal norms.

Michael W. Apple (2006, 2009) argues that neoliberals are the most powerful element within the alliance supporting conservative modernization, and efficiency and an "ethic" of cost-benefit analysis are the dominant norms. Furthermore, he stresses that the idea of the "consumer" is crucial when we want to discuss educational reforms, and the idea of "consumer choice" is the guarantor of democracy. Furthermore, he argues that the metaphor of the consumer and the supermarket are actually opposites here, and markets ultimately will distribute resources efficiently and fairly according to effort. Other scholars also acknowledge the significant influence of neoliberalism and neoliberal policies on education in various country contexts (Hill 2001, 2009; Peters 2001; Carney 2003; Harris 2007; Hershock et al., 2007).

Some scholars argue that neoconservative perspectives focus on a resurgence of business values, market-oriented reforms, and the need to return to a common culture that ultimately makes schools more efficient and more responsive to the private sector (Elliott and MacLennan 1994; Apple 2006; Brown 2006). But there is more to the neoconservative standpoint than this argument. Neoconservatives are also concerned about the preservation of traditional values in society, promoting moral education, and defending the traditional definition of the family which is the fundamental unit of society. The neoconservative emphasis on the return to traditional values and "morality" has struck a responsive chord with mainstream society in different global regions (Raulo 2000; Tatto 2003; Barone 2004; Sidorovitch 2005; Zhao 2007; Tan 2008). This perspective is reflected in a recent book edited by David Aspin and Judith Chapman (2007), *Values Education and Lifelong Learning: Principles, Policies and Programmes*, with contributing chapters on peace education, self-reflection, the Eastern notion of cooperation and communal responsibility in the moral education process, democratic citizenship, responsibility of teachers and administrators to practice moral leadership, and being ethically centered. Another prominent neoconservative book is William Bennett's (1993) *The Book of Virtues*, which aims to provide "moral tales" for children to "restore" a commitment to "traditional virtues" such as patriotism, honesty, moral character, and entrepreneurial spirit. Neoconservatives are concerned about defending the right of freedom of religion, speech, and traditional social norms. Education is one of the primary sectors involved in the preservation and furthering of neoconservative values.

Domination, exploitation, and ideology critique of Marxism are key issues associated with the Left. Neo-Marxism can be discussed from two perspectives: one is derived from Louis Althuser (1972) and the other from Antonio Gramsci (Mayo 2009). The appeal of an ideological state apparatus by Althuser is regarded as structuralist Marxism that follows Marx's critique of the base/superstructure model and focuses its attention primarily on social reproduction. The crucial issue from Gramsci's (1999) theory is cultural hegemony that is attributed into cultural Marxism. Several contemporary sociology of education theories support this perspective (i.e., critical theory, cultural studies, and critical pedagogy) and are influenced by Marxist and Neo-Marxist theories. These perspectives constitute what is known as the Neo-Left.

Education is an ideal political nexus for the Neo-Right vs. Neo-Left debate to unfold and this dialectic is reflected in EPAM. This education policy reform framework provides an opportunity for equity-based education to reach its ultimate destination—excellence. But this is not an easy path to forge and is often challenged and sometimes marred by internal and external forces along the way.

CONCLUSION

Along with the predominant influence of globalization, international competition, and the fast pace in which technology and other changes occur, CIDE continues to flourish in the twenty-first century. In this article we reviewed multiple CIDE perspectives based on geography, economy, and theory. A critical discussion of Confucian and Taoist thought in this discourse was introduced emphasizing the latent undercurrent Eastern educational thought has on CIDE.

Both the Tai-Ji Model and Education Policy Analysis Model (EPAM) were presented to emphasize new areas of theoretical and policy reform developments in CIDE research and education reforms. Determining which social theory to base a CIDE research project, study, or dissertation on should be an eclectic process and highly determined upon several factors identified in this article. A careful examination of culture, language, history, geographic context, and economy are needed to make a theoretical selection. Using the Tai-Ji Model in the theory and research methods selection or filtering process is helpful for identifying additional and alternative ways of viewing CIDE research and educational phenomena. In some cases one theory is sufficient to base a study upon; in other situations multiple theories are required to fully represent complex phenomena. The Tai-Ji Model enhances theoretical scope and sheds additional light into CIDE's theoretical closet.

The four internal criteria of *equity, excellence, choice,* and *efficiency* serve as the nucleus of EPAM. *Globalization* and *localization* and the *Neo-Right* and the *Neo-Left* serve as perennial dialectics that provide the internal criteria a space to work within. Equity is the key axis upon which all other internal criteria hinge; therefore we emphasize its crucial role in addressing key issues in educational reforms like multiculturalism, social justice, and critical pedagogy. All of these issues focus on the equity of educational opportunity. Placing added emphasis on equity should not diminish in any way the importance of the remaining three criteria. We position excellence as the goal or objective for all educational reform efforts. Similarly, we emphasize the need for reforms to increase student autonomy in relation to school choice, and place measures for responsible and efficient allocation of limited educational resources.

Simply examining the internal dynamics of educational reforms prevents many from looking outside the box at the extrinsic forces that are so eminent in educational reform today—globalization, localization, the New Right, and the New Left. The dialectic of globalization and localization has a huge influence on educational reforms.

Finally, we conclude that the dialectics from the East and the West and other perspectives are of imminent importance in CIDE research. They reflect the diversity of a complex world and the essential role that education plays in advancing theoretical progress in the social sciences. The Tai-Ji Model and EPAM can serve an important role in advancing this ongoing education initiative toward advancing theory and striving for excellence.

REFERENCES

Abdi, Ali A., Korbla P. Puplampu, & George J. Sefa Dei, eds. (2006). *African Education and Globalization: Critical Perspectives.* Lanham, MD: Rowman and Littlefield, Inc.

Althuser, Louis. (1972). "Ideology and Ideological State Apparatuses." In B. R. Cosin (Ed.), *Education: Structure and Society* (pp. 242–280). Harmondsworth, UK: Penguin Books.

Apodaca, Clair. (2002). "The Globalization of Capital in East and Southeast Asia: Measuring the Impact on Human Rights Standards." *Asian Survey, 42*(6), 883–905.

Apple, Michael W. (2006). *Educating the "Right" Way: Markets, Standards, God, and Inequality*. 2nd ed. New York: Routledge.

Apple, Michael W. (2009). "Can Critical Education Interrupt the Right?" *Discourse: Studies in the Cultural Politics of Education, 30*(3), 239–251.

Aspin, David N., & Judith D. Chapman, eds. (2007). *Values Education and Lifelong Learning: Principles, Policies and Programmes*. Dordrecht, The Netherlands: Springer.

Ayodele, J. B., & I. O. Akindutire. (2009). "The Production of Quality Teachers to Boost the Efficiency of Nigeria's Education System." *Research in Education*, (81), 43–52.

Barone, Thomas N. (2004). "Moral Dimensions of Teacher-Student Interactions in Malaysian Secondary Schools." *Journal of Moral Education, 33*(2), 179–196.

Bennett, William. (1993). *The Book of Virtues: A Treasury of Great Moral Stories*. New York: Simon & Schuster.

Best, Steven, & Douglas Kellner. (1991). *Postmodern Theory*. New York: The Guilford Press.

Bigalke, Terance W., & Deane E. Neubauer. (2009). *Higher Education in Asia/Pacific*. New York: Palgrave Macmillan.

Billingsley, K. Lloyd, ed. (1994). *Voices on Choice: The Education Reform Debate*. San Francisco: Pacific Research Institute for Public Policy.

Bosker, Roel J., Bert P. M. Creemers, & Sam Stringfield in collaboration with Interuniversitair Centrum voor Onderwijskundig Onderzoek. (1999). *Enhancing Educational Excellence, Equity, and Efficiency: Evidence from Evaluations of Systems and Schools in Change*. Dordrecht; Boston: Kluwer Academic Publishers.

Brown, Wendy. (2006). "American Nightmare: Neoliberalism, Neoconservatism, and De-Democratization." *Political Theory, 34*(6), 690–714.

Burbules, Nicholas C., & Carlos Alberto Torres, eds. (2000). *Globalization and Education: Critical Perspectives*. New York: Routledge.

Carney, Stephen. (2003). "Globalisation, Neo-liberalism and the Limitations of School Effectiveness Research in Developing Countries: The Case of Nepal." *Globalisation, Societies & Education. 1*(1), 87–101.

Chapman, Christopher, Geoff Lindsay, Daniel Muijs, Alma Harris, Elisabeth Arweck, & Janet Goodall. (2010). "Governance, Leadership, and Management in Federations of Schools." *School Effectiveness & School Improvement, 21*(1), 53–74.

Cheng, Sheng Yao. (2009). "Quality Assurance in Higher Education: The Taiwan Experience since the 1990s." In Terance W. Bigalke and Deane E. Neubauer (Ed.), *Higher Education in Asia/Pacific: Quality and the Public Good*. New York: Palgrave Macmillan.

Cheng, Sheng Yao, & W. James Jacob. (2005). "Toward the Future of Education: The EPAM Approach to Education Reform." *Journal of Education Research, 129*(1), 145–154.

Coleman, James S. (1990). *Equality and Achievement in Education*. San Francisco: Westview.

Cronin, Peter. (2008). "What's in a Name? The Dilemma of South-South Transfer." *Society for International Education, 5*(1), 1–12.

Crossley, Kathy, & U.S. Department of Education. (1990). *Excellence in Education: Blue Ribbon Schools Program. Schools Recognized 1982–83 through 1989–90*. Washington, DC: U.S. Department of Education.

Deem, Rosemary, & Gail P. Kelly. (1984). *Excellence, Reform and Equity in Education: An International Perspective*. Buffalo, NY: Comparative Education Center, Faculty of Educational Studies, State University of New York at Buffalo; Ontario Institute for Studies in Education, Toronto.

Devine, Nesta. (2004). *Education and Public Choice: A Critical Account of the Invisible Hand in Education*. Westport, CT: Praeger Publishers.

de Wit, Hans. (2002). *Internationalization of Higher Education in the United States of America and Europe: A Historical, Comparative, and Conceptual Analysis*. Westport, CT: Greenwood Press.

Donner, Henrike. (2008). *Domestic Goddesses: Maternity, Globalization and Middle-Class Identity in Contemporary India*. Aldershot, UK; Burlington, VT: Ashgate.

Economist. (2006). "Think Global, Act Local." *Economist, 379*(8480), 73–74.

Elliott, Brian, & David MacLennan. (1994). "Education, Modernity and Neo-Conservative School Reform in Canada, Britain and the US." *British Journal of Sociology of Education, 15*(2), 165–185.

Forsey, Martin G. (2010). "Publicly Minded, Privately Focused: Western Australian Teachers and School Choice." *Teaching & Teacher Education, 26*(1), 53–60.

Friedman, Thomas L. (2004). "Think Global, Act Local." *New York Times,* June 6, 13.

Gillies, Donald. (2008). "Quality and Equality: The Mask of Discursive Conflation in Education Policy Texts." *Journal of Education Policy, 23*(6), 685–699.

Gramsci, Antonio. (1999). *Selections from the Prison Notebooks of Antonio Gramsci.* Trans. Quintin Hoare and Geoffrey Nowell Smith. New York: International Publishers.

Guillen, Mauro F. (2001). "Is Globalization Civilizing, Destructive or Feeble? A Critique of Five Key Debates in the Social Science Literature." *Annual Review of Sociology, 27*, 235–260.

Harris, Suzy. (2007). *The Governance of Education: How Neo-liberalism Is Transforming Policy and Practice.* New York: Continuum Press.

Hatoss, Aniko. (2009). "Imagining Multilingual Schools: Languages in Education and Glocalization." *Studies in Continuing Education, 31*(2), 203–206.

Hawkins, John N. (2007). "The Intractable Dominant Educational Paradigm." In Peter D. Hershock, Mark Mason, and John N. Hawkins (Eds.) *Changing Education: Leadership, Innovation and Development in a Globalizing Asia Pacific* (pp. 137–162). Dordrecht, The Netherlands: Springer and Comparative Education Research Centre, University of Hong Kong (CERC).

Hawkins, John N., W. James Jacob, & Wenli Li. (2009). "Higher Education in China: Access, Equity and Equality." In Donald B. Holsinger and W. James Jacob (Ed.), *Inequality in Education: Comparative and International Perspectives* (pp. 215–239). Dordrecht, The Netherlands: Springer/CERC.

Hershock, Peter D., Mark Mason, & John N. Hawkins, eds. (2007). *Changing Education: Leadership, Innovation and Development in a Globalizing Asia Pacific.* Dordrecht, The Netherlands: Springer/CERC.

Hill, David. (2001). "State Theory and the Neo-Liberal Reconstruction of Schooling and Teacher Education: A Structuralist Neo-Marxist Critique of Postmodernist, Quasi-Postmodernist, and Culturalist Neo-Marxist Theory." *British Journal of Sociology of Education, 22*(1), 135–155.

Hill, David. (2009). "Does Capitalism Inevitably Increase inequality?" In Donald B. Holsinger and W. James Jacob (Ed.), *Inequality in Education: Comparative and International Perspectives* (pp. 59–85). Dordrecht, The Netherlands: Springer/CERC.

Holsinger, Donald B., & W. James Jacob, eds. (2009). *Inequality in Education: Comparative and International Perspectives.* Dordrecht, The Netherlands: Springer/CERC.

Hyer, Karen E., Bonnie Ballif-Spanvill, Susan J. Peters, Yodit Solomon, Heather Thomas, & Carol Ward. (2009). "Gender Inequalities in Educational Participation." In Donald B. Holsinger and W. James Jacob (Ed.), *Inequality in Education: Comparative and International Perspectives* (pp. 128–148). Dordrecht, The Netherlands: Springer/CERC.

Inkeles, Alex, & Donald B. Holsinger. (1973). "Education and Individual Modernity." *International Journal of Comparative Sociology, 14*(3&4), 157–162.

Inoue, Kazuma, & Moses Oketch. (2008). "Implementing Free Primary Education Policy in Malawi and Ghana: Equity and Efficiency Analysis." *Peabody Journal of Education, 83*(1): 41–70.

Ish-Shalom, Piki. (2006). "Theory Gets Real, and the Case for a Normative Ethic: Rostow, Modernization Theory, and the Alliance for Progress." *International Studies Quarterly, 50*(2), 287–311.

Jacob, W. James. (2006). "Social Justice in Chinese Higher Education: Issues of Equity and Access." *International Review of Education, 52*(1), 149–169.

Jacob, W. James, & Sheng Yao Cheng. (2003). "Toward the Future of Education: The EPAM Approach to Educational Reform." Paper presented at the American Education Research Association National Conference, Chicago, 23 April 2003.

Jacob, W. James, & Sheng Yao Cheng. (2005). "Mapping Paradigms and Theories in Comparative, International, and Development Education (CIDE) Research." In David P. Baker and Alexander W. Wiseman (Ed.), *Global Trends in Educational Policy* (pp. 221–258). New York: Elsevier.

Jacob, W. James, & Donald B. Holsinger. (2009). "Inequality in Education: A Critical Analysis." In Donald B. Holsinger and W. James Jacob (Ed.), *Inequality in Education: Comparative and International Perspectives* (pp. 1–33). Dordrecht, The Netherlands: Springer/CERC.

Jacob, W. James, & Yafflo W. Ouattara. (2009). "HIV Education in Emergency, Conflict, and Post-Conflict Contexts." *Prospects, 39*(4), 359–381.

Jacobsen, K. H. (2009). "Patterns of Co-Authorship in International Epidemiology." *Journal of Epidemiology & Community Health, 63*(8), 665–669.

Kim, Jiyun, Stephen L. DesJardins, & Brian P. McCall. (2009). "Exploring the Effects of Student Expectations about Financial Aid on Postsecondary Choice: A Focus on Income and Racial/Ethnic Differences." *Research in Higher Education, 50*(8), 741–774.

Lin, Y. 2009. *The Wisdom of Confucius II.* Taipei: Cheng Chung Book Co.

Maddison, Angus. (1983). "A Comparison of Levels of GDP Per Capita in Developed and Developing Countries, 1700–1980." *Journal of Economic History, 43*(1), 27–41.

Mangieri, John N. (1985). *Excellence in Education.* Fort Worth, TX: Texas Christian University Press.

Maslak, Mary Ann. (2009). "Using Enrollment and Attainment in Formal Education to Understand the Case of India." In Donald B. Holsinger and W. James Jacob (Ed.), *Inequality in Education: Comparative and International Perspectives* (pp. 240–260). Dordrecht, The Netherlands: Springer/CERC.

Mayo, Peter. (2009). "Editorial: Antonio Gramsci and Educational Thought." *Educational Philosophy & Theory, 41*(6), 601–604.

Mbabuike, Michael C. (2004). "The Unfolding North/South Relationship: Africa in the Scheme of Things." *Signs: Journal of Women in Culture and Society, 29*(2), 614–617.

Mok, Ka Ho, ed. (2010). *Paradigm Shift or Business as Usual: The Search for New Governance in Higher Education in Asia.* New York: Palgrave Macmillan.

Mok, Ka Ho, & David Kin-keung Chan, eds. (2002). "Introduction." Ka Ho Mok and David Kin-keung Chan (Ed.), *Globalization and Education: The Quest for Quality Education in Hong Kong* (pp. 1–19). Hong Kong: Honk Kong University Press.

Paulston, Rolland G. (1999). "Mapping Comparative Education after Postmodernity." *Comparative Education Review, 43*(4), 438–463.

Paulston, Rolland G. (2000). "Imagining Comparative Education: Past, Present, and Future." *Compare, 30*(3), 353–367.

Peters, Michael. (2001). "Environmental Education, Neo-liberalism and Globalisation: the 'New Zealand experiment'." *Educational Philosophy & Theory, 33*(2), 203–216.

Peters, Susan J. (2009). "Inequalities in Education for People with Disabilities." In Donald B. Holsinger and W. James Jacob (Ed.), *Inequality in Education: Comparative and International Perspectives* (pp. 149–171). Dordrecht, The Netherlands: Springer/CERC.

Phillips, David, & Michele Schweisfurth. (2008). *Comparative and International Education: An Introduction to Theory, Method and Practice.* London: Continuum.

Portnoi, Laura M., Val D. Rust, & Sylvia S. Bagley, eds. (2010). *Higher Education, Policy, and the Global Competition Phenomenon.* New York: Palgrave Macmillan.

Raulo, Marianna. (2000). Moral Education and Development. *Journal of Social Philosophy, 31*(4), 507–551.

Rees, Nina Shokraii. (2000). *School Choice 2000 Annual Report.* Washington, DC: Heritage Foundation 2000.

Rostow, Walt Whithman. (1960). *The Stages of Economic Growth: A Non-Communist Manifesto.* Cambridge: Cambridge University Press.

Rust, Val D. (1996). "From Modern to Postmodern Ways of Seeing Social and Educational Change." In Rolland G. Paulston (Ed.), *Social Cartography: Mapping Ways of Seeing Education and Social Change.* New York: Garland Publishing.

Rust, Val D. (2004). "Postmodernism and Globalization: The State of the Debate." Paper presented at the Comparative and International Education Society Annual Conference, Salt Lake City, Utah, 10 March 2004.

Rust, Val D., & W. James Jacob. (2005). "Globalisation and Educational Policy Shifts." In Joseph Zajda (Ed.), *International Handbook on Globalisation, Education and Policy Research: Global Pedagogies and Policies* (pp. 235–252). Dordrecht, The Netherlands: Springer.

Sarroub, Loukia K. (2008). "Living 'Glocally' With Literacy Success in the Midwest." *Theory Into Practice, 47*(1), 59–66.

Scott, Janelle T. (2005). *School Choice and Diversity: What the Evidence Says.* New York: Teachers College Press.

Shen, J., Z. Fu, Z. Xu, S. Hao, J. Sun, & Ren min ti yu chu ban she. (1988). Tai ji quan quan shu (Di 1 ban. ed.). Beijing: Ren min ti yu chu ban she: Xin hua shu dian Beijing fa xing suo fa xing.

Sewpaul, Vishanthie. (2006). "The Global-Local Dialectic: Challenges for African Scholarship and Social Work in a Post-Colonial World." *British Journal of Social Work, 36*(3), 419–434.

Sidorovitch, Anna. (2005). "Moral Education in Contemporary Belarus: Return to a Soviet Past?" *Journal of Moral Education, 34*(4), 479–489.

Stromquist, Nelly P. (1996). "Mapping Gendered Spaces in Third World Educational Interventions." In Rolland G. Paulston (Ed.), *Social Cartography: Mapping Ways of Seeing Social and Educational Change.* New York: Garland Publishing.

Stromquist, Nelly P., & Karen Monkman, eds. (2000). *Globalization and Education: Integration and Contestation across Cultures.* Lanham, MD: Rowman & Littlefield Publishers, Inc.

Tan, Charlene. (2008). "Two Views of Education: Promoting Civic and Moral Values in Cambodia Schools." *International Journal of Educational Developmen,t 28*(5), 560–570.

Tatto, Maria Teresa. (2003). "Examining Mexico and US Values Education in a Global Context." *Journal of Beliefs & Values: Studies in Religion & Education, 24*(2), 219–237.

Tong, K. M. (1970). *Educational Ideas of Confucius.* Taipei: Youth Book Store.

UNESCO. (1995). "Cultural Production: The Gap between Developed and Developing Countries." *UNESCO Sources No. 74,* 12.

UNESCO. (2001). *Inclusion in Education: The Participation of Disabled Learners.* Paris: UNESCO.

United Nations Population Division (UNPD). (2009). *World Population Prospects, The 2008 Revision.* New York: UNPD.

Uvalic-Trumbic, Stamenka, UNESCO, and International Association of Universities (IAU). (2002). *Globalization and the Market in Higher Education: Quality, Accreditation and Qualifications.* Paris: UNESCO.

Vranish, P., Rose, S., Clark, J., Slattery, J. E., Bucy, A., Hambrook, J., et al., (2010). "School Choice is No Panacea." *American School Board Journal, 197,* 14–15.

Wallerstein, Immanuel. (1974). *The Modern World-System: Capitalist Agriculture and the Origins of the European World-Economy in the Sixteenth Century.* New York: Academic Press.

Watson, Hilbourne A. (2002). "Globalization as Capitalism in the Age of Electronics: Issues of Popular Power, Culture, Revolution, and Globalization from Below." *Latin American Perspectives, 29*(6), 32–43.

West, Anne, & Annamari Ylonen. (2010). "Market-Oriented School Reform in England and Finland: School Choice, Finance and Governance." *Educational Studies, 36*(1), 1–12.

World Bank. (2009). *HIV and AIDS Strategic and Operational Planning Capacity Building Workshops in Five Global Regions.* Washington, DC: World Bank.

Wu, Xiaoxin. (2008). "The Power of Positional Competition and Market Mechanism: A Case Study of Recent Parental Choice Development in China." *Journal of Education Policy, 23*(6), 595–614.

Zhang, Dainian, & Edmond Ryden. (2002). *Key Concepts in Chinese Philosophy.* New Haven: Yale University Press.

Zhao, Yong. (2007). "China and the Whole Child." *Educational Leadership, 64*(8), 70–73.

ROGER BOSHIER

17. *KIA KAHA* (STAY STRONG)

How New Zealand Maori Use Adult in the Context of Higher Education

LEARNING OUT-OF-SCHOOL

The idea education should be "universal and lifelong" was at the center of the British Ministry of Reconstruction 1919 Report on Adult Education (Final Report 1919). At first, the notion of lifelong education stalled but, after World War II, many reform efforts focussed on the need to foster learning throughout society. In newly independent nations and industrial centres undergoing rapid change it was no longer viable to depend on classrooms in universities or schools to produce personnel capable of building a better world.

By 1946 leaders were seriously contemplating ways to build a "learning society" because nobody could afford to have schools and universities monopolising education and learning. Instead, in a learning society, learning and education would be the preoccupation of all citizens and settings (Faure 1972). Above all, there had to be more determined attempts to link learning in nonformal and formal settings. Although universities are bastions of conservatism they would hopefully participate in building a learning society.

Having regard to the foregoing, the purpose of this study was to: (1) critically reflect on the continuing inability of mainstream higher education to dissolve boundaries between formal and nonformal settings for learning, and (2) highlight the theoretical dimensions of Maori wananga (indigenous university) attempts to use a nonformal setting as a fundamental principle of higher educational planning and practice.

Lifelong Education in the Learning Society

As shown in Figure 17.1, the learning society can be visualized by drawing a vertical line on a page. At the bottom are young, and at the top, old people. This is the lifespan aspect of the learning society. Draw a line across the page so it bisects the vertical. This is the horizontal or lifewide aspect of the learning society. On the left, nonformal and, on the right, formal settings for learning and education. Formal settings are age-graded credential-awarding schools, colleges, universities and similar settings usually under control of the Ministry of Education. Non-formal are out-of-school settings for learning and education such as *marae* (community centers, churches, prisons, and the workplace).

John C. Weidman, W. James Jacob (eds.), Beyond the Comparative: Advancing Theory and Its Application to Practice, 315–332.

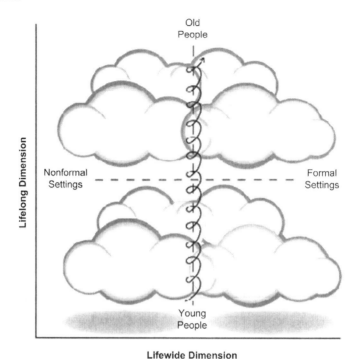

Figure 17.1. Vertical and Horizontal Dimensions of the Learning Society.

This mapping yields four equal-sized zones encompassing learning and education for young and older people in formal and nonformal settings. At the top are zones concerning education for older people in formal (e.g., universities) and nonformal settings (e.g., community centres, churches or marae). Zones at the bottom encompass the learning and education of young people in formal and nonformal settings.

In a well-balanced learning society there would be a more or less equal distribution of resource and effort around these four zones. A learner would be able to swim back and forth, learning in a formal setting today and a nonformal one tomorrow. There would also be some recognition of learning occurring in informal settings. The emphasis would not be on where a learner gets educated. Rather the focus would be on what is learned. There would be also being a more relaxed attitude about prerequisites. Education does not occur in linear or compartmentalized ways and learners would be able to secure access to higher levels without always having done (often irrelevant) prerequisites.

Vertical Integration

The vertical axis (young to old) is the lifespan aspect of the learning society. This is the idea learning and education should occur throughout life, from cradle to grave. Unfortunately, there are psychosocial and structural barriers impeding the ability of people to opt in and out of education throughout their lives. Structural barriers are bad but psychocultural factors just as worrying. Equal opportunity does not automatically translate into equal participation because audiotapes inside people's heads send negative messages about returning to education as an adult. Regrettably, some Maori carry self-deprecating messages in their heads. Pakeha worldviews are "mainstream;" Maori have "other" values. Pakeha knowledge is for the "real" world; Maori knowledge is a "cultural artifact," based on "myths," "legends," or "heritage." Indigenous forms of collectivism are "unrealistic" in the context of twenty-first century urban-industrial capitalism.

Horizontal Integration

Horizontal integration in the learning society refers to the need to foster learning and education in a plethora of settings. It is intolerable to have a situation where education secured in formal settings results in prestigious credentials, and that gained in nonformal settings attracts few credentials and no status. This is because what is learned is more important than where knowledge was acquired. There should be a more relaxed attitude about and celebration of what is learned in nonformal settings such as marae.

Typically, education in formal settings is paid for by government, well organized, assigned adequate resources and results in credentials. Education secured in nonformal settings is largely unorganized, struggles with meagre resources and is regarded as "alternative" or outside the "mainstream."

What Edgar Faure (1972) and other architects of the learning society envisaged was not a dismantling of formal settings. What was needed (then and now) was a more pluralistic and accessible array of opportunities for learning and education throughout the life cycle. For Maori, learning in formal classroom settings will likely be prefaced by a happy bout of learning in a nonformal setting.

Writers like Christopher Knapper and Arthur Cropley (2000) point at the need for universities to acknowledge the importance of learning in nonformal settings and lessen their obsession with classroom teaching. But, all over the world, formal settings are still the coin of the university realm. Formal and nonformal settings are like two railway lines that never meet. Despite vast flotillas of deans, vice-deans, provosts, pro-vice chancellors and their assistants, universities are still largely incapable of engaging with nonformal settings. Calls to build learning communities with no boundaries between the formal and nonformal have been dismissed as overly utopian or "unrealistic."

NEW ZEALAND UNIVERSITIES ON THE DEFENSIVE

From 1984 until 1999 New Zealand was subject to a radical experiment in free market economics. An economic miracle didn't occur. Prior to 1986, 15-to-25 year old New Zealanders were making a median income of NZ$14,700 a year. By year 2000 the same group were making NZ$8,100 and youth suicides were higher than in comparable countries. As well, living standards plummeted and 70 percent of households were worse off than counterparts ten years earlier. Cabinet briefing papers spoke of "a sense of unease about the country's social fabric . . . the fraying state of the nation's families, children and the socially excluded" (*Sunday Star-Times* 2000, C2).

Smacking the Disadvantaged

"Efficiency" and the "free market" meant already disadvantaged—young Maori and Pacific Islands women—were even more seriously jeopardized (Peters et al., 1994). After 1984 the rationality of the marketplace would prevail and investments in tertiary and higher education had to have demonstrated links to the workplace. It didn't work. Society "lost cohesion and continuity . . . industries closed, communities withered, people have moved out of employment, change has been so constant many people are disoriented. People wander through life relating to no social group wider than the family, and often not even that" (Jesson 1999, 211). The notion of the privatised student neglecting social and community responsibilities while hell-bent on building a career, fostered narcissism and a "stuff-you" attitude (Marshall and Peters 1990). None of this was congruent with Maori collectivism or iwi rights and responsibilities.

By 1987, influential members of the government Treasury decided education was a commodity to be placed on the "free market." This advice became the centrepiece of reports and Acts of Parliament (the *Education Act* of 1989, the *Education Amendment Act* of 1990, and the *Education Amendment Acts (4)* of 1991). There would be a shift from the liberal humanist ethos of the 1970s to a technocratic ideology—accompanied by nastiness, a collapse of conviviality and over-emphasis on surveillance and accountability.

Maori suffered more than most during 1980s "reforms." For the first time since 1950s bodgies and widgies (imitators of British teddy boys) appeared, New Zealand socially disruptive gangs were built around ethnicity. Architects of 1980s reforms warned neoliberalism would produce winners and losers, urged citizens to regard the world as their stage and endorsed individualism as a better option than messy collectivism promoted by Maori. Since then, New Zealand Labour, National (Tory) and coalition governments have tried to repair damage resulting from 1980s radical rightwing restructuring of New Zealand society. Today, the situation is not helped by soil erosion, earthquakes, mine tragedies and other disasters. By 2011 many social problems remained. Most Maori are still impoverished and reside on the margins of society.

Squashed Here, Pops Up Over There

During the tumult of restructuring adult educators promoting the value of nonformal settings grew accustomed to budget cuts and neoliberal attacks. They mostly sighed and carried on. When adult education was flattened by a foot from above it tended to pop up elsewhere. In 2009 there was another round of insults and NZ$80 million worth of cuts to adult and continuing education. Adult educators had heard enough, made banners, and on 4 August 2009 staged a protest march in rain-drenched Wellington streets.

Outside the Parliament buildings community educator Valerie Morse was arrested for trespass, opposition Members of Parliament made speeches, activists handed over a petition with 53,334 signatures and television news used words like "adult education" in "nonformal settings." It was an extraordinary moment in the history of New Zealand adult education to see protest banners claiming "Learning Is For Life!" "Don't Let The Sun Set on Night Classes!"

Throughout Organisation for Economic Co-operation and Development (OECD) countries, adult education has been undercut by mean-spirited neoliberal versions of lifelong learning. But, while the New Zealand government eviscerated Pakeha forms of adult education, a Maori wananga made it a primary pillar of curriculum reform and community engagement. Just when it looked like adult education and nonformal settings were on life support, they popped up in new and energetic ways. Like hobbits emerging from a hillside, adult education appeared in new guises. This time it wore a Maori cloak.

BIRTH OF THE *WANANGA* (INDIGENOUS UNIVERSITY)

Pakeha-dominated universities are encouraged to adopt Maori names. Hence the University of Auckland is Te Whare Wananga o Tamaki Makaurau. Maori wananga do not have reciprocal naming rights and must exercise care when using the term "university." Even so, they grant bachelors, masters and doctoral degrees. In popular parlance and, particularly when engaging with foreigners, wananga describe themselves as indigenous universities.

Te Whare Wananga o Raukawa in Otaki opened as a tribal university in 1981.The idea of establishing additional wananga was mooted at a 1987 *hui* (meeting) at Poroporo marae. As a result, students and staff at the University of Waikato created plans for a wananga in the old sawmill at Whakatane and Awanuiarangi got started in 1992.

The *Education Amendment Act* of 1990 defined wananga as places committed to "teaching and research that maintains, advances and disseminates knowledge and develops intellectual independence and assists the application of knowledge regarding mahuatanga Maori (Maori tradition) according to tikanga Maori (Maori custom)." Today, there are three wananga—Raukawa, Awanuiarangi and Aotearoa—offering undergraduate, graduate degree and iwi-development programs.

These are significant institutions. In 2005, Te Wananga o Aotearoa was the largest educational institution in New Zealand with about 40,000 students. Each wananga embraces *Pakeha* (or world) knowledge while foregrounding indigenous views and ways of behaving. The emergence of wananga was the big story of late twentieth century education and three of them now enrol about 60 percent of Maori tertiary students (Durie 2009). This chapter focuses on how adult education pervades iwi-development at one wananga.

Three-Legged Stool in Whakatane

Awanuiarangi leaders want to maintain sufficient levels of flexibility to foster social transformation (Awanuiarangi Meeting 2010). The main campus is in Whakatane—a small resort-town in the relatively isolated eastern Bay of Plenty on the North Island of New Zealand. While some local people are Ngati Awa, the area is also home to descendants of those arriving on the Mataatua canoe.

Whakatane has historically depended on farming, paper production, fishing, and, during the last decade, tourism. As a result of global warming and paper production, there are pressing environmental issues. On most socioeconomic indicators, the eastern Bay of Plenty is one of most deprived places in New Zealand.

Whakatane was chosen as a wananga site because of socio-economic deprivation, influential local citizens, the relatively large number of Maori living nearby and absence of other opportunities for tertiary or higher education. There is a bush-clad hill overlooking a tidal estuary. The wananga is close to the Pacific Ocean and has links to indigenous peoples and educators in other countries—most notably Canada, the United States, Australia, and Pacific Island nations.

In Maori, *whare* refers to a "house" and *wananga* to "learning place." Not all wananga are the same. *Awanuiarangi* is literally a "house of learning." It officially opened on 10 February 1992 and was deliberately constructed to prepare people for workplaces of the twenty-first century while nurturing active citizens, addressing local problems and fostering social transformation.

Although identified with local Ngati Awa, it welcomes students from all parts of New Zealand. Its undergraduate and graduate degree programs replicate standards at the University of Auckland. What makes it unique is the lavish use of adult education methodologies within the context of higher education. Awanuiarangi is a wananga (indigenous university) built on three legs: (1) undergraduate studies, (2) graduate studies, and (3) iwi-development. Traditional Maori world views put emphasis on *whanau* (the extended family), the *hapu* (cluster of families), the *iwi* (tribe or, in North America parlance, band). The fundamental idea embedded in these concepts concerns reciprocal rights, responsibilities and relations. At Awanuiarangi, iwi-development is not a peripheral extension, continuing education, outreach, community engagement or service-learning activity tagged onto mainstream campus programs. As one component of a three-legged operation, adult education in a nonformal setting is at the heart of wananga planning and priorities.

Marae-based iwi-development represents an attempt to serve communities by dissolving boundaries between formal and nonformal settings. Adult education is at the heart of holistic (or 360-degree) wananga notions of learning-for- development and is regarded as an integral part of higher education. New Zealand iwi range in size from 100 to 80,000 persons. The Ngati Awa iwi at Whakatane consists of about 19,000 registered persons. Most live near Whakatane; others reside in Auckland, Wellington, and Waikato. Some people have affiliations with more than one iwi. Through their *whakapapa* (geneaology), Maori are linked to whanau, hapu, iwi, mountains, lakes, rivers, and lands of tribal areas.

Now the task is to describe the theoretical and operational contours of marae-based iwi-development orchestrated by Awanuiarangi. This will be accomplished by analyzing iwi-development within a cartography of theory developed by Gibson Burrell and Gareth Morgan (1979) and elaborated by Rolland G. Paulston (1977; 1996).

The Learning-Marae

Just as there are learning-villages, learning-districts, and a learning-mountain in other countries, there are attempts to build learning-marae in New Zealand. On a learning-marae the task is to:

Educate Leaders. Community leaders need to know what distinguishes fluid and broad notions of lifelong learning from older, narrower and dysfunctional notions of education and training.

Do An Inventory of Resources. Create an inventory of community resources for learning. Focus on who knows what and who needs to learn. Identify learners, teachers (in the broad sense of the word) and settings for learning.

Create Partnerships and Links. Identify informal and formal partnerships. Ask about the extent to which these—along with new ones to be developed—can be harnessed for learning.

Contact the Diaspora. Many marae have members living in urban areas. Many have resources, skills and contacts needed back home on the marae.

Deploy Technology. Networking is important and digital technologies useful. Hence, identify local resources—such as computer or Internet-savvy young or old people—and bottlenecks—such as non-welcoming Internet policies inhibiting connectivity and learning.

Foster Social Justice. Involve groups prominent because of their previous lack of participation in community life. Secure the cooperation and leadership skills of role models who are socially-motivated and have a facility for working with at-risk citizens for whom learning is potentially life transforming.

Make Learning a Social Process. Many Maori have unhappy memories of school. Some think learning is an individual and gruelling endeavour. On the learning-marae there is a festive and convivial atmosphere.

Conduct Research. Merely declaring oneself a learning marae will not suffice. Any serious attempt to become a learning-marae will, to a large extent, depend on its ability to understand itself. Hence, it should stimulate research—some traditional and theory laden. But, as well, there's a need for participatory and narrative forms of enquiry utilizing community members as researchers and drawing on a broad range of local (not just university, college or professional) resources.

There are about 2,000 marae in New Zealand, most in the North Island. A marae consists of a meeting house (suitable for sleeping and other activities), a *pae pae* (the speaking area out front), and grounds for welcomes, farewells, sport, ceremonies, and other outdoor activities. Because *kai* (food) is a centrepiece of Maori life, kitchens and eating areas are nearby.

The marae is a spiritual and cultural home—even for descendants who long ago moved to other places. Despite political rivalries and family fractures, everyone supports the marae. Marae are neat and tidy and a critical site for dialogue concerning collective issues facing the community. Marae are named by and after ancestors. Ancestor stories are frequently heard there. Although primarily a site for political solidarity, marae have also historically functioned as places of learning. In Horace Belshaw and Apirana Ngata's (1939) report on adult education they identified the marae as a crucial site for learning. Forty years later Ranginui Walker (1980) did much the same. The marae is a site for learning and there has always been a need to build social capital as a means to iwi-development.

The New Zealand government claims to be interested in fostering Maori access to education (Ministry of Education 2010). But there are collisions between those advocating techno-rational or others advancing socio-cultural solutions to so-called Maori "underachievement." Advocates of techno-rational forms of education claim Maori need "skilling," or "upskilling" so as to enter the workforce.

Advocates of socio-cultural solutions want to build pathways into higher education by using nonformal settings to foster confidence in and awareness of a Maori identity. Advocates of socio-cultural approaches to development do not denigrate workplace skills or city-based universities. But, by foregrounding the psychological need for Maori to dig where they stand, this group frequently collides with those who consider education a technical, scientific, or politically benign process of information-transmittal. Awanuiarangi regional coordinators operate from a socio-cultural perspective and talk with and listen to iwi members. Although marae have unique needs, there are communalities in what they say. Hence, regional coordinators find there is typically a need for learning about:

- *Waiata* (Traditional songs)
- *Tikanga* (Maori customs and social behaviour)
- *Whakapapa* (Geneaology)
- *Raranga* (Weaving)
- *Karanga* (Call of welcome)
- *Whakairo* (Carving)
- *Whaikorero* (Speechmaking)

- *Mau Rakau* (Weaponry drills)
- *Karakia* (Spiritual procedures and prayer)
- *Te Reo* (Maori language)

These topics rarely lead directly to jobs in the workforce. But they build social capital and knowledge, confidence, attitudes and skills needed for further education. Most important, they foster enthusiasm for learning.

Awanuiarangi stresses the need to draw out local resources. Hence, the emphasis is on facilitating learning. Organizers hire credible local people to run learning events. A typical program involves waiata. Singing is an integral part of Maori culture and anyone making a speech had better be ready to follow it with a song. Because of urban migration, an ageing population and churches, iwi members sometimes know more Anglican hymns than Maori songs. A popular iwi development program aims to rectify this situation and contains clear guidelines concerning the need to sing but also discusses the origins and significance of waiata. An iwi-development program focussed on waiata would consist of three noho (components) and involve locals and iwi members who travelled long distances to the marae.

PROGRAM

The program typically starts with a powhiri (welcome) on a Friday night. This would be followed by kai (food), an orientation, breakout groups and instructions about practising and learning the history of waiata. Throughout Saturday there would be presentations, songs and discussion. In the evening there would be activities designed to clarify whether waiata are intended for celebration or times of sorrow. During Sunday sessions there would be a consolidation of what was learned on Saturday and, after kai, wind-up activities and a farewell. This Friday to Sunday sequence would typically be repeated three times and there are learning tasks to complete between meetings.

Harnessing Nonformal Settings for Higher Education

Canadian universities (such as Memorial University and the University of Saskatchewan) have a long and distinguished history of invoking nonformal settings and working with rural people. In Nova Scotia, the St. Francis Xavier University Antigonish movement involved nonformal settings like kitchen study clubs, credit unions, and producer cooperatives where pedagogy was almost entirely informed by principles of adult education. The Antigonish Movement was orchestrated by a university but is today one of the glittering icons of Canadian adult education. By 2011, the University of British Columbia was putting a major emphasis on service learning for undergraduates. This involves building reciprocal links between what is being learned in nonformal and formal settings (www.aplaceofmind.ca).

Mainstream university attempts to work with rural Maori began in the 1930s but produced less than satisfactory outcomes (see Belshaw and Ngata 1939; Walker

1980; Spoonley 2009). When Maori extension workers (such as Maharaia Winiata, Matiu te Hau and Koro Dewes in Auckland or Bill Parker in Wellington) spent time at rural marae, bosses wondered about how these trips contributed to the university mission. Did marae visits produce articles for refereed journals? When academics go to the marae are they doing "real" work? When receipts for travel expenses were presented there were often struggles over the meaning of "university business."

By 1963, Auckland University had lost patience with Maori rural work and, after orders from above, it ceased (Walker 1980). In the city the task of the Maori academic was "to give lectures on Maori society . . . to middle-class mums of Remuera and Pakeha liberals who came to get their instant fix of Maori culture" (Walker quoted in Spoonley 2009, 72). Against this neglect of rural marae, contemporary Awanuiarangi iwi-development programs take on added significance.

The next task is to examine roles occupied by learners, the nature of nonformal settings, iwi-development pedagogy and what is known about outcomes flowing from marae-based learning.

Farm-Gate Learners

At one time most New Zealand Maori lived in the countryside but, after World War II, urbanization, government policy and a lack of rural jobs brought them into cities and towns. Today, 70 percent of Maori live in urban areas; 30 percent in the countryside. Most Maori did not acquire their knowledge in classrooms and many had unhappy encounters with school systems and teachers. Older Maori were strapped for speaking their language at school. Pakeha also had unhappy encounters with formal education. For these and other reasons, New Zealand has an unusual number of "farm-gate intellectuals," self-educated people who excel on the world stage without the benefit of higher education (Boshier 2002).

New Zealand has had a greater impact on international arenas than its size and location might suggest. It habitually punches above its weight and is known abroad because of formally uneducated people like Edmund Hillary (international development), Bill Hamilton (marine jet drives), Bruce Farr (yacht design), Richard Pearse (heavier-than-air flight), John Britten (motor cycles), Grant Dalton (yacht racing), Arthur Lydiard (athletics), Kiri te Kanawa (opera), and Peter Jackson (film director).

Many eminent New Zealanders—like Sir Edmund Hillary—have grave misgivings about school and a spectacular lack of accomplishment at university. Almost all are farm-gate intellectuals. The might use technology and go to libraries but have little respect for disciplinary boundaries, are often generalists, suspicious of orthodox wisdom and have considerable respect for what's heard across the gate. Farm-gate intellectuals are part of a radical humanist anarchist-utopian tradition (see Paulston 1977) with roots in the colonial experience—where there was a lack of access to formal education matched by a pressing need to work together and learn from mates (women and men).

There are many Maori farm-gate intellectuals in New Zealand. A good example is the late Hone Tuwhare, perhaps Aotearoa's most distinguished poet. A Ngapuhi from North Auckland, he spoke Maori until age nine and had a father who encouraged him to appreciate words. Tuwhare (1964) apprenticed as a fitter in the Otahuhu railway workshops and got involved in union work. His first collection of poems—*No Ordinary Sun* (about the atomic bomb over Hiroshima)—appeared in 1964 and received widespread acclaim. Tuwhare had no tertiary or higher education and, apart from assistance from mentors, was entirely self taught. Much originality came from his Maori perspective and lyrical response to sea and landscape. Another extraordinary and multitalented mostly self-educated Maori farm-gate intellectual is Selwyn Muru—film-maker, artist, broadcaster, sculptor, musician, orator, writer, painter, and lecturer.

Much Maori knowledge about farming, fishing, weather and social relations resides in farm-gate learners and iwi-development is designed to draw it out. By foregrounding local knowledge, Awanuiarangi unmasks local talent and builds capacities. Most important, it nurtures adaptive behaviour and acts as an antidote to globalisation by celebrating the local.

Formal, Nonformal, and Informal Settings

Many former colonies securing independence after World War II realized school systems were incapable of responding to local needs. Realizing this, policy analysts stressed the need to foster education in nonformal and informal (as well as formal) settings. These are not perfect concepts but, as shown in Figure 17.2, people learn most from informal settings, a considerable amount in nonformal and a lesser amount in formal settings. Lifelong education greatly depends on fostering interaction between formal and nonformal settings for learning. Nonformal and formal are more systematically organized than informal settings.

Formal Settings. Formal settings for learning include schools, colleges and universities. Learners in formal settings are usually differentiated according to age and control is vested in Ministries of Education or comparable agencies. They are organized in a systematic fashion and learning in formal settings usually involve a sequence of activities and leads to paper credentials.

Nonformal Settings. These are out-of-school settings for learning. The teaching and learning process in nonformal settings is sometimes quite orthodox and formal. Hence, the label "nonformal" refers to the setting, not activities occurring therein. There are many more nonformal (out-of-school) settings for learning than there are schools, colleges and universities. Examples of nonformal settings for learning include community centres, workplaces, government departments, the military, churches, prisons, farms and factories. They are organized in a systematic fashion and learning in nonformal settings usually involves a sequence of activities. A Maori marae is a nonformal learning setting.

Informal Settings. Learners acquire huge amounts of knowledge, attitudes and skills from the everyday settings of daily life. Most people get up in the morning and, if fortunate, have access to numerous sources of knowledge. Informal settings are those where people learn from "daily experience and exposure to the environment."

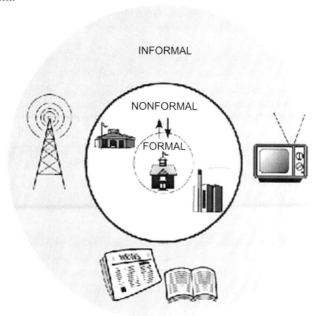

Figure 17.2. Interrelationships between Informal, Nonformal, and Formal Settings for Learning.

During one iwi-development program facilitators noticed a Maori gang member observing the marae from a nearby hill. Hearing singing, he came off the hill and concealed himself behind a fence. Seeing him, organizers sent someone to invite him to participate in what remained of the program. They cite the safety of the marae as the reason for his willingness to join. Other organizers talk about the tendency of elderly people to first loiter at the back of the hall but gradually move forward until they are up front and leading the community in *waiata* (singing) or *whaikorero* (speech-making) (Awanuiarangi Meeting 2010). It was the same when Awanuiarangi bought young men from Ruatoki village to acquire carpentry skills and social capital needed to tackle the problem of dilapidated housing in rural areas.

Learning spaces have special meanings for Maori (Robust 2006; C. W. Smith 2007) and marae activities are embedded in awareness of whakapapa (geneaology) and community. As one iwi-development worker put it "our history, our ancestors are on the marae. We are connected to the past. This is not like learning from a textbook" (Awanuiarangi Meeting 2010). Learning on the marae has many advantages:

- It honours local perspectives.
- The marae is a place for reciprocity so it is hard to distinguish the teacher from the taught.
- The marae is culturally familiar and thus a safe place for learning.
- It is easy to make arrangements for kai (food).
- There is an emphasis in tikanga—Maori ways of doing things.
- The marae is a place for celebration, humour and laughter.
- The marae is a powerful instrument for identity formation.
- Marae events are held under the eyes of ancestors.

Pedagogy

In Maori society there is a major emphasis on family and mokopuna (children) attend marae functions. On the marae there are childcare arrangements and three (or even four) generations of a family can be present. As a participant from the Mangaroa (Hawke's Bay) marae wrote about iwi-development "the whanau are here, the children are here . . . it helps to see them . . . running around and parents and grandparents and great-grandparents all learning together" (Eastwood 2007, 8). When urbanized family members come home to participate in iwi-development, there is a chance to reconnect with whanau and tikanga fading under the stress and distance of city living. In the past, the trip to the home marae was triggered by death of a relative. Coming home to learn new things—or get a refresher on something learned long ago—makes for an enjoyable journey and renewal of resolutions about pursuing further education.

Iwi-development programs typically involve a balance of individual study, small group work, large group discussion, singing and laughter over the kai table. Architects of marae-based learning characterize what happens as "knowledge recovery" and "learning *with* people" (Awanuiarangi Meeting 2010). "Knowledge recovery" is in the New Zealand Tertiary Education strategy vision statement. Hence, "acknowledging and advancing Maori language, culture and identity is important in providing a basis for Maori success in all forms of education" (Ministry of Education 2010, 7).

Facilitators are urged to resist the temptation to teach. Instead, the task is to design a cumulative sequences of games and group activities involving learners. As the program expands, Awanuiarangi will be obliged to mount programs where facilitators from rural areas share their experience. Although some facilitators are trained teachers they do not do a better job than the untrained. This is because it is hard for trained teachers to set aside the urge to teach. Above all, pedagogy tries to be participatory and respectful.

OUTCOMES

Not long after wananga were established there were scandals over money, hiring and the importation of literacy programs from Cuba. Scandal triggered media eruptions. Today, teething problems of earlier years have abated and, by 2010 Awanuiarangi had a program for unemployed youth from remote and impoverished villages where dilapidated houses needed urgent attention. Participants in the house refurbishing program learn about solidarity and the political economy of life in remote rural regions. Along with applied skills they build confidence and social capital. Because of their ability to engage with the hard-to-reach of an earlier era and wananga willingness to dissolve boundaries between nonformal and formal settings, more Maori are on their way into tertiary and higher education.

When an iwi learning event is over the marae must submit a written statement describing the significance of what happened. Most send in photographs to support the written statement. These Wellington-prescribed reporting requirements have provided wananga with data concerning marae-based learning and its role as a mechanism for recruiting Maori into other (such as degree-granting) programs. Regarding outcomes, marae officials, ministry observers, and regional coordinators have all observed the following:

An increasing tendency for participants in marae-based learning activities to make enquiries concerning other opportunities for learning in nonformal or formal settings.

An escalating number of requests for more marae-based programs—to a point where demand exceeds the Awanuiarangi capacity to respond.

A plethora of letters and reports from marae administrators—saying things like: "Doing this within my own marae means I am not embarrassed to learn or make mistakes." "Here if we make a mistake we can laugh about it. The marae is right for my way of learning."

THEORETICAL CONTOURS OF MARAE LEARNING

By adopting a socio-cultural approach to iwi-development Awanuiarangi has added a new dimension to the cartography of social theory created by Burrell and Morgan (1979) and elaborated by Paulston (1977; 1996). Figure 17.3 is my rendering of Burrell and Morgan's (1979) cartography of social theory which, with a nod to the maritime character of Whakatane, contains four paradigms sufficiently distinct to characterize them as islands. The utility of this model has previously been demonstrated in, for example, studies on HIV/AIDS, fishing vessel accidents, and faculty development, environmental education, and international development and was the backdrop to many of Rolland Paulston's social cartographies.

The horizontal axis concerns ontology. All educational development programs arise from an objectivist or subjectivist view of reality. The vertical axis concerns

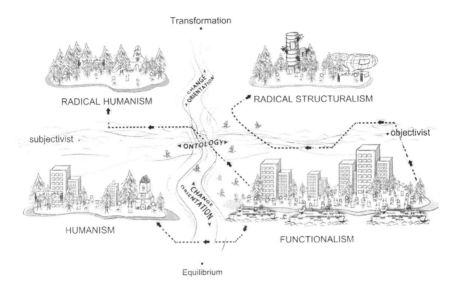

Figure 17.3. Map of Theory Informing Different Kinds of Learning and Education.

the "change orientation"—the extent to which development challenges or reinforces extant power relationships. At the lower end of the vertical axis are equilibrium-oriented theories; at the upper end are conflict-oriented theories.

Ontology and change-orientation axes lie in an orthogonal (right-angled) relationship to each other. Treat ontology like latitude and the change orientation like longitude on a nautical chart. Four islands created by the two axes embrace multiple theoretical alternatives.

The two islands in the bottom of the picture embrace theories whose postulates tend to have an unproblematized view of the world and perpetuate the status quo. Those above the ontology (horizontal) axis contain postulates putting a high priority on social transformation. Islands on the left side foreground human subjectivity. Those on the right assume there is an objective world which exists outside human consciousness. Most orthodox Maori development programs are built on functionalist foundations. Inhabitants of the radical humanism island live closer to nature than people in other locations. At Awanuiarangi the main task is to detach iwi-development from the techno-rational banalities of functionalist orthodoxy and be open to "other" theories.

Functionalism

Functionalism provides an essentially rational explanation for social affairs. This island is crowded because it is the dominant ideology of twenty-first century science and governance. Its epistemology tends to be positivist. Functionalists want practical solutions to practical problems and are usually committed to gradualism and maintenance of equilibrium. Functionalists attempt to apply models derived from natural sciences. They see educational development as a process of building skills and competencies and, as such, have a pragmatic interest in applied methodologies and outcomes.

Humanism

Theorists located on the humanist (or interpretivist) island are subjectivists in that reality is what it is construed to be. Great effort is devoted to adopting the frame of reference of the participant. Humanist theory dwells on meaning-making and ways of reading social situations. In an iwi-development program informed by humanism, there would be a lot of sharing and reflection-on-experience but few changes to oppressive structures.

Radical Humanism

The radical humanist island is the home of Awanuiarangi iwi-development workers and theorists who want to upset extant power relationships. Those residing on this island are anchored within a subjectivist ontology and are usually anti (or post) positivist. Radical humanists want to overthrow or transcend existing social arrangements. Radical humanism is more political and action-oriented than humanism.

Radical Functionalism

The radical functionalist island is the least populated. Radical functionalists share fundamental assumptions buttressing functionalism but are committed to the overthrow of oppressive social structures which build false consciousness. Radical functionalism concerns modes of domination, deprivation and contradictions within an objective social world. Within this paradigm are theorists who focus on contradictions within society while others dwell on power relationships. But common to all theories on this island is the notion social structures are characterized by conflicts and, within these, lie the basis of development.

FROM FUNCTIONALIST ORTHODOXY TO RADICAL HUMANISM

Iwi-development at Awanuiarangi is deliberately based on Maori subjectivity and aimed at social transformation. Hence, it flows from a need for cultural revitalization (Paulston 1977) and is a clear manifestation of radical humanism as envisaged by Burrell and Morgan (1979).

Other educational theories nested in a radical humanist paradigm include critical theory, Paulo Freire's (1972) notions of conscientization, some forms of feminism, critical pedagogy, deschooling, anarchist-utopian forms of self-directed learning, popular education, post-colonial perspectives, resistance theory, and the Moeawatea critical service learning heritage conservation process in New Zealand (Boshier and Harré 2008).

Unlike abstract theory advocated by "armchair revolutionaries" (G. Smith 2009) iwi-development anchored in radical humanism has a strong action component. Whether radical humanist forms of iwi development produce better outcomes than functionalist orthodoxy, remains to be seen. In the meantime, Awanuiarangi is standing on solid ground by offering educationally disadvantaged rural Maori a framework for lifelong learning and creating pathways into credentialed forms of higher education. Just as important, it is fulfilling a dream of the early architects of lifelong education who envisaged a day when formal and nonformal settings would sing, dance and take kai together.

REFERENCES

Awanuiarangi Meeting. (2010). Notes of a meeting with senior administration and iwi-development staff held at Awanuiarangi, Whakatane, 22 February 2010.
Belshaw, Horace, & Apirana Ngata. (1939). *Report of the Young Maori Leaders' Conference.* Auckland: Auckland University College.
Boshier, Roger W. (2002). "Farm-gate Intellectuals, Excellence and the University Problem in Aotearoa/New Zealand." *Studies in Continuing Education, 24*(1), 5–24.
Boshier, Roger W., & Dave Harré. (2008). "Critical Service Learning in New Zealand/Aotearoa." In G. Strohschen (Ed.), Challenges and Solution in the Development and Delivery of International Adult Education Programs (pp. 139–155). Dordrecht, The Netherlands: Springer.
Burrell, Gibson, & Gareth Morgan. G. (1979). *Sociological Paradigms and Organizational Analysis.* Portsmouth: Heinemann.
Durie, Mason. (2009). "Towards Social Cohesion: The Indigenisation of Higher Education in New Zealand." Paper presented at the 2009 Vice Chancellors Forum, Kuala Lumpur, 15–19 June 2009.
Eastwood, Elizabeth. (2007). *Marae-Based Learning: Feedback from Communities.* Whakatane, New Zealand: Te Whare Wananga o Awanuiarangi.
Faure, Edgar. (1972). *Learning to Be.* Paris: UNESCO.
British Ministry of Reconstruction. (1919). *Final Report of the Adult Education Committee.* London: British Ministry of Reconstruction.
Freire, Paulo. (1972). *Pedagogy of the Oppressed.* New York: Continuum.
Jesson, Bruce. (1999). *Only Their Purpose is Mad: The Money Men Take Over New Zealand.* Palmerston North, New Zealand: Dunmore Press.
Knapper, Christopher, & Arthur Cropley. (2000). *Lifelong learning in Higher Education.* London: Kogan Page.
Marshall, James, & Michael Peters. (1990). "Children of Rogernomics: The New Right, Individualism and the Culture of Narcissism." Sites, 21, November 4–6.
Ministry of Education. (2010). *Tertiary Education Strategy, 2010–2015.* Wellington, New Zealand: Ministry of Education.
Paulston, Rolland G. (1977). "Social and Educational Change: Conceptual Frameworks." *Comparative Education Review, 21*(2–3), 370–395.
Paulston, Rolland G, ed. (1996). *Social Cartography: Mapping Ways of Seeing Social and Educational Change.* New York: Garland Publishing.
Peters, Michael, James Marshall, & Lauran Massey. (1994). "Recent Educational Reforms in Aotearoa." In E. Cox, K. Jenkins, and J. Marshall (Ed.), The Politics of Learning and Teaching in Aotearoa-New Zealand (pp. 251–272). Palmerstone North, New Zealand: Dunmore Press.
Robust, Tui. (2006). "Developing Indigenous Structures in the University: Another Era or Another Error?" PhD Diss., Department of Education, University of Auckland, New Zealand.
Smith, Cheryl W. (2007). "He pou herenga kit e nui: Maori knowledge and the university." PhD diss., Department of Education, University of Auckland, New Zealand.
Smith, Graham. (2009). "The Problematic of Indigenous Theorizing: A Critical Reflection." Paper presented at the annual conference of the American Educational Research Association, San Diego.

Spoonley, Paul. (2009). Mata Toa: The Life and Times of Ranginui Walker. Auckland: Penguin.
Sunday Star-Times. (2000). "Clark Finds New Energy," Sunday Star-Times, January 23, C2.
Tuwhare, Hone. (1964). *No Ordinary Sun*. Auckland: Blackwood and Janet Paul.
Walker, Ranginui. (1984). "Maori Adult Education." In Roger Boshier (Ed.), Towards a Learning Society: New Zealand Adult Education in Transition (pp. 101–120). Vancouver: Learning Press.

ENKHJARGAL ADIYA DIFFENDAL AND JOHN C. WEIDMAN

18. GENDER EQUITY IN ACCESS TO HIGHER EDUCATION IN MONGOLIA[1]

The increasing proportion of entering students has been one of the most outstanding events in the recent evolution of higher education. In particular, the extension to more inclusive groups including female students and less privileged social class students is becoming a worldwide phenomenon. Over the past decade and a half, higher education expansion has been most dramatic in the newly independent republics of the former Soviet Union and Mongolia (Magno and Silova 2008).

Mongolia, while maintaining its independence, nevertheless adopted a Russian style education system and shared a number of cultural characteristics with the countries of Central Asia (Kazakhstan, the Kyrgyz Republic, Tajikistan, Turkmenistan, and Uzbekistan) that were part of the Soviet Union (Weidman et al., 2004). However, the development of higher education in Mongolia had its own unique qualities. There was no historical experience of higher education; its development started from scratch by establishing completely new institutions and universities. The first modern type of higher education institution—the National University of Mongolia—was established in 1942 in Ulaanbaatar.

This chapter explores reasons for the lower participation of males than females in Mongolian higher education. It explores the cultural and societal norms that affect gender equity in access to higher education in Mongolia (Weidman et al., 2004) as well as economic factors such as opportunity costs and deferred income (Becker 1993). In 2004–2005, 62 percent of Mongolian undergraduates were female, a pattern that has existed since the early 1990s (Davaa et al., 2005). Only Kazakhstan and Kyrgyzstan among the republics of Central Asia have a similar predominance of females enrolled in higher education (Weidman et al., 2004). Interestingly, this is a phenomenon also shared with the contemporary United States (Lewin 2006).

CONTEXT AND PROBLEM

Current Situation of Higher Education in Mongolia

Prior to 1992, higher education in Mongolia was totally controlled by the state. "The government owned, financed and operated all higher education institutions in Mongolia" (Weidman and Bat-Erdene 2002, 132). In the 1990s, as Mongolia began to build democracy and started to shift from a centrally planned to a market

John C. Weidman, W. James Jacob (eds.), Beyond the Comparative: Advancing Theory and Its Application to Practice, 333–353.

economy, the country started reforming the entire education system. This included fully shaping the Mongolian higher education subsector in terms of ownership, governance, funding, and academic curriculum.

Mongolia is similar to several other Asian countries in experiencing significant growth in higher education enrollments, in part due to the expansion of the private sector. It is, however, unique in that the public sector was effectively privatized in 1993 when the Mongolian government began requiring public higher education institutions to begin charging tuition at levels sufficient to cover the entire of cost of academic staff salaries, thus generating a large reduction in the government's budget for higher education. The Government of Mongolia found higher education to be the most promising sector for cost sharing and shifted a part of its fiscal burden to institutions and recipients of services (i.e., students). Consequently, all students are required to pay fees and there is relatively little difference in the fees for public and private higher education institutions. Direct funding of universities and colleges ceased in 2003. Currently, 95 percent of public institutions' budgets come from the tuition fees of students (Davaa et al., 2005) and the only support provided by the government to higher education is through the State Training Fund which provides loans and scholarships to students. About 60 percent of students obtain loans and grants on the basis of merit and need. In this changing environment, higher education institutions have been challenged to embrace global forces and compete for resources, particularly for research funding, qualified faculty members, and students (Davaa et al., 2005).

It is estimated that 80 percent of Mongolian secondary school graduates continue into postsecondary education (Davaa et al., 2005). According to 2005–2006 statistical information, out of 170 higher education institutions operating in Mongolia, 116 (68 percent) are private and 109 (64 percent) are located in Ulaanbaatar, the capital city of Mongolia, where one third of the population is concentrated (Ministry of Education, Culture and Science of Mongolia [MECS] 2007). It has only been in the last 15 years that these 116 private institutions have been established (Davaa et al., 2005). About 82 percent of private and 61 percent of public institutions were not accredited by the Mongolian National Higher Education Accreditation Agency established in the late 1990s.

Due largely to concerns about quality of the rapidly expanded private higher education subsector, a sample model of higher education standards of Mongolia was approved by the MECS in 2001. The initiative identified objectives for Bachelor of Arts programs and specified universal and minimum requirements for graduates. It also put forward critical issues such as democratization of training, resolving problems from different points of view (pluralism), foreign language competence, computer skills and teamwork skills. The curriculum in support of master's degree programs has been developed even though the quality of Master of Arts and PhD training lags behind international standards. In general, higher education is transitioning to concentrate on introducing new teaching methods and technology, moving from the traditional professor-centered approach to student-centered approaches including problem-solving/teaching, and developing active student participation. A quality assurance and quality assessment system for evaluation of higher education curriculum and syllabi has not yet been established completely in Mongolia. National accreditation has focused on institutional rather than academic program accreditation.

Important issues such as setting up and implementing criteria for academic programs are another problem area for the higher education subsector. Universities do not have a system for accurate student assessment such as an advanced management database, which would include development and distribution of locally designed software for management, student registration, and institutional data collection in accordance with international standards (Davaa et al., 2005).

Since the abolition of traditional higher education system planning following the transition from a socialist to democratic government, bachelor's degree programs have been required to be more relevant to contemporary societal needs and the integration of Mongolia into regional economies. Graduates with qualifications that are no longer relevant to the labor market and new government jobs face difficulties. A better fit between degree programs and the labor market would reduce that anxiety of graduates when seeking employment and strengthen the role of the higher education subsector in making a contribution to securing social sustainability. Minimum requirements for communication skills, foreign language competence, teamwork, and computer and information technology (IT) knowledge required by the labor market have been identified as challenges for bachelor's degree programs.

Reverse Gender Gap in Higher Education in Mongolia

Until the early 1990s, under the Soviet-style economic system, 60 percent of the students in higher education in Mongolia were male (Lin-Liu 2005). But with the collapse of communism and the return of livestock to private ownership, young males could resume their traditional role as herders and contribute to family income. Furthermore, changing times resulted in the closure of the government's vocational and technical training schools, largely due to mismatch between what was being taught and job requirements in the emerging market economy (Davaa et al., 2005). Since the socialist era, enrollment rates of girls have been higher than boys for primary, secondary and tertiary education (see Table 18.1). Since the beginning of the transition period, there has been what the United Nations calls a widening "reverse gender gap" in secondary and tertiary education; though enrollment rates of both boys and girls decreased. In secondary education in 2000, gross enrollment rates of girls were 20 percent higher than those for boys (United Nations Development Fund for Women [UNIFEM] 2001). In 2005, for instance, while approximately equal numbers of girls and boys started primary school, 57 percent of the high school graduates were female (Davaa et al., 2005). However, as it is illustrated in Table 18.1, recently the ratio of girls to boys in both primary and secondary education has been steadily falling. This indicates that the gender gap is narrowing slowly at all levels of education, to the point where the ratio of girls to boys in secondary education was just 1.03 in 2006 (Government of Mongolia 2007).

Table 18.1. Gender Dimensions in Mongolia, 1990–2006

Gender Dimensions	1990	2000	2005	2006
Ratio of girls to boys in primary schools	1.03	1.01	0.98	0.98
Ratio of girls to boys in secondary education	1.33	1.20	1.11	1.03
Ratio of female to male students in higher education	1.72	1.72	1.53	1.53
Proportion of women in the population engaged in wage employment in non-agriculture sectors	51.10	50.40	53.10	53.90
Percentage of women elected to national parliament	24.90	11.80	6.60	6.60
Percentage of women candidates in parliamentary election	7.70	10.90	13.70	–

Source: Government of Mongolia (2007).

The main reasons for the growing gender gap during the political and economic transition period in education of the 1990s had been the withdrawal of boys from school to assist in income-earning activities, mainly herding, and the collapse of the vocational education system. Ironically, male-oriented education for jobs that no longer existed influenced the reverse gender gap in Mongolia (Mongolian Education Alliance 2005). Rather than studying, males became more involved in trade in the capital or a smaller town or young men remained in the countryside raising livestock to feed their families. Moreover, the tradition of parents passing on material possessions like livestock and land to sons is strong in Mongolia. But parents also believe that daughters should have some resources of their own rather than be left to their own devices or married off to another family, which happens in many other Asian cultures. As a result, the preference to send daughters to college led to a "reverse gender gap," with women now making up 60.5 percent of all students at Mongolian universities (MECS 2008). The trend is particularly distinctive because Asia is typically considered a place where women are less valued than men.

However, the narrowing gender gap in education does not necessarily mean that gender inequalities in various spheres of society are narrowing simultaneously (Nozaki et al., 2009). In the labor market, although women's share of wage employment in the non-agricultural sector is near parity with men, inequalities in gender relations in the workplace persist (Government of Mongolia 2007). The impressive educational achievements of women have not generated comparable financial returns as evidenced by their under-representation among top management in business and in decision-making positions (UNIFEM 2001; Government of Mongolia 2007). Women are also discriminated against because of societal expectations that women would leave the labor force in order to start a family (UNIFEM 2001).

From 2000 to 2005, the number of bachelor's degree students in government owned educational institutions increased by 46.3 percent while the total number of those studying in private institutions grew 240 percent (Davaa et al., 2005). During the same period of time, the total number of bachelor's degree students in higher education institutions increased by 70.1 percent, among whom 62 percent were female students (Davaa et al., 2005). In general, female students outnumber males at all levels of education in Mongolia, a pattern that has existed since the early 1990s (MECS 2007). Furthermore, among master's and PhD degree students, female students are in the majority (see Table 18.2).

Table 18.2. Gender Balance by Education Level, 2006–2007

Education Level	Total	Female Students	% of Female Students
Diploma students	4,193	2,952	70.4
Bachelor's students	129,833	77,897	60.0
Master's students	6,286	4,115	65.5
PhD students	2,099	1,219	58.1
Total	142,411	86,183	60.5

Source: MECS Statistics (2008).

Interestingly, the proportion of female students in higher education has been decreasing slowly from 2000 to 2007. As illustrated in Figure 18.1, the total proportion of female students in higher education in 2000 was equal to 63.2 percent while this number in the academic year 2006–2007 was equal to 60.5 percent (MECS 2008).

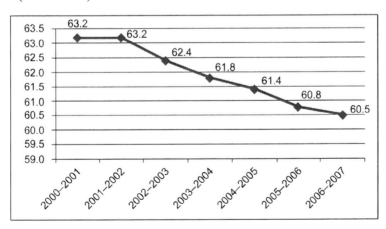

Figure 18.1. Percentage of Female Students in Higher Education, 2000–2007.
Source: MECS (2008).

Furthermore, the female-to-male student ratio in higher education has been slowly decreasing from 1.72 in 2000 to 1.53 in 2006 (see Table 18.1). The proportion of male students in higher education increased from 39.2 percent in 2000 to 39.5 percent in 2006. According to the *Mongolian Second National Report on Implementation of Millennium Development Goals (MDGs)*, the greater number of female students in higher education is due to a higher proportion of girls among graduates of secondary schools as well as to "traditional differing upbringing of girls and boys in Mongolian families" (Government of Mongolia 2007, 43).

The Mongolian higher education system also manifests gender segregation by fields of study (Nozaki et al., 2009). Female students studying in service fields have increased by 7.7 percent while the proportion tends to be decreasing in other fields. Students studying in social science and humanities fields constituted 51.8 percent of all students in the academic year of 2004–2005 compared to 43.8 percent in 2000–2001. Female students have always been over represented in these fields. Table 18.3 shows the gender distribution of Mongolian undergraduates by field of study in 2000 and 2004.

Table 18.3. Bachelor's Degree Students in Mongolia by Professional-Occupational Areas, 2000–2004

Index	Occupational Classification	2000–2001		2004–2005		% Increase in Total 2000–2004
		Total	Female (%)	Total	Female (%)	
1	Medicine	3,346	83.1	6,406	79.2	91.5
2	Language, history, philosophy	5,121	79.4	11,285	78.5	120.4
3	Education	8,706	80.9	11,167	76.6	28.3
4	Social work	0	0	807	76.1	–
5	Journalism	1,062	78.0	1,766	75.4	66.3
6	Biology, chemistry	822	74.6	860	71.0	4.6
7	Business, management	11,183	67.2	24,804	67.7	121.8
8	Politics, sociology	5,645	65.5	9,327	65.3	65.2
9	Mathematics	893	62.9	1,430	61.0	60.1
10	Production technology	9,743	40.7	6,103	59.2	−37.4
11	Agriculture, forestry	2,686	58.4	2,781	59.1	3.5
12	Law	3,134	62.5	6,574	57.3	109.8
13	Art (artist)	2,040	46.1	2,959	46.4	45.0
14	Physics, geography	1,452	41.7	2,308	42.5	59.0
15	Tourism	606	63.2	1,623	39.1	270.0
16	Software, hardware	1,381	42.8	2,991	36.5	220.0
17	Engineering	2,994	70.6	8,930	34.9	300.0
18	Construction, architecture	214	35.0	3,081	25.7	1,339.7

Source: Davaa, et al., (2005, Table 7.14).

Clearly, most fields have a predominance of females, with the notable exception of fields that are computer-related (software, hardware), engineering, construction, and architecture. However, the number of females approaches males in physics and geography, while exceeding them in mathematics. The largest proportion of females is in medicine, a pattern common in Russia and most former Soviet Republics.

Conceptual Framework

Drawing from models of human capital theory (Becker 1993) and socioeconomic effects on college choice (McDonough 1997), the study considers several sets of influences on the choice of whether or not to enroll in higher education, including pressures from family and peers, prior experiences with education, attractions of income producing activities, and anticipated consequences of completing higher education, including foregone earnings. These factors are construed as complex and interacting, not linear or entirely deterministic.

This chapter explores reasons why the gender imbalance favoring females persists in Mongolian higher education, especially since in all spheres of life, including politics and certainly business, males dominate in leadership positions. The primary focus is on social and cultural norms that encourage females to continue their education past the secondary level. This varies by province (*aimag*), with the female imbalance more prevalent in rural than in urban areas.

Ethnic and religious differences are mentioned in the research literature but are not addressed in the present research because of the relative high homogeneity in Mongolia on these dimensions. Mongolia is a predominantly Tibetan Buddhist country, but there are also small groups of Christians and Muslims. Finally, as suggested by research in the United States (McDonough 1997), it is very important to examine socioeconomic differences in access. In the most affluent families, gender differences seem to be minimal but males from middle and lower income families are less likely to enroll in college than their female siblings.

Another special area of focus will be on economic factors influencing college choice, which might have a strong influence on the current gender situation in Mongolia. Economic factors are especially important because Mongolia was a socialist country for 70 years and it was not until the beginning of the 1990s that Mongolia began its transition from a centrally planned to a market economy.

In addition to changing economic conditions, the support of parents and family members is a crucial factor. At the moment, little is known about family and peer influences on higher education attendance in Mongolia and there is not much systematic information about labor market opportunities for highly educated females and males. The gender imbalance favoring female enrollment in higher education is a phenomenon also shared with the contemporary United States (McDonough 1997; Lewin 2006). Hence, the research contributes to a broader understanding of shifting gender equity patterns in higher education enrollment in Mongolia with implications for the United States as well as other countries around the world.

To date, there has been very little research on gender differences in Mongolian higher education, an issue that has been ignored at the policy development and implementation level. Since we are studying factors related to gender disparities in

Mongolian higher education, the study is particularly important because it addresses a phenomenon identified by the Government of Mongolia (2007) as a target for taking short-term actions necessary for implementing the third goal of the United Nations MDGs: to promote gender equality, to empower women, and to increase their participation at the decision making level. Finally, we contribute to social cartography by mapping conceptually both the qualitative data analysis process that we employed and the patterns of relationships among the various dimensions of gender phenomena in Mongolia.

RESEARCH DESIGN

This is a qualitative study, an approach that is particularly effective in allowing for improved understanding of particular events, roles, interactions, or social situations (Creswell 2003), making it appropriate for investigating a new and changing socioeconomic environment in Mongolia which has led to the current gender imbalance in higher education. During summer 2007 (phase one) and fall 2008 (phase two), open-ended interviews were conducted with 42 respondents: 31 Mongolian university students, three college-age out-of-university respondents, three representatives of local nongovernmental organizations (NGOs), three people from different international organizations and two university professors. The intention of the respondent selection process for all three phases of this study was to cover all stakeholders including students, professors, parents, policy makers, representatives from local NGOs and international organizations and college-age out-of-university young people by involving as many people as possible who would have knowledge and experience about the gender situation in higher education.

For the first phase of data collection in summer 2007, university student respondents who had male siblings of university age or older who did not enroll in higher education were identified in order to gain information about reasons for the siblings' non-attendance. After interviewing 34 respondents during phase one, respondents started to repeat the same ideas adding no new information. For the second and third phases of data collection in summer 2008 and 2009, interviewees were chosen who could provide information about certain issues brought up by previous informants as a reason for lower participation of males than females in Mongolian higher education. We followed the chain of contacts in successive years in order to identify and accumulate information about critical issues. Gender balance and representation from most regions of the country were sought in the selection of respondents.

This approach had the advantage of (1) reducing the need for in-country travel by conducting the research in Ulaanbaatar where virtually all of the country's universities are located, (2) providing access to respondents from across the vast nation, (3) being able to collect data on both college attenders and non-attenders in the same family, and (4) hearing opinions of other stakeholders about the current situation on gender equity in higher education.

Interview questions covered reasons for higher education enrollment, including personal motivation and family influence as well as economic factors. Structured around seven open-ended questions, the 60-to-90-minute interviews explored the academic and private life experiences of respondents in relation to gender equity and access to higher education. Most interviews were conducted in the Mongolian language, taped, and translated into English by the Mongolian co-author of this research.

DATA ANALYSIS

Upon completion of the individual interviews, all were translated into English, transcribed and put into soft and hard copy. The qualitative technique of inductive data analysis (i.e., identifying categories, patterns of response, and the drawing of connections between units of data) was used to analyze the data. According to J. Amos Hatch (2002, 161), "Inductive thinking proceeds from specific to the general. Understandings are generated by starting with specific elements and finding connections among them." The inductive qualitative data analysis model shown in Figure 18.2 was developed for this research.

According to the model, the qualitative data analyzing process has four major phases, each with three or four sub-processes: noticing, collecting, thinking (Seidel 1998), and writing. Before each phase began, all transcripts were read thoroughly in order to develop a solid sense of what was included in the data set, what was used so far and what was ignored and left redundant. Because each reading brought new insights to the research, data were re-read before beginning each phase.

At the beginning of the "reading" phase, all transcripts were read carefully so we could become familiar with dimensions of the data set and start making decisions about how we would disassemble the data into analyzable parts. This process requires that all the data be examined interview-by-interview, line-by-line, and word-by-word. Hatch (2002) called these analyzable parts "frames of analysis," used to identify starting points in the data analysis process. As data analysis continued, it was not unusual to find that these frames could shift and change. Coding involves identifying tentative labels through which data can be grouped and analyzed. While there are many different approaches to coding, the present study treated codes as "condensed representation of facts described in the data" (Seidel and Kelle 1995). Essentially, the coding procedure facilitates the process of identifying and naming interesting facts in the data set. Additionally, codes serve to summarize, synthesize, and sort the many observations appearing in the data (Seidel 1998). As data are coded, the process of breaking up, separating or disassembling research materials into manageable pieces, parts, elements or units starts.

The "collecting" phase begins the process of bringing order to the data, which means reassembling the data set based on a coding scheme. According to Danny Jorgenson (1989, 4), "the researcher sorts and sifts data, searching for types, classes, sequences, processes, patterns or wholes. The aim of this process was to assemble or reconstruct data into a meaningful or comprehensive fashion." This stage involved conceptual ordering, the organization of data into discrete categories according to their properties and dimensions. These categories stem from the data, as filtered, of course, through the researcher's lens, but the data have to "speak" to a category before one can be established. As sets of categories became established they were defined more precisely through a process of discovering domains of analysis, developing a set of categories of meanings or domains that reflects relationships represented in the data. This process is different from the previous step because domains are established by combining some categories in order to explain those facts or categories based on emerging relationships. According to Hatch (2002, 165), "Domains can be categories that are understood by large numbers of people with common cultural understandings, or they can be categories that are developed within smaller groups with specialized interests and needs." Domains are established that showed relationships among concepts, senses or meanings (Spradley 1979).

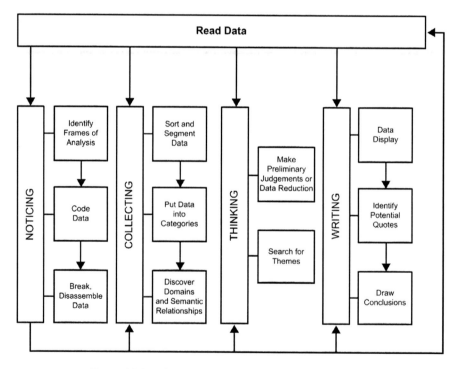

Figure 18.2. Inductive Model for Qualitative Data Analysis.
Source: Adiya (2010).

The "thinking" phase involved making preliminary judgments or decisions about which domains were important to the study and which were not. Matthew Miles and Michael Huberman (1994) call this a "data reduction" process.

According to them, the major challenge in practical qualitative research is data reduction because everything looks important, especially at the outset, and the analyst wants to get it all: "data reduction refers to the process of selecting, focusing, simplifying, abstracting and transforming the data that appears in written up field notes and transcriptions" (Miles and Huberman 1994, 10). The purpose of this process was to narrow the focus of analysis by studying domains and deciding which domains were most relevant, forcing choices about which aspects of the assembled data should be emphasized, minimized, or set aside completely. Themes were developed after careful examination of each domain and the connections between them. The goal of this activity was to look across a broad spectrum of the data and bring pieces together to explain the phenomenon under study. According to James Spradley (1979), in order to look for themes we should look for relationships among relationships in addition to similarities and differences. Essentially, "themes should emerge that provide a basic framework for understanding the social setting being studied and for writing up your description and analysis of that setting" (Hatch 2002, 176.)

The final phase was the process of "writing." Data display is the most important element in the writing stage of qualitative analysis. Data display goes a step beyond data reduction to provide an extended piece of text or a diagram, chart, or matrix that provides a new way of arranging and thinking about the more textually embedded data. Data displays, whether in word or diagrammatic form, allow the analyst to extrapolate from the data enough to begin to discern systematic patterns and interrelationships. At the display stage, additional, higher order categories or themes may emerge from the data that go beyond those first discovered during the initial process of data reduction (Miles and Huberman 1994). Hatch (2002, 176) refers to data displays as a master outline expressing relationships within and among domains that should logically follow what the researcher has done so far. Joseph Novak and D. Bob Gowin (1984, 15) called a data display "a schematic device for representing a set of concept meanings embedded in a framework of propositions." Generally, data displays are conceptual maps used to frame a research project, reduce qualitative data, analyze themes and interconnections in a study, and present findings.

For the present study, we developed a social map that illustrates how people we have interviewed for this particular study see why there is gender imbalance in Mongolian higher education (see Figure 18.3). According to Rolland G. Paulston and Martin Liebman (2000, 8),

applied to comparative education, social maps as a distinct mode of visual representation may help to present and decode immediate and practical answers to the perceived locations and relationships of persons, objects and perceptions in the social milieu. The interpretation and comprehension of both theoretical constructs and social events then can be facilitated and enhanced by mapped images.

343

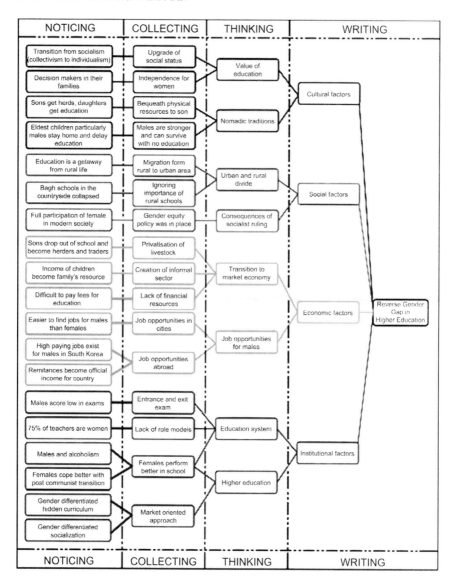

Figure 18.3. Mapping the Reverse Gender Gap in Mongolian Higher Education.

Once the data display had been developed, text supporting the findings was identified by re-reading data for the last time. According to Hatch (2002, 178) "identifying potential quotes in the data is important to getting ready to write, but it is also a good final check to see if sufficient data is evident to give you confidence in making your final report." The last activity was drawing conclusions by stepping back to consider what the analysis meant with respect to the research issues.

Verification, integrally linked to conclusion drawing, entails revisiting the data as many times as necessary to cross-check or verify emergent conclusions. "The meanings emerging from the data have to be tested for their plausibility, their sturdiness, their 'confirmability'—that is, their validity" (Miles and Huberman 1994, 11). Validity encompasses a set of overall concerns about the extent to which the conclusions being drawn from the data are credible, defensible, warranted, and able to withstand alternative explanations.

FINDINGS

While a number of themes emerged from this study, four have been identified as most important for understanding why gender imbalance persists in Mongolian higher education (Figure 18.3). Their descriptions are enriched by a sampling of interview comments and text as well as data from other relevant documents.

Theme 1. Cultural Factors

The findings of this study show that cultural factors have a clear impact on the gender imbalance in Mongolian higher education. Unlike most other Asian countries, Mongolian families prefer to send girls rather than boys to higher education if they have to make a choice due to problematic circumstances (i.e., limited financial resources, need for manual help, need for extra income in the family, etc.). Traditionally, women's role in the nomadic life style has been as important as men's (UNIFEM 2001). Mongolian females have played an indispensable role and assumed responsibility in the family economy, and therefore, their education has been seen as crucial.

Often rural Mongolian males are left behind in education because of social and economic demands in the countryside as well as attachment to a lifestyle that nomadic people in Mongolia have led for many centuries. For 3,000 years, the people of the steppes have adopted a pastoral way of life, moving constantly in search of best pastures and campsites. The herds were privatized after the collapse of the socialist system and one family of herders could own up to 2,000 head of livestock. Privatization of livestock brought a new division of labor, with the family becoming the working unit rather than large collective farms. Because families can keep the income from farm products, nomadic parents allow girls to stay in school while often pushing boys to drop out of school to help with livestock. Results from the *Mongolian Dropout Study* conducted in 2005 by the Mongolian Education Alliance indicate that a majority of those who leave secondary school are boys, with 71.4 percent of boys dropping out of school to work with the herds. The report also states "the lack of means of family subsistence had a more direct effect on boys than girls" (Mongolian Education Alliance 2005, 66). According to this report, parents consider the boys a "working force" to help the family, especially because the kind of work they do—looking after cattle and livestock, carrying baggage for fees, selling goods, gold panning, land digging, et cetera—earns more money.

Girls, on the other hand, if they are engaged in working and earning some money sell home-made food like traditional steamed and fried dumplings (*buuz* and *khoshur*) at markets or engage in small retailing. Girls are also regarded as more sensitive to any kind of pressure and violence and it is safer for them to stay in school. According to one respondent, "higher education for girls is some kind of ticket for a successful future with fewer mistakes." Thus, education is a kind of support mechanism and protection for girls. The report on drop outs also notes that girls do not quit schools to earn money but let parents, mostly mothers, work.

The decision to provide for children's education despite economic hardship may be strongly motivated by tendency of parents place a high value on education including the parents, who have not gone beyond secondary education. In most cases, parents who support children financially during their studies in higher education institutions have financial hardship themselves. The current tuition at Mongolian state universities and colleges varies by academic program type, averaging about US$300. Programs in high demand are more expensive than programs with lower demand. The tuition for medicine and pharmacy is the highest because of the length of study (five to six years) and other associated costs. Around 25 percent of students obtain "tuition fee" loans or grants from the government.

Annual non-tuition costs—food, accommodation and other personal expenses—are US$532 for students living with parents, US$892 for students living in dormitories, and US$1,972 for students renting a private apartment (Gantsog and Altantsetseg 2003). Compared to the average salary of people employed in Mongolia (around US$100 per month), college related expenses are high. Many parents struggle to send their children to universities, especially those who are the sole financial supporters for students. In fact, in most cases parents' incomes are much lower than tuition fees and living expenses required by their children who are students in higher education.

There is a general perception among Mongolian parents, including less educated parents, that higher education for their children is the only way to upgrade one's social status and live a life with fewer struggles. For that reason, college education seems to be some kind of door to a better life with better jobs and, most importantly for them, better income. Interestingly, most nomadic parents in Mongolia who had been working all their lives looking after livestock and had a strong work ethic tied to manual work desired that their children continue in school, asserting strongly that schooling and higher education is their only chance for a secure economic future.

For both parents and children in Mongolia, no matter what their social status, education is desired. Almost without exception, respondents in our study had a desire to continue their education in order to gain increased control over their own lives. Our female respondents did "not embrace the fantasies that they will be taken care of by men," and consequently, they see education as a bridge to "freedom." Thus, it was not surprising to see that most Mongolian families see higher education for girls not only as a way of gaining financial and social independence but also as a way of gaining gender independence. This can be seen from one respondent's comment that "parents were ready to do anything to get us to university." Another respondent commented "in my generation people believe that if they do not get university education, they get nothing."

For some Mongolian families, supporting educational attainment serves as just as tangible a resource as passing on material goods. There seems to be a tendency among Mongolian families to bequeath physical resources—livestock and assets—to their sons while daughters get more intangible resources such as education. Mongolians prefer to empower women through knowledge. Men, they believe, have power and enough physical strength to survive with or without an education and can make a livelihood in more ways than women can. All respondents in our study expressed that they experienced family influence on their decision to enroll in higher education.

Theme 2. Social Factors

From the interviews, it became clear that social factors have a great impact on life choices and, consequently, on college choice. Interview respondents named two important social factors that contribute to the reverse gender gap in Mongolian higher education. The urban and rural divide that exists in Mongolia at the moment, particularly internal migration from the countryside to the cities, and the Mongolian government's neglect of rural schools were named as the most important factors influencing the feminization of higher education. Interestingly, some respondents also talked about the consequences of socialist rule in Mongolia for over 70 years prior to the transition to a market economy as one of the main reasons for the gender imbalance in Mongolian higher education.

The rural life of nomadic people, moving in search of best pastures and campsites for their livestock, is humble and simple, without most modern conveniences such as running water, sanitation facilities, electricity, etc. Urban life, on the contrary, has all the attributes of modern development that exist in big cities everywhere around the world. Since life in the countryside is tough and urban life is regarded as easier, many modern nomads wish for a life other than herding for themselves and their children; as a result they migrate to urban areas.

Related to the rural and urban divide, respondents named the collapse of *bagh* (rural settlement) schools in remote areas together with dormitories as one of the most important reasons why there are fewer males than females in Mongolian higher education. Right after the collapse of the socialist system in the mid and late 1900s, many small primary schools in *baghs* were shut down during structural adjustment reforms advocated by the World Bank, among others, which led to a significant reduction in the proportion of Mongolian government expenditures on the social sector, including education, health and social welfare. Boarding facilities for nomadic children attending school in villages, towns (*soums*) and provinces (*aimags*) were closed during the 1990s, but were re-opened later.

Schools and dormitories are important for herders' children because schools, for the most part, are fixed location resources. Children must live in dormitories because their nomadic families may reside hundreds of miles of away from settled areas. While children spend most of the year in dormitories, they go home twice a year: once during winter vacation, which usually coincides with lunar new year, the biggest holiday for herders, and during summer vacation for a full three months. In some cases, children spend hours on horseback to get to the dormitories twice a year, which can be particularly brutal in hot summers and cold winters.

Facing the pressures of family and work, rural Mongolian students must often attend classes in less than ideal facilities. Many schools and dormitories in remote rural areas suffer from poor sanitation and overcrowded dormitories, further discouraging children from staying in school. To this day, many rural schools and dormitories are not sufficiently heated during long cold winters because of the high cost of fuel. As result of the urban and rural divide, migration and closure of rural schools, males continue to drop out more than females at the secondary school level. Other factors include the need to work or help at home, distance from school, lack of transport, family moving or emigrating, and teacher or school conditions.

Theme 3. Economic Factors

A wide range of employment opportunities became available for Mongolian boys in both rural and urban areas of the country in conjunction with the shift from a centrally planned economy to a market economy (Mongolian Education Alliance 2005). Particularly in rural areas, as farm lands and the rural economy move towards growth and reform, families find it more economically rewarding to keep boys in farming rather than sending them to school (UNICEF 2004). This is especially likely to happen with the eldest son who feels he is responsible for the well-being of younger siblings and the family as a whole (UNIFEM 2001). This is one reason why boys tend to choose a path of earning money rather than "spending their parents' money on higher education," especially for families from lower socioeconomic backgrounds. Sons from these families want to start working to earn money and be independent at an early age so they do not burden their parents with worries about the cost of gaining an education.

In urban areas in Mongolia, as the economy transitioned and the service economy grew, it became possible for males to get relatively high paying jobs that did not require higher education. Mongolia's development during the 1990s witnessed a sharp contraction in manufacturing as formerly state owned enterprises collapsed and government employment was reduced. This resulted in large numbers of redundant workers in the formal employment sector. Women and men who were formerly secure in government enterprises and public service became unemployed and underemployed or entered the informal economy. Boys tended to become engaged in earning money right after graduation or even before completing secondary school (Mongolian Education Alliance 2005). Many Mongolian families became involved in different types of business activities, particularly cross-border trading activities, buying and reselling different types of goods from Russia and China. This included buying raw livestock materials including wool, cashmere, rawhide, skins and meat in urban areas from nomadic people and then reselling them in Ulaanbaatar, the capital city. Other people bought inexpensive items such as food, clothing, fabric, furniture, construction materials and other things from

Erlan, a Chinese town located on the border between China and Mongolia, and sold it in Mongolia in order to profit on the price difference.

Different types of vending in the streets also evolved, with the informal sector playing an important role in the transition economy (Morris 2002). Trade also involves a lot of manual work, with siblings often teaming up to save on travel costs. According to the United Nations Development Programme's (UNDP) Sub-Sector Review of Microfinance, 30 percent of Mongolia's Gross Domestic Product (GDP) is attributed to the informal sector, with 30 percent of the employed population's primary income derived from the informal sector (UNDP 2005).

Another important reason why Mongolian males do not enroll in higher education is related to the availability of high paying employment opportunities existing for men in other regional countries, including the Republic of Korea which is estimated to have a Mongolian population of 30,000 (Tsogtsaikhan 2008). Considering that the population of Mongolia is 2.6 million, at least one out of every 100 Mongolians is working in the Republic of Korea. The Government of South Korea estimates that one out of every two urban households in Mongolia has a family member working in South Korea. Furthermore, there is still a large number of Mongolians seeking to go to South Korea for work. The main purpose of people working in Korea is to make money for their families and their country. Many of the approximately 9,500 Mongolian nationals living in South Korea are illegal immigrants doing the most difficult, dangerous, and dirty work—referred to as the "3Ds"—in small- and medium-scale factories. Since the work that is available there for immigrant workers is related to heavy industry, which requires manual labor, Koreans want recruited workers to be men, particularly young men, who can perform heavy work (Tsogtsaikhan 2008). However, working abroad requires young Mongolian men to forego the opportunity to enroll in higher education, something they seem glad to do because of the relatively high salaries they are paid.

Many Mongolians immigrate to other counties including Germany, the United States, Japan, Hungary, the Czech Republic, the United Kingdom, and others to look for better financial opportunities. It is estimated that around 130,000 Mongolians live abroad (Tsogtsaikhan 2008). At this rate, Mongolia is likely to turn into a country heavily reliant on remittances. According to the World Bank, inward remittance to Mongolia, which is officially recorded at US$182 million, made up 7 percent of total GDP in 2006 (World Bank 2008). The true size of remittances, including unrecorded flow through formal and informal channels, is believed to be larger.

Theme 4. Institutional Factors

Interesting outcomes of this study are related to institutional factors explaining feminization of Mongolian higher education. Interview respondents pointed out that factors related to structural problems existing in the Mongolian education system, including tertiary education, have effects on reverse gender balance in higher education in Mongolia. Most interview respondents expressed the belief that females perform better in school and cope better with the post communist transition. It is interesting that most of the respondents tied men's underperformance in school and struggle with the transition period to problems with the education system.

Female respondents expressed their ideas about male students' underachievement in school using strong language such as "lazy," "not committed," "laid back," "irresponsible," "not diligent," and so on. Boys' underperformance in schools may be related to socioeconomic conditions within the country. With the transition from a centrally planned to a market economy in the last 15 years, many families had low salaries. Parents had been busy with their own problems and paid less attention to the academic performance of their children. A professor from the National University of Mongolia we interviewed believes that girls were better able to cope with the post communist transition because they were not expected to do the hard labor associated with tending livestock.

Some education experts emphasized that the school system itself encourages young people to leave before they reach the university level. Women's dominance simply reflects their success all the way through the three major sets of exams, in Grades 5, 8 and 10. Since there are not enough schools—especially in the countryside—to allow everyone to enter Grade 9, there is intense pressure on students to get high grades on exams in Grade 8. One male respondent, a third-year undergraduate studying chemistry at the National University of Mongolia, said that by the time he was in Grade 10, he was one of only seven boys in a class of 29. Now he is one of three men in a class of 17. He adds that as a result of underachievement in secondary school, boys do not get high enough scores on entrance exams for higher education institutions.

The university professor believes that sifting out students in Grade 8 is wrong. According to him, "because boys are usually more mobile, they tend not to show the best results at school during their teenage years." Furthermore, he added "boys usually become more responsible in the final grades of secondary school. Therefore, it is too bad if they drop out of school at Grade 8. The more accurate and concentrated ones stay, and as a rule, they are girls." He also said that "women also perform better than men at places like the National University of Mongolia." He added: "looking over the scores on a recent entrance exam in the Mongolian-language department, eight of the top ten students are women. In economics, women are seven of the top ten students; in science departments, women account for about half of the top ten." When we asked why the gap exists, he answered "Perhaps women are more hard-working." "Boys are lazy" seems to be the typical explanation among parents and female respondents attending university. Boys also lack role models in schools, where 75 percent of the teachers are women (MECS 2008). There are critiques that the education system itself, with mostly women teachers, does not motivate male students to study hard.

Some of our respondents said that bad companions who were involved with drinking and crime were also reasons for boys to drop out of school and not continue to higher education. Boys are especially vulnerable to getting distracted, becoming involved with and being influenced by bad companions. That is why, once influenced by bad companions and becoming addicted to drinking, some Mongolian men unconsciously choose other paths of life rather than higher education. Alcohol dependence rates in Mongolia are very high and alcoholism is becoming quite common, especially in rural areas (Ministry of Health [MOH]/World Health Organization [WHO] 2006). A recent WHO-sponsored alcohol use survey found that 22 percent of men and five percent of women were dependent on alcohol. Mean alcohol consumption among men was three times higher than for women (MOH/WHO 2006).

DISCUSSION

The findings of this research show that the reasons for lower participation of males than females in Mongolian higher education are complex. The findings suggest that many of the reasons for the reverse gender gap in higher education are closely related to Mongolia's continuing transition from a centrally planned to a market economy. Some of the reasons are related to unique traditions and a nomadic lifestyle that Mongolians have led for centuries. In addition, the consequences and structural elements of the socialist period have had an impact on gender equity in higher education.

The findings of this research suggest that the reverse gender gap in education has long roots and feminization of the higher education subsector has not happened over night. This gender gap starts in secondary education, with many more girls than boys dropping out at this level. Common reasons for boys dropping out of school are privatization of livestock and family poverty. It seems that lack of motivation or interest, in addition to underperformance in school, contributes to adolescent boys dropping out of school. Other factors include the need to work or help at home, distance from school, lack of transport, family moving or emigrating, influence of friends who are themselves drop-outs, teacher or school conditions, and foregoing education for employment either at home or abroad.

Consequently, it is important to preserve access to education and retain students from poor families, especially boys. The government needs to take action to eliminate child labor and have policies to support children from poor families to ensure access to education and retention in school to prevent poverty from being transmitted from one generation to another, creating a permanent "underclass" of poor and unemployed. Excluding the poor from education represents a loss to society and to the economy. The government needs to strengthen the education "pipeline" through improvements in primary and secondary schooling, especially for poor and disadvantaged male students.

While men are out trying to find work in a variety of different types of jobs associated with a burgeoning market economy in order to earn money to help their families, Mongolian women are acquiring education and skills that are necessary for longer term prosperity. The findings of our study show that there are many institutional, economic, social, and cultural reasons behind this phenomenon. In the future, joblessness, inadequate education and inability to support themselves and their families among Mongolian men might damage the gender balance in society even further. In particular, if this situation of gender imbalance in higher education and society continues long enough, it may negatively affect social life, especially family life.

Raising awareness of the existing gender imbalance in higher education is important for policy makers because the issue lies on the intersection of many fields, including education, health and labor. It is important for educators, political leaders, and the media to concentrate time, resources, and attention on the male students who are in greatest danger of being left behind in the educational pipeline, unable to meet the demands of the market economy for highly educated workers. Meanwhile, Mongolian society will be under pressure to lower the "glass ceiling" for highly educated women, allowing them to assume positions commensurate with their advanced educational qualifications.

NOTE

1. This chapter is a revised version of a paper originally presented at the Annual Conference of the Association for the Study of Higher Education (ASHE), Vancouver, British Columbia, Canada, 7 November 2009.

REFERENCES

Adiya, Enkhjargal. (2010). "Gender Equity in Access to Higher Education in Mongolia." PhD diss., Administrative and Policy Studies, School of Education, University of Pittsburgh, USA.

Becker, Gary S. (1993). *Human Capital: A Theoretical and Empirical Analysis, With Special Reference to Education.* 3rd ed. Chicago: The University of Chicago Press.

Creswell, John W. (2003). *Research Design: Qualitative, Quantitative, and Mixed Methods Approaches.* Thousand Oaks, CA: Sage.

Davaa, Suren, Pagma Batrinchin, Sambuu Altangerel, Densmaa Dungerdorj, & Batjav Bayartsetseg. (2005). *Higher Education Study Team Report.* Ulaanbaatar: Ministry of Education, Culture and Science (MECS).

Gantsog, Tserensodnom, & Altantsetseg Sodnomtseren. (2003). *Globalization, WTO and Mongolian Higher Education.* New YorK: International Policy Fellowships, Open Society Institute. Available online at: http://www.policy.hu.

Government of Mongolia. (2007). *Implementation of Millennium Development Goals. Second National Report.* Ulaanbaatar: Government of Mongolia.

Hatch, J. Amos. (2002). *Doing Qualitative Research in Education Settings.* Albany, NY: State University of New York Press.

Jorgensen, Danny L. (1989). *Participant Observation: A Methodology for Human Studies.* Newbury Park, CA: Sage.

Lewin, Tamar. (2006). "At Colleges, Women Are Leaving Men in the Dust." *The New York Times, CLV.* No. 53, July 9, 635.

Lin-Liu, Jen. (2005). "Mongolia Reverse Gender Gap." *The Chronicle of Higher Education, 51*(22), A39.

Magno, Cathryn, & Iveta Silova. (2008). "Divergent Trends in Higher Education in the Post-Socialist Transition." *International Studies in Education, 9*(1), 6–10.

McDonough, Patricia M. (1997). *Choosing Colleges: How Social Class and Schools Structure Opportunity.* Albany, NY: State University of New York Press.

Miles, Matthew B., & A. Michael Huberman. (1994). *Qualitative Data Analysis.* 2nd ed. Thousand Oaks, CA: Sage.

Ministry of Education, Culture and Science (MECS). (2007). *MECS Statistics.* Ulaanbaatar: MECS. Available online at: http://mecs.pmis.gov.mn.

MECS. (2008). *MECS Statistics.* Ulaanbaatar: MECS. Available online at: http://mecs.pmis.gov.mn.

Ministry of Health/World Health Organization (WHO). (2006). *Epidemiological Study on Prevalence of Alcohol Consumption, Alcohol Drinking Patterns and Alcohol Related Harms in Mongolia.* Ulaanbaatar: Ministry of Health/WHO.

Mongolian Education Alliance. (2005). *The Mongolian Drop Out Study.* Ulaanbaatar: Mongolian Education Alliance.

Morris Elizabeth. (2002). *The Informal Sector in Mongolia: Profiles, Needs and Strategies.* Bangkok: International Labour Organization.

Nozaki, Yoshiko, Rima Aranha, Rachel Fix-Dominguez, & Yuri Nakajima. (2009). "Gender Gap and Women's Participation in Higher Education: Views from Japan, Mongolia, and India." In Alexander W. Wiseman and David P. Baker (Ed.), *International Perspectives on Education and Society: Gender, Equality, and Education from International and Comparative Perspectives,* Vol. 10, (pp. 217–254). Bingley, UK: Emerald Group Publishing.

Novak, Joseph D., & D. Bob Gowin. (1984). *Learning How to Learn.* New York; Cambridge, UK: Cambridge University Press.

Paulston, Rolland G., & Martin Liebman. (2000). "Social Cartography: A New Methaphor/Tool for Comparative Studies." In Rolland G. Paulston (Ed.), *Social Cartography: Mapping Ways of Seeing Social and Educational Change* (pp. 7–28). Pittsburgh: University of Pittsburgh Book Center.

Seidel, John V. (1998). *Qualitative Data Analysis.* Colorado Springs, CO: Qualis Research. Available online at www.qualisresearch.com.

Seidel, John V., & Klaus U. Kelle. (1995). "Different Functions of Coding in the Analysis of Data." In Klaus U. Kelle (Ed.), *Computer Aided Qualitative Data Analysis: Theory, Methods, and Practice* Thousand Oaks, CA: Sage.

Spradley, James P. (1979). *The Ethnographic Interview.* New York: Holt Rinehart, and Wilson.

Tsogtsaikhan, Bolormaa. (2008). *Demographic Changes and Labor Migration in Mongolia.* Singapore: Pacific Economic Cooperation Council (PECC). Available online at: http://www.pecc.org.

United Nations Children's Fund (UNICEF). (2004). *Mongolia: Fostering Partnerships with Parents.* New York: UNICEF. Availabale online at: http://www.unicef.org.

United Nations Development Fund for Women (UNIFEM). (2001). *Women in Mongolia. Mapping Progress Under Transition.* Ulaanbaatar: UNIFEM.

United Nations Development Programme (UNDP). (2005). *Sub-Sector Review of Microfinance in Mongolia.* Ulaanbaatar: UNDP.

Weidman, John C., & Regsuren Bat-Erdene. (2002). "Higher Education and the State in Mongolia: Dilemmas of Democratic Transition." In David W. Chapman and Ann E. Austin (Ed.), *Higher Education in the Developing World: Changing Contexts and Institutional Responses* (pp. 129–148). Westport, CT: Greenwood Press.

Weidman, John C., David W. Chapman, Marc Cohen, & Macrina Lelei. (2004). "Access to Education in Five Newly Independent States of Central Asia and Mongolia: A Regional Agenda." In Stephen P. Heyneman and Alan J. DeYoung (Ed.), *Challenges for Education in Central Asia* (pp. 181–197). Greenwich, CT: Information Age Publishing.

World Bank. (2008). *Migration and Remittances Fact Book 2008.* Washington, DC: World Bank.

MARK B. GINSBURG, PEGGY NSAMA CHAKUFYALI, KALIMA
KALIMA, BENNY MWAANGA, AND WINNEHL TUBMAN

19. PROMOTING EVIDENCE-BASED POLICY
PLANNING AND IMPLEMENTATION
IN EDUCATION IN ZAMBIA

INTRODUCTION

Over his long and illustrious career at the University of Pittsburgh, Rolland G. Paulston focused his keen intellect toward charting the theoretical and methodological terrains on which academic and professional work in the field of comparative and international education took place. Initially, this took the form of a typology that grouped theories of educational change under either an equilibrium or a conflict paradigm (Paulston 1976, 1977), and then later a two-dimensional, four-celled typology, differentiating functionalist, radical functionalist, radical humanist, and humanist perspectives (Paulston 1980). Subsequently, Paulston's energies moved toward the task of locating various social theories on two- and sometimes three-dimensional "maps" (Paulston 1994, 1996).

Thus, it is not surprising that one of Paulston's intellectual passions was to "type" or "map" each person whom he worked with—and many others whom he mainly came to know through their writings—to a particular place in various two- or multidimensional spaces. For instance, Pauston labeled one of us as a radical functionalist, even though Ginsburg (a colleague of Paulston's in Pittsburgh from 1987–2004) perceived his work as more in line with versions of critical theory, which could be situated in the paradigmatic territory Paulston defined as radical humanist. Similarly, Carnoy (2006, 563) reports that "Rolland Paulston, spent many years classifying methodological approaches in comparative and international education. . . . Paulston liked to call my own work radical functionalism."

It is important to note that Paulston also highlighted (via his typing and mapping) differences in methodological approaches. However, this work appears to be less well known to colleagues outside of Pittsburgh. For instance, Rust and colleagues (1999, 87) write that in the 1970s and 1980s Paulston and other "conflict theorists successfully challenged the so-called equilibrium paradigm . . . ; however, [they] were more concerned with theory than research methodology, and [thus] . . . failed to raise fundamental considerations regarding research methods." Nevertheless, in addition to teaching for many years a course entitled "Theories of Educational Change," Paulston also taught a course on "Evaluation of [International] Education Projects." In this latter course, he introduced students to the epistemological roots of various evaluation methodologies, grouped under

John C. Weidman, W. James Jacob (eds.), Beyond the Comparative: Advancing Theory and Its Application to Practice, 355–370.

positivist and constructivist labels, as well as reminding students that projects and evaluations were grounded in one or the other social theory paradigm.

His concern with categorizing or mapping methodological approaches is mentioned briefly in some of his early work mainly focused on presenting typologies of social theories. For example, Paulston (1976, 39) states:

> Where functionalists view education change from the needs of total social systems, and conflict-theory adherents explain reforms as a function of power rather than need, a non-Marxist dialectical [read as constructivist] perspective provides no *a priori* answers . . . . Rather, the dialectic is an empirical approach, a way of knowing suitable for . . . [recognizing] many types of duality that appear in continually changing social wholes, from complementarily and mutual implication to ambiguity, ambivalence, and polarization.

And about the time that Rust and colleagues wrote the above-quoted comment, Paulson collaborated with an Argentine student/colleague to map approaches to evaluation (Paulston and Gorostiaga 1998; Gorostiaga and Paulston 1999). In their social cartography of this professional field they focus on seven evaluation approaches, noting that "[m]ethodological and political implications can be suggested using two dimensions: the participatory versus expert-based dimension (considering the level and scope of stakeholder participation) and the constructivism versus ontological essentialism [read as positivism]" (Gorostiaga and Paulston 1999, 25).

Ginsburg does not recall Paulston ever "typing" or "mapping" him based on his research methodological orientation. However, he believes that Paulston would have classified him as working within the constructivist or critical ethnographic tradition, given the nature of the research that many of his students and he undertook while he was a faculty member at the University of Pittsburgh (e.g., see Ginsburg 1995; Ginsburg and Tidwell 1995; Al-Harthi and Ginsburg 2003; Megahed and Ginsburg 2003; Cordova and Ginsburg 2006).

In this contribution to the Festschrift in honor of Rolland Paulston, we describe our approach to and selected findings from an evaluation of a multi-pronged, U.S. Agency for International Development (USAID)-funded "reform" project in Zambia. We conclude by imagining how Rolland might map this team effort.

EQUIP2/ZAMBIA AND INTEREST IN EVIDENCE-BASED DECISION MAKING

The Educational Quality Improvement Program (EQUIP2/Zambia, 2004–2008 and 2008–2011) is a USAID-funded activity to provide "technical assistance to the Ministry of Education (MOE) to improve the quality of basic education throughout Zambia.[1] EQUIP2/Zambia works collaboratively with the Ministry to build its capacity help it achieve its goals, and fulfill its mandate of providing life-long quality education for all citizens" (AED et al., 2008). More specifically, EQUIP2 seeks to strengthen MOE capacity in institutional management, school health and nutrition, HIV/AIDS workplace programs, information management systems, information and communication technology, monitoring and evaluation, and policy and research. Among the goals to be achieved with support from EQUIP2/Zambia are:

- Provide technical assistance and capacity building to enhance the policy formulation and analysis efforts of central and provincial officials and staff;
- Support the institutional strengthening of national, provincial, district and school structures to provide quality education;
- Assist the MOE's Directorate of Planning in developing a monitoring and evaluation system for tracking the education sector objectives;
- Build the MOE's and the education sector's research capacity;
- Improve a system for collecting and processing the annual school census data; and
- Strengthen information gathering and flow and the use of evidence-based decision making in the MOE at all levels. (AED et al., 2008)

EQUIP2/Zambia operated in a national and international context in which there were increasing calls for using data and other information in policy planning, and implementation decisions, activity which requires productive and cooperative working relations between researchers and decision makers (Ginsburg and Gorostiaga 2003). The push was for "evidence-based" decision making, "analytically based" decision making (Auriat 1998), "evaluation utilization" in decision making (Cousins and Leithwood 1986), "knowledge use" in decision making (Dunn 1986), and "research utilization" in decision making (Weiss 1991). That is, rather than only drawing on assumptions and theories, communication and argumentation, tradition, or experience, decision makers should make systematic use of official statistics, research and evaluations studies when establishing or reforming policies, developing or refining plans, and implementing or adapting policies and plans.

In the case of Zambia, as early as 1996 the Ministry stated that it "will support and inform its decision-making . . . by a more systematic use of research" (MOE 1996, 179). More recently, in 2006 it called for "conduct[ing] focused policy relevant studies and reviews in response to identified policy gaps [and] . . . improv[ing] information management systems that are responsive to the needs of the education and training sector at all levels" (GRZ 2006, 153). And in 2010 it once again emphasized that "[i]n order for policy makers and practitioners to effectively and efficiently implement the strategies and programmes to achieve the objectives they need to have reliable evidence to inform their decisions. This requires the regular collection and maintenance of data as part of a management information system as well as periodic research studies on high priority topics" (GRZ 2010, 18).

FOCUS OF THE RESEARCH AND METHODOLOGY

The study briefly reported here was part of an "outcomes survey" designed to inform project staff, Ministry officials, and USAID personnel about the degree of and reasons for progress in enhancing the effectiveness of various aspects of the functioning of the education sector.[2] Specifically, the questions we address here are:

M.B. GINSBURG ET AL.

1. To what extent do stakeholders perceive that the effectiveness of the following aspects of the Zambian education system (at the district, provincial, and national levels) has improved between 2005 and 2009:

   a. engaging in *policy planning and implementation* (PPI)?
   b. conducting *monitoring, evaluation, and research* (MER)?
   c. developing and using an *education management information system* (EMIS)?

2. Why do stakeholders perceive that this improvement in effectiveness of the Zambian education system (at the district, provincial, and national levels) occurred between 2005 and 2009?

3. To what extent do variations in perceived improvements in the effectiveness in MER and in EMIS explain variations in perceived improvements in PPI at the district, provincial, and national levels in Zambia?

To address these research questions we directed a team of field researchers to collect data in April 2009 from 327 respondents,[3] including national-, provincial-, district-, and school-level Ministry of Education personnel as well as representatives of cooperating partners (i.e., bilateral development agencies) and civil society (i.e., key Zambian NGOs involved in education). We sampled education personnel in 27 of the 72 districts, three from each of Zambia's nine provinces. Education personnel and other respondents were asked to rate the effectiveness of certain aspects of the system above and/or below them (but not their own level). In the end this yielded perceptions of district-level effectiveness from 65 provincial- and school-level respondents; 118 perceptions of provincial-level effectiveness from national- and district-level respondents as well as respondents from colleges of education; and 54 perceptions of national-level effectiveness from provincial-level personnel, university staff, and civil society and international organization representatives.

The questionnaire included a set of items which were combined to form a scale for each aspect of the education system under study. See Tables 19.1, 19.2, and 19.3 for specific items used to form each scale and the reliability of each scale for responses focused on the district, provincial, and national levels.

For each item, respondents were asked to indicate their perception of effectiveness for a specified level both for 2005 and for 2009, using the following response categories:

1. = not at all effective
2. = somewhat effective
3. = effective
4. = very effective
5. = extremely effective

In addition, respondents were encouraged to write in their explanations of why they thought this level of the education system had or had not become more effective in the specified area of functioning between 2005 and 2009.

Table 19.1. Items for Measuring Perceived Effectiveness in
Policy, Planning, and Evaluation (PPI)

Items	National		Provincial		District	
analyzing and interpreting policies	X		X		X	
developing (***-level) policies	X		X		X	
developing annual work plans	X		X		X	
long-term educational planning	X		X		X	
implementing policies and plans	X		X		X	
involving civil society/community in planning and other decisions	X		X		X	
Delegating decision-making authority to lower levels of the system	X		X		X	
Reliability (Cronbach's alpha)	2005 .89	2009 .81	2005 .85	2009 .89	2005 .89	2009 .87

To answer the research questions 1a, 1b, and 1c, we analyzed the data using a t-test to assess the significance of the difference between the respective means for 2005 and 2009.[4] To answer research question 2, we undertook a content analysis of the responses to the open-ended questions on the questionnaires. To answer research question 3, we used linear regression analysis to detect the size and the significance of the effects of the independent variables (MER and EMIS) on the dependent variable (PPI).

FINDINGS

Our presentation of the findings is organized around the three research questions.

Changes in Effectiveness

The findings related to the first set of research questions are presented in Tables 19.4, 19.5, and 19.6. With respect to the perceived effectiveness in the education system's functioning in the area of PPI (see Table 19.4), we observe that on average respondents reported that between 2005 and 2009 the system at each level improved about a half of point (0.5 or 0.6) on the five-point scale. The perceived movement at the district, provincial, and national levels of effectiveness was from somewhat below "effective" (2.6, 2.8, and 2.9, respectively) to somewhat above effective (3.1, 3.3, and 3.5, respectively), though less than "very effective" (4.0). Although at each level the difference between 2005 and 2009 perceptions of effectiveness was significant, we should note that these represent rather modest gains over a four-year period (0.5 equals one eighth of the total scale range).

Table 19.2. Items for Measuring Perceived Effectiveness in Monitoring, Evaluation, and Research (MER)

Items	National		Provincial		District	
monitoring/evaluating implementation of policies and plans	X		X		X	
using data (generally) to inform decision making	X		X		X	
establishing an agenda of priority research	X		X		X	
supervising contracted research	X		X		X	
designing and conducting research	X		X		X	
setting targets	X				X	
selecting and defining indicators	X				X	
discussing target with stakeholders	X				X	
analyzing and interpreting data	X		X		X	
communicating findings from research	X		X		X	
Reliability (Cronbach's alpha)	2005 .92	2009 .92	2005 .93	2009 .93	2005 .93	2009 .94

Table 19.3. Items for Measuring Perceived Effectiveness in Education Management Information Systems (EMIS)

Items	National		Provincial		District	
collecting data for Annual School Census	X		X		X	
assuring the quality of Annual School Census data	X		X		X	
analyzing and interpreting EMIS data	X		X		X	
using EMIS data in making decisions	X		X		X	
producing & distributing Education Statistics Bulletin	X					
producing and distributing the Ed*Assist CD	X					
providing training programmes to ensure stakeholders are able to make use of the EMIS data			X			
building capacity within schools to collect data for ASC and make use of school profile & school records for decision making					X	
Reliability (Cronbach's alpha)	2005 .90	2009 .92	2005 .91	2009 .87	2005 .90	2009 .91

Table 19.4. Perceived Effectiveness in the Area of
Policy, Planning, and Implementation (PPI)

Level	Year 2005	Year 2009	Difference	Significance
National Level	2.9	3.5	+0.6	<.001
Provincial Level	2.8	3.3	+0.5	<.001
District Level	2.6	3.1	+0.5	<.001

With respect to the perceived effectiveness in the education system's functioning in the area of MER (see Table 19.5), we observe that on average respondents reported that between 2005 and 2009 the system at each level improved just under a half of point (0.4) on the five-point scale. In the case of the national level, the movement was from somewhat below "effective" (2.7) to somewhat above "effective" (3.1). In the case of the district and provincial levels, perceived effectiveness remained between "somewhat effective" (2.0) and "effective" (3.0), with the 2005 figures (2.3) being closer to the former and the 2009 figures (2.7) being closer to the latter. Although at each level the difference between 2005 and 2009 perceptions of effectiveness was significant, we should note again that these represent rather modest gains over a four-year period (0.4 equals one tenth of the total scale range).

Table 19.5. Perceived Effectiveness in the Area of
Monitoring, Evaluation, and Research (MER)

Level	Year 2005	Year 2009	Difference	Significance
National Level	2.7	3.1	+0.4	<.001
Provincial Level	2.3	2.7	+0.4	<.001
District Level	2.3	2.7	+0.4	<.001

With respect to the perceived effectiveness in the education system's functioning in the area of *developing and using an* EMIS (see Table 19.6), we observe that on average respondents reported that between 2005 and 2009 the system at each level improved about a half of point (0.4 or 0.5) on the five-point scale. In the case of the national level, the movement was from just above "effective" (3.1) to midway between "effective" and "very effective" (3.5). In the case of the district and provincial levels, perceived effectiveness moved from somewhat below "effective" (2.7 and 2.9, respectively) to somewhat above "effective" (3.1 and 3.4, respectively). Although at each level the difference between 2005 and 2009 perceptions of effectiveness was significant, we should note again that these represent rather modest gains over a four-year period (0.4 equals one tenth of the total scale range).

Table 19.6. Perceived Effectiveness in the Area of Developing and Using
an Education Management Information System (EMIS)

Level	Year 2005	Year 2009	Difference	Significance
National Level	3.1	3.5	+0.4	.002
Provincial Level	2.9	3.4	+0.5	<.001
District Level	2.7	3.1	+0.4	<.001

Reasons for the Changes

Our second research question draws on the qualitative data provided by some respondents who indicated on the questionnaire what factors they believed facilitated or inhibited improvement in effectiveness in a given area of the education sectors functioning. Across the aspects of the education system (policy planning and implementation; monitoring, evaluation, and research; and developing and using EMIS), the following categories of facilitating factors were mentioned:

1. Enhanced individual capacity and commitment
2. Increased number of personnel
3. Improved guidelines and procedures
4. Increased financial resources

Another facilitating factor, involving members of civil society, was mentioned in relation to PPI and MER, but not EMIS. Also, across the three aspects of the education system, the following categories of inhibiting factors were identified:

1. Additional capacity building needs
2. Centralized system remains
3. Limited monitoring and coordination
4. Limited/poor communication
5. Insufficient funding

To illustrate, respondents at all three levels of the system mentioned increased staffing levels and civil society involvement in explaining why they perceived improvement in effectiveness in the area of PPI:

- National: "Staffing in departments increased to an adequate level" and "There was a greater involvement of the civil society in the Joint Annual Review meetings."
- Provincial: "There were more trained personnel filling positions" and "There was greater community participation in planning and implementation."
- District: "There were more staff to give proper attention to such activities" and "The involvement of boards and the community in planning has helped improve the effectiveness in the districts."

As another example, respondents at all levels of the system emphasized communication as a key inhibitor to greater improvement in effectiveness in relation to MER:

- National: "Unfortunately, there is little awareness on research being carried out."
- Provincial: "There is not enough communication of findings to the lower levels [of the system] after the research has been conducted."
- District: "There is not enough communication of findings to the lower levels after research reports have been written."

With respect to increased effectiveness of the system in the aspect of developing and using EMIS, respondents at all levels of the system mentioned enhanced financial human resources and capacity building as key facilitators:

- National: "There are adequate financial resources to manage EMIS" and "The availability of technical assistance has helped build the capacity of staff at the lower levels."
- Provincial: "There were more financial resources available" and "Capacity building helped improve the effectiveness of the province in EMIS systems use and interpretation" and
- District: "Increased funding has made it possible to deploy more staff" and "There was a lot of capacity building involved."

The Effect of MER and EMIS on PPI

Figures 19.1–19.3 present in path diagram form the results of the regression analysis, which address the third research question.[5] First, we observe that the two independent variables, the scales measuring perceived effectiveness in MER and developing and using an EMIS are strongly and significantly correlated for the national, provincial, and district level data (.77, .62, and .72, respectively, in 2005 and .81, .60, .71, respectively, for 2009). This means that to a relatively great extent if respondents perceived the system as more effective on one aspect, they also tended to see the system as effective on the other aspect. This multicolinearity also makes it more complicated to interpret the regression coefficients (betas) that identify the strength of the impact of each independent variable on the dependent variable (perceived effectiveness in the area of PPI). In particular, while we focus on the direct effects on PPI of one of the independent variables, while controlling for the other independent variable, we should also consider the indirect effects (i.e., MER→EMIS→PPI and EMIS→MER→PPI).

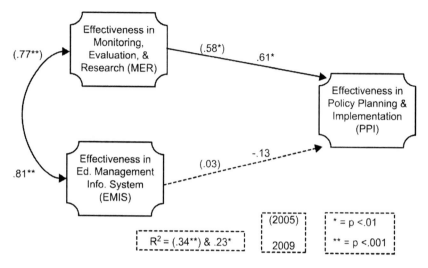

Figure 19.1. Relationships between Measures of Effectiveness of EMIS, MER, and PPI: National Level.

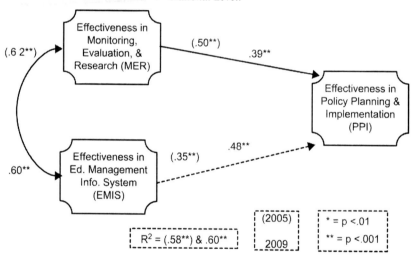

Figure 19.2. Relationships between Measures of Effectiveness of EMIS, MER, and PPI: Provincial Level.

Second, the figures show that MER has a significant and moderately strong effect on PPI at all three levels (national, provincial, and district) for both years (with betas equal to .58, .50, and .40, respectively for 2005 and .61, .39, and .37, respectively, for 2009). This provides clear and consistent evidence that perceived effectiveness in the area of MER has a direct effect on (or at least a relationship with) perceived effectiveness in the area of PPI, even when controlling for the effects of EMIS.

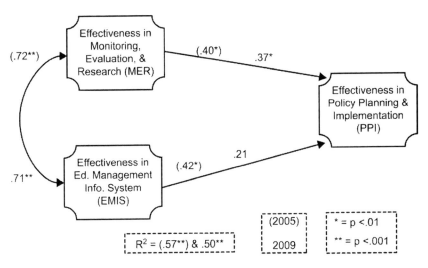

Figure 19.3. Relationships between Measures of Effectiveness of EMIS, MER, and PPI: District Level.

Third, the figures show that EMIS does not have a consistent, significant effect on PPI, when controlling for the effect of MER. Note that at the national level both the 2005 nor 2009 coefficients are small and not significant (.03 and -.13, respectively); at the provincial level both the 2005 and 2009 coefficients are moderately strong and significant (.35 and .48, respectively); and at the district level only the 2005 coefficient is significant (.42). This indicates clear evidence that, when controlling for the effects of MER, perceived effectiveness in the area of developing and using EMIS does not have a direct effect on perceived effectiveness in the area of PPI, although EMIS does directly affect PPI at provincial level. The situation at the district level is less clear, though it seems to be more similar to the provincial than the national level (the beta for 2005 is significant and the coefficient for 2009 just misses being significant).

DISCUSSION OF FINDINGS

The findings suggest that respondents perceived the effectiveness of all areas of functioning at the three levels of the education system to be significantly, but modestly, higher in 2009 compared to 2005. We cannot say for sure that such improvements are attributable to technical assistance and capacity building of the USAID-funded EQUIP2/Zambia. While the project sought to contribute to capacity building, developing/refining guidelines procedures, promote civil society involvement, and provide some supplementary funding—all things that respondents mentioned as facilitating improvement in effectiveness, there were also other projects and other international organizations supporting Zambia during this period. We should also note that the inhibiting factors (e.g., poor communication and limited monitoring and coordination) were also areas on which EQUIP2/Zambia and other international organization-supported initiatives focused, though clearly without complete success.

Moreover, variations in perceived effectiveness in the MER area and—to a lesser extent—perceived effectiveness in the area of developing and using EMIS accounted for a significant and substantial amount of the variation in the PPI area of functioning at each level of the education system. While our design does not allow us to draw unequivocal "causal" conclusions,[6] it appears that respondents saw improvements in the effectiveness in one area (PPI) as being relatively highly dependent on improvements in the effectiveness in the other areas (especially MER).

CONCLUSION

We conclude by imagining how Paulston might map this team effort. We begin with an admission that perhaps Paulston might get a migraine or indigestion[7] in trying to locate this work on one of his maps. Indeed, he might find that our work is all over the (theoretical and methodological) map. At the same time, we think that this initial headache or stomach upset would lead to a sense of relief—and perhaps excitement—because of our attempt to "embody" ideas from different paradigms in an evaluation of a project that was designed to support Zambia's goal of using data to inform policy/practice decisions.

If Paulston had a chance to read our work, we think he would be initially surprised, perhaps even dismayed,[8] that one of the members of our team (Ginsburg) had traveled such a great distance on the maps of social theories. As mentioned in the introduction, Paulston generally located Ginsburg's writings in the 1980s and 1990s under the conflict theory category of radical functionalism, which emphasizes "power, exploitation, [and] contradictions . . . [and in which] formal education is . . . viewed as a part of the ideological structure which a ruling class controls to maintain its control of knowledge and, thus, its privilege and cultural hegemony" (Paulston 1977, 386). Based on the above-reported evaluation study, Paulston might map our work as more in line with the functionalist paradigm or, more specifically, as reflecting a systems theory perspective within the equilibrium paradigm. As Paulston (1977, 383) writes:

> From the systems perspective, the need for change arises with evidence of system 'malfunctioning.' . . . [R]esearch and development . . . largely concentrates on the change process in isolation . . . [without attention to] who determines the 'malfunction.' . . . [Little, if any, attempt is made] to identify, include, and operationalize contextual variables, such as competing ideologies, power, [and] vested interests . . . ."

Locating our work closer to a functionalist than a conflict paradigm seems appropriate. That the work represents a different perspective than Ginsburg's other writing may reflect (a) a shift in Ginsburg's orientation, (b) the search for common theoretical ground within the team, and/or (c) the nature of the client/audience for the evaluation study (Government of the Republic of Zambia, USAID, and other multilateral/bilateral "donors"). However, we would note that in the background—and, therefore, less visible but not invisible—is a focus on issues of power. For example, two of the items used to measure the scale of "effectiveness in policy planning and implementation" are: (a) involving civil society/community in planning and other decisions and (b) delegating decision-making authority to lower levels of the system.

Paulston might also be surprised to see in this evaluation study such a strong emphasis on quantitative data and a survey research grounded in a positivist epistemology. Part of his surprise about Ginsburg's involvement in this type of study stems from the fact that, during his career just prior to and during his time in Pittsburgh, Ginsburg mainly pursued inquiries grounded in a constructivist or interpretivist methodological tradition. However, it is likely upon deeper reflection that Paulston would be less surprised, given that Ginsburg regularly taught a course in Pittsburgh on Disciplined Inquiry, which introduced and promoted positivist as well as interpretivist approaches and that Ginsburg's dissertation (Ginsburg 1976) and some of his early-career publications (e.g., O'Shea et al., 1976; Ginsburg and Redican 1980; Spatig et al., 1982) reflected a positivist epistemology.

Moreover, when he examined our methodology more closely, we are sure that Paulston would notice our effort to collect and analyze a mixture of quantitative and qualitative data. While it turned out that the open-ended questions did not yield as rich data as was hoped for, we tried to mine respondents' or participants' understandings of the reasons that change in effectiveness in the system's functioning occurred but only to a limited extent. And Paulston might call attention to the fact that our "quantitative" data were also based on subjective interpretations by people in different positions in relation to different levels of the system. That is, we invited them in 2009 to give us their perceptions of how "effective" various aspects of the system were in 2005 and 2009. We left to respondents both the definition of effective and the degree to which such obtained at two points in time.

However, regardless of whether he would be surprised, we are certain that Paulston would not be dismayed by our somewhat eclectic methodological approach. For instance, in his commentary on Psacharopolous' (1990) argument that only positivist forms of research have value in planning and other decision making in education, Paulston (1990, 396) offers "some markedly different proposals also seeking to improve the rigor and relevance of research on education by encouraging tolerance, and the utility of multiple approaches in knowledge production and use." Similarly, in his co-authored piece mapping approaches to program evaluation, one reads that "We think that it is very important to consider the possibility of combinations [of approaches] and even to consider the seven new approaches as part of a 'rich tool kit' for evaluators today" (Gorostiaga and Paulston 1999, 25).[9]

In closing, we would note that it would be much better if we did not have to imagine what Paulston would say about our work, but could actually share a draft with him for the depth and breadth of his insights. However, at least one of us was fortunate enough to have had the opportunity to do that over a number of years.

NOTES

1. In addition to this and other project funded by USAID, the Zambian government's efforts to improve educational quality was supported by other bilateral organizations, including the Embassy of Ireland, Japanese International Cooperation Agency, and Netherlands Development Organization. UNESCO, United Nations Children's Fund (UNICEF), United Nations Development Programme (UNDP), and the World Bank also are engaged in support of the education sector in Zambia.
2. Here we give attention to three related aspects: (a) policy, planning, and implementation; (b) monitoring, evaluation, and research; and (c) developing and utilizing education management information systems. In the larger evaluation study (Nsama Chakufyali et al., 2009) we also focused on: (d) budget-related activities; (e) building, maintaining, expanding, supporting, and using ICT resources; (f) developing health-related programs; and (g) implementing continuous assessment of students.
3. In fact, we collected data from 413 individuals, but not all of them were asked to answer questions dealing with the three aspects of the education system considered here.
4. For questions 1a, 1b, and 1c as well as question 3 we used a p value of less than or equal to .01 as the criterion of significance.
5. Note that the R^2 for each equation (for each level and each year) is moderately large and significant. For 2005 and 2009, respectively, the values of this statistic are .34 and .23 at the national level, .58 and .60 at the provincial level, and .57 and .50 at the district level. This indicates that a reasonable proportion of the variance in PPI is explained by the combination of the two independent variables (MER and EMIS).
6. When we collect a second wave of data in the fall of 2010, we anticipate being in a better—but not perfect—position to look at cause and effect.
7. These physiological metaphors are used here, in part, to recognize that Paulston, particularly in his latter career, was a strong proponent of "embodying" one's intellectual work.
8. We say dismayed because although Paulston sought in his work to be relatively heterodox, giving voice and providing space to multiple perspectives, he noted that "my personal bias is toward conflict theory" (Paulston 1976, 39). This self-categorization is thus similar to the earlier quoted classification by Rust and colleagues (1999), though in conversations Ginsburg had with him later in his career and when he mapped himself (see Paulston and Liebman 1996, 15), Paulston tended to locate his perspective closer to radical humanism or even humanism than to radical functionalism.
9. Ginsburg and colleagues (1996) make a similar point that the methodological choices in conducting research and evaluation studies are not necessarily mutually exclusive.

REFERENCES

Academy for Educational Development (AED), American Institutes for Research (AIR), and Research Triangle Institute (RTI). (2008). "EQUIP2/Zambia 2008–2010 Program Description." Proposal for Cooperative Agreement No. 690-A-00-04-00095-00. Washington, DC: AED, AIR, and RTI.
Al-Harthi, Hamood, & Mark B. Ginsburg. (2003). "Student-Faculty Power/Knowledge Relations: The Implications of the Internet in the College of Education, Sultan Qaboos University." *Current Issues in Comparative Education, 6*(1), 5–16. Available online at: http://www.tc.columbia.edu/CICE.
Auriat, Nadia. (1998). "Social Policy and Social Enquiry: Reopening Debate." *International Social Science Journal, 50*(156), 275–287.
Carnoy, Martin. (2006). "Rethinking the Comparative—and the International." *Comparative Education Review, 50*(4), 551–570.
Cordova, Victor, & Mark B. Ginsburg. (2006). "Hegemony, 'Mediated' Campus Struggles, and Political (In)Action: Extracurricular Political Socialization of Prospective Educators in Mexico." In Thomas Clayton (Ed.), *Rethinking Hegemony* (pp. 133–148). Albert Park, Australia: James Nicholas Publishers.
Cousins, J. Bradley, & Kenneth A. Leithwood. (1986). "Current Empirical Research on Evaluation Utilization." *Review of Evaluation Research, 56*(3), 331–364.
Dunn, William. (1986). "Studying Knowledge Use: A Profile of Procedures and Issues." In George M. Beal, Wimal Dissanayake, and Sumiye Konoshima (Ed.), *Knowledge Generation, Exchange and Utilization* (pp. 29–42). Boulder, CO: Westview Press.

Ginsburg, Mark B. (1976). "An Investigation of the Determinants of Various Modes of Community Participation in School Affairs: Implications for the Post-Serrano v. Priest Era." PhD diss., Graduate School of Education, University of California, Los Angeles, USA.

Ginsburg, Mark B. (1995). "Contradiction, Resistance and Incorporation in the Political Socialization of Educators in Mexico." In Mark B. Ginsburg and Beverly Lindsay (Ed.,) *The Political Dimension in Teacher Education: Comparative Perspectives on Policy Formation, Socialization, and Society* (pp. 216–242). London: Falmer Press.

Ginsburg, Mark B., & Jorge M. Gorostiaga, eds. (2003). *Limitations and Possibilities of Dialogue among Researchers, Policy Makers, and Practitioners: International Perspectives on the Field of Education.* New York: RoutledgeFalmer.

Ginsburg, Mark B., Leopold E. Klopfer, Thomas Clayton, Michel Rakotomanana, Judy Sylvester, & Katherine Yasin. (1996). "Choices in Conceptualizing Classroom-Anchored Research and Linking It to Policy/Practice to Improve Educational Quality in Developing Countries." *Research Papers in Education, 11*(3), 239–254.

Ginsburg, Mark B., & Bede Redican. (1980). "The Basis of Student Peer Group Structures." *Research in Education, 23,* 57–73.

Ginsburg, Mark B., & Monte Tidwell. (1995). "Political Socialization of Prospective Educators in Mexico." In Carlos Alberto Torres (Ed.), *Education and Social Change in Latin America* (pp. 127–142). Albert Park, Australia: James Nichols Publishers.

Gorostiaga, Jorge M., & Rolland G. Paulston. (1999). *Mapping New Approaches in Program Evaluation: A Cross-Cultural Perspective.* Working Paper Series No. SRF-1999-01. Pittsburgh: Institute for International Studies in Education, University of Pittsburgh.

Government of the Republic of Zambia (GRZ). (2006). "Chapter 16: Education & Skills Development." In *Fifth National Development Plan, 2006–2010.* Lusaka, Zambia: GRZ.

GRZ. (2010). "Chapter 16: Education & Skills Development." In *Sixth National Development Plan, 2010–2014.* (Draft, 29 April 2010). Lusaka, Zambia: GRZ.

Megahed, Nagwa M., & Mark B. Ginsburg. (2003). "Stratified Students, Stratified Teachers: Ideologically Informed Perceptions of Educational Reform in Egypt." *Mediterranean Journal of Educational Studies, 8*(2), 7–33.

Ministry of Education (MOE). (1996). *Educating Our Future: National Policy on Education.* Lusaka, Zambia: MOE, Republic of Zambia.

Nsama Chakufyali, Peggy, Mark B. Ginsburg, Kalima Kalima, Benny Mwaanga, & Winnehl Tubman. (2009). *Annual Outcome Survey, 2009.* Lusaka, Zambia: EQUIP2/Zambia and Zambian Ministry of Education.

O'Shea, David, C. Wayne Gordon, & Mark B. Ginsburg. (1976). "Desegregation in the Los Angeles School District: Report of a Public Opinion Survey." *Educational Research Quarterly, 1*(1), 1–17.

Paulston, Rolland G. (1976). *Conflicting Theories of Social and Educational Change: A Typological Review.* Pittsburgh: University Center for International Studies, University of Pittsburgh.

Paulston, Rolland G. (1977). "Social and Educational Change: Conceptual Frameworks." *Comparative Education Review, 21*(2–3), 370–395.

Paulston, Rolland G. (1980). "Education as Anti-Structure: Non-Formal Education in Social and Ethnic Movements." *Comparative Education, 16*(1), 55–66.

Paulston, Rolland G. (1990). "From Paradigm Wars to Disputatious Community." *Comparative Education Review, 34*(3), 395–400.

Paulston, Rolland G. (1994). "Comparative and International Education: Paradigms and Theories." In Torsten Husén and T. Neville Postlewaite (Ed.), *The International Encyclopedia of Education.* Oxford: Pergamon.

Paulston, Rolland G. (1996). *Social Cartography: Mapping Ways of Seeing Social and Educational Change.* New York: Garland Publishing.

Paulston, Rolland G., & Jorge M. Gorostiaga. (1998). "Nuevas Ideas para la Evaluación Educativa en América Latina?" *La Educación: Inter-American Review of Education, 129,* 49–76.

Paulston, Rolland G., & Martin Liebman. (1996). "Social Cartography: A New Metaphor/Tool for Comparative Studies." In Rolland G. Paulston (Ed.), *Social Cartography: Mapping Ways of Seeing Social and Educational Change* (pp.7–28). New York: Garland Publishing.

Psacharopoulos, George. (1990). "Comparative Education: From Theory to Practice, or Are You A:\neo.* or B:*.ist?" *Comparative Education Review, 34*(3), 369–380.

Rust, Val D., Aminata Soumaré, Octavio Pescador, & Megumi Shibuya. (1999). "Research Strategies in Comparative Education." *Comparative Education Review, 43*(1), 86–109.
Spatig, Linda, Mark B. Ginsburg, & Dov Liberman. (1982). "Ego Development as an Explanation of Passive and Active Models of Teacher Socialization." *College Student Journal, 16*(4), 315–325.
Weiss, Carol H. (1991). "The Many Meanings of Research Utilization." In Don Anderson and Bruce J. Biddle (Ed.), *Knowledge for Policy: Improving Education through Research* (pp. 47–68). London: Falmer Press.

SHOKO YAMADA AND JING LIU

20. BETWEEN EPISTEMOLOGY AND RESEARCH PRACTICES

*Emerging Research Paradigms and the Tradition
of Japanese Comparative Education*

INTRODUCTION

This chapter analyzes the epistemological debates among the members of the Japan Comparative Education Society (JCES). Changing perceptions about the location of the academic field of comparative education will be considered against the sociopolitical context which has surrounded comparative educationists since the 1990s. The authors also investigate to what extent such epistemological debates have affected the actual research practices that are observable from the articles published in the JCES journal, *Comparative Education*. (To differentiate the Japanese *Comparative Education* from the journal which is published in the UK under the same title, it will be abbreviated as *CEJ* from now on.) Even a casual glance at *CEJ* reveals that there have been many special issues groping for the answers to the existential questions of comparative education, such as the current situation, prospects, reviews, reflections, and so on. A characteristic of comparative educationists is to continuously query their own academic identity. At the same time, it is noticeable that the JCES members were rather silent—at least in the *CEJ*—about their epistemology for about a quarter century after the special issue, which was the first issue of *CEJ* in 1975. Then, from the 1990s, suddenly the journal started to put together special issues on epistemology: for example, volumes 17, 19, 20, 22, 25, 26, and 27.[2]

The articles in the special issues or topical research collections are different in nature from those of the "general" category because they were contributed by invited authors for particular purposes set by the review committee. An analysis of these articles reveals topics and themes that the members of the review committee considered that organized discussion is necessary. The epistemological discourse among comparative educationists in Japan of course reflects that in the English language. At the same time, things written and spoken in Japanese often show a unique divergence from mainstream English-language discussions. There are many Japanese researchers who are trained overseas and regularly exposed to English literature. They themselves also publish in English. At the same time, Japanese appears to provide a different academic space for Japanese comparative educationists from those whose language of communication is English. Although many people

John C. Weidman, W. James Jacob (eds.), Beyond the Comparative: Advancing Theory and Its Application to Practice, 371–393.

belong to both circles, they shift their mode of presentation and communication when they are in a Japanese-language space. Therefore, it is important to examine the epistemological discussion in Japanese comparative education circles against contemporary discussions outside of Japan. An analysis of the special issues and topical research collections in *CEJ* will shed light on the uniqueness of Japanese epistemology while also echoing various global commonalities.

On the other hand, the articles in the "general" category are submitted by the authors to be reviewed. They reflect the types of research which the review committee considers to be suitable for publication in *CEJ* in terms of their approach and perspectives, in addition to the quality of data and analysis. The selection of the submitted articles is, therefore, not necessarily connected to epistemological discourse which was demonstrated in the special issues and topical research collections. Whatever the discussion about academic nature or the identity of the comparative educationists, there are types of articles appreciated in *CEJ* that are quite consistent regardless of the rise and fall of the epistemological debate.

To understand the background of the epistemological debates that became active after 1990 and their relationship with the research practices of JCES members, we have categorized the "general" articles that appeared in *CEJ* between 1990 and 2009. This was done according to criteria such as geographic focus, methods utilized for data collection and analysis, unit of analysis, and the focus of the level and kind of education. The categorized articles were then analyzed to see the patterns and trends of research practices among JCES members. What was revealed by this analysis was a tendency of *CEJ* to collect articles which are descriptive of the educational practices of a particular society and foster an attitude of close observation among the authors. In other words, the journal attracts articles which capture education in the web of culture, religion, history, and other aspects of the social life of people in particular contexts, instead of evaluating the effectiveness or the function of education (especially schooling) seen from the side of the service provider or outsiders. The types of articles in this general category have been rather consistent, which do not necessarily correspond to the view which was repeatedly raised in the special issues—that comparative education research has to go one step further than mere foreign studies—and relate education of the research sites with that of Japan to "examine its [Japan's] unique characteristics" to be truly "comparative" (Ichikawa 1990; Ishizuki 1999; Shibuya 2001; Takekuma 2001). To do a thorough study of a foreign education system requires a deep understanding of the society in question, which is valuable in itself. However, given the fact that there are repeated discussions to make comparative education "comparative," one has to admit that there is a disconnection between the practice of researchers who publish in *CEJ* and the issues pointed out in the special issues and topical research collections. It would require further research to fully investigate the reasons of such a disconnection or the time lag between epistemology and practice. However, in this chapter we have attempted to grasp the trends of comparative education in Japan as closely as possible to reality by segregating the two dynamics visible from the analysis of articles collected in special issues and the "general" category.

In addition to the solicited articles in *CEJ*, we have also categorized articles about education in foreign countries published in other journals. The purpose of this analysis was to consider the nature of comparative education beyond the boundary of a particular academic society and its journal, namely JCES and its journal *CEJ*. Research on educational practices and policies in other societies is conducted in various fields such as area studies, sociology, economics, anthropology, and history, to name a few. In our analysis, we have focused particularly on articles whose geographic slant is developing countries. To highlight the nature of articles published in *CEJ*, we also reviewed two journals that collect articles concerning developmental issues in less developed regions. The reason for this concentration was our understanding that education development or assistance for developing countries was one of the factors which brought about changes in the discourse on comparative education in the 1990s. "Development" concerns the change for betterment or the attitude to observe the process of such change, which was not common in comparative education before. Therefore, it was also assumed that articles that appeared in development-related journals would reflect a different research paradigm from those in *CEJ* even though they are about education in developing countries.

"Development" or "international development cooperation" was one of the research themes that emerged in the 1990s, together with other issues such as globalization and gender. Reflecting the fact that Japan became one of the top providers of official development aid (ODA), the demands for research and experts in the field of education development grew quickly. In fact, *CEJ* picked up on the emerging issue of "development" in special issues and topical research collections in 1995 (No. 21), 1996 (No. 22), 2000 (No. 26), and 2005 (No. 31). Therefore, the comparison of the characteristics of articles in *CEJ* and development-related journals is to capture the nature of changes from the 1990s onward and to locate the research conducted to tackle the emerging issue of comparative education in a broader academic context. Through this analysis, we hope that the characteristics of JCES and *CEJ* will be clarified in relative terms.

Classification of journal articles has been done by various researchers in the field of comparative education as a means to find patterns in research focus and methodologies. Rolland G. Paulston (1993) conducted a textual analysis of articles to examine the emergence of paradigmatic and theoretical conceptions. It is an interesting analysis which, constructed from the analysis of individual articles, attempts to find the concentration, divergence, and timeline changes of theories and paradigms. It was Val D. Rust and his colleagues (1999) who moved on from the simple grouping of articles by the countries/regions of focus to methods of data collection and analysis, levels of economic development of the countries/regions researched, and utilization of qualitative and quantitative approaches. They reviewed *Comparative Education Review* (*CER* [United States]), *Comparative Education* (*CE* [United Kingdom]), and the *International Journal of Educational Development* from when each journal was founded to 1995 (the numbers of categorized articles are 947, 675, and 347 respectively). Rosalind Latiner Raby publishes an article each year to review the patterns of research themes and the geographic focus of published articles of the year, using the catalog of *CER* articles (for example, 2009). In the British journal *CE*, Angela Little (2000) published an article in a special issue in which she categorized 472 articles published in *CE* between 1977 and 1998 by geographic focus, objectives, and the existence of comparative perspectives (one country study or a comparison of multiple cases). Further, Cook and colleagues (2004) conducted a questionnaire among Comparative and International Education Society (CIES) members regarding their perceptions on research stance, theories, and the methodologies they rely on.

In Japan, there have also been several efforts to map the research paradigms and find patterns in the research practices of JCES members. Examples of such efforts include "Catalog of JCES Members' Articles and Literature," which has been published three times since the 1960s (1967, 1980, and 1993); and "40 Years' History of Japan Comparative Education Society" (2004). In addition, the Research Information for International and Comparative Education (RICE) is "the database which gathers outline information about literature and data on comparative education research in Japan and educational activities conducted by international organizations and countries around the world" (JCES 2010). Toru Umakoshi (2007) reviewed comparative education research and teaching programs in universities to examine research trends in the 1990s. Yuto Kitamura (2005) has categorized the articles published in the *CER* according to their geographic focus when looking for the relationship between comparative education and development studies.

There have been a number of works, both in English and Japanese, categorizing comparative education publications. However, there has not been much effort to look at the relationship between English-language and non-English-language discourse. A different language creates a different academic space. Still, the echoes of the mainstream discussion are far from negligible. Therefore, by coding and mapping the changes in the pattern of Japanese comparative education research, this chapter attempts to expand the basis of academic discourse. There have not been many publications about research trends outside of Europe and North America. For example, English-language articles about East Asia are few, and those that exist are mainly about mainland China and Hong Kong (Shu and Zhou 1990; Chen 1994; Bray 2001). Regarding Japan, one of the few English publications in this category is the one by Akira Ninomiya (2007) which reviews the changing geographic focus by categorizing titles of oral presentations at the JCES annual meetings and articles. Given such a gap in knowledge, one of the objectives of this chapter is to share what is discussed and written in Japanese with a wider English audience for the sake of a "comparative" perspective. The authors also hope that this provides an opportunity for scholars who predominantly communicate in English to objectively review their own epistemology.

EPISTEMOLOGY OF COMPARATIVE EDUCATION IN ENGLISH AND ITS IMPLICATIONS FOR THE DISCOURSE IN JAPAN

Comparative educationists have repeatedly discussed the definitions, subjects of research, methodologies, and theories of their academic field. The major questions include: whether comparative education should cover wider areas comprehensively or narrow the focus so that comparative education will have a clear boundary as an independent science or a discipline (Holmes 1972; Hansen 1977); whether researchers should spend more energy elaborating theories or accumulating practical research that is applicable to actual educational work and policies (Masemann 1982; Sheehan 1983); what the roles of universities are for training researchers and for the advancement of the research in this field; and how to draw the line between comparative education research and studies of education in foreign countries done within the domains of other education fields, such as economics of education, sociology of education, educational psychology, and pedagogy (Zajda 2003; Ninnes and Mehta 2004; Schriewer 2009). The academic boundaries of comparative education were contested not only on the disciplinary front, but also in terms of the issues they treat. There has also been a lot of debate about the differences between international education, multicultural education, and comparative education. Often a result of serious debate is whether a national society of comparative education should have "international" in its name or not. The current Comparative and International Education Societies in the United States and the United Kingdom did not include "international education" in their scope in the earlier time (Bray 2010). In Japan, there have been heated debates about the inclusion of "international education" but even today this has not been incorporated. All in all, one may say that these questions and debates reflect the sense of uncertainty about academic boundaries among comparative educationists.

A quick review of the articles that have appeared in *CE*, *CER*, and *CEJ* reveals that many special issues have been published to discuss the characteristics of this academic field and its past, present, and future. Curiously, such existential debates arose at similar time periods across each respective country. It first occurred in the latter half of the 1970s (*CEJ*, No. 1, 1975; *CE*, 13, No. 2, 1977; Altbach and Kelly, 1978); around the 1990s (*CEJ*, No. 16, 1990; No. 17, 1991; No. 19, 1993; No. 20, 1994; *CER*, Vol. 34, No. 3); and around 2000 (*CEJ*, No. 25, 1999; No. 27, 2001; *CE*, Vol. 36, No. 3, 2000). Such a synchronicity of discussion indicates epistemological reflection in one part of the global comparative educationist circle would be caught and spread in the other parts of the circle.

One of the obvious echoes of the discourse in Japan with those of the United States and the United Kingdom was that of the issue of "development" in economically poorer regions and countries. In 1990, the World Conference on Education for All (EFA) was held in Jomtien, Thailand, and the delegates of 155 countries and representatives of 150 organizations agreed on a common set of goals for educational development around the world. It was the beginning of a new era, and the first time in the history of educational development in which the international community agreed to work in collaboration for the same goals. *CER* published a special issue in 1990 centered on an article contributed by George Psacharopoulos (1990), an education economist based at the World Bank, whose rate-of-return analysis played a significant role in the shift in the trends in educational assistance from higher to primary-level education. At the beginning of the article, Psacharopoulos boldly states that it does not matter whether your theoretical stance is neo-Marxist, structural functionalist, or something else; what matters is one's position on a substantive issue and proposal for solving problems—in his case, in developing countries. Among the few scholars who contributed pieces in response to Psacharopoulos was Paulston (1990), who argued that oversimplification and an exclusive reliance on hypothesis testing would overlook the heterogeneity of realities and accumulated knowledge in the field of comparative education.

The Jomtien Conference and the increasing presence of aid organizations in education research has had an impact on comparative education circles and stirred debate in various places, including Japan. Reflecting its strong economy, Japan became the top ODA provider in 1989 and started to increase aid projects in the field of education. Such a change in the ODA environment created new demands for more, and new kinds of, comparative education research. As the authors will discuss later, it was from the 1990s onward that "development"-oriented educational research emerged. On the one hand, the global discourse on "development," with its strong focus on basic education, has caused a significant change in Japanese comparative education research. On the other hand, such "development" discourse did not cause fundamental changes in the epistemology of comparative education; in other words, it did not affect the dominance of a conventional paradigm within the JCES. There was an article titled "Research Themes in Educational Development and Educational Cooperation Aid" (Ushiogi 1995) in a special issue of *CEJ* in 1995. Also, in 1996, a solicited article titled "Structural Adjustment by the World Bank and Educational Reform Process: The Case of Education Sector Adjustment in Ghana" (Hamano 1996) appeared in *CEJ*. Aside from these limited cases, most of the papers regarding aid policies, projects, and topics related to these development activities were published outside of *CEJ*, although the authors of these articles were, in many cases, members of the JCES.

Here lies a significant divergence of Japanese epistemology from English-language circles. The mainstream of Japanese comparative education is country studies, with a clear effort not to link it to any agenda or theory, but to be precise in description. While there has been heated discussion about theories such as modernization, world-systems, structuralism, and postmodernism in English literature throughout the post-World War II period (Arnove 1980; Eckstein and Noah 1985; Welch 1985), Japanese comparative educationists seem not to have needed the theoretical framework to demonstrate their sophistication or draw boundaries from other academic fields. This is odd given the fact that *CEJ* has published various special issues on its content, methodologies, and subjects to be taught to comparative education students, which shows a convergence with the mainstream English-language discourse. One of the explanations of this lack of effort to theorize is that in comparison to Europe and North America, comparative education research in Japan has been less influenced by diplomacy and policies of the government and funding organizations. Comparative educationists in Europe and America have depended on research grants from the government and international organizations in competition with other researchers in the social sciences. As Joel Samoff (1999) has argued, academic fields that cannot divorce themselves from funding from such sources tend to concentrate on the "hot" issues of diplomacy and/or aid. In post-World War II Europe and North America, theories such as modernization, world-systems, and dependency developed against the background of postcolonial relationships between industrialized and newly independent countries. Research that was to compete for funds from governments and international organizations—whether in comparative education or another field—were to theorize themselves along these lines. This was how comparative education in these societies was inherently "development-oriented" and based on the theories and ideologies reflecting the atmosphere of the time (Epstein 1983, 1991; Steiner-Khamsi 2006). Compared to that, research in Japan, at least in top research institutions, has been well subsidized by the government without much control or expectations for short-term contributions. It was only after the 1990s when more development-oriented research with similar theoretical framework as Europe or America started to be demanded, reflecting the change of Japanese diplomatic position.

PRACTICES OF JAPANESE COMPARATIVE EDUCATION SINCE THE 1990S

Based on the observation of the convergence and divergence of epistemology between English-language and Japanese discourse, let us now turn to the practice of comparative education researchers in Japan.

Table 20.1 indicates the geographic focus of articles that appeared in *CEJ* between 1990 and 2008. Conventionally, in terms of geography, a large number of comparative educationists focused on North America and European countries such as the United Kingdom, Germany, and France; another large group specialized in East Asia. Such tendencies are still obvious as articles on East Asia/Pacific and North America/Western Europe constitute 104.3 percent (55.6 and 48.7 percent respectively) of the articles in *CEJ*.[3] One of the causes of such a concentration was that Japanese comparative education began with the "borrowing" of ideas and learning from good practices in the supposedly advanced systems of Western countries (Morishita 2010). Also, after World War II and until the 1970s, aside from official purposes, overseas travel was restricted for ordinary Japanese citizens. Therefore, the number of countries from which Japanese researchers could collect detailed and reliable information and statistics were limited. According to Shogo Ichikawa (1990), such limitations in information access made researchers focus on Western countries—whose information is available through the Organisation for Economic Co-operation and Development (OECD) and some international sources—and neighboring East Asian countries.

After the 1990s, Japanese researchers started to emphasize the value of research on education in various places from global perspectives, moving away from their own Eurocentrism. Also, as mentioned earlier, with the end of the Cold War and rapid globalization, concerns grew about research on emerging issues such as gender, development, and globalization. However, at least in terms of geographic distribution, actual research practices have not changed in the mainstream of the JCES.

Table 20.1. Geographic Focus of Articles in CEJ and JID and JICE

Total No. of Articles Categorized**	CEJ		JID and JICE*	
	261	%	130	%
Arab countries	3	1.1	5	3.8
Sub-Saharan Africa	7	2.7	59	45.4
Latin America/Caribbean	9	3.4	14	10.8
Central and Eastern Europe	9	3.4	1	0.8
Central Asia	4	1.5	0	0.0
East Asia/Pacific	145	55.6	39	30.0
South and West Asia	11	4.2	10	7.7
North America/Western Europe	127	48.7	4	3.1

Journal of International Development (JID) and *Journal of International Cooperation in Education (JICE)*
** The percentages of articles coded for each region will add up to more than 100 percent because there are articles which touch upon more than one region.

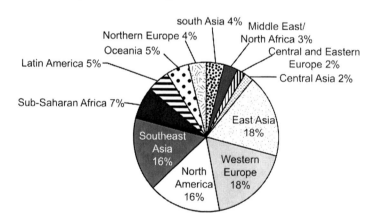

Figure 20.1. Geographic Focus of the JCES Members (N=229).

Figure 20.1 shows the geographic focus of the JCES members based on responses to a questionnaire.[4] Even though they still constitute a large group, JCES members who selected Western Europe, East Asia, and North America as their geographic focus totaled only 52 percent (18 percent, 18 percent, and 16 percent respectively) which highlights a notable difference from 104.3 percent, the proportion of the articles on these regions published in *CEJ*. It indicates the fact that, although there have been a growing number of comparative educationists whose geographic focus is different from conventional ones, most of their works were not published in *CEJ*.

JCES members do not necessarily publish in *CEJ*. Considering the consistent tendency of the articles selected in the "general" category of *CEJ*, against the growingly diversifying geographic research focus of the JCES members, one can assume that a large part of the JCES members look for the journal in which they can publish outside of *CEJ*, the journal of JCES.

Based on such assumptions, the authors compared *CEJ* articles with the educational papers that appeared in two other journals in the field of development studies. We selected these journals because of the perception that the research demanded by ODA organizations has created a new dynamic and increased the number of JCES members in the last 20 years. As shown in Table 20.1, in total, 130 education-related articles were found from two journals—the *Journal of International Development* (issued by the Japan Association for the Studies of International Development, 36 volumes) from the journal's launch in 1993 to 2007 and the *Journal of International Cooperation in Education* (issued by the Center for the Study of International Cooperation in Education, Hiroshima University, 23 volumes)[5] from the journal's launch in 1998 to 2008.

Comparison of Articles in CEJ and Development-Oriented Journals

In the following, the authors will discuss the findings from a comparison of articles in *CEJ* and two development-oriented journals according to the following criteria: (1) proportion of references cited in local languages; (2) unit of analysis; (3) research method; and (4) level/kind of education focused on.

Prior to the discussion of the characteristics of research approach and methods, it must be pointed out that the selection of research sites clearly shows different patterns between *CEJ* and the development-oriented journals, *JID* and *JICE*. In terms of regional focus, the authors of the *JID* and *JICE* are more diverse, with an uneven concentration on Sub-Saharan Africa (52.2 percent). This heavy emphasis on Sub-Saharan Africa is partly caused by the institutional orientation of the research center at Hiroshima University that publishes one of the sample journals. It is also explained by the global consensus to assist developing countries whose basic education enrolment is low, and in many cases are in Sub-Saharan Africa. Putting aside Sub-Saharan Africa, the areas covered in *JID* and *JICE* are still diverse, with a higher proportion of articles than *CEJ* devoted to Latin America/Caribbean and South and West Asia. The differential characteristics in country selection are also visible when one classifies the articles by the economic levels of the countries studied.[6]

Table 20.2 shows the breakdown of the articles on developing countries by their economic levels.

Table 20.2. Articles in CEJ and JID and JICE With a
Geographic Focus on Developing Countries

	CEJ		*JID* and *JICE*	
Total number of articles on developing countries*	58**	%	63***	%
Low Income Countries	13	22.4	59	93.7
Lower Middle Income Countries	51	87.9	20	31.7
Upper Middle Income Countries	22	25.6	4	6.3

* The percentages of articles coded for each region will add up to more than 100 percent, because there are articles which touch upon more than one region.
** 58 articles on developing countries constitute 22.2 percent of 261, total number of the *CEJ* articles coded.
*** 63 articles on developing countries constitute 48.1 percent of 130, total number of the *JID-JICE* articles coded.

Among *CEJ* articles only 22.2 percent (58 articles) focused on developing countries that are categorized as low, lower middle, and upper middle income countries. Out of 261 *CEJ* articles classified, those focusing on low income countries comprised only 22.4 percent (13 articles). Among the three categories of developing countries, lower middle income countries received the most attention (51 articles) in *CEJ*. This supports our earlier argument that studies on East Asia have been—and still are—dominant in Japanese comparative education. In contrast, even though it was predictable from the nature of the journals, 48.1 percent (63 articles) of 130 articles chosen from development-oriented journals were on developing countries, out of which the lion's share (93.7 percent) was taken by the researchers on low income countries.

In the following section, we discuss the findings from a comparison of the contents of the two types of journals. Differing from the above analysis, which included all education articles regardless of their focus countries, the articles used for the following analysis are only those that deal with developing—low income, lower middle income, and upper middle income—countries. This was made in the interest of having a common basis of comparison.

1. Languages of the Literature. One aspect of the tradition transmitted among generations of scholars in comparative education programs at Japanese universities was the one in which novice researchers are, before anything, expected to immerse themselves into the foreign society they chose as their lifetime field of study. By doing so, they come to understand the society's sociocultural background, such as the norms of school and childhood and the relationship between ethnicity and education, which are the foundations of education systems (Murata and Shibuya, 1999). To be able to do that, language acquisition is indispensable. Setsuo Nishino (2001) states that it is a fantasy to assume that one can learn about foreign societies through the internet or secondary sources by using only a lingua franca such as

English (see also Otsuka 2005). For these conventional comparative educationists, proficiency in the local language and extensive fieldwork are the foundation of academic work. Given such traditions, we considered that the language(s) of the literature cited in the articles would be a good indicator to see if an article is written by a researcher who is trained in established Japanese comparative education programs or someone new who is either trained overseas, started their career as practitioners, or originally trained in another discipline or academic field.

Figure 20.2 shows the percentage distribution of the local language literatures cited in the articles. In the case of *CEJ*, more than 70 percent of the articles cite local language literatures to varying extents; whereas, in *JID* and *JICE*, the majority of articles rely on English and Japanese literature only.

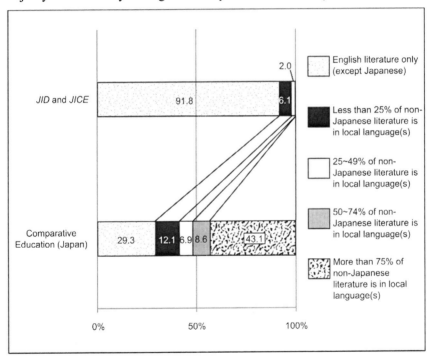

Figure 20.2. Languages of Literature Cited in Different Types of Journals (Except for Japanese).

The examples of the *CEJ* articles which cited only English and Japanese literature are Atsushi Takei (1995), Takashi Hamano (1996), and Nobuhide Sawamura (2004), who wrote about India, Ghana, and Kenya respectively. Although these countries are all known for their diversity of languages, these articles referred to none of the local-language literature. These three papers also have similarities in their selection of themes that are linked with aid programs or policy reform; in other words, they are "development-oriented." The field of educational development or development aid is greatly linked to an agenda set by the international community, and the impact of the interventions is often measured by common indicators. Under such circumstances, researchers are to be conversant with the latest issues which are, most of the time, accessible in English or a few official UN languages.

In terms of *JID* and *JICE*, the inclination to English literature is more obvious. As Norihiro Kuroda (2005, 5–6) notes

> one of the motivations for [development studies] is practical needs to acquire know-how to promote international educational cooperation (aid). [Because of this], themes of research selected among this group of scholars tend to be highly practical and driven by policy or development. . . . While creating and accumulating know-how, it is also important [for articles in development studies] to [translate and] share the information about educational aid by other donor countries and international organizations.

2. Unit of Analysis. Based on the cube model of units of analysis by Mark Bray (1995), we came up with ten items according to which we have classified articles. They include: (1) individual (learner and/or parent); (2) family; (3) classroom; (4) school and/or educational institution; (5) local community; (6) region of a country; (7) single country; (8) comparison among countries; (9) regional (international) comparison; and (10) the world as a whole. The smallest unit of analysis is the individual (the far left in Figure 20.3), and the unit becomes bigger toward the right end of the bar.

Compared with the articles in development-oriented journals, those in *CEJ* have a more microscopic focus. For instance, 12.4 percent of articles in *CEJ* take the individual (learner or parent) as the unit of analysis. Among *CEJ* articles, the first six units which are smaller than a single country constitute 72.2 percent of all articles. Only 3.1 percent of all the *CEJ* articles focused on a unit larger than a single country. On the other hand, among the articles in development-oriented journals, only 31.3 percent focused on units smaller than a single country. More than half the articles in these journals (53 percent) took a single country as their unit, with most of them writing about national education systems. Here, one can point out the clear contrast between articles in *CEJ* and development-oriented journals—*JID* and *JICE*—in their choice of the units of analysis; while *CEJ* articles tend to be microscopic, development-oriented articles are more macroscopic, focusing mostly on a country or units larger than a country, often comparing systems across countries or regions. In the Japan Comparative Education Society, there has been repeated criticism from within that merely studying a country's education system is not "comparative." The fact that more *CEJ* articles utilize a microscopic/smaller unit approach can be understood as a sign that mainstream comparative education is departing from its conventional form of foreign systems study to be more nuanced and context-sensitive area studies.

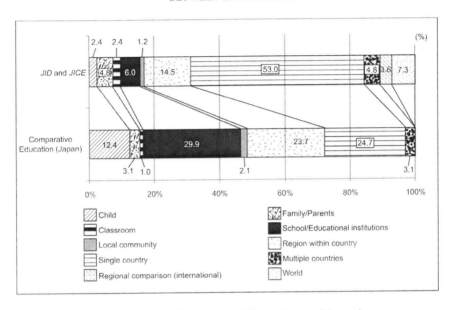

Figure 20.3. Unit of Analysis in Different Types of Journals.

3. Research Method. For the research method, we developed 12 categories for classification, referring to the frameworks used by Little (2000) and Rust and his colleagues (1999) in their respective article mappings. Although the coding was done with 12 categories, in the interest of clarification and simplification, in the process of analysis we regrouped them into six according to the closeness of the nature of the research methods. The combined categories were: (1) field-based (interview, participant observation, questionnaire, document collection); (2) non-field-based (secondary statistics); (3) content analysis (curriculum, textbooks); (4) evaluation (project evaluation, report); (5) historical (pre-World War II, post-World War II, contemporary history); and (6) theoretical (literature review, theory analysis). Research is not analyzed and testified by a single method but by combining several methods. Therefore, in this study, we selected up to three categories that are the most important in the respective articles. Also, research always starts with a review of the existing literature, such as academic articles on a similar topic, reports, data, and other materials. However, the literature review in our coding does not refer to that conducted for establishing the basic framework of the research. Only the articles which included a literature review for the sake of analysis were categorized as using a literature review as their research method. In this type of article, the literature review itself tends to be the main research method and the authors tend not to conduct fieldwork to collect primary or secondary data on the ground.

As Figure 20.4 shows, field-based research methods such as interviews, participant observation, and questionnaires are used by more than half (55.5 percent) of the authors of *CEJ* articles.

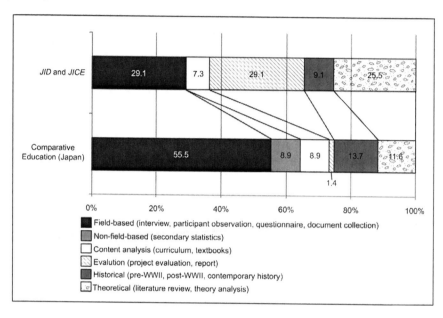

Figure 20.4. Research Methods by Different Types of Journals.

On the other hand, development-oriented journals use less than 30 percent. As mentioned earlier, the mainstream comparative educationists of JCES, who often identify themselves with "area studies," emphasize fieldwork as an important means of acquiring primary data; as Yutaka Otsuka (1994) calls it, "Fieldwork for data creation." In contrast to the dominance of fieldwork among the *CEJ* articles, development-oriented journals have as much evaluation-type research as fieldwork. This is to assess the impact of development projects and policies, which are closely related to the operation of development assistance. The third popular research method among development journals is that categorized as "theoretical," which consists of papers which are based on an analysis of theories and literature, without field-based data collection.

4. Level/Kind of Education Dealt with in the Article. Articles were also classified according to the level/kind of education they focus on. The following nine categories are used: (1) basic education (primary and junior secondary education); (2) upper secondary education; (3) tertiary (university, polytechnic, post-secondary); (4) early childhood education; (5) informal/home education and family education; (6) nonformal education and social education; (7) the education system as a whole; (8) life-long learning; and (9) formal vocational and technical education.

The most noticeable pattern in Figure 20.5 is the dominance of basic education, which takes the largest share in both kinds of journals but especially so in development-oriented journals, taking nearly 60 percent. The series of EFA conferences and related initiatives became the normative power to converge the policies and practices of aid organizations and the governments of developing countries to prioritize basic education. In 2002 the Japanese Ministry of Foreign Affairs, for the first time in its history, developed an overall aid policy in the field of education, named the "Basic Education for Growth Initiative." It is natural to consider that such a major move for assisting basic education development had a significant effect on the research on education in developing countries, especially among researchers who are development-oriented.

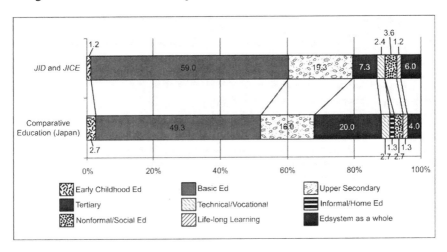

Figure 20.5. Focus Level/Kind of Education in Different Types of Journals.

Another noteworthy pattern in the research focus is the relatively high proportion of higher education in *CEJ*. It was 13 points higher than development-oriented journals (20 percent and 7.3 percent respectively). Higher education reform is currently a popular topic among comparative educationists, not only in Japan but globally. This is also noticeable from the number of sessions on this level of education in the CIES annual meetings. Higher education reform is a very real and worrying topic among university-based researchers. Also, there is an increasing demand for research on higher education systems and reforms in other countries, and the demand for collaboration with these overseas institutions is also high. On the other hand, with an almost exclusive focus on basic education in the global aid discourse from the 1990s, development-oriented researchers were less involved in this field. The motivation for their research come from the offices of aid organizations or governments of developing countries rather than the Japanese Ministry of Education, Culture, Sports, Science and Technology (MEXT) or the universities they belong to. The international aid community has begun to search for the next step after EFA, and there is a possibility that research on senior-secondary and higher education will increase in the next few years. That may cause changes in the distribution of research themes among articles in the development-oriented journals that are yet to be seen.

Research Orientation among Comparative Educationists in Japan

So far, we have attempted to demonstrate the different characteristics between articles in *CEJ* and development-oriented journals by their research methods, unit of analysis, language of literature, and the focus levels/kinds of education. This is circumstantial evidence that indirectly hints at the research orientation and the objectives of researchers, governing their way of data collection, analysis, and writeup. However, it was not clear how the differences in the methods and selection of themes relate to approaches in which the researchers analyze and present outcomes in their articles. Therefore, in this last section, we will present the findings from the article classification by research orientation. For this analysis, we coded articles according to two aspects: (1) whether the article is written with the motivation to contribute to reforms; and/or (2) whether the author's perspectives are closer to that of an educational service provider or that of a society and individuals who accept the education system and schools. This coding was done by looking at the introduction, conclusion, and overall perspectives expressed in the articles. To avoid the judgment of a particular researcher to affect the quality of data entry, after the initial coding by members of the research team, the team regularly held meetings to discuss and agree on the category of research orientation assigned to respective articles.

The results of this classification are presented in the four quadrants along two axes (Figure 20.6), and the diagrams were created both for the articles in *CEJ* and the development-oriented journals for the sake of comparison. The horizontal axis indicates the existence or lack of recommendations or suggestions which would impact education policies or the practices of educational development. When there were recommendations or reformist comments in the article, especially in the concluding section, the article was classified as "reform-oriented." The vertical axis shows the research orientation of the article by highlighting the difference between those that intend to closely describe the reality of the society in which education is only one aspect of a comprehensive social life, and those that concentrate on certain aspects of educational service provision.

First, the vertical axis refers to perspectives either from society or from the system and shows that 37.93 percent (22 articles) of *CEJ* articles are society-oriented. The articles used for this analysis are the same as the other analysis, namely, 58 for *CEJ* and 63 for *JID* and JCES. At 25.40 percent (16 articles), there was not much difference in the proportion of articles in development-oriented

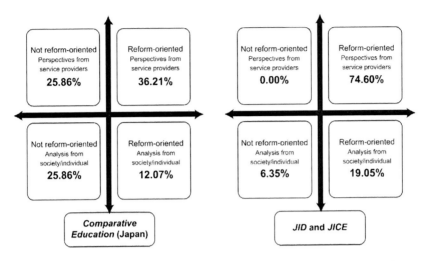

Figure 20.6. Contrasting Research Orientations between Two Types of Journals.

journals in this category. Also, 62.07 percent (36 articles) in *CEJ* and 74.60 percent (47 articles) in development-oriented journals were written from the perspective of service providers. In both types of journals, further research was conducted from the perspective of service providers and there is not much difference between *CEJ* and development journals in this sense. As mentioned earlier, the analysis of *CER* articles after the 1990s demonstrates that many of them are written with a microscopic approach by researchers who most likely begin their academic careers from learning the local language and immersing themselves in the social context. This was a clear contrast from the macroscopic articles in development-oriented journals. Regardless of such an "area studies" type of approach, the perspective of the *CEJ* articles are still that of service providers which may be considered to be a legacy of the era when comparative educationists studied foreign education systems to "borrow" some ideas for Japanese practice. Arguably, development researchers widely share the belief that education and literacy will contribute to the creation of an equal and fair society. Against this background, it is understandable that *JID and JICE* authors are more likely to write from the system perspective.

A very clear difference between *CEJ* and development-oriented articles was the existence—or lack of—reform orientation. The horizontal axis of the diagrams shows that 48.28 percent of the articles in *CEJ* have a policy recommendation or reformist comments. In contrast, 93.65 percent of the articles in development-oriented journals have that kind of motivation. In *JID and JICE*, there is no article in the fourth quadrant, which stands for "no reform orientation from a service-provider's perspective." The stronger willingness among development researchers to contribute to policies or reform can be explained by their perceived role of "showing the standard or knowledge useful for policy-making regarding international educational development and assistance" (Kitamura 2005). Kitamura expresses his conviction as a development researcher that they must make a "conscious effort of making policy recommendations with empirical data" (250). In the case of *CEJ*, even articles written from the service-provider's perspective have little orientation toward reform. For example, Takahiro Nanbu's (1996) *CEJ* article illustrates the mechanism which caused the regional research gap in Chinese higher education institutions. The theme itself can be the analysis of the impact of policy—the author did not show any sign of policy recommendation in his writing.

There are also cases in which the premises of discussion are different. The following two examples can provide clues for readers to see such differences. They are both classified in the third quadrant, "without reform orientation and with perspective from society." One is Mina Hattori (1996), and the other is Seiji Utsumi and colleagues (2006). While Hattori focuses on traditional practices and education in a religious community, Utsumi and colleagues investigate the reason d'être of a "small school" as a form of schooling adapted to traditional society. Both are of the type of research which does not draw practical policy recommendations. Also, they do not look at modern formal education (school education) while considering the meaning of education in the contemporary world through a society's unique history and culture. However, the two are different in the way that Utsumi and colleagues focus on the "conditions for the modern education system to be accepted" in traditional society, while Hattori examines the cultural transformation in traditional society caused by the expansion of the modern school system. In development studies, there is little discussion about the meaning of modernization itself or its location in traditional societies. Because of the different premise, the understanding of issues and the way of constructing the arguments are different between the comparative educationists in development and area studies. Such contrasts in attitude toward modernization through schooling are different in nature from the debates about theories such as modernization, dependency, or world-systems. The issues of debate in Japan have not been so much about how to construct the framework of research theoretically, but rather from whose perspectives to do the research and for whom to present the findings.

CONCLUSION

Traditional comparative educationists in Japan emphasize the importance of a fine description of the reality of the countries studied but are not necessarily interested in contributing to policy-making or reform of the education system. To examine this characteristic more closely, we mapped the articles of three journals according to two axes regarding the orientation toward reform and the perspectives from which the articles were written. The authors' analysis confirmed the contrast which has been perceived—and has recurred—as the issue of debate between two groups of comparative educationists: those who have been identified with "area studies" and are the mainstream of JCES and those who are symbolically linked with "development studies" and whose numbers started to increase in the 1990s.

The articles in special issues of *CEJ*, which were written by the leading authorities on comparative education in Japan, have repeatedly pointed out the limitations of conventional "foreign studies"-type research and the necessity of revising research paradigms and methodologies. There have also been several special issues since the 1990s regarding the emerging issues of comparative education such as globalization, development, and gender. However, our study revealed that regardless of the epistemological discussion, the research papers solicited and reviewed for *CEJ* have more or less maintained the same conventional type. A close and comprehensive understanding of education in the web of social context is most valued while issue-based papers tend to be undervalued (and often rejected in the review process) in *CEJ*. The contrast of the nature of articles between *CEJ* and development-oriented journals was not caused by disciplinary differences because the authors in both cases are, more often than not, members of JCES. Therefore, it is not enough to point out the different nature of the two camps and confirm that perceived differences were real. What is actually happening here is the drawing of boundaries within the comparative education circle in Japan. The flip side of the many discussions about the academic core and framework of comparative education both in Japan and in English-language circles was the elasticity and ambiguity of what counts as "comparative education." In other words, the core issue surrounding the debate over the boundaries of comparative education is often a matter of power rather than academic authenticity. It also has to be pointed out that although "development studies" is often considered as *the* emerging group of comparative educationists, it is not necessarily so. The number of JCES members has almost doubled in the last two decades, and researchers focusing on developing countries may be influential enough to look as if they symbolically represent the non-conventional type of researchers. Still, in terms of numbers, people focusing on developing countries are in the minority.

Lastly, one of the objectives of this chapter was to call attention to non-English circles that have their own histories and value systems, although publications and presentations in the English-language set the tone of discourse in the global circle of comparative educationists. As our analysis of epistemology and the practice of Japanese comparative education have demonstrated not only convergence but also divergence from the mainstream, there are diverse comparative education circles around the world which are similar but somewhat different in nature. Comparative education is an academic field whose members share a sense of insecurity and constantly question their identity and academic boundaries. However, such epistemological debates in English are restricted by their own frame of imagination. With this chapter, we would like to propose an expansion of the scope of imagination and reconsider the epistemology from the periphery—non-English comparative education circles. As we understand, extending the academic imagination to be more holistic is one of the messages of Paulston (1976; 2000).

NOTES

1. This research was conducted as a part of the larger research project, "Reconstructing educational research on/in developing countries: A fusion between area studies and development studies (project leader: Shoko Yamada)," which has been enabled by a grant-in-aid from the Japan Society for Promotion of Science. The criteria for article categorization were discussed among all researchers

involved in the project, although the analysis presented here is strictly by the authors. In addition to the researchers who commented on this study in the process, the authors would also like to express their gratitude to the indispensable contributions of two former students at Nagoya University—Norihide Furukawa (PhD student, Indiana University), and Takayo Ogisu (PhD student, Michigan State University)—and Hiromi Uemura (Nagoya Management Junior College).

2. The titles of the special issues and topical research collections of this type are as follows: Volume 17 (1991) "Review and Prospect of Comparative Education Research"; Volume 19 (1993) "Teaching Comparative Education: Consideration on its Contents and Methods"; Volume 20 (1994) "30 years of Comparative Education Research: Its Research Trends and Future Prospects"; Volume 22 (1996) "Women, Development, and Education: Consideration on the Issues for Comparative Education"; Volume 25 (1999) "New Development of Comparative Education: Its Possibilities and Prospects"; Volume 26 (2000) "Examining the Location of International Educational Cooperation within Comparative Education Research"; and Volume 27 (2001) "Frontier of Education Research as Area Studies."

3. Regional categories follow those of the World Bank's World Development Indicators.

4. The questionnaire was conducted in November 2009, as a part of the research project mentioned in note 1 above. 699 questionnaires were distributed to JCES members who joined the society by 2007 and agreed with the public access of their contact information. The JCES secretariat authorized the team to use the information strictly for the purposes of the questionnaire only. Its objective was to know the research orientations and perceptions of JCES members. Given the space limitations here, this chapter will not discuss the questionnaire data in detail.

5. The *Journal of International Cooperation in Education* is different from the *CEJ* and the *Journal of International Development* in the sense that it was not published by an academic association but a university institution. Among formerly national (now corporatized) universities in Japan, there are a few graduate schools that teach and research various issues regarding international development. They were established in the early 1990s because of the perceived urgent need to produce Japanese professionals in this field. These graduate schools and research centers in Nagoya, Kobe, and Tsukuba publish journals in the wider development area. However, the journal at Hiroshima University was selected for the current research because of its exclusive focus on and a large pool of articles on educational development. With its historical background, this journal can be considered as one of the barometers which can show the trends of research on educational development and educational cooperation (Kuroda 2005).

6. As per the regional category, country groupings by economic level also follow that of the World Development Indicators. According to this grouping, there are three levels of developing countries: low income, lower middle income, and upper middle income.

REFERENCES

Altbach, Philip G., & Gail P. Kelly, eds. (1978). *New Approaches to Comparative Education*. Chicago: University of Chicago Press.

Arnove, Robert F. (1980). "Comparative Education and World-Systems Analysis." *Comparative Education Review, 24*(1), 48–62.

Bray, Mark. (1995). "Levels of Comparison in Educational Studies: Different Insights from Different Literatures and the Value of Multilevel Analysis." *Harvard Education Review, 65*(3), 472–491.

Bray, Mark. (2001). "Comparative Education in Greater China: Contexts, Characteristics, Contrasts and Contributions." *Comparative Education, 37*(4), 451–473.

Bray, Mark. (2010). "Comparative Education and International Education in the History of *Compare*: Boundaries, Overlaps and Ambiguities." *Compare, 40*(6), 711–725.

Chen, Shu-Ching. (1994). "Research Trends in Mainland Chinese Comparative Education." *Comparative Education Review, 38*(2), 233–253.

Comparative Education (CE). (1977-). Oxford, UK: Taylor & Francis.

Comparative Education (CEJ). [比較教育学研究]. (1975-). Tokyo: Toshindo.

Comparative Education Review (CER). (1970-). Chicago: University of Chicago Press.

Cook, Bradley J., Steven J. Hite, & Erwin H. Epstein. (2004). "Discerning Trends, Contours, and Boundaries in Comparative Education: A Survey of Comparativists and Their Literature." *Comparative Education Review, 48*(2), 123–150.

Eckstein, Max A., & Harold J. Noah. (1985). "Dependency Theory in Comparative Education: The New Simplicitude." *Prospects, 15*(2), 213–225.

Epstein, Erwin H. (1983). "Currents Left and Right: Ideology in Comparative Education." *Comparative Education Review, 27*(1), 3–29.

Epstein, Erwin H. (1991). "Editorial: Ideological Orthodoxy and Comparative Education." *Comparative Education Review, 35*(3), 401–405.

Hamano, Takashi [浜野 隆]. (1996). "世界銀行による構造調整と教育改革過程－ガーナにおける教育部門調整を事例として－" ["Structural Adjustment by the World Bank and Educational Reform Process: The Case of Education Sector Adjustment in Ghana"]. 比較教育学研究 [*Comparative Education*], 22, 153–166.

Hansen, W. Lee. (1977). "Economics and Comparative Education: Will They Ever Meet? And If So, When?" *Comparative Education Review, 21*(2&3), 230–246.

Hattori, Mina [服部美奈]. (1996). "イスラームにおける通過儀礼と宗教教育に関する序論－インドネシア・西スマトラ州パリアガン村における事例研究" ["A Study on the Rites of Passage and Religious Education in Islamic Society: A Case Study of Pariagan Village in West Sumatra, Indonesia"]. 比較教育学研究 [*Comparative Education*], 22, 139–152.

Holmes, Brian. (1972). "Comparative Education as a Scientific Study." *British Journal of Educational Studies, 20*(2), 205–219.

Ichikawa, Shogo [市川昭午]. (1990). "比較教育再考－日本的特質解明のための比較研究のすすめ－" ["Comparative Education Reconsidered: Recommendation of Comparative Studies to Untangle Japanese Characteristics"]. 比較教育学研究 [*Comparative Education*], 16, 5–18.

Ishizuki, Minoru [石附 実]. (1999). "教育学研究における比較・国際教育学の役割" ["The Role of Comparative and International Education in Educational Research"]. 比較教育学研究 [*Comparative Education*], 25, 16–27.

Japan Comparative Education Society (JCES) [日本比較教育学会]. (1967). 会員の研究論文・文献一覧』第1号 [*Catalog of JCES Members' Articles and Literature*], Vol. 1.

JCES [日本比較教育学会]. (1980). *Kaiin no Kenkyuuronbun, Bunken Ichiran* [*Catalog of JCES Members' Articles and Literature*], Vol. 2.

JCES [日本比較教育学会]. (1993). *Kaiin no Kenkyuuronbun, Bunken Ichiran* [*Catalog of JCES Members' Articles and Literature*]. Vol. 3.

JCES [日本比較教育学会]. (2004). 日本比較教育学会40年の歩み [*40 Years' History of Japan Comparative Education Society*]. Tokyo: Toshindo.

JCES [日本比較教育学会]. (2010). 比較. 国際教育情報データベース（略称：RICE） [*Research Information for International and Comparative Education (RICE)*]. Hiroshima: JCES. Available online at: http://wwwsoc.nii.ac.jp/jces/rice/index.shtml.

Journal of International Cooperation in Education. (1998-). Hiroshima: Hiroshima University.

Journal of International Development Studies. (1993-). Kanagawa, Japan: Bunkyo University.

Kitamura, Yuto [北村友人]. (2005). "比較教育学と開発研究の関わり" ["Relationship between Comparative Education and Development Studies"]. 比較教育学研究 [*Comparative Education*], 31, 241–252.

Kuroda, Norihiro [黒田則博]. (2005). "日本における国際教育協力研究の展開" ["Evolution of the Studies on International Educational Cooperation in Japan"]. 比較教育学研究 [*Comparative Education*], 31, 3–14.

Little, Angela. (2000). "Development Studies and Comparative Education: Context, Content, Comparison and Contributors." *Comparative Education, 36*(3), 279–296.

Masemann, Vandra Lea. (1982). "Critical Ethnography in the Study of Comparative Education." *Comparative Education Review, 26*(1), 1–15.

Morishita, Minoru. (2010). "Trends and Challenges of Japan Comparative Education Society: Its Diversity of Research Paradigms and Approaches." Paper presented at the Comparative and International Education Society 54th Annual Conference, Chicago, 3 March 2010.

Murata, Yokuo [村田翼夫], and Megumi Shibuya [渋谷恵]. 1999. "比較教育学と地域研究(1)東南アジア地域研究の立場から－" ["Comparative Education and Area Studies (1): From the Perspective of Southeast Asian Studies"]. 比較教育学研究 [*Comparative Education*], 25, 55–60.

Nanbu, Takahiro [南部広孝]. 1996. "現代中国における研究活動の地域間較差－普通高等教育機関自然科学系分野を中心に－" ["Regional Disparity of Research Activity in Present-Day China: A Focus on Natural Science Research in Ordinary Higher Education Institutions"]. 比較教育学研究 [*Comparative Education*], 22, 127–138.

Ninnes, Peter, and Sonia Mehta. (2004). *Re-Imaging Comparative Education: Postfoundational Ideas and Applications for Critical Times*. New York; London: RoutledgeFalmer.

Ninomiya, Akira. (2007). "The Japan Comparative Education Society (JCES)." In Vandra Masemann, Mark Bray, and Maria Manzon (Ed.), *Common Interests, Uncommon Goals: Histories of the World Council of Comparative Education Societies and its Members* (pp.128–138). Dordrecht, The Netherlands: Springer.

Nishino, Setsuo [西野節男]. 2001. "「イスラーム文化圏」の教育研究" ["Educational Research on the 'Islam Cultural Zone'"]. 比較教育学研究 [*Comparative Education*], 27, 41–54.

Otsuka, Yutaka [大塚豊]. (1994). "教育の地域研究（主に非西洋）" ["Area Studies of Education: With a Focus on Non-Western Areas"]. 比較教育学研究 [*Comparative Education*], 20, 41–48.

Otsuka, Yutaka [大塚豊]. (2005). "方法としてのフィールド－比較教育学の方法論検討の一視点－" ["Field as a Method: A Perspective for Examining Methodologies of Comparative Education"]. *Comparative Education Studies*, 31, 253–265.

Paulston, Rolland G. (1976). "Presidential Address: Ethnicity and Educational Change: A Priority for Comparative Education." *Comparative Education Review*, 20(3), 269–277.

Paulston, Rolland G. (1990). "From Paradigm Wars to Disputatious Community." *Comparative Education Review*, 34(3), 395–400.

Paulston, Rolland G. (1993). "Mapping Discourse in Comparative Education Texts." *Compare*. 23(2), 101–114.

Paulston, Rolland G. (2000). "Imagining Comparative Education: Past, Present, Future." *Compare*. 30(3), 353–367.

Psacharopoulos, George. (1990). "Comparative Education: From Theory to Practice, Or Are You A:\neo.* or B:*.ist?" *Comparative Education Review*, 34(3), 369–380.

Raby, Rosalind Latiner. (2009). "Whither Diversity in Publishing? A Review of the 2008 Comparative Education Review Bibliography." *Comparative Education Review*, 53(3), 435–449.

Rust, Val D., Aminata Soumaré, Octavio Pescador, & Megumi Shibuya. (1999). "Research Strategies in Comparative Education." *Comparative Education Review*, 43(1), 86–109.

Samoff, Joel. (1999). "Institutionalizing International Influence." In Robert F. Arnove and Carlos Alberto Torres (Ed.), *Comparative Education: The Dialectic of the Global and the Local*. Oxford, UK: Rowman & Littlefield Publishers.

Sawamura, Nobuhide [澤村信英]. (2004). "ケニアにおける初等教育完全普及への取り組み－無償化政策の現状と問題点－" ["Efforts towards Universal Primary Education in Kenya: The Current Situation and Issues in Fee Abolition Policy]. 比較教育学研究 [*Comparative Education*], 30, 129–147.

Schriewer, Jürgen, ed. (2009). *Discourse Formation in Comparative Education*. Bern, Switzerland: Peter Lang Pub Inc.

Sheehan, Barry A. (1983). "Comparative Education: Phoenix or Dodo?" Comparative and International Studies and the Theory and Practice of Education. Proceedings of the Annual Conference of the Australian Comparative and International Education Society, Hamilton, New Zealand, 21–24 August 1983.

Shibuya, Hideaki [渋谷英章]. (2001). "地域教育研究の可能性－「地域教育事情」からの脱皮－" ["The Possibilities of Educational Area Studies: A Departure from 'Foreign Education Studies'"]. 比較教育学研究 [*Comparative Education*], 27, 16–28.

Shu, Hangli, & Nanzhao Zhou. (1990). "Comparative Education in Asia and Its Prospects." *Prospects*. 20(1), 65–78.

Steiner-Khamsi, Gita. (2006). "The Development Turn in Comparative Education." *European Education*, 38(3), 19–47.

Takei, Atsushi [武井敦史]. (1995). "インド・アンドラプテデーシュ州における初等教育計画に関する一考察－初等教育援助のあり方をめぐって－" ["A Study of the Andhra Pradesh Primary Education Project (APPEP) in India: An Analysis of Assistance Given to Primary Education"]. 比較教育学研究 [*Comparative Education*], 21, 121–132.

Takekuma, Hisao [竹熊尚夫]. (2001). "比較教育学と地域教育研究の課題" ["Issues on Comparative Education and Educational Area Studies"]. *比較教育学研究* [*Comparative Education*], 27, 5–15.

Umakoshi, Toru [馬越徹]. (2007). *比較教育学：越境のレッスン* [*Comparative Education: Lessons for Crossing the Border*]. Tokyo: Toshindo.

Ushiogi, Morikazu [潮木守一]. (1995). "教育開発・教育協力援助の研究課題" ["Research Themes in Educational Development and Educational Cooperation Aid"]. *比較教育学研究* [*Comparative Education*], 21, 7–14.

Utsumi, Seiji [内海成治], Nobuhide Sawamura [澤村信英], Mao Takahashi [高橋真央], and Madoka Asano [浅野円香]. (2006). "ケニアの「小さい学校」の意味—マサイランドにおける不完全学校の就学実態—"["The Meaning of a 'Small School' in Kenya: The Reality of Enrollment in Incomplete Schools in Masailand"]. *国際協力論集* [*Journal of International Cooperation in Education*], 9(2), 27–36.

Welch, Anthony R. (1985). "The Functionalist Tradition and Comparative Education." *Comparative Education, 21*(1), 5–19.

Zajda, Joseph. (2003). "Discourses of Postmodern Globalization: The Future Role of Comparative Education Research." *Education and Society, 21*(1), 99–113.

NOTES ON CONTRIBUTORS

Enkhjargal ADIYA DIFFENDAL served as Managing Director of the Institute for International Studies in Education (IISE), University of Pittsburgh, where she also received her PhD in 2010. Prior to coming to the United States, Enkhjargal had undertaken both teaching/research and higher education administration tasks at the National University of Mongolia. She also worked as a consultant for different international and local projects in Mongolia. Her research interests and experience are in the areas of higher education management, research methods, policy analysis, program evaluation, international development, social theory, and multicultural education.

Supriya BAILY is Assistant Professor at George Mason University in the Initiatives in Educational Transformation Master's Program for practicing teachers. Her areas of research include gender and power, young adults and nonformal education, and teacher's perceptions of international students. She received her PhD in International Education from George Mason University. Her recent publications include book chapters related to educating young adolescents and the role and place of peace education in India and forthcoming journal articles related to women and empowerment. She has presented papers at numerous national and international conferences. Additionally, she has spent over 15 years in the field of international development working with women's rights groups, peace, and justice organizations, as well as grassroots efforts supporting Tibetan and Burmese refugees in India. She continues to consult with nonprofits in the area of curriculum development and training.

Roger BOSHIER is Professor of Adult Education at the University of British Columbia, Vancouver, Canada. A New Zealander by birth and disposition, he is actively engaged with educational politics in his homeland and has a particular interest in farm-gate (self-educated) intellectuals and sociocultural factors explaining why New Zealand film-makers, adventurers, engineers, and racing sailors excel in international arenas. He was raised in Ngati Kahungungu Territory on the east coast of New Zealand where, in a 1769 outburst of market forces, Maori grabbed Captain Cook's cabin boy and traded him for valuables carried by the British naval captain. Boshier has also been elaborating lifelong education theory and assisting the large-scale effort to build learning villages, towns, and cities in China.

Katherine T. CARROLL holds a PhD in Comparative Education from Loyola University Chicago and teaches undergraduate and graduate courses in education policy, leadership, and foundations at Loyola and at Concordia University Chicago, part-time. She has published studies in *Education Review* (2003) and in *Comparative Education Review* (2005), with Erwin H. Epstein. Her book-length study of the impact of postmodern thought in comparative education, *Does Postmodernism Compare? An Analysis of the Use of Postmodern Constructs in*

Comparative Education Studies was published in 2008. Her research interests include education frameworks in totalitarian states and the foundations of education policy in the United States.

Peggy Nsama CHAKUFYALI is a Lecturer in the Department of Educational Administration and Policy Studies in the School of Education at the University of Zambia, having received her MA in Education from the University of Zambia.

Pochang CHEN is Chair Professor in the Department of Education at National Tainan University in Taiwan. Chen is also the current President of the Taiwan Higher Education Society. He served as Dean of the National Academy of Educational Research, President of National Hualien University of Education, Dean of the College of Education at Tamkang University, and President of the Taiwan Association of Sociology of Education. Chen received his PhD in the Department of Education at National Taiwan Normal University and became a Visiting Scholar at the University of Missouri and Institute of Education at the University of London. He has published dozens of journal articles and book chapters and has great influence on educational reforms both in Taiwan and other Asia societies. The topic of his current research interests are higher education, educational reform, and sociology of curriculum.

Sheng Yao (Kent) CHENG is Associate Professor in the Graduate Institute of Curriculum Studies and Center for Teacher Education at National Chung Cheng University in Taiwan. Cheng is also Director of Institute for Disadvantaged Students' Learning at CCU; Board Member of Chinese Comparative Education Society-Taipei; Program Chair of the Comparative and International Education Society (CIES) Higher Education Special Interest Group; International Advisor of the National Center for University Entrance Examinations (Japan); Co-Director of Global Education, Training, and Leadership Institute; Affiliated Faculty Member of the University of Pittsburgh Institute for International Studies in Education; and Executive Editor of *Journal of Comparative Education*. Cheng received his PhD in the Division of Social Science and Comparative Education at UCLA in 2004 and the topic of his dissertation focused on the politics of identity and indigenous schooling between Taiwan Aborigines and American Indians. Cheng's recent research interests include higher education, comparative education, sociology of education, and international educational reforms.

Jennifer R. CRANDALL is a Doctoral Student in the Social and Comparative Analysis in Education Program at the University of Pittsburgh. Her research interests include education policy and access, retention and equity in higher education. The goal of her dissertation work is to move beyond broad racial comparisons that obscure heterogeneity and explore the intersections of ethnicity, class and gender. Prior to joining the University of Pittsburgh, she worked as a grantee for associations and institutions in Russia and India on English language teaching curriculum development and instruction. She has taught in the United States, South Korea, Nepal, and the Slovak Republic.

Joan DEJAEGHERE is Assistant Professor of Comparative and International Development Education in the Department of Organizational Leadership, Policy and Development at the University of Minnesota. Her scholarship examines the intersections of gender, ethnicity, and citizen status and how they materialize as inequalities in education. Several of her publications examine inequalities in education using perspectives from globalization and transnationalism. Her recent publications include: "The Making of Mexican Migrant Youth Civic Identities: Transnational Spaces and Imaginaries" in *Anthropology of Education Quarterly* (2010) (with K. McCleary); "Critical Citizenship Education for Multicultural Societies" in the *Inter-American Journal of Education for Democracy* (2009); "Citizenship as Privilege and Power: Australian Educators' Lived Experiences as Citizens" *Comparative Education Review* (2008), and "Intercultural Dimensions of Citizenship in the Australian Secondary Curriculum: Between Critical Contestations and Minimal Constructions" in Stevick and Levinson's, *Reimagining Civic Education: How Diverse Societies Form Democratic Citizens* (2006).

Erwin H. EPSTEIN is Professor of Cultural and Educational Policy Studies and Director of the Center for Comparative Education at Loyola University Chicago. Prior to his tenure at Loyola, he was Director of the University Center for International Studies and Professor of Humanistic Foundations of Education and of Rural Sociology at The Ohio State University. He is a former Editor of the *Comparative Education Review*, a former President of the Comparative and International Education Society, and a former President of the World Council of Comparative Education Societies. He serves currently as Historian of the Comparative and International Education Society. His research has focused on, among other topics, comparative theory, US administration of education in the Hispanic Caribbean, and the impact of education on national identity in socio-culturally marginal communities especially in Latin America.

Irving EPSTEIN is Associate Dean of the Faculty and Professor of Educational Studies at Illinois Wesleyan University. His publications include the edited volumes, *Chinese Education: Problems, Policies and Prospects* (Garland, 1991), *Recapturing the Personal: Essays on Education and Embodied Knowledge in Comparative Perspective* (Information Age, 2007), and the six volume *Greenwood Encyclopedia of Children's Issues Worldwide* (Greenwood, 2007) in addition to numerous articles and book chapters. From 1988–1998 he served as an Associate Editor of the *Comparative Education Review*, and from 2006–2011, he served as Coeditor of the *ASIANetwork Exchange*. He is most proud of his service on the Advisory Board of the Scholars at Risk Network, an international consortium of universities dedicated to the preservation of academic freedom around the world.

Tom FRIEDRICH is Assistant Professor of English and Director of Freshman Composition at the State University of New York at Plattsburgh. He holds a PhD in Literacy Education from the University of Minnesota. His research on teacher identity and response to student writing has been published in *The Indo-Pacific Journal of Phenomenology* and *Handbook of Writing Research*.

Mark Ginsburg is a Senior Advisor for Research, Evaluation, and Teacher Education in the Global Education Center, Academy for Educational Development, supporting projects in El Salvador, Egypt, Equatorial Guinea, Ethiopia, Pakistan, Rwanda, and Pakistan. He is also a Visiting Professor in the International Education Policy program at the University of Maryland and serves as Coeditor of the *Comparative Education Review*. He previously was a faculty member at the University of Aston (Birmingham, England); the University of Houston (Texas, USA); and the University of Pittsburgh (Pennsylvania, USA).

Esther E. Gottlieb holds a PhD from the University of Pittsburgh, and a MA from Case Western Reserve University. Her wide experience in educational planning, economic development, and teacher training includes working at Kibbutzim College, Tel Aviv, West Virginia University, and consulting in Bosnia, South Africa, and Cuba. She joined The Ohio State University International Affairs in 2002 and is now involved in internationalizing the students' learning experiences. She is Adjunct Associate Professor of Education Policy and Leadership and teaches Education in Global Perspectives and Internationalizing across the Curriculum. Her research in comparative and international education has focused on discursive practices of reforms and policies, and most recently examines the discourse of "becoming/being world-class." Gottlieb's publications include "Global Rhetoric, Local Policy: Teacher Training Reform in Israeli Education," *Educational Policy* (1991); "Appalachian Self-Fashioning: Regional Identities and Cultural Models" in *Discourse: Studies in the Cultural Politics of Education* (2001); an edited volume with J. Craig Jenkins, *Identity Conflicts: Can Violence be Regulated?* (2007); and "World-Class Education for Economic and National Security: The Story of a State on the Verge" (forthcoming).

Jason Hilton is a Social Studies Teacher and a Doctoral Student in the Administration and Policy Studies Department within the University of Pittsburgh School of Education. He has experience working with interviews of both children and adults within the education setting. His academic interests include social theory, social justice, and praxis for change.

Halla B. Holmarsdottir is an Associate Professor in Multicultural and International Education at Oslo University College, Norway. She holds a PhD in Education and Development from the University of Oslo. Holmarsdottir is currently the scientific coordinator of the Gender Equality, Education and Poverty (GEEP) project funded by the Norwegian Ministry of Foreign Affairs. Her academic competency is within both humanities and social science disciplines, which has contributed to an interdisciplinary approach in her work. Since 2005 she has served as the UNESCO liaison representing the World Council of Comparative Education Societies (WCCES). In this capacity she has participated in numerous High Level meetings and NGO forums. More recently she has co-edited (with Mina O'Dowd) the collective volume *Nordic Voices: Teaching and Researching Comparative and International Education in the Nordic Countries* (2009) published by Sense and she is currently working on a new book entitled: *Gendered Voices: Reflections on Gender and Education in South Africa and Sudan*.

W. James JACOB is Director of the Institute for International Studies in Education at the University of Pittsburgh's School of Education, and is the former Assistant Director of the Center for International and Development Education at UCLA. His research focuses on program design, implementation, and evaluation; HIV/AIDS multisectoral capacity building and prevention; and higher education organizational analysis in developing countries with geographic emphases in Africa, East and Southeast Asia, and the Pacific Islands. He has authored numerous articles and books and serves as Coeditor of Palgrave Macmillan's *International and Development Education* Book Series, Sense Publishers' *Pittsburgh Studies in Comparative and International Education* Book Series, and as Associate Editor of the journal *Excellence in Higher Education.*

Kalima KALIMA is a Lecturer in the Department of Educational Psychology, Sociology, and Special Education in the School of Education at the University of Zambia, having received his MEd from the University of Zambia.

Amanda KENDERES has extensive international experience. Her developmental years were spent living in countries such as Greece, Morocco, and South Korea. She is presently a Doctoral Candidate in the Social Science and Comparative Education Program at the University of California, Los Angeles. In 2009–2010 she served as the Administrative Director of the Center for International and Development Education at UCLA.

Moosung LEE is Assistant Professor of Educational Policy and Leadership at the Hong Kong Institute of Education. He holds two master's degrees from Seoul National University and Oxford University and a PhD in Educational Policy and Administration from the University of Minnesota. His doctoral studies were supported by competitive scholarship awards (e.g., Fulbright Scholarship, UNESCO Fellowship, and Doctoral Dissertation Fellowship). He has been enthusiastic about studying contemporary educational issues facing socially-marginalized groups such as ethnic minority adolescents and immigrant workers. His research has been published in the *British Journal of Sociology of Education, Cambridge Journal of Education, Urban Education, International Journal of Lifelong Education,* and *Comparative Education,* to name a few. Some of these studies have been selected as a best paper by several US-based academic societies such as American Educational Research Association (i.e., Special Interest Group of Leadership for Social Justice), and the Committee of Adult Education Research Conference.

Jing LIU is a Doctoral Student in Graduate School of International Development, Nagoya University, Japan. His research interests include international education development, comparative education, education for internal migrant children in urban China, school choice in urban China, and education policy studies. In 2009, he served an internship at the Assessment, Information Systems, Monitoring and Statistics (AIMS) Unit of the UNESCO Office in Bangkok. He served as a Visiting Scholar in the University of Pittsburgh Institute for International Studies in Education in the first six months of 2010. His master's thesis is titled "Education for Migrant Children in Beijing from Access to Quality" and was presented at the Comparative and International Education Annual Meeting in 2009, Charleston, South Carolina. Currently, Liu is working on his dissertation research design which focuses on school choice in public school in urban China based on the analysis of discourse on *Ze Xiao*.

Maureen W. MCCLURE'S work focuses on educational strategy and mapping. She specializes in large-scale crises in education and their shorter and longer-term consequences for a next generation. She is currently Associate Professor, former Chair of the Department of Administrative and Policy Studies at the University of Pittsburgh, Senior Research Associate at the Institute for International Studies in Education (IISE), and Director of the Global Information Networks in Education (GINIE) Project. She has worked with global policy teams in USAID, UNESCO, UNHCR, and UNICEF, working with national governments on education strategic policy during and after crises. The World Bank, the Asian Development Bank, and The British Council have also supported her work. She is a past member of the US Technical Planning Panel for Education Finance at the National Center for Education Statistics. She has an MBA, a MS, and a PhD from the University of Rochester, with a specialization in education strategy.

Benny MWAANGA currently works for the Academy for Educational Development as the Monitoring and Evaluation Advisor for the EQUIP2/Zambia Project. He previously worked for Africare-Zambia as the Monitoring and Evaluation Officer for the Reaching HIV/AIDS Affected People with Integrated Support and Development (RAPIDS) Program and for the Cooperative League of USA (CLUSA)-Zambia as the Monitoring and Evaluation Specialist for the Smallholder Enterprise and Marketing Program (SHEMP). He is also pursuing an MSc in Public Policy Management at the University of London, having received his BA in Education at the University of Zambia.

Laura NORTHROP is a Doctoral Student in the Social and Comparative Analysis in Education Program at the University of Pittsburgh. She previously worked as a middle school teacher, a PreK-adult reading specialist, and a research assistant on several statewide teacher professional development projects to improve reading instruction in the classroom. Her research interests include reading instruction, assessment and policy, and the economics of education.

Mina O'DOWD is Professor at Lund University in Sweden. She was awarded her PhD in International and Comparative Education by Stockholm University. O'Dowd has conducted both school-based research and policy-oriented research over the years. O'Dowd is the immediate Past President of the Nordic Comparative and International Education Society (NOCIES). She is a former member of the International Advisory Board of *Compare* and is currently a member of the International Advisory Board of *Research in Comparative and International Education.* O'Dowd's work is distinguished by its focus on the philosophy and sociology of education and a special interest in methodological and theoretical issues in education research. Her most recent publications are "The God that

Failed. Lifelong Learning: From Utopianism to Instrumentalism," *The Bulgarian Comparative Education Society, Conference Proceedings*, Vol. 7, 2009, ed. James Ogunleye, Bruno Leutwyler, Charl Wolhuter, and Marinela Mihova; and "The Bologna Process: Is It an Education Reform?" in *Papers in Memory of David N. Wilson: Clamouring for a Better World*, ed. Vandra Masemann (Rotterdam: Sense Publishers, 2010).

Gary W. J. PLUIM has coordinated education and other programs for several Canadian NGOs in Tanzania, Guyana, and Vanuatu. His previous publications and presentations include "Theorizing the NGO in a Post-aid Context" (2009); "Democratic Accountability in Education for Development: How Canadian NGOs Claim Participatory Legitimacy" (2009); "Small, Canadian NGOs in Education for Development: Agents of Hegemony or of Local Solidarity?" (2008); and "Efficacy of Education-Oriented NGOs: The Role of Organizational Culture" (2007). Pluim holds degrees from Queens University, the University of Waterloo, and the Ontario Institute for Studies in Education at the University of Toronto (OISE/UT). He is currently a Doctoral Candidate in Comparative, Development and Education and an Instructor in International and Global Education at OISE/UT. His research examines the international NGO intervention in post-earthquake Haiti, and focuses specifically on perceptions of participation in education reconstruction.

Richard E. RODMAN is Professor of International Education at the SIT Graduate Institute and its Program for Intercultural Service Leadership and Management. His interests center on international education theory-to-practice, access and quality, experiential education, intercultural communication and contact. He has development education experience in project design, management, with activities in more than 60 countries, most notably the years in basic school reform in Lesotho and southern Africa. Rodman directed international education and global leadership development for the Presbyterian Church (USA) denomination. As an Academic Dean at Warren Wilson College, he created an education abroad program with a focus on academics, work, and service. He has sat on the Board of Trustees of the Lebanese American University, American Community School of Beirut, United Board for Christian Higher Education in Asia, the International Partnership for Service Learning, and is a member of the Editorial Board of *Abroad View.*

Val D. RUST is Professor of Education at UCLA. He has recently been the Director of the UCLA International Education Office, the head of the Social Sciences and Comparative Education Division in the Department of Education, and the Associate Director of the Center for International and Development Education. He has served as the President of the Comparative and International Education Society.

Lou L. SABINA is a Doctoral Student in the Social and Comparative Analysis of Education program at the University of Pittsburgh, with a supporting field in the Katz Graduate School of Business. Lou previously served as a high school business, mathematics, law, and computer science teacher and then as an elementary school administrator. Lou currently teaches part-time for Point Park University and Butler County Community College in their business and education departments. Lou's research interests include succession planning for school leaders, human resources in education, merit pay and its effects, principal training providers, and the principalship itself, both domestic and abroad. His dissertation investigates administrator stress and burnout.

Nelly P. STROMQUIST is Professor of International Education Policy in the College of Education at the University of Maryland. Her research interests focus on the dynamics among educational policies and practices, gender relations, adult literacy, and social change, which she examines from a critical sociology perspective. At present, she is following the processes of globalization and their impact on higher education. She has written several books and numerous articles. Her most recent books include editing *The Professoriate in the Age of Globalization* (Rotterdam: Sense Publishers, 2007) and writing *Feminist Organizations and Social Transformation in Latin America* (Boulder: Paradigm, 2006). She is a former President of the Comparative and International Education Society and a 2005–2006 Fulbright New Century Scholar. She has served as Associate Editor of the *Comparative Education Review* and is on the Editorial Board of various journals in the US, the UK, Spain, South Africa, and Brazil.

Winnehl TUBMAN is a Program Officer in the System Services Center, Academy for Educational Development, supporting monitoring and evaluation activities for projects in Equatorial Guinea, Liberia, and Zambia. She holds an MA in International Educational Development from Teachers College, Columbia University.

Lisa VU is a Doctoral Student in the Comparative and International Development Education Program at the University of Minnesota, Twin Cities. She holds an MA from Teachers College, Columbia University. Her scholarly interests are in the areas of migration, development, and the role of diaspora members in the educational development of the country of origin. As part of her dissertation work, she plans to investigate educational projects in Vietnam that were initiated by Vietnamese Americans.

John C. WEIDMAN is Professor of Education at the University of Pittsburgh. He was Chair of the Department of Administrative and Policy Studies from 1986–1993 and 2007–2010; and Director, Institute for International Studies in Education (IISE) from 2004–2007. His visiting appointments include Guest Professor at Beijing Normal University in China (2007–2012), UNESCO Chair of Higher Education Research at Maseno University in Kenya (1993), and Fulbright Professor of the Sociology of Education at Augsburg University in Germany (1986–1987). He has worked on comparative education management, finance, reform, strategic planning, and policy analysis projects in Indonesia, Kenya, Kyrgyzstan, Laos, Mongolia, Vietnam, Saudi Arabia, South Africa, and Uzbekistan. Results from this work have been published in journals, edited books, and research monographs. He is Coeditor of the *Pittsburgh Studies in Comparative* *and International Education* Book Series from Sense Publishers and the journal, *Excellence in Higher Education,* launched in December 2010 in cooperation with the Consortium of Indonesian Universities-Pittsburgh (KPTIP).

Shoko YAMADA is Associate Professor of Comparative Education and Educational Policy Studies at the Graduate School of International Development, Nagoya University, Japan. She has conducted research on educational policy making and implementation in Africa and Asia. Currently she is leading a research project which reviews paradigms and practices of comparative education research in Japan. Her publications include: "Educational Borrowing as Negotiation: Reexamining the Influence of American Black Industrial Education Model on British Colonial Education in Africa." *Comparative Education.* Vol. 43, No. 1, 2007; "Making Sense of the EFA from a National Context – Its Implementation, and Impact on Households in Ethiopia," in *Education for All: Global Promises, National Challenges,* ed. Baker and Wiseman, Elsevier Science Ltd., 2007; and *Multiple Conceptions of Education for All and EFA Development Goals: The processes of adopting a global agenda in the policies of Kenya, Tanzania, and Ethiopia,* author edited, VDM Verlag, 2010.

Yukiko YAMAMOTO is a Doctoral Candidate in the Social and Comparative Analysis in Education Program, within the Department of Administrative Policy Studies at the University of Pittsburgh. Her dissertation analyzes various current education policies for youth unemployment through the lens of human capital theory to explore how self-employment can help to solve job shortage problems. In her dissertation, she used social cartography methods to analyze the literature on entrepreneurial education, with implications for policy. Her work in the private sector in Tokyo and in the public sector in the United States led her to pursue a career in the area of education policy which addresses labor market needs. She has also taught Japanese at the University of Pittsburgh.

Rolland G. Paulston (1929–2006)

Short Biography and Significant Contribution[1]

Source: Photo courtesy of Christina Paulston. This photo was taken in 1991 by Roger Boshier at Bath Island in the Gulf of Georgia, British Columbia, during one of Rolland Paulston's several trips to meet with colleagues at the University of British Columbia, Vancouver, Canada.

Rolland Paulston was a former President of CIES (1975) and Professor at the University of Pittsburgh's School of Education. He earned his Bachelor's degree in art history and geography at the University of California, Los Angeles and his master's degree in economic geography at the University of Stockholm (Sweden). After teaching social studies in Los Angeles and Tangier, Morocco, Paulston earned his Doctorate in Comparative and International Education at Teachers College, Columbia University. In 1968 he began teaching at the University of Pittsburgh, was granted the position of full Professor in 1972, and remained an influential figure in comparative education there until his death in 2006.

In one of Paulston's early works, an evaluation of the contributing factors to the results of teacher-centered educational reform in four schools in Peru, he critically tested the prevailing notion that education is the logical choice for carrying out change and development in society. In order to understand why the reform worked in some schools and failed in others, Paulston focused on the point of contact, or the "interface" of the movement; the teacher and the community. Instead of relying on a structural functionalist or neo-Marxism perspective to observe these interactions based on hierarchies or class, Paulston instead focused on multiple variables including community values (i.e., religion), self-perception of national/local identity (i.e., language, ethnicity), and the teacher's own sense of identity in relation to the community. Paulston concluded that the teacher-centered approach to educational reforms is more successful when the teacher and school are more closely aligned to the main cultural characteristics of the community. Infusions of financial resources, technical experts or teacher training were effective only in contributing to the failure of reform in a school. This characterization was prescient and incisive, essentially foreshadowing the problems of the participatory development movements of the following decades that was "discovered" and noted by scholars and agencies thirty years later. Traditional dualist approaches would have only reiterated assumed distinctions based on class or bureaucratic hierarchies. Paulston's inclusion of human interactions based on cultural relations added more voices and perspectives to his evaluation, thus adding more accuracy, validity and applicability to his findings.

Paulston is best known for his work in "social cartography." For Paulston, rigid, reductionist perspectives like structural functionalism are not useful in understanding the "true" reality in a given field of observation or study. Additionally, Paulston found that equilibrium theories (i.e., evolutionary, neo-evolutionary, and structural functionalist) of social and educational reform movements are largely descriptive with very little to offer by way of predictive capabilities. Conflict or transformative orientations (i.e., neo-Marxist, cultural revival, and anarchist utopian) or are more useful in describing and predicting social and educational reform movements, but are sometimes simply not realistic enough for concrete results. Thus, the comparativist is left between alternating either/or theoretical constructs that leave too may gaps or exclude too many non-aligned perspectives and voices. Enter social cartography.

Paulston relied significantly on Foucauldian analysis of history to inform his theory of social cartography. His application of Foucault's postmodernism to comparative education led him to assert that a postmodern (deconstructive) analysis was the best means by which to understand educational policy analysis, and this is best articulated through the process of social cartography. This process allowed the comparativist to map the spatial relations in which competing perspectives were situated, providing a better way to understand the manner in which they negotiated that space in relation to each other. By admitting multiple "voices" in any given discussion the comparativist is able to apprehend a more representative picture (or map) of the theoretical space in which s/he is working, including the identification of his/her space on that map, an important part of the process for Paulston.

Paulston's career was marked by a persistent and consistent desire to compare, educate and transform not just education but the educators and comparativists themselves. Always keen to improve the field of comparative education, he even issued a challenge to his fellow colleagues in a speech delivered at a meeting of comparative education scholars in Canada in 1976. After identifying the problems, limitations and failures of the comparative education field and listing possible solutions for them, he adamantly encouraged his colleagues to comparatively address the political and ideological characteristics of ethnicity as a social construction with the force of a social movement. He called for more "rigorous study of ethnogensis" which he felt would improve comparative education theory and scholarship as well as result in a more democratic and humane society. Paulston targeted himself, too, with his criticisms and challenges, working and reworking his approach through social cartography over many years, and addressing the dynamism and fluidity of ethnicity as a social force in educational reform.

NOTE

1. The author of this brief bio on Paulston is Matthew Hayden. For the original source, see Cieclopedia.org, "Rolland G. Paulston, 1929–2006," New York: Teachers College, Columbia University, 2008 (available online at http://www.cieclopedia.org).

INDEX

A
Adams, Don (Donald) K., xxii, 2, 3, 24, 168
Africa, 11, 51, 55, 56, 65, 83-84, 194, 204-212, 257, 298, 378, 379
see also *individual countries*
African (higher education), 56, 83-84, 205
Afrocentric, 263
Algeria, 96
American (university), 55
Anderson, C. Arnold, 24, 62
Apple, Michael W., 239
Arab countries, 378
archeology, 37, 38, 40
Aristotle, 24, 185, 201, 212, 297
Arnove, Robert F., 27, 61, 100-101, 117, 118, 120-122, 124-125
Asia, 64, 297, 334, 336, 345
see also *Central Asia, East Asia, South Asia, individual countries*
Asia Pacific Education Review (APER), 71-72
Australia, 236, 297, 299, 320

B
Baudrillard, Jean, 33, 44
Biraimah, Karen, 117, 121-122
Blacks, 187, 403
Bologna Process, 107
Bourdieu, Pierre, 98-100, 109, 118
Bray, Mark, 56, 59, 60, 382
Brazil, 174, 178, 183, 185, 226, 299
Burrell, Gibson, xxii, 4-5, 15, 22-24, 26-27, 154, 321, 328

C
Canada, 297, 299, 320
capability approach, 82, 83-84, 201
capacity building, 87, 357, 362-363, 365

capital
cultural capital, 96, 98
economic capital, 97
social capital, 322-323, 325, 328
Caribbean, 378-379
Carnoy, Martin, 115, 117-122, 124-125, 355
Central and Eastern Europe, 378
Central Asia, 64, 333, 378
Centrality (degree, closeness, and betweenness), 116-121, 128, 155-156, 162, 203
Chaos Theory, 5
China, 65, 107, 153, 257, 282, 296, 299, 305, 348-349, 374
Chinese, 103, 166, 300, 348, 388
citation network analysis, 10, 113-144
cliques, 10, 122-124, 128
Cold War, 3, 257, 299, 377
collegiality, 242, 245-246, 248
colonialism, 96, 297
de-colonization, 160, 263
neo-colonial(ism), *see* neo-colonial(ism)
colonized, 285-286
commercialization, 104
Communities of Practice, 77-78
Comparative Education Review (CER), 3, 4, 7, 13, 25, 31, 32-35, 59, 63, 71-72, 88, 114-115, 116, 125, 128, 276, 373-375, 387
Comparative Education, Japan (*CEJ*), 13, 80, 371-393
Comparative Education, UK (*CE*), 71-72, 373-375
Comparative and International Education Society (CIES), xix, 2, 32, 50, 59, 146, 238, 374
CIES Presidents, 116-128
CIES Presidential Addresses, 116-128

CPSIA information can be obtained at www.ICGtesting.com
Printed in the USA
LVOW07s0756120914

403781LV00001B/6/P